Vital
Signs

GREGG LEVOY

Vital Signs

THE NATURE AND NURTURE OF PASSION

JEREMY P. TARCHER/PENGUIN | A MEMBER OF PENGUIN GROUP (USA) | NEW YORK

Jeremy P. Tarcher/Penguin
Published by the Penguin Group
Penguin Group (USA) LLC
375 Hudson Street
New York, New York 10014

USA · Canada · UK · Ireland · Australia
New Zealand · India · South Africa · China

penguin.com
A Penguin Random House Company

Most Tarcher/Penguin books are available at special quantity discounts for bulk purchase for sales
promotions, premiums, fund-raising, and educational needs. Special books or book excerpts also can
be created to fit specific needs. For details, write: Special.Markets@us.penguingroup.com.

Library of Congress Cataloging-in-Publication Data

Levoy, Gregg.
Vital signs : the nature and nurture of passion / Gregg Levoy.
p.   cm.
ISBN 978-0-399-16323-4
1. Interest (Psychology).   2. Curiosity.   3. Creative ability.   4. Emotions.
5. Self-realization.   I. Title.
BF323.I5L49   2014   2014026846
152.4—dc23

Printed in the United States of America
1   3   5   7   9   10   8   6   4   2

Book design by Ellen Cipriano

Contents

Introduction

Chase down your passion like it's the last bus of the night.

—TERRI GUILLEMETS

I USED TO BE a reporter for the *Cincinnati Enquirer,* back in my twenties, and among my favorite stories was one I wrote about the Ringling Bros. and Barnum & Bailey Circus coming to town.

In a fit of journalistic zeal, however—and therefore shortsightedness— I let one of the animal trainers convince me that riding bareback on an elephant at the head of the circus parade through downtown Cincinnati would add *color* to my story.

Contrary to my jungle-book fantasy of being airlifted onto the elephant's back while standing on its trunk, the only way to actually get up there was to use a ladder, and the only way to *stay* up there during the parade was to hang on to the elephant's ears.

Those who've ridden elephants bareback probably know about this already, but elephant ears have an extremely disagreeable habit of flapping a lot, especially when they're hot. And it was high summer. So the only way to stay up there was to remain extremely flappable, otherwise I'd have been thrown, and it was probably ten to fifteen feet to the ground—a concern that, to be honest, *paled* in comparison with my concern about how stupid I looked up there, desperately hanging on to this animal's buffeting ears, wearing my business clothes, because the animal trainer had sprung this brilliant idea on me right before the parade, and with my pants scrunched up *above* my knees.

I was the first thing anybody saw in that parade, and I'm fairly certain I did not capture the theme of "The Greatest Show on Earth."

But in looking back on my elephant ride, and on what I've learned since then about what's involved in living passionately and courageously, that experience had a lot in common with the experience of following passions—in that I was caught by surprise and carried off by something much bigger than me; in that it was nerve-racking and thrilling simultaneously; and in that the elephant couldn't have cared less. By which I mean that I've discovered an unsettling truth: my soul doesn't seem to care what price I have to pay to live passionately.

This seems like a design flaw to me. But my security, my popularity, my vanity, even my happiness don't seem to matter to my soul. It's not interested in whether I live a comfortable life. It's not interested in making me rich or famous. It's not interested in whether people even like me or not. What *does* seem to matter to it, though, is staying up on the elephant and being willing to go for the Ride—the one that ensures that someday if my life flashes in front of my eyes, it will at least hold my interest.

PASSION IS WHAT DISTURBS and confounds the safe and settled in your life, the tendency to try to lock yourself into geosynchronous orbit around some form of security, no amount of which will ever adequately compensate you for giving up your passions or selling your soul, though it may allow you to suffer in nicer surroundings.

Passion is the impulse toward growth, which, by its nature, protests boredom and ennui, refuses to bump mindlessly along on the conveyor belt, and has little patience for the "been there, done that" attitude that there's nothing new under the sun. It's what stirs your interest in life, helping you awaken from the trances and entrapments of the everyday, which block the natural migration of your energies.

Whether passion takes the form of colorful intensity or contemplative alertness, it contributes to a vibrant life, a keen awareness of where the pulse is, and a determination to plug into that place. It helps you stay engaged with the world and enjoy it as a function of the primary calling of *all* creatures—maximum aliveness.

In fact, passion is a survival mechanism, because your attachment to life depends on your interest in it, your sense of wonder and reverence, enthusiasm and gratitude, *participation*. It also depends on your ability to resist the torpor of dailiness, with its hypnotic routines and its soothing illusion that there's always tomorrow—a lamp of Aladdin merely awaiting your caress—and that you have plenty of time to make your dreams come true and your passions come alive, even though years may continue to slip by Rip Van Winkle–like and you occasionally awaken with a growing uneasiness and a sense of being unrecognizable even to yourself.

Part of the reason so many people are fascinated nowadays with vampires and zombies is our collective fear of being sucked of our life force, drained of our vitalities, and left in a bloodless and catatonic state.

This fear may not be so much one of dying, or even being eaten alive, as much as one of being turned *into* a zombie. And most of us know, or have known, the experience of feeling like the living dead. Being at a job that, like a vampire, sucks the life out of you. School years spent staring zombielike into space and dreaming about the pleasures of the flesh or perhaps about freedom. Evenings spent clocking your statutory 4.8 hours of daily television. Being in a relationship in which you feel like a mere ghost of your full vital self. Long, dull stretches of life through which you've staggered like the walking dead. And most of us also know the fear of losing our minds and our identities that can come with simply growing old and suffering dementia. Given enough time, life itself devours our brains.

But even if we haven't sent out a new shoot in years, or haven't strayed much beyond the cadaverous light of the television and computer, the hunger for passion reminds us that we're still vivid with life force, our souls shouting at the turned backs of resignation and boredom and time being torn off the calendar unused.

Just as there are parts of us we put to sleep over the course of life— passions ignored, pleasures denied, emotions censored, powers hidden— there's another part that wants to bend down and kiss our sleeping selves awake.

During the aerial bombing of London in World War II, damage to the

Natural History Museum allowed light and moisture to enter the buildings, and mimosa seeds that had been brought over from China in 1793 and stashed in wooden collection cases suddenly awoke from their 150-year sleep and began sprouting. We, too, are revivable. No matter how long or deep the sleep, the soul is always willing to awaken.

Granted, the work of coming-to is formidable, whether individually or collectively. A lot of people feel deeply disengaged from life, from themselves, and from a sense of purpose or passion. A 2012 Gallup poll of employees in 142 countries found that, on average, 87 percent of them are either "not engaged" or "actively disengaged" (63 percent and 24 percent, respectively), and only 13 percent were "engaged." In the United States alone, this adds up to roughly $550 billion a year in lost productivity.

Passion equals productivity, and lack of passion sabotages it, and that goes for both work and non-work modes of expression—which makes you wonder what the engagement/disengagement figures would be on school life, family life, social life, and spiritual life. "While complying can be an effective strategy for physical survival," says Daniel Pink in *Drive*, "it's a lousy one for personal fulfillment."

"Not engaged" means you're checked out, but "actively disengaged" means you're busy acting out your unhappiness and dispiritedness, spreading the virus among your colleagues, family, and friends, to say nothing of the body politic of which you're a cell. What it means, as one business columnist puts it, is that if you're part of a rowing team out on a river, one of the team members is rowing his or her heart out, five are just taking in the scenery, and two are actively trying to sink the boat.

But while dispassion is contagious, passion is equally catching. Some years ago, I was invited to facilitate one of my Callings workshops (based on my last book, *Callings*) for the environmental organization Earthstewards Network. As I was unpacking my car in the parking lot before the workshop began, a man pulled in, parked his car, got out, and motioned me over. He told me that he'd taken one of my workshops a year before and wanted to share with me the passion that had emerged for him as a result. "I'm going to start my car," he said, "and I want you to bend down and smell the exhaust."

This was certainly among the stranger requests I've had in my time, but the exhaust that came out of the back of that fellow's car smelled exactly like a McDonald's. He explained that he'd recently invented a process capable of turning used french fry oil into nonpolluting fuel for automobiles. In fact, he called it "McFuel." And he was about to embark on a one-year pilgrimage driving his car around the country to drum up media attention for his new breakthrough, which, needless to say, relies on an abundant and renewable resource.

It reminded me that people—their enthusiasm and ingenuity—are amazing and that you never know who's watching you. One person's passion can have a profound effect on the unfolding of another person's passion, without the first person even being aware of it. So, it thus matters greatly that every one of us is out there doing our proverbial thing and expressing our passion for life, interconnectedness being what it is, the Web being what it is, the mechanics of inspiration being what they are.

This certainly goes for anyone in a position of leadership or stewardship, especially relative to children and young adults. Whether you're a parent, teacher, minister, mentor, manager, coach, counselor, politician, or CEO, this much is certain: *your* passion is critical to *their* engagement.

There's a reason some of the world's great stories, like Sleeping Beauty and King Arthur and the Holy Grail—of which there are versions all over the world—speak to the idea that when the king or queen sleeps, those around them also sleep, and the kingdom sleeps. But when the king and queen awaken, those around them also awaken, and the kingdom begins to flower. It's an idea embedded very deeply into the mythologies, and thus the psychologies and philosophies, of the world, and what it tells us is that our individual work is also the work of the world, and that when we insist on our own aliveness, we stake a claim for everyone's.

Among my favorite stories from the Colombian novelist Gabriel García Márquez is the story of a man trying to solve the world's problems. His young son comes into the room and asks if he can help. Touched by his son's concern but impatient to get on with his task, the man takes a map of the world, rips it into little pieces, and gives it to the boy, telling him that he can help by piecing the world back together. The boy doesn't have a clue what the world looks like, but he takes the pile of paper off to his room.

Two days later, he rushes into his father's study. "Father! I've put the world back together." And indeed the shreds of paper have been meticulously taped together. His father is stunned and asks how he did it. The boy turns the map over and says, "On the back was a picture of a person, Father. I put the person back together and then turned it over and the world was back together!"

VITAL SIGNS is about what inspires passion and what defeats it. How you lose it and how you get it back. And ultimately it's about the endless yet endlessly fruitful tug-of-war between passion and security, the wild in you and the tame, your natural self and your conditioned self.

My prior book, *Callings*, is primarily about finding your vocational passion, and *Vital Signs* expands that exploration into the art of *living* passionately in all arenas of life—adventure and discovery, creativity and self-expression, relationships, service, and spirituality. While *Callings* is geared to *doing* what you love, *Vital Signs* is geared to *being* in love with life. Not just attaining *a* passion, but cultivating the *skill* of passion. Not just passion as a place you get *to*, but a place you come *from*.

Vital Signs also speaks to those who've been living through years of a Great Recession and a Code Orange world, which has driven many people to batten their hatches and hunker down. Those stresses highlight the many downward-pulling forces of everyday life that can siphon your vitality and make it hard to keep your fires burning.

The restorative lies in determinedly tapping into those places where your life force wells up to the surface even during dry spells and downturns, so you can not just survive but also thrive—and crucially, take your power back during those times when you feel disempowered, starting with a clear sense of what *choice* in any given moment will lead you toward or away from your sense of aliveness.

Each chapter in *Vital Signs* is a core sample, an intimate biography of one of the strategies you can employ to gain or regain passion—including the search for wonder and awe, the quest for novelty, the urge toward self-expression, the hunger to reconnect with inner and outer wildness, the desire to keep passion alive in your relationships, and the role that risk-taking plays in the ripening of passion.

In exploring what's healthy and essential about these strategies, as well as what's potentially unhealthy and maladaptive about them, this book offers a kind of mug shot of passion—so we'll know it when we see it—and an expansive menu of possibilities for how to discover and rediscover it.

The book also affirms the importance of courageous inquiry into our *dispassion*—when we're numb, depressed, stuck, or bored—so we'll recognize *that* when we see it too. Because behind these debilitating conditions is our rightful inheritance of vitality and our incredible capacities.

Vital Signs is also a kind of natural history of passion as it expresses itself in the human experience, following its tracks back to the dens of family, culture, religion, gender, genetics, and primal reflex. It looks at what psychology and science, as well as spirituality and myth, art and literature, history and philosophy, have to say about passion. And of course it shares the personal stories of people who've claimed and reclaimed their passion and aliveness, propelled by the understanding that being alive without *feeling* alive is like eating food with no taste to it and that we should insist on living in a world—on *creating* a world—that enlivens us rather than deadens us.

Among the most consistent and compelling lessons these people have shared with me (and that I've learned myself) about the call to live passionately are the following, which I'll flesh out in lavish detail in the pages to come:

- Passion can be cultivated—turned on as well as turned off. It's not in the either-you've-got-it-or-you-don't department. And this cultivation happens most readily at the level of the gesture and the moment, not the five-year plan.

- Passion is in the risk, in the willingness to step from the sidelines onto the playing field. The act of courage itself, even a single bold step beyond the comfort zone, is the defibrillator that strikes the heart awake like a clapper to a bell.

- Passion breeds passion, and disinterest breeds disinterest. If we lack passion in our own lives, for our own lives, our other relationships—our partnerships, friendships, communities, classrooms, corporations, and congregations—will be denied that energy.

- Passion isn't necessarily about happiness, nor is it always a peak experience. It can just as readily involve fury, fright, or sorrow—righteous anger, for instance, or the adrenaline rush of a thrill sport, or the melancholy pleasure of watching the evening sun sink into the ocean. Andrew Solomon, in his book *The Noonday Demon: An Atlas of Depression*, writes, "I can see the beauty of glass objects fully at the moment when they slip from my hand toward the floor."

- Passion is intimately related to health. To the degree that passion is vitality, denying ourselves our passion contributes to diminished vitality, and not just in a psychological sense. Much illness is the result of not paying attention to the prescriptions handed out by our own inner lives.

- Passion is more than exuberance; it's *endurance*. It's sometimes shoulder-to-the-wheel stamina and patience on the order of years. If our creative inspirations, for instance, or even our infatuations aren't balanced by long hours at the workbench, they don't truly come to fruition.

A few years ago, some work took me to Orlando, Florida, and I spent a few extra days at the nearby Atlantic coast. One early evening I was watching the news in bed when a small box appeared in the corner of the screen showing footage of a rocket being launched and a caption explaining that it was a Navy satellite taking off from Cape Canaveral.

It took a moment before it dawned on me that I was just up the beach from Cape Canaveral. I bolted out of bed and ran outside, and there it was, barely a thousand feet off the launchpad and close enough that I could see flames shooting earthward from the bottom of the rocket, which gleamed white atop a cone of fire and a thick column of smoke that reached all the way to the ground.

Barely eight minutes later, it was in orbit around Earth and I was still standing barefoot on the lawn of that B&B, amazed, watching the smoke drift out to sea and marveling at the hard-won bodies of knowledge in a dozen disciplines—mathematics, metallurgy, physics, propulsion, chemistry, computer science, rocketry, robotics, astronomy—that had to be laminated together over centuries to pull off that feat, and pondering the costly trials and errors, the lives devoted and sometimes sacrificed, the interlinkings of science and politics. All of it was powered by insatiable curiosity and indomitable passion.

I also thought about my father, who lit those very fires in me with his enthusiasm for science and discovery and his sense of wonder, and who would love to have seen that sight.

Vital Signs is about striking a match to your exuberance and vitality, and discovering what passions give you reason to get out of bed in the morning, if not run outside in your bare feet.

1

Eyes Wide Open

Cultivating Wonder

Let us worship the spine and its tingle.

—VLADIMIR NABOKOV

YEARS AGO I SAW the Italian tenor Luciano Pavarotti perform with the Cincinnati Opera—not because I like opera, but because I wanted to see Pavarotti, the most popular classical artist in the history of the recording industry and a member, along with Plácido Domingo and José Carreras, of the great operatic triumvirate the Three Tenors, all believed to be the best of that generation.

It was a packed house, and at the end of the concert, I witnessed something I'd never seen before, not even at a Rolling Stones or Michael Jackson concert: a ten-minute standing ovation, complete with thunderous chandelier-shaking applause, high-pitched whistles, and inarticulate howls. The tuxedoed gentleman with a distinguished white beard sitting next to me grabbed onto the back of the velvet-upholstered chair in front of him and jumped up and down like a madman, with both of his feet leaving the ground at the same time. People were delirious. Inflamed. Very nearly a mob.

Even without a working knowledge of opera or much of a basis for comparison, it was impossible not to recognize that Pavarotti's voice was heart-stoppingly beautiful, like nothing I'd heard in my life, and his presence like that of a great matador. And this level of mastery, of beauty and charisma, is absolutely bewitching, has us jumping up and down in our wingtips and tuxedos in stark contrast to our dignified breeding. We find ourselves recapitulating the fate of Actaeon, a hunter who spied the goddess Artemis, queen of the beasts, bathing naked in the forest, and upon being discovered was turned into a stag. We become so seized by beauty and awe that we're struck speechless, and all we can do is stamp and bray.

In her book *Cultivating Delight*, Diane Ackerman describes a stone in her front courtyard, beneath a hawthorn tree, which has the word "Wonder" carved into it. Next to it is another stone, carved with the words "Carpe Diem"—seize the day. "Two faces of the same thought," she says. Wonder and passion are a binary star, intimately orbiting each other, and together exerting a unique gravitational force. Sometimes we seize the moment, and sometimes it seizes us.

In *Blue Arabesque*, the author Patricia Hampl describes how she was hurrying to meet a friend at the Art Institute of Chicago's cafeteria, and though she was running late, she was stopped in her tracks by a painting she saw in her peripheral vision, a Matisse called *Woman Before an Aquarium*. But, she says, "I didn't halt, didn't stop. I was stopped. Apprehended, even. . . . I was simply fastened there."

This is one of the features of wonder: it's gripping. You're stopped in your tracks, riveted to the spot, your gaze held. Consider the lingo of the awestruck: *spellbound, captivated, transfixed, rapt in wonder, entranced, arrested, stunned, mesmerized,* and at the further extremes, *petrified*. The world swirls by you, a river around a rock. Your workaday life is forgotten—appointments, deadlines, to-do lists, a friend waiting for you in the cafeteria.

But this is not captivation as imprisonment. It's a moment when being apprehended sets you free, a moment that steps out from the march of time and unclasps you from the commonplace.

There is, of course, no universally agreed-upon checklist of awe-inspiring experiences. You either swoon at the opera or the art museum or you don't. You either get worked up about feats of engineering and groundbreaking new theories or you don't. Your mouth either drops open when you watch a baseball player pitch a perfect game or it doesn't.

I remember years ago listening to a radio interview with Bill James, the guy who created *Baseball Abstracts*, a mind-boggling statistical evaluation of Major League Baseball. He referred to statistics that could put an actuary into a coma as "living poetry" and said it was "a poetry that marches to the even drumbeat of Pete Rose's .310 .310 .310 or relaxes in the stressed and unstressed syllables of Willie Davis strolling through his prime in trochaic indifference."

Obviously, wonder isn't something that happens out there, but *in here*; a function of the observer, not the event. Yet the experience of wonder is universal and speaks of our hunger to be *moved*, to be engaged and impassioned with the world, to take pleasure in it, to be attuned to it, and to be fascinated by it. To be grateful for it.

Wonder is both a response and a stimulus. It's our reaction to being moved, and it's our *desire* for it. Our desire to feel radically alive rather than bored and disinterested or so caught up in the toils and troubles of daily life that we miss out on its multitudes of marvels. It's our desire to part the curtain and get a load of the grander scheme, from what's around the next corner to epiphanies about the nature of things. And it asks us to continually turn the stones in our own yards in search of these enlivening moments.

I was sitting at my desk one recent overcast afternoon when just such a moment was spliced into my day. A pinhole opened in the cloud cover, and a bolt of sun suddenly spotlighted a patch of dark mountain on the far side of the valley. It caught my eye, and I heard myself say, "Whoa" (yet another expression of stoppage).

The taxonomy of wonder begins here, with the mere tickle, with surprise and puzzlement as cheap thrills, and it moves through the jolt and the jar, the gape and the gawk, the boggle, the epiphany, and finally to the awe that's four-fifths terror—watching a tornado bearing down, scuba diving while sharks circle around you, or seeing the ground rolling in waves during an earthquake, as my mother once did near Mexico City, forever undermining her trust in terra firma.

So along this spectrum from simple arousal to holy terror, "Whoa" is a fairly modest claim to wonder. But it shows up on the radar screen—shows that my old brain is lighting up properly when nerve cells in my eyes register something moving against a still background. It shows that the sense of wonder is to some degree biologically driven, a survival instinct related to surprise and curiosity and an investigative scanning of the environment—all subsets of the urge to explore.

Like any good animal with a functioning startle reflex, we're tuned to respond strongly to unexpected and anomalous intrusions into our environment, anything from bolts of light and rustlings in the undergrowth to earthquakes, avalanches, shooting stars, synchronicities, and snow in summer.

Unlike most animals, we're also inclined to deliberately seek out anomalies, if not enchantment and astonishment, and this impulse needs regular maintenance and retuning lest we slip into a state of passivity. I recently traveled partway around the world to sit slack-jawed in front of the only mountain I've ever seen move. My twin brother, Ross, and I went to the highlands of Costa Rica, and one afternoon we sat at the foot of Arenal Volcano—fastened and fascinated, binoculars glued to our faces for five straight hours—close enough to see and hear enormous boulders hurtling down the mountainside, jarred loose by lava pushing out from inside. Many of them were the size of washing machines or Dumpsters and glowing red-hot, each a giant ember.

It was unusual to see the mountain at all, given the sombrero of clouds that normally hangs over its upper reaches, but that day we saw a constant avalanche of blazing boulders, which, on their way down the five-thousand-foot mountain, picked up so much speed that they bounced in arcs of one hundred or two hundred feet, every bounce kicking up a violent plume of dust and ash.

Wonder sets itself over and against the still background of daily life, the routine and orderly, the familiar and predictable—those unravelers of awe—and even against the endless irritations of life that tend to build up our calluses and desensitize us to its marvels.

At the end of Hermann Hesse's novel *Steppenwolf,* the protagonist gets a drubbing from the ghost of Mozart, one of his heroes, who plays for him Handel's *Concerto Grosso in F Major* on the radio and chides him for his tormented reaction to the music's disfigurement by the horrid little instrument. Mozart challenges him to find the spirit of Handel's divine music behind the tinny distortion and to continually seek the beauty and sublimity of the world despite its noxious intrusions.

To live passionately, the painter Pierre Bonnard once said, is one of the basic human desires and an artistic necessity. "What I wanted, at all costs," he said, "was to escape the monotony of life."

This isn't to denigrate monotony altogether. A certain amount of it is an earthly requirement. Before life will come forth, before it will take root or take wing, it has to have some guarantee of nature's stability. And nature largely cooperates. It's mostly steadfast, its laws administered with an even hand and its changes delivered by slow drip. This makes it safer to come out of the shell, the sea, the cave, or the ground, knowing that the laws of light and gravity, the proportions of chemistry, and the ground beneath your feet will stay the course long enough for you to do your business and get back to the burrow by nightfall.

For some, the very reliability of it all is the wonder. It's not the exception but the rule that astonishes—the regular and orderly. The fourteenth-century theologian Nicole Oresme, commenting on what were then called "monstrous births" (conjoined twins, hermaphrodites, and the like), professed that it's considerably more amazing how often nature does *not* fail in the staggeringly complicated business of manufacturing a human being than how often it does fail.

Still, in an age when so many people can, with the push of a button, offset the inconveniences of nature—for instance, being cold, dark, wet, hungry—as well as avoid those intrusions of the anomalous that actually help keep us on our toes, wonder acts as a kind of backup generator to restimulate our interest in the world.

It's a corrective for the conventional and habitual, for the fact that day-to-day life offers so few helpings of raw experience, of intensity and aliveness, and of novelty, which is really as close as digging a rock out of the ground and cracking it in half. You'd be the first human being ever to lay eyes on the inside of that rock, and it would be the first time the inside of that rock had ever seen the light of the sun.

Even when life *does* offer a heaping platter of raw experience, wonder is still easily curbed by convention and conformity, and our uprisings of enthusiasm are routinely put down by the need to go by the book. The first man on the moon, for example, was so busy making sure that such a Great Moment in History was treated with—pardon the expression—gravity that his awe was scripted into oblivion. It was left to the second man on the moon to express the wonder of the place itself: "Beautiful. Beautiful." he said. "Magnificent desolation."

But it was the third guy who *really* captured it: "Whoopee!"

Becoming Adult-erated

One winter several years ago, I conducted a weekend Callings retreat at a conference center in western Massachusetts, and when I arrived, I found out that there was another retreat being offered there the same weekend, on the subject of tracking. The two retreats, it turned out, were essentially about the same subject: the search for signs. In the other retreat, attendees were seeking signs indicating the presence of animals. In my retreat, we were seeking signs indicating the presence of callings.

We shared meals together in the dining hall, so I had a chance to talk with the participants from the tracking retreat over the course of the weekend, and what struck me most was how excited they were just about the *signs* of the animals, not even the animals themselves. Frankly, they never even *saw* the animals—it was the middle of winter in Massachusetts, for one thing—but I've never seen a group of grown-ups so excited about the subject of poop in my entire life.

I found this inspiring, though, and shared it with the people in my own retreat. If we can cultivate that quality of enthusiasm just for the hunt, I told them, just for the act of tracking our lives, paying attention to them, approaching them with wonder and curiosity, our lives are bound to reveal things to us that they won't reveal if we're not interested. They simply won't give up their secrets if we don't offer them some devoted curiosity.

And animal tracks are like signs of any kind: they lead to something. In his book *The Tracker,* Tom Brown Jr. says, "A first track is the end of a string. At the far end, a being is moving, a mystery that leaves itself like a trail of breadcrumbs, and by the time your mind has eaten its way to the maker of the tracks, the mystery is inside you."

The psychologist Abraham Maslow considered fascination the simplest version of the peak experience, and the kind of fascination that propels our enthusiasm for the hunt is akin to the mind-set of wonder that Buddhists call beginner's mind: one of profound innocence and openness, even if you think you've seen it all. It's a mind-set that views life as if through the eyes of a child, who eagerly sits in the splash zone at the killer whale show, keeps a mind open for business and a runway cleared at all times for incoming adventure, and hasn't yet learned the grossly overrated art of being cool and nonchalant, of being the knower rather than the wonderer.

Unfortunately, it's easy to become "adult-erated" and thus spoiled for the world, to lose the attitude of *youthfulness*, while the pleasures and enthusiasms we keep from ourselves turn to sorrows that eventually find their way to the eyes and mouth and set their heavy sacks down there.

It's an attitude that's often lost on youths themselves. I see it regularly at colleges around the country where I present Callings seminars—old people of twenty who seem to have passed through the membrane from youth to adulthood with little of their joie de vivre intact. They've lost much of their sparkle and initiative and ceased demanding great things of themselves, or even interesting things. And they often seem frozen in the headlights of having to declare a major, choose a vocation, make a living, and generally face the stern exigencies of an uncertain future, in the process of which they suffer precocious senility and become prematurely arthritic in their outlook on life.

A grown-up is often just the husk left over at the end of childhood.

Astronomer Carl Sagan once described the difference between visiting a kindergarten class and a high school class to talk about science. The kindergartners were avidly curious, endlessly enthusiastic, and natural-born scientists who had never heard of a dumb question. The high schoolers were jaded, the joy of discovery and the sense of wonder largely lost to them. And they were terrified of asking a dumb question.

According to *Newsweek*, research shows that preschool children ask their parents an average of a hundred questions a day—"cries to understand the world," Sagan said—which of course would test the patience of even the most committed parent or teacher. Often, the adults simply wish it would stop, and unfortunately for the children, it does. By middle school, they've largely stopped asking questions, which, not coincidentally, corresponds with a sharp decline in their sense of motivation and engagement.

And often their mental health. According to a Hofstra University study, young people who are immersed in activities and have a passion to help others tend to be more grateful, more hopeful, and happier, and to report higher life satisfaction, self-esteem, and grade point averages.

THE REASONS WHY CHILDREN'S enthusiasm for learning and discovery and their spirit of wonder often devolve into a sense of passionless duty to achieve and comply are complicated. Some reasons are social and bureaucratic, some personal and parental. But none of them are developmental. The passion for learning doesn't naturally wane as we get older. Something gets in the way.

Actually, it's a multitude of somethings: the social value placed on short-term gratification, the challenge of competing with internet attention spans, low expectations, the substitution of internal motivation for grade-grubbing, the sense of irrelevance and meaninglessness that teenagers often feel toward what's being taught, a grading system that makes many students feel like they're second-rate learners, and an environment where submissiveness and lack of power are the norm, which includes the atmosphere of physical and emotional bullying so common in schools, and in adolescence.

For teachers, there are also forces aplenty that undermine passion and ideals: administrators who prefer to run classrooms from the front office, skeptical fellow teachers, standardized tests that don't take the individual into account, indifferent parents, disruptive students, increasing class sizes, and decreasing funding.

Despite all this, though, and aside from the nearly limitless tactical options available for helping kids stay engaged in learning, Robert L. Fried in *The Passionate Learner* argues for the meta-practice of taking a *"stance"* toward kids by which we view them as naturally enthusiastic learners. This will make us look for and encourage their will to learn, which many kids display far more readily outside school than in the classroom.

Fried relates the story of how the principal at his son's high school once sat down with a group of graduating seniors and asked them to tell her where in their lives they worked the hardest and did their best thinking. They listed their jobs, hobbies, music, sports, friendships, and volunteer activities. None of them mentioned school. Their *independent* learning was more spirited than what they were exhibiting inside the classroom.

"Teachers are amazed to discover, in students from whom they see very little as far as classwork or homework is concerned, the energy and discipline that those same kids put into taking apart a car in the family garage and putting it back together; or serving as assistant manager at a local fast-food restaurant; or organizing a charity drive for a church; or putting together a band, finding a place to practice, and getting gigs," Fried writes. "What teachers get to see, mostly, is not students' enterprise and enthusiasm, but their compliance or lack thereof."

And don't dismiss these involvements as extracurricular activities that students choose to participate in, Fried says. Academic rigor is also a choice. "Students *choose* to absorb, or to repel, the instruction we offer them."

To captivate students and instill in them the kind of wonder that leads to wondering, which leads to curiosity, which leads to knowledge and sometimes wisdom, educator Kerry Ruef developed The Private Eye, a curriculum program designed to encourage those mental habits central to the scientist and the artist: wide-eyed looking, thinking by analogy, and a sense of the mysterious, which Einstein considered "the most beautiful thing we can experience" and the source of all true art and science.

The Private Eye—as in both investigative and physiological—aims to trigger what Kerry calls "the little explosions of excitement" that are the experience of wonder and "the fizz in the mind" that helps arouse the passion for exploration and learning, which so often get knocked off the rails early on.

Her motive is to "rescue the brain" and invite it back to what it was doing "before it was interrupted by being made wrong, by the control of unimaginative institutions and teachers, who are not famously investigative, by too much rote memorization and regurgitation of facts, and by the distractions of daily life—all of which cause a massive depression to settle in by around third grade, in both students and teachers."

Piloted twenty years ago in the Seattle public schools, Kerry's "intervention" has by now been shared with several million students across the country; tens of thousands of teachers; more than fifty universities, which use it in their science-methods courses; and museums, which offer it as educational outreach.

Its tools are simple. It begins with close observation of anything, from seeds and sponges to the palm of your hand, using a jeweler's loupe, which not only cuts out peripheral vision—i.e., distractions—so that people can concentrate but also, by magnifying the world, helps to make it a little strange, subtly breaking down expectations and stereotypes.

Specimens are then further magnified, and the imagination further stretched, by the posing of a simple question: What does it remind you of? What else? What else? What else? This introduces thinking by analogy, the main tool of the inventive mind. A third grader in one of Kerry's classes, louping a seahorse, turned her answers into a poem: "Seahorses / like spines on a blackberry bush / cobwebs in a cave of bats / like a swiggly lizard smoking a cigar / like the skeleton of a giraffe."

Follow-up questions include "Why is it like that?" and "If it reminds me of X, might it function like that too?" Both of these introduce people to the scientific method: theorizing and testing your theories. If the surface of a leaf reminds you of hair or fur, might it function in the same way, and how might you test that hypothesis?

First, Kerry says, students are "visually wowed." Then they begin to make connections, find unexpected likenesses, make guesses, and test them. And all of it amplifies and prolongs the wonder, and expresses what Kerry calls "the native language of the brain. The natural sequence is from wonder to wondering and back, and it's a self-reinforcing pleasure."

Not that it doesn't benefit from external reinforcement and role-modeling. In fact, the zest for learning is encouraged when teachers and parents approach children as learning *partners*, not just as buckets in which to dump their credos and curricula. As the poet William Butler Yeats once said, education is not the filling of a pail, but the lighting of a fire.

In teaching kids about the natural world, for instance, biologist Rachel Carson, in *The Sense of Wonder*, suggests that adults adopt the child's viewpoint and not expect the child to adopt theirs. Don't go around naming everything and testing the child on what he or she has learned. Don't bury the world under a load of facts and explanations. Minimize the teaching and explaining, she counsels. Approach the world with senses and emotions more than thinking and analyzing—a sense of the beautiful, an excitement for the new and unknown, a feeling of sympathy, fellowship, respect, and love, and the kind of awe and humility that prompted the Nobel Prize–winning physicist Richard Feynman to proclaim, "Nothing is 'mere'!"

Skillful teachers find ways of meeting not only the schools' but also the students' learning goals, which start with their being respected—for who they are and what they know, what's important to them, and what they're capable of. Granted, respect is a two-way street, but *we* go first. It's the grown-ups who start the ball rolling in that department. Or don't.

This requires power sharing, which isn't usually on the menu in teacher-centered classrooms and top-down organizations. "But a class might agree on the rule that if you feel bored and want to stop doing something that other people (including the teacher) think is important," Fried says, "then you must take responsibility for coming up with an activity at least as challenging.

"Another rule might state that if at least half the class feels an activity is boring (after trying it for a while), the teacher should ask for suggestions from the kids on how to make it more interesting and worthwhile."

One third-grade teacher Fried interviewed said this: "In science, with the topic of 'sound,' I tell the kids that we're going to study sound because we're supposed to, but that they get to decide what we actually *learn* about it. . . . '*You* are the designers of this unit,' I tell them. 'We'll learn the things that you are interested in.'"

Another teacher, working up a unit on the period in history during which America was settled by Europeans, made it relevant and meaningful to his sixth-grade class—mostly Asian American and African American kids—by having them trace the history of their own family's arrival in Boston, thus drawing the connection between their family's particular emigration and that of earlier settlers, which brought the subject to life for them in a way textbook learning couldn't and culminated in a community presentation before a large audience of parents.

It's a potent motivator to give kids the opportunity to share their work with real audiences, give them real jobs to do, ways to apply their classroom learning to challenges in their own communities. A chemistry teacher might challenge her students to create a pamphlet on good nutrition to be placed in doctors' waiting rooms. A high-school Spanish teacher could help her students overcome their shyness about using the language by having them teach it to elementary school kids. An English teacher might decide that every major writing assignment should have an audience outside the school, in the form of writing letters to the editor, or complaints to manufacturers about shoddy products, or stories written about significant people in their own family history or community.

The history teacher described his class to Fried as "electric with energy, the kids' hands shooting up in response to every question, eager to argue every point, ask questions, seek clarity, and tackle an academic challenge of real magnitude." And as for why the atmosphere in that class was filled with little explosions of excitement, it starts with that particular teacher's own passion for both the students and the subject matter—"Passion is cool"—and the fact that he never made it a secret that his class was all about kids becoming *powerful*, through the use of their minds and the development of their intellect.

"The kids reflect that vision," the teacher said, "in the way they use words like *perspective* and *voice* and *stereotype* and *ignorance*, in the way they applaud respectfully when a student says something they think is especially intelligent, and in the way they act so unself-consciously about using their minds in class."

Keeping the Fires Burning

It probably isn't lost on kids, either, the degree to which we *ourselves*, as their role models, are engaged in independent learning outside our own nine-to-five lives. Do *we* remain interested and involved in the issues of the day? Do we read books though there are no tests to take, sign up for adult-ed class, or even just look up unfamiliar words in the dictionary?

The fact is, *our* enthusiasm is critical to the development of *theirs*. I remember my father telling me, as I headed off to college, that I'd be better off choosing professors than courses, because those who were passionate about what they taught could make even the driest subject come to life, and me along with it.

What makes the biggest difference in the quality of the learning experience for students is a teacher's passion, says Fried. "More than knowledge of subject matter, more than variety of teaching techniques, more than being well organized or friendly or funny or fair. Passion. Passionate people are the ones who make a difference in our lives."

But when we as teachers and parents, coaches and mentors, are no longer learning, we're no longer teaching, because we've left behind the ability to role-model the art of discovery, the love of learning and being intellectually active. We no longer help students become "hunter-gatherers of insights, just passive consumers of pre-packaged information," as Fried puts it.

We lose the ability to inspire by example. We can still palm off information, but it's once removed from the true purpose of education, which is to bring out the passion for learning, not just shove in the data, which will begin to fade from memory the moment the test is over. As the philosopher Alfred North Whitehead once said, "The justification for university is that it preserves the connection between knowledge and the zest for life."

The commitment to being a lifelong learner is thus critical to sustaining passion in our children and in ourselves, because it keeps us engaged with life over the long haul. In fact, we're more likely to *have* a long haul if we stay engaged, since we're more likely to want to stick around if we take a keen interest in life.

And we're more likely to be successful. For his best-selling book, *The Corner Office*, Adam Bryant, a columnist for the *New York Times*, interviewed over seven hundred leading American CEOs and asked them, "What qualities do you see most often in those who succeed?" Number one on their collective lists: "passionate curiosity."

By nurturing curiosity, the world becomes endlessly fascinating, with dolls inside of dolls inside of dolls, and you realize—not with dismay but anticipation—that you understand almost none of it, a fraction of a fraction. Even many of the things you encounter every day, you barely fathom. Why does your skin wrinkle in the bathtub? How do spiders avoid getting tangled in their own webs? What holds clouds up if water is heavier than air?

When you're a lifelong learner, you take nothing for granted. You're always poking into things and wondering what makes it all tick. You're on intimate terms with search engines, consider ignorance bliss because it's the beginning of discovery, and continually remind yourself that the world is dynamic, not static, and that you're a part of the world.

You understand that education isn't something that stops when you receive a diploma, that learning doesn't have to culminate in a test, and that boredom in school isn't necessarily your fault (even if you *are* part of the Snapchat generation), though it *is* your responsibility, especially as an adult, to address in your life the meaningless and tedious, the routine and repetitive—all those activities that lead to boredom, which author Saul Bellow described as "the pain of unused powers, the pain of wasted possibilities or talents." Boredom that, for adults as surely as for high school students, has them cutting class and dropping out.

It's only under the pressing thumb of age that some of us manage to come around again to a beginner's mind, holding life up to the light like a color slide and appreciating the precious ordinariness of the world. It's only then that many of us blessedly cease to care what others think of us, and once again are able to enjoy little or no distinction between the private self and the public self, be charmed by the simplest things, and feel at home in the present, like rabbits and foxes.

In *A Private History of Awe*, Scott Russell Sanders says that we enter the world empty of ideas and full of sensation, and if we live long enough to lose memory and language, we'll leave the world the same way. But in between, he says, we should aspire to be like small children who, when they aren't asleep, are utterly awake, with all instruments turned on.

But this is challenging, given some of the ground rules for grown-ups: the ways we're expected to act, the behaviors that, were we children, wouldn't elicit so much as a batted eye from others but that in grown-ups are considered strange, even suspect. I remember the astonishment I felt during one of my first assignments for the *Cincinnati Enquirer*, a story about the Kenner toy company, which was headquartered there. As I was being escorted into the back offices to meet the production manager of its new *Star Wars* line of toys, we passed a couple of guys in suits and ties who were down on their hands and knees in the hallway, playing with toy rockets, toy robots, and toy cars. They were even making explosion, acceleration, and screeching-brake noises. Which probably shouldn't have surprised me, given that these were employees of a company whose corporate mascot was something called Gooney Bird.

Years later, shortly after moving to North Carolina, I was walking along an old dirt road near my house when I stopped to admire a big open pasture surrounded by forest. A man pulled up in a pickup truck, with the name of a company printed on the door, and asked, "What are you looking at?" Intuition told me he had some proprietary relationship to the pasture, and he gave me the clear impression that he thought it odd that a man would stop to stare at an empty meadow.

"I'm looking at North Carolina," I said, explaining that I'd just moved from southern Arizona, where there are no green meadows and no forests, and that they were novelties to me. I tried to sound innocent, and then tried not to sound like I was trying to sound innocent.

He seemed satisfied with my answer and drove off. I turned back to my reverie. A few minutes later I heard a car pull to a stop behind me and a voice ask, "What are you looking at?" I let out a short burst of a laugh, made up of equal parts humor and exasperation, and as I swung around, I said, "You're the second person . . ." It was a police officer. I figured the first fellow wasn't, after all, entirely satisfied with my answer. But I repeated it, almost verbatim, and he, too, drove off.

One arena in which I continually work to re-up my beginner's mind, despite the odds, is in the willingness to be clueless. I like being the knower as much as the next guy, and don't particularly relish looking foolish, but I seldom pass up the opportunity to ask a question when I don't know the answer and want to, even when it makes my companions squirm. Questions are my stock in trade as a reporter and as a teacher, and my father long ago taught me that without questions, there's no discovery; and without discovery, there's no learning.

Earlier this year, for instance, I watched the Super Bowl with some friends and kept asking questions whose answers were apparently obvious to others: Are they allowed to grab onto each other's clothing? Why are some fumbles pounced on and others avoided? Why do they frown on dancing in the end zone after scoring a touchdown? Afterward, one friend said she felt embarrassed for me, asking such clearly amateurish questions in front of a bunch of football fanatics, and I couldn't imagine why. It seems to me there's no shame in not knowing something, even if some wrongheaded gender decree says that real men are supposed to know about sports, cars, and power tools, none of which are subjects with which I'm conversant. It actually didn't enter my mind that others might be judging me for knowing jack about football, and even if they did, it would have nothing whatsoever to do with *me*.

Most of those watching the football game with me that night don't know much about *writing*, but I wouldn't think to judge them for it. For that matter, most people don't know much about *most* things, given the sheer variety of subjects there are to know about in this world.

Certainly, many of those who attend my Callings workshops around the country are faced with the need to cultivate cluelessness, because many of them are baby boomers who've spent twenty to thirty years in some line of business that no longer works for them, and come midlife, other parts of them want airtime—often passions or talents they've sidelined in making the choices they made.

After doing anything for twenty or thirty years, you're going to have gained a measure of mastery in it; a sense of competence, identity, and stability; a network of colleagues; a regular paycheck; a lifestyle to which you've become accustomed and perhaps would like to *remain* accustomed. And it can be a stinker to be a rookie again and have to start from scratch in a whole new arena, to ask the most basic questions. And without the willingness to be clueless—and a hardy commitment to growth—you're not likely to do what your life is calling you to do, and your passions will likely remain benched.

THE MAN WHO TAUGHT the tracking workshop at the Massachusetts conference center, Paul Rezendes, was called toward just such a turnaround in his life—though *commanded* is probably a better word. It was a vocational redirection that took him from being the leader of a motorcycle gang to being an animal tracker and spiritual teacher, a journey that began with and returned to the cultivation of beginner's mind.

As Rachel Carson says about cultivating a sense of wonder, every child needs at least one adult with whom to share the experience of nature, and for Paul, that adult was his mother. "She was my first teacher in the language of nature, who took me into the woods near my house as soon as I could walk and taught me a sensitivity to all living things and a wonder at creation. The forest became the scene of many of my childhood adventures, but also the setting for the beginning of my spiritual search, and where I started questioning what my place was in all this beauty."

Unfortunately, the mind-set that had him going about in a state of wonder and compassion, all bright-eyed and bushy-tailed, was sufficient to get him beat up on the playground with some regularity. So he did what most of us do under such circumstances—he shut down. His bright eyes narrowed and his bushy tail got tucked between his legs.

"Boys have to demonstrate how tough they are, so if I ran across a group of boys torturing a frog or something, my brother was smart enough to keep his mouth shut, but I spoke up. And I'd get called a sissy and get beat up. So eventually I turned my back on the truth and learned how not to object, how to fit in, how to be tough, how not to care. I just went to an extreme."

He became the leader of a motorcycle gang he started in Fall River, Massachusetts, called the Huns, which eventually became a chapter of the Devil's Diciples (the misspelling intentional, according to their website, "so as to distance ourselves from religious affiliation"—on the incredibly off chance that someone might actually be confused). For ten years, starting in the early 1960s, Paul led what he describes as "a violent, criminal life." But it was a kind of double life too. "I was a gangbanger and notorious street fighter who meditated and read Socrates on the sly, who talked about the psychological self, cosmic consciousness, egoic structures, and wholeness."

It was also a life that caught up with him when he got busted for possession of an illegal firearm and three shopping bags full of marijuana, intent to sell. But it was his ticket out. Motorcycle gangs are like the Mafia, he said. You need a damn good reason to leave. And the prospect of a prison sentence (suspended) gave him a reason his fellow gang members could understand—the need to lay low.

Thus the considerable effort required to reactivate his sense of wonder and his beginner's mind began, as personal growth so often does, with a crisis. "Heroes ain't born," Redd Foxx once said. "They're cornered."

When Paul first came out of gang life, he turned to the Catholicism of his youth, which isn't the contradiction it would seem. "They're both authoritarian systems. It's just spiritual pride instead of machismo pride."

Then, on the recommendation of a friend, he became, of all things, a Hatha Yoga teacher, founding two ashrams over the course of ten years, which ended when he discovered his wife having an affair with one of his students.

Eventually he found his way back to the woods. "It's the one thing that never left me, or that I never left, and that kept me connected to any kind of sanity." Following the tracks of animals, he said, "I began to synthesize the lessons of nature and spirituality that would direct the rest of my life."

Out of his experience of trading one wild life for another, gangbanging for animal tracking, he wrote a book called *The Wild Within*, a quality he refers to as "the larger sense of who we are," and whose tracks we obliterate with our ideas and images of who we *think* we are, or need to be, and with the continual lapses in attention that put us out of touch with ourselves and our surroundings, with the Maker of the Tracks, and with the core instruction all spiritual traditions teach to those wishing to fulfill their potential: Sit down and shut up. Be quiet and listen. Be still and know.

It's the primary mandate and meditation in Paul's tracking and stalking classes: pay attention. To every footfall, every breath, every sound you make, every nuance of landscape, wind, and light. Move from the realm of thought to the realm of senses, from the mind of the tracker to the mind of the animal—the coyote silently following the deer through fresh snow, the deer snapping to attention at the slightest shift of wind that brings with it the smell of coyote; the hawk eyeing the rabbit from above, the rabbit watching for the shadow of the hawk, whose shape it can distinguish, on the ground, from that of every other bird.

Tapping into the larger sense of who you are requires paying heed to your environment with a Sensurround wakefulness, Paul says. It requires taking an interest in the world again, and in yourself. Whether you're in the forest, the office, or the street, he says, stop once in a while, stand very still like a tree or a lamppost or a hunter, and just observe. What you're after is a moment when your mind isn't elsewhere, a moment when—especially for you urban guerrillas and concrete-jungle animals—you step out from behind that protective bubble of "Don't mess with me."

Stand on a street corner while waiting for the light to change and listen to the rumble of engines; the rattle of tailpipes; and to car radios, sirens, the Doppler effect of passing jets, honking horns, shoes hitting pavement, snippets of a dozen conversations, the sizzle of burning tobacco in someone's cigarette, a shout, a laugh, a baby's cry, a car door slamming, the banging of lumber at a construction site, the screeching of tires—little of which you truly hear until you stop and notice how much you tune out, pulling your collar up around your senses.

With this level of awareness, Paul says, you're keenly attentive to the world—once again—alive to the subtlest movements within and without, to the demands of this moment and the possibilities of the next. And with it, you're back in touch with the world and your place in all this beauty.

The Envy of Angels: Everyday Awe

Try designing a system capable of suspending a billion pounds of water in midair with no strings attached.

It's called a cloud, and someone who'd never seen one would undoubtedly find it fascinating. But try working up enthusiasm for clouds when you've lived with them every day of your life and forgotten—or more likely, never knew—how amazing it is that even a modest-size cloud, an "everyday" cloud like a cumulus a half mile high and wide, weighs as much as 3,500 747s at 400,000 pounds each (empty), almost 1.5 billion pounds total, according to the U.S. Geological Survey. A good-size cumulonimbus cloud, a thunderhead five or six miles on each side—an everyday summer cloud in, say, New Mexico—weighs nearly 14 billion pounds. One cloud.

Even the word *billion* is just another everyday thing. The McDonald's near my house proclaims, "Billions and billions sold." But if you counted off one number every second, day and night, it would take you thirty-two years to count to a billion. It would take you twelve days just to count to a million. And even if you had literally all the time in the world, the entire age of the universe, you couldn't count to a quintillion, which would take you thirty-two billion years.

It's axiomatic that we should try to find wonder in our own backyards, should learn to re-sacralize the world by falling back in love with the ordinary and everyday. But the everyday is actually the *hardest* place to find wonder and to become re-impassioned about, because its wonders have usually long since been drained away by familiarity.

To overcome the anesthetic effect of familiarity with ordinary things, to look with renewed wonder at something you've looked at a thousand times—your own body, the sky, your kid—thereby turning the commonplace uncommon again, what's usually required, to paraphrase Marcel Proust, isn't new vistas but new eyes. And those eyes don't even have to be yours. You can reintroduce yourself to the charms of your town by seeing it through the eyes of a visitor and to the wonders of the world through the eyes of your children. You can look at your husband through the eyes of another woman, your wife through the eyes of another man.

Those eyes don't even have to be mortal. In the Wim Wenders film *Wings of Desire*, the story unfolds through the eyes of a couple of middle-age angels in trench coats who've spent eternity witnessing but not partaking of human life. One day, one angel says to the other: "It's great to live only by the spirit. . . . But sometimes I get fed up with my spiritual existence. Instead of forever hovering above, I'd like to feel there's some weight to me, to end my eternity and bind me to the earth. At each step, each gust of wind, I'd like to be able to say 'Now.' 'Now and now' and no longer say 'since always' and 'forever.'"

This being bound to Earth, all the particulars of earthly life that unfold in the now and the now are what makes us human and, from the angel's point of view, enviable.

In another scene, the angel comes upon a man who's just had a terrible motorcycle accident and is dying, and to comfort him recites in his ear all the particular things the man has loved in life: "The fire on the cattle range, the potato in the ashes, the boathouse floating in the lake, the Southern Cross, the Far East, the Great North, the Wild West, the Great Bear Lake, Tristan de Cunha, the Mississippi Delta, Stromboli, the old houses of Charlottenburg, Albert Camus, the morning light, the child's eyes, the swim in the waterfall, the stains from the first raindrops, the sun, the bread and wine, hopping, Easter, the veins of the leaves, the color of stones, the pebbles on the stream bed, the white tablecloths outdoors, the dream of a house inside the house, the loved one asleep in the next room, the peaceful Sunday, the horizon, the night flight, riding a bicycle with no hands, the beautiful stranger, my father, my mother, my child."

You can also look at things from new angles. I recently went to the Smithsonian's National Air and Space Museum in Washington, D.C., and hanging next to the Wright brothers' airplane in the main lobby is the *Mercury* capsule that took John Glenn and his *Right Stuff* into man's first Earth orbit. But seeing the little cone-shape capsule, no bigger than a VW bug and surrounded by gawking tourists, was a little like watching the first *Star Wars* movie after thirty years of increasingly sophisticated special-effects films; it seemed primitive and even a little cheesy with its waxy astronaut mannequin inside.

But when I wandered around to the back side of the capsule, I saw something that took it *far* out of the realm of being merely a museum display. That side was blackened like burnt toast, and as I stared at it, I slowly realized that what I was looking at was the actual residue from its fiery reentry into Earth's atmosphere, and that this little canister, which could just as easily have become a casket, a crematorium, participated in one hell of a spectacle, to say nothing of the awesome vulnerability of the man inside.

Similarly, if you're watching a sunset—and what could be more common than a sunset—stare not at the sun, but at the earth, and you'll begin to make out what's *really* going on, which is not the sun setting but the earth rising, spinning hugely in space. You'll begin to make out its actual motion and remember that you live on a planet hanging in midair.

Anything familiar experienced in an unfamiliar *context* is also likely to be an enlivening anomaly. A scene in Vladimir Nabokov's novel *The Gift* describes a man crossing a street when, struck by a burst of light that ricochets off his temple, he sees a rectangle of sky being unloaded from a van—a dresser-with-mirror reflecting sky and trees "sliding and swaying not arboreally, but with a human vacillation." Here is the everyday sky, but in a wholly unusual and fleeting context, down here on the ground, being unloaded from a van.

Merely walking is suddenly made marvelous whenever I hit one of those moving sidewalks at the airport, with the wonderfully athletic sensation it gives me of instantly doubling my speed and seeing the scenery comparatively *fly* by.

Slowing down also does the trick. A few years ago, I spent a day by a small, crystal-clear pond nestled in a tiny granite bowl high in Northern California's Trinity Alps. The pond was perhaps a hundred feet long by thirty feet wide, and I could easily throw a stone from one end to the other. I decided to walk around the pond *really slowly*, a walking meditation, an experiment in seeing the world at a snail's pace. I took one step every minute, by my watch.

It took me three hours to get around that little lake. Normally it would have taken a couple of minutes. But I also felt like I really *saw* the place, and certainly saw the fibrillating restlessness and impatience inside me that occupied about half my time on that little stroll, and easily that much of my life in general; the needlings of a lifetime of being industrious, goal-oriented, and hyperactive. But I stuck with it. I saw flowers so small I would never have even noticed them on an ordinary walk, the peculiar geometries of rotting wood, the melting and dripping of leftover snow, birds—and thoughts—flitting by at what, from my glacial pace, seemed like supersonic speed.

And I remembered reading, in a book called *Wanderlust*, about a peculiar fashion in mid-nineteenth-century Paris, in which strollers sometimes took turtles for walks in the parks, the better to slow their pace and maximize the connoisseurship of their amblings.

After coming out of the mountains, I drove down to Santa Cruz to visit my brother Ross. One afternoon we sat at an outdoor cafe and watched a man who's locally famous for walking one of the town's main streets, Pacific Avenue, every day and very, very slowly, taking one baby step every five seconds or so. It can take him the better part of an afternoon to get from one end of the avenue to the other, barely half a dozen blocks, but I imagine he sees a lot of things that pass by the rest of us in a blur.

Ross told me that he once stopped to talk with the man, who used to be a NASA electrical engineer, and when Ross asked him what he does at intersections if the light changes while he's in middle of the street, the man shrugged and said, "I walk faster."

Sound, too, is utterly prosaic until you add a new element, like distance, whereupon it suddenly reveals a whole new facet: its speed. On Earth it's roughly Mach 1, 750 miles per hour, or a second to reach from ground level to the top of the Empire State Building.

Annie Dillard once described walking to the edge of the Sea of Galilee, in Israel, and seeing, across a cove, a man splitting wood. "I heard a wrong ring," she says, watching the man's ax clang at the top of his swing rather than the bottom. She continued to watch the distant, silhouetted figure. He drove the ax down again; she could see the wood split and drop to either side, but in silence. When he bent straight and raised the maul again with both arms, she heard it ring, "as if he was clobbering the heavens."

Talking to people on the phone is easy to take for granted until you get a phone call like the one I received from my older brother, Marc, while I was living in New Mexico: "Hi, which house is yours?"

"What?"

"This is Marc. I'm flying over Taos on my way to New York. Which house is yours?"

I ran outside and saw a jet flying high overhead, and tried to picture my brother's face pressed to the window, calling me quite literally from out of the blue.

Or you could just take a nap. After all, is there anything that rouses the imagination more than *sleep*, with its promise (or so neuroscience tells us) of half a dozen dreams a night? What novel or theater is equal to the phantasmagorical and allegorical empire of dreams, with their scenarios of wingless flight and talking animals? What movie or opera sets by your slippers every morning such tales of wonder and intrigue, in which your day-to-day perplexities are run through an outlandish costume shop, and your everyday conundrums are paraded around in startling metaphors? And how close to home all these hidden intelligences.

Another option is to pay a visit to somebody else's everyday life. Few things mollify the hunger for wonder like travel, through which we're immersed in discovery and launched into the learning curve. With a little disposable income, you can drive to the airport, park in the long-term lot, and get on a plane headed to someplace where no one knows your name, where the landscape, the language, and the constellations are all unfamiliar. A plane is taking off for such a place every few minutes of every day. You can find a menu on any international flight monitor: Cairo, Caracas, Istanbul, Kathmandu, Marrakech, Nairobi, Rangoon, Tangier, Timbuktu, Ulaanbaatar.

There are even places in the world whose names *alone* trigger flights of fantasy and an outbreak of wonder in the mind: the Spanish Steps, the Snows of Kilimanjaro, the Valley of the Kings, the Spice Islands, the Nile, the Left Bank, the South Seas, the West Indies, the Silk Road.

Ultimately, what we need to do is get out from behind the desk and the chores from time to time and create opportunities for our souls, wheezing like engines that won't turn over, to encounter wonder, to put ourselves in its path, and deliberately create a little estrangement from business as usual.

You might take a magnifying glass on your walks, or seek out displays of mastery and genius, or stop and stare whenever you enter grand lobbies and atriums, or get a season pass to a museum, or bookmark NASA's Astronomy Picture of the Day website (apod.nasa.gov), or listen to TED

Talks. Mostly it's a matter of figuring out what triggers wonder and awe in you, what fascinates you, and simply doing more of it.

The invariable mark of wisdom, Ralph Waldo Emerson said, is to see the miraculous in the commonplace, and anything that counters the tendency to take life for granted is an active ingredient in both wisdom and wonder, as is an appreciative bent toward life in general and the life you have in particular, and your willingness to be mystified and not need to pin down every butterfly. Just because we can pontificate in lengthy scientific treatises on the origin of the universe or the nature of DNA, just because we can trace the massive genealogy of consciousness and name God, doesn't make these phenomena any more commonplace, nor should it diminish the awe we feel about them. They're still fully functioning miracles.

Abraham Maslow, who popularized the term "self-actualization," didn't generally believe in a big bang theory of it, in which peak experiences suddenly bring us into being as the people we've always imagined ourselves to be or deliver us to transcendence on the back of some great white stallion of revelation. Toward the end of his life, he talked about a kind of time-release version of the peak experience that he called the *plateau* experience.

The plateau experience is a sort of ongoing peak experience that is more calm and less climactic, more a discipline than an event, and that we only slowly and painstakingly teach ourselves to experience by choosing to sacralize life. We witness it in the deepest and most mindful ways by paying exquisite attention to it, by exposing ourselves to inspiring people, great music and art, and the raptures of nature, and by living in a more or less permanent state of being turned on. Maslow called it "holding classes in miraculousness."

It is, of course, challenging to keep that love light burning when you're perpetually on the treadmill, and particularly when you're *suffering*—from illness, poverty, heartbreak, meaninglessness. Yes, there's fascination even in suffering. Dark nights of the soul and trials by fire are every bit as rich in it as days of wine and roses. Yes, the scope of life doesn't necessarily narrow just because you're confined to a sickbed or even a prison. The poet E.E. Cummings wrote a book called *The Enormous Room* while in jail. And yes, the way out of suffering is probably *through* rather than around. But it's asking a lot.

Still, looked at rightly, any item from your litany of complaints or your daily to-do list can potentially become a portal back to a sense of wonder if not sacredness—Zen and the art of doing the dishes, Zen and the art of being sick. David Steindl-Rast offers a beautiful example from his book *Gratefulness, the Heart of Prayer*: "Suppose, for example, you're reciting Psalms. If all goes well, this may be a truly prayerful experience. But all doesn't always go well. While reciting Psalms, you might experience nothing but a struggle against distractions. Half an hour later you are watering your African violets. Now, suddenly the prayerfulness that never came during the prayers overwhelms you. You come alive from within. Your heart expands and embraces those velvet leaves, those blossoms looking up to you. The watering and drinking become a give-and-take so intimate that you cannot separate your pouring of the water from the roots' receiving, the flower's giving of joy from your drinking it in. And in a rush of gratefulness your heart celebrates this belonging together. As long as this lasts, everything has meaning, everything makes sense. You are communicating with your full self, with all there is, with God. Which was the real prayer, the Psalms or the watering of your African violets?

"Wherever we come alive," Steindl-Rast says in another part of the book, "that is the area in which we are spiritual. To be vital, awake, aware, in all areas of our lives, is the task . . . and the goal."

WE REFER to the "sense of wonder" because the senses play such a vital role, and they have as impressive a scope as the wonders themselves. The naked eye, for instance, can see down into the microscopic realm, can actually make out certain of the amoebas, those single-celled protoplasmic shape-shifters that go by vaguely mythic names like Proteus and Pelomyxa, and which you can find in any backyard pond.

The naked eye can also see out to a distance of nearly three million light-years, out to the Triangulum Galaxy on a clear night far from the city. A *single* light-year being equivalent to almost six trillion miles—times three million—we're prodigiously farsighted.

But our senses are also limited. The human eye can see only a very narrow band of the world's available light—the visible being but a single octave in the full keyboard of the electromagnetic spectrum, which stretches from mile-long radio waves that would require eyes the size of satellite dishes to see, down to the staccato bursts of gamma rays. Still, within that narrow chink of discernible light is a stunning range of wonders, some of them way over our heads, and some right beneath our feet.

The beauty is that we can greatly extend our senses, and thus our apprehension of wonders and our passion for the world, by utilizing new *lenses*, and we have an arsenal at hand—magnifying glasses, binoculars, microscopes, telescopes, amplifiers, stethoscopes, cyclotrons, satellite dishes, radioscopes.

A simple magnifying glass can transform a sprinkling of sand on the palm into a field of boulders, and the bark of a tree into a maze of canyons. On my inaugural outing a few years ago with a new magnifying glass, which I now carry almost everywhere I go, I found one of the iridescent blue dragonflies that populate the forests in this part of the country expired in an abandoned spiderweb—a perfect opportunity to examine him up close, which I spent the next twenty minutes doing.

His finely veined black wings were tattered like the sails of a galleon ripped by cannon fire, his eyes the very definition of "bug-eyed"—two globes of compound eyes on either side of his head, like black billiard balls, the largest eyes in the insect world, with nearly thirty thousand individual facets, through which I would appear as a mosaic. He had three pairs of legs, two pairs of wings, and two pairs of genitalia, including a clasper at the back of his blue chassis for grabbing females by the neck during mating.

That same afternoon I used the magnifying glass to inspect spring flowers in my backyard—phlox, pansies, irises, lilies, fuchsias, azaleas, roses—like hundreds of Chagall paintings, Tiffany lamps, Kurosawa films, Einstein theorems, Neruda poems, Blakean visions, Fabergé eggs, and *effortlessly* brought to life, compared with the animal gruntings and flop sweat discharged by my own creative endeavors. I could spend a lifetime and never come up with anything of such drop-dead design and elegance as the simple velvet face of a flower.

Through any schoolkid's microscope you can marvel at the squirming animalcules in your own spit, or the wigglyworms and flagellates in a drop of water from the birdbath out back—thousands of creatures jellied and hydra-headed, coiled and ciliated, tubed and tentacled, beaded, honeycombed, spiraled, ridged, grooved, pajamaed in fluttering silks, or heaped together like the spools and springs of a smashed clock.

Even a common dustball from beneath the couch is a small galaxy under a microscope. What we nonchalantly refer to as dust is really a goulash whose ingredients list reads like a recipe for a witch's brew: flakes of skin and spores of mold, volcanic ash from days of old, flea eggs, filaments of asbestos, the digits and droppings of insects, tire meltings, sea salt, pollen, pavement grit, fabric and hair fragments, tissue and toilet paper shreds, and sand particles blown in from Africa—all collectively referred to by dust mites as lunch.

And it doesn't just stay under the couch. Every cubic foot of air in our houses has roughly three hundred thousand bits of flotsam held aloft by air currents. And there are as many creatures crawling across the plains of our skin and swimming through the kelp beds under our arms and between our legs as there are in any equatorial swamp or forest canopy.

Through the medium of a television, you can even channel the big bang. According to Bill Bryson in *A Short History of Nearly Everything*, a certain percentage of the shimmering static on TV is cosmic radiation emanating from the big bang itself, the ultimate reality show, the original word from your Sponsor. So when nothing else is on, he says, or when programming stops in the wee hours, you can always watch the Creation.

IN *THE SNOW LEOPARD*, Peter Matthiessen talks about "coming down" from a literal high, a two-month pilgrimage in the remote pyramidal reaches of the Tibetan Himalayas, during which he heard not a single engine, read not a single letter from home, passed through villages that hadn't changed appreciably since the eighth century, and had been so far removed from civilization as he knew it that his mind quieted to a whisper and notions of past and future receded enough to offer him a taste of enlightenment if you define enlightenment as "*Now!*"

However, the lower in elevation he went and the closer to the world he left behind, the more irritable he became. At one point he nearly decked one of the locals for an unwitting intrusion. "I had lost the flow of things and gone awry," he said, "sticking out from the unwinding spiral of my life like a bent spring."

He experienced what every spiritual seeker before him and after him must eventually come to: the challenge of bringing your vision over into daily life, integrating and sustaining it, pushing your expanded self through the eye of a needle. The desire to make room in our lives for wonder and awe, and the passions they can release in us, will always have to contend with agents of decay and distraction, the foremost being the hoodoo of habit and routine, which relentlessly conspire to break the spells of enchantment.

Like all life and all revelation, wonder decays. It decays from childhood to adulthood. It decays from first encounter to subsequent encounters, and from infatuation on. Like the content of dreams, much of what we bring back from our forays into the realms of wonder is fleeting if not unfathomable. Certainly our discoveries will try to attach themselves to the womb walls of daily life, get a foothold and bloom, but many will end in miscarriage, flushed from consciousness by the demands of Monday morning.

"Somewhere a philosopher is erasing 'time's empty passing' because he's seen a woman in a ravishing dress," the poet Stephen Dunn writes. "In a different hour he'll put it back."

I once sat in on a weekend trapeze class at a retreat center in Texas, designed, like fire-walking workshops, largely as a fear-fighting tool—"If you can do this, you can do anything." On the last day, I overheard a participant say to one of her classmates, "Well, I'll be fearless for a week." (Which would, of course, be precisely the week to take some long-needed risks.)

Certainly at the higher registers of wonder—the kind of elusive and mystical encounter Matthiessen was seeking in the form of the snow leopard—the challenge of preserving expanded states of mind is even more difficult, because it involves breaking through not just the crust of everyday apathy but also the armor of the ego. And the ego can't be shattered as easily as is implied by a famous Zen parable about individual consciousness being the air inside a sealed glass jar and cosmic consciousness the air around it, and all we have to do is break the glass to experience mystical reunion and rejoin the stubborn molecules of self with the Boundless and Inexhaustible.

For one thing, the ego is master of the boundaries and won't so readily participate in its own death. Nor is there one swift blow that's guaranteed to shatter all our illusions, one dose of Maya-Be-Gone that will dissolve our trances once and for all. If nothing else, they tend to regrow once we "come down."

Trying to sustain beginner's mind past the beginner stage of life, trying to continually renew our willingness to be moved and keep remembering that the wondrous is embedded in the ordinary, is like trying to live each day as if it could be your last. They're both true—the mundane *is* miraculous and you *could* die today—and they're both excellent meditations that would undoubtedly enrich your life. But they're both hard to pull off for more than a little while at a time. We're habituated to take things for granted. They don't call it the *force* of habit for nothing. It takes real work to see the universe in a grain of sand and heaven in a wildflower. Forgetfulness, on the other hand, is no discipline at all.

"Life is a spell so exquisite," the poet Emily Dickinson wrote, "that everything conspires to break it." So we need a few counterspells, something to help us maintain the enchantment and cut through the distractions—a word that means "to be pulled apart."

Consider the following advice from Hasidic rabbi Abraham Heschel: "We are trained in maintaining our sense of wonder by uttering a prayer before the enjoyment of food. For daily wonder we need daily worship: three times a day we say, 'We thank You for Your miracles which are daily with us, for Your continual marvels.'" And this, I think, is the crux of it. We sustain wonder the same way we sustain spiritual traditions—with regular discipline and worship.

This isn't to say that daily prayers, like anything overly familiar (even wonder) can't be dispatched so perfunctorily that they're gutted of meaning. I uttered them myself every day of summer camp for years when I was a kid, the pre-meal blessing: *Baruch atah Adonai Eloheinu melech ha'olam hamotzi lechem min ha'aretz.* But it was just a thing to get done before eating. We could as easily have said "Rub-a-dub-dub, thanks for the grub" for how sincere we were in worship. How many people really understand the miraculousness of food and the complicated chain of events that brings it to the table? Carl Sagan: "If you wish to make an apple-pie from scratch, first you must invent the universe."

And if wonder can devolve into routine, it can also devolve into escape, leading us not so much toward engagement as disengagement. For example, humans have always liked their holidays from the everyday, their ventures down the rabbit holes of amazement and into wonderlands of alternative consciousness, whether mystically or mycologically inspired, whether brought on by travels or novels. Sometimes these journeys are merely dis-tractive, something to get your mind off your troubles and chase down with beer and pretzels, and sometimes they're bids for genuine off-the-grid transcendence, a piercing of the veil and a crossing of the Jordan.

But either way, what goes up must come down, and what goes out must come back. And if we don't make peace with ordinary life, if we don't resolve to live in an everyday world that inspires us rather than deflates us, we become not so much pilgrims as fugitives.

Emerson once said this of travel: "At home I dream that at Naples, at Rome, I can be intoxicated with beauty and lose my sadness. I pack my trunk, embrace my friends, embark on the sea, and at last wake up in Naples, and there beside me is the stern Fact, the sad self, unrelenting, identical, that I fled from. My giant goes with me wherever I go."

The desire to be intoxicated is strong in us, though, and wonder and awe can be like any high, a wallop of arousal in which the brain dumps large amounts of psycho-juices into the bloodstream—dopamine, epi-nephrine, serotonin—sending an urgent message over the wires: Do it again! But this time, don't settle for Naples. How about the North Pole?

For some, this can be compounded by an expectation that upon reach-ing the top of the world or the bottom of the ocean, the foot of the pyra-mids or the grave of Jim Morrison, you're going to have an epiphany. You're going to be swept with waves of profound emotion and gratitude and fig-ure out Something Important. And maybe you will and maybe you won't. But if you don't, then the ante is upped. Next time, you'll need a stronger dose, a higher mountain, a deeper descent, a bigger thrill—something that raises *more* hair.

At its extremes, the hunger for wonder and awe can mutate into the need for shock and fright. I once saw a series of photographs of a roller coaster that goes 120 miles per hour straight down and into a corkscrew. The last photo shows a young woman coming off the ride, her blue jeans soaked clear through at the crotch and a shaky smile on her face.

Wonder is highly commodified nowadays. Impresarios use it to fill cir-cus tents. Religions rely on it to pitch kingdoms to come. Corporations sell new technologies by showcasing "the wonders of science." So it's not hard to find someone willing to give you your fix, sell you a potion to help you tap the vast fallow fields of your sensorium, or take you to any awe-inspiring corner of the world you like.

But when the remotest Himalayas and the wreck of the *Titanic* become available as package tours, when you can reach the summit of Mount Everest and call your wife in New York on your cell phone to tell her about it, when consumer culture offers *"adventures* in macrame" and *"new frontiers* in baking" and "a *revolution* in toilet paper," wonder and awe are in danger of being drained of their majesty.

Thunderstruck: On Passion and Perspective

I gave a lecture in London a few years ago, which gave me an opportunity to visit the British Museum, home to arguably the largest collection— some say plunder—of classical antiquity in the world.

I was especially enamored of a long corridor in the Assyrian collection whose walls are lined with elaborately sculptured stone slabs that in the ninth century B.C. lined the throne room of the king's palace in the Meso-potamian city of Nimrud. The nearly floor-to-ceiling bas-reliefs are covered with warriors and winged bulls, chariots and horses, eagle-headed men and human-headed lions that until the mid-1800s were buried beneath the sands of the desert and hidden from the sight of humanity for thirty centuries.

But standing in the cold light of the British Museum, staring down that avenue of stone walls, with interpretive plaques and barrier wires and crowds of people, it was hard to grasp how utterly astonished and dazzled the explorers who first unearthed them from the yellow deserts along the Tigris River must have been. To say nothing of the astonishment of the crowds of Arabs who assembled at the dig site each day to see what sensa-tional finds would turn up next: sphinxes, black marble obelisks, weapons and armor, giant alabaster vases, stone monsters with the heads of vultures, the bodies of men and the tails of fish, colossal sculptures of winged lions with the bearded heads of men—the logo of the Assyrian Empire—thirteen pairs of them, each up to seventeen feet tall and weighing ten tons.

And all of it exhumed in the era of the pick and shovel. Not the bulldozer and the forklift, not infrared photography, aerial surveying, remote sensing, and carbon dating.

Perhaps what most stirred the imagination of Europe, though, were the hundreds of clay tablets lining the palace library's shelves, each covered with a hieroglyphic-like script, which scholars called cuneiform but at the time couldn't decipher. When they finally cracked the cuneiform code a few years later, they were suddenly able to restore the language and history of the Assyria of the Old Testament—everything from its grammar and dictionaries to its laws and religions, including treatises on botany, astronomy, astrology, metallurgy, geology, and geography. All the records of an empire submerged beneath the sand for over three thousand years.

Finally they understood what they were looking at: a city referred to in the book of Genesis as Calah, one of civilization's first great cities, where the perfumes of Arabia were exchanged for the tapestries of Anatolia, the spices of Phoenicia for the pearls of Oman, and the silks of China for the purple dyes of Tyre, a gram of which was worth more than twenty grams of gold.

And what a strange and implausible destiny the relics of Calah have had, to go from adorning the palace walls of Assyria to being buried for 150 generations beneath the plains of the Fertile Crescent, then being unearthed, hauled across the desert on oxcarts, packed onto rafts buoyed by hundreds of inflated goatskins, and floated down the Tigris River to the sea, then getting shipped around the bottom of Africa to a land no Assyrian even knew existed, and finally being enthroned anew in the austere aisles of the British Museum.

The Arabs in whose backyard this drama unfolded often feasted and danced all night at the site of the reappearing city of ancient Nimrud, sometimes dashing like madmen into the trenches, amazed and terrified at the strange figures emerging from the desert, throwing off their clothes and shouting war cries. One sheik exclaimed, "Wonderful! Wonderful! What has been all our lives beneath our feet without our having known anything about it. A palace underground. Wonderful! Wonderful!"

The author Annie Dillard says of a backyard reverie, "I had been my whole life a bell and never knew it until at that moment I was lifted and struck." As in thunder-, awe-, dumbstruck. And all three are certainly characteristic of the more amplified forms of wonder, like astonishment and mystification and the sense of sublimity. Of incomprehensibility and whatever's beyond the making of sense, beyond your ability to speak rationally of it. What takes words right up to their timberline.

Sublime and metaphysical experiences enthrall us precisely because they stupefy and overwhelm us, because they're literally inexpressible, leaving us not just tongue-tied but also fallen entirely from our faith in language. When the journalist Harry Reasoner was asked on TV to share his reaction to seeing the Great Wall of China in 1972, he said, "It's . . . uh . . . it's one of the two or three darndest things I ever saw."

We value these experiences *because* they're so mystifying, *because* they knock us on our asses. In fact, reverence itself grows out of an understanding of just such limitations, and a quite literal understanding: that there's always something we stand under, always something over our heads. It explains why Orthodox Jews wear yarmulkes and why Turkish sultans once entered the great Byzantine mosque of Saint Sophia in ancient Constantinople wearing hats in the shape of Muhammad's foot—to remind them that there's always Someone above them. It's sometimes referred to as knowing your place, and it's an acquired taste.

Being made to feel small takes some getting used to, whether the dressing-down comes at the hands of sniffy maître d's, imperious biographies, or gods and goddesses. But there's a different, perhaps even agreeable way to feel diminished, and that's in the presence of the magnificent and almighty as it manifests in, say, nature, because there's really no *comparing* yourself with it. There's no personal affront or sense of failure. No one looking down an upturned nose at you or throwing a gauntlet at your feet.

This hasn't always been the case. Mountains, for instance, are a standard source of wonder and sublimity nowadays, and in many cultures always have been. Not so in Christian Europe. The ancient Romans found them desolate. People in the Middle Ages considered them warts on the planet. A seventeenth-century phrasebook listed among their attributes "insolent, ambitious, uncouth, inhospitable, shapeless, ill-figured, sky-threatening and forsaken." And Martin Luther believed them to be part of God's retribution for man's disobedience in the Garden. Even social philosophies have often considered the "high" to be suspect and the "low" to be preferable: "Every valley shall be exalted," the Bible says, "and every mountain shall be laid low."

And if mountains have not always been revered, even *reverence* of mountains has not always been revered. In *The Way of All Flesh*, Samuel Butler pokes fun at one of his characters, a Mr. Pontifex, whose first glimpse of Mont Blanc, the highest mountain in Europe, causes him to hemorrhage awe: "My feelings I cannot express. I gasped, yet hardly dared to breathe, as I viewed for the first time the monarch of the mountains. . . . I was so overcome by my feelings that I was almost bereft of my faculties, and would not for worlds have spoken after my first exclamation till I found some relief in a gush of tears. With pain I tore myself from contemplating . . . this sublime spectacle."

This hyperventilating appraisal, though, is actually a pretty close approximation of my own reaction to seeing the Andes in South America—an *extremely* agreeable diminishment. I had gone to Peru to do some mountain biking and trekking in the Cordillera Blanca, part of the snowcapped spine of the Andes that winds through central Peru and home to twenty-seven peaks above twenty thousand feet. Outside the Himalayas, they're the world's tallest mountains. But never having seen anything higher than the Alps, which top out at about fifteen thousand feet, I found myself staring dumbfounded at the enormous physicality of the Andes, whose glaciered massifs are simply so *huge*. It's a sight to humble the hairiest thunderer of an ego, but as long as you don't feel competitive with mountains the way some people do, it's an utterly pleasurable way to be humbled.

The category in my brain called "Mountain" was so thoroughly challenged, even negated, by the vastness and novelty of the Andes that it was given the chance to expand to accommodate this new arrival, and that expansion was exhilarating.

It happened again later that same summer back in the States, when I watched the Perseid meteor shower. A couple of friends and I were lying on big plastic lawn chairs tipped back onto the ground, and among the meteors we saw was one that streaked, large and low, from one horizon to the other—in two seconds flat! I have never seen anything move that fast. The closest has been when I'm flying and see another jet heading in the opposite direction in the flight lane below me. The combined speed of the jets gives me a visual aid to what 1,000 miles per hour looks like (the speed of Earth's rotation). But this was a peek at what *132,000* miles per hour looks like. It physically startled me.

So here's another of the benedictions of wonder: it's a stimulus to contemplations grander than the everyday, to perspectives that the earthbound and time-bound often crave. It's a look at the bigger picture, which is always getting bigger because the universe is always expanding.

If you sat on a beach and pushed the heel of your hand through the sand, you'd create a trough lined by ridges where the sand was shoved aside. Recently I sat on the flank of just such a ridge created when an Ice Age glacier pushed its way down a mountainside twenty thousand years ago in what is now Colorado, dragging boulders the size of bungalows along like they were pebbles. That sage-scented ridge, however, was two thousand feet high, and its partner on the other side of the valley was a mile away.

Spilling down the valley between them was an enormous carpet of coniferous forest where the glacier used to be, and meadows filled with moving herds of elk. Predators were nowhere in sight, but their handiwork was scattered across the valley—the stripped carcasses of elk, their bones still bearing the teeth marks of lion and bear, the skin and fur on their legs peeled down like ladies' stockings. Up the valley were snowcapped peaks whose perpetual ice fields looked like blotches of white paint splashed from above.

It was a fine day in the warm interglacial, and it would be a thousand generations before the white tide rolled back in and covered the land with two thousand feet and ten thousand years of winter, and for a few hours on that lovely afternoon—and in very few other ways—I was able to apprehend something of the size of the force that makes mountains and that puts me in my rightful place in the universe, a *glimpse* of the magnitude at which evolution is constantly working, with world-creating, world-destroying gusto.

On the wall in a nearby cabin where I'd gone for a weeklong retreat was a depiction of yet another order of magnitude—a National Geographic map called "The Physical World," which showed not the usual patchwork of countries in playful kindergarten colors but just the geographical features, the deserts, ice caps, plains, valleys, and mountains of Earth, including those under the oceans. It was one continuous landform, some of it above water level, some of it below. And it was apparent that Mount Everest is not only the highest mountain on Earth but also the cap of a monstrous escarpment that starts thirty thousand feet deep at the bottom of the Mariana Trench. It stretches up the flank beneath the East China Sea, across China itself, and onto the Tibetan Plateau, where Everest sits at twenty-nine thousand feet—forming a mountain over sixty-five thousand feet tall.

Sitting on the front steps of the cabin at night, I looked out into a solar system that was halfway through its pilgrimage between the arms of the Milky Way, which it traverses every quarter of a million years. This means that 125,000 years from now, the night sky is going to look like a Jackson Pollock painting and be so bright as to obliterate the constellations and no longer suffice to hide prowlers at their doings.

It reminded me of the final scene in the movie *Men in Black*, in which Earth is a marble in a game of marbles played by gargantuan aliens; or the parting shot in the movie *Antz*, the camera panning slowly back until the anthill in which the movie's entire drama took place is now seen against the voluminous backdrop of Central Park and the skyscrapers of New York.

Among the benedictions of perspective, of the Big Picture, as hinted at by the cultural, spiritual, and especially natural wonders of the world, is that although we may be small in relation to it, we also have a *place* there. And whether the marvels that lead us toward that bigger picture are under our feet or over our heads, they can serve to lift us up like a bell and strike us with a new appreciation for the largeness and richness of life, with new intensities of perception and new depths of feeling and significance.

Perhaps it's no coincidence that we use the term *peak* experiences to describe these high points and turning points in our lives, or that *astonishment* comes from a word meaning "to stun with a thunderbolt," as in being thunderstruck. It's at these times that we're momentarily taken outside ourselves and connected to a larger frame of reference.

IF WONDER AND AWE typically begin with the new barging in on the old while it's dozing, a sudden gust through an open window that scatters your thesis papers across the room, then it works as surely at the cultural level as at the personal. Entire *eras* have been characterized by the titillating trespasses of the unexpected and anomalous, by the hunger for novelty and fascination, and by the exhilarating and unnerving expansion of our worldview. Our current era is undoubtedly one of these, as was the era referred to as the Age of Wonder, a.k.a. the Renaissance.

Christopher Columbus's voyage west in 1492 instigated a couple of centuries of radical amazement, as Europe was flooded with wondrous new *stuff* brought back by explorers from the far-flung empires of the New World—the Americas, Asia, India, Africa, and the Middle East. The very existence of these zoological, geological, botanical, cultural, and anthropological marvels hauled into question the egocentricity of the European worldview. The scientific revolution of the time simultaneously hauled into question the centrality of the world itself, compliments of the discoveries of Copernicus, Galileo, and Bacon, who proved that Earth wasn't the center of the universe.

People's sights were turned toward whole new -cosms, both macro and micro. Telescopes brought a new order to the heavens. Microscopes brought into view the teeming universes of the tiny. The printing press spread the news far and wide.

Europeans, says Stephen Greenblatt in *Marvelous Possessions: The Wonder of the New World*, experienced several centuries of something like the startle reflex seen in infants—"eyes widened, arms outstretched, breathing stilled, the whole body momentarily convulsed." Columbus himself used the word *wonder* so many times in his journals and dispatches that the king of Spain suggested he be called not Almirante (the Admiral) but Admirans (the one who wonders).

It must have been a giddy time. How far and fast the horizons were being pushed back and the maps redrawn, how completely people's conceptions of size and scale, height and depth were being altered. How the parochial imagination must have reeled at seeing, for the first time, mummies and the giant vertebrae of whales.

In fact, it was to accommodate and advertise all this marvelous new stuff that museums were born. Starting out as collections called wonder cabinets, or cabinets of curiosities, they were anything from a literal cabinet or closet to an entire building stuffed with all manner of rarities and curiosa: shrunken heads, the skeletons of mastodons and conjoined twins, the enormous horns of rhinoceroses, astrolabes, alligator skins, Amazonian dugout canoes, Javanese bridal costumes, and the contents of Egyptian burial chambers. It was an endless treasury from whole new continents that Europeans came to think of as their own personal cabinets of curiosities, when they weren't thinking of them as their personal coffers and fiefdoms. Their journeying to new worlds was, in a sense, a chronicle of the colonization of the marvelous and the commodification of wonder.

The world's ruins speak eloquently of these ages of wonder, of whole epochs when the inspiring of awe was national passion and pastime, and heroic scale the order of the day. I'm among those who ardently seek out places where this is on grand display, and the job in London was a perfect excuse to indulge that appetite with a side trip to one of the places that most monopolizes the imagination of ruin-lusters like myself: Italy, a country whose language even has a tense called *passato remoto* to refer specifically to events in the very remote past.

I spent a month there, wandering day and night through the world's highest concentration of UNESCO World Heritage sites and through the magnificent ruins of the Roman Empire, whose power terrified kings, including the kings of Assyria, and made a hundred nations bow at the waist. Italy's ruins enthrall me the same way dinosaurs enthrall me—that such a thing once existed!

To stand amid the colossal ruins of Italy is to be set down on an alien world and survey the remains of a vanished race. And to travel in Italy is to see entire ages deposited in sedimentary layers, one enameled on top of another—the pagan above the Stone Age, the medieval above the pagan, the modern above the medieval, the ghosts of one age lodged with the ghosts of previous ages. Around every corner are bolts of unexpected illumination.

Italy is an object lesson in a kind of beauty and ornateness largely gone from the world, a piercing contrast between the ravishing craftsmanship in stone, wood, and mosaic that graced its ancient buildings—reminding us what can happen when people build with eternity in mind—and the comparatively dreary and uninspired architecture of our own time.

Just the skeletal remains of the old temples and triumphal arches are more splendid than most modern buildings with all their flesh and blood intact, and remind me that death and beauty are not strangers to each other; they share a wall.

These monuments were built not just for beauty or practicality, though, but also for impact, for propaganda. They were designed to awe and intimidate, to stun and stupefy when approached from ground level looking up, throwing the awestruck into shadow, or doubt, and built to impress the gods as well as the mortals. The pyramids of Giza, the Parthenon in Athens, the Great Wall of China, the Temple of Karnak—they were all meant to be *beheld* and to demonstrate the virility of their makers and their empires. And size *does* matter. It's no coincidence that in the literature of wonder and awe, the phrase "the sheer size" appears routinely, whether the wonder is natural or architectural, grand canyons or grand cathedrals, the world's largest ball of twine or the enormity of the world's suffering.

And the world is *full* of the remnants of these literally monumental creations. Full of the toppled and fox-haunted ruins of Roman arenas, Chinese royal tombs protected from grave robbers by automatic crossbows, Turkish fortresses where pashas once reclined on divans and clapped their hands for goblets of sherbet, Indian palaces in whose courtyards rajas played Parcheesi with human pawns, and Greek temples with their marble gods whose noses and fingers made target practice for the bored soldiers of countless armies.

Not that a ruin has to be grand to speak to us of wonder and rouse the passion for living that's often borne of perspective, of a glimpse at the big picture reminding us that this is our precious nick of time and that we'd better make the most of it. Old graveyards will do it. So will log cabins set agreeably in yellow meadows, and ramshackle horse-and-buggy wagons floating like derelict schooners in the waving grasses along country lanes.

Or the mere stones that pave the streets of old Roman hill towns, which are often embedded with fossil shells that appear as if floating at the surface, advertising in limestone, alabaster, and marble that oceans and mountains trade places from time to time and that on this spot fish once swam by at eye level.

The enormous brethren of these shells that float in the paving stones of Italy—the fossil bones of mastodons, for instance, or the skulls of dinosaurs—have also been a stimulus to the human imagination, providing our forebears with the inspiration for some of their most striking myths, like the gold-guarding griffin, half lion and half eagle, which sprang to life from the tales of Scythian gold miners who, prospecting in the Gobi desert, found the beaked skeletons of Protoceratops. The stone bones of mammoths found on the island of Samos were reconfigured in the Greek imagination as the war elephants that Dionysus employed in his battle with the Amazons. And on Crete the titanic skull of a mastodon was found, with its great nasal cavity in the center, from which a trunk once emerged, as well as a story of a race of one-eyed giants known as Cyclops.

IN THE LATE WINTER OF 1790, a Frenchman named Xavier de Maistre was under six weeks of house arrest for a dueling incident in Turin, confined to his room in an old apartment building, a room thirty-six paces in circumference if you hugged the wall, and a detention, he said, that, were it up to him, he would have chosen to execute during Lent rather than Carnival.

In his wide-ranging ruminations on that forty-two-day confinement, called *A Journey Around My Room*, he says, "The authorities have forbidden me to roam around the city, a mere point in space. But they have left me with the whole universe. Immensity and eternity are mine to command. It is not in their power to prevent me from exploring at will the vast space that always lies open before me."

Once again, here is captivation not as imprisonment but its opposite. The quest that's triggered by wonder, by the baffling of the mind or the transfixing of the spirit (or the body, in de Maistre's case), has the potential to magnify the world in the way Wendell Berry meant it when he said that the impeded stream is the one that sings, in the way Einstein meant it when he said that "once you can accept the universe as matter expanding into nothing that is something, wearing stripes with plaid comes easy."

This magnification starts with the way wonder arranges itself on the face—eyes wide, mouth agape—and runs through those mind-expanding epiphanies that can occur in mystical, psychotherapeutic, or psychedelic encounters; in powerful healings, synchronicities, or crises; through peak experiences, prolonged fasting, solitude or prayer, travel, ecstatic dancing in the Sufi or Hasidic traditions, or the deliberate frustration of the logical mind by Zen koan.

The rupturing of ordinary perception leads us to consider that the world isn't what we thought it was. What we believed matters most doesn't. And we're far more powerful than we imagined. Or far less. But either way, the experience has the effect of latching a capo onto us and raising our pitch.

These experiences are like random mutations in nature, unexpected buds from which grow entirely new evolutionary branches or whole new species of behavior. From then on, we're a different creature. We temporarily escape the small self that's always fishing in the shallows and head out into the deep pelagic waters. And our lives are split down the middle, into B.C. and A.D., into marking our lives by the time that came Before Comprehension and the time that came After.

I had one of these experiences on the north coast of Scotland when I was in my late twenties, shortly after a personal crisis—losing the one and only job I've ever lost. I was sitting on a cliff at the edge of the North Sea, looking out over an ocean that was the only thing between me and the Arctic Circle. The terrain was wild and isolated, with moors covered in purple heather sweeping in from behind me and dropping abruptly into the blue-green water, and gulls wheeling by in lavish arcs on the wind.

Looking out over enormous bulwarks of rock anchored like battleships along the coast, I was suddenly—though what is *suddenly* when it took my whole life to get to that moment?—struck by the understanding that the same force that lifted those ramparts out of the sea just as easily pushes up a daisy, and just as surely created me. I came off the same conveyor belt as those moors and that frigid ocean.

I stood up and slowly turned around in a circle, a kind of circumambulating meditation at the edge of the cliff, taking in all the various and glorious substantiations of that animating force, in rock, flower, sea, and sky, in the gulls riding the thermals and the bleached skull of a sheep laying nearby, which now sits on a shelf in my office with a feather quill pen sticking out of the bullet hole in the back—a kind of memento vitae.

And when wonder leads on to *wondering*, we find ourselves pursuing the kinds of questions and possibilities that further enlarge our universe, starting with the three-pound universe inside our heads. That is, the practical product of wonder is knowledge—assuming you follow the trail of bread crumbs that wonder leaves behind—and knowledge enlarges the brain. It expands the cortex and builds new neural connections, new pathways that weren't there before.

It may be confined to a nutshell, but the brain offers lots of room for expansion, though not for the reason most people think—the misconception that we aren't utilizing 90 percent of it, that it's just sitting there like a large vacant lot awaiting the developers.

The brain has been created by natural selection, like every organ in every creature, and neuroscientists consider it extremely unlikely that evolution would fashion a body part so metabolically expensive to maintain, that uses such a huge amount of the body's energy reserves, only to let 90 percent of it sit idle. It would be equivalent to installing half a dozen engines on an airplane and only using one of them to fly.

Furthermore, electrical stimulation of the brain during neurosurgery hasn't turned up any part that's dormant. Neuropsychologist Barry Beyerstein, of the Language and Brain Lab at Simon Fraser University in Vancouver, says, "There is no cerebral spare tire waiting to be mounted in service of one's grade point average, job advancement, or the pursuit of a cure for cancer or the Great American novel."

Wonder can offer us the adaptive benefit of free cognitive upgrades, reorientings that help us sync the models in our heads about how the world works with the way the world *actually* works. For example, I'd been living in New Mexico for several years, often wandering for miles along the dry washes that snake through the deserts and canyons, before I saw my first flash flood. One day I watched with textbook awe (wonder and fear) as a storm up in the mountains turned a dry arroyo into a boiling river of brown water six feet deep within *minutes*, and bounced an old washing machine along with it at twenty miles per hour. Cognitive upgrade: I never looked at those withered waterways the same way after that, and I kept a warier eye out for even distant storms upstream. That is, better investigative scanning of the environment.

The 1991 fire in the Oakland, California, hills offered another opportunity for an upgrade. Fueled by a five-year drought and stiff Santa Ana winds, it left behind a landscape reminiscent of old photographs of Hiroshima and Nagasaki—*thousands* of homes reduced to smoldering foundations and liquefied girders. I wandered through the ravaged neighborhoods a few days after the fire was put out, and I remember standing dumbfounded in front of a melted motorcycle.

Scenes of widespread devastation readily provoke the experience of awe, but the most terrifying aspect of the fire, at least to me, were the reports from authors and professors at the University of California, Berkeley, of the loss of books in progress. My brother Marc, a professor at Stanford, was not at all sympathetic. He said there's no excuse anymore for losing manuscripts like that, when they can so easily be backed up and stashed in a safe-deposit box. Cognitive upgrade: I made a copy of my then first book in progress and put it in a safe-deposit box, and have done so with every book I've written since, and all my computer files of anything I'd be devastated to lose.

Among the first cognitive makeovers I ever experienced at the hands of awe was in a college course I took called Human Sexuality, whose final exam was a sex-role-change party. Our assignment: come as you're *not*.

My girlfriend at the time helped dress me up as a vamp, a seductress in a long brunette wig, dangly earrings, makeup, a gauzy white peasant shirt, a prodigiously padded bra, lots of bangles and jewelry, skintight blue jeans, and bare feet—and I surprised myself with the enthusiasm with which I threw myself into the role, only partly due, I think, to the fact that we were being graded on how authentically we embodied whatever guise we took on that night and how much risk we were willing to take with it.

Sexual identity is a very fluid affair, I discovered that night, especially when your grade depends on it, and especially with a change of wardrobe, a little permission to play-act, and a little wine. Okay, more than a little. But it turns out that the clothes do indeed make the man . . . do things he wouldn't normally do.

A few years ago, a friend hosted a New Year's Eve party and made available to the revelers a collection of her wigs of all styles: punk, shag, Afro, glitter, blonde bombshell, you name it. And I was impressed by what the simple act of putting on a wig evoked in people. As the night progressed and people's inhibitions *re*gressed, that party became populated by a constantly shifting kaleidoscope of personalities and interactions, punctuated by regular outbursts of laughter and surprise. And it wasn't just that people *took on* the personas represented by various wigs, but that the wigs seemed to draw out of them different personas, potentialities that were already there, latent.

I saw, once again, that entirely different facets of personality—which are always in there waiting for an entrance cue—can be brought to the fore by the simplest change of attire or setting or company. I carry myself very differently, for example, when I'm wearing cowboy boots than when I'm wearing sneakers or sandals. I exude a very different vibe when I'm wearing a five o'clock shadow (what a friend calls designer stubble) than when I'm clean-shaven. I'm a different guy when I'm wearing a pompadour wig than when I'm wearing a Rod Stewart shag.

As a reporter, I've certainly seen how chameleon-like I can be, unconsciously adopting some of the speech and gestural patterns of the people I'm interviewing, or rather adapting mine to theirs. Whether I do this for the sake of rapport building or approval seeking I'm not entirely sure.

What I remember most about the sex-role-change party was latching onto one of my classmates who came as a monk (which was very much *not* how he was). I spent half the evening, it seems, stroking his hair, whispering coarse suggestions in his ear, and damn near lap-dancing him. And in retrospect I probably did that because, among all the characters at that party, he was the safest. His sexuality was enfrocked and embelted, and his grade required that he stay in character. So he was a blank canvas for me, and I splattered my assumed sexuality all over him. I could play it up without having to be defensive.

At midnight, by design, the party came to a close, and we sat in a circle to debrief and to grade one another.

I got an A, and a cognitive upgrade: an eye-opening education in the astonishing suppleness of human sexuality. Of my *own* sexuality. We're all infused with a great many spices.

ROUGHLY TWO HUNDRED THOUSAND years ago, our Stone Age selves, the Neanderthal, became the first creatures on Earth to bury their dead, and not just with dirt but with ceremony and provisions for an afterlife—tools, weapons, clothing, food.

Their Paleolithic gravesites scattered across Europe and Asia are evidence that they had devised ways of explaining the inexplicable to themselves—the fact of death and the question of what happens after it—to comfort themselves in their deepest mystifications. It's proof that even in our embryonic minds we understood that the world was governed by powerful forces that could be not just comprehended but also controlled. And it's proof that religion is really, really old.

In fact, if wonder is the impetus for art, science, and philosophy, it's also the spur for spirituality. If awe and amazement are vivid enough, they tend to lead to those passions we call worship and devotion, since faced with the vast and incomprehensible, it's natural to consider the infinite—whether in the presence of birth or death, miracles or mountains, whether out on the ocean or under the great wilderness of the night sky.

Theologian Rudolf Otto, in his book *The Idea of the Holy*, calls this response the numinous; the primitive and felt sense of something "wholly other" in the world, of something *there*, tremendous and uncanny, not approachable or apprehensible with senses or intellect, something we hungrily seek out experiences of and audience with in the form of deities, the supernatural, the sacred, and the transcendent. We naturally contemplate what powers might have stage-set the whole affair, asking "What force could possibly . . .?" and "How, then, shall we live?" What way of living is compatible with such grandeur and mystery and improbability? (Certainly a grateful and spirited one.)

From an evolutionary point of view, the human brain is wired to look for the causes of unseen events—the snap of a twig, a rustle in the underbrush—so that we're prepared to respond effectively. The brain works to figure things out, to help us feel our way through the unfamiliar and unpuzzle the puzzling. And religion is one of the outgrowths of this inclination to seek *agency*, to explain to ourselves events in the primordial world more complex than just the snapping of twigs—the appearance of meteors and eclipses, the movement of the stars, the disappearance of migrating animal herds, sickness and death, and our ever-eager existential questions, from "Why are we here?" to "What happens after we die?"

As an emotional response to the awesome and inscrutable, to what psychologist William James called the unseen order, wonder is not only every bit as old as religion; it's also one of its handmaidens. To the degree that we allow ourselves to wonder at the enigmatic, to submit to our own awe, we establish contact with a larger frame of reference, a "higher" order of things, and the recognition or remembrance—so essential to spirituality and science—that there are hidden worlds.

"Open for me a door the size of a pinhole and I will open for you the supernal gates," a book of Jewish mysticism called the *Zohar* quotes God as saying. Interestingly, the Hubble Telescope recently focused on precisely a pinhole-size patch of space and found there 1,500 *galaxies.* Now multiply that by however many pinhole-size patches of space there are in the night sky.

"My sense of God," Einstein said, "is my sense of wonder about the universe." Or as the poet William Blake more bluntly put it, "Unless the eye catch fire, the God will not be seen. / Unless the mind catch fire, the God will not be known."

Not that the mind and the eye are the only organs capable of catching fire, of being moved or enlarged by wonder. So is the heart. Wonder is indeed a response to "something moving"—something that moves us—whether displays of love, beauty, power, passion, mystery, talent, rarity, vastness, compassion, courage, even cruelty. And this response is likely to be emotional as well as visual, an affair of the heart as much as one of the senses. (And the inhibition of a sense of wonder may be symptomatic of an inhibition of feelings in general.)

Not that all the wonders of the world are architectural or artistic, physical or metaphysical. Often they're behavioral. Sometimes it's no more than a stunning gesture. Last year I lectured at a church in which the minister introduced to the congregation a man whose son was to be baptized that day. He asked the father to stand up with the baby, whom he lifted high above his head, a gesture that unexpectedly brought tears to my eyes, it was so powerfully exultant, so exquisitely theatrical.

Sometimes, too, we find ourselves astonished by, and hungry for, stories about our own moral beauty and generosity, unexpected kindnesses, and incomprehensible changes of heart. Like the skinhead who recants and begins teaching love and tolerance, the woman who visits her daughter's murderer in prison, or the famous 1914 Christmas Truce along the western front in World War I, when thousands of German and Allied troops, in direct defiance of orders, laid down their arms and met in the no-man's-land between their opposing trenches to sing carols, exchange souvenirs, play football, and help each other bury their dead—a shining moment of sanity and brotherhood amid the carnage of war.

Among the most moving examples of awe-inspiring behavior I've run across is the story of Aaron Feuerstein, a legend in the corporate world and the annals of compassionate action. The third-generation owner and CEO of the Malden Mills textile factory in Lawrence, Massachusetts, when it burned to the ground in 1995, in the largest fire the state had seen in a century, Feuerstein decided not to take the three hundred million dollars in insurance money and retire, as some people thought he should. ("What would I do with it?" he asked. "Eat more? Buy another suit? Retire and die?")

Instead he rebuilt the factory right there in Lawrence rather than down south or overseas, as much of the textile industry had done in search of cheap labor. With an additional twenty-five million dollars of his own money, he also decided to "do the right thing" and pay the salaries and benefits of all three thousand of his suddenly unemployed workers during the three months it took to rebuild, even while he was filing for bankruptcy.

For guidance he turned to the Torah, the book of Jewish law. "You are not permitted to oppress the working man," Feuerstein paraphrased. "It would have been unconscionable to put 3,000 people on the streets and deliver a deathblow to the cities of Lawrence and Methuen. Maybe on paper our company was worthless to Wall Street, but I can tell you it's worth more." Feuerstein became that rarest of ducks: the businessman as national hero. The press and the politicians adored him. President Clinton invited him to the State of the Union address as an honored guest, and he received twelve honorary degrees from universities around the country.

Wonder is an appeal to intimacy, as is religion (the word means "to reconnect"). We're called to enlarge our embrace so that we're continually increasing our circle of acquaintance and affection. It's an emotion like love, which draws us toward something or someone even as it unnerves us. Cultivating the sense of wonder is therefore cultivating not just an inspired and passionate worldview but also an *ethical* worldview, since what we love we care for, and what's considered sacred is more likely to be treated that way.

Trading Faith for Wonder

Whether your sense of sublimity arises from encounters with God or nature, faith or science, both are perfectly capable of stupefying with their mysteries, and both are sources of wonder and awe that can offer the critical and vitalizing advantage of a transcendental outlook on life.

Most people probably draw on some combination of both conceptual frameworks, but others sometimes feel forced to choose.

For as long as he could remember, Jay Valusek felt himself caught between these two seemingly contrary outlooks and ideologies. And though he had always looked to both science and Scripture to help him articulate his passion and awe for life—to, he says, "find my place in the world"—he was seldom able to resolve the tensions between them. Early in life he made a conscious choice to accept God and set science on the back burner, "to turn toward God all the awe and wonder, all the sense of mystery and majesty that I felt about the world and about nature, and to do it without proof," he says. "As a scientist, though, that just sits in the back of your mind and never goes away."

Not even when, in his late teens, he joined the Way International, "a charismatic creationist, literalist, fundamentalist, healing, preaching, save-the-world kind of group," for which he served as missionary and leader for nine years—while simultaneously majoring in geology in college. "I arrived in school as a creationist. A literal six-day creationist, and within two semesters I abandoned it completely and started studying geology, paleontology, cultural anthropology, archaeology, astronomy, cosmology, and eventually became a petroleum geologist."

After college, though, he taught theology and Christian living in the Episcopal Church, followed by twelve years on the contemplative path, all of it accompanied by concerted and unsuccessful efforts to fulfill what he believed was a call to the ministry. "I went so far as wanting to become a monk, and actually had a hand-tailored monastic robe made for myself. But all my attempts failed, one after another. Traumatic failures."

One cold November night in 2003, after what he describes as "a long, slow, gradual dissolution," which he chronicles in his book about the experience, *The Secret Sorrow*, he sat down with a pad of paper and for three days continually asked himself, "What do I know about God?" He listed one hundred items, most of which are not for the easily offended. They included:

"The mere fact that theologians still write elaborate proofs of the existence of God, after thousands of years, proves that God's existence is not obvious."

"I prefer the image of God that I know to the Mystery that exists beyond the image."

"Faith in the God of scripture requires a radical trust in the documents themselves. When my confidence in the holy writings is shaken, the images they portray begin to fracture. In the widening cracks, if you look closely, you will see only darkness."

"Unbelief in the face of God's unknowability is an entirely reasonable response. Skeptics, therefore, may be closer to the mystery than we [believers] are."

"We feel isolated. We reach out. And what do we know better than our own humanity? So we make God in our image. It's so obvious, how did I miss it for so long?"

What these conundrums added up to was "nada," as he puts it. The same nada that Saint John of the Cross described finding at the summit of the metaphorical Mount Carmel, where he expected to encounter God. Except that in Jay's case, it wasn't the Nothing that led to Everything, but the Nothing that led him away from the mountain altogether, to seek his place in the world within the world itself, not beyond it, and without the need for an anthropomorphized supernatural being. "I lost faith in God," he says, "because when I went out to not just think about God, and study God, and see what everyone else said about God, but to *meet* God, there was no-one there.

"Every example I could think of, every experience where I believed that 'God said this' or 'God did that,' could, using the principle of Occam's Razor—the simplest explanation is usually the most plausible—be more easily explained by *me* making choices, or me arriving at conclusions that made sense to me. All those years when I thought God had been speaking to me and guiding me, I realized I'd actually been talking to myself, guiding myself by my own inner wisdom, comforting and challenging myself. I was 'God' most of the time; life and accident and happenstance were God some of the time; and traditional or modern concepts and ideas *about* God were God the rest of the time.

"I was so startled and disturbed by what I wrote that I knew I had finally touched upon the truth, at least *my* truth. While I felt as if I still 'believed,' I also sensed that I was trying just a bit too hard to believe. And then . . . I just didn't anymore. When I honestly reviewed my experience of God, I became aware that God was mostly absent, and every moment of presence was at best ambiguous. The concept of God eventually came to feel *off* to me. I feel like I saw through it.

"I could no longer sustain my belief in the reality of God. There just wasn't any evidence. And I was still enough of a scientist to require something more than wishful thinking. All the old beliefs I had relied on to make sense of the world, that had given my life meaning, simply vanished. I awoke from the dream of God."

By doing so, he joined a long line of people who have had their faith in the God of their upbringing undone by data and reason, by "the facts," by following Buddha's advice to not accept what's handed down to you by teachers and traditions but test it out for yourself.

He's no longer a theist but counts himself one among a breed of non-theists called religious naturalists, who claim as their own Albert Einstein, theologian Paul Tillich, and E. O. Wilson, the father of sociobiology, as well as many from mainstream denominations—Christians, Quakers, Buddhists, though they won't be your standard models.

Religious naturalists believe that the wonder they feel at "God's creation" is no less "wonder-full"—in fact more so—for leaving God out of the equation and going with a fact-based rather than faith-based approach to life, which still leaves intact their religious impulse—that hunger for connection to something greater than themselves that appears to have been factory-installed in us by social evolution, if not, as some believe, by genetics.

Jay now redirects that impulse toward the physical world rather than the metaphysical one, toward nature rather than God, but he continues to be religious in the sense of honoring what is holy, the sacredness that's endemic to all life and not merely concentrated in deities. He is simply more attracted to the Light than to the Lamp. And the issue isn't even whether God exists or not. It's that at some point in his life, he simply chose to switch allegiances, to redirect his sense of wonder from the Creator to the Creation. And he's found that doing this has increased rather than decreased his sense of awe, wonder, compassion, humility, reverence, and gratitude, and his passion for life.

The Creation, he finds, is a far richer trove than the creation stories we make up about it, and nature every bit as worthy of hallelujahs as God, and you can get your hands on it. Religion, on the other hand, has typically taught that what is holy is taboo, unknowable in any direct sense—in fact, dangerous. The ancients believed that if gods or goddesses were to appear to mortals in their true forms, the sight would incinerate us, as happened to Semele, mother of Dionysus, when she asked to see Zeus in his full immortal splendor and was granted her wish. In Exodus, God tells Moses, "No man can see me and live." And the Ark of the Covenant and the chalice of the Holy Grail are both considered to be sacred *and forbidden*.

Jay now prefers his mysteries embodied rather than disembodied, and he has found that his passion for pursuing mystery at all is given plenty of fodder by the natural world, of which he feels himself a more intimate part than ever before. As the naturalist and author Chet Raymo says, "I no longer require answers to the Big Questions. I want instead answers to the Little Questions. How does a hummingbird hover?" Or as Peter Mayer sings in "Holy Now": "Wine from water is not so small / But an even better magic trick / Is that anything is here at all / So the challenging thing becomes / Not to look for miracles / But finding where there isn't one."

Historically, when humans made sacrifices, what we sacrificed was the fatted calf, our best sheep, the cream of the crop—i.e., something we wanted for something we wanted even *more*, which was the good graces of our gods and goddesses. But Jay's purpose has been just the opposite. He sacrificed his relationship with a god in order to make his earthly life more sanctified. He gave up the supernatural for the natural. He gave up the prospect of heaven and immortality—and a landlord he was taught he could petition for an extension of his lease on life—for the more certain benedictions of the only life we *know* we have.

And the finite life has encouraged him to straighten out his priorities more insistently than an infinite life. "What I lost was eternal life, but what I got was *this* life, here and now. If there's no eternal life, when do you live? You live now. I have a kind of faith in the present that I didn't have then, and I feel like I'm finally living *here*. I also look back and realize that I squandered millions of present moments because I believed there was an infinite amount of time. I didn't have to pay attention to *this* moment because there was an eternity of them. Not anymore."

Still, his is a perfect case in point that faith is not so easily extinguished, nor is any array of arguments against it likely to sway a believer to unbelief. Only personal experience, trial and error, and perhaps a buildup of the kind of devotional disappointments Jay experienced over the years, and, especially for a scientist and empiricist like him, the ever-increasing difficulty in accepting *any* assertion based on nothing more than faith.

Interestingly, the doctrine of Vitalism, which holds that what separates living from nonliving entities is a vital force, a spark or spirit often called chi or élan vital or *prana*, is a concept largely rejected by contemporary scientists. But on behalf of intellectual consistency, it seems they would then have to dismiss out of hand any number of traditional if not ancient practices—those, say, which claim that illnesses are caused by disturbances or imbalances in the body's vital force.

So into the dustbin would go not just homeopathy, hands-on healing, shamanism, and prayer, but also all the healing and holistic systems of the Orient—Chinese medicine, Ayurvedic medicine, yoga, acupuncture, chakra healing, tantra, Reiki, feng shui, even the martial arts—since they're all based on a belief in the flow of a life force, which is impossible to isolate in the laboratory.

But dismissing the belief systems of half the world (and most of human history) just because the ingredient at their core is an X-factor, immeasurable, something you have to take entirely on faith, would be ironic, to say the least, when the same thing can be said of religion. Yet many scientists who scoff at the notion of Vitalism still go to church on Sundays. Forty percent of them, according to a 1997 study out of the University of Georgia, which took its sample from a general directory called *American Men and Women of Science.*

(Interestingly, another survey from that same year and reported in the science journal *Nature* surveyed over five hundred members of the prestigious National Academy of Sciences, among whom only 7 percent believe in God. Conclusion: The greater scientists' educational attainment and the higher their scores on intelligence and achievement tests, the less likely they are to believe in God. Which is also true of the general population.)

Nonetheless, what Jay calls "the Christian leg of my spiritual journey" came to an abrupt end when he was forty-nine years old, followed, naturally, by what Saint John called a dark night of the soul. Except that for Jay, the night didn't end with daybreak: "Day never followed. I waited, believe me. But no light ever dawned again, other than the light of awareness that I had apparently spent my entire life living an illusion. It was shattering. The most wrenching experience of my adult life. And what died was not just a mental construct, but also my hope for immortality.

"The five years I spent mourning God's death were largely about this for me: I am going to die, and no-one is going to keep me alive. But how do you let go of the one thing you've been told all your life will keep you alive forever? That was the biggest loss for me about the death of God. Though strange as it may seem, I *wanted* to believe, at last, that I am going to die, so that I might begin to live more fully and passionately, more gratefully, more wildly and freely while I'm still alive."

Curiously, though, he chose to stay in suspense about what would be left in the aftermath of God's departure, rather than seek premature resolution. He stopped teaching contemplative prayer, gave away hundreds of books on Scripture, theology, church history, liturgy, spirituality, and the contemplative life—his sacred texts now became those of science and poetry—and took up the teaching of mindfulness meditation and the study of Buddhist psychology. He also found comfort—and a new community—in an unusual group of people, the members of a philosophical discussion group called Socrates Cafe, based on a book of the same name; these are people for whom questions, in true Socratic style, are more important than answers.

Meeting in cafes, bookstores, schools, churches, community centers, and even prisons, people in these philosophical jam sessions tackle life's big and little questions. Jay started and facilitated a bimonthly group in the Colorado town where he then lived, and it became his community for three years. It wasn't just a hankering for kindred spirits but also an act of self-care. When people turn from a belief in God, they often turn as well from the communities of faith that went along with that belief, and community involvement seems to be the primary reason why studies show a connection between religion and health. It's not so much the religious beliefs themselves, but the sense of community and social support.

"'Longing for God' is the name I always gave for the desire not to feel separate from everything," Jay says. "To transcend this lonely sense of self, this narrow self-consciousness. And the way that I find my place again, and weave new threads of attachment to the world as it is, is by remembering that I'm a part of all this. The idea that we're stardust, that we came from the stars, some people think that's just romantic and meaningless. But to me it's an anchor in reality. And the sense of beauty and wonder and awe at being part of this larger thing, which I used to call God, I now call the universe. Not in some cosmic metaphysical sense, but the actual, scientific universe. It's awe-inspiring to me to think of my place in the grand tree of evolution, the grand mystery of reality as it is.

"When I go up on a mountaintop and look up at the night sky and turn in a circle, which I do reverently, with my arms open—among my new 'religious' rituals—I'm looking at the Source. I came from there. Every atom in my body was forged in a supernova, or in the Big Bang. And they coalesced and went through this amazing, awe-inspiring, mysterious, brain-numbing series of events that are apparently unique in the entire universe, which led to us. Which led to me.

"Life doesn't get less precious without God. It gets *more* precious. And nature is now my Ground of Being, the Source from which I was separated, the Beloved I long to be reunited with. I go into nature and just open my senses and just feel, and it'll bring tears to my eyes. The epic of evolution is a perfectly firm basis for an inspiring and meaningful view of my place in the universe."

Captivated or Held Captive: Wonder and Credulity

When I was in my mid-teens, my two brothers and I held a rudimentary séance to explore the possibility of disembodied spirits, which I felt certain existed as a result of a recent experience involving a few friends and a Ouija board. We sat in a circle in the dark of Ross's bedroom, holding hands. "If there are spirits with us," my older brother, Marc, gravely intoned, "give us a sign." A moment later, a book fell over on the dresser.

After we regained our composure, we started in again, Marc once again invoking "the spirits." This time, the desk chair started to move.

Since I was already primed by my mystifying experience with the

Ouija board, it's hard to convey the utter shock, almost dread, I felt when things started to go bump in the night. When I believed that actual *ghosts* were in the room with us. When my whole worldview, firmly cemented after fifteen years in a family full of scientists, engineers, detectives, nonfiction writers, and New Yorkers, suddenly didn't seem nearly as solid as I thought.

We took a break, during which I ran breathlessly downstairs to tell my mother, whose scoff I should well have expected. Her rallying cries are Aristotelian logic, Cartesian causality, and the Puritan work ethic, not occult rituals and incantatory juju (though oddly enough, shortly after Marc got married, my mother began carving a fertility statue out of marble, in hopes that it would effect a grandchild. She says that within weeks of finishing it, Marc and his wife announced that they were pregnant, whereupon my mother, quite pleased with herself, revealed her metaphysical machinations. When I heard about it from Marc, I called this woman and demanded to know who she was and what she'd done with my mother.).

My brothers and I reconvened our séance upstairs, and this time, after a long, expectant silence, a straw donkey about the size of a toaster—a gift to Ross from a relative who went to Mexico or Morocco or somewhere—started floating across the room from its perch on a high shelf. I couldn't have been more shocked if the thing had begun to *talk*. Suddenly I heard a pop like the sound of a string snapping, and the donkey dropped partway to the floor and spun around. When I got up to turn on the light, my brothers erupted in laughter.

Unbeknownst to me, they'd rigged the room with a system of strings and pulleys that allowed them to make objects move or fall or even float. And amazingly, neither of them even remembers this incident. Marc claims that "the scientist in me must have blocked it out," though it was the scientist in him who had concocted the scheme.

In Shakespeare's *Hamlet*, the appearance of the ghost of the murdered king provokes Hamlet's friend Horatio to say, "O day and night, but this is wondrous strange!" To which Hamlet replies, "And therefore as a stranger give it welcome. There are more things in heaven and earth, Horatio, than are dreamt of in your philosophy."

The unexpected suddenly arises in the midst of ordinary day and night, appearing in its binary form, wondrous and strange, and with it comes the call to give it welcome.

But judiciously.

Just because wonder can help us drop anchor over the unseen realms doesn't mean we should go overboard. We need to cultivate the wonder of childhood without the credulity of childhood, the kind of unthinking, unblinking naïveté that puts us out of contact with our critical faculties and that at its extremes has us subscribing to tabloid wonder: interviews with Bigfoot's love slave, helpful hints on how to tell if your senator is an alien or your toilet a portal to the underworld, flash bulletins from scientists readying themselves to open Pandora's box, shocking news from the front lines of biblical archaeology about the discovery that pizza was delivered at the Last Supper.

During my visit to the British Museum, I saw, tucked away on a shelf in the Enlightenment Room (as in the era, not the state of mind), one of the frauds that occasionally found their way into the old cabinets of curiosities: a merman, the bottom half fish, the top half monkey—sewn together.

My brother Marc once participated in an archaeological dig behind the Temple of Castor in the Roman Forum, and during that week a colleague from Oxford University uncovered a marble block just below the surface, thought to be part of the ancient sewer system. But the colleague didn't want to have his picture taken with it out of concern that it might not be "in situ," in its original place—i.e., authentic—and any photo of him posing with such a questionable find could be professionally incriminating, casting a shadow of doubt on his archaeological IQ. Marc, on the other hand, not being in the field himself, had no such qualms and gleefully had his picture taken with it, down on his knees in the dirt, grinning like any ten-year-old with his first bicycle or his first trout.

As the archaeologist understood, though, wonder and awe can be potentially disabling, leading to that peculiar infectious disease known as being so open-minded your brains fall out.

Max Weber, one of the founders of sociology, considered "the disenchantment of the world" not a fall from magic but a freedom from magic, which he defined as magical thinking, nonscientific causal reasoning. In other words, superstition. A roof collapses on a man while he's sleeping, and it's chalked up to a spell that had been cast on him rather than the termites that have been chewing on his roof beams for months. A tsunami that wipes out a village is ascribed to the wrath of gods rather than to shifting tectonic plates far out at sea.

Weber was inclined to remind people that being enchanted, charmed, bewitched, spellbound, mesmerized, enraptured, entranced, or enthralled originally meant something very different from what they mean nowadays. They meant being overpowered, even enslaved. Not captivated but held captive. Not occupied as in absorbed, but occupied as in taken over, as in an occupied country. We can be hijacked by our own passions.

The expression "Holy moly!"—a standard reaction to wonder and surprise—is a holdover from that era. It refers to a magic herb called moly, which the god Hermes gave Ulysses to ward off a spell cast by the sorceress Circe that would have turned him into a pig. "Holy moly!" is thus an invocation of *protection* against enchantment.

I could have used a dose of it on my trip to Italy, actually. Traveling to a place like Italy tends to make me susceptible to the curse of the picturesque, the spell of the quaint and the charming. I went from one photogenic locale to another and another, my eyes pinwheeling in my head, trying to blot out from awareness the ugly and unswept, the slums by the railroad tracks, the trash heaped behind the pastel-hued buildings, the graffiti all over the medieval walls, the satellite dishes sprouting like a plague of mushrooms from the tiled roofs—any rude elements that might have detracted from my rapture had I stooped to notice them.

But being under the sway of the picturesque, I tried not to. It helped that my critical faculties were largely knocked senseless with awe. I set my receiver to "selective perception" and my camera to "creative photography," and I tried to capture scenes from only the most appealing and romantic angles, sans tourists, trash, traffic, and telephone wires, anything that might have undermined the impression, the illusion, that I had traveled back to a time when beauty in perfect aesthetic and mathematical proportion was unravaged by the ravages of time and tackiness.

I also tried to keep my mind untroubled by the inconvenient fact that most ruins, as wondrous as they are in their picturesque ebb, aren't ruins because of benign neglect but because they were murdered. Sacked, pillaged, and plundered, with their inhabitants slaughtered, enslaved, or scattered to the winds, their walls smashed and burned, their temples defiled by defecating soldiers, their tumultuous vitality brutally extinguished.

Sometimes they were drowned, like Sybaris, the capital of the Greek colonies that lay between Italy's heel and toe 2,800 years ago, and from which we get the word *sybaritic*, as in the love of luxury and pleasure. The entire opulent city was drowned and buried when the inhabitants of the rival city of Croton, famous contrarily for their sobriety and physical strength, sent an army of one hundred thousand men led by a professional boxer and, by literally changing the course of the nearby river Crathis, inundated Sybaris entirely. To this day it lies fathoms deep under alluvial mud, despite the concerted efforts of archaeologists to unearth it.

But it's easier to soft-focus my way through their picturesque settings and nostalgic reveries than to turn my enchantment toward an examination of the lurid histories of these wonders of the world, which is, to a great extent, the history of human savagery, staggering in scale and increasing in frequency. In the 2,500 years from 1000 B.C. to A.D. 1500 there were roughly 200 wars, one every 12 years or so. In the 400 years from 1500 to 1900 there were 450 wars, better than 1 every year. And in the little more than 100 years from 1900 to the present there have been over 350 wars, more than 3 every year.

Awe is usually associated with the unexpected, but in this case it's the *habitualness* of the behavior that awes us and awakens astonishment's twisted sister, horror—our own monstrous cruelties with their brutal and inscrutable logic, our inconceivable arrogances and insensitivities, the genocides that prompted the United Nations in 1946 to condemn acts that "shock the conscience of mankind."

The truth is, I often find myself having to muscle my way into a mood of reverie when I'm visiting ruins. Past these insights. Past herds of sightseers and their incessant shutterbuggery. Past the cyclone fences, ticket offices, and plaintive cries of street hawkers selling tacky whirligig toys and plastic pyramid replicas. All of it threatens to break the spell of wonder under which I'm trying to fall, the lovely hollowness of that departed life that I'm trying to fill with my own fascination.

It's like watching the movie *Ben-Hur* and seeing one of the gladiators wearing a wristwatch, or *Dances with Wolves* with that jet contrail slicing through the prairie sky and a bottle of Gatorade tucked into the protagonist's saddle. Gorged with crowds of camera-humping tourists and trinket-peddlers, Hard Rock Cafe T-shirts and bright red buses going by in the background, a palace ruin whose marble chambers Augustus or Kubla Khan once paced, a temple on whose grass-grown steps Plato once sat, can seem like an amusement park.

It's a grotesque distortion of the fact that standing before me is not just a tourist attraction, not just something to take overexposed pictures of for the folks back home, but the Lost City of the Incas, whose priests blew kisses at the rising sun every morning. Or the Roman Colosseum, where elephants fought tigers, entire naval battles were re-created in the great flooded stadium, and on one spring day in A.D. 107, five thousand pairs of gladiators, each chained together at the waist, fought to the death before one hundred thousand screaming Roman fans.

The distortion is further amplified by the fact that in the age-old contest between romantics and archaeologists—between those who love ruins for their beauty and the display of fate's extremes and those who love them for their glimpses into the antiquarian past—the scientists have largely prevailed. In hopes of preserving the past, they've literally deflowered most of the world's ruins, denuding them of all the flora that, according to centuries of ruin lovers, gave them much of their picturesqueness.

An eighteenth-century traveler once described Italy's exfoliated ruins as evoking in him "the feeling one has before a beautiful naked body." But by the time I first saw them in the twentieth century, they sometimes struck me as more akin to plucked chickens. My ideal of the perfect ruin includes twining ivy and the roosts of owl and raven, to say nothing of silence and solitude.

It was only at the enormous thirteenth-century remains of an old ironworks deep in the coastal mountains behind Amalfi that I had a ruin all to myself for the whole day, one far from the beaten track, unscrubbed and unlabeled, wildly whiskered with trees and vines sprouting from its walls and innermost courtyards, the surrounding forest pressing in from every direction.

And there's no doubt about it: the solitude and the undoctored ruin accentuated the sense of enchantment and the nearly pleasurable sadness that ruins can evoke. It made the magic of the place far easier to feel, the sense of a then and a now and of the forces that work both gently and ruthlessly on all things born and built and hoped-for.

NONE OF THIS is to suggest that holy moly might not come in equally handy in our dealings with the modern world, especially the enchantments of science, not just pseudoscience or magic or trips to Italy.

Take the computer. On one hand, it's certainly an unmitigated wonder, a bona fide outlet for our desire for magic, in the sense of being granted wishes. You type in a word, do a search, and out of the rabbit warren of human knowledge and data storage the thing you seek is suddenly conjured up on your screen. Clicking on a link is no different from saying "Open sesame!" There's even a Command key. As a writer old enough to have spent many an afternoon hunting down arcana in the public library, I never cease to be amazed at the invocational power of the computer.

On the other hand, spellbinding wouldn't be an inappropriate description of its hold on many of us, and like being spellbound, we can forget the distinction between reality and virtual reality. (Same with television. Viewers wrote 250,000 letters addressed to the fictional Marcus Welby, M.D., during his five years on TV.) You can get lost in the maze. There's a distinct correlation between enchantment and enthrallment. There's an ever-present danger that enchantment will turn from being a balm to being an escape, a psychological opium haze.

The poet John Keats even went so far as to claim that Isaac Newton robbed the rainbow of its poetry by reducing it to its prismatic colors. He wrote that science "will clip an Angel's wings, / Conquer all the mysteries by rule and line, / Empty the haunted air, and gnomed mine— / Unweave a rainbow."

What Newton actually did was darken his study and let a small beam of light in through a hole in a shutter. In its path he placed his infamous prism, which split the light into its component colors and spread them across a wall, showing, for the first time, that white light is an amalgam of different colors.

But if his experiment trimmed any angel's wings, it also created a whole host of new angels, including the science of spectroscopy, by which we've come to know the natural history of stars—their color and chemical makeup, their temperature and size, their luminosity, their *future*. We've also learned that they're the nuclear furnaces in which our own atoms were forged—the oxygen in our lungs, the nitrogen in our DNA, the calcium in our teeth, the iron in our blood, the silicone in our implants.

Did Newton really unweave the rainbow or did he weave a new set of illuminations? Did he really conquer the mysteries of light and spoil everybody's fun or did he offer whole new mysteries to wonder at and to inspire passionate new poems?

Even if science is responsible for unraveling any rainbows, it certainly isn't *modern* science. The process of what Weber calls demagification started 2,500 years ago with a fellow named Thales, considered the father of science, who attempted to find naturalistic explanations for things rather than supernatural and mythological ones, even if some of those attempts were so far-fetched as to seem almost superstitious by modern standards. For example, he hypothesized that earthquakes occur because the earth floats on water and is occasionally rocked by waves.

It was another of the early scientists, Democritus, who came up with the first atomic theory, which we tend to think of as belonging to our own time. In explaining that all matter is made up of imperishable elements, he coined the word *atom*, meaning "indivisible," though that, too, turned out not to be the case.

The technological world is anything but bereft of enchantment. In the cloud-cuckoo-land of quantum science, parallel lines meet, curves get you from one place to another quicker than straight lines, time expands and contracts, and electrons jump from point A to point B without traversing the distance in between. It's only missing mad hatters entertaining guests down in rabbit holes. I read recently that scientists can now attach satellite tags to fish, which make daily records of their travels and then, after six months, automatically detach themselves from the fish, float to the surface, and upload their data to a satellite, which can then be downloaded to a scientist's computer.

Science has opened up so many new worlds of enchantment, in fact—the microscopic, the astronomic, the genetic, the quantum, the computerized, the subterranean, and submarine—that it might even be fair to say that it's provided us with *more* enchantment, not less. The telescope, Galileo claimed, brought more wonders into the world than any discovery in human history, drawing the stars themselves within reach. (Though it's curious how frequently scientists refer to Earth itself as "an insignificant planet of a humdrum star lost in a galaxy tucked away in some forgotten corner of a universe." Forgotten by whom? Humdrum by what standards?)

Scientists do leave a bit to be desired in their descriptions of the wonders they unveil. When poets talk of the sun, they invoke the father of shadows, the dew's undoer, tinted with a thousand fires. Scientists refer to a class G2V yellow dwarf. I've read some of my brother Marc's professional journal articles on computer graphics, and they're almost literally Greek to me. I understand nothing except his byline: "The Fourier projection-slice theorem states that the inverse transform of a slice extracted from the frequency domain representation of a volume yields a projection of the volume in a direction perpendicular to the slice."

The truth is, *mystery* comes from a word meaning "to close the mouth," so words and graphs and flowcharts—for that matter, explanations of any kind, whether they emanate from the laboratory or the pulpit—can go only so far in answering our frequently asked questions. The rest is adjudicated by faith and contemplation.

GIVEN MY IGNOMINIOUS introduction to the world of the paranormal at the hands of my two brothers, it was with no small irony that when I was given the opportunity to revisit that domain of disembodied spirits and youthful credulity, barely a decade later, I took it.

I had the chance to interview a medium—then known as a trance channeler—someone who claims to access the spirit world the way a computer accesses a database, drawing into conversation various "entities," which some people call spiritual guides, others call emissaries from the collective unconscious, and still others call poppycock.

Communication with spirits requires you to entertain a simple proposition: that the human personality can survive independently of the body. This evokes in me two powerfully contrary dispositions: the skeptical and the hopeful.

The truth is, I *want* to believe in the famously exotic realms of the psyche—the extrasensory, telepathic, clairvoyant, shamanic, and mystical. I *want* to believe in kingdoms beyond this small daily life, in signs and wonders, in love conquering all and mind over matter, in miracles and the power of prayer to heal, in the existence of life on other planets. I want to believe in "Do what you love and the money will follow," though they never tell you how much, or when, or even whether it will follow *you*. I want to believe in forgiveness. I want to believe I'm on a path and not merely wandering aimlessly through the world. I want to believe that at the end of life I'll be reunited with my loved ones. And with my hair.

It was at this crossroads where wonder, desire, and doubt all meet—and with the memory of that adolescent séance lodged firmly in my craw—that I encountered a trance channeler named Kevin Ryerson, whom I'd recently seen playing himself on ABC's metaphysical miniseries *Out on a Limb*, based on Shirley MacLaine's best seller of the same name. He was also a consultant on the movie *Poltergeist II*, a collaboration that raises some interesting cinematic questions. Should channeled entities get screen credits? Are they required to be members of the Screen Actors Guild?

While Ryerson was in high school in Sandusky, Ohio—a town featured in two episodes of *The Twilight Zone*—he was administered an occupational profile test that told him he'd make a great dock foreman. But by the time I met him in the early 1980s, he was a trance channeler used by a variety of "discarnates" as something of a human telephone, talking with whoever came for a two-hour session, whether a New York City cabbie (they *haven't* seen it all), the mayor of Cleveland, Elisabeth Kübler-Ross, or Shirley MacLaine, who worked with Ryerson in putting together two of her books and whose acquaintance had proved to be a blessing and a curse, he said, gathering about him not only renown and mystique but a vocal coterie of critics demanding that he "prove it!"

Ryerson, soft-spoken and boyish at age thirty-six, hosted four entities, an unlikely cast of dramatis personae. At first glance they seemed like comic strip characters from the ethereal plane. The most prevalent was Tom Mcpherson, a rascally Irish pickpocket who had lived during Shakespeare's time and was working off his errant karma by being of service to people as a storyteller and an astrologer.

John, son of Zebedee, was a two-thousand-year-old scholar of the Essenes, a Hebrew sect widely believed to be the authors of the Dead Sea Scrolls.

Obadiah was a one-hundred-fifty-year-old Jamaican herbalist with an accent far deeper, Ryerson said, than any octave he himself could reach.

The fourth was Doctor Shangru, a one-hundred-year-old Hindi physician and homeopath who has since been replaced by free agents Japu, a Buddhist monk from the Indus Valley, and Atun Re, an ancient Egyptian priest and, improbably, former head of the Egyptian army.

I arrived for my private session at Ryerson's San Francisco apartment, expecting at least some measure of Hollywood razzmatazz—the temptation is enormous. But Ryerson's brand of spiritism involved no quaking furniture or sudden inexplicable gusts of wind. For one thing, pickpockets like Mcpherson don't make grand entrances; it's bad for business. Ryerson simply turned on a tape recorder, settled into a chair, and within three minutes was "under," a state he likened to deep meditation. He claimed to simply move aside so that the entities could speak through him as one would through a ham-radio set—heard but not seen.

If there was anything wondrous about the experience, it wasn't actually my encounter with Ryerson's entities, or even with Ryerson. It was the soul-searching prompted by his instruction to come prepared with a list of questions I might want to ask of God if I were granted the opportunity.

I dove into the task with a sincerity that surprised me, given my largely agnostic upbringing. But to rally my own consent if not enthusiasm for the exercise and to get myself over the imaginal hump of picturing an actual conversation with the Supreme Being, I had to personify God in a way that was far more representational than I actually believe God to be. So I alternately pictured the big bearded fellow Michelangelo painted on the ceiling of the Sistine Chapel and the statue of Zeus at Olympia, one of the Seven Wonders of the Ancient World and one of the deities about whom the writer Albert Goldbarth says, "He sits on a throne, with all that implies: stature, image, buttocks."

I ended up filling two pages with questions, all the "who, what, when, where, and why" of my dreams and dramas, all the knock-knocks and explorations that animated my days. Questions are magic words that invoke the spirit of discovery and wonder, and asking the questions out loud is the open sesame.

This is a lesson I learned at the altar of my father's knee. His great passion was science, and his favorite game to play with me and my two brothers was something he invented called the Alien Game, in which he was a visitor from another planet (which we had suspected all along), and we were his guides on Earth. We would go out into the neighborhood, down by the shore, or into the city, and he would ask questions and we would try to answer them. He'd point up into the sky, for instance, and ask, "What are the white formations that move through your atmosphere?"

We'd all say, "Clouds!"

He'd ask, "What are they composed of?"

We'd all say, "Water!"

He'd ask, "How does the water get up there, and what holds it up, and what makes it move?"

In no time at all, it would become apparent to us Earthlings that clouds weren't the only things over our heads. But it also showed us, very early on, that the more we persist with our questions about life, the more marvels and mysteries open themselves to our curiosity and confusion, and the more vistas open before us. We learned the power of questions to spark our imaginations as well as to draw knowledge both from us and to us, which comes in handy in exploring and explaining the inner world as well as the outer world.

"People travel to wonder at the height of the mountains," said Saint Augustine, "at the huge waves of the seas, at the long course of the rivers, at the vast compass of the ocean, at the circular motion of the stars, and yet they pass by themselves without wondering."

The word *mirror* and the word *miracle* share the same Latin root, which means "to wonder at," and it's important to locate wonder not just out there in the world, always fanning its plumage, but also within ourselves. By turning exclamatory wonder in our own direction—marveling at our gifts and heroisms, our passions and compassions, the sensual and athletic marvels of the body, the imagination at work even while we sleep, the questions that animate our days, the fact that we're here at all—we help wonder condense into wisdom and bloom into gratitude.

2

Questing

The Happiness of Pursuit

SCHEHERAZADE WAS THE QUEEN whose stories make up *The Arabian Nights*, and I believe we all share her fate.

Scheherazade became the wife of the sultan of Persia, who had a decree that every woman he married would be killed on the morning after the wedding—a man with a serious intimacy problem. She wanted to put a stop to this, so on the day of their wedding, she began telling the sultan a story, but stopped just short of the finish. The sultan agreed to let her live one more day to see how the story turned out.

The next day, she finished the story and started another, stopping, once again, just short of the climax. Again the sultan let her live one more day to see how *that* story unfolded. After 1,001 nights and 1,001 stories, the sultan fell in love with Scheherazade and the killing stopped.

Scheherazade reminds us that the commitment to forward momentum is a lifesaving virtue, and that it's critical not to fall too far out of sync with life, which *moves*. That is, if we stop telling *our* stories, we're dead. If we stop the narrative from moving forward, stop doing the life-giving thing, stop doing what Scheherazade's storytelling ultimately did—create passion where there wasn't any—we're dead, in a soul sense.

The world, too, owes its forward-leaning impulses, its progress, and its passion, to the spirit of questing—even restlessness—within us. To the part of each one of us that eventually grows weary of the status quo and hungry for a challenge, and that feels born to run—to move, explore, experiment, travel, climb, create, investigate, invent, pioneer, and discover. To grow. "Perhaps the world progresses not by maturing," says novelist Julian Barnes, "but by being in a permanent state of adolescence, of thrilled discovery."

Maybe the world even owes some of its sanity to this part of us. "If you stopped all the time, you'd go crazy," a friend, Vince, once said, describing road trips he used to take with his family. He was one of ten kids, and his father had drilled a hole in the floorboard in the backseat and inserted a length of pipe attached to a funnel for the kids to use when they had to relieve themselves. We make better headway—and mileage—when we build up some momentum, and we're less likely to go stir-crazy.

The philosopher Blaise Pascal once said that all of our miseries derive from not being able to sit quietly in a room alone—but surely some of our miseries derive from too *much* time sitting alone in a room, legs pulsating under the desk, running in place. Our orbits can so easily narrow down to the use of a few beaten paths, a handful of faculties, the company of the same people and the same ideas, a small wedge of experience that excludes whole universes of pleasure and whole continents of people, while the larger life that's always out there accuses us of mere contentment.

When he was in his twenties, the travel writer Bruce Chatwin (whose surname means "the winding path" in old Anglo-Saxon) was an art expert at Sotheby's, a job he found increasingly distasteful. One morning he woke up blind. The doctor said there was nothing organically wrong with him. "You've been looking too closely at pictures," the doctor told him. "Why don't you swap them for some long horizons." So he went to Africa. His eyes recovered by the time he got to the airport.

In her book *New*, Winifred Gallagher refers to neophilia—the enthusiasm for novelty that's at the heart of the exploratory urge—as being the quintessential human survival skill, whether we're adapting to climate change on the primordial African savanna or coping with the computer-ization of modern life and what she calls our desk-tethered world; whether we're exploring uncharted terrain, investigating new artistic techniques, poking around at the further reaches of a scientific theory, or probing the endless possibilities of intimacy.

Some of us are neophiliacs and some neophobes—people who shy away from novelty, if not outright fear it—and most of us fall on the broad spectrum between.

Neophilia's grand design is to help us learn and create, as well as adapt to the moving target that is the world, both then and now. "It's all about anticipation, desire, *wanting*," says Gallagher.

Researchers looking for the traits that characterize people who tend to flourish over the years have found that such people tend to score high in novelty seeking. They also score high on persistence, which might seem to be incompatible but isn't. Gallagher considers the two an ideal combin-ation. "Don't go wide and shallow," she says. "Use your neophilia to go deep into subjects that are important to you."

The main character in Walker Percy's novel *The Moviegoer* is, by his own admission, a neophobe—a model citizen, model tenant, creature of habit, regular as a monk, who takes pleasure in doing all that's expected of him, though he once dreamed of doing something great.

But throughout the book, he describes being routinely stopped in the middle of his middlebrow days by a reverie about what he calls "the search," which he never quite articulates but which seems to be of a vaguely spiritual nature, and which he believes anyone would undertake "if he were not sunk in the everydayness of his own life," having con-demned himself to being "an Anyone living Anywhere," settling for what he calls "the Little Way."

To be aware at all of the possibility of the search, he insists, is to be "onto something," and not to be onto something is to be in despair. But he also feels that the search itself has spoiled the pleasure of his tidy life and plays on him the miserable trick the romantic continually plays on him-self: setting just beyond reach the very thing he seeks.

The question at the heart of questing, of course, is whether you'll ever attain the thing you seek, and that depends on what you're seeking and whether you're looking for it in the right places or the wrong places. And sometimes you don't even know what you're after when you set out on a quest, and only discover it *by* setting out, or when you come back to port, and maybe not even then.

Pat Henry's neophilia took her on an eight-year odyssey that put her into the record books as the first American woman—and at fifty, the oldest anywhere—to sail solo around the world (via the canals rather than the capes), and her story illuminates the complexities of "the search."

With a cast-iron constitution and a venturing spirit that makes most of us look like we're chained to a stump, she single-handed her way over forty thousand miles of not just seven seas but eleven (the Pacific Ocean, Coral Sea, Arafura Sea, Java Sea, Andaman Sea, Indian Ocean, Arabian Sea, Red Sea, Mediterranean, Atlantic, and Caribbean), following a kind of migratory urge she calls "questing"—and others might call an adventurous euphemism for restlessness.

It began at the tender age of three, when she wandered away from her grandmother's homestead in South Dakota searching for the proverbial pot of gold and was found several hours later in the local bar being fed ice cream by some of the regulars.

"All my life, what's drawn me is always change, and freedom, and the horizon which speaks to me of *something more*, some delight that I can't wait to see," she recently told me. "I always want to be on my way to somewhere, and not necessarily somewhere locational. It could be some new knowledge or challenge, something to figure out, something to learn, some problem to solve. I'm never content to keep doing the same thing. Life happens best on the days when I don't know what to expect—a state that's guaranteed if I keep moving."

Pat claims she took the trip to rebuild her confidence after a business failure, though the confidence required for a solo circumnavigation of the world suggests that hers was still in good fighting form. To say nothing of the number of complex skills needed to make good on that level of questing: handling a thirty-foot sailboat alone, knowing every nut and bolt and beam aboard ship, being able to take engines apart and put them back together (sometimes in mid-ocean and mid-storm), deciphering navigational charts and occasionally steering only by the stars, having the sheer nerve to sail across seas famous for their piracy and cut across shipping lanes like those near Singapore, which is like trying to run across a six-lane superhighway. And taking on constant storms—not the metaphorical kind but the meteorological—in which she was literally fighting for her life and in the middle of which she could honestly say to herself, "I love this! This makes me feel alive."

What James Joyce said of his protagonist in *Portrait of the Artist as a Young Man* could readily be said of Pat: "There was a lust of wandering in his feet that burned to set out for the ends of the earth. On! On! his heart seemed to cry. . . . He was alone. He was unheeded, happy and near to the wild heart of life."

One of the questions that underlies the passion for such journeying is whether it's done for the sake of encounter or escape, and in fact a few people wondered, occasionally aloud, whether Pat was running not so much toward something—freedom, adventure, the horizon—as away from something.

It's the most common accusation leveled against the restless: that there's something they don't want to face or don't want to feel. And though the unexamined life is definitely still worth living, contrary to the grumpy counsel of Socrates—and though running away is wisdom, not folly, if what you're running from is toxic—sometimes the allegation is true. Sometimes restlessness *is* avoidance, a kind of motion sickness in which you use activities like travel, job hopping, relocation, promiscuity, and upward mobility as distractions from deeper explorations and commitments—the emotional equivalent of channel surfing. At the far end of the questing spectrum is dromomania, literally a passion for running, wanderlust, even what's referred to as pathological tourism. It's what drove Forrest Gump on his crisscross-country jog.

The anthropologist Loren Eiseley once said that even the venture into space is meaningless unless it coincides with an interior expansion, a growing universe within, and one of the great clichés of restlessness and endless questing is that wherever you go, there you are. Even if you moved to another *world*, you'd take your inner world with you.

You can go from port to port, job to job, and affair to affair, always trying to chase down paradise, a dream job, a soulmate, or a grand unified theory, but you're still going to see the same inner sky no matter what new worlds you discover. Furthermore, travel itself forces on you a highly concentrated dose of your own personality and approach to life—to change, freedom, stress, surrender, and the unknown—and ultimately highlights rather than obscures what's already there. And all that glitters in such glamorous and peripatetic lives isn't necessarily gold. Sometimes it's the shimmer on the surface of mirage, the tinsel sheen of your own fantasies and ambitions. Life on the road, for example, can be famously lonesome.

The timing of Pat's departure certainly made people wonder. It came directly on the heels of that business failure, the foundering of an import-export company, which ended up such a financial mess that the IRS came after her; in fact, it pursued her literally around the world, threatening to seize her property and bank accounts, except that she no longer had either. She didn't even have a usable credit card to take on the trip, just some cash, which ran out quickly, forcing her to rely on painting watercolors to earn money. She made friends in every boat club in every port and managed to stage small showings of her work, which she sold for an average of fifty dollars apiece, though a more elaborate show in Singapore netted her ten thousand dollars.

When I asked Pat if her questing *is* in any part the search for a fix, she reluctantly spoke about "a history of ephemeral relationships," though whether they were a cause or a consequence of her questing wasn't clear. "I don't know that there isn't a little hole I'm trying to fill. I'm not much of a team player. In relationships, I tend to either take over or back out. I came up to the States recently [she lives in Puerto Vallarta, Mexico] to take some tango classes, and they say tangos are three-minute love affairs. I can handle that."

One of those ephemeral relationships was with her father, a man she saw all of twenty times in her whole life. She was one year old when Pearl Harbor was bombed and he was shipped off to war. While overseas, he fell in love with another woman, leaving Pat's mother to raise her alone, but not before she struck a kind of devil's bargain with him. He could have his divorce under one condition: he agree never to see his daughter again.

Children, being naturally self-centered, assume everything revolves around them, including the failures of their parents, so Pat grew up feeling that if only she were "good enough," her father would have fought to see her—which may explain some of her drive and restlessness, and certainly explains a dramatic confrontation she had on the last day of the voyage.

Her boat, *Southern Cross*, was finally docked in Puerto Vallarta after eight years at sea, the marina staff abuzz with congratulations and champagne and well wishes from family, friends, and editors at newspapers like the *New York Times*. As she sat alone belowdecks, she was suddenly overcome with what she describes as an emotional explosion. "I shouted, 'There! Now did I do enough?'"

There was no one in the cabin with her but the ghost of her father, and tears poured out. "It was a huge surprise to me," she wrote in her book about the journey, *By the Grace of the Sea*, "but there he was. Until that moment, I had no idea to what extent his role in my life had influenced not only that voyage but my constant push to measure up, to reach higher and higher, to keep questing."

A Revolt Against the Fixed

"I travel not to go anywhere, but to go," Robert Louis Stevenson wrote in *Travels with a Donkey in the Cévennes*. "I travel for travel's sake. The great affair is to move."

Seventy-five years later, when Jack Kerouac climbed into his fin-tailed car to head out on the road, he said the same thing: "We were leaving confusion and nonsense behind and performing our one and noble function of the time, move." (Never mind that the confusion and nonsense were largely self-inflicted and that he created a good deal more of it on the road.)

The author Richard Ford even wrote in one of his novels that "all of America's literature, Cotton Mather to Steinbeck . . . was forged by one positivist principle: to leave, and then to arrive in a better state."

It seems to me that only a roving mind and a busy body are really adequate to this world, anyway, which is spinning on its axis at 1,000 miles per hour, in an orbit around the sun at 65,000 miles per hour, in a solar system traveling at 540,000 miles per hour around the galaxy, in a galaxy charging through space at 670,000 miles per hour, in a universe expanding at 160,000 miles per hour per megaparsec, whatever that means.

What it means to you, personally, is that even when you're sitting peacefully in the lotus position, you're moving at a million and a half miles an hour, which you won't notice, of course, unless something happens to hit your windshield.

Motion, in fact, is required for matter to even exist, since electrons orbiting nuclei a million billion times in the blink of an eye accounts for solidity in the universe. Likewise, motion is essential to a life of substance, and action is the active ingredient in making our passions coalesce and creating form out of what's unformed in us.

Restlessness is as old as the world, something we all knew back when we were zygotes. The lime in our bones and the salt in our blood are inheritances from what poets call the restless sea. Every womb is the primordial water, every fetus a fish. Every one of us swims up onto land and stands upright, and so does the bottom of the sea. There's marine limestone at the top of Mount Everest.

The psalmist admonishes us to lift our eyes unto the hills, for they are solid and enduring beside the fleeting blur of our own lives. But the truth is, the hills are moving too, and they're mortal. Restlessness isn't as old as the hills; it's older. It's a restless universe presided over by a restless Spirit, the ultimate multitasker, but one who still pays exquisite attention to detail, is not lacking in commitment, and puts the lie to the notion that there's a contradiction between being busy and being wise. "The hinges on the wing of an earwig," the theologian William Paley said, "are as highly wrought as if the Creator had nothing else to finish. We see no signs of diminution of care by multiplicity of objects, or distraction of thought by variety."

Paley is referring to one infinitesimally small moving part on a creature manufactured by the billions every year—a perfect set of hinges practically every time, with no inventors, no architects, no mechanical engineers, contractors, carpenters, masons, plasterers, electricians, inspectors, or caterers. To say nothing of all the other design elements with which each hinge has to coordinate itself to ensure flight and survival: wing struts of an exact tensile strength, a leathery sheath of upper wings and a gauzy layer of lower wings working in perfect contrapuntal rhythm, and microscopic ligaments that hold them to the chassis of a body containing cockpit, navigation, and landing gear.

And this is one part of one creature among millions of species, including ours and the staggering multiplicity of our own moving parts, like the simple ball-and-socket hinge that lets us get out of bed in the morning and make bacon and eggs, run triathlons, paint Sistine Chapels, and send rocket ships into the nether regions of space to take pictures and deliver Chuck Berry songs to whoever might run across them out there.

We are, Paley rightly claims, looked after, and by a restless and busy Creator who still finds time to come around to the garden and sweep the path, trim the hedges, and tidy the place up a bit.

THE RESTLESSNESS that's at the heart of questing can encompass anything from garden-variety hyperactivity to the kind of headlong busyness that characterizes such a large swath of human activity. It can range from travel fever to the kind of passionate intensity typical of creative and exploratory types, who are seldom satisfied with the status quo or their station in life, and from the feeling of being unsettled within yourself to an ever-present hunger for personal growth and spiritual refinement.

And though evidence for the hand-me-down nature of restlessness is strong, there are cultural suspects as well: a foundational (and spreading) Western mythos that says expansion is inevitable and preferable and that the way to a better life is to keep moving, coupled with a baffling multitude of outlets for our restlessness, all of consumer culture's weapons of mass distraction, brought to us by up to three thousand marketing messages a day per person in the United States. We're surrounded by nearly endless options and replaceable parts, a global marketplace supersaturated with goods and improvement plans, and freedom and leisure and, for a lot of us, the money to make good on them. And these forces tend to interact with our inherent restlessness in mutually reinforcing ways.

But in searching for the origins of restlessness, if not the journeying urge, you have to eventually set aside the feather quill pen of cultural studies and take up the cudgel of carbon dating and genomics, which remind us that we all come from nomadic stock. Mobility is the rule in human history. Sedentary life is the exception. In the brainstem of every human being is a revolt against what's fixed, and a deep migratory urge. Ten thousand years of settlement isn't enough to undo the several *million* years that forged our hunter-gatherer genome, and trying to do so is playing against the house.

In other words, restlessness is not just a function of the peculiar bead-and-feather work of the individual personality, or the parents to whom you were born. It can't be explained away as wanderlust or attention-deficit/hyperactivity disorder or by the fact that you clocked twenty thousand hours in front of the television by the time you reached voting age, thus bestowing on you a *Sesame Street* attention span. It's not just an ailment brought on by civilization, industrialization, democracy, the automobile, sugar-frosted breakfast cereals, or a consumerism gone runny in the intestines. It's shared by people who aren't hyperactive, aren't Western, and didn't have disappearing daddies and fidgety forebears. And it doesn't always mean you're running from something.

Dogs still turn around in circles before lying down, a holdover from their days in the savanna grass. Horses still get up on their feet an hour after being born so they're ready to move with the herd in the morning. And we still carry the residue of our nomadic heritage. We have genes selected for curiosity and novelty, limbs that were made for walking, long childhoods during which to practice exploration, and brains designed to think imaginatively. So it's no surprise that we're often beleaguered with sudden shouts of wanting that order us to our feet.

The hunger to quest is also self-propelling. The drive for discovery leads to pleasure—the satisfaction of the urge to explore, the scratching of an ancient itch—and in turn that pleasure spurs the urge for more discovery.

Unfortunately, it also spurs constraint, especially for children who are new to the art of questing. They may be compelled by millions of years of genetic programming to explore the world with relish, to stick their fingers into every nook and cranny and submit all evidence to taste testing, but though the world is filled with many delights, it's also filled with many deterrents, and typically more red lights than green lights.

In *The Biology of Transcendence*, Joseph Chilton Pearce cites a study in which the mothers of eleven- to seventeen-month-old children expressed verbal restraints ("No," "Don't") on the average of every nine minutes, often accompanied by physical restraint or punishment. And with few exceptions, children will choose to preserve the bond with their caregivers over their own will to explore. The child's resistance is eventually broken down, along with their exploratory urge, and we call it socializing.

"Inhibition is a form of depression," says Pearce. "The same hormones are involved."

Some children, however, come in with an extra dose of wandering in their genes—compliments of a chromosomal variant called the exon III 7-repeat allele, linked to both attention-deficit/hyperactivity disorder and folks with migratory ancestors.

Genetic demographics show that the gene—which mutated into existence about forty thousand years ago, a period characterized by major human migrations and explorations of the planet—is also present in highly varying percentages in different populations worldwide. Researchers have looked at the frequency of this gene in eighteen indigenous populations spread along the routes humans took from Africa to Europe, Asia, and the Americas, and the farther away from Africa they are, the more likely they are to have the gene—up to 85 percent among native South Americans whose ancestors are thought to have migrated across Arctic ice bridges long gone, but only 0 to 2 percent among South Asians.

Another of the active ingredients in restlessness is hyperactivity, which is also largely born, I think, not made. I saw this on the pediatric wing of a hospital in New York where my mother went for surgery a few years ago. Wandering the corridors one afternoon during my weeklong visit, I stumbled on a scene I've seen only in movies—the baby ward. On one side of its glass partition were newborns, and on the other side their mooning relatives.

Babies arrive here straight from the cosmic pipeline, still stoned on transfiguration, only minutes or hours from having finished the spectacular journey into being, their eyes squinting at the light of an alien world and their lungs gulping air once breathed by dinosaurs. Here they're processed, registered, sorted (their tags read, "Hi, I'm a Boy" or "Hi, I'm a Girl"), and prepared for shipping and distribution. What I noticed was that some of the babies were lying quietly in their swaddle, and others were twitching like beetles on their backs—not unlike my mother did during her week in the hospital.

And not unlike, my mother claims, *I* did during my entire childhood—a chip off the old block. This probably explains why my parents slipped Ritalin into my morning milk, why I routinely got sent to the principal's office for drumming "Wipeout" on the desks, why I went to four different colleges, why as a reporter I was a generalist and not a specialist, why I became a freelancer who, in keeping with tradition and definition, has allegiance to no king or kingdom, and why I worked *hard* to stay married for twenty years. I'm even restless in my sleep.

I've never been one to be lastingly satisfied where I was planted or heed the advice of my elders to settle down. I dislike having my momentum disrupted—hate getting caught at red lights or being interrupted while I'm reading, never pick up the phone, seldom come to a complete stop at stop signs. I sway back and forth when I stand still, vibrate my legs like tuning forks under the table, practice mime gestures and dance routines while waiting for the toast, tap out syncopated rhythms on any available surface, and explore endless variations on the theme of fidgeting, an integral part of my exercise regimen. And not just mine. A National Institutes of Health study found that fidgeting burns calories (anywhere from one hundred to eight hundred a day), is largely genetic, and is something that translates rather handily from body movements to general attitude.

Writing is even a fitting profession. Even its quietest moments are full of bustle. I can sit peacefully in my office chair—twisting back and forth of course—and be in a squall inside my head, launching sentences into heavy surf, calling up whole worlds and destroying them in a single paragraph, and yet birds can walk by on the windowsill three feet from where I'm sitting and not be alarmed.

Last night a gnat landed on my writing pad and was so unperturbed by my advancing pen that I was able to draw a circle around it as I passed. The gnat remained momentarily in the circle, like an actor in a spotlight, then exited. I followed it around the page, drawing circles around it, and I saw in the growing spatter an analog of my restless and questing life. I wondered: if I look closely enough, through a strong-enough microscope, would I be able to make out its footprints on the cellulose, any trace of its passing, the way paleontologists sometimes find the fossilized footprints of hominids along primeval mudflats?

I've also moved twenty-three times in thirty-eight years, something I find no precedence for in my immediate family, only my phylogenetic family (wandering Jews). I'm not an army brat, the son of diplomats, corporate gypsies, migrant workers, or anyone in the witness protection program. Neither of my brothers has moved around this often, though Ross had a childhood passion for collecting stamps, those emblems of the world's far-off places. My mother was born in Brooklyn and until only recently (when my brothers and I moved her into a nursing home in California) lived within twenty miles of it her whole life. My father always lived in the same town on Long Island, except for a stint in the Air Force during World War II, when he was stationed in Brazil and helped direct planes to North Africa. And my grandparents made the *great* move from the old countries to the new, from Russia and Germany to America at the turn of the last century—compared with which all my own moves seem *cosmetic*—but once in the New York City area, they never moved out.

To inhabit a place means to make it a habit, and I've simply never made a habit of anywhere I ever lived. I'm always passing through. I'm also told that when you multiply this behavior by the forty-three million Americans who move every year, it gets to be bad for the environment and community life. If you don't claim a place, it's tough to care about it.

Such moving around sometimes feels like attention-deficit disorder on a grand scale—some people go through jobs, businesses, cars, communities, schemes, relationships; I go through homes. But this isn't to say I haven't enjoyed the moving around. It's been richly adventurous and an outstanding teacher in the arts of adaptability and resilience, which life sorely tests and which are among the beatitudes of questing.

Every move also tells me that I'm not where I was, that change is possible, and that anything can happen. I've lived on the East Coast and the West, a stone's throw from Canada and from Mexico, in the city and in the country, in conservative towns and in liberal ones, in the mountains and by the sea, in the deserts and in the forests. The variety has been extremely welcome stimulation.

It's also been a fine education in the rigors of nonattachment, since moving, by definition, always compels me to let go of something or other, whether stationery and business cards, houses and homes, or familiarity and the comfort or contempt bred by it. Still, things have a way of piling up wherever they encounter a stationary object, like leaves blown against a fence, and a house is a stationary object, even if you live in it for only a year and even if it's a mobile home or a houseboat. When was the last time you saw a houseboat on the open sea?

Ironically, each move has been a notch up on an ever-increasing gradient of complexity—especially as I transitioned from renter to homeowner, from single to married, from a run-down studio apartment with a panoramic view of an alley and an air-conditioning duct to, at one point, a three-bedroom suburban house with a pool, and as the sheer gross tonnage of my possessions correspondingly increased, despite my attempts to live tentwise.

Once upon a time, everything I owned fit in a car, with room left over for a hitchhiker, two if it was raining. Moving meant little more than giving somebody thirty days' notice and packing the car. Now it's a job I have to hire out, and it involves moving vans that were too big to even negotiate the hairpin turns that led to the last house I owned.

Most wandering people travel light, living in tents and on saddles, and their primary possessions—herds—move by themselves. The nomadic life tends to work against the desire to accumulate things, and vice versa. I, on the other hand, shoulder from watering hole to watering hole a four-poster bed and a grand piano. After my last move, some friends sent me a farewell card with a picture of a backpacker walking into the wilderness with all his household belongings piled on his back, everything from a television, satellite dish, and extension cords to a cheese grater. Even his dog was heaped like a pack mule. This is a state of affairs about which I ultimately feel mixed, the nomad and the settler in me constantly vying for supremacy, constantly at the bargaining table.

Nomads such as the Aborigines believe that goods malign their possessors unless the goods remain moving, unless they keep up a wandering life themselves and don't make us their owners and curators but merely their distributors. But hauling all the goods along with us every time we move is probably not what they have in mind. Though being settled is certainly not one of the load-bearing beams of American life—we move on average every five years, change jobs every four, and each month two million of us change jobs—most of us are certainly not nomads in the original sense.

When I saw the movie *Gabbeh*, about Iranian nomads, it struck me that for all their wandering, they didn't seem at all restless to me, not in the feverish way that, say, Westerners embody the term. What *we* do falls into the intermezzo between nomad and settler, between being hunter-gatherers and being canner-preservers. We wander repeatedly, but from settlement to settlement.

. . .

TWO YEARS AGO, I received a most literal object lesson in how things can pile up in our lives and not merely get in our way but also drag us down, working at utter cross-purposes to our desire to stay fleet of foot and in the flow.

My mother had a dining room table that no one had seen for nearly twenty years, though it sat right in the middle of her dining room. This was because for twenty years she had used it as a cross between an archive and a landfill, effectively burying it beneath ever-accumulating and occasionally landsliding heaps of paper—magazines, newsletters, bills, bank statements, coupons, charity appeals, concert stubs, birthday cards, newspaper articles, advertisements, copies of itineraries for vacations she took back in the 1990s, baby pictures of her grandchildren who are now paying off college loans, and handwritten personal letters from back in the day when people actually wrote such things.

You could have taken a core sample from any quadrant of that dining room table and had a complete geological record of the past twenty years of my mother's life, along with her slowly composting state of mind.

Ross and I had flown to New York to visit her, though our true mission was to assess her condition, to determine what, if any, elder care she might be needing. This was because we'd been receiving alarming phone calls from strangers. "Your mother is standing here in the post office and doesn't understand why we won't cash a check for her," a postal clerk said.

"Your mother just left here after dropping off her taxes," said the wife of her accountant, "and she doesn't know a receipt from a refund anymore. And she shouldn't be driving."

"Your mother came downstairs today and told me she doesn't have any food, so I took her shopping," the superintendent of her apartment building said. "You boys need to get out here."

"Just keep her alive until Sunday," Ross said to him. "We're on our way."

The first of these phone calls came about two years ago, when my mother's longtime physician called to introduce herself, to tell us we'd likely be in contact more and more over time and that my mother, who was then eighty-two, was failing roughly 50 percent of her cognitive tests—what year is it, what kind of car do you drive, who's in the White

House, what's in the news? ("I don't know," my mother had said to the last one, "but it's all bad.")

Certainly we'd been noticing her faltering memory for some time, her tendency to ask the same question half a dozen times in ten minutes, her decomposing language skills, which of late had reduced her to using the term "the thing . . . you know, the thing" to describe whatever she couldn't find the right word for, and the ominous proliferation of little red rubber bands around everything in sight, including refrigerated items like Tupperware containers and jars of pickles.

And we certainly couldn't help but notice the heaving mounds of rummage where her dining room table used to be, and which appeared to upset my mother every time she looked at it, prompting her to wave her hands helplessly in the air and turn her head as if from the scene of an accident.

"Mom, why don't we go through all that stuff and clear it out," Ross suggested on our first night in New York.

"Oh no no no no no no no . . ." my mother said. "No. Uh-uh. Don't touch it."

The next afternoon, when my mother couldn't find a bill that may or may not have been paid, Ross proposed that it might be entombed somewhere in the dining room and that perhaps we should at least have a look at what's there. "Besides," he said, "all those piles are clearly stressing you out. Why suffer any more?" But my mother only let out a long, worried groan, cast a cowed glance in the direction of the dining room, and shook her head. "Uh-uh. Another time maybe. Are you boys hungry?"

On our last night in New York, Ross and I were sitting in the kitchen, making our way through one of the six wedges of brie that were in my mother's refrigerator because the superintendent—who had taken her to the grocery store last week when she believed she had run out of food, though it turned out she had merely run out of chocolate—had gone shopping as if the end-time were upon her.

My mother walked up to us with a small stack of unopened mail wrapped tightly with a red rubber band, which she had wrested from the glacial creep at the western edge of the dining room table, and said, "Help me go through this."

"Sure," I said as nonchalantly as possible, and when we had succeeded in separating wheat from chaff, I said, "Well, that's one less thing to worry about. Wanna knock off another little stack from the dining room? If it's too upsetting, we can just stop, okay?"

My mother led the way, walking slowly into the dining room the way an animal trainer might enter the cage with the tigers in it, holding a chair and a whip, then just stood there with who knows what flashing through her mind. Ross and I came up behind her, and after a moment's collective pause, he reached for a stack on one side of the table. "No!" my mother said sharply, then softened. "Let's start at the other end. That's where the older stuff is."

As we waded in, I noticed the muscles at my mother's jaw bunching.

In exactly one and a quarter hours, we made our way through that entire landscape of litter, twenty years' worth of stockpiling, my mother continually shaking her head and saying, "Why did I keep all this? What was I thinking?" We tossed 95 percent of it into paper shopping bags, easily a dozen of them, and when I asked what she wanted us to do with them, she surprised us all by saying, "Put it in the incinerator"—an order that I didn't waste a split second carrying out, lest she have a relapse.

When I returned from that mission, I found her leaning reverently over the newly excavated dining room table, whose surface she had literally not laid eyes on in two decades. She had a bottle of Windex in one hand and a paper towel in the other and was massaging the glass tabletop as if it were a holy relic.

Our lives sometimes call on us to clean house, to clear the decks and shake off the dust. To wade through the accumulated piles, garbage bags at the ready, and get to the bottom of things, remember who we are and what we're here to do and get on with it, or simply travel lighter. Things, and habits, have a way of piling up and getting underfoot, both in the house and in the psyche, and they can end up inhibiting our momentum and troubling our minds.

Settling for Less

For all its charms and comforts, domestication is a walling-in, and once walled in, we tend to lose our sense of the natural timetables of migrations, ripenings, and seasons that used to set us afoot, and which characterized our first few hundred million years of evolution. People are constantly shorn of these instincts by culture, but just as constantly, generation after generation, we're born with them. They're indefinitely stubborn. They can't be bred out of us like seeds can be bred out of grapes and melons.

The call of the road doesn't go away. If it isn't answered or even acknowledged, if it isn't given *some* rein—physically or psychologically—it can shape-shift into disquietude, busy mind, and outburst, what Morris Berman in *Wandering God* calls a "rogue element," a mocking rhizome at the root of our tree house.

In the movie *The Great New Wonderful*, Olympia Dukakis's character and her husband spend their days in a mind-numbingly stale routine in a high-rise apartment outside New York City. Every evening, while he watches TV, she sits at the kitchen table and creates an elaborate collage of all the places she yearns to travel to, and then she puts the finished collage in a hall closet along with what appear to be dozens more of them all stacked up, forty years' worth.

One day, while he's out smoking his after-dinner cigarette on the patio, she snaps. Bursting out the balcony door, she charges at him and tries to push him over the railing.

There's often just as thin a line between repression and depression. When animals are deprived of their freedom and natural habitat, as they are in zoos, for instance, they slowly go out of their minds, like the panther in Rainer Rilke's eponymous poem, whose "rhythmical easy stride . . . circles down to the tiniest hub, is like a dance of energy around a point in which a great will stands stunned and numb." Lions sleep up to twenty hours a day, but when those few hours come around and they're ready to roam, robbing them of it is enough to bring their souls to a standstill.

In their dreams, even our pets twitch with the hunt, though when they wake up they're still lying on the floor of an apartment in the city or a house in the suburbs, where they and their owners, animal and human alike, live in brooding forgetfulness of the origin of their needs.

Culture is what comes between an animal and its environment; sometimes it's a buffer, but often it's a barrier. The transition to sedentary life and a fixed address had, and has, a calcifying effect on the kind of kaleidoscopic worldview that characterizes the wild kingdoms and the lives of hunters and children, which may be some of what we're after with our questing. We literally settle for less.

The sedentary life is also bad for our health, contributing to a host of maladies—cardiovascular disease, diabetes, osteoporosis, stroke, hypertension, depression, obesity—that together account for up to 75 percent of the deaths in industrialized countries.

The tradition of the caravan has always been at odds with the tradition of the pyramid, and we've been caught in their cross-fire ever since we put up the first wall. In fact, the first archaeological evidence of what looks like war happens to coincide with the rise of agriculture and herding in the Mesolithic, twelve thousand or so years ago—because with settlement and the stockpiling of food and possessions, some people found it easier to steal than to hunt and forage. As a Bedouin proverb says, "Raids are our agriculture." War began as theft.

Settlers and nomads have always eyed one another suspiciously, even as they've exchanged envies. The settlers sometimes wish they could wander like gypsies, and the wanderers sometimes find themselves peering through the settlers' living room windows to see what they're missing. In his essay "Finding the Place," Wallace Stegner perfectly captures the contrary urges and agendas of nomads and settlers. "My father was a boomer, a gambler, a rainbow-chaser, as footloose as a tumbleweed in a windstorm. My mother was always hopefully, hopelessly, trying to nest."

Or take the story of Cain and Abel. Cain, the farmer, settler, builder of the first city and committer of the first murder, slew his brother Abel, the shepherd and nomad. Ironically, Cain's punishment was to become "a fugitive and a vagabond," the latter coming from a word meaning to wander. But a shadow wanderer, someone not so much on the road as on the run, an outsider to the goings-on of civilized folk.

(Suspicion toward the journeying life received another linguistic boost seven or eight hundred years ago when a trickle of morality seeped into the meaning of the word *err*, which originally meant to wander or journey and then turned it into "going wrong." Not just wandering, but wandering from the proper path, from regular and orderly conduct.)

Some people consider the story of Cain and Abel a fable to explain the origin of the wandering desert tribes of the time, whose life was considered cursed. In contemplating the first nomads in the historical record—a Semitic band called the Amorites who lived five thousand years ago in what is now Syria—a Sumerian poet wrote about:

> *A tent dweller buffeted by wind and rain*
> *Dwelling in the mountain . . .*
> *Who in his lifetime does not have a house;*
> *Who on the day of his death will not be buried.*

The urge to journey works against the urge to stay put and sink roots, settle down and raise a family. Granted, we like the comforts of home, the conveniences of technology, the recognition of the local shopkeepers so we don't have to continually show them our driver's licenses, and the stability of the pyramid, the stablest form in all of architecture and a picture of which I had on my business card during the years I was engaged in the caravan profession of freelance writing.

But we don't crave just security and certainty. We also crave their opposite—passion, spontaneity, novelty, discovery, an adrenaline rush, a push to the limits, a mad dash across an open field (when was the last time you *ran?*), the bedlam of love and creativity, the full range of emotions, a locker at the bus station. We like the world to occasionally be unpredictable and full of surprises, despite our sensible lifestyles. We like to feel *alive.*

But the wandering instinct, the exploratory urge, has to make some kind of peace with domestication (and vice versa). In the natural and nomadic worlds, it does. For example, nomads and migrating fish and fowl all take to the road, but the roads are usually the same, the journeys predictable and only recalibrated in the face of drought, disaster, or the encroachments of the "civilized" world.

In animals, the compulsion to fly away is balanced by the compulsion to return, and there's always a return. Some birds even migrate for ten thousand miles and return to the same exact *tree* they departed from, and turtles have been known to swim from Australia to California and back, fifteen thousand miles, and crawl up onto the same beach they left from thirty years before. Sometimes the civilized world even helps out: migrating birds have occasionally rested in mid-ocean on the decks of ships.

The sequence of departure and return works not only in the natural world but also in the creative one—which won't come to fruition if our wanderings and woolgatherings aren't matched by long hours at the work table. We may gain inspiration on the road, that all-important experience that is the flax we'll need to weave into gold, but at some point we have to come off the road, leave our comrades back at the pub, and lock ourselves in the study or the studio to work the loom.

The cycle of separation and return also works in the mythic world. Stories of the "hero's journey," from Bilbo to Buddha, show us that leave-taking is an essential, perhaps *the* essential task. We have to leave the village or the castle or the farmhouse in Kansas and strike out across unknown territory. But that's only Act I of a two-act play. The departure sets in motion an eventual return to the village bearing the hand of the princess or the head of the demon in a sack, which redeems the kingdom (at least until the demon's son or daughter grows up and comes for a reckoning).

To the degree questing is about growth and transformation, it won't be a full-fledged hero's journey if you don't make good on that phase of it called the Return, which involves bringing the fruits of your labors back to the community in the form of action, insight, wisdom, vision, leadership, service, or at least a better mousetrap.

Patterns of domesticity, however, are very hard to break. The task of leaving the village is considered heroic for a good reason. In the movie *Papillon*, Steve McQueen and Dustin Hoffman play a couple of prisoners trying to escape from the Devil's Island penal colony—a real place, operated for one hundred years by the French. I've seen it myself. It's a tiny dot of an island off the coast of French Guiana in South America.

In one scene, McQueen's character, Papillon ("butterfly" in French), is released from a long stretch of solitary confinement. One of the habits he developed while in solitary was counting off the number of steps he could take in any direction, which was five. He's now standing outside the cell, and slowly begins walking down the corridor, counting off the steps.

On the fifth step, he stops, looks around bewildered, and takes a *sixth* step, on which he says, "Well, son of a bitch," then passes out cold.

It's a beautiful illustration of how literally overwhelming it can be to take even a single step beyond what's familiar, even when what's familiar is a *prison*. How easy it is to "go unconscious."

I'm always amused by a bumper sticker I see everywhere around the country on my travels: "No Fear." I know it's only a pitch for a clothing line, but I don't buy it. Fear is a biological imperative. It's hardwired in any creature that has a brain. The fight-or-flight mechanism is a perfect example. I saw one of these bumper stickers in Arizona a few years ago that had a slight alteration in it, made, I think, in the name of credibility. It said, "*Some* Fear." And some fear is appropriate when you're up against the work of stepping outside the box.

No Cure for Curiosity

> The most exciting phrase in science, the one that heralds new discoveries, isn't "Eureka!" but rather "Hmm . . . that's funny."
>
> —ISAAC ASIMOV

Something that resides in the Garden has been a goad to our passion and restlessness ever since we put ashore: the tree with the apples. We've been outfitted with hungry and irrepressible minds, but we're easily haunted by what we don't know, which towers over us, beckoning with fruit and trilling alien music from the high branches. There are a million mysteries hidden in the pockets of this world alone, a thousand cryptograms scrawled on the walls of the body, a thousand more in the heart, and as inscrutable to us as the far side of Jupiter.

"I do not know what I may appear to the world," said Sir Isaac Newton, considered by many to be the single greatest genius humanity has ever produced, "but to myself I seem to have been only a boy playing on the seashore and diverting myself in now and then finding a smoother pebble or a prettier shell than ordinary, while the great ocean of truth lay all undiscovered before me."

Indeed, humans have so far window-shopped only seventy worlds—planets, moons, the sun—out of *trillions*, and have landed a grand total of twelve people on but one of them, and only recently have any of our spacecraft even begun to leave the sheltered cove of our solar system and enter the open ocean of interstellar space. What there is to know is unfathomably huge and the resources we bring to bear on it modest to the point of hilarity. The knowledge we've amassed in our entire human history might seem to us illuminata, but it's little more than a nightlight to calm children on their way to the bathroom in the dark.

We especially want the answers that can't be given us, and this stokes not just passion but also dissatisfaction. For instance, we know a great deal about the *how* of things—how the world works, how it came into being, how it evolves through time and space. But we don't know the *why*. The primary causes of things, not the secondary causes. Why are we here, for what purpose? And as long as the why eludes us, we're frustrated, even as we're roused to rummage and explore, even as we're inspired to dialogue with deities and to look deep within for some of those answers. Nor are we any more foolish for asking the questions than we are for taking on the bottomless oceans of space in a tin skiff.

I remember an exchange between two of my step-siblings, brother and sister, while we were sitting in the car waiting for the grown-ups. Regarding some conundrum I no longer recall, she asked him, "Why?" and he said, "Because." She asked again, "But why?" He said, "Because." "Why?" "Because." "Why?" "Because." And it went on like that for so many rounds that by the time the grown-ups got to the car, she was hitting him.

This may sum up the way of our deepest inquiries about meaning and purpose. "Why are we here?" "Because." We may never get a better or a more concise answer than that. And we may not even get that. It turns out that not every why even *has* a because. Quantum mechanics has shown, experimentally *proved*, that there can be effects without causes. Contrary to the classical laws of physics and compliments of something called a quantum fluctuation, matter and energy can spontaneously pop into and out of being from the void—including, some people think, the universe itself. It turns out that not only is there such a thing as a free lunch, but as physicist Stephen Hawking once said, the entire *universe* may be a free lunch.

And who hasn't occasionally been so baffled by the mysterious ways of cause and effect that you question your most basic assumptions about the universe and how it operates while glimpsing the magic, the *possibilities*, that are constantly afoot there?

A few years ago, a speaking engagement took me to Cincinnati, where I lived in my twenties while working for the *Cincinnati Enquirer*. In some of my off-hours I wandered a neighborhood called Mount Adams (once affectionately referred to as Mad Adams), the old artist's section high on a hill overlooking downtown. At one point, I walked past an Irish pub where, thirty-five years before, I had sat in a back booth and composed a forlorn love letter to a girlfriend who was away on a trip to New York. I remembered describing myself to her as feeling like a lime slice stuck at the bottom of a beer glass. An instant later, I looked down and saw a *lime slice* lying in the gutter.

Now, by what manifestational sleight of hand, through what cosmic wormhole, did that lime slice end up in the gutter at exactly that moment in time? How do these things happen? What do they *mean*? Would that lime slice have been there if *I* hadn't been there?

A few months later, on the very day I signed divorce papers, a picture my ex-wife had painted of a black cat in a garden, which had been hanging on the wall for twenty years, fell and crashed to the floor, shattering all over my dining room. On that exact day.

The astronomer Carl Sagan once undertook a research project that highlights the challenges of trying to nail down cause and effect, if not satisfy our endless curiosities in any absolute way. He had set out to study the roots of the nuclear arms race, which led him back to World War II, which had its origins in World War I, which grew out of the rise of nation-states, which emerged at the very beginning of human civilization, itself a by-product of the earliest domestication of plants and animals, an outgrowth of our history as hunter-gatherers. Et cetera. Before long, Sagan was digging into the events of ancient ages, hip-deep in the musty suppositions and relics of the first humans, as well as in the futility of finding either an ultimate starting point or an ultimate conclusion.

As children we learn that stories have beginnings ("once upon a time"), middles ("when suddenly"), and endings ("happily ever after," or at least "riding off into the sunset"). But it's never that simple. Any story is just an outtake, a coming-in in the middle of a sentence. There's something that preceded the beginning and something that proceeds after the ending. Once upon a time? What about the time before that? Happily ever after? What about five years down the road when the fairy dust has worn off? In the history of anything, it's impossible to draw a starting line and declare, "This is where it all began." Even the big bang leaves a lot of unanswered questions. What was there before the explosion? If it was nothing, then what did it explode out *into*? And who lit the fuse?

Same with personal history. I can nail down a birth day, but the meter didn't really start running at birth. Before that, I spent the better part of a year stitching my birthday suit. Before that, there were a series of rendezvous. Before that, there was just the *idea* of me, threading its way through other people's lives. And those lives wouldn't have come to be without a matrix of still other lives and other circumstances—wars, migrations, famines, revolutions, individual fortunes—all of them randomized by the ever-present influences of chance and mutation. Even the barest sliver of history would require an eternity of bedtime stories and a wing of the public library.

This may in part explain why the Anbarra, an Australian aboriginal tribe, encourage their children *not* to be curious—an uphill battle if ever there was one—but to understand that information will be revealed to them when it's deemed appropriate (the logic of initiation rituals). The Anbarra don't even have a word for "why." They're taught to simply accept things as they are, which is a fairly good definition of wisdom, assuming it works, and among the usual prescriptions for ceaseless desire.

Most people would find the Anbarra's solution insufferable, although Loren Eiseley was probably right in saying that even if we were to know tomorrow the answer to "Why?"—were to suddenly penetrate the secret of the universe, assuming there is one—we would in all likelihood grow bored on the day after. And it's no coincidence how often you hear the words *bored* and *restless* in the same sentence.

Desire is simply more powerful than satisfaction, certainly more lasting, and the restless often spend their days pitching between the two. Pursuit-of-happiness theory says, "I feel empty, but once I get X, then I'll be happy," as Berman puts it. Wheel-of-suffering theory says, "Once you get X, then you'll want Y." In other words, there's no cure for curiosity. There's only palliative and, as the Anbarra demonstrate, deflection.

Actually, there is a cure for curiosity. Mortality makes everyone put down their pencils, brings the curtain down on all of our explorations, though the whiff of it is also a stimulant. We know that there'll come a time when not so much as a single nerve impulse or blood cell, not a breath, a muscle, a thought, or a desire will ever again move from here to there; that life is short, death is long, and we need to make our moves while we can. There'll be plenty of time for rest in the grave, unless we depart life sufficiently unreconciled about something to leave behind a hungry ghost to wander the world.

Those who work closely with the dying are familiar with something called terminal restlessness, an amalgam of end-of-life symptoms that involves a host of seemingly purposeless movements: thrashing, twitching, and fidgeting. Among the explanations for it are psychological ones, such as a "crisis of knowledge" brought on by the understanding that death is imminent, and the frantic attempt to finish unfinished business.

Anyone midlife or older, leaning into mortality's headwind, probably recognizes this urgency to get done whatever they want to get done before the clock strikes twelve. They may even struggle with the perception that the world is getting bigger, not smaller. That the scope of what remains to be explored and experienced only grows: entire bandwidths of cultures and countries they'll never see, books they'll never have time to read, projects they'll never get to sink their teeth into, things they should say to people that they're not saying.

I recently Googled the phrase "things I want to do before I die" and came up with dozens of lists people have compiled. I could have written any one of them. Wander through the attic of the Smithsonian, see the temples of Angkor Wat and the Paleolithic art in the caves at Lascaux, accompany an archaeological expedition to find dinosaur eggs in Mongolia, read all the Pulitzer Prize–winning novels, live in Greece for a year, help Habitat for Humanity build someone a house or a school in Timbuktu, tour the Carrera marble quarry in Italy from which Michelangelo got his marble, trek the Himalayas and raft the Grand Canyon, see the northern lights, scuba dive into the ancient city of Heracleion off the coast of Egypt, descend twenty thousand leagues under the sea in a bathysphere, become fluent in Spanish. Here's one from an intake form I filled out at a dentist's office last year: in answer to the question "What improvements would you like to make to your mouth?" I wrote, "That every time I open it, kind words come out."

I sometimes feel like someone in a supermarket sweepstakes, racing through the aisles trying to stuff as much into my cart as I can before the timer goes off. Being a reporter, I know this by now about deadlines: they get things done.

I also know that the pursuit of not just experience but also knowledge is an intoxicant, and that the same goes for scientists and scholars, archaeologists, explorers, detectives, and anyone with a beginner's mind still on active duty. Years ago my brother Ross and I fell into a speculative conversation about what superpower we'd choose to possess were we given the chance. Ross's initial response: the ability to speak any language on Earth. Mine: the power to lay my hand on any book and instantly absorb everything in it.

One of the reasons I went into journalism was to satisfy my endless curiosity, even pay the rent with it. For anyone else, a research profession like writing would be like doing homework for a living. But the thrill of the chase has been an integral part of the pleasure I've derived from it, the primary impetus for adventure in my life, and it's given me some extraordinary homework assignments over the years: riding bareback on the elephant at the head of the circus parade, helping birth a foal on a Kentucky horse farm, watching twins being born, holding an anteater in my lap at the Cincinnati Zoo, attending a nude party in San Francisco, drumming with Mickey Hart of the Grateful Dead, seeing the rings of Saturn through an observatory telescope, and scuba diving into an undersea research habitat in the West Indies that would have turned Jules Verne green with envy.

I also know that though all the hustle and bustle can certainly have its drawbacks, another of its merits is that it helps slow down the timer. Or rather, my perception of time. When it involves not just fidgeting and antsiness but real movement and intention, restlessness leads to two distinct outcomes: novelty and variety. And the more any given day or week is composed of these two elements, the longer it feels.

For instance, it's early autumn while I'm writing this, and I'm in a state of some shock that summer is over already. It just began and it's over and the trees are starting to change. Four months, gone like *that*! And I know why. I spent the entire summer working on a book proposal in a state of laser focus. Meaning that I spent the summer in a very circumscribed routine: mornings at my desk, lunch, afternoons at my desk, a hike, evenings either at my desk or reading, with very few detours.

When I fall into this kind of routine, every day a ditto of the one before it, time absolutely rockets by. And it didn't help that I ran across a quote last week—one of those passages that tolls for thee—that said something like "if you spend your whole life in stuffy rooms, searching and research-ing, you can suddenly find yourself too old to enjoy life." As any writer knows, it's hard to avoid searching and researching, and stuffy rooms.

But whenever I inject novelty into my days, or quit the routine alto-gether and hit the road on vacation, assignment, or speaking engagement, time slows way down. It's a fairly clear pattern and one I've tracked for years. The more I move around, the more variety and novelty I have in any given day or week or year, and the more leash I give to my curiosity and wanderlust, the slower time seems to flow.

To be fair, there can be a time-related *drawback* to restlessness too. Years ago I interviewed a man named Bernard Murchland, a professor of art and aesthetics at Ohio Wesleyan University, on what he called the Ten Commandments of Creativity, his notion of the essential ingredients in the creative personality. One of them is restlessness. Creative types, he said, are never satisfied with the present state of affairs, theirs or anyone else's, and are constantly caught between trying to change the way things are and having to accept them in their present condition.

In other words, they spend a good deal of their time living in and for the future, and not, as the saying goes, being here now, though being in the present (a classic hallmark of enlightenment) may not be all it's cracked up to be. There are cases on record of people who, through accidents and ill-nesses, have lost all but very short-term memory. They live only in the present moment, which may sound appealing to those whose ambition is to be here now, but on closer examination would be hugely problematic for, say, relationships.

If you shared a meal with such a person and got up to leave the room, you would cease to exist. You wouldn't be able to build a body of accumu-lated affections, an inventory of intimacies. You would become a stranger every time you came back from an errand to the grocery store or a trip to the basement, which might spice up your sex life but probably wouldn't lend itself to building trust over the long haul.

On the other hand, with nothing but short-term memory you'd never have to watch reruns on TV and you could hide your own Easter eggs.

. . .

I RECENTLY RAN across a letter someone wrote (and posted on the internet) after watching an episode of *Dr. Phil* in which he said, "The way to achieve inner peace is to finish all the things you've started and never finished." Here's the letter:

> *So I looked around my house to see all the things I started and hadn't finished, and before leaving the house this morning, I finished off a bottle of Merlot, a bottle of White Zinfandel, a bottle of Bailey's Irish Cream, a bottle of Kahlua, a package of Oreos, the remainder of my old Prozac prescription, the rest of the cheesecake, all of the Doritos, and a box of chocolates.*
>
> *You have absolutely no idea how freaking good I feel right now. Dang, that Dr. Phil is smart!*

The truth, of course, as anyone who's reached or passed midlife probably knows, is that contrary to popular belief, you can't finish all your earthly business, and anything is *not* possible. You can't actually hitch your wagon to a star. Without the kind of massive budget and infrastructure that only governments tend to possess, you can't shoot for the moon. And the energy it takes to *fuel* your passions may simply not be in the batteries to the same degree it was when you were younger.

In fact, maybe there's a point in life at which it's natural to tire of all your passions, all their storm and stress, all their demands on your time, energy, and vigilance, and maybe this explains why some people, especially the old, seem to prefer comfort to excitement. Perhaps I'm still under the illusion of relative youth when I say that I can't imagine feeling this way, and believe that though there's a certain amount of slowing down that does take place, a tempering of the fight and the drive in us, losing interest in the world is purely optional, and successful aging is a state in which we maintain our curiosity about life and an eagerness to follow where it leads.

On the other hand, the writer David Shields talks about his father, who at ninety-seven seems "bored beyond belief, virtually without a single interest or enthusiasm other than continued existence, day after day after day." And he wonders whether, as our bodies break down, they become the primary focus of our attention, usurping all other interests.

By the time you reach midlife, though, you've probably experienced something of the limitations of time and talent, the breakdown of expectations, even the shattering of lifelong illusions—you're sadder perhaps but wiser—and this wisdom can bring you back into right relationship with yourself and the world. Maybe you have to surrender what James Hollis in *The Middle Passage* calls the infiniteness of your aspirations, and maybe it's a surrender that feels like defeat, but it's really a kind of liberation. You know better where you stand with life, and you understand that postponement of your remaining passions is less and less a viable option.

The kind of thinking that characterizes this phase of life, though—which is realistic thinking—cuts out a lot of static. It cuts down on the magical thinking of childhood, and the heroic thinking of adolescence and young adulthood, and helps you focus, in the way Samuel Johnson meant it when he said that when you know you're to be hanged in a fortnight, it concentrates the mind wonderfully.

Given our infinite aspirations—the multiform nature of the self, the sheer possibilities of life—it's impossible to live out more than a fraction of them, to illuminate more than a few facets. This defines one of the inherent tragedies of human life, but the more facets we're able to bring to light, or at least the more depth we're able to bring to those facets we devote our attentions to, the richer our lives will be, as well as the lives of anyone who comes across that reflected light.

That humans evolve in response to changes in their environment is perhaps the central tenet of the anthropological and evolutionary sciences, and we can extrapolate from this to our own individual lives. If we wish to continue evolving and not end up in some Darwinian dead zone, we have to keep responding to change. We can't hide in a cave and hope the changes will blow on by. We have to take them on, whether they're developmental or circumstantial. We have to deal.

It's vital to cultivate, and maintain, a feel for what wants to emerge in our lives, what's trying to happen at any given turning point, in any given moment or situation or relationship. It's a skill that's especially important in a world increasingly operating on internet time, because lack of *responsiveness* in this kind of climate is the equivalent of wearing cement shoes, particularly in terms of personal or professional growth. And then you find yourself having encounters like the one I had years ago with my thirteen-year-old niece, who was standing in front of me, rolling her eyes, and saying—as only a thirteen-year-old can say—"That is so last week!" And this from a seventh grader who still had stuffed animals on her bed. Which is so sixth grade.

But old dogs can most assuredly learn new tricks. The consensus among dog trainers is that it's utter nonsense that you can't teach old dogs new tricks. In fact, most of them are eager to be physically and mentally stimulated, as long as it doesn't involve backflips. What's called "shrinking world syndrome" isn't a function of just incapacity but also our assumptions about aging, whether in our dogs or in ourselves.

Because old dogs can't keep up as friskily as they once did, we tend to take them on fewer walks and fewer outings to the dog park, play with them less, stop training and teaching them new tricks, stop looking for new ways to connect with them, and we eventually just let them molder in a heap by the fire or the front door. But if you think old dogs prefer just lying around, the question is, have you given them a choice?

Among the calls of getting older is regeneration and renewal, and there's precedence for it in everyone's life. In other words, you've been here before, at the place of dreaming your life, needing and wanting to experiment with it, trying things out, taking risks, finding out who you are. It was called adolescence, and some researchers even call the last third of life the second adolescence. Only this one doesn't come with an entire institutionalized structure designed to encourage the passage from adolescence to adulthood, i.e., an educational system. There's no degree program in maturity. We're on our own and have to design our own curriculums.

The Power of Walkabout

While strolling the grounds of a retreat center near my home, I found a labyrinth made, uncharacteristically, of cement, engineered by someone who either reckoned the spiritual journey harder on the feet and more blinding to the eyes than those who build their labyrinths out of earth, or who just wanted to minimize the weeding.

Rather than walking the labyrinth the way you're supposed to, the long and winding road and all that, I just took three or four giant steps right into the center and had to laugh out loud when I found there not the usual altar with offerings of stones, feathers, flowers, and prayers—a miniature Wailing Wall—but a large wing nut embedded in the cement, "made in Taiwan." I wondered what would happen if I unscrewed it. Is the universe held together with nothing more than a wing nut and a prayer?

My base-stealing maneuver aside, the labyrinth reminded me that movement is one of the essential vehicles of spiritual transport—used by shaking Shakers, quaking Quakers, whirling dervishes, walking meditators, holy rollers, trance dancers, labyrinth walkers, and seventh- and eighth-century Celtic seafaring friars known as *peregrini*, from which we get the word *peregrination*, as in "journeying." On behalf of the homeless Christ, they would set themselves adrift in rudderless and oarless skin boats, with no particular destination, believing that God would guide them safely to their place of resurrection.

If restlessness is only about running away from something, is only distraction and avoidance, then how to explain the psychology of pilgrimage, the search for god-self precisely *through* walkabout, and an institution some believe was designed to compensate for the lack of migration? Maybe even moving twenty-three times in thirty-eight years is just a pilgrimage in installments.

Also, among the most common symptoms of spiritual awakening, as in ecstatic trance or dance, is physical activity including vibrating, shaking, and contractions. The encounter with the sacred always seems to involve shuddering. In fact, spirituality itself, which Robert C. Solomon in *Spirituality for the Skeptic* describes as "the thoughtful love of life," requires an active emotional life (emote meaning "to move out"), as well as impassioned engagements and quests. These, of course, can sometimes tip over into instability and insatiability, a kind of possessiveness that has us flailing around in life, whacking at piñatas, but spirituality isn't only about peace of mind, tranquility, and contentment. "It is a passion," Solomon says, "the passion for life and for the world. It is a movement, not a state."

To physicist and psychologist Arnold Mindell, founder of process-oriented psychology, restlessness is *literally* about movement—rest less— and sometimes the question we have to ask ourselves is "What wants to move and where does it want to go?"

In working with clients, he hones in on restlessness as a physical phenomenon first, a dream in the body that's trying to come true, something about that person's life that's trying to happen. So he follows the body. "If someone comes in and tells me they're depressed, but their feet are constantly moving, I'll say, 'I'm not sure you're depressed. I think there's a lot of energy you're not in contact with. Let's follow your feet.' I worked with a woman from Dublin recently, and when I asked what her feet would do if they were free to do what they wanted, she got up and did a jig. She realized there was a whole lot of excitement she didn't feel permitted to show in public."

Some spiritual traditions consider stillness of mind among the ultimate attainments, and refer to a peripatetic mind as monkey mind, but this, says Mindell, "suggests they don't like monkeys very much. Why anyone would want to have a peaceful mind is beyond me. It would be boring. Quiet mind is wonderful if it quiets down in order to open up to spontaneity and creativity, but you don't have to have a quiet mind to do those things. It's right there in front of your feet."

Or perhaps *in* your feet. There's a medical condition known as restless legs syndrome, and one in ten Americans has it—over thirty million people. It's characterized by difficulty in resting or sleeping, disturbing sensations in the legs that patients describe most frequently as "creepy" and "crawly," and the compelling urge to move. In fact, the medical literature says that actually getting up and moving usually offers immediate relief. As the actress Tracey Ullman once put it, "Restless legs syndrome is God's way of telling me I've got places to go."

As for why the relief is only temporary, the philosopher Johann Goethe said that being harassed by restless sleep is usually a function of stagnation in some quarter, which, if confronted, would alleviate the problem. Prescription drugs, of course, tackle the symptom but not the source.

The source of stagnation in Dan Rhodes's (not his real name) life was centered in two quarters—his sense of calling and his sense of sexual identity, or "sexual imprisonment," as he calls it—and he used his own restlessness and nomadic nature to attempt to liberate himself and find his "place of resurrection."

For ten years Dan had worked as a professor at a conservative Christian university in the South. But in 2010 a colleague outed him to the board of trustees, referring to him in a letter as a "celibate homosexual in leadership."

College policy disallowed any kind of sexual activity outside marriage, in particular homosexual activity—though not orientation. In other words, "Don't ask, don't tell, don't act out."

Dan had *never* acted out. In fact, he remained a virgin until he was forty-four. But in the couple of years prior to what he apocalyptically calls "the Letter," he had tentatively begun to share his secret orientation with a handful of trusted friends at the college, one of whom turned out not to be so trustworthy.

The college president supported him, the board got behind him, but the colleague made it clear that he would out Dan to the wider community unless he resigned. Which he did. "Which forced me back into the closet," he says, "and reinforced the shame of it all, the internalized homophobia." Ironically, the year before, Dan had published a book (under a pseudonym) called *Superheroes, Saviors and Sinners Without Secrets*, whose cover is a photograph of an empty canoe on the shore of a lake, and the second chapter of which kicks off with a quote from a producer of the movie *Spider-Man 2*: "There is nothing more destructive to the human soul than the secrets, the sins we keep from others."

What Dan had been doing up until the day he was outed is referred to by the gay community as "passing," though the term entered the lexicon by way of the African American community and refers to those who pass themselves off as someone they're not, or at least someone other than who they understand themselves to be. It has historically referred to light-skinned blacks passing as white, gays passing as straight, Jews passing as Gentile, writers disguising their identity or gender behind pseudonyms, but probably includes *all* of us at some point or another. Padding your résumé, getting cosmetic surgery to pretend to be younger than you are, having an affair while passing for faithful, being an undercover cop or investigative reporter, living out someone else's life rather than your own, sweet-talking a contractor who's over budget and past deadline when you'd really like to bean him but you want the work to continue.

We all put on masks from time to time and act in ways that are contrary to our true nature and values. And at some level we can all relate to the experience of being in the closet, hiding our authenticity in a dark room and not bringing to light the full spectrum of our aliveness. Passing, not coincidentally, also refers to dying. And coming out means telling the truth.

The objective of passing is usually to gain social acceptance and opportunity, to avoid rejection and persecution, or, in Dan's case, to elude that abomination passage from Leviticus ("Thou shalt not lie with a man as with a woman," the penalty for which was death) and the widespread intolerance it begat. The fact is, we live in a world of very real inequalities with very real repercussions, and to whatever degree passing raises the moral issue of deception, the question is, do we judge the passer for engaging in it or the system for making it necessary?

Not that passing doesn't have its own repercussions. Just to get through an average day, people like Dan have to rely on an arsenal of subterfuges that would drive most people to drink. Conversations they have to side-step, jokes they have to laugh at though they're offended, feigning interest in subjects they have no interest in, even the invention of fictitious romances to avoid suspicion. There are milestones they can't celebrate with coworkers, tragedies they can't get support for, the burden of secrecy they bestow upon any confidantes, and the crying need for a purifying rationale to justify to themselves why they're passing.

And it takes a toll. The strain of having to separate your public and private lives has been shown to increase rates of substance abuse, depression, anxiety, hostility, and poor self-esteem. "Passing demands that you become invisible," says Michelle Cliff in Claiming an Identity They Taught Me to Despise. "It demands quiet. And from that quiet—silence. And silence, over time, atrophies the voice. It's a loss with such grave consequences that it's a form of dispossession."

In order to repossess himself, Dan created a project that he called his "Year of Living Passionately," a bucket list of experiences and vocations he'd always wanted to explore, as well as a handful of personal themes that needed delving into, such as identity, fear, adventure, and deep listening, all of them related to the challenge of "figuring life out." After a year of preparation, he embarked on a "global research expedition" in search of "truth, meaning, and hopefully a job." He conceived of it mostly as a career quest during which he would immerse himself in different vocations and locations throughout the year, paid for with savings and by working along the way for room and board.

"I wasn't planning on it becoming a coming-out process, or that I'd become more comfortable with myself as a gay man, but that's what happened." As did clarification of what he considers his greatest gift, which he describes (without even noting the irony) as "drawing people out."

After being in the closet for most of his life, it was no wonder he wanted to hit the road, just to be moving and exercising his freedom, just to be out of the closet and in the great outdoors. He helped himself *come* out by *going* out, into the world and beyond his comfort zone. He used restlessness to help him settle on a path.

"One thing I knew all too well was the feeling of being trapped. Most of my life I'd been dreaming of escape. Not just escape *out of*—out of enslavement, out of an oppressive sense of depression and isolation—but an escape *into* something. Into myself. Toward finding myself rather than losing myself. And I'd never been more desperate. I wanted clarity, but I *needed* resolution, redemption, and restoration of heart."

Toward that end, his "Year of Living Passionately" enterprise took him, among many places, to the West Coast to work in the movie industry, to the East Coast to spend time at a monastery, to Greenland to work with an aboriginal rights organization, and to a South American village to work with a vocational school.

During this particular stint, he reconnected with an old college friend who had initially condemned his homosexual leanings but now matter-of-factly encouraged Dan to "accept yourself" and introduced him to someone who had reconciled his Christian faith with his homosexuality.

"That was an emotional high and a revelation to me," says Dan, "finding out that it wasn't a contradiction, confronting the belief that homosexuality is a sin and displeasing to God, and reworking those ideas in my own mind."

Among the highlights of his travels was the time he spent exploring his ancestral roots in Eastern Europe, in particular tracking down the village where his great-grandfather came from and at one point getting down on his knees and kissing the ground. "I didn't expect that as an emotional response, but I remember feeling so much more grounded, in my identity, in who I was. The whole year was largely about clarifying my sense of identity, and this brought it to a much deeper level than just sexual identity or vocational identity."

In his journal for that stretch of the trip, he quoted the poet Daisy Rinehart's "The Call of the Open Sea": "I am tired of sailing my little boat / Far inside the harbor bar / I want to go out where the big ships are / Out on the deep where the great ones are."

In the course of his yearlong walkabout, Dan traveled to fifteen states, eight countries, and five continents. He fractured one toe, herniated one disc, pinched one nerve, and broke one middle finger. And he learned one great lesson: "to fall back in love with my life."

That life, however, took a few unforeseen and discouraging turns in the years that followed his return from the road. To make a long story short, he's back in the closet. At least professionally.

"The process of coming out did not go as well as I expected, the freelance photographic work I'd hoped to develop once I got home didn't pan out, and my job search in higher-ed fell flat. I must have applied for hundreds of positions over the past four years, with almost no interest. My funds dwindled, and so did my spirits and resolve. I thought coming out was supposed to be liberating and life-changing. Not so much."

As a last-ditch effort, Dan put his name in for a position at a conservative nonprofit out west, but when they offered him the job, he turned it down, seized by a desperate urge to not return to an environment where he had to hide his newly excavated identity. Months passed with no other offers, and when the nonprofit pursued him with renewed interest, he broke down—"just to survive financially and psychologically"—and took the job. Even his therapist at the time suggested that employment trumped authenticity, in the service of pulling himself out of the hole of depression into which he'd fallen.

"This is certainly not a storyline I would ever have predicted or wished for myself, but I'm surviving. The people are very nice, the work is a good fit for my skills, it's meaningful and satisfying, and I get to do my 'drawing people out' work through mentoring and leading groups of clients and students abroad. But I would lose my job if they knew I was gay. So I'm living a double life again, complete with flashbacks to my experience at the university.

"But I've gotten used to it. In fact, I'm quite practiced at it, and could even imagine sustaining this situation, though I wonder what I could accomplish without these limitations, and lament how much energy I'm wasting on coping with it. On the other hand, it's also forced me to be creative in ways I wouldn't otherwise be. So I go back and forth.

"I hate it when songs and movies and books wrap things up so neatly, as if life were a sitcom. I think life is much more complicated than that, much more a mystery than a manual. I was not healed to the core by my 'Year of Living Passionately,' but I live with hope. I despair of relationships, but I long for love. I am weak, but strong."

The Tonic of Boredom

In a poem called "The Cemetery by the Sea," French writer Paul Valéry describes how the wind suddenly ruffles the immobile surface of the water, and his own impassive mood, breathing into him a fresh vitality and reminding him to reengage with the challenges of life, in particular his poetry, which he had silenced for twenty years and only recently returned to. "Into the waves with us, and out alive! The wind is rising! . . . We must try to live!"

I recently experienced a similar intervention, a ruffling of my own immobile waters, in this case in the form of a dream.

I had been in a slough for months, a boggy state of dispiritedness in which I felt as close to the state of depression as I ever get, not being particularly prone to it. I was sleeping too much, feeling lazy, bored, and disconnected from everything and everyone—lacking initiative and yet restless. Feeling *off*. And I couldn't get to the bottom of it until I had the following dream:

I was walking down an old disused road on some property I owned, its pavement cracked, grass growing up all over it, and I came to an old stone wall by the side of the road with a sign attached to it that I couldn't decipher because the lettering kept mysteriously shifting around. I thought

I saw the word *Gregg*, which changed to the word *egg*, which changed to something else and something else.

As I was trying to figure out what the sign said, I looked down the road half a mile and suddenly saw an enormous black dragon fly into view, heading straight for me. It sent me skittering like a rabbit in desperate search of a hole in the ground. But there was nowhere to hide.

Suddenly the dragon was directly above me, looking down with its huge tyrannosaurus head and blazing amber eyes. But its teeth weren't flashing—the sure sign of a predator's intent—and it wasn't breathing fire. It was only looking down at me while I tried to fight it off with *a safety pin*. Finally, out of sheer fright, certain that I was about to be eaten, and with a distinct sense of incredulity that no god was emerging from the machinery to rescue me at the last second, like in the movies, I woke up.

The gist of it was that I was on a road that hadn't been used for a long while, couldn't make out the writing on the wall, though it appeared to have my name on it, and there was a fateful encounter with a primal creature that would not be denied, and whose mere presence woke me up.

What immediately came to me in interpreting the dream was that the dragon was my writing. My *real* writing. Not the book-reporting, interviewing, and third-person research writing I'd been doing a lot of at the time—essentially taking dictation—but the freewriting practice I meant to be doing alongside it, and wasn't. Not the dainty sniffing of other people's flowers, but the fierce pollinating of my own, shoving my snout into their flowery groins, smearing my whole body with their perfumes, and flying fully-laden back to the hive.

What I needed to be doing, the dragon was telling me, was the kind of writing in which I free myself from other people's ideas and go down the Old Road, the path of raw unfiltered psyche, memory, and voice, the one with the sign along it that has the name *Gregg* on it, followed by the word *egg*, which is something that hatches, that comes forth with new life. I needed to turn my questing nature outward *and* inward.

The dream reminded me that I'd been avoiding this road for some time, playing it safe—thus the absurdly inadequate safety-pin defense. It reminded me that I felt cut off from my own creativity in doing all that cautious and academic writing—and this in the midst of putting together a book on *passion*—when what the dragon wanted was for me to breathe fire and eat elephants for hors d'oeuvres.

But it woke me up, literally and figuratively, and over the following months I regained my momentum, reacquainted myself with that abandoned road—my *own* voice—and the boredom and depression lifted.

And this wasn't just about breathing fresh creative vitality back into my work or my life, but also about straight-up health care. Much illness, I think, is simply the result of not paying attention to what we know, not listening to the prescriptions given out by our own inner lives, by our dreams at night, and the dreams in the body. The word *symptom* means "a sign"—of what? The word *pathology* means "the logic of pain"—what's the logic?

According to a report in *Scientific American*, easily bored people are at higher risk for depression, anxiety, drug addiction, alcoholism, compulsive gambling, eating disorders, hostility, anger, poor social skills, bad grades, and low work performance. And it turns out that you *can*, in a sense, be bored to death. A University College London study of 7,500 people over the course of twenty-five years found that those who complained of high levels of boredom in their lives were 40 percent likelier to have died from heart disease or stroke by the end of the study than those who found life more entertaining, mostly because they tended to turn to unhealthy habits like drinking and smoking to alleviate their boredom. As Abraham Lincoln once said, "If they decide to turn their back on the fire and burn their behinds, then they will just have to sit on their blisters."

Interestingly, the day after the dream, I read a passage from Rainer Maria Rilke that said, "Perhaps all the dragons in our lives are princesses who are only waiting to see us act, just once, with beauty and courage."

They don't always wait, though. Sometimes they hunt us down. And they do because they're hungry. Boredom is a kind of hunger—a signal that we're starved for stimulation and engagement, for novelty, for *meaning*. And if we don't use boredom as a tonic to catalyze our quests and our creativity, it can easily become a narcotic that paralyzes them, blocking our forward momentum and short-circuiting our exploratory impulses. There's a reason we refer to being bored *stiff*. It's the opposite of being in the flow.

Granted, passion isn't a constant condition, and all quests have their stops and starts. "There is no such thing as a life of passion any more than a continuous earthquake, or an eternal fever," said Lord Byron. "Besides, who would ever shave themselves in such a state?" Life is a continual swinging between the poles of ardor and languor, action and passivity, and short of striking a Faustian bargain—trading your soul for the everlastingly beautiful moment of your choice—it's important to make peace with the come and go of it. Life simply has a certain amount of boring in it, and novelty and excitement naturally tend to devolve into familiarity.

Everyday boredom—whether in relation to a tiresome course of study or a tedious movie—is typically characterized by monotony, confinement, predictability, and the lack of an activity's sense of value. It's usually cured by the passage of time—you eventually reach the cashier, the clock strikes five, you finally wrap up yet another boring errand/class/chore/commute/conversation—or by the introduction of a little novelty, which can be bundled into your days in countless ways.

Get up on the *other* side of the bed for a change, turn the bathroom faucet on with your *other* hand, wander around while brushing your teeth, listen to five minutes of music before jumping on the computer in the morning, sit at a different side of the table for breakfast, drive to work by a slightly different route, buy an item at the grocery store you've never bought before, order something other than your usual at the restaurant, sit in a different pew at church or synagogue than you normally do, rearrange one piece of furniture in your house.

Unfortunately, the modern world and the wired life compound-fracture our attention spans in a thousand ways, making it increasingly difficult to cope with even small stretches of idleness: standing in the checkout line, waiting for a movie to begin, sitting in traffic or in a waiting room—those unexpected snatches of precious time during which we might, once upon a time, have daydreamed or reflected, composed a few lines of poetry, or just enjoyed a small eddy in the midst of our otherwise swirling days.

Many of us saturate even these mere moments with digital busywork disguised as productivity and communication. Motorola, to hawk its cell phones, even coined the term "microboredom" to describe these apparently insufferable moments of free time, which, of course, the electronic and entertainment industries are happy to help you fill with their latest and greatest. I've even seen little TV screens installed above urinals and gas pumps.

And of course daily life is rife with colorless routines, including those everyday maintenance tasks without which things would quickly become disgusting—brushing your teeth, taking a shower, doing the dishes, changing the sheets, taking out the trash, vacuuming the house—though repetition isn't *inherently* boring. If it were, children wouldn't delight in hearing the same story read to them dozens of times, and actors and musicians wouldn't be able to stomach delivering the same lines and the same songs in performance after performance.

In fact, in every field of endeavor, repetition is essential to the gaining of an experience that is thrilling to most people—mastery. And without passion, there isn't the perseverance required for mastery, or to ride out the repetitiousness, if not see the beauty in it. Author Malcolm Gladwell even calculates that mastery in most endeavors requires at least ten thousand hours of dedicated practice. The math: ninety minutes a day for twenty years.

Anyone who's ever played in a band or acted in a play knows that the ratio of time spent rehearsing compared to that spent performing is something like 90:10, but it's largely passion that accounts for people's willingness to abide by that equation, to practice the same lyrics or the same lines for thousands of hours for the chance to share them publicly barely a tenth of the time. And the fact that they don't mind that formula is also a pretty good diagnostic tool for determining that they're on the right path after all.

Some people even believe that passion itself won't grow without the resolute practice of building capabilities and striving for mastery, or as I once heard someone say, "There are no thrills until you've got the skills."

A notch up from the boredom of everyday routine—and which we see especially in the vocational and educational arenas—is the boredom that results from eager and capable minds being put in dull circumstances. Or from the absence of life goals for which you feel any passion. Or from having them but doing nothing about them. Or from doing work that's literally "de-meaning," lacking any sense of meaning or purpose.

A quest implies a goal, and ideally an interesting one. The word *interesting* originally meant "important," so if you do what's important to you, it should, by definition, be interesting to you. Some kinds of boredom can certainly be a function of ignoring what's important to you, and what makes a goal feel important and worth your precious time is the meaning you attach to it, the purpose it serves in your life, and the *needs* it satisfies—creative expression, service, community, joy.

I read a story recently of a couple who retired, sold their house, and took to the road in an RV to enjoy their golden years. After only a few months of it, they got bored to the point of a near-death experience, so they hooked up their traveling with "habitating"—joining a subculture of RVers called Care-A-Vanners, who help Habitat for Humanity build houses all around the country. By connecting their leisure with service, they suddenly infused it with purpose and a renewed sense of—you'll pardon the pun—drive. It's no coincidence that the word *travel* shares roots with the word *travail*, which speaks of exertions, of purpose, and not merely destination.

Like boredom itself, purpose can be situational or existential, one that animates a particular project and ends when the project ends, or one that animates your whole life and ends only when *you* do. Either way, it contributes to the undoing of ennui, gives you a reason to get out of bed in the morning licking your chops, helps carry you through the hardships of the journey, and engages or reengages you with passion.

This goes especially for those macro-purposes that define and drive your life, not just your to-do list, and that require you to ask some of those ultimate questions of purpose and meaning that humans have been noodling over ever since we first splashed down here. And not the purpose of life, but the purpose of *your* life. Not the meaning of life, but the meaning of *your* life.

The greater the blank where a sense of meaning should be, and the greater the gap between what you want and what you believe is *possible* for you, the greater your sense of futility and apathy are likely to be. There's a reason we refer to "yawning" chasms. And such chasms can open up before anyone whose passion and power, whose sense of purpose, are being squelched or bypassed.

Everyday boredom is like seasickness—it stops as soon as you hit solid ground, as soon as the immediate cause is removed. But when boredom has started leaving its toothbrush at your house, when it no longer feels circumstantial but existential, and you realize that what you're bored with is your own company ("the phone call is coming from *inside* the house"), then a more systemic response is called for than merely waiting it out or plugging into your iPod.

If boredom is still there after you turn off the TV, return from your travels, come down from your highs and parachute jumps, or awaken from sleep, you're dealing with a different issue. The kind Carl Jung was referring to when he said that neurosis is "the suffering of a soul which has not discovered its meaning." The kind that finds us contenting ourselves with inadequate answers to the questions of life. The kind that finds us turning a blind eye to our passions and running from the dragons in our lives rather than facing them.

Here we experience the loss of a sense of meaning and aliveness, which tends to occur when our innate, passion-driven movement into the world is somehow obstructed. A character in a Russian novel called *Oblomov* speaks of feeling "the narrow, pitiful little pathway of his own existence was being blocked by a great boulder . . . so that always he would be prevented from entering life's field and sailing across it with the aid of intellect and of will . . . Brain and volition alike had been paralysed."

Accompanying this state of suspended animation is often an emotional, a sensual, or a spiritual barrenness that's a loss of passion not just for the tasks at hand but for life itself. This is closer to what the French mean by *ennui*, the Germans by *unlust*, and the scientists by *hyperboredom*, and what the famous existential crisis is all about. It's life pinched of purpose and meaning. It's a chronic emptiness and profound failure to grasp The Point of It All. It's an energyless and feelingless state that's often indistinguishable from depression. At its extreme, it causes people to go through life in a kind of zombielike trance, their days filled with the numbness of marking time and treading water. As I once heard someone say, "I just want to lie down and keep on going."

Ennui is a more metaphysical malady than boredom, yet it derives from a Latin word referring to an outright hatred of life itself. And more than a few researchers on the subject of boredom—certainly the advanced stages of it—have noticed that it has a kernel, or a core, of aggression in the threat of mutiny if we fully allow ourselves to recognize not only our boredom but also the source of it. Theologian Paul Tillich called boredom "rage spread thin." And writing about the lot of women in Victorian England, Patricia Meyer Spacks, in her book *Boredom: The Literary History of a State of Mind*, declares that "to reject as uninteresting what conventional life has to offer constitutes a psychic act of profound hostility." Which is sometimes a *good* thing.

Inside boredom and ennui are frustration, but it's what we *do* with our frustration that determines the outcome of our dissatisfactions, certainly when it comes to ennui. The age-old remedy of getting busy is most useful for ameliorating the effects of simple boredom: doing things to remove yourself from the cause of it, if you can. And you can't always. If you're stuck in coach class on a flight from New York to LA, you've just got to sit tight and read your book. It may be a distraction, but it's also a solution. You're *doing* something about it. When airports move baggage claim farther from arrival gates, flyers' satisfaction increases, because apparently people don't mind walking so much as they mind waiting.

In Valéry's book *Soul and Dance*, he highlights the logic of this in a scene in which Socrates asks a physician if he knows of a cure for the ennui that saps the soul, drains all desire and hope from it, and chases off "the gods who are in our blood." And even with ennui, the physician prescribes action, but especially those actions that get the blood and the gods flowing and set the body in motion, even if they're only on miniature quests around our room or around our neighborhood. It matters little what they are. Start small. Spin around in your office chair. Rake the yard or trim the hedges. Go down to the playground and swing on a swing. Run at the waves, flail your arms at flocks of birds, take someone by the hand and go dancing.

When dealing with existential boredom, though, with the windless inertia you experience when your life has come to a standstill and your willpower has become neutered, attempts at mere distraction are often second-best solutions, temporary fixes that don't really get to the bottom of it and thus redirect your life so that there's no longer something to distract yourself *from*. They're like placebos—you think you're getting the real thing, but you're not—and though you may feel better for a time, they just end up veiling your boredom and preventing you from dealing with the real hungers that are beneath it.

The world is full of quick fixes that don't fix anything, and methods of protesting our virility rather than genuinely feeling it, but which we gratefully avail ourselves of—the full spectrum of mass media and social life; a cornucopia of drugs, foods, and internet identities; catalogs full of toys; and tourist attractions.

If you're applying them to simple boredom—you're stuck in line at the bank or having a slow month—they'll probably do the trick. But if it's hyperboredom—you're bored with yourself, your life, your career, your marriage—it will likely still be there after a shopping spree at the mall, an affair, or even a trip around the world, which will be just temporary diversions from something that needs a far more down-reaching solution.

And if we consume culture to fill up the empty places in us, we should remember that consumer culture also bites back. While we consume it, it consumes us, gobbling up our precious time, depleting our resources, and occasionally devouring our initiative.

Television and computers, for example, are sometimes referred to as technologies of *fixation*—antithetical to the questing spirit—featuring a kind of sensory deprivation in which awareness of the surrounding environment only gets in the way. You sit immobilized in a room, other people are generally tuned out, only two senses are operating and those only within a very narrow range, you're staring at fluorescent light for hours on end and largely unaware of how many pretzels and Oreos you're eating. And it's more than a little disconcerting when you run across studies out of Harvard University with titles like "Fluorescent Light Induces Malignant Transformation in Mouse Embryo Cell Cultures."

Certainly there's plenty that's beneficial about these technologies: the computer as a research tool, distance learning and educational TV, online community-building, PBS and NPR, video games that enhance creativity and problem solving, e-books that help save trees, families that are scattered to the winds but can get together online to connect. As with anything, it's not technology that's the problem, but how it's used.

It becomes problematic when we use our computers/TVs/video games/cell phones/Facebooks (or for that matter sex, drugs, and rock 'n' roll) as substitutes for intimacy, distractions from personal problems that need solving, proxies for bonding with your children, surrogates for socializing with real people face-to-face, diversions from reading and self-reflection, replacements for going outside to play or exercise and interact with the actual environment, and deterrents from active rather than just passive engagement with life.

When your primary source of daily excitement and drama is watching *Game of Thrones* and *Survivor* reruns, it's time for an upgrade on your approach to life. As a mentor of mine used to say, "Quit watching the news. Go out and *make* some."

The seemingly uninhibited nature of popular culture, says Ernest van den Haag in *Passion and Social Constraint*, "the uproarious din, the raucous noise, the shouting," are often attempts to "drown out the shriek of unused capacities, of individuality repressed and bent into futility." The kind of boredom that undergirds much of this raucousness, van den Haag believes, will not be assuaged by any number of distractions. "Even the Second Coming would become just another barren thrill to be watched on television until the next newscast comes on. No distraction can cure boredom, just as the company so unceasingly pursued cannot stave off loneliness. Bored people are lonely for themselves, not, as they think, for others. We miss the individuality we've lost."

Sometimes we appear to be living it up when the truth is that we have a radioactive core of despair that's simply being held in check by the cooling towers of our bustling lives. And sometimes our questing is propelled more by boredom than by enthusiasm—and it's hard to tell whether our pursuits are driven by passion or the search for it.

I read Henry Miller's *Tropic of Cancer* a while back, and much of the sex and boozing therein—and there's a lot of it—seems desultory, aimless, and angry, but at a visceral level I understand it. What seems on the surface as mechanical as working an assembly line, a thing mean and restless, is actually the search for, if not the actual finding of, an antidote to the dehydrated life. The life of mentalizing and moralizing, of too much constipation by thinking and not enough extravagance of feeling, of too much sitting, staring, wishing, planning, laboring, subsisting, censoring, reasoning, rationalizing, too much blasted efficiency, too much time in the harness, and too much time worrying about being bored rather than being *boring*.

Any exultation done to excess, of course, done with malice or apathy, done without sense or sensibility, is its own desiccation, but I think what Miller is trumpeting is raw, immediate personal experience. Encounter and exposure. Immediacy and vulnerability. "Let the dead eat the dead," he says. "Let us living ones dance about the rim of the crater, a last expiring dance. But a dance!"

When it comes to passion, though, there's a difference between being called and being driven. A University of Quebec professor named Robert Vallerand distinguishes harmonious passion (characterized by a flexible persistence toward activity and more of a flow-state) from obsessive passion (persistence at any cost, the activity controlling the person rather than the other way around, and self-esteem and identity largely wrapped up in performance).

Those who are motivated by harmonious passion, he says, are more psychologically well adjusted than obsessives, and better able to satisfy (both in and out of work) what many researchers consider the three primary human drives: autonomy, competence, and relatedness. They're simply more fulfilled, spend their time immersed in more positive emotional states, and are less inclined to push themselves in ways that may be injurious, as in sports, which can turn acute injuries into chronic ones.

The harmoniously passionate also adjust better to the cessation of their passionate work lives (i.e., retirement), experiencing less anxiety and depression, and more vitality, than those who can't control their urge to work and can't live satisfactorily without it.

But both the harmonious and the obsessive, Vallerand adds, are better adjusted than those without passion at all.

Sacred Drift

Most people opt to avoid boredom at all costs, but creative people often find it a motivating force. Goethe believed it to be "the mother of invention" as well as "the mother of the Muses," and though a noxious weed, as he put it, also a spice for the digestion. "Boredom! Thanks be to you," he wrote. "You pushed into my hand the beloved but dull quills. You forced me to write, and sent me a page of joy."

The same dilemma has confronted every writer who has had to fill the empty page, every painter who ever stepped up to an empty canvas, and every parent called to respond to a child's plaintive cries of "I'm bored"—how do I fill the time and the space?

Nietzsche thought of boredom as the "windless calm" that precedes a blustery voyage. The anthropologist Ralph Linton contends that boredom drives all cultural advance. And meditators of all stripes think of boredom—the restlessness and sensory deprivation that often attend that practice—as one of the disciplinary whistle-stops on the way to enlightenment. The year I had to commute an hour between Santa Fe and Albuquerque to teach journalism classes at the University of New Mexico was the year I discovered audio books. Used rightly, boredom can become the instrument of our deliverance, the chutes and ladders that take us to new heights and new depths.

Saint John of the Cross spoke eloquently of dark nights of the soul, which aren't just about getting through life's rough patches but also about doing the hard human work of disentangling from worldly fixations and uniting with the Creator. It's a process that typically involves the traversing of a void and a period of meaninglessness, and since both situational and existential boredom are microcosmic versions of this journey, they're potentially gateways to a more creative life, part of an enlivening process rather than just a deadening process. They can be a stage in transformation, not a hindrance to happiness. You just have to stop reaching for the remote and avoiding the void.

The philosopher Søren Kierkegaard proposed a creative approach to combating boredom that's akin to crop rotation. It doesn't require that you constantly cultivate new fields, but that you tend to one field and continually rotate the crop, which is yourself. To become a fruitful inventor of new outlooks. To stay and be different.

Whenever I read stories of people who insist on rebuilding their homes on the banks of the very rivers or seashores that just flooded them out, I shake my head in disbelief and grumble about *my* taxes going to pay for *their* literal bailouts. Why not move to higher ground? But they always say the same thing: because it's our home. It's where we live, not someplace else.

But maybe they bring back with them a fertile new frame of mind, an understanding that there's a philosophical advantage to staying put—that rebuilding their houses in plain sight of the river is an aid to contemplation, a daily reminder of the precipitousness of life. Not its uncertainty, but its certainty—that it comes and it goes. Maybe having that fitful river in their backyard helps them acknowledge their true position in the scheme of things, and relieves them of the job of carrying the world on their shoulders when in fact it's the world that carries them, as casually as a whale carries a barnacle.

And maybe this is ultimately an enlivening meditation for them, even a kind of purification. Maybe it helps ream out the ego and allows them to accept life on its own terms, not rose-color it with fantasies and false securities—a kind of negative capability that points them toward the positive. "Once we overcome the No in our surrounding conditions," says Tillich, "we reach a Yes that is livelier than ever before."

ACTION IS OFTEN boredom's remedy—undoing your sense of helplessness by acting rather than being acted upon—but especially with the deeper kinds of boredom, the vaccine is more likely to be *insight*. If you dig a bit, you can probably identify the thwarted desire or vitality that boredom is masking, the stone that's been thrown onto your path, which will still bring you back to the need for action, but at least it will be *informed* action. And action rather than distraction.

Maybe the medicine we need for our boredom and ennui is of the homeopathic variety—like curing like—in which we approach boredom by boring in, drilling down into ourselves until we get to the root of our dispassion. When you're losing traction with the road, you turn *into* the skid, not away from it.

The point is to use boredom for what it was designed for, which is, ironically, to grab your attention. And by turning your attention *toward* your boredom, your inertia and impassivity, rather than reaching for the latest from Netflix, you stand to be enlightened by it. In Rilke's poem "The Archaic Torso of Apollo," a man is studying an ancient statue and suddenly intuits that the statue is also studying him, and he ends the poem by declaring, "There is no place that does not see you. You must change your life."

Research out of York University in Toronto confirms a positive correlation between people's proneness to boredom and their lack of emotional awareness. A study conducted there by psychologist John Eastwood found that it's possible to predict how susceptible people are to boredom, and how difficult it is for them to cope with it, based on their emotional literacy—that is, the amount of attention they pay to their thoughts and feelings and their capacity for examining and identifying their moods. If we study our boredom, and let it study us, we may find that it's full of wisdom.

It may be a stubborn nutshell that we'd prefer to smash with a rock rather than pry slowly apart to find some seed of contemplation, but submersion is the only solution that's guaranteed not to be a distraction. And boredom may end up surprising you with its kaleidoscopic underwater terrain, fascinating in the way fractals are fascinating, though repetitiveness is their very essence. Besides, the sooner you hit bottom—and there's only up from there—the sooner you'll reach the surface again.

In the movie *Smoke*, the manager of a cigar store takes a photograph of his shop from across the street every morning. He has over four thousand of them. One of his customers, idly leafing through his photo albums, says, "They're all the same." But of course they're not. A closer look reveals subtle changes in light, weather, and people from picture to picture. Same with boredom. If you're willing to look closely, it can be surprisingly interesting, containing all manner of weather patterns.

For several years now London has hosted something called the Boring Conference, in the suitably dreary month of November—to sold-out crowds every year. It features keynote speeches on supermarket self-service checkouts (with a special emphasis on "unexpected items in the bagging area"); lectures like "My Relationship with Bus Routes" and "Listening to Paint Dry," in which the speaker recites all 415 of the colors listed in a paint catalog; and breakout sessions on shipping forecasts, discontinued IBM cash registers, car park roofs, the carriage numbering system on the London underground, and toast, complete with PowerPoint images of toast slices ranging from the untoasted to the burnt-black, to demonstrate "the confusing, non-regulated series of toaster settings on the market." The lunchtime buffet table features sliced white bread, digestive biscuits, dry crackers, and cucumber slices skewered on cocktail sticks.

In similar fashion, the Dull Men's Club is a website that includes reporting on such tinder-dry topics as the Duct Tape Festival in Avon, Ohio; the winner of the Shed of the Year award; celebrations of Rest Area Month and the Park Bench Appreciation Society; and for your listening pleasure, the "Sounds of Cement," featuring the rhythmic sounds of cement mixers.

These organizations are dedicated to the principle that even the stodgiest of subjects can become intriguing if considered—and presented—in the right way, that the mundane can be seen as beautiful, and that with just a dash of irony, the tedious can be made at least enjoyably tedious.

In some ways, that's the very same logic behind mindfulness practice—taking ordinary, everyday activities (breathing, sitting, walking) and, by subjecting them to watchful and impartial attention, coming to know their richness. Ditto with thoughts, feelings, sensations, and states of mind like boredom. By bringing presence of mind to a condition we normally equate with an absence of arousal, we can suddenly make it engaging.

The emptiness at the core of boredom, certainly ennui, would seem to be qualitatively different from the emptiness that mindfulness practitioners, meditators, and mystics seek, which is filled with presence rather than absence, an expression of spirit rather than a depression of spirit. But maybe they're the same, and it's only how you look at it. Maybe just a quarter turn to the right or left and the emptiness that's the bane of the bored can be seen as the boon of the Buddhists. You feel empty? How wonderful.

Maybe it's like the difference between loneliness and solitude. They're both forms of aloneness, but one is sour and the other sweet. Aloneness can be framed as forlornness and exile or reframed as refuge, privacy, and certainly authenticity in the sense that you're most authentic, most yourself, when you're all alone. And emptiness can be reframed as spaciousness.

Mindfulness practitioners would probably tell us that the antidote to loneliness isn't necessarily company; it's *sitting* with loneliness. Rather than go with the desperate unthinking drive of it, the urge to fill up the hole by any and all means available, instead sit at the edge of it and ponder its dimensions, it's "hole-iness." Notice that emptiness is not at all nothingness. There's a lot of there there—light, space, potential.

Take it on as a contemplation, a vision quest right there in your own bedroom, one that's not about distraction but investigation, not about destruction (end the emptiness) but creation (write it down, dance it up, draw it out, sing the blues, compose a piece called "Suite for Weeping Violins"). Using creativity to combat ennui follows the logic that if you can't beat it, join it. Sink a well and draw up creative juices.

Parents are often counseled that when their children come to them complaining of boredom, they should avoid rushing to help them simply fill the time and get back to busyness-as-usual. Rather, they should stop what they're doing and focus on the child for five minutes, using the time to just connect, chat, and snuggle, whereupon most children will probably get the refueling they need and be on their way. Or you can inspire them even more quickly by offering to enlist them in housework or yard work to ameliorate their anguish.

We should use the same tactics with ourselves. Don't rush to fill up the empty spaces. Just give yourself some attention. Pull your bored self up into your lap for a little quality time.

In the months prior to writing my last book—before I even knew I was going to begin writing a book—I had several dreams of a man kneeling on the ground, holding a large, empty bowl on his shoulders, and waiting. For what, I didn't know. There was just a man holding a bowl, and months of waiting.

What eventually ended up filling that bowl were the pages of my book, which needed the bowl's emptiness, and the man's patient anticipation, to start flowing. But I not only had to sit with the emptiness for a while before it would reveal its purpose—rather than rushing to fill it—I also had to kneel before it. Not as a penitent awaiting punishment, but as a man awaiting knighthood. Or kneeling in prayer, or proposal.

And it wasn't just the bowl that was empty. Earlier that year I'd moved from San Francisco to Taos, New Mexico, which required that I empty my life of much of the Familiar—my home and surroundings, my friends and family, my teaching jobs and income. For eight years prior to moving, I'd been a freelance writer for magazines and newspapers, but as soon as I ensconced myself in the desert, work inexplicably dried up. Editors stopped returning my query letters. Those who did weren't interested in my ideas. Assignments drained away. My freelance career simply unraveled.

What had always worked no longer worked, and I couldn't figure out why. What conspiracy of luck and destiny and the ever-confounding material world made this happen? How could my willpower—which had proven itself seaworthy on a hundred, a thousand voyages—suddenly fail me? How could cause-and-effect cease to operate in the usual manner? I work hard and smart and things happen; it's that simple. Only it wasn't that simple anymore.

I tried redoubling my efforts, literally working twice as hard and long, but it was met with a resounding zilch. Dead silence at the other end of the line. I shouted and stomped my feet, rattled my empty cup across the bars, and nothing happened, except that in the course of a couple of months I went through a gauntlet of all the classic stages of grief and loss— shock and denial, anger, bargaining with the Almighty, depression, and finally a bitter acceptance that I just had to get on with it. I also made a few unscheduled stops at panic, self-pity, Ben & Jerry's, scheming, sleeplessness, and diarrhea.

However, throughout it all, I also kept hearing a small voice telling me that there was something afoot, something I wouldn't understand for a while; that my cup was emptying for a reason that reason couldn't fathom. It reminded me of the jigsaw puzzle pieces I kept finding on my travels over the course of one particular year, during a time when I was impatiently seeking clarity about my professional direction, and which I took to be clues that I needed to be patient and trusting, that the pieces of a larger puzzle were slowly coming together. Which they eventually did.

The Law of Watched Pots told me that I couldn't control things with impatience and that I just had to wait, not even knowing what I was waiting for, and in my panic I was forgetting how critical emptiness is to the creative process—the pauses in music, the negative space around a sculpture, the come-on of the empty canvas and the blank page.

Having to wait is, of course, one of the prime instigators of boredom, but it can also be a path out of it. But waiting *actively*, not passively. Tuning in, taking notes, maybe even kneeling in prayer. To wait, after all, means to watch. "Pay close attention to the most tedious thing you can find (Tax Returns, Televised Golf)," novelist David Foster Wallace wrote, "and, in waves, a boredom like you've never known will wash over you and just about kill you. Ride these out, and it's like stepping from black and white into color. Like water after days in the desert."

THE LACK OF such fruitful emptiness in our lives can make it hard for our passions and callings to reach us, since they have a hard time getting through when they get nothing but a busy signal. We may need to occasionally stop what we're doing and just float in the slack tide for a spell, in the state of what Sufis call sacred drift, resisting the temptation to reach for a quick fix.

The world, unfortunately, isn't always so friendly to work stoppage and considers almost illicit the kind of idleness required by introspection, meditation, contemplation, mindfulness practice, soul searching, wandering, even napping—though it seems to make an exception for that night-of-the-living-dead trance people get into in front of the TV. It's hard to carve out even a moment just to float, gaze, amble, daydream, and let your friends drum their fingers in the cafeteria.

Our ability to sit still and behold things—within or without—has taken a licking at the hands of a fitful world. For example, before the age of cameras and cell phones, travelers who wanted to capture images of what they'd seen often learned to sketch, so they could draw, and truly absorb, what they saw. However, with cameras and cell phones have come push-button memory and a reduced intensity of presence with what we're observing. Those who've spent half their vacation behind the lens of a camera may know the discomfiting sense that they're once removed from their own holiday, taking *pictures* of things rather than actually seeing them and being present to them. Countless times I've seen people pull up to a vista, get out of their car just long enough to snap a picture, then drive off. Sometimes they don't even get out of the car. They just stick the camera out the window and do a drive-by.

I read a story in the *New Yorker* some years ago in which the author, Adam Gopnik, talks about his three-year-old daughter who has an imaginary playmate named Charlie Ravioli. There's nothing unusual about a three-year-old having an imaginary playmate, except this one is always too busy to play with her. Whenever she calls Charlie Ravioli on her toy cell phone, she always gets his answering machine and has to leave a message.

A few months later, her father discovers that she's now leaving messages with someone named Laurie, who turns out to be Charlie Ravioli's assistant, someone he's apparently hired to return his phone calls for him.

Perhaps I'm being overly sensitive, but when our three-year-olds' imaginary playmates are too busy to play with them and start hiring agents to fend off the insistent phone calls of the children who imagine them to begin with, maybe it's time to move away from New York. Or rearrange your priorities. Or something.

The compulsion toward busyness is a pretty good definition of workaholism, which is one of our very few socially sanctioned addictions—the experts just call it a process addiction instead of a substance addiction—and one of the very few you can put on your résumé. You can't do that with most addictions. But even if all of our works are good works, even if all of our busyness is in the service of worthy and noble causes, when the means to those ends is an addictive process, the end result is probably a *loss* of soul and a *depletion* of spirit.

ONE OF THE DRAWBACKS of the passionate life, too, is that it can sometimes keep us in such hot pursuit of our earthly affairs, running from one excitement and urgency to the next and the next, that we seldom take our noses off the grindstone of details and take in the bigger picture, or question the validity of constantly shoveling coal into the furnace. "Enthusiasm shares a border with fanaticism, and joy with hysteria," writes Kay Redfield Jamison in *Exuberance*. "Exuberance lives in uncomfortable proximity to mania."

I had a firsthand encounter with this when I spent an afternoon wandering through the Metropolitan Museum of Art in New York and found myself bleary and spent after only a couple of hours—from the sheer overload. From what Henry James called the aesthetic headache brought on by submitting yourself to any bewildering and exhausting accumulation of art or culture, whether it's a wander through the two million works at the Met or through a city like Rome or Paris. Too much aesthetics is anesthetic.

There's even a medical condition known as hyperkulturemia, characterized by dizziness, nausea, and even hallucinations brought on by exposure to too much art. It's also called the Florence syndrome, in homage to that city's staggering catalog of art treasures. A recent issue of *Firenze spettacolo* actually lists the sites to avoid if you're susceptible. The top three: Michelangelo's statue of *David*, the Giotto frescoes in Santa Croce's Cappella Nicolini, and Botticelli's painting *Primavera* in the Uffizi Gallery.

My own case of hyperkulturemia was induced by the cramming into gallery room after gallery room at the Met, in wing after wing, absolute

logjams of artwork mounted shoulder to shoulder and eye level to ceiling—
combined with a central fact of both museums and all-you-can-eat restaurants: your eyes are bigger than your stomach. It was an atmosphere of
such overkill that my energy was quickly drained and my awe declawed.
(How, I wonder, do you clear the palate between paintings in a museum,
or even poems in a collection of poetry, so that they maintain their
singularity, their eachness, without sloshing and blurring together—the
equivalent of wine tasters taking a bite of bread between mouthfuls?)

What began with a delicious, kid-in-a-candy-store sense of anticipation, with the feeling of being at the start of a five-thousand-year journey
through the human hunger for self-expression, slowly but surely turned
into an aesthetic headache that found me slumped on the gallery couches
and seeking refuge in the cafeteria. I was less winded mountain-biking at
sixteen thousand feet in the Andes than by a tranquil stroll through
the Met.

Love's Driving Force

The ancient Greeks spoke of *pothos*, meaning a longing for the unattainable and incomprehensible, a word into which is rolled both desire and
regret. On a vase in the British Museum, Pothos is shown as the chariot
driver for Aphrodite, goddess of love—literally love's driving force.

It's also the part of desire that's never satisfied by consummation. It's
that part of the human psyche that exists only to draw us on—not toward
something, just onward. It's an old leather map whose margins swim with
sea serpents and the swollen face of the north wind howling in one corner,
but it's not a map to some far-flung treasure hidden in a crevice of the
world, some ancient cave scattered with scrolls or a temple room lined with
illuminated texts. It's more like Ken Kesey's Magic Bus roaming around
America in the 1960s, its destination sign simply reading "Further."

The Latin root of *desire*, according to Connie Zweig in *The Holy Longing*, means "ceasing to see," which could certainly refer to being blinded by
our ambitions, but also suggests that what we're ultimately after is something we cannot see, something not material but immaterial.

When my friend Judith came to see the twenty-second house I lived in, a few years ago, and stood in my third-floor office with its sliding glass door leading onto a deck and a prodigious mountain vista, she declared, "This is the pinnacle." Referring not to the place the room occupied at the crow's nest of the house, but to what she concluded must be the fulfillment of a writer's dream: a quiet loft in an upper story with an awe-inspiring view.

But the moment she said it, I knew she was wrong. There's always another pinnacle, and Pothos is always sitting out at the curb honking his horn. In fact, when I first saw the vista myself, I said, "All it needs is a snowcapped peak in the background."

But the fact that Eros is the only human desire named after a god (another Greek god of love and longing) suggests that whatever restlessness we feel isn't just our doing. It's beyond the gluttony of ego and willfulness, beyond the search for pinnacles and perfection and flyaway fathers. It's more than the product of society and its discontents. It's also powered by divine fiat. Not just mortal ambition but also sacred passion. It's what drives religion and science alike: the desire to part the curtain and behold the mystery, or at least get our hands on a splinter from the cross or one of Buddha's teeth.

The human story is full of god-induced wanderings: Adam and Eve's exile from the Garden, Cain's vagabondage, Ulysses's Poseidon-driven decade at sea, the Jews' forty-year sojourn in the desert. God's first word to Abraham was "Go!" With no more information than that. Abraham was seventy-five years old, and God told him to get out of town, no destination, just go, and that by doing so, he'd be blessed. The blessing was simply in the going. And Greek mythology tells that the gods created each human with two sexes but became threatened by their power and convinced Zeus to hack them in two. The search for a soulmate is a kind of nostalgia.

Maybe so is my serial search for home. Maybe it's a quest for something I once had and lost, which is the very definition of the religious experience, *religare* in Latin meaning "to repair a lost connection." At the risk of overanalyzing, I wonder if my parents' divorce when I was nine had something to do with all of my wayfaring. With the gleaming blade of a few soft-spoken words, my father was largely cut out of my life, along with the house I grew up in.

In fact, I was on the road at the time, in the back of the family station wagon on the way to a vacation in Vermont, when that first great departure of my life was formally announced, and I remember it the way I remember where I was when I heard that John F. Kennedy had been shot, which had happened only a month before. And ever since that day, and my parents' divorce shortly after, I've been going back to it like a tongue to a missing tooth, feeling for what isn't there anymore.

Much of the rapping I've done in rap groups, the journaling I started in my late teens, the therapy I've taken on over the years, even the days I recently spent poring over my mother's personal papers in cleaning out her apartment, has been a continual returning to the scene of the crime, an endless circumambulation around a mountain, crossing paths now and then with Sisyphus on his ups and downs. Trying to figure it out, to understand what happened and why.

It's been a kind of cosmology, or ballistics—a study of the aftermath of an explosion, a tracking of its residues. And somewhere in my mind, I picture that all the light from that winter day, the whole of the day's scattered earthlight, including the light bounced from the snowy streets, from the windows of the station wagon and the skis on the ski rack and my nine-year-old self, from all the road light, rock light, glass light, and water light of the world on that day—it's all just now reaching the star Mu Arae, fifty light-years away. And in the telescopes that Araeans use to study their patch of space, I'm still a small boy and my parents are still married.

Nonetheless, my father left home shortly after that fateful car ride, and soon after that, the rest of us left home for a new home, and a new father figure, and not a word was spoken about it from then on. But two dreams were sired: the dream of the child of divorce and the dream of the exile. One dream really: to go back.

Which can't be done. In *The Last Voyage*, Giovanni Pascoli writes about Ulysses, who, grown old and restless and drawn on by migratory birds, moves not forward into what time remains for him but backward. He tries to retrace the great Odyssey of his youth but finds all the heroic hurdles reduced to trifles, if he finds them at all. Circe's enchanted isle is abandoned, the sorceress long gone. The Sirens have all stopped singing, and the bones of those who fell under their spell long since returned to dust. The ancient cave of the Cyclops is empty.

As with visiting a house you grew up in as a child, everything seemed smaller and less momentous. He suffered from a nostalgia that wasn't the hunger for home that the ancient Greeks meant by the word—the one that drove him through *The Odyssey*—but a hunger for the road. And not the road ahead but the road behind. The vanished adventures of youth.

Nor was he the only one incapable of retracing those steps. I myself harbored a decade-long dream to follow in the footsteps of Ulysses and write about it, which ended abruptly when I called a professor of Greek history at the University of New Mexico and was told that it would be impossible because the islands mentioned in the Odyssey don't correspond to actual places. Only Ithaca, the birthplace of Ulysses.

Freud had a different take on the role of family in the drive to wander. He believed that the psychic force behind the urge to travel is the child-hood desire to escape home and family, and that when one finally acts on it, crosses the sea and attains the cities or lands one has long dreamed of, the feeling is virtually heroic, and startling: so all this really *does* exist.

I'm struck by how often I've said to myself, in my many moves over the years, that "there's no perfect place," an admission that that's precisely what I've been searching for. In emotional parlance, the place where the broken world is remade, the tribe regathered, and the wounds healed. I do know better, of course, and my twenty-three consecutive failures to arrive at this perfect place ought to clue me in that it's not something I'm likely to find in the "Homes for Sale" section of the newspaper.

I recall an exchange I had with the clerk at a coffee shop, during my most recent house-hunting adventure. On the counter was one of those fortune-telling eight balls. I picked it up and asked if I'd find the house I was looking for. The eight ball said, "Outlook Good."

"Yes!" I said, pumping my fist in the air.

"Yes what?" the woman behind the counter asked.

"Yes, I'm going to find the house I'm looking for." When I described it to her, this perfect house, she said, "I spent a year looking for that house, and finally gave up and just rented."

Nor would I be likely to find that house even if I *could* go back to the moment before the blade fell, because the family that was split apart by my parents' divorce was *not* a perfect place. That's why it split apart. But maybe by continually reenacting a single rite of passage—leaving home—I'm hoping to set the stage for a homecoming to that imagined and flawless place.

Or perhaps I'm secretly hoping *never* to find it. The author Milan Kundera once said that vertigo is not the fear of falling but the *desire* to fall, the voice of the emptiness below that tempts and lures us. Similarly, I wonder whether those who are propelled through life by restlessness, or any insatiable desire, secretly hope not that their desire finds satisfaction but that it doesn't, lest they suffer a crisis of purpose. Desire itself is the intoxicant, not the fulfillment of it. "The suspense is killing me," a friend once said of an infatuation. "I hope it lasts."

Leave-taking, though, can sometimes feel more like repetition-compulsion than heroic journey. It can fail to transmute lead into gold and can simply transfer our problems and shortcomings to a new address, over time making our cumulative wanderings seem like little more than the crazy skitterings of a bug at a lightbulb.

The parallel is apt. Nocturnal moths navigate by moonlight, and as long as the moon is at a certain angle relative to them, they know they're going in a straight line, or as straight a line as moths are capable of, the straight line a drunkard walks during a sobriety test. But when you're navigating by an object that's as far away as the moon, you can fly all night and it doesn't get any closer. So when moths pass a lightbulb or a lighted window, which mimics the light of the moon, they can zoom right by it and think they've just flown past the moon. They backtrack, trying to reorient themselves, and this, some say, is the wild dance we see.

But it's a drunken courtship, the failure of any addict to distinguish the knockoff from the real thing, that screws up their navigational skills. They get stuck in jagged orbits around false gods or hurl themselves repeatedly against invisible barriers, often becoming trapped or incinerated. I've cleaned out many a light fixture and found their dried corpses. Nor do the bodies of the fallen dissuade others from filling in the ranks. The only thing that stops the confusion is when the light goes out or the sun comes up.

Pothos drives all impossible dreamers, wanderers, seekers, and lunatics (literally the moonstruck). But he also tells us that the objects of our desires—whether person, place, or thing—are ultimately just stand-ins for the Unattainable, for an experience of perfect union, or self-transcendence, that keeps drawing us on and on through life, only dimly aware that no perfect place, no romantic love, no earthly paradise, no Olympic gold medal, no controlled substance—no "It" in "Making It"—will fill the Void.

This isn't to say it isn't filled for brief and rapturous moments when we fall in love or gain the promotion or land in the new world or have an orgasm—which, of course, explains much of the impetus for restlessness and the hunger for discovery. Then, for moments or hours or days or months, the walls come tumbling down, the angel sheathes his flaming sword, and we're back in the Garden. For a visit. Paradise is just a breather between quandaries, happiness an interval between the problem solved and the problem to come.

Those who are always at the glass, always leaving hot condensed breath on the partition at the baby ward while waiting to see the Star of Bethlehem, forget that the window onto the divine is also the partition *between* the divine and the mortal, and it's shatterproof. And a good thing. All the religious literatures argue that what is holy is also taboo. You can't look directly at the gods and live (unless they've taken on mortal guise). The painting on the ceiling of the Sistine Chapel in Rome captures this: God and Adam are always reaching for each other, but never touching. Restlessness is the passion at the core of spiritual life, creative life, scientific life, and faith, but it can't be resolved once and for all. Longing is a human proclivity; quenching it is not.

Something You Cannot Possibly Do

Think of the birds that migrated back to Atlantis,
circling the empty sea.

—ALBERT GOLDBARTH

Ross and I—suntanned after weeks in the desert sun of North Africa, our bodies striped where the sun was blocked by wristwatches and sandals— each sit atop a saddle shaped like a doughnut, wedged around the hump of a camel. Our Berber guide, Mohammed, brought these sturdy "ships of the desert" to port at the edge of the Sahara Desert by forcing them onto their knees so that we could climb aboard.

When the camels rise, he told us, it will be back legs first, which will pitch you forward in your saddle, so lean backward. To sit astride a camel is to be higher off the ground than when sitting on a horse, not as high as when on an elephant, and without stirrups to counter your body's full weight as it grinds your perineal tendon—the one that hurts after a long ride on a narrow bicycle seat—against the top of the camel's hump, which protrudes from the hole in the saddle.

But to ride atop a camel as it winds among undulating dunes—whose sinewy ridges snake off into the distance, whose scalloped edges atomize into mists of fine sand like the crests of ocean waves blown into spray by the wind—is to stand at the prow of a ship in rolling seas, the world hugely expanded by the simplicity of elements stretching out in all directions, at the far reaches of which are places you've read about since childhood, like Timbuktu, fifty-three days away by camel, Mohammed told us, at the far end of a string of oases that have defined trade routes here for thousands of years—at the far end of the very caravan route on which we were then setting out.

After a few hours, I found it hard to imagine sitting on a camel for fifty-three days, especially the one-humped. At least with the two-humped, I could nestle in the saddle between them, and there'd be something resembling back support. But with only one hump, I had little choice but to sit on top of it—a most literal pain in the ass—but it was either that or walking on mountains of sand, which Mohammed did for hours on end, barefoot.

Near sunset on the first day, we came around a bend in the desert and stared up at an enormous dune, burnt a deep orange and the height of a thirty-story building, at the base of which is one of those oases on the way south to Timbuktu. In this case, it was little more than a patch of palm trees and a clutch of oleander in bloom, beside which was a Berber encampment that was to be our home for the night and home already to a handful of nomadic families whose camels were hunkered down beneath the palms and whose children ran out to greet us.

It was a scene straight out of Central Casting, an outtake from *Lawrence of Arabia, Ali Baba and the Forty Thieves, Sinbad the Sailor,* or the imaginative life of any Westerner asked to conjure a living cliché from *The Arabian Nights.*

Our tent camp was constructed of brown wool blankets anchored—if anything can be said to be anchored in the constantly shifting sands of the Sahara—with long wooden stakes and built, like most Moroccan homes, around a central courtyard, daily life facing inward rather than outward, the sand carpeted over with Berber rugs and impaled with torches on long poles.

While waiting for a pot of mint tea to heat up (the locals drink their national beverage in tall glasses stuffed with mint leaves still on the stalk and saturated with enough honey to make Southern-style sweet tea seem bland by comparison), my brother and I hiked to the top of the great dune above the oasis, to survey the vastness and the solitude. From there, our entire camp at the base of the dune was easily blotted out by a fist, and the whole of the dunelands we had cameled through that day merely a cove at the edge of a far greater ocean of dunes called the Western Sand Sea, which stretched deep into neighboring Algeria and which was home to no human villages and no roads.

That night we played drums with the Berbers late into the night and slept outside under the stars.

I awoke in the middle of the night and wandered barefoot into the desert to relieve myself, then stood transfixed for a quarter of an hour, partaking of the surreal. A half-moon illuminated a desert tableau so exotic and otherworldly that I had trouble actually placing myself there, and heard myself ask, "Am I really standing under the moonlight at the edge of a nomad's camp in the Sahara Desert? Are those really camels over there sleeping by an oasis? Am I really that close to Timbuktu, the capital of the Middle of Nowhere, the one and only Ends of the Earth?"

I was there because I'd wanted something out of the box and a world away from anything familiar, not dulled and diluted by fifty years of Thomas Cook Tours. When I travel to foreign countries and cities, even exotic ones, much of what I encounter are variations on familiar themes: buildings and streets, merchants and shops, monuments and museums, mountains and rivers. This, however, was something entirely different and offered wholly unfamiliar categories of experience: living with nomadic people, caravan routes and desert oases, sand dunes the size of skyscrapers, camels as the primary mode of transport, and a language whose alphabet I couldn't even read.

But standing there in the Saharan moonlight in my bare feet, I realized that as far off the main drag of my life as it was, it was still only partway to someplace I've been trying to get to with all my wandering and questing, a place beyond just getting away from it all—an oases in my mind blooming with freedom, transcendence, *release.*

And yet, standing alone in that Arabian night, I wondered whether all my quests to attain this place of delicious remoteness and sublimity, away from it all and yet at the center of it all, were just a desert mirage, a phantasm of the thirst-crazed. Not only can I not get there from here, I heard myself say, but I can't get there from anywhere, because nowhere isn't a place and doesn't have a middle. And Earth is round—it doesn't have ends. And Timbuktu, I just discovered, now has an international airport.

In *The Lost Ones,* one of novelist Samuel Beckett's various hells, the protagonists are eternally trapped within a world consisting of a flattened cylinder with rubber walls, "vast enough for search to be in vain, and narrow enough for flight to be in vain." Their only desire, climbing, is accommodated by the presence of the only object in their universe: ladders. Their simian impulse is driven by an age-old rumor that there is, somewhere, an exit. It's a vision of endless seeking balanced by endless frustration, one that would warm an existentialist's heart, but not an optimist's.

This search, not unlike that in *The Moviegoer,* surely has me "onto something," something more than vaguely spiritual, but it also tends to blow sand into my sandwich and continually sets just beyond reach the very thing I seek. But if restlessness is the story of the struggle between the life we have and the life we want, spirituality is what we do with that unrest—along with philosophy, psychology, literature, and art. These are our attempts to figure it out and explain it to ourselves, to make sense of—peace with—the hope and pain our passions evoke. And ideally, to get to the bottom of the hungers that drive our questing, like Aphrodite's chariot, and turn them toward their true goal, though you could ride all night and get no closer to it.

The secret of life, the sculptor Henry Moore once said, is "to have a task, something you devote your entire life to, something you bring everything to, every minute of the day for your whole life. And the most important thing is—it must be something you cannot possibly do!" So we go in search of the Garden. We leave the sheltered cove and set coordinates for the unattainable. We try to change the world, though weeks can go by and nothing happens. Heaven is there to help us keep our chins up. And if we're lucky, our questing brings us back to what may be the great work after all: falling in love with an *ordinary* life, lived on *ordinary* holy ground.

I manage to make landfall there from time to time. I find that there are moments now and then, scattered throughout any given year, when I'm temporarily relieved of all my longings and all my questing, often when I'm sitting somewhere beautiful and my work and my worries are else-where, out of sight and for a little while out of mind, the tangled world briefly unknotted and my henhouse of a mind briefly unruffled. And the thought settles on me that this is enough. Just this. Lying here, feeling peaceful, the setting utterly simple and lovely—just trees and ground, or just sand, sea, and sky. And I understand that not only is it enough, it's also the prize. The hokey pokey that it's all about—just Being There. And it's like loosening my belt a notch. It's like when the refrigerator, which I hadn't even noticed before, suddenly turns off, and my body, which I also hadn't noticed, suddenly relaxes.

In the decade following college, when I worked at the Cincinnati paper, I prided myself on having a sense of direction in life, being on the go, hav-ing goals and going after them with a determination that once prompted a grocery store clerk to say, "You frown too much and walk too fast. Slow down. You'll live longer" (I was twenty-two at the time). Even when I was just walking to the sandwich shop around the corner from my office, to order the same sandwich I always ordered—turkey and cheese on rye with lettuce, mayo, mustard, and tomatoes—I always walked there with a union march of a stride.

One day I left work early and drove to a state park north of town. Instead of walking the familiar trails, though, I bushwhacked for several miles deep into the forest, and when I couldn't hear the sounds of civiliza-tion anymore, I stopped and spun around in circles until I toppled over on the ground. When I got up and tried to get my bearings, I realized I'd lost them. Happily lost them.

The points on the compass were just ideas in my head. Retracing my steps was impossible. I couldn't even tell from which fold in the forest I'd stumbled onto that spot, though I knew how I'd gotten there, to the point of *wanting* to lose myself, wanting to walk around aimlessly for once, free of ambition and the burden of purpose.

I also knew that somewhere out beyond the edge of the forest I held down a job like it was a squirming animal, or maybe it held me down. I knew I was wired to "go places"—my father told me—so every decision was calculated, every outing an errand, every vacation an assignment, every day a step closer to a place I've never gotten to and never will.

But the mind-set that allowed me to let go the way I did in the forest that day, wanting to be lost and found simultaneously, may be the same place I've been trying to get to. The poet Jalal ad-Din Rumi tells the story of a man paying homage to Allah, until a cynic points out that he's never gotten an answer. The devotee stops praying and falls into a confused sleep. A spirit comes to him in a dream and asks why he stopped, and the man says because he never got an answer. The spirit then says:

> *This longing you express is the return message.*
> *The grief you cry out from draws you toward union.*
> *Your pure sadness that wants help is the secret cup.*
> *Listen to the moan of a dog for its master.*
> *That whining is the connection.*

This isn't to say there aren't situations in which the holy ground over there is better than the holy ground over here. You hate your job, you quit to do something more in sync with who you are, you feel better. You live in a run-down studio apartment with a view of an alley, you move into nicer digs, you feel better. You're in an abusive marriage, you leave, you feel better. You're not disappointed because you aren't in an abusive marriage anymore or don't still work at a crummy job. Some philosophical flip-flop isn't going to make you indifferent to the real difference it makes. It's just that now that you've gotten X, you'll want Y.

The Declaration of Independence promises the *pursuit* of happiness, not the achievement of it or even the enjoyment of it. According to a 2002 survey by the New Road Map Foundation, started by the authors of *Your Money or Your Life*, the percentage of Americans who say they've achieved the American dream is 5 percent among people earning less than fifteen thousand dollars a year but only 6 percent among people earning more than fifty thousand dollars a year.

Nonetheless, from the moment we hit the snooze button in the morning to give us a few more minutes alone with our dreams, the chase is on. Get up, get out of bed, drag a comb across your head, get the kids off to school, get some exercise, go to work, sit in traffic, go shopping, pay the bills, clean up the house before company comes, make dinner, do the laundry, return phone calls, go through stacks of paperwork, read the kids a bedtime story, and by then the day's gone in a blur of habit and routine and the gumminess of domestication, and the days fly by this way, and your life flies by, and the hole in the hedgerow leading to the secret garden grows smaller and smaller, and eventually you can't remember if it even exists or if you just imagined it.

A STUDENT in one of my retreats once asked me to estimate my ratio of good days to bad days. I knew he wanted a numerical appraisal, not a lot of qualifications and relativities, so off the top of my head I said, "Sixty to forty, good days to bad." There was a pause you could have played a round of golf in, and then he nodded once, firmly.

He seemed satisfied with my response. But in retrospect, I should have qualified it.

What's a good day? A day I'm aboveground? Then I have 100 percent good days. A day I remember to be grateful for something? Then it's 70 percent. A day I'm satisfied with my accomplishments? Then it's 50 percent. A day I believe I'm fine just the way I am, with no need to change or prove a thing? Ten percent.

I know this reflects a substantial failure of some kind, but at the core of the human soul, I think, is not just a chewy nougat of kumbaya but also an emptiness. And yet, this thing we've devoted our lives to and cannot possibly do—lifting ourselves up from our fallen grace—is part of our pure sadness and whining that may draw us toward home.

3

Call of the Wild

I got to light out for the Territory ahead of the rest,
because Aunt Sally she's going to adopt me and sivilize me,
and I can't stand it. I been there before.

—HUCKLEBERRY FINN

JAY GRIFFITHS is an environmental journalist who lives on the outskirts of a small village in Wales and has been described as an "immersionist." Starting in her mid-thirties, she spent seven years following what she calls "the feral angel" wherever it led, into the wilds of the world and into the company of those who live there.

It was a journey that began by being lost, in what she describes as a wasteland: a long and dark depression. "No animation, no vivacity," she says in her ravishing book about the odyssey, *Wild: An Elemental Journey.* "The body is without dynamism, flair or potency." She had been unable to shake it for months, during which, she said, "I couldn't walk, couldn't write, and it felt like I couldn't survive the violence of my unhappiness. I had a repeated image in my mind of a little night-light guttering in the wind."

One spring morning as she sat crying in her rented London flat, the phone rang. It was an anthropologist whose work she was familiar with, and who knew and admired her work, but who she had never met. When he asked how she was, she said, "I'm drowning." Whereupon he invited her to meet him in Peru that September to meet with some shamans he knew, who, he believed, were adept at curing such maladies of the mind. She said yes.

Why don't you think about it for a few days, he said. It's an expensive trip, a big journey.

No, she said. "I knew a lifeline when I was being thrown one."

So over the next several months, she learned Spanish, emptied her bank account, waxed her boots, and left. Not so much in search of wild places but of the *quality* of wildness—"pure freedom, pure passion, pure hunger."

"I was homesick for wildness," she says. "We may think we're domesticated, but we are not. We're schooled in the cautious life and tamed from childhood on, but we're feral in pheromone and intuition, feral in our sweat and fear, feral in tongue and language. . . . Our strings are tuned to the same pitch as the earth, our rhythms are as graceful and ineluctable as the four quartets of the moon. We are—every one of us—a force of nature.

"I was educated—as we all are—to stay inside, within the bounds of my tribe (physical bounds and intellectual bounds) and to stay within the protected zone, to let the traffic of routine smother desire for the real outside. I was taught—as we all are—to be scared of the prowling unknown, of the wild deserts of Beyond."

As for the wild deserts of Within, she calls it "my elemental self," the part of her that wants to feel the world "exquisitely and physically and in reality," as she put it during our interview, "not on screens or through camera lenses; that wants an immediate experience of life, not a literally mediated one that involves go-betweens." In the book, she argues that this elemental self is rooted in "Freedom . . . an intrinsic part of wildness. Freedom is not polite. It doesn't knock or telephone first. It slams its hand down on your desk and says *Dance*.

"I wanted to put my cheeks against a glacier," she writes, "to drink direct from hot springs, to see vistas untamed . . . to feel the wind in my hair, the crusts of mud under my fingernails, the sun on my naked body." As she said to me, "I wanted to escape the chloroformed world." (Without going *too* far, that is. She still purchased travel insurance and a return ticket.)

She wanted nothing to do with the heroics of the solo expedition, though. There was no mountain she wanted to conquer, no desert she wanted to be the first woman to cross. "I simply wanted to know something of the landscapes I visited and wanted to do that by listening to what the knowers of those lands could tell me if I asked."

She spent the next seven years shuttling back and forth between the U.K. and the far-flung corners of the world, relying on contacts with anthropologists and letters of introduction from indigenous people living in England, as well as a research grant and eventually a book advance of thirty thousand pounds.

First she lived among the Aguaruna in Amazonian Peru, for whom the principles of deep ecology and the Gaia hypothesis are old news, and whose shamans taught her to see the world through feral eyes, starting with a respect for dreams. Shamans "were magnets to dreams. If you were a dream, it would be their sleep you'd swim toward, their minds you'd yearn to be dreamt in."

At night, she wrote her notes while hunched over in near-complete darkness to avoid attracting bugs with a light or lantern, and when one of her indigenous guides saw her dilemma, he caught a firefly, gently looped a thread around its body, and tied it to the tip of her pen so its green glow would illuminate her notebook.

She lived in the vast white-light reaches of the Arctic with Inuit tribes who make spears from narwhal tusks and boats from walrus skins stretched over driftwood, whose translucence enables them to see down into the green sea through the bottom of the boat. She saw the seas freeze over and ate whale meat with soy sauce. She learned there that "all landscape is knowledgescape," that going out into the wilds is a necessary human initiation, and that for young people lost in life's bleak expanses, the land is medicine. "Troubled youth" she told me, "are jousting at petty or parental authority and need real authority: ice, fire, thirst, hunger, predator. Nature is far wilder than their rebel wildness, more complex and tougher."

She lived among Papuans in the Highlands of West Papua, a mountain range so remote that the few maps she could find of the area specified "Relief Data Incomplete" and "MEF indeterminable"—maximum elevation in feet unknown—and from whom she learned that freedom is "the absolute demand of the human spirit."

And in the Australian outback town of Alice Springs, she asked an aboriginal painter what he felt when he was out on the land, and he immediately took a great deep breath, exhaled, and said, "You feel that you can *breathe* and you're alive."

All these experiences, she said, had the effect of not only casting off her depression but also shedding life of much of its complexity, boiling it down to a simplified and clarified modus vivendi. "Things now fall into two categories for me: those on the side of death and the wasteland and those on the side of life and the wild."

She also spoke of the importance of self-induced wildness, what she calls "derangement"—literally going counter to the line or row, the rank or file. But you don't have to head into the wilds of West Papua to de-range yourself. You can "go native" in your own backyard. Her recommendations: "Sex, drugs and rock 'n roll, according to your own compass."

She mentioned everything from a glass of red wine to an afternoon in the garden to the kick of creativity, through which we encounter the unknown and the unexpected. She applauded the reading of poetry you've never read before, taking classes out of sheer curiosity rather than utility, and "making sure that at 40 you're not espousing the same opinions you had at 20." She spoke of cultivating "a nomadic mind," being always a student, always learning and discovering, putting the *quest* back in *questioning*.

And to the degree that wildness is a state of being on the alert like an animal—"mental stupor is not a state of wildness"—she insisted that anything from deep meditation to extreme sports can take you there.

"One of the reasons I wrote the book," she said, "was to say to people yes, yes, yes, yes, yes. This is in you, and you know it. Vitality is a human birthright, and this tight, narrow world isn't all there is. We have a primal allegiance to wildness, to really live, to snatch the fruit and suck it, and to just bugger off for a while."

Her own journey of buggering off began with depression, but ended with levity, with time spent in a Buddhist monastery in the Gobi Desert of Outer Mongolia, where she learned from a resident monk that you can bicycle on the ice and fall off laughing. "At the core of life is levity," she says, "and the force of levity is stronger than the force of gravity. Rising is ultimately easier than falling, because all that's alive has an upward swing, and the strength is there in us."

We may be educated, as Jay says, to stay inside the bounds of the cautious life and the protected zone, but to educate actually means to bring *out*, to draw forth the gifts of our true nature, if not our elemental selves. Despite the implorings of the domesticated self, the indoor self, we want what's untamed in us, what scratches at the back door wanting out. And with good reason: in the Native American O'odham language, the term for wildness is linked with the words for wholeness, health, and aliveness.

What Fights the Saddle

The novel *We* by Yevgeny Zamyatin is a portrayal of the cautious life at its extremes. It tells of an utterly controlled society of "mathematically infallible happiness," in which every moment is tightly scheduled and nothing unexpected ever happens. Every bite is chewed fifty times, the Railway Guide is hailed as great literature, and all decisions are filleted of emotion and based on absolute rationality—on what the author, using an unexpectedly wild metaphor, refers to as "the purest mountain air of thought."

The ambition of the One State that rules over all this is "to unbend the wild, the primitive curve, and straighten it."

Toward this end, its members (referred to as numbers, not people) live in perfectly angular glass houses in a perfectly angular glass city, all of it surrounded by the thick glass of the Green Wall, outside of which is, well, they don't even like to think about it. When the protagonist, D-503, asks, "Who are they?" of the gentle, hairy creatures he sees outside the Wall one day, he is told, "The half we have lost." And when, near the end of the novel, he's briefly smuggled outside the Wall, it completely unnerves him. "I was frozen. I could not make a step, because under my feet was not a level surface, not a firm level surface but something revoltingly soft, yielding, springy, green, alive."

Even the oceans have succumbed to the State's unbending efforts. D-503—a mathematician so tightly wound that he remembers being frightened of irrational numbers as a child—proudly boasts that the ancients used to allow the ocean to beat monotonously at the shore twenty-four hours a day, while the millions of kilograms of energy residing in the waves went only to heighten the sentiments of lovers. "But we have extracted electricity from the amorous whisper of the waves," he says. "We have transformed the savage, foam-spitting beast into a domestic animal."

One of the few elemental forces the One State is incapable of domesticating is fog, which occasionally settles over the city, and which D-503 professes to hate. "That means you love it," a rebellious friend tells him. "You're afraid of it because it's stronger than you, you hate it because you're afraid of it, and you love it because you can't subdue it to your will."

That's because what is wild is, by definition, willful. As in self-willed, self-regulating. And we love what is free, even as it defies us.

What is wild is what confounds the settled, whether in thought or action, person or place. It's what slips through the net and fights the saddle. It's whoever is ornery for life, glowing from within with a kind of bioluminescence. It's the part of each of us that dreams of the open range and dies in captivity.

Thoreau said that in *wildness*—not wilderness—is the preservation of the world. He didn't say *wilderness* because he didn't *mean* wilderness; he meant the breaking of rules, David Rothenberg argues in *Wild Ideas*, the insurgent life in the midst of your peers. Meaning this: Walden Pond is and was a mile from downtown Concord, and a train passes close by its shore to this day, as it did in Thoreau's time. "That nearness is the wild in it. To buck civilization right in its midst. To find a deep surge of nature right inside us."

What we're after isn't the wildness that's divorced from cultivated life and exists only in outbacks and hinterlands, belonging only to other species and other eons—though we seek that, too, sometimes. We're after the wildness that exists alongside daily life, at the edges of "Concord." That wild kingdom brought to you by an insurance company in Nebraska.

We might find it in the dreams that switch on when the conscious mind switches off, which are among our last remaining protected wildernesses, since the conscious mind can't fence them.

It surfaces in those rich and raw emotions that occasionally manage to claw their way out of the bag of behavioral restraint and in those moments when you act with spontaneity—from the Italian word *sponte*, meaning, once again, "willful," "of one's own accord," "obeying natural impulses."

It's the questioning of authority, the fantasy of going native that interrupts your workday, your envy of the hippies with their backpacks, the imagination that smuggles you over the walls of the schoolhouse and the cubicle.

It's Take Your Dog to Work Day.

It's wherever you turn against the tide, spurning the conventions of culture if not propriety, deliberately leaving the barn door open—radical acts being those that, by definition, go to the *root* of a thing.

It's roof rot and bathroom mold and Freudian slips, those little whistle-blowers from the unconscious. It's carnival season and crimes of passion and God laughing at your five-year plan. It's the desire to *live*, in spite of dark thoughts to the contrary.

It's rhythm. When your foot pulses while you're listening to music, that's the will of rhythm coming through, and rhythm is the sound track of the natural world, of the whole earth story. It's the pulse of waves on the primordial shore and the beat of your heart, the cadence of katydids and the pax de deux of apogee and perigee, rise and fall, sun up and sun down, breath in and breath out, the opposites that never-endingly attract and repel, the downbeat of dying and the backbeat of the baby's cry.

It's also the future, which is wild, is like fog. You can't see into it and can't control it. You can plant seeds or bury them for later, but there's no guarantee someone else won't dig them up, or that they'll germinate and bear fruit, or even that come next season, you'll remember where you planted them. The arts of prophesying and prognostication are little more than blowing on dice and rubbing magic lamps. Even weather forecasting and medical prognosis—attempts to bridle nature with science—are rid-dled with uncertainties.

The Ainu people of Japan ritualize the proximity of the wild and the domestic by keeping a fire pit in the center of their houses, positioned so that the sun streaming through the eastern door each morning touches the fire. They say the sun goddess is visiting her sister the fire goddess, and that you should not walk through these sunbeams lest you break their contact.

The intuition that the bond between wild and tame, natural and human, should not be severed is an ancient one, woven deep into our psyches. But between us and the wild is also a divide, an evocative and dis-turbing border called the frontier—the edge, the brink, the fringe, the limits of your culture's jurisdiction over you and your free will. It's the line you sometimes have to cross to reclaim your passion for life.

But frontiers aren't just out there. Some say the inward equivalent of the wilderness is the unconscious, with all its willful and unkempt energies, all its suppressed desires and dreams, and that our primal intuition of danger out at the edge of the encampment, past the pale of settlement, has its counterpart at the edge of the psyche, where Reason, which normally sits astride bronze stallions in town squares and city plazas, can barely get a leg up. Here, the rules of politesse and protocol thin out, and we're swayed only by wind, not public opinion.

"The depths of mind," says poet Gary Snyder, "are our inner wilderness areas, and that is where a bobcat is *right now.*"

IT'S THE UNCERTAINTIES within *human* nature that Yevgeny's One State attempts to batten down. When D-503 unexpectedly falls in love with his rebellious friend, I-330, in helpless defiance of official protocol, he finds himself overcome with *feelings*, begins noticing that he now walks down the streets swinging his arms absurdly, out of sync with his steps, and one night even has a dream—of flowing sap—which wakes him in terror. He immediately checks himself into a medical clinic.

"You're in a bad way," the doctor tells him. "Apparently you have developed a soul."

"Is it . . . very dangerous?"

"Incurable."

Though actually it turns out not to be, as the Benefactor of the One State has hit upon a remedy for bouts of soul and willful individuality, an operation to excise from the brain the seat of infection—imagination.

An imaginectomy would make perfect sense, of course, to anyone whose ambition is unbending the wild and straightening people out, since they would naturally be unhinged by a force that's so frequently coupled with the adjective "runaway." The imagination is, by definition, free from worldly constraints, winging about in flights of fancy rather than housebound like reason and knowledge. (Einstein: "Knowledge is limited. Imagination circles the world.")

But an imagination that's vivid is, true to the word, alive, and life tends to move in wiggles, not in straight lines. *We* are the primary exception, constantly creating straight lines, which we then have to toe, or fall in. Rigid people, said philosopher Alan Watts, feel some basic disgust with wiggles. They want to get things *straight*. But life wiggles, nature swings her hips, and Earth itself wobbles on its axis.

In the thirteenth and fourteenth centuries, an insurgent philosophy called the Brethren of the Free Spirit believed that Scripture sanctified sensual pleasure, free love, and the conducting of mass in the nude. Its practitioners also believed that spirit was indwelling rather than external, and divinity best expressed through natural instincts and urges.

A Catholic mystic named Henry Suso, speaking *against* the Brethren, described a vision he had in 1330 of a spirit:

> SUSO: What is your name?
> SPIRIT: I am called Nameless Wildness.
> SUSO: Where does your insight lead?
> SPIRIT: Into untrammeled freedom.
> SUSO: What do you call untrammeled freedom?
> SPIRIT: When a man lives according to all his caprices without distinguishing between God and himself and without before or after.

He meant it as a denunciation, but "without before or after" sounds like a depiction of living in the moment, which is another way of saying enlightenment. And "without distinguishing between God and himself" sounds like a description of immanence, the lack of a sense of separation between the sacred and the mortal. And both of these phrases are fine descriptors of wild mind, of consciousness grounded in nature, the kind of aliveness and presence that characterize the lives of animals, from whom we're either descended or arisen, depending on your viewpoint.

But it's Suso's use of the word *caprices* to describe freedom—living according to our caprices—that's the clincher. It comes from the Italian word *capriccio*, meaning "curly." As in wiggly, kinky, twisted. As in Beethoven's *Rondo a capriccio* in G major, whose tempo is "allegro vivace," cheerfully lively. As in our desire to dance a rondo around the maypole every spring, that utterly universal urge to celebrate the triumph of light over darkness and life over death, to throw off our woolens and follow "the throb of it," as Willa Cather says, "the restlessness, the vital essence of it everywhere."

Beginning a thousand years before the birth of Christ, pagan rites celebrated the Saxon dawn goddess Eostre, from whom we get the direction east and the holiday Easter, whose date is still determined by the old moon cycle. It's here that the astrological year begins with, appropriate to the east, a fire sign, Aries. Here that the fertility goddess Demeter is reunited with her daughter Persephone, who's been consigned to the underworld for half the year. Here that Passover is observed, commemorating our release from bondage, and here that Easter is celebrated, first with a stripping of altars, an extinguishing of candles, an emptying of the fonts of holy water, a silencing of bells, and then with the lighting of candles and bonfires, the strewing of flowers and eggs, the singing of hymns, the consuming of feasts, the rumpus of carnival and parade, and the last time many folks will be seen in church until Christmas.

Our own embeddedness in the round of seasons reminds us that, like all nature, we and our wildness are big on caprices, on circles and cycles, curvature and chaos. But we're also big on control. And wildness—inner or outer—frightens us, and has for a very long time. Our creation stories alone give us away—at least the primary creation story in Western cosmology. In all the Abrahamic religions, the ancient image of paradise is the Garden of Eden, and a garden, as Jay Griffiths notes, is an expression of the will of the gardener, not the garden. Our most cherished fantasy of paradise is one in which things are tame, not wild.

Paradise comes from the Persian *apiri-daeza*, meaning a walled orchard. That is, a tamed wilderness, one that's tilled, terraced, mulched, pruned, sprayed, seeded, weeded, fertilized, composted, landscaped, and harvested. Not one that's left to its own devices and designs, but one that's controlled. So when we yearn to get back to the Garden, we're actually yearning for a life of control, not freedom.

And although it's technically a garden, paradise isn't always conducive to growth. Eve herself gave birth to nothing while in Paradise, only afterward and outside the walls.

Breaking the Spell

The human psyche is a dirt floor covered with carpet remnants we call civilization, but beneath it are the ur-emotions and proto-instincts of a billion years of outdoor education gone a little fusty in the head from too much recirculated air. We have canid teeth and old circadian rhythms, deep and supersensual intelligences, and a brain that, having spent 99 percent of its developmental time in the wild kingdom, doesn't quite know what hit it.

But we also haven't forgotten these bonds, and we're drawn to reconnect with wildness, with our instinctive self and its intimacy with natural rhythms, native intelligences, and untamed vitality. This could take the form of wilderness sojourns, creativity, sudden leaps of mad religion and free spirit, a half-wild impulse to light out for the Territories, take up the drums, turn off the mind and turn on the body, trust our intuitions, or just generally follow that fierce little pagan within, the feral angel.

Maybe, as Thoreau suggested, the wild is just the surprise element that exists in experience, like parrots that speak human language. There's a reason we talk about being be*wild*ered. And the way back to it is through disorientation if not discomfiture, which he considers high aspirations. It behooves us, he said, to find ways to be caught off guard and shaken up, to be estranged in the sense of exposing ourselves to the strange and unfamiliar through encounters with wild animals and foreign visitors, radical geographies and old books whose worldview and sensibilities—whose *smell*—are of another era.

The first (1908) edition of *The Wind in the Willows,* by Kenneth Grahame, has on its cover an illustration of Pan, goat-god of the mountain wilds, who, in a chapter called "The Piper at the Gates of Dawn," appears to two of the anthropomorphized characters, Mole and Rat, while they're out in the wilderness. The encounter provokes in them very mixed emotions:

"'Rat!' he [Mole] found his breath to whisper, shaking. 'Are you afraid?'

"'Afraid?' murmured the Rat, his eyes shining with unutterable love.

'Afraid! Of *Him?* O, never, never! And yet—and yet—O, Mole, I am afraid!'"

At that moment the morning sun blazes over the horizon and catches the two of them full in the eyes, dazzling them. When they've regained their vision, Pan has disappeared, leaving them "as they stared blankly, in dumb misery deepening as they slowly realized all they had seen and all they had lost."

But with his departure, Pan bestows on them the gift of oblivion, of forgetfulness, so that their normal life, their "home" life, won't forever be haunted by the encounter with their true nature and their true home.

The thing is, that spell of benevolent amnesia doesn't always take. Some of us anthropomorphized animals—perhaps all of us at some level—still hear the pipes, still remember that beautiful otherness, that nature which is deeper than the one we call human.

To even use the term "human nature" admits that the two are entwined, that we're a subset of the larger category called Nature, which includes everything from the endless escarpments of outer space to that call we sometimes wake up at three a.m. to answer, padding to the bathroom in our slippers. And Nature is vivace in the extreme, savage and sensuous in full measure, liberal with the color palette, ready to colonize every available niche, utterly intent on life, spawning and spilling over, unconstrained by timidity, taboo, shame, superstition, or self-consciousness.

And the kind of freedom our wild nature prefers is the untrammeled kind, a word used with exactitude in the Wilderness Act of 1964, which created America's legal definition of wilderness as land "untrammeled by man." But *untrammeled* doesn't mean untrampled. It means unrestrained. A trammel was originally a fishnet, and has come to mean anything that hinders, and the wild is anything that's unhindered.

Or helps to unhinder. If the unconscious is the in-house version of the wilderness, among its mightiest inhabitants is one known since antiquity as the daimon. The ancient Romans called it the genius (from which we get the word *genie*) and it's a guiding spirit that *everyone* possesses, though for most people it's bottled up. Etymologically, it means a distributor of destinies. Practically speaking, it's the rememberer.

According to Plato, the soul, on its passage into mortal existence, chooses a life path, and the Fates choose for us a daimon to help us realize that path. But then, just before embodiment, the soul sips from the River of Forgetting, and all memory of the life path is obliterated, along with any memory of past lives or what happened between lives. But what's forgotten isn't lost, and it's by turning to your daimon, your genius, that you're able to recall your destiny.

Surely the whole procedure could have been made easier by not wiping the slate clean there on the banks of oblivion, but there seems to be something vital, or so the story tells us, in the *effort* of remembering what you've forgotten. And daimons are formidable allies in the work to be done, and formidable enemies if we turn our backs on them. (That started happening, in large part, when Christianity got hold of them. The notion that one should listen to an inward guide didn't sit well with theologians who insisted that the only true authority was an outward guide—a singular God with a single master plan, not a personal god delivering a personal destiny. Daimons were downgraded to malevolent spirits called demons.)

The psychologist Rollo May, author of *Love and Will*, insists that daimons represent "the urge in every being to affirm itself, assert itself, perpetuate and increase itself." May writes, "Its source lies in those realms where the self is rooted in natural forces which go beyond the self and are felt as the grasp of fate upon us."

There are few descriptions of the workings of the daimon more eloquent than a passage in Jack London's novel *The Call of the Wild*, in which the "hero" of the story, the dog Buck, hears for the first time the sound of wolves. "Life streamed through him in splendid flood, glad and rampant. . . . It was the call, the many-noted call . . . sounding in the depths of the forest. It filled him with a great unrest and strange desires. It caused him to feel a vague, sweet gladness, and he was aware of wild yearnings and stirrings for he knew not what."

The daimon, like the willful soul it's meant to superintend, doesn't like taking no for an answer, won't accept clock time, nine-to-five schedules, excuses, or admonitions to sit still and stop fidgeting. It doesn't want to get in line, bow to the rules, and do as it's told. It won't give up without a fight. In its spare time it likes to read myths and fairy tales, as they're great sources of nourishment for wildness, advocating for the integration, not the suppression, of the turbulent energies of humanity.

In fact, the wildness of our once-upon-a-time lives certainly found its way into these legends, whether Norse sagas, Siberian shamanic tales, or Greek epics like *The Odyssey*. The raw materials for these original action-adventure stories were perilous journeys, otherworldly encounters, heroic ordeals, or treacherous passages through dark woods or clashing rocks. And the point of them wasn't just an adrenaline rush or a little escapism from the desk job. It was transformation. From cowardice to courage, folly to wisdom, woundedness to wholeness, and sleep to awakening. They didn't speak of merely physical journeys so much as psychological ones, of our formative face-offs with limitation.

I drew a picture of my daimon once. It was an elaborate, technicolor oil-pastel drawing, a foot by a foot and a half, which I did as part of a two-year attempt to chronicle in pictures my passage through a calling that began when my ex-wife, Robin, came to me one day, out of the blue, and said, "I want to move to the country," and like a good New Yorker, I said, "What country?" It turned out to be a move from San Francisco to a hamlet north of Taos, New Mexico, called Arroyo Seco—"dry creek" in Spanish.

Robin, a painter, had suggested that in addition to writing about the experience—that is, processing it mentally—I draw pictures of it, following Goethe's observation that "we talk too much. We should talk less and draw more," and following a bit of advice from the Jungian psychologist James Hillman: "When you ask, 'Where is my soul? How do I meet it? What does it want now?' the answer is 'Turn to your images.'"

Images are far more ancient emanations from the human psyche than language, and far more visceral articulators of the soul's untrammeled will. They emerged at a time when humanity was on the brink of self-consciousness, poised between worlds, between the animal and the human, the Old Stone Age and the New. Back when we were *all* hunters, we drew pictures of the creatures we sought, in the hope that this would lead us to them, or them to us. Our images were a way of drawing near to wildlife. And they still are.

That drawing journal was *filled* with elemental, almost Paleolithic images. The first ones I did—my initial response to hearing the call to leave city life for country life—included the picture of a man staring petrified over the edge of a cliff, another of him disappearing into a ring of fire, and finally an image of him swinging a club in frustration.

My indecision emerged as a triptych—in the first drawing a man is pushing against a boulder, in the second he's pushing against his reflection in a mirror, and in the third he's tearing himself in two with his own hands. (See next page.)

My fear and frustration with the chaos unleashed by the call came out in a series of monster drawings that years later, when I began sharing the pictures in my Callings retreats, prompted Robin to say, "You're not going to show those to people before bedtime, are you?"

My decision to finally follow the call came as a portrait (significantly, twice the size of all the preceding drawings) of a man with wings for arms, leaning out over a cliff and just past the point of no return, but looking upward this time not downward. In the background is an exploding volcano.

At precisely this point in my process, a friend gave me a drawing *she*

did, her perception of what I was then going through: a picture of Jonah in the belly of the whale, surrounded by flames—an amalgam of trial by fire and dark night of the soul. And precisely nine months after finally moving to the country, I drew a picture of a man with the body of Hercules pulling himself out of the ground, his bottom half still submerged in the earth.

The final drawing in the series was of a man kneeling on the ground, hoisting on his shoulders an enormous urn into which is being poured, from a vine-covered goblet suspended high in the air, a waterfall. It was a perfect simulacrum of the response I ultimately made to that call: a writing project that became the *Callings* book.

As graphic and illuminating as the drawings were, they were matched in revelatory power by a discovery I made shortly after I finished them:

Joseph Campbell's work. He's the mythologist who, in a series of interviews with Bill Moyers in the 1980s, helped popularize the concept of "the hero's journey," as well as the bumper sticker FOLLOW YOUR BLISS.

After reading his description of the classic stages of the hero's journey—the call, the refusal of the call, the road of trials, the allies, the obstacles, the supreme ordeal, the receiving of the gift, and the return to the community bearing the gift—I went back to my drawings and was stunned by how closely my personal journey matched, even chronologically, the age-old hero's journey that's the basis of every myth and fairy tale humans have ever told, and the prototype for how people typically respond to callings. It gave the whole notion of archetypes, those ancient and universally recurring patterns in the human experience, a huge boost in credibility in my mind, and taught me to trust my daimon, no matter what his marching orders.

I knew nothing of daimons, though, when I drew a picture of my own—the only other drawing in the lot that was double-size, and the portrait of a singularly wild creature.

In the foreground is the diminutive figure of a man in profile, his arms raised in the air, his eyes closed, his mouth turned up in a smile, facing a brilliant sunlight coming from outside the picture. His shadow snakes along the ground behind him and slowly rises up, larger and larger, higher and higher, until it becomes a great green brute towering overhead, whose grin is a chasm filled with crooked shark teeth, whose eyes are two roaring furnaces. And though it's obvious he could devour the man in a single bite, he's clearly smiling too, and lit by the same sun.

The only reason the man can turn his back on this Goliath with impunity is that he's made his acquaintance. Daimons turn into demons only when they're ignored or repressed. And the ancient Greek word for happiness is *eudamonia*, meaning "a well-pleased daimon." (To see the rest of the drawings from the journal, visit www.gregglevoy.com.)

The Wilds of Meditation

Clearly we don't have to look far to find our own wildness, and indeed the mind itself is famously wild. But so is perhaps the most common technique we use to manage it, meditation, which is eminently wild in both origin and effect.

Meditation arose among hunting cultures of the Himalayan foothills as a direct descendant of the stilling and centering tactics essential to all hunters, animal and human, and it aims not ultimately for control but for acceptance—to remove all controls, all editing and taming, and simply to allow and observe the mind being what it is, a force of nature.

Camping out alone in the Allegheny Mountains, Gerald G. May, author of *The Wisdom of Wilderness*, once lay wide-eyed in his tent while a bear prowled his campsite. He describes a fear more intense than anything he experienced even in Vietnam, and says that he was completely present to it, beyond all coping, because there was nothing to do.

"I have never before experienced such clean, unadulterated purity of emotion," he says of the encounter. "This fear is naked. It consists of my heart pounding so loudly I'm certain the bear must hear it, my breath rushing yet fully silent, my body ready for anything, my mind absolutely empty, open, waiting. I have never felt so alive."

Like any strong emotion, he says, fear can make you exquisitely conscious of living, perfectly aware of being in the moment. But it can only do that on those rare occasions when you don't try to fight it, run away from it, cope with it, suppress it, or in any way try to domesticate it. "Wild, untamed emotions are full of life-spirit, vibrant with the energy of being. They don't have to be acted out, but neither do they need to be tamed. They're part of our inner wilderness."

In entering that wilderness through meditation, you enter a backcountry of silence, which, like the actual wilderness, is for most people a great unknown, and like a solo journey into the wilds, something you tough out.

In the dark and solitude, you're exposed to the entire elemental life of the human psyche, the endless flow and bluster of passions, angers, joys, lusts, worries, inspirations, doubts, and fears. The entire avalanche of mind and its ferocious need to fill up empty spaces with torrents of talking and thinking. And with the departing storms you begin to make out that border where human time meets geological time, where minutes feel like hours and hours like eons.

Whether you meditate sitting, standing, walking, or dancing, you face into the question of what will happen next. And in this regard, meditation is like the asteroid that ushered out the dinosaurs and gave the mammals underfoot a shot at prominence. The thunder lizards of everyday consciousness are sidelined and other life-forms are given an entrance cue, parts of you that are normally overshadowed. "We can make our minds so like still water," William Butler Yeats once said, "that beings gather about us to see their own images and so live for a moment with a clearer, perhaps even a fiercer life because of our quiet."

An acquaintance of mine told me that the people she knows who meditate regularly are particularly gifted at spontaneity, at "dancing with the moment." Having practiced the ferocious art of being *in* the moment, they're better equipped to go *with* the moment.

And who better to teach us the meditative arts of being in the moment than animals, with their thinkless presence. I read that when the actress Helena Bonham Carter was tapped to play the character of Ari in Tim Burton's remake of *Planet of the Apes*, she studied for the part by attending six weeks of "ape school" to learn simian movements, under the tutelage of Cirque du Soleil acrobat Terry Notary. "Humans are so distracted," Notary says. "Apes just focus. If they're eating a grape, they're into it. And when they're done, they go on to something else 100 percent. That's living moment to moment. Finding your inner ape is really, truly living."

And you want wild? Try a *ten-day* sitting meditation, during which most of your cultural struts are kicked out from under you and compared with which most of the wilderness outside is about as menacing as a petting zoo.

Ironically, in most such retreats, your standard-issue freedoms are curtailed to press you into a deeper kind of freedom. You're required to give up the freedom to move around at will, set your own schedule, even choose your own food. You relinquish all personal items (cell phone, keys, wallet), social contact with other meditators (including speech and eye contact), physical and sexual contact with anybody, even proximity to members of the opposite sex, who are kept segregated. You're to have no contact with the outside world, engage in no reading, writing, talking, intoxicants, or music, and to suspend all other spiritual and healing practices.

According to one teacher of Vipassana (the word means "pure watchfulness" in India's Pali language), you're to remain "aware but equanimous" of the fact that you're in excruciating pain, due to sitting cross-legged for anywhere from ten to eighteen hours a day, and indifferent to your recurring fantasies of sex and hamburgers, as well as the general blather of the mind. The latter will have you thinking about anything but the formidable meditative tasks at hand, including, as one meditation blogger I ran across put it, "Analyzing every film I've seen over the past ten years, why I've always hated my grandmother's furniture, and what my second-grade teacher's perm looked like." In some of the more ascetic meditation retreats, you even sleep on a wooden table and a wooden pillow with a notch cut out for your head, which is exactly as comfortable as it sounds.

The prevailing wisdom among longtime meditators is that if you can't get out of something, get into it, bearing with and bearing witness to whatever emotional, physical, and sensory hoopla presents itself to your awareness, without looking away. But stick with it and meditation can bring you to the *other* aspect of wilderness—its serenity, its self-willed and self-regulating balance.

We praise the wilderness for its wildness, but we often seek out wild places for inner calm and spiritual clarity, for the simple reason that among the endowments of wilderness is vast stillness and, when sufficiently removed from the din of humanity, vast silence, in which the Larger Voices that want to come through us are easier to hear than in the city, with all its aural and moral cacophony.

In Hebrew, the word for wilderness is *midbar*, referring to a place without speech, "beyond words." But it's also a place where, by falling silent and listening, we hear a deeper speech, that of the divine. Which means there's no such thing as a godforsaken wilderness. It's in wilderness that we're most likely to hear God.

The Israelites spent forty years wandering through this place beyond words, during which they reconfigured themselves from slavery to freedom and coalesced into a people—a religion, a nation, and an identity. They also received the Torah—the words of God that non-Jews call the Old Testament. For the Jews, wilderness is a central metaphor for understanding who they are and what they must do.

In my mid-teens I began a meditation practice, initially using a candle flame as the focusing agent. But I changed my regimen after an experience I had in my early twenties. I was driving through the Southwest one afternoon and found myself sitting at the edge of a cliff overlooking Canyonlands National Park, in southern Utah, gazing into its red-rock maze of canyons and mesas, marveling that such an enormous volume of space could be so *quiet*. Not a bird, not a cricket, not so much as a sigh of wind.

I'd never "heard" such radical silence before and decided that I had to get down into it. Within an hour I had my backpack on and was on my way. I lasted three days. It wasn't that I ran out of patience for the silence. I was driven out by the howling at night—which was only coyotes but I didn't know that. Being from New York, I'd never heard coyotes before and thought they were wolves, whereupon a childhood full of monster movies took hold in the back of my mind.

But when I got home, I incorporated that glorious silence into my meditation practice, substituting the candle flame with the sound I heard "ringing" in my head in the Southwest—a clear, high-pitched note, dog-whistle high-pitched. And even outside of meditation practice, I'm still able to summon that sound when it's not so quiet, and I still use it to settle and focus my attention and to recapitulate the serenity that I consider one of the great benedictions of wilderness, and a great boon to anyone whose propellers are choked with the floating debris of the ten thousand things.

There's a reason sages are characterized, if not caricatured, as living in remote mountain reaches or in caves, and the desert associated with spiritual search, as in the tradition of the Desert Fathers and the Temptation of Christ. Buddha gained enlightenment while sitting under a tree. Muhammad received his first revelation of God in a cave in the mountains. Jonah was carried to redemption in the belly of a whale. And in all the world's mythologies, those who undertake a hero's journey—or who simply seek to avoid imprisonment and gain political freedom—do so first by swapping the comforts of home for zones unknown, wildlands of one kind or another.

And it's no coincidence that humanity's formalized journeys to the Source—our vision quests and walkabouts—continue taking us back to the wilderness for the rendezvous. It's the very scene of Nativity, of the Chaos that our holy books tell us preceded Creation and that in its original Greek simply meant "to be wide open." Chaos doesn't mean disorder. It means unshaped life, the very essence of potential.

Not that the outward-bound quest to reach your potential, or just calmness and clarity, doesn't first pass through a few stations of the cross. In the desert, the soul stands solitary before its gods and its demons, who are nothing if not wild. As I once heard a climber say, "Mountains cut the crap." But the wilderness also seems to have a meditative effect on the human psyche over time, able to absorb and contain its ferocities better than human community.

On a few memorable occasions in my own life, I've gone to the woods or the mountains, filled with the usual rages that pile up in the soul over time, dug a hole in the ground with my bare hands, and *screamed* into it, then covered it with dirt. I've walked away from these episodes appeased, the god of anger propitiated with a sacrifice of shouts. Besides, I figure the body of Earth can handle those energies better than my own body.

If you're contemplating following suit, I recommend only that you choose a spot well out of earshot, so you don't frighten anyone (not that the animals won't be startled) and have the search-and-rescue folks or the sanatorium folks coming after you. The Irish have a saying about these things: all conversations with a potato should be kept in private.

The Wilderness Effect

My garage and my attic are probably like a lot of people's—packed with boxes full of stuff, a significant percentage of which falls into the category of "Well, you never know. . . ." Though after hauling it around for decades, you probably *do* know.

In one of the boxes in my attic is a moldy old backpack, though it's been twenty years since I last went camping, since I walked out into the solitude of the wilderness and stayed there long enough to start waking at sunrise and sleeping at sunset and to remember that this is natural, long enough that the animals started doing whatever they were doing before I arrived.

The backpack is a link to a neglected part of me, and the fantasy of return, and I'm not ready to let go of it yet, any more than I want to sit down at the piano someday, like I saw a friend do recently, and slam the lid down in frustration because too many years have gone by without playing and it's lost to me.

Standing in the garage during my last move, contemplating once again whether to take the backpack or leave it (I took it), I felt that same sting of loss. I saw in my mind's eye a jumbled flickering of memories, images, and decisions that illuminated how I got so caught up in the game that I lost my taste for sleeping outside and being immersed in the wilderness.

My generation (the baby boomers) may have been the last one to spend such a large percentage of its youth and young adulthood in the great outdoors, though the older we've gotten, the more we've cut back on visiting hours, thereby joining the ranks of succeeding generations, who spend most of their time inside (Americans as a whole spend 90 percent of their time indoors, according to the Environmental Protection Agency).

But our disengagement from the outdoors isn't just a function of getting older, though not wanting to subject our lower backs and bum knees to the rigors of wilderness outings and fifty-pound backpacks has something to do with it. It's more a matter of having gotten so inadvertently caught up in the business of life and the mechanics of keeping the wheels turning that we live in a kind of exile from the natural world.

We go months or years without touching a tree or knowing what phase the moon is in, without seeing an animal in the wild or submerging our bodies in running water that doesn't emanate from a showerhead, without even walking on the *ground*. Not the sidewalk, the street, the marbled foyers of an office building, the linoleum aisles of a supermarket, the concourses of an airport terminal, or a carpeted apartment in the city—but the actual ground.

I had a sobering conversation with my brother Ross many years ago. We were comparing notes on the various sensual and natural pleasures and passions we'd let slide over the years, wondering where they went, or where we went. It wasn't that some of them hadn't been replaced with new pleasures, but many of them were victims of a certain amount of neglect. At the time they included, between us, guitar and piano playing, dancing, camping, massage, kayaking, skiing in the mountains (which were only two hours away), swimming and boogie-boarding in the ocean (which was two blocks away), and lovemaking with our respective partners (who were only arm's length away).

We cataloged with sad precision the years of cultivating footpaths *around* the piano, *near* the garden on our way to work, *under* the kayak, which was hanging in the garage collecting Olympic-size spiderwebs—and how, when we occasionally came to and reached for the guitar or the girl-friend after so much time away, they'd grown a bit cold to the touch.

It's tragically easy to lose contact with the body, and the body of the earth, and the sensation of being at home in both. Too easy to suffer from what author Richard Louv calls "nature-deficit disorder," summed up by a fourth grader he quoted as saying, "I like to play indoors better 'cause that's where all the electric outlets are."

But as my brother and I did for each other that day years ago, it's good to be reminded of "the half we have lost," if not the price we have paid, and of the benedictions this lost life can offer to our sense of aliveness.

A hundred studies have confirmed the healing properties of nature, and why, as Louv puts it, nature experiences should be taken out of the leisure column and put in the health column, if not outright taken as med-ical deductions. And you don't even have to go outside to benefit. Sitting on your couch and watching fish in an aquarium will lower your blood pressure, pulse rate, and muscle tension. Having a hospital room with a view of a park rather than a parking lot will help you heal faster, leave the hospital sooner, use less medication, have fewer complications, and cost yourself and the health care system less money. Prison inmates whose cells face onto farmland get sick 25 percent less often than those whose cells face the prison courtyard. Office workers with windows looking onto trees or lawns experience less frustration at work and more enthusiasm for it than those without such views. And the mortality rate of heart-disease patients with pets is a third that of those without.

And all this without even stepping outside to savor the age-old con-nection between lying down in green pastures and having your soul restored—to be refreshed by the sight of inexhaustible vigor, as Thoreau put it. Nature is surely the place where aliveness is most abundantly dis-played and in greater variety than anywhere else. It's a master teacher in the ways and means of vitality with its relentless drive for life—its muscu-lar shovings down into the soil and up toward the sun, its vigorous cam-paigns of copulation and comingling, thirst and hunger, endless bloomings and blossomings, and the endless decayings that make way for more bloom-ings and blossomings.

But if nature displays death, too, more abundantly than anywhere else, nowhere is it also more evident that death is *related* to aliveness. Someone's demise is someone else's dinner. Snowfields melt into rivers that nourish the valleys and riparian communities. Mountains are ground down into soil in which the forests make their stand.

In nature, the utility of death is obvious, the fact that it's not merely an ending but a prelude, and not theoretically or theologically but practically, visibly. Death and decay are put to immediate use, plowed right back in to feed life's appetite for itself. Life continually emerges from death, so every day is resurrection day, and the world continually spins, so every day is a revolution.

A back-to-the-garden crusade called the Eden Alternative is also a revolution, dedicating itself to transforming eldercare for the 1.7 million Americans who presently reside in long-term care facilities, by introducing the presence of animals, plants, and children. It offers elders the opportunity to give and receive care and companionship, providing an antidote to what founder Dr. Bill Thomas—a self-described "nursing home abolitionist"—calls the three plagues of the elderly: loneliness, helplessness, and boredom. "We imbue daily life with variety and spontaneity," he says, "by creating an environment in which unexpected and unpredictable interactions and happenings can take place."

The Tioga Nursing Facility in upstate New York, for example, has a dozen dogs and cats, four hundred birds, a giant rabbit, and a potbellied pig all living on the premises, and gets regular visits from a Shetland pony named Nutmeg. As for the children, Tioga renovated an adjacent building, opened four classrooms, and several days a week brings a hundred kindergartners onto the nursing home grounds for intergenerational activities. Many Eden-registered facilities also have on-site day-care centers for their staff, along with after-school programs and summer camps.

As for the gardens of Eden, many facilities also have flower or vegetable gardens that are wheelchair accessible, featuring (very) raised beds, benches, and shade.

There are currently over three hundred Eden Alternative facilities, and since converting to the Eden philosophy they've seen a drop in mortality rates, infection rates, staff turnover, and the use of medication. The Texas Long Term Care Institute, at Texas State University, conducted a two-year study of the Eden Alternative across six homes with over seven hundred residents, and yielded the following results: a 60 percent decrease in behavioral incidents, a 57 percent decrease in pressure sores, a 48 percent decrease in staff absenteeism, and an 18 percent decrease in the use of restraints.

According to a staffer in one Northern California facility: "We had a woman here who was so severely depressed nothing could reach her. No drugs, no therapy, nothing. Then the facility put a cockatiel across from her room. Ever so slowly, she started to take an interest in that bird. Then she got out of bed on her own for the first time so she could see it better. Then she crossed the hall and started talking to the bird. Then she started talking to other residents and to the staff. Her depression was gone. A simple bird had done what no drugs, no therapists, nothing else could do."

ROBERT GREENWAY has spent more time in the wilderness than almost anyone I've ever met short of the indigenous, and done more than most to quantify what he calls the "wilderness effect." A self-described "nature boy," who at eight years old had an animal museum in the basement of his house ("snakes in jars, snakeskins, spiders, etc.") and at twelve had a thriving gardening business with twenty-five customers, Robert became a garden writer for *Sunset* magazine, was a founding dean of ecologically based Franconia College in New Hampshire, and developed a training program for the Peace Corps using wilderness experience.

In 1963, he coined the term "psycho-ecology" to explore the emotional bond between humans and nature, though its initial adherents weren't crazy about being called psycho-ecologists, and the term "ecopsychology" was born, a movement more than a settled field, and one devoted to defining sanity as if the whole world mattered.

During twenty-two years at Sonoma State University in Northern California, starting in the late 1960s, he taught ecopsychology and developed the first graduate program providing wilderness therapy training in the United States. In the spirit of his belief that "wisdom keeps school outdoors," he also took more than fifteen hundred students into the wilderness for anywhere from two to four weeks at a time, and sometimes went there by himself for up to three months.

To mollify nervous deans and department heads, and because many students returning from these sojourns were often incoherent about what had happened to them out there, Robert began conducting formal research into the wilderness experience, which, under the tutelage of ecopsychology, is more than "the wonderful but naive practice of simply escaping into the wilderness." It's a journey carefully structured to resemble a rite of passage, with its triune architecture of separation-initiation-return—leaving behind what's familiar, reworking yourself, and returning to the community renewed.

Similar to what research on meditative and psychedelic experiences has revealed, Robert found that the wilderness effect involves dropping below cultural mind-sets into a deeper experience, and that the many forms of pleasure that tend to get numbed by especially urban living—bodily, perceptual, aesthetic, spiritual—also tend to come back to life in natural settings. These forms contribute to an expanded sense of self—what "deep ecologists" call an ecological self.

Time spent outdoors can vaccinate against nature-deficit disorder as well as, to some degree, narcissism, since your primary reference point is less likely to narrow down to *you*. And though nature is certainly among our most accessible means for contemplating metaphysical superlatives like infinity and eternity—a look into the night sky at outer space, for example, which the astronomer Fred Hoyle reminds us would be only half an hour away by car if you could drive straight up—it's not the only way to gain the bigger picture. So is spiritual practice, service, the study of history or cosmology, even just sitting before the pulpit of your grandfather's life and listening to the old stories.

However you manage it, says the poet Denise Levertov, once you lose track of your own obsessions and self-concerns and give yourself over to the parallel world of nature, "something tethered in us, hobbled like a donkey on its patch of gnawed grass and thistles, breaks free."

The sort of non-goal-oriented awareness heightened by entering the wilderness emotionally as well as physically, along with the outgassing of everyday concerns and timetables, helps people feel expansive and rejuvenated, reconnected to themselves and others.

Of the seven hundred people Robert interviewed in his research on the wilderness experience, 90 percent reported an increased sense of "aliveness, well-being and energy"; 90 percent said that it helped them break an addiction; 77 percent described a major life change upon their return, 38 percent of which "held" for five years; 76 percent reported a dramatic increase in the frequency and vividness of dreams; and 82 percent told of a change in dream *context* from urban to natural settings, generally within three or four days of entering the wilderness, which prompted Robert to remark that though we've had ten thousand years of culture, it's only four days deep. (On a weeklong solo retreat in Rocky Mountain National Park a few years ago, during which I slept in a cabin but spent twelve hours a day in the wilderness, I actually forgot my phone number after exactly four days.)

Robert defines the wilderness experience not just by heading out into nature but by leaving culture behind, and believes that the more of it participants can leave behind, the better. The point is to unplug, decompress, and retreat from the world to advance the spirit and meet nature with what D. H. Lawrence called "sheer naked contact." Sometimes literally.

Once, in a remote corner of the desert in southwestern Utah, I took off all my clothes, even my shoes and wedding ring, and walked completely naked a mile out into the desert, along the washes, across the red rocks, beside a creek that had sprung up after a storm earlier in the day. I just wanted to feel my creatureliness, dispense with anything that reminded me that I was separate from nature.

I sometimes feel the urge to not just simplify my life but also devolve altogether, unstitch the Frankenstein beast, roll back down the mountain like Sisyphus's grindstone and be left alone in the furry arms of entropy. After billions of years of multiplying and dividing, clawing my way onto solid ground and surviving among the fittest, some part of me wants to undo it all, to unspool and slide oozingly back into the sea, "to crawl deep into her on all fours," as the poet Albert Goldbarth put it, "and curl up there in the mamaswamp."

For an hour out there in the desert, I saw not a single thing around me or on me to suggest the existence of human culture, except for the mind that was cataloging the experience. And it was exhilarating, even though it became starkly evident to me how vulnerable the naked human is out there, with no claws, fangs, fur, hooves, or camouflage—which certainly helps explain why we cling so maniacally to culture.

Leaving it behind, though, Robert says, means not just leaving the city and the suburbs, not just cars and careers and daily schedules, but books, cameras, tape recorders, telephones, iPods, and even writing materials if you can stand it. Even your watch, since clock time is a very different animal from wild time, according to Jay Griffiths in another of her books, *A Sideways Look at Time.*

Wild time is that which passes when you're indifferent to time, when you're involved in anything that releases you from the fenced-in yards you normally reserve for time—the minutes, hours, days, weeks, months, and years that you clock-watch and count down, and which, as you get older, seem to slip by like the furrows in a field you see from a speeding car.

Meditators know that the wildest stretch of time is the moment—a mere point in time but enormously expansive. In fact, it's as close to eternity as we get, argues Jay, though eternity isn't actually a span of time at all, but the *depth* in the moment. In it, we're swallowed up and absorbed by something larger than ourselves, which expands to accommodate us, just as a sponge expands when absorbing water, or a bumper increases in kinetic energy when absorbing an impact.

Once in the wilderness, Robert says, people shouldn't compare it with "the culture out there," nor focus on their sense of opposition to it or their judgment of it, which he considers just another form of dualism. So no talk of the military-industrial complex, patriarchal oppression, Judeo-Christian tradition, multinational greedmongering, etc. Not even discussion of movies or media or your awesome camping equipment.

Moses may have led his people into the wilderness to separate them from their oppressors, but separating them from their *oppression* was another story, and it explains why he kept them in the wilderness for forty years. It took that long for those who knew the oppression itself to pass away and for the golden calf to melt down. "The monument must become liquid again," writes Diane Ackerman in *Cultivating Delight*, "must be broken down to its elements and re-formed into another shape."

The monument, though, is made of tough stuff, and the wilderness effect, Robert says, tends to either dissolve upon returning to the ordinary world, or put you in direct conflict with it. Among his interviewees, 53 percent reported becoming depressed within two days of returning.

"I think the depression is an important clue," he said during my visit to his farm at the edge of the Olympic Mountains in Washington State. "The connection with nature greatly raises your energy level. But obviously this connection is broken or blocked in the human-created world to which we return, the world that split us off from nature to begin with. And when you feel your opened self closing back up, it's painful."

Part of the pain, he said, is separation from the pack, from the small tribe-like communities that are formed among people on extended wilderness trips. "Sitting around fires at night, intimacy with a small band of others and with celestial events—these things are familiar to us, and not that far below our cultural programming."

He described watching students struggle to integrate themselves back into high school or college, "starting as shining beacons standing out in the crowded halls, then dimming and paling until, within two weeks of their return, they were indistinguishable from their fellow students. I began to realize that I was inadvertently creating a drama of profound conflict. On the last day of one of the wilderness trips, a student said, 'Give me one reason why I should go back?' And the only reason I could come up with was 'Because you agreed to on the first day of the trip.'"

Another time Robert was summoned by the manager of a local supermarket to do "an intervention" with one of his students, who a few days after returning was found slumped on the floor in the paper-products aisle, babbling incoherently and laughing hysterically about the absurd number of brands of toilet paper, the sheer consumptive-overload bottomless-pitness of it all, and the terrible economic disparity in the world that it represented.

As a result of observing people's frequently fiery reentries back into the world—which does *not* change in their absence—Robert began requiring yoga and meditation practice as part of his students' preparation for the wilderness experience as well as during the trip and after their return. He found that it almost entirely eliminated homecoming depression. These regimens, he believes, help stabilize the wilderness effects of expanded, goalless awareness and "non-dual frames of mind," which can ameliorate the sense of split. *Yoga*, after all, means "to unite."

THE IDEA OF CULTURE and wilderness as two separate entities—the notion that you can leave one behind and enter the other—would have seemed incomprehensible to archaic people, and it still does to many of their living relatives among the indigenous. According to the environmental ethicist Andrew Light, no word in any indigenous North American language has been identified as meaning what people nowadays mean by the word *wilderness*, something separate from culture, something alien. The indigenes just call it *home*. So there's no way of "leaving home." Nowhere on Earth they can go and not be in their element. No wilderness, and thus no way of being "lost in the wilderness."

Ironically, this mind-set, this *feeling* about the world, is what people are often after in their longing for wildness and their time spent in wilderness and among indigenous people who have no word for wilderness. They want an experience of feeling at home on Earth once again, to be able to crawl back into the lap of this grand old crone of a world and heal the split. And they want to feel part of the force that put it *all* here, nature and culture, termite mounds and skyscrapers—the force that scooped us all out of the brine and the methane and blew a shot of psycho-activating wake-me-up into our nostrils.

They want an experience of living in Primordial Standard Time, which is native to both the young life of the human individual and the young life of the human race. It's a developmental phase in which there's no distinction between human and nature, in which, as John Lennon put it, "I am he as you are he as you are me and we are all together."

It was the time before duality split us down the middle and sent us on a never-ending scavenger hunt for unity and the innocence of an earlier world, for the aboriginal intuition that sacredness is fused to all things, not concentrated in any one form, so that contemplating the kingdoms within a clump of soil is every bit as devotional as church attendance, and tree hugging is as much a meditation on what's greater than ourselves as prayer. It was the time before dualistic thinking became a recipe for every kind of imperialism in the world. Step one: divide. Step two: conquer.

Maybe the hunger for wildness is in some measure the hunger to recapture a bit of our own Paleolithic consciousness, the native intelligence by which subject and object are rolled back into one. And though we know we can't go back again, that we have to go forward into time, we can still relearn the arts of seeing the world through the eyes of wonder and reverence and not just calculation, still regard nature as source and not just resource, swaying forests and not just board feet, mountain meadows and not just ski resorts, understanding that harmony is as valuable as productivity, and good manners the least we can offer our host.

The Tame and the Wild

It takes some doing to arrive at the place of unity, or even just balance, and meanwhile there's the old tug-of-war between our wild side and our tame, the seesaw between natural and artificial. As the writer Sark puts it, being tame is what we're taught—put the crayons back, stay in line, don't talk too loud, keep your knees together—but being wild is what we are.

What the Ten Commandments and the Seven Deadly Sins and the One State all understand about human nature is that our wild desires, so recently emerged from the forest and risen up from four legs onto two, need some restraining. We're still in possession of vestigial fangs and promiscuous appetites, our blood a hot soup of chemical commands and coarse whisperings that run counter to the party line. And though it hardly seems like a fair fight—millions, arguably billions of years of genetics and instinct set against a few ten thousand years of tradition and the finger-wagging minions of conscience—culture is still a hard habit to break, or even balance out.

Some people define *neurosis* as the experience of being split between two warring factions: your intrinsic, essential natural self, whose third-base coach is the daimon; and your socialized, conditioned self. Or perhaps it's a triangle, a rivalry, in psychological parlance, among the id, the ego, and the superego. I want, I can, and I should. The pleasure principle, the reality principle, and the moral principle. "I Want to Hold Your Hand," "You Can't Always Get What You Want," and "Think (What You're Trying to Do to Me)."

Hermann Hesse's *Steppenwolf* is the portrait of a man who suffers an irresolvable duality between two natures, that of a man and that of an animal. The man is hungry for contact with, and acceptance by, society, and the wolf is starved for the isolation and freedom of the steppes, his nature "the free, the savage, the untamable, the dangerous and strong," and his worst nightmare—confinement.

At one point the protagonist realizes that he's the coincidence and conflagration of not just two competing natures but hundreds, maybe even thousands—a constantly shifting kaleidoscope of different selves, different breeds of men and women, animals and spirits, all jumbled together and jostling for position—and that a human being is an exceptionally rich elixir, seasoned with a thousand herbs.

When he's in the throes of his Steppenwolf nature, he rages against "the slumbering god of contentment" and "all the countless hours and days that I lost in mere passivity and that brought me nothing." He's full of wild longings and overpowering emotions, a fury against the toneless, flat, sterile life. "I have a mad impulse to smash something, a warehouse, perhaps, or a cathedral, or myself, to commit outrages, to pull the wigs off a few revered idols, to provide a few rebellious schoolboys with the longed-for ticket to Hamburg."

Among his observations on the making of a steppenwolf: "It might, for example, be possible that in his childhood he was a little wild and disobedient and disorderly, and that those who brought him up declared a war of extinction against the beast in him."

Thus we have neurosis, which may be one of the unavoidable prices we *all* pay for membership in civilization, or just in a family, swinging back and forth, suppressing our wildness and yearning for it, living a dual life, or two half-lives side by side. We know ourselves to be civilized while knowing our needs are not. We stick to the indoors like domesticated animals, but we leave our steaming breath on the windows. We understand that we're in possession of instincts and intuitions, but we ignore them.

I saw this played out one day this summer at a swimming hole near my house, which has a world-class rope swing attached to a tree that overhangs the river. From a spot high on the bank, you can swing out in a good thirty-foot arc that at its far end suspends you fifteen feet above the water. The only obstacle is a large log at the water's edge, near the bottom of the arc, but you just have to tuck your legs up a little to miss it.

On this particular afternoon, a group of high school kids were lined up at the rope swing—all except for one young woman who clearly wasn't interested. But one of her friends kept goading her, telling she should do it, it's great fun, it's totally safe, don't be a weenie.

He eventually succeeded in pressuring or shaming her into ignoring the call of the wild—her intuition—and when she finally took the plunge, she didn't lift her legs high enough to clear the log at the bottom of the arc, and smashed both her shins into it really hard, and then did a face-plant right into shallow water.

Her pride was *not* the only thing she hurt. Both her shins swelled up and turned bright purple, and she spent the next half hour writhing around on the ground.

How often it seems that the two-by-four approach to consciousness-raising is the only way we learn to mend the split between native intelligence and social pressure, which in most cases isn't experienced as a cure so much as a crisis, putting us at odds with not only our peers but also sometimes our entire upbringing.

The midlife crisis is a good example, and to my mind largely a function of who you really are catching up with who you thought you should be, the authentic self catching up with the socialized self—sometimes quite literally. Lenny Bruce used to tell the story of a child born to a pair of brilliant astrophysicists who gets lost in the woods and is raised by a pack of wild dogs. He eventually finds his way back to civilization and goes on to graduate with honors from MIT. But a year later he's killed chasing a car.

As for reconciling our warring factions, the "neurotic" struggle between our myriad natures, consider a scientific metaphor that speaks to the utility of collision, of bringing together seeming opposites, and, rather than rushing to judgment or taking sides, instead witnessing their concussive debate in full consciousness, with all instruments turned on.

The Large Hadron Collide in Geneva, Switzerland, which is both the largest particle accelerator and the largest scientific instrument on Earth, drives protons around its seventeen-mile circumference at 99.99999 percent the speed of light, or eleven thousand revolutions a *second*—around a seventeen-mile track! These particles are then collided with particles going in the opposite direction at the same speed, and enormous digital cameras take pictures of the results, which physicists say approximate the conditions of the universe a billionth of a second after the big bang—a flashback of monumental proportions.

When atoms are smashed together in accelerators, they set off a fireworks display of weird science, a shower of particles with sci-fi names like gluons, muons, leptons, bosons, quarks, and antiquarks. To particle physicists, these are the objects of their desire, the truth that is beauty, and they flash into and out of being in an instant so brief that in many cases they are inferred rather than seen directly. Yet physicists hope these little beauties will help them reveal the innermost mechanisms of the universe, will lay themselves down like bread crumbs leading to a grand unified theory that explains every process in nature and that answers every question of ultimate mystery that's bewitched scientists, poets, philosophers, and theologians for five thousand years.

Astronomers believe the big bang began as just such a proto-speck, and the search for that primogenial dot of origin is what has them endlessly bushwhacking through the jungles of the cosmos, down thirteen billion years of time and space in search of the Starting Point. And smashing atoms together is among their best vehicles for finding it.

So, too, perhaps, our own individual searches for what in Zen is called our original face, our true nature. Collision is useful. Friction and confoundment are tools of the trade. If atom smashing is a demolition derby at high speeds to see what parts fall out, perhaps the work of holding the paradoxes in our own lives operates in similar fashion. We allow the animal and the human, the wild and the cultivated, to collide and see what parts fall out—and to try to capture their fireworks before they disappear.

SOME FRIENDS OF MINE recently thought that they'd lost their cat. Strictly an indoor cat, Racket got out the back door and didn't return for three days. They'd already lost two cats to the great outdoors and were wracked by every horrible scenario of how a house cat could die out there: run over by a car, killed by a dog, eaten by an owl. They were sitting in their living room late one night when Racket came back, mewling at the back door.

By way of not repeating the experience, they said the cat would now be monitored closely to ensure that he never got out again, though he'd now been to Paree. Unwilling to risk losing him, they pulled rank, denying him his needs in favor of theirs, as any parent has to sometimes. But this quarantine didn't last very long, as they were struck by a bout of conscience. They decided that though they might lose him, he should be allowed to live out his days as he was designed to and that his freedom was more important than their sense of security, as any parent also has to understand at some point. Otherwise, we create diminishing returns, turning our loved ones—turning ourselves—into the equivalent of a zoo animal, pacing neurotically in front of the bars, literally going stir-crazy.

A few years ago I found *myself* on a steep learning curve on that one, the contest of wills between wildness and domestication, between the desire to allow a wild thing to be its natural-born self and the desire for a little order in the court and the attempt to prevent too much of the outdoors from being tracked indoors and all over my carpeting.

Robin and I had taken on an eight-week-old puppy—a long-coated white German shepherd we named Issa (pronounced "eesa"), which began a long and untidy process of deconstructing her wildness, about which I felt decidedly mixed.

Literally overnight we separated her from her mother, her siblings, and her home—her entire pack—and brought her to live with an alien species. And in the process, we had to commit a most unwild act: we had to cage her. She was shipped to us from Washington State, which required, though we didn't realize it at the time, that we break one of the cardinal rules of crate training (i.e., housebreaking) a puppy—do it slowly and gradually—by sticking her in a crate for a ten-hour flight to North Carolina. It's the equivalent of learning how to swim by being thrown into the deep end, and it had the effect of traumatizing her and making crate-training impossible, triggering a full-blown panic every time we attempted it.

Once she was here, the majority of our verbal communications in her direction took the form of commands and inhibitions: "Come," "Sit," "Stay," "Stop," "Lie down," "Heel," "No jumping," "Quit barking," "Drop it." Of course you need all that to ensure that an animal gets along in polite society and—since Robin wanted Issa to be a therapy dog—behaves reasonably well at the children's hospital and the nursing home and doesn't go after the tennis balls that the old folks attach to the bottoms of their walkers to make them glide more easily on linoleum.

But I noticed I took a certain secret pleasure in her willfulness and disobedience. I liked the fight in her. I liked having an *animal* in the house. (On the other hand, it's a good thing the young are adorable. It surely prevents a lot of parents from burying their progeny in the backyard or throwing them into the stew. And in an ironic contrast to the wildness Issa brought into our lives, we considered buying one of those robo vacuum cleaners that operates by itself, to offset the fact that she was a long-haired shepherd who shed in great and terrible profusion.)

But if Issa had to tame her wildness to get on with the hominids, we tried to meet her halfway, tapping into a well of wildness we were unfamiliar with, including the need to play alpha dog, attune ourselves to her unique signals, and even imitate her littermates by yelping and turning from her when she bit too hard, or snarling like her mother would when she's not given enough space and doesn't want to be suckled anymore.

Sometimes when Robin or I were caught up in anxiety or argument, Issa would start chewing furiously on a squeaky toy, which seldom failed to break the spell. Sometimes the three of us would throw our heads back and howl together like wolves, the moon in our throats. Sometimes we'd smell the pads of her feet after she'd been running in the forest, inhaling the faintly sweet odor that was part her and part not-her. And Issa's needs themselves were so elemental—eating, running in the woods, curling up with the pack—and so clearly articulated that we found ourselves inspired by her emotional simplicity, as opposed to the Rubik's Cube of our own emotional lives.

Issa also helped to literally *ground* us, get us down on the ground in our bodies, on all fours, out of our minds, out of the office and the studio, away from our plans and schemes, our man-made troubles, our higher brains. And there's great native intelligence in this, I think—perhaps the primordial intuition that life proceeds from the ground up, that dirt itself is the launching pad for resurrection.

Some anthropologists even believe that the urge to bury the dead may be a spin-off from the agricultural experience that if you plant something in the ground, it will grow. Or simply an invocation of the resurgence of nature that we've borne witness to every spring since we were first set down here.

We can also take a lesson from the Greek giant Antaeus, son of Gaia (Mother Earth), who challenged all passersby to a wrestling match, which he invariably won, and who met his match only in Hercules, who figured out that Antaeus drew his strength directly from the earth and was invincible only as long as his feet were on the ground. He defeated the giant by lifting him off the ground until his power drained away—a bit of age-old wisdom about the price of losing contact with Earth and our own earthiness.

The tug-of-war between wildness and tameness, though, extends well beyond the merely human arena and into the rest of the natural world, none of whose denizens are permitted a completely uninhibited existence.

We may think of wild things as willful and unrestrained, living according to their own laws and beyond the clutches of constraint—the opposite of the domestic—but this is true only up to a point. We refer to the *laws* of nature because nature, too, operates within limits and is rife with restrictions on its own passions and exuberances. There are habitable zones and uninhabitable zones, aridity and drought, predation and pecking orders, diseases and diebacks, competition and consequences.

You're free to be you, as long as you obey the ground rules of physics, thermodynamics, causality, and entropy. As long as you don't try your hand at flying when you don't possess wings, or attempt to bud before the frosts are finished, or take on the alpha male while you've still got fuzz on your antlers. Nature has rules and regulations every bit as uncompromising as those civilization has devised. Not cruel, though, just stringent.

And if we think of nature's wildness as unpredictable and inscrutable, we forget that humans are the most unpredictable of *all* creatures. By introducing the one and only neocortex—that rind around the primordial pulp, home of whim and war—our brains evolved well beyond the fixed, predetermined patterns of behavior that characterize other species. The more developed the neocortex, the more the animal will think for itself and respond to the world in all kinds of baffling and mercurial ways.

Technically speaking, though, the wildest parts of us—all of us—are the most deeply programmed, the most stable and predictable: survival, instinct, arousal, emotions, reflexes, the self-ruling works of the body; our biorhythms and timetables. Deep nature is really quite orderly.

Maybe it's not the freedom, after all, that we desire and envy about wildlife, but the *harmony*. And maybe it's those who seek to leave all habit and routine behind who are actually the ones flying in the face of nature.

Besides, structure isn't the enemy of aliveness. Rigidity is. Inflexibility. The refusal to relinquish control and adapt to changing conditions, outside or inside. And they're constantly changing. The world, as Heraclitus observed twenty-five hundred years ago, is ever-living fire, in measures being kindled and in measures going out.

Controlling Interests

A few days before flying to New York to accompany my mother to the hospital for hip-replacement surgery some years ago, I read a story about an aging physicist who had taken to wearing enormous padded boots, several sizes too large for him, in the belief that he was in constant danger of falling through the gaps between molecules into the chasms of empty space. A stroll from the living room into the kitchen became as death-defying as walking the girders of a skyscraper under construction.

The night before the surgery to replace her right hip, my mother sat me down in the kitchen of her apartment and pushed a folder two inches thick across the table. She told me to prepare for battle, prepare to make a scene and wave powers of attorney around to ward off any number of worst-case scenarios: the surgeon sending in a pinch-hitter at the last minute, the anesthesiologist giving her a general anesthetic instead of the spinal she insisted on so she could be awake during the surgery, and the nurses giving her, as she put it, heroin instead of morphine.

The folder, which I was to carry in the hospital at all times, included her living will and power of attorney, a copy of her patient's bill of rights, multitudes of hospital forms, paperwork for her three kinds of medical insurance, the phone numbers of everyone she knows, a copy of her driver's license, a transcript of the interview she conducted with the surgeon about her procedure, which he more or less patiently submitted himself to, and literature on the surgery itself, including a stockholders' prospectus on the company that manufactures the ball-and-socket mechanism with which the surgeon would be replacing my mother's arthritic hip.

It was, of course, an understandable and intelligent spasm of vigilance in the face of a trip through the health care system—the third most fatal disease in the United States, medical treatment itself—in which the squeaky wheel tends to get the most grease, having an advocate in your corner is a critical advantage, and controlling behavior a life-saving inclination.

And yet it was also more than that. On the way to the hospital, we had to negotiate four locks on her front door (two chains and two deadbolts) and two security systems on her car (ignition code and steering wheel boot). And this in a wealthy Long Island suburb, in a secure garage. It lent her anxieties the dimensions of a more common affliction: the fear of being out of control, transferred to the material world and disguised as a deadbolt, or a to-do list. It also highlighted her lifelong fear of falling through gaps in her best-laid plans and well-constructed safety nets, falling victim to forces beyond her control, natural or man-made—the willfulness of life itself, the wild cards of other people, and, as in this case, the wild animal of her own body, which had suddenly turned on the lion tamer.

I was all set to congratulate myself for having fallen far from the tree, but when I returned home, I was shocked to hear a little Freudian slip I'd inadvertently left on the outgoing message of my answering machine before heading to New York. I *meant* to leave a message that said, "Hello, this is Gregg Levoy. I'll be out of the office until August 25." Instead I left a message that said, "Hello, this is Gregg Levoy, I'll be out of control until August 25."

The morning after I got home, I also did what I usually do when returning from a trip: I dove headfirst into work to try to catch up, to steady an in-basket that was predictably—perpetually—at flood stage. As usual I overdid it, straining my back and prompting Robin to resort to a little trick she'd devised to signal that I was overdoing it: stringing police cordon tape across my desk.

I've always counted among the most disturbing revelations of adulthood those times when I've seen in myself the habits and mannerisms of my parents that I'd sworn an oath not to repeat. And suddenly I began to notice, and soon couldn't *stop* noticing, the similarities between my mother's modus operandi and my own. I saw my bench-pressing work habits, my tendency to overprepare for things, my habit of using logic as a flak jacket against incoming emotions, and the elaborate constellation of tactics I apply toward impression management, toward snake-charming other people's opinions of me.

A friend recently reminded me of another tactic: Her company had brought me to Ohio to teach a seminar, and the night before it, a group of us went out to dinner at an Italian restaurant. When it came time for dessert, people started negotiating with one another about who was going to share whose—not my MO when it comes to dessert, especially being a twin. So I said to the waiter that I wanted chocolate cake with a side order of barbed wire. The day after the workshop, my friend drove me back to the airport and said she thought the comment was indicative of a "larger issue" in my life.

I've been told before, and with far less diplomacy, that, like the denizens of the One State, I keep a wall around myself, an invisible circle of wagons, and though I'd like to point out that I'm a twin and that boundaries are the critical hyphen between I and Thou, it's been over forty years since anyone asked, "If I pinch *him*, will *you* feel it?"

In all fairness, I also saw the upside of my control tactics, though their efficacy depends on whether I do them in moderation or overdo them: my perfectionism and drive for excellence, my ability to concentrate on a project with laser focus and sustain it for years, my determination to suffer creatively and not just neurotically, and all the personal strategies for winning and coping that were laid down in the soft mud of my formative years.

Call it what you want—the will to conquer, the drive for mastery, being a control freak—we're all wired with the urge to sling saddles across life, to make the wild world a little less wild. The problem is that control works often enough that it's hard to tell when it *stops* working and instead clamps its teeth down on our vitality.

Actually, the whole *universe* is wired for control. After the big bang sent shrapnel flying out in all directions, it was only because expansion met gravitation that anything began to cohere—galaxies, solar systems, planets, bodies of any sort. Without the bronco-busting force of gravity, nothing would have held together, but would have just continued on its merry rampant way. Or as John Travolta's angel puts it in the movie *Michael*, "I invented standing in line. Before that, everyone was just wandering around."

In taking an inventory of my own control-freakishness, it wouldn't be fair to say that I get it all from my mother, though she's certainly my primary West Coast distributor. The struggle for control is in the germ plasm of the human experience and has been ever since we were first turned loose down here to wrestle with the dirty angel of mortal life. It's got its own wild roots. For one thing, it's a natural reaction to helplessness—even a baby's cry is an attempt at control, a strategy to manage hunger and pain—and according to Barbara Ehrenreich in *Blood Rites*, a certain *kind* of helplessness.

The longest-standing precursor of our fear of being out of control, she says—as well as of our relationship to power in general—is the literally prehistoric terror of being preyed on by animals that were initially far stronger and more skillful than we were. The memory of that experience, left over from the evolution of primates, is still with us. It's in our fight-or-flight response and even our immune system, both of which evolved precisely to combat deadly enemies and keep us alive.

Before "man the hunter" was "man the hunted." Before we had dominion over the animals, they had dominion over us. Whatever sovereignty we have or imagine we have over the natural world was certainly not handed to us on a platter. Our forebears paid for it with the literal pound of flesh. The desire for dominance, for power and control over our lives if not our deaths, is the result of one of the primary traumas in the young life of humanity: being devoured by a monster, the fear of which is, to this day, one of the standard-issue nightmares of childhood.

I learned this lesson vividly in high school, during my one and only foray into the wilds of babysitting. Either I was desperate or the couple who hired me was, but I spent the evening with a three-year-old girl and a six-year-old boy. My first inkling that this wasn't my line of work came when the little girl suddenly started dropping her pants. She'd follow me from room to room dropping her drawers and grinning like a hyena.

Her brother refused to go to bed at bedtime, and I tried every form of persuasion short of binding and gagging him. Finally, I had him in his pajamas, in bed, under the covers, and I was slowly backing out of the room the way you back away from a puppy you're training to "stay." Just before hitting the light switch, I said to him, in my desperate and untutored state, "I want you to stay in bed this time. If you don't, the animals on your blanket are going to come alive and eat you." Then I turned off the light and closed the door.

Then I heard a bloodcurdling scream.

I didn't realize, or forgot, that deep in the forests of childhood is a primitive terror of being devoured by animals, by the thing under the bed. Studies from the time even before television, with its outpouring of monsters and stalkers and shows like *When Animals Attack*, tell us that wild animals are near the top of the list of things children are afraid of, even when their suburban environments bring them into contact with nothing wilder than cats and dogs. In fact, phobias are usually triggered by things that were potentially dangerous in our *ancient* environment—snakes, spiders, rats, heights, enclosed spaces—and they're rarely provoked by modern artifacts like knives, guns, cars, and electric can openers.

Needless to say, the little boy was wide awake when his parents came home at eleven p.m., as was his sister. And for this I got paid $1.50 an hour. But I also got an unforgettable crash course in the human fear factor—how buried deep in each of our aft-brains is a visceral and primordial terror of our own helplessness, of being overpowered, if not devoured, by life.

I WAS in the intensive care unit when my mother came around. She'd received only the spinal block but was so heavily sedated in addition to it that she was effectively knocked out. I stood by her bed and, caught between seeing her with the eyes of an adult and the feelings of a child, looked down at this formidable woman swaddled like an infant, remembering the time a friend who was privy to my sense of intimidation around my mother said, "What are you so afraid of? She's a little old lady."

As if.

As if little old ladies are by definition harmless, congenial bakers of pies and crocheters of doilies, rather than descendants of Kali, who wears a necklace of skulls and eats trolls to freshen her breath.

My mother had been a regal beauty, fiercely independent and opinionated, who broke the child labor laws by going to work at thirteen years old to compensate for her father yanking her allowance every time she misbehaved, which was frequently, and who became one of the first women stockbrokers on Wall Street in the mid-1960s, a state of affairs that drove my stepfather into jealous rages. In the photograph of her graduating class at the F. I. duPont & Co. school for account executives, she's standing front and center, wearing a white knee-length dress, one foot in front of the other like a fashion model, in a sea of men in black.

It was a career she greatly preferred to motherhood, which made her feel, as she once told me, "trapped, bored, and restless," and is a role with which she *still* has difficulty identifying. Whenever she leaves a message on my answering machine, she invariably refers to herself as "mother person," which sounds like one of those tip-offs that someone is an extraterrestrial, along with complaining about gravity a lot and messing up your TV reception whenever she walks by.

When my mother finally came out of her surgical stupor, the first words she said, and kept saying, were "I can't believe it's over. I can't believe how easy it was. I can't believe it." It was certainly easy compared with the week that followed, which, like soldiering, was composed of long stretches of boredom punctuated by short bursts of terror, as when her morphine ran out and I couldn't find a nurse.

Mostly she spent the first two days dopey with painkillers and immobilized in one position—no small thing for a hyperactive—lying on her back with her legs strapped on either side of a large foam cushion to prevent her from inadvertently popping the new ball out of its socket and having to go back into surgery. I was impressed that she withstood the temptation of the television, which she didn't turn on once in the two weeks she was in the hospital and rehab.

Mostly I sat by her hospital bed and watched her drift in and out of sleep and restlessness, taking the rare opportunity to observe my mother up close and in repose. Her skin had the look of old cellophane, and all around the site of the IV needle, blood pooled darkly like air pockets under lake ice. When she gestured with her arms, the loose flesh under her biceps swam like two moray eels; and when she slept, the muscles around her mouth and jaw were sometimes so tight her chin looked like an apricot pit.

During that week, we probably amassed the highest concentration of intimacies she and I have ever shared in a relationship not generally characterized by them. I held her hand while she was gurneyed into the operating room; she blew me kisses at the end of each day. I lifted her head so she could puke after surgery; she presented me with a panoramic vista of her backside when her hospital gown had a wardrobe malfunction and accidentally fell open.

More difficult for my mother than the restlessness, though, even the vulnerability, was struggling to control her temper with the hospital staff. Bad service normally sets my mother's teeth on edge (actually, most things set my mother's teeth on edge; she has a lifelong habit of teeth grinding that requires her to wear a plastic nightguard when she sleeps). I've sat in restaurants with her on numerous occasions while she scolded the staff for service that was less than prompt and efficient, which one can do with impunity in a restaurant.

Not so in a hospital, where it can be life-threatening to not be nice to the staff, who are sufficiently shorthanded and overwhelmed that it's clear they have little patience for rebuke. A woman in a room around the corner screamed her head off for over an hour one afternoon and no one came to even look in on her. When I mentioned this to a nurse, she rolled her eyes and walked away. I've never seen my mother so courteous in the presence of such spotty service. It was just another form of control, really—honey instead of vinegar—but it certainly had the desired effect.

This is control's appeal, and its power: it gets things done and helps unbend the wild, at least to a degree, whether our strategies of control are discipline, planning, perfectionism, workaholism, violence, seduction, generosity, guilt-tripping, anger, or supplication. And it's not just manipulation; it's mastery. It's not just control but also choreography. It's about making things happen, working the world, staying one step ahead of the surprise element, keeping a lid on disorder, and feeling like we've got life by the proverbials instead of the other way around. And the payoffs we're after are what they've always been: survival or perceived survival, power, and securities physical, financial, or emotional.

Control is also about the *satisfaction*—a word meaning "to be surrounded by fruit"—that comes with mastery, with learning to control the ball, shape the language, manage the team, stay healthy, and keep the wolf *outside* the door. Discipline gets books written and careers off the ground. Conscience reins in the wild horses of human impulse and helps grow community. Socialization—from toilet training to table manners—is the superintending force that turns children into functioning and hopefully moral adults. Creativity and technology are a honing of the elements into form and function.

The Ukrainian artist Nikolai Syadristy's work beautifully personifies the link between control and mastery. To create his micro-miniature

sculptures, which are so small that you need a two-hundred-power magnifying glass to even see them, he has learned to control his nervous system,
blood flow, and breathing, and touches his carving instruments to the
sculptures *only in between heartbeats,* to prevent his hand from trembling.

His sculptures include a swallow's nest filled with baby birds carved
from a poppy seed; an entire chessboard that fits on the head of a pin; a
caravan of camels next to a pyramid, all made from flecks of gold and all
of which fit into the eye of a needle; a jug, two wineglasses, a tea tray, and
an apple all carved from a grain of sugar; and a sailing frigate whose riggings are four hundred times thinner than a human hair.

To be sure, the desire for control is either constructive or destructive,
depending on whether you can find the optimum balance between force
and flexibility, holding on and letting go. Where we get into trouble is in
distinguishing what we have control over and what we don't, and the belief
that mastery will automatically bestow on us a sense of being in control of
our lives. "If I'm the master of my own fate," I once heard someone say,
"why do I feel so out of control?" And you may be the proverbial author of
your own life, but as any author knows, the act of sending work out into
the world is referred to as submission.

What we don't have control over are birth and death, race and gender,
the weather, the price of gas and food, interest rates, what other people
think of us, and most of the body's internal functions, including dreams.
Dreaming itself—"a wide realm of wild reality," Lord Byron called it—is
the result of a loss of control. While we sleep, the sentries between the
conscious and unconscious doze at their watch, and the delineations that
regulate life and keep the gravy from mixing with the cranberry sauce lose
their edges, as do the borders between fantasy and reality, moral and
immoral.

What we *do* have control over is how we react to the things we don't
have control over. In other words, our responses, opinions, interpretations,
and decisions. If we spent as much energy trying to respond intelligently to
the uncontrollable as we do trying to manhandle it, we'd probably kick up
a lot less dust and be a lot less saddle sore at the end of the day. "The only
argument available with an east wind," the poet James Lowell once said,
"is to put on your overcoat."

The absurdity of refusing to relinquish the reins, to make peace with what we *don't* have control over, is adroitly captured in movie called *Enchanted April*, in a scene in which an austere English dowager, staying for a month at an Italian villa, is pacing nervously around her room and asking herself, "Why do I feel so restless?" Suddenly she stops and says, "Something is going to happen, and I'm not going to let it."

This could be the motto of the entire anti-aging industry, everything from potions and lotions to cryogenics, which are based on the belief that we can rein in or even ward off aging and dying—that is, that we can control nature. We can. But only a little.

It could also be the motto of the Army Corps of Engineers in *its* approach to controlling nature. For example, just over the mountains from where I live in western North Carolina, the Mississippi changes course roughly every thousand years, jumping its banks and heading off in entirely new directions across an arc of floodplain almost two hundred miles wide, always with the intention of getting to the Gulf of Mexico by the most expedient route.

However, in the interval since the last relocation, a nation was built, large portions of it hugging the banks of the river. And that nation can't afford the inconvenient whims of nature. A shift that to the river would be little more than rolling over in bed would turn New Orleans and Baton Rouge into sleepy bayous cut off from the freshwater and inland shipping that sustain them.

The Army Corps of Engineers made a film years ago, outlining its plans to prevent the Mississippi and the cumulative drainage of all of Middle America from changing course, and the narrator said, "This nation has a large and powerful adversary. We are fighting Mother Nature."

"Might as well bully the comets in their courses," Mark Twain said of the Mississippi River Commission's attempt to similarly stifle "that lawless stream."

The same goes for people. Most of us resist being controlled, whether from within or without (though describing someone as wild is usually code for someone who's not out of control but rather out of *our* control. When a kid is willful and disobedient, we say he is a wild child. We're commenting not on his bestial nature but on his literally unruly nature—doing what he wants, not what he's told.)

I recently went to a twentieth wedding anniversary party for some friends, and when it came time to herd the guests toward a group photo, a woman I'd never met came forth and effortlessly assumed the role of director, with a practiced and determined charm. When a friend of hers later told me that she's an event planner, I said, "I'm not surprised, given how natural she was at . . ."—and then I stalled momentarily, searching for a discreet word.

"Control?" she said.

And how fortunate, I added, that she had found a profession that allows her to utilize that skill in such a useful and socially sanctioned way.

A few weeks later I talked to the event planner about her work, and at one point she mentioned that her boyfriend, who works for her, had moved in with her—downstairs. They share the main house and the master bedroom, but two days and nights out of the week he has to retire to the downstairs apartment to give her solo time and to "allow him to live the way he wants down there." She says, "If it bothers me, if it's too chaotic or things are messy and broken, I just may not go down and visit him very often. And that's where he'll keep our dog when we get a dog, because I don't want the dog hair up in my space."

She was married once, in her early twenties (she's now fifty-seven), and when I asked about it, her eyes bugged out and she let out a big sigh. "Oh. That. Was not good. That man was the most controlling man on earth. He ran my life. He decided what clothes I was going to wear, what kind of car I was going to drive, where we'd go on vacation, what kind of house we'd live in, and he controlled most of the money. After five years, he said, 'I have another girlfriend,' took all the money out of our joint savings account, gave my car to his new girlfriend, and left me pregnant.

"After that, I said, 'Never again.' Never would I put myself in the position where I was not in control. Nobody was going to do that to me again. And making that vow may have made me hard. May have made me undermine the other men in my life. I've certainly asked myself over the years why I haven't had a relationship that lasts."

Probably because people naturally rebel against being trammeled, and whenever possible will apply to it a healthy dose of Newton's third law of motion—equal and opposite reactions. In a nod to the human inclination to resist control, students of the psychologist B. F. Skinner—who believed you could shape human behavior by shaping reward systems—came up with what they called the "Harvard Law of Animal Behavior": "Under controlled experimental conditions of temperature, time, lighting, feeding and training, the organism will do as it damn well pleases."

Up to a point, though, control is good for us. Studies of hospital and nursing home patients, prisoners, and people living under totalitarian regimes all confirm that being deprived of control over one's life lowers morale and heightens mortality. In the 1970s, anesthesiologists found that letting post-op patients dole out their own doses of painkillers gave them more effective pain relief, with fewer doses, and what pain they did have was experienced as less intense.

Even if we can't dole out our own pain relief, though, merely *believing* we can has a placebo effect, and more than a few studies have shown that just the *illusion* of control lessens stress and hastens healing. Maybe this explains why my mother not only left rehab two weeks before her doctors expected but also sent the home-care nurse packing after a single day and was walking a mile a day within the week. It turned out she was only half kidding when she told the surgeon on the Monday morning of her operation that she was hoping to make a doubles tennis match that Friday.

But control is good medicine only in the right doses, and the wisdom to know the difference between too little of it and too much is the punch line of the serenity prayer—which a lot of people read not as the search for the serenity to accept the things they cannot change but as the search for serenity by trying to change the things they cannot *accept*. Again, it's hard to tell when it's working for us and when it's working against us.

I spend a lot of time on the road, teaching and lecturing, and my first order of business on reaching a hotel is always to unpack and put everything away, right down to the toiletries in the bathroom and the flashlight and writing pad by the bed in case I'm awakened by dreams in the middle of the night. It's a routine that anchors me in an unfamiliar city, establishing a headquarters for field operations. First, clothing and shelter; then, hunting and gathering.

It's a routine that works well for settling into hotel rooms, but not for settling into new homes, which I've done every other year, on average, for thirty-eight years—because it takes a month to really settle into a new home, to climb out of the black hole of boxes and logistics and checklists and the various and confounding requirements of insurance companies, motor vehicle departments, and utility companies. There's simply no way to get immediate gratification. But because that's my goal, I often end up blowing a gasket.

In the face of whatever's overwhelming, it's natural to look around for something to give us a feeling of control, or at least dance routines with stenciled footprints on the floor. But patterns of control, certainly an overdose of it, can backfire. In a children's book called *Anthony the Perfect Monster*, Anthony works very hard to be the perfect child, always doing what he's told, eating his spinach, and controlling his temper. But one night Anthony cracks from the strain and with one hiccup becomes a little monster who rants and raves and won't wear his raincoat.

Sometimes such a snap brings on not just the opposite of control but its antidote: yielding, submitting yourself to whatever you've been wrestling to restrain, which can free up the energies that were previously bound up in the attempt at restraint and can restore some of life's diminished vigor. An orgasm, for example, is a collapsing of control, but it's also an outpouring of raw vitality through the body.

In a short story called "The Neurosis of Containment," Rikki Ducornet describes a character who always lays out her combs and brushes in order of size, and her shoes as if they were obedient schoolchildren. Her landlady says, "Suppose it all *means something*. . . . Suppose those shoes and those brushes in their rigorous rows, and the perfectly folded linens in the upper-left-hand drawer, were the key to your inviolable soul. . . . Saying more about you than anything you could possibly say about yourself?"

What it spoke of was something she felt compelled to hold in check inside her and control with a severe morality—sexual longing. One night it burst out of her in the form of an overpowering fantasy of a rendezvous on a moon-flooded lawn with two tall, beautiful young men with enormous velvety black wings, who tell her they're there because she dreamed them, called them.

Yielding has the power to free up our obstructed energies and bring us back to life, and sometimes it simply allows life to flow unimpeded along its natural course. Recently I was told a story about someone's grandmother who, at ninety and on her deathbed, surrounded by a few close friends and relatives, seemed unable to let go. At one point, her daughter said, "Mom, you can leave now. We've let you go," at which point she came out of her semi-comatose state and reached into the air, as if to brush aside cobwebs, and said, "I can't. There are strings." Her husband of sixty years began to cry and said, "I can't let you go." But with his release of grief, he released his hold on her, and minutes later she died.

Unfortunately, there's no official checkpoint where healthy, adaptive control crosses the border into anxious control that's likely to end in an emotional hernia, where striving becomes strife, and a certain ambidexterity in both exercising and surrendering control is in order; knowing when to hold 'em and knowing when to fold 'em. Discerning one from the other probably comes down to the old Gospel criteria: by their fruits you shall know them. What does your intuition tell you, your body, your dreams, your friends, the results you're getting, the price you're paying for those results?

Discernment is tricky business. As with the event planner, something may look affirmative but end up bearing bitter fruit. Or, like my hotel behavior, something may look a bit neurotic, may make you feel like you're climbing around in the lower branches of the bodhi tree, but the goal may actually be positive and life affirming—an experience of yourself as safe and secure. It's hard to tell, though, when you're hunched over your desk like a galley slave at the oars, or you're constantly grumbling about all the jokers in the deck or about life's chronically unfinished business, which will probably remain unfinished as long as a single electron inside you still spins around the maypole. Nothing "settles the matter" because matter won't be settled.

Control, though, is like ego. It's gotten a bad rap. From a spiritual point of view, ego and will are both supposed to be transcended, as in "thy will be done," though trying to overcome either one is like trying to drain mirages of their water—they can't be eliminated, only seen through. But in its uncorrupted form, ego is just what helps you pick yourself out of a crowd and stabilize life. And will is simply the desire to shape the world that helps us turn clay into pottery, raw minerals into plows and pacemakers, and difficult childhoods into serviceable adulthoods.

It can also prevent your car from getting stolen and help keep the boogeyman from the door. There was evidence, in fact, that all the deadbolts on my mother's apartment door—that her controlaholic tendencies—had succeeded, on at least one dramatic occasion, in doing just that. The metal doorjamb, where many of her neighbors have attached mezuzahs—tiny scrolls to remind them of God's presence—is dented all along its length by ax blows that were painted over. They were administered by my stepfather—a psychologist—after my mother locked him out during a fight. "You should have seen the *door*," she said.

A fundamental fact about the nature of control, if not the definition, needs to be kept in mind, though: it's about exerting authority over, curbing, and constraining, and when allowed to cell-divide unchecked it exerts a throttling effect on life, certainly love and passion, and even soul in the sense that Socrates meant it when he said soul is closer to movement than fixity, and loss of soul the condition of being stuck.

Control is restraint on movement, and because complete control would be complete restraint, control itself has to be controlled if there's to be movement at all, certainly vitality. If life is entirely stabilized and secured, it's by definition lost, its development arrested, the same way water isn't itself anymore when bucketed.

It's no coincidence that the term addicts use to describe their prime objective is a "fix," which suppresses their emotions, constricts their freedom, and binds them to their addiction. Similarly, to be "fixated" is to be stuck, unable to evolve. You're possessed of a focus so rigid that instead of being an act of true will, it's an act that enslaves the will and locks up its energy.

The chronic vigilance required to maintain it is also a hatchery for ulcers and insomnias, especially if you tend to get your knickers in a knot whenever things aren't predictable and orderly, which they often aren't, and when your attempts to control life turn into not just habits but also life paths: lashing yourself to a job you hate to have security and avoid putting your true passions to the test; surrounding yourself with people who aren't your equal so you minimize rejection; hiding your light under a rock so you don't outshine your parents or siblings; avoiding intimacy altogether to avoid being controlled or feeling out of control.

The truth is, trying to control life doesn't usually bring us the security we want. Nor does it bring us exemption from other people's incursions and exploitations, or undisturbed sleep. Actually, it tends to bring on exhaustion, because trying to control life requires a tremendous investment of energy, and it's ultimately impossible. Life's contraption has a thousand confounded moving parts, each with a mind of its own and purposes we're not privy to, and it's utterly indifferent to the dream of happiness.

Frederick Taylor, the father of scientific management and industrial efficiency—a control freak if ever there was one—used to strap himself into a harness-like device of his own design at night in an effort to tame the nightmares that nonetheless plagued him his whole life.

The famous poem "Invictus," written by Englishman William Ernest Henley, who was "bloody but unbowed" by tuberculosis, is a paean to the spirit of doggedness. The last lines of the poem argue, "It matters not how strait the gate / How charged with punishments the scroll / I am the master of my fate: / I am the captain of my soul." And this rugged sentiment certainly appeals to the cussed spirit within us that fancies itself indomitable, capable through sheer willpower of overcoming all manner of obstacles. And indeed we do have considerable powers in determining the course of our own fate and the set of our jaw in response to adversity. Far more power, in fact, than we typically give ourselves credit for.

But/and life has its own considerable powers, and they're not arrayed with our personal pleasure or dominion in mind, and are heedless to our proclamations of defiance and our determination to triumph over all obstacles.

Which is the better part of valor, then—proceeding through the gate with a "failure is not in my vocabulary" attitude or knowing full well that failure is distinctly possible but you're going to proceed anyway and do your best to captain your soul should the Fates turn against you?

An unconquerable spirit isn't always to be desired or envied either, because it sometimes comes as a matching set with unconquerable arrogance. I once read the story of a young soldier who was captured by the enemy and forced to walk a gauntlet of men who beat him with their rifle butts as he passed. To prove himself superior, he held a blade of grass between his teeth as he walked the line, at the end of which, bloodied but unbowed, he took the grass from between his teeth and held it up for all to see—it had not a mark on it. His name was Joseph Stalin.

Being in control, though, even when we *can* achieve it, isn't the same as having peace of mind. Actually, our attempts to get a fix on life put us at odds with it, because at its most intrinsic levels—the cellular and molecular, the microscopic and atomic—life is gaga with randomness and motion, couplings and collisions a billion times a second, every body a busy body out on the dance floor doing the twist and shout. There's just no way to get a grip on it. The historian Henry Adams believed that "chaos is the law of nature, order is the dream of man." But we act as if we could simply unhinge our jaws like a snake swallowing an egg and swallow chaos whole, then just spit out the hard parts.

The author John Gardner once said this: "Stars torment my wits toward meaningful patterns that do not exist." That is, stars appear to us like paint spatters against a dark canvas, on which we trace like a connect-the-dots game all the figures of myth and zodiac. The stars, though, aren't scattered across a flat plane but across a sphere, not across two dimensions but three (four if you include time). And in the four-dimensional universe we actually live in, these pretty pictures don't exist. They're fables we've hung on pegs in the sky, fantastical creation stories we've conjured up by campfire light and set spinning in our heads.

But we're insistent pattern seekers. There's even a branch of psychology called constellation work, used precisely to explore the patterns in a person's life. And connecting dots helps make the capricious world a bit more manageable, helps us alphabetize and classify and fix our ever-shifting positions. It brings a little order to the chaos that's an inherent part of life, and whose effect on the best-laid plans you don't have to look far to see.

Spring was in full swing here in North Carolina when I flew to California for business one year. The landscape was halfway from brown to green, whole mountainsides at the lower elevations covered with a chartreuse sheen of new growth, from the ground cover to the canopy, with bright runnels of it creeping up into the folds of the high mountains. The neighboring houses, whose proximity is rudely revealed when the leaves fall, were finally beginning to disappear behind the expanding foliage, returning my privacy.

The day before I returned from my trip, a sudden cold front brought spring to a screeching halt. Literally overnight, every leaf cell on every tree on every mountain as far as the eye could see froze and ruptured, turning all that bright green into hanging clumps of rotten vegetable matter like the slime I sometimes find in bags of lettuce in the refrigerator.

I was astonished that a force as driving and widespread as spring could be stopped so abruptly in its tracks in a single night. It took three months for spring to regain its footing; three months of looking at a blotchy quilt of sickly browns and pale half-greens that reminded me daily there wasn't a thing I could do about it but reflect on the fact that chaos operates as ruthlessly and indifferently on the natural world as it does on the man-made one. But I also knew that in the gluey core of every plant out there was a similar indifference, a mindless determination to prevail and rein-vent, and not a shred of grief or impatience.

Where any overwhelming or even terrifying reality presses in on people but can't be changed—impending disaster, imprisonment, war, death, even meaninglessness—it's human nature to escape into, if not depression, then fictions that deny our impotence. We take flight into a kind of idolatry in which we worship the false god of our own omnipo-tence, the belief that we're in control and know what's best for us, when a straightforward look at the state of the world might indicate that we do not.

Despite flying the Jolly Roger of fearlessness, we're all soft and pink on the inside, and conceding this is the first baby step in the twelve-step pro-gram: admitting we're powerless over our addictions (which is not, the twelve-steppers tell us, the same as admitting we're powerless as individu-als). So perhaps a degree of *hopelessness* is in order and could be a huge relief, because in it is parole from the grinding intensity of striving for control over life and pretending we can train Leviathan to roll over and play dead.

I was in Costa Rica a few years ago facilitating a weeklong retreat, and during orientation the sponsoring organization's on-site coordinator expressed the hope that the various retreats being conducted that week would help participants' lives to be "better and better." A woman in the back of the room raised her hand. "What if we like our life just the way it is?" The coordinator, apparently flummoxed by this notion, said, "Well, um, we want it to be even *better*."

Which is fine. We all want to improve our lives, if not the world, and no one would have been attending those retreats if they didn't. But some-times the better part of wisdom isn't in the philosophies of improvement but in acceptance. In *The Inferno*, by Dante Alighieri, the damned are unable to see the present but can foretell the future—showing that if we're constantly absorbed in trying to improve our lives, we might forget to live them as they are, here and now, for better and for worse, wild or tame.

Freud once counted three historical blows to human narcissism that, looked at through the right lens, can help us gain some of that healthy hopelessness. The first was the Copernican revolution, which placed Earth not at the center of the universe but merely floating among its multitudes of flotsam and jetsam. The second was the Darwinian revolution, which informed us that we're not so much descended gods as elevated apes. And the third was his own "discovery" of the unconscious, which told us that we're not even the masters of our own house, our own minds, but are governed by psychic forces of which we're not even aware, no less in control.

And yet, as author Stephen A. Mitchell writes in *Can Love Last?* the loss of our sense of self-importance and self-governance has come with an enormous payoff, introducing us to a greater truth that ultimately enlarges and enlivens us rather than diminishes us: "the awesome, mind-rattling universe of which we are a part," or the fact that we're participants in something colossal and magnificent.

As with so many of our resistances to life, what we defend against so vehemently often turns out to be far lesser than what becomes available to us once we stop manning the barricades. "What we're called upon to give up," says Mitchell, "is a certain kind of hubris. What we gain is participation in something much richer and more complex than we ever took ourselves to be."

And it *is* humbling to admit we don't have as much control over our lives and our fates, or even our feelings, as we imagine and prefer. And we prefer it and strive for it in direct proportion to how out-of-control our lives and our fates feel to us. But the more we struggle for control, the more we reinforce an illusion—the more vitality we lose.

Life in all its discommodious glory doesn't offer anything like ultimate safety or security, to say nothing of wholeness or completion. But it seems there's no end to the hope that some paradisal place exists that runneth over with these things. And no amount of either personal or collective failure to attain them ever seems to turn us aside from this ancient and long-suffering hope of security and transcendence, this dream at the heart of religion and addiction alike, love and war, even science and technology.

Anyone who's ever bought a computer thinking that it would simplify life and control the chaos, knows the hollow ring of that hope. Anyone who believes the promotional literature that technology or faith can tame the elements and regulate acts of God should by now surely have gotten to the fine print. Anyone who still thinks the answers to the questions of certainty and meaning that trouble us in our sleep are out there somewhere, who thinks the Garden can still be gotten to on foot or by ship, who thinks that life's secret would tumble from the mind of the Maker if only there were more federal funding—certainly it's dawned on such a person that the road to the Garden doesn't pass through the world of forms, but through the human heart and soul.

Wired for Wildness

When I teach weekend and weeklong retreats, people sometimes ask if we can take a particular day's class outside. I tried it a few times in the beginning but found that people's attention immediately began to wander, understandably, in the face of squirrels chasing one another around tree trunks, the wind in the willows, and the temptation to sprawl out in the grass and drink in the sunshine. So I now pass on these requests.

Humans are *designed* to respond sensually to the elements, to follow movement in the bushes and branches, sniff the air, adjust to changes in light and temperature, and it can be hard to get a lick of work done out there under these circumstances. The people who design office buildings and classrooms know what they're doing by minimizing the "distractions"—painting the walls white, soundproofing them, keeping the temperature constant, the light bland and uniform, the air processed, and the animals outside. It cuts down on competing stimuli and sensory flights of fancy. And though most people would probably prefer to spend their office hours working than adjusting to changes in temperature and light, in a larger sense it diminishes our capacity to *adjust* to the world.

But our bodies were crafted for the outdoors by millions upon millions of years of evolution, and our seeking, questioning minds were polished in the tumbler of vast journeying. We have senses tuned to the subtleties of nature, reflexes ready to run or rumble at the slightest sound, a deep well of know-how, sights calibrated for treetops and horizons, and souls calibrated for freedom.

And not only our bodies and senses but also our souls and spirits—which we consider animating forces in human life—are elementally and etymologically wild. Among the oldest roots of the word *soul* is a Germanic word meaning "belonging to the sea," because that was supposed to be the stopping place of the soul before birth and after death. And to the ancient Greeks, who used the same word for "alive" as for "ensouled," both soul and spirit meant "to blow," as in wind or breath. So any practice that brings awareness to the *breath*—meditation, yoga, dance, tantra, martial arts, chanting, singing, even athletics—will also bring on increases in soul and wildness.

I recently ran across a passage in an ecology textbook stating that "human beings evolved over the course of some five million years," which is like saying that Christopher Columbus discovered America. As if nobody was living there prior to his arrival. We didn't begin evolving five million years ago. That's just when we branched off from the other primates.

Before that, we branched off from the mammals. Before that, the vertebrates. Before that, the invertebrates, the single-celled, the soup, the stars. Our wild heritage goes *way* back. We weren't cobbled together over the course of merely five million years, but all thirteen billion of them. We have a thousand afterimages of evolution flickering in the backs of our minds, and the lint of stars stuck in our belly buttons.

In a geology exhibit at the Smithsonian Institution's National Museum of Natural History, inside a teardrop-shaped glass vial no bigger than a lapel pin, is a speck of diamond dust, microscopic crystals that were found inside a meteor that crashed in Mexico in 1969, forged in the supernova explosion that created the solar system. Above it is a small plaque that says, "The oldest material you will ever see." That is, the oldest thing you will ever see is an element found inside your own body—carbon—and one that's the chemical basis of all known life.

We may constantly hie ourselves toward the future, hungry for upgrades and transcendence, for godbodies and supermind, for a time when our vestigial organs are no longer reminders of the unrecognizable creatures we once were but merely financial gain for surgeons. But the modern mind that conceives of such things is campfire whittlings compared to the foundry works of our ancient heritage. If the body and emotions spent all day in the oven on low heat like a Thanksgiving turkey, the intellect was dropped into the toaster like a Pop-Tart.

Not that the human brain is a mere afterthought. Once the more-or-less modern human split off from the lineage of the man-apes, the brain grew at a fantastic pace, faster than any organ in the history of life—adding onto itself the equivalent of a tablespoon every hundred thousand years. Which may not seem like much at first glance, but in every one of those fluid ounces were storm surges and bolts of lightning, the upthrusting tectonics of intellect and moral agency, and the rising floodwaters of reason. And though all of it fits neatly into a space barely bigger than a coconut, a supercomputer capable of counting a thousand synapses a second would take ten thousand to fifteen thousand years to count all the synapses in the human brain.

That brain is actually a layer cake of three brains packaged together in a box, created in utero in the order in which they appeared in evolution: the reptilian in the first trimester, the mammalian in the second, the neo-cortex in the third. The reptilian and mammalian brains, though, have far more job experience on planet Earth than the "higher" brain, which hasn't climbed nearly high enough in just a few million years to escape a genome that took billions of years to manufacture and that was passed down to us through an ancestry that includes the primate, mammalian, reptilian, amphibian, ichthyian, and bacterial, and that, by some estimates, now changes barely 1 percent every hundred thousand years.

Neocortex means "new bark," which tells us that the trunk of the tree is firmly planted in the animal kingdom. In fact, it's those "animal know-ings" like instinct and reflex that kept us in the game long enough to even allow a higher brain to evolve. And there's not as great a distance between human and nonhuman as we'd like to think. Not only do we share roughly 96 percent of our genes with chimpanzees and 85 percent with mice, but we also share 50 percent of them with *bananas*.

On my office wall I have a mask that I brought back from Central America a few years ago, carved by a member of the Boruca tribe named Francisco Morales. It depicts a *diablito* (little devil), which is what the Spanish conquistadors called the indigenous people they met, and the mask is a fusion of one-third human, one-third animal, and one-third plant. There are fewer firm boundaries, fewer no-fly zones between Us and Them than we imagine.

The truth is, we're sphinxes. We have the heads and intellects of humans but the bodies and emotions of animals, and there's a reason our wild and mythic imaginations have for thousands of years conjured and carved in stone an endless pet-parade of creatures half human and half animal. Satyrs and centaurs, sirens and fauns, mermaids and werewolves and Teenage Mutant Ninja Turtles, angels with their wings and devils with their horns and hooves, and of course Medusa, whose hair is a nest of vipers. (The cartoonist Gary Larson once depicted her holding a mouse just beyond the vipers' reach, with a caption reading, "Medusa teasing her hair.")

Annie Dillard has written about a visit to a maternity ward during which a baby was born with gill slits in his neck, like a shark, and a long tail, thick at the top like a kangaroo's but naked, and which the attending pediatrician had to untuck from between the baby's legs to learn its gender. A chimera. An amalgam of fish, mammal, and human. A reminder of where we really came from, and that once upon a time we breathed through gills the warm water of shallow seas and hung by our tails from the tree of life. We swim and crawl and swing through all of evolution in the womb, and sometimes we retrace our steps.

Furthermore, most of the cells in the human body aren't even human. They're microbial, by a factor of ten to one. There are as many as one hundred trillion microorganisms in the human intestine alone, to say nothing of the skin, ears, nose, and mouth. And as for being fruitful and multiplying, they can drink us under the table. They're so abundant that even slaughtering them by the millions, which you do every time you take a shower, doesn't even make a dent. A single bacterium will reproduce itself twice every hour, leaving behind a million generations before you even hit retirement age. And every one of us hosts between five hundred and one thousand different species of these fruitful multipliers. A human being is actually a *composite* of species.

Nor are they invasive species. We co-evolved with them and couldn't survive without them, though they know nothing about us, who we are, where we live, what we do for a living, what our five-year plans are. The personal "I" of which we take such pride is insignificant to them. (And what greater "I" is the vast sea in which *we* float and go about our business?)

And if the animals live inside us, we've taken up residence inside them as well. Huddled in the skins of bears and in dwellings made from the bones of mammoths covered in hide, we've lived quite snugly through entire ice ages. Once, people even believed that these very animals lived inside the body of Earth. During his voyage to South America in 1833 aboard the *Beagle*, Charles Darwin investigated a deposit of mastodon bones protruding from the side of a cliff in Argentina. When he asked his guides how they thought the bones had found their way to that unlikely spot, they told him that clearly the huge mastodon had been a burrowing animal.

It turns out, though, that our most direct and intimate access to "the wild" isn't the woods at the edge of town or even the bird feeder in the backyard. It's the body. The body that for each of us is our own personal animal, not just a rickshaw to carry the brain around in. "Our instincts, our motives, our biology, our basic needs—pure animal," says Diane Ackerman.

We might think nature is behind us or beneath us, or out *there* somewhere, but it isn't. A dinner date is courtship behavior. Office politics and sibling rivalry are the competition for resources. There are times when Ross and I are sharing a meal, and if he sees me eyeballing something on his plate, he'll actually growl at me, like a dog, his lips curling back in a snarl, his eyes narrowing to slits. There's something about us, it seems, always stirring at the corner of the eye, moving with a vaguely familiar stealth, or grace, and casting the shadow of a panther or an ape on the alley wall.

In *Primal Love*, Douglas Gillette talks about a group exercise he does called the ape-embodiment exercise, a series of physical and vocal activities designed to get people out of their heads and into their animal bodies and souls. Part of it involves pairing people up and going through a regimen of primate behaviors together—gazing, grooming, grimacing, begging, playing, confronting and making up, dominance and submission, etc., all the while making animal sounds: whining, growling, barking, screeching, hooting.

At each step of the exercise, Gillette also has them share their emotional reactions to these prehuman exchanges to encourage them to integrate their humanness, with its capacity to reflect and analyze, with their animal selves. It gives people a chance to experience some of the deeply underlying impulses that govern us all, the raw nature within us that's operating below the civilized surface all the time, and which has critical implications for what's *really* going on between us.

The fact is, we're rich with the reflexes of animals: snapping our heads at a sudden noise, taking an intuitive liking or disliking to someone, feeling vertigo at the edge of a cliff, stretching our muscles after a nap, having a Pavlovian response to the smell of food, getting a thump of adrenaline in the gut in a moment of fear or danger.

We're the inheritors of an ancient body that truly came up through the ranks. The nine months we each spend in utero demonstrate this. It's a recapitulation and condensation of the entire process of evolution over billions of years, taking us from one-celled organism to fish to mammal to man and woman. We're all shape-shifters of the highest order, carrying within us the innate knowledge of how to make radical change. As our dreams sometimes show us, we once knew how to breathe underwater and swing through the air with the greatest of ease. But perhaps they're not so much dreams as memories. Perhaps when the day-guards are off duty, we swim past the breakers and back out toward the briny deep of animal life.

Not just in our dreams and memories but also in our animal bodies is more wildness than we know. There are wetlands in our lungs and swamps in the gut and bowels, electrical storms in the brain and thunder in the heart, roving predators and perpetual dark, and sixty thousand miles of bloodred river. And on the outside, the remnant of a pelt—the hair on the back of your hands and across the top of your toes, the coarse hairs on your chest and the fine hairs in the small of your back, and a runnel of it running like a line of ants from your navel to your crotch.

However far removed you may feel from the natural world, tottering in high heels or hidden away in a carpeted office under fluorescent lights on the thirty-third floor of an office building scraping the sky over a city of twenty million, you can be taken out of the forest, but the forest can't be taken out of you. The context of our lives in the past is wilderness, says environmental author Paul Shepard, "and our genes look expectantly for those circumstances that are their optimal ambiance, a genetic expectation that is unfulfilled in the world we have created."

This might explain why wilderness today is usually something we escape to, a place to which we go for solace and serenity, silence and perspective, initiations and visions, and to test ourselves. No one goes to the city for a vision quest. People don't test their mettle by climbing skyscrapers, or decompress from the stresses of life by camping out near the interstate. The wild nature that selected our genes is required to satisfy some of the emotional and psychological needs that were also programmed by those genes.

Raising Cain

We are probably as close to the wild state as we'll ever get when we're born. We then face the Bambi-meets-Godzilla scenario of trying to hang on to our instinctive selves in the face of the world's knuckle-rapping oversight, the "civilizing" effects of parenting, schooling, bibling, and gendering that, without necessarily meaning to, ensure we'll leave behind much of what is vital in us by the time we take our position at the grown-ups' table.

Nonetheless, as any daimon will tell you, it remains our true nature to affirm and assert ourselves, to be self-initiating and self-determining. And this passionate and independent spirit is the core of what Chris Mercogliano calls inner wildness.

Chris is the author of *In Defense of Childhood: Protecting Kids' Inner Wildness* and for thirty-five years directed and taught at the Albany Free School, in New York, the oldest inner-city independent alternative school in the country. Alternative, that is, to what he calls the compulsory, factory-style, standards-driven model of education, which he considers to be the largest single agent of "childhood domestication," whose guiding principle is control and whose net effect, as Thoreau once observed, is to make a straight-cut ditch out of a free, meandering brook.

And it's that way because it was intended to be that way. The father of educational psychology, Edward Thorndike, once said, "There can be no moral warrant for studying man's nature unless the study will enable us to control his acts."

Chris defines inner wildness as a "luminescent spark" and an "elusive essence that strives mightily to resist the control of others." This wildness struggles to keep itself lit amid the damping effects of modernity that, he claims, are slowly squeezing the novelty, independence, adventure, exploration, challenge, expression, wonder, innocence, and physicality—the juice, the aliveness—from the lives of children (and the adults they become). Even as it makes those lives longer, healthier, and more prosperous.

This is where the Free School comes in. With no mandatory classes, grades, or standardized tests, the kids (ranging in age from two to fourteen) are free to choose what they want to do, when they want to do it. "Every day they come to school," he told me, "it's *their* day. 'What do I want to do?' It's all based on their interests, their excitement, their motivation. Nobody's laying it out for them. They want fascination, novelty, stuff that's going to *move* them."

Not surprisingly, what tends to move kids is usually play. Lots and lots of play. Days, weeks, months, and years of play, while reading writing and 'rithmetic collect dust on a shelf. This, of course, sends a lot of parents and teachers into paroxysms. But true learning, Chris insists, is more the result of active engagement than of passive storage and formal instruction. It occurs spontaneously, mostly through play, fantasy, and experimentation, what he calls "wild learning." And it's propelled by an inner vital force that the pioneering educator Maria Montessori called *horme*, derived from the ancient Greek personification of energetic activity, Hormes, and from which we get the word *hormone*, a chemical that *stimulates*.

Wild learning—"this whole freedom thing"—is an educational philosophy that in actual practice, Chris admits, is "a pain in the ass." It's certainly messier and more chaotic—more democratic—than the conventional approach, with the frenetic kids bouncing off the walls right next to the contemplative kids trying to read a book, and requiring everyone to hash it out as a community. But wild learning doesn't necessarily equate with wild behavior. "People are concerned that if you let 'em run wild," he said, "they'll grow up wild, but the truth is, if you give them the chance to express their wildness, they'll eventually settle down and learn to manage their own energies quite satisfactorily."

In the book, Chris adds, "When highly active children can run, jump, climb, yell, dance, dig holes in the sandbox, and hammer ten-penny nails into two-by-fours in the wood shop to their hearts' content, they gradually settle down and develop the ability to modulate their energy level." This is not to say, he told me, "that inner wildness is always expressed in yelling and dancing. A quiet, contemplative person can express it just as adamantly through art, imagination, or a deep sense of wonder. But for both kinds of people, the trouble begins when you stifle them, when you suppress their need to move and do and explore, and try to force them to pay attention when the desire and excitement are missing."

Kids whose inner wildness is respected and cultivated, though, are inherently civil, he insists. A *Lord of the Flies* scenario—based on William Golding's novel about a group of schoolboys who turn savage when marooned on a deserted island—is not at all inevitable. It bears mentioning that Golding was the schoolmaster at an elite Church of England grammar school when he wrote that novel, and it's not hard to imagine that a bunch of upper-crust English boys who were raised by surrogates in a rigid, competitive, and emotionally parched atmosphere would turn barbarous in the absence of adult supervision.

Chris flatly states that this would *not* be the outcome were the inhabitants of that island students from the Free School, who are not only loved and touched and trusted and spoken to honestly but also permitted and encouraged in "the Tom Sawyer/Huck Finn archetype—brash, willful, naughty, rambunctious, aggressive, and always dirty." (When I exhibited those behaviors in school, as an eight-year-old, I was sent first to a school psychologist and then to a neurologist, who reported that I was "hyperactive, wild, frequently in mischief and relatively insusceptible to restraints, discipline and control.")

When I joked with Chris that the public high schools must *love* getting his Sawyeresque kids (since most eventually transfer there), he said, "Actually, they do. Because they're responsible and independent. They're thoughtful and think for themselves. And they pursue instruction rather than waiting for it. At the classroom level, it's nice for any teacher to have a kid who's thinking, problem solving, and doesn't have to be bribed and prodded, who's really there, participating."

Not that Free Schoolers don't occasionally make them squirm. Chris recalled the story of a former student, a fifteen-year-old girl, who confronted the new principal of Albany High School a few months into his tenure. She walked right up to him in the courtyard and said, "Dr. So-and-So, I thought you might want to know what the students here are saying about you—a lot of really negative things. And do you know why? Because we never see you. We don't even know who you are. You're invisible. We don't know anything about you. I just thought you'd like to know. And by the way, my name's Eve."

Ten minutes later, the principal got on the PA system, interrupting all classes, and said that it had recently come to his attention that he had neglected to introduce himself, and then he spent the next fifteen minutes doing just that.

The primary payoff of wild learning is the creation of that precious commodity called intrinsic motivation—spontaneous interest in and exploration of a subject—which tends to shrivel in the face of extrinsic reinforcers like grades, bribes, threats, deadlines, directives, punishments, imposed goals, even praise and rewards, as well as parents who overparent. Which I hear a *lot* about when I guest lecture at colleges around the country.

Staff and faculty call it hyper-parenting, hothouse parenting, death-grip parenting, and helicopter parenting, referring to mothers and fathers who are always hovering nearby, ready to swoop in to rescue their progeny and fight their battles for them, which prevents kids from making their own decisions and learning from their own mistakes, and works against strengthening the muscles of inner wildness.

By the time kids have endured fifteen or twenty years of the extrinsics of standard education and overparenting, their internal motivation has often lost a good deal of its stuffing. Of his visits to college campuses to talk to education classes, especially at the public universities (what he calls the factory schools), Chris says: "It's sad and scary. The kids are like robots. Nobody's thinking for themselves. They're bored. They're used to being bored. They seem to expect to be bored. Generating engagement from them is a real challenge, and I'm good at it. But I look out and see all those dead faces and dead eyes and a chill runs through me."

Without intrinsic motivation, he says, "you end up not knowing yourself, what you want, why you want it. You can't think creatively or solve problems. You're dependent on other people. And this isn't what the world needs. I hear corporations saying, 'We don't want people who can just follow directions. We want people who can *make* directions, self-starters, creative thinkers. We don't want people who are passive, dependent, rigid and rule-bound, who lack confidence and have a hard time improvising."

Nature has a word for those who are rigid and fail to improvise: extinct. But nature also provides at least temporary relief from the zoofication of kids and the domestication of childhood. When Free School students are taken to the school's 250 acres of wilderness outside the city, within *minutes*, Chris says, you can see them begin to shed their urban and suburban skins and come alive. "Their eyes glisten with wonder, their bodies become more relaxed and their movements more fluid."

It's good for their schoolwork too. Though as many as 50 percent of American school districts have cut back on recess in deference to liability issues and the work ethic of a test-crazy culture—it used to be half an hour twice a day; now some schools are being built without even a playground— studies show that kids are actually more attentive in the classroom after recess than before it. In schools without *any* recess, the amount of instructional time lost to fidgeting adds up to the amount of time it takes to have recess in the first place. A compilation of over two hundred studies on exercise and cognitive functioning also found that physical activity boosts learning, both academic and social. But barely 4 percent of elementary schools and 2 percent of high schools even *offer* phys ed anymore.

This might explain the No Child Left Inside Act, an arguably desperate measure introduced by Congressman John Sarbanes, a Democrat from Maryland, which aims to funnel more federal funds toward getting kids outdoors. The House bill, which is still in committee, calls for better environmental-education training for teachers across the country; a beefed-up environmental curriculum at the local, state, and university levels; and more federal grants to, in Sarbanes's words, "help young people become more engaged in the natural world." The more they're taught to enjoy it, he believes, the more they'll learn to sympathize.

Without such initiatives, both political and personal, the vitality of childhood and the inner wildness of us all is in danger of becoming an endangered species, an increasingly fragile filament in our lives. J. M. Barrie, author of *Peter Pan*, once spoke of "a little something in us which is no larger than a mote in the eye, and that, like it, dances in front of us beguiling us all our days. I cannot cut the hair by which it hangs."

All Hail the Beast Within

My stepfather used to have a Luger with which he would sometimes crouch in an upstairs window and try to pick off the fighting tomcats that would snatch the goldfish from our backyard pond.

This is one of the images that came to me some years ago as I tried to puzzle out how to handle a small dilemma.

I had discovered a mouse one evening as I sat at my typewriter and watched impassively as it made its way along the wall in the kitchen, like a small toy car. Naturally, I decided to get rid of it, but soon discovered that there were only two kinds of mousetraps in the hardware store around the corner from my house. One was your basic Last Supper affair—cheddar cheese, spring-loaded. It was guaranteed, as my friendly neighborhood hardware store man told me, to "break their little bones." It cost a buck fifty.

The other was an aluminum box about the size of a toaster, with a small tunnel running through it at floor level and designed to be placed two inches from a wall. Mice, being agoraphobic and possessed of only modest eyesight, keep close to walls for security. I know the feeling. I slept most of my childhood that way.

When a mouse, feeling its way by its whiskers, finds an opening in a wall, it instinctively slips in. Hence the hole in the aluminum box. The mouse crawls in, tripping a pressure-sensitive plate, and a paddlewheel sweeps him into an empty chamber. The cost of such beneficence, with its prospect of setting the mouse free in the field beside my house, was $17.50. I was not exactly beating a path to the checkout counter to pay $17.50 for a mousetrap, but I also didn't want to kill it, and now I was haggling over the price of compassion.

As a boy—as were most boys—I was a squoosher. I squooshed an appalling number of caterpillars, ants, worms, flies, and spiders during my formative years, both in and outside my house. This impulse was, I think, an assertion of my meager dominion, or my competitive urge misplaced. A friend even suggested that it's a primal instinct (a bored and aimless one, perhaps) that puts me on red alert and prompts me to attack when another creature invades my territory. But I think it's overaddressing the issue to imply that some saber-toothed twitch of the brain stem is what prompts me to pulverize spiders in my living room, a territory boundaried by carpeting, quadraphonic coaxial speakers, and a welcome mat.

More likely, this behavior is a reaction to growing up in a home where everything had its place, and any animal that stepped out of line or slipped into the house uninvited was fair game. The message was clear: there's no bargaining in the pecking order. Every portal into the house had a screen, we had a pest spray or a rolled-up magazine for every genus and species, the dogs belonged downstairs, and my stepfather, of course, had the Luger.

I remember when this king-of-the-hill disposition I'd inherited began to change. It was the year my parents got divorced, when they sent me to spend the summer at the farm of some friends in rural Pennsylvania. The two boys in the family took me hunting one day with their BB gun. I was the city kid who had never hunted before, and when I shot a sparrow in the high branches of an elm on my first try, I felt a surge of accomplishment and bravado. But when I picked up my prize by its wing and saw the dark red blood dripping from its head—not insect green or yellow this time, but red like mine—I felt a sudden, sickening regret.

As I came in close to my own pain that summer, and for a long time thereafter, I slowly began to see pain everywhere. Gradually, I've been trying to cease administering it. I sense there's a diminishing curve of insensitivity as a man gets older.

So I don't strip the leaves off twigs anymore as I walk along the sidewalk, and I work around the ant colony when I'm clearing the backyard. Sometimes I feel so isolated from the proverbial web of things, living in the city or the suburbs, that a part of me is even glad to have something resembling an ecosystem around. The spiderwebs in the windows do wondrous things with the light that slips in at sunset. Also, I can't shake the feeling that somewhere there's a tally being kept of these things—my cruelties and my compassions—and that it will make a difference somewhere down the line when I go to cash in my chips.

Besides, there's a very real question in my mind of relativity. Who's the pest here: me or the mouse? To a germ, I'm sure, even health is a form of disease.

In the end, there was no real dilemma. I had made up my mind. I intended to loosen the grip on my assumed sovereignty and make good on my preference for life. And if I paid an arm and a leg for a mousetrap, such was the price of the rodent not taken.

As I stood in the checkout line at the hardware store, an elderly man tapped me on the shoulder. "Good for you," he said, surveying my $17.50 mousetrap. "You'll probably come back as a mouse."

GENESIS CALLS FOR HUMANITY to care for the Creation, but it also contains that troublesome "dominion" passage: "Be fruitful and multiply, and fill the earth and subdue it; and have dominion over the fish of the sea and over the birds of the air and over every living thing that moves upon the earth."

It isn't hard to see which dictum we've followed more faithfully, and certainly among the reasons we might feel separated from the wider and wilder world is that we have a long-standing habit of placing ourselves above it. And this habit keeps us at arm's length from not only our own wildness, but also the passions and vitalities contained within it.

The modern mind is full of what John Muir called "indoor philosophy," which is flamboyantly egotistical (rather than ecotistical) in its assumption that humans are the crown of creation, the center of attention, the conclusion of the story toward which the universe has been drawing for thirteen billion years, and the reason everything else was put here. As if evolution spent billions of years sitting around in the dressing room primping and plucking its eyebrows, just waiting for its cue to entertain us.

It's not so hard to imagine, though, that locusts might presume humans were put here to provide for *them*, that viruses and parasites might consider the human body *their* earthly paradise in which to be fruitful and multiply, to fill and subdue, or that nature in general might deem us merely a means to its own self-reflection.

I understand that, to some people, to entire religions, this is a kind of heresy, the belief that nature was *not*, in fact, put here to be our personal delicatessen, lumber yard, and filling station, a platter of finger foods we can pluck from at our whim; or that the animals are not necessarily ours to do with as we please, to carry our burdens, pull our plows, guard our homes, produce our milk, offer up their flesh for our dinner tables, and provide useful moral instruction (lions on courage, bees on the virtue of hard work, etc.); or that our relationship with the natural world that birthed us should not be largely utilitarian.

The trouble is, questioning this assumption of dominion compromises our fantasies of power and eminence. It unmakes the make-believe that we're bigger than we actually are in this age-old world, with its towering cliffs, overhanging gods, fanged opponents, and immensities of what there is to know. ("You never conquer a mountain," mountaineer Arlene Blum says. "You stand on the summit a few moments; then the wind blows your footprints away.") It drains the mirage that we're the point and purpose of it all. The fact is, we're just a whistle-stop along its endless track.

This was beautifully captured by the gothic cartoonist Gahan Wilson in an old *New Yorker* cartoon showing a long staircase stretching diagonally from one end of the frame to the other. On it stand various representatives from human evolution, starting with some indistinguishable proto-wriggler at the bottom of the stairs and moving through mammal-fish and hairy nibbler and tree swinger and knuckle dragger, and ending with a man in a suit and tie gazing wide-eyed up the stairs to where they disappear out of sight. The hominid next to him says, "I was wondering when you'd notice there's lots more steps." And what will the *next* figure in this sequence look like?

Our intuition that we're not at the top of the stairs probably explains why we compulsively practice our swaggers in the mirror, crowd ourselves into swarming colonies and gated communities, and barricade ourselves behind pretend dominion. It's sobering to think that the entire machinery of human life, all the spinning plates of our busy lives, are just hamster wheels spinning inside the orbits of larger wheels spinning inside still larger wheels out to the farthest edges. And it's hard to believe that among the two million species so far cataloged, we're the only one that if removed from the planet altogether, would benefit all the *other* species (domestic pets notwithstanding).

It's as hard to swallow as the uprising that Copernicus and Galileo provoked when they proved that the universe didn't revolve around Earth, which rocked more than a few statues in the town squares.

I'm often amused by how earnestly people seem to need to distinguish themselves from the animals by declaring that "we're the only species that": is self-reflective, seeks meaning and purpose, engages in ritual and ceremony, creates art, is responsible for our behavior, thinks about the past and the future, gets embarrassed or has reason to, takes so long to grow up, wears makeup, goes camping, uses Cuisinarts, whatever.

Plato may have been the first to start this game when he announced that humans are the only creatures who are naked and walk on two legs, whereupon Diogenes showed up at the lecture hall carrying a plucked chicken, which he set loose, declaring, "Here is Plato's man." Plato then amended his definition to include "having broad nails."

We seem intent on distinguishing if not disassociating ourselves from the animal kingdom—and our own inner wildness—with an eagerness that smacks of overcompensation. Perhaps we're trying to prove that we're finally stronger and smarter than the bullies and predators who, for most of our lives on Earth, were far superior to us in terms of strength, speed, and sense-ability. Or maybe it's just the desire to put some distance between us and our own wild if not uncontrollable selves.

Some cultures, like the Balinese, believe so strongly that it's undesirable to be animalistic that at puberty every child has his or her canine teeth—vestiges of a wilder nature and what dentists call carnivora—ceremonially filed down. And this among the same people who gave us the word *amok*, as in "running amok," which the author Elizabeth Gilbert describes as "a battle technique of suddenly going insanely wild against one's enemies in suicidal and bloody hand-to-hand combat."

When people act barbarously, we call them animals; when they act compassionately, we call them humane. We like to claim the higher ground and fob off our darker impulses onto the animals and the "savages." But by depicting our ill manners as animalistic, we denigrate the animals and misrepresent ourselves.

If by *civilized* we mean well bred and refined, then the beasts have it all over us. They're exquisitely attuned to their environments, their senses have remained polished over time rather than become dulled, and they're enlightened if you define *enlightened* as "being in the moment."

To say, for instance, as the ancient Romans used to, that "man is wolf to man" is an insult to a gregarious and cooperative creature, and one so famously loyal that our forebears chose to domesticate them as protectors and friends. And it's balderdash to say, as Teddy Roosevelt once did of war, that "all men who feel any power of joy in battle know what it is like when the wolf rises in the heart." Wolves don't rise up in communal viciousness and march off to war. It was the supposedly civilized nations that slaughtered sixty to seventy million of each other's citizens in the thirty years from the beginning of World War I to the end of World War II. Wolves and sharks are Muppets compared with this.

By human standards, says Mary Midgley in *Beast and Man*, wolves are paragons of steadfastness and good conduct: "They pair for life, they're faithful and affectionate spouses and parents, they show great loyalty to their pack and great courage and persistence in the face of difficulties, they carefully respect one another's territory, keep their dens clean, and rarely kill anything they don't need for dinner."

When we talk about "the law of the jungle," we usually mean ruthless and unrestrained competition, with everyone out solely for his or her own advantage. But the phrase was coined by Rudyard Kipling in *The Second Jungle Book*, and he meant something very different. His law of the jungle is a law that wolves in a pack are supposed to obey. His poem says, "The strength of the Pack is the Wolf, and the strength of the Wolf is the Pack," and it lays out the basic principles of social cooperation—an admirable mixture of individualism and collectivism.

And why, when we speak about our iniquitous behavior, do we assume it emanates from "the beast within" rather than just from our everyday human selves, which is, after all, the case. We identify cold-bloodedness, lawlessness, murderous rage, and sexual perversion with the behavior of beasts, but if a grizzly were to go around murdering its own or trying to mate with mountain lions, it wouldn't be a bear, and wouldn't last long as a species. Partly we do this because the "beast within," as Midgley points out, conveniently solves the problem of evil. It's an alien creature that somehow slipped past our defenses and got into the house.

But there's no beast within any more than there's a god of war. We're it. The demons that Buddha and Jesus encountered in their respective wildernesses—the personifications of avarice, arrogance, and illusion—weren't *out there*. They're not predators that come with the territory. They come stowed away in the folds of our frocks. The scariest thing out there is *us*.

What we really mean by the "beast within" is behavior we don't want to admit to in ourselves, and in classic psychological fashion project onto someone else. We're then eager to exaggerate the differences between us and them, which is undoubtedly a good thing, since it highlights how mortified we actually are by our own behavior.

And if there's no such thing as a lawless beast outside us, there's not likely one inside us either. It's far more accurate to say that the beast within is that part of us that obeys the natural laws that help us operate if not flourish in the world—our instincts and sensory awareness, our deepest intuitions about what to move toward and what to move away from—those wild gifts that can help bring us in line with our truest nature.

In *The African Queen*, Katharine Hepburn upbraids Humphrey Bogart by telling him, "Nature, Mr. Allnut, is what we are put in this world to rise above."

Not surprisingly, Hepburn's character is a missionary, and as such holds dear a belief congenital to Western religion: that spiritual life should take us up and out from nature, and that it's the antidote to our instincts and emotions, our animal wants and sensual passions. An antagonism is set up between the two, with spirit transcendent. Heaven is above and beyond Earth, and hell is inside it, as opposed to the indigenous belief that the natural world and the spiritual are one and the same.

Most religions, certainly the Abrahamic, are rise-above theologies. We yearn more hungrily for heaven than for earth. We prefer Easter's themes of resurrection and ascension to Lent's themes of fasting and retreat into the wilderness. We point our religions and our hopes toward afterlife rather than mortal life, the hereafter rather than the here and now, the promised land rather than the one we actually got, and the eternal happiness assumed for the immortal soul rather than the messy conundrums of life in a body.

The religious practice of "mortifying the flesh" (literally putting it to death) is one form of this belief in the value of inhibiting and overcoming our natural inclinations. Colossians 3:5 even says, "Put to death what is earthly in you." (The current conquest of nature, with its accompanying eco-catastrophes, appears to be an attempt to do just that, and there are certainly parts of our own selves that we abuse, neglect, erode, bulldoze, trash, and pave over. In both cases, reclamation is in order.)

In most biblical references, wilderness is analogous to wasteland. It's a place of thirst, hunger, deprivation, and danger. Barren and wind-scorched, it's the haunt of evil powers and welcome refuge only for outlaws and fugitives. Deuteronomy speaks of the "howling waste of the wilderness," and Luke of the "voice of one crying in the wilderness." It's the repository of God's curses, not God's blessings—the place of banishment. And not just for humans.

Among the rituals historically performed during Yom Kippur, the Jewish Day of Atonement, two goats were chosen, one to be sacrificed and the other to become the scapegoat, literally the escape-goat, the one that escaped sacrifice but was symbolically heaped with all the sins of the people and then banished to the wilderness, where sins presumably feel at home.

Interestingly, by allowing the goat to live, we were admitting that immorality and wrongdoing can be dismissed but not eradicated, suppressed but not extinguished. Psychologically speaking, our imperfections are still alive but cast into a wilderness, exiled to some *deserted* part of our psyches—though sometimes, then as now, the goat inadvertently wanders back to town.

To be sure, our iniquities have become far too numerous and heavy to bear on the back of a goat, so we've turned our sights on larger beasts of burden—minority groups, practitioners of different religions and political beliefs, whole nations, entire races of people. The Jews would know.

And though most people assume that our alienation from nature was a long, slow process of enculturation and domestication, some forms of it were actually done at gunpoint. My great-grandparents were forced from their land and villages in Russia by their own government, as were the American Indians, farmers who are evicted from the land by economic hardship, and, at least in this hemisphere, black people who were snatched from their homelands, shipped to the Americas, and forced to work the land, enslaved to the soil of an alien nation.

Still, the word *culture*, which we so eagerly employ in the service of distinguishing ourselves from whoever we imagine is *lacking* in culture, is utterly nature-based, sprung from the word for *cultivation* (as in "agriculture"), which itself comes from the word for *till*. As the Indian philosopher and physicist Vandana Shiva said, "The wild is not the opposite of the cultivated. It's the opposite of the captivated."

However high-minded we get about it, culture is *soiled*. It's about dirt, mud, and mire. It's about the dust from which we came and to which we'll return. It's earth-based, biological. Yogurt culture is every bit as cultured as human culture. Dirt is Source—womb and tomb and the ecotone between them that we call a life. Maybe those with the most dirt under their fingernails are really the wisest. Maybe we should quit trying to wipe all traces of it from our environs and straining for dust bunnies under the couch.

Technically speaking, then, it's the heathens and the hillbillies—the children of the heaths and the hills—who are the most cultured. It's the savages whose name means merely people "of the wood," the pagans who lived in a *pagus*, a rural precinct, and the villains who were simply peasants living in farming villages, whose faith usually lay outside the monotheistic triad of Christianity, Judaism, and Islam, and whose gods were an especially wild bunch. Fully alive and theatrical, full of the passionate powers of creation and destruction, they were richly emotional and sensual, and ever eager to hurl thunderbolts, whip the seas into froth, and turn the mortals into stones and trees.

Among the most celebrated of these was Dionysus, the Greek god of wine and theater and one of the twelve Olympians; he was known as the Liberator for freeing humans from their everyday selves through spiritual or physical intoxication, sensuous experience (the senses aroused by art, music, or ceremony; the life of the spirit as seen through the senses), or sensual experience (pleasure seeking for its own sake, delicious meals, voluptuous sexual encounters, altered states).

But it's the fading of Dionysus from the scene that speaks so poignantly of the triumph of the rational life of the mind over the nonrational wisdom of the senses (I hesitate to use the word *ir*rational, besotted as it is with implications of foolishness).

Some people believe that the conquering of Dionysian ecstasy has been a necessary evil, a compensatory urge in the human psyche that's helped nurture the rational—the disciplined and analytical side of us that's been so useful in the flowering of science, law, and culture. The trouble is, the urge to purge the ecstatic appears to have gotten out of hand, and a balancing act is in order.

For those who've lost their senses, lost touch with the elemental world and elemental pleasures—whether individuals or cultures—a treaty needs to be struck between the rational and nonrational, the indoor and the outdoor life. All work and no play makes Jack a dull boy.

The loss of Dionysian ecstasy is largely the story of how the ecstatic if not antic behavior of these revelers was suppressed by the stern and patriarchal followers of the Roman, Jewish, and Christian religions of the time, who downgraded Dionysus from the god of wine to the god of drunkenness, and eventually curtailed and then outright prohibited the revelries of this "cult" (all religions begin as cults: a charismatic leader and his or her followers). They deemed it a threat to their authority and their conviction that women shouldn't occupy leadership positions, which they did quite floridly under Dionysus.

Interestingly, Dionysus is often depicted with goatlike features and qualities, and many scholars believe that he, and especially his comrade Pan, were prototypes for the devil. Pan with his horns and cloven hooves, his shaggy loins, was the consort of satyrs and nymphs, fauns and dryads and maenads, all the wild children of nature. And he was famous for a lustiness that early Christians considered debased.

The author Tom Robbins, in his novel *Jitterbug Perfume,* calls Pan "Mr charmer, Mr irrational, Mr instinct, Mr gypsy hoof, Mr clown, Mr body odor, Mr animal mystery, Mr nightmare, Mr lie in wait, Mr panic, Mr bark at the moon, Mr internal wilderness, Mr startle reaction, Mr wayward force, Mr insolence, Mr nature knows best."

Nonetheless, in the time-tested tradition of suppression, in which the gods of one faith are turned into the demons of the next, the panpipes were swapped for a pitchfork, the horns and hooves were kept, and Satan was born. This lent a very bad name to the beasts. Demons almost universally possess horns, claws, tails, fur, hooves, scales, and the leathery wings of bats, and their lairs are usually outdoors or underground.

It also left Pan, now consigned to the status of dirty old man, laughing with the derision of one who, as D. H. Lawrence put it, "feels himself defeated by something lesser than himself."

Disturbingly, there's only one story in all the annals of Greek mythology about the death of a god, and that god is Pan—though anyone who's spent time in the deep woods or the deep psyche knows that the reports of his demise are greatly exaggerated. The human psyche is still every bit the dark wood in which Dante awoke to find himself lost. It's every bit the leviathan that roused Ahab's vengeance and the sea over which he sailed, hell-bent. And it still storms with the longing and libido that endow us with passion, pleasure, poetry, and children. Pan is alive and well and living inside your head.

Still, it's interesting to consider that the word *deadpan* means "lacking in emotional expressiveness," "passive," and "detached," which is what happens to us when we lose touch with our wildness. Lawrence believed that we've long been living in deadpan times and that the death of Pan has come at the hands of "the engines or instruments which . . . intervene between man and the living universe, and give him mastery." But then what, Lawrence asks? "A conquered world is no good to man. He sits stupefied with boredom upon his conquest. We need the universe to live again, so that we can live with it."

This need may help explain our fascination with the indigenous. These are nature's last remaining wild children, who still live in a living universe, whose gods are still nature spirits, and who haven't entirely succumbed to the engines and instruments that so frequently intervene between humans and their own vitality, though most are well on their way.

Maybe it's a fascination with ourselves at a wilder stage in our development—our childhood—and with desires that "civilized" folks have sought to repress, the possibility of a fully sensuous and passionate relationship to the world. Maybe it's our response to what author Linda Hogan refers to as "the call to origins," the same impulse that propels scientists into the darkest corners of the universe in search of not only our origins but also our fate.

All spiritual traditions, including the Western, speak of the melting of the self into larger frames of reference, into a pressed-to-the-bosom intimacy with the natural, oceanic, universal, and all-embracing. This yearning is at the heart of our enthrallment with indigenous peoples, with whom we civilized types have an extravagantly conflicted relationship.

We have two clumsy conceptions of human wildness, of "the primitive" (which just means "primary," "original"). One is the noble savage: nature's gentleman, innately intelligent, unsullied by the corruptions of civilization, peaceable, egalitarian, sexually liberated, and eco-friendly. The other is the caveman: nasty, brutish, and short, whose knuckles drag on the ground and who speaks in monosyllables.

On one hand, we recoil from the rawness of "primitives," their nakedness, their vulnerability to the savageries of both the wilderness and the modern world, and their belief that penis gourds represent the height of fashion.

On the other hand, we swoon with Gaugin's descriptions of South Sea paradise, eagerly follow Conrad's dispatches from the heart of darkness, can't get enough of the adventures of Tarzan and Indiana Jones, and marvel at National Geographic accounts of Papuan tribes who use the heads of their dead fathers as pillows to charge their dreams with ancestral power.

We playact them on Halloween, and co-opt their jewelry and tattoos. We hang their dream catchers from our rearview mirrors and their carved masks on our walls, their horns and tusks, lolling tongues, flaring nostrils, and bulging eyes speaking to us of wildness and abandon, and the fleeting intuition that we may not entirely belong to Western civilization. Or at least that we have a foot in both camps and an origin far more mysterious and fearsome than we imagine.

These wild ideas are counterarguments to our urban and suburban sensibilities, in which our walls are painted in Martha Stewart signature colors and our shelves strategically positioned with knickknacks. They tell us that though we may get no closer to wildness in our everyday lives than Amazon.com and Brut cologne, another part of us wants to run with the wolves and sleep on a pillow of skulls to help us siphon the dreams of forebears.

ONE AFTERNOON LAST YEAR, I stood in a mountain meadow near my house and watched as a herd of horses on an adjacent ridge, several dozen of them, turned and came running toward me. I was caught between being riveted to the spot, full of wild excitement and anticipation, and wanting to run like hell from what was, after all, a thundering herd of large mammals heading directly for me.

I stayed where I was as the horses raced down the hillside, disappeared momentarily into the gulch between the two ridges, and suddenly appeared right in front of me. I felt the pounding of their hooves through my feet and my heart flapping in my chest. As the herd came closer, the horses slowed and spread out all around me, then stopped and just stood staring at me, and me at them. I reached out my arms, and several of them walked right up to me and allowed me to run my hands along their necks and flanks, along their muscular jaws—for whole minutes. It was as close to physical ecstasy as I've ever come. And it was unnerving.

This probably explains our ambivalence toward encounters with wildlife, even domesticated wildlife the size of a tractor. Animal encounters are among our fondest means to ecstasy and communion with wildness in the world, but wild things are also the closest thing to aliens that this planet provides, and meeting up with them unexpectedly can send a good thump of adrenaline through us.

Even just being *looked* at by wild animals, or coming across their tracks, can be electrifying. "To come upon a grizzly track is to experience the wild in a most intimate, carnal way," says Jack Turner in *The Abstract Wild*, "an experience that's marked by gross alterations in attention, perception, body language, body chemistry, and emotion. Which is to say you feel yourself as part of the biological order known as the food chain."

You feel yourself reach across what has become an almost implacable divide for many of us—that between the human and animal—the ten thousand years since our respective footprints crossed paths in the mud of ancient waterholes. You feel a rush of pleasure and danger.

And if you're like most people, you treasure the memory of these encounters even when they scare the daylights out of you, and twenty years later you still recount them with the kind of lurid fascination people normally reserve for reminiscing about great earthquakes and floods. Like the time I was circled by sharks and barracudas while scuba diving in the West Indies. Or the time I came to a rocky rise in New Mexico's Sangre de Christo Mountains at the exact moment a black bear came up to the same ridge from the opposite side, each of us scaring the archetypal crap out of the other.

Not that animal encounters have to be hair-raising to thrill, nor even require that you go outside to meet *them*. You can invite wildlife into your backyard by offering them the usual creature comforts—food, shelter, water, and a place to raise their young—and then enjoy them through the safety of your living room window.

But whether you run into them by accident or tease them out with backyard snacks, these encounters can inject a vivifying dose of drama and awe into our everyday lives, connecting us with the larger life that always surrounds us and contributing the prime ingredient of a truly sound ecological life, if not ecological policy: *personal relationship* with wild nature.

I know an environmentalist who once asked a friend of his, a city planner who worked for the Russian government, how they could get more people involved in saving the environment. "First," his friend said, "I think it's important that one fall in love."

That is, with the Earth. That is, before issues of strategy and implementation can be addressed, it's important to address issues of passion and compassion. Because if you don't have passion, where's your *com*passion going to come from? And under the sway of love, the experience of self isn't confined to just "in here" but also encompasses "out there," and the boundaries between the two soften if not dissolve.

As Freud put it, "A man who is in love declares that 'I' and 'you' are one, and is prepared to behave as if it were a fact." And what the world needs now, to borrow an old phrase, is not just love sweet love, but also people who feel oneness with the larger "you" of Earth and are willing to behave as if it were a fact. And as if they had a long-term love affair in mind rather than a roll in the hay.

One reason a sustainable conservation ethic has had difficulty getting off the ground is that natural selection has programmed us to live in physiological time, human-scale time, not multigenerational time, no less ecological and evolutionary time. We're a shortsighted bunch, and only with a measure of education and reflection can far-off events have an emotional impact on us.

But we also have a long-standing and very personal relationship with the natural world, a genetic predisposition for wildlife. Edward O. Wilson, the father of sociobiology, calls this feeling for living forms and systems "biophilia," a term he borrowed from the psychologist Erich Fromm, author of *The Art of Loving*, who first described it as the passionate love of life and all that's alive.

Biophiliacs are devoted to furthering growth, whether in a person, a plant, an idea, or a culture. They love the adventure of living more than the certainty, and appreciate the whole as much as the parts. And though both Wilson and Fromm believe biophilia is innate, these days it also needs to be *activated*.

In attempting to activate my own inner biophiliac and hone my passion for life, I've found animals to be a great inspiration. Their appearance in my dreams alone has helped me unravel countless mysteries. The eagle that landed on top of my head, the bees that stung me in both ears, the whale that chased me to the bottom of the sea, the thirsty bear to whom I gave water, the deer I hunted while wearing a loincloth, the raging black bull I let out of its corral, and later tamed, the dragon I escaped only by waking up in the middle of the dream.

A dear friend of mine, Pripo Teplitsky, once told me a story about how an animal helped turn his life around. He was working as a corporate executive in his twenties, a job with which he became increasingly disenchanted—"Not my passion," he said—and one afternoon, while helping set up a conference room for a company presentation, he saw a spider frantically trying to get away from him, and sensed, almost, its panic and claustrophobia. Rather than leaving it to fend for itself, he chased after it with the intention of taking it outside.

After ten minutes of scrambling around on his hands and knees in the conference room, in his Armani suit, with his colleagues wondering what the hell he was doing, he finally caught the spider, cupped it in his hands, took it outside, and released it in the grass. "In that moment," he said, "I felt what I imagined the spider was feeling—finally free—and when I turned around to go back inside, I suddenly knew I was going to quit my job."

Animals themselves role-model authenticity, never straining to be what they're not, never making choices contrary to their nature. And such *grace*. The curvaceous savagery of stalking cats, the sinuous stride of giraffes, the schools of fish and flocks of birds that by the thousands all turn and catch the sun in the same split second, the band of devil rays I once saw while diving in Central America, gliding like enormous black butterflies out at the ghostly edge of invisibility.

And part of this grace, I think, lies in their complete lack of self-consciousness (so unlike myself), their utter disregard for appearances, with the exception of those times when they're involved in mating behavior and showing off is the order of the day. But animals don't even make the connection between sex and reproduction, so it's not like they're out there trying to make good Darwinian sense of their lives, concerned about or even conscious of improving the stock. They're just acting on the straightforward desire for sex and pleasure.

Maybe our own wildness is that part of us that cares nothing for appearances and is still capable of acting on the desire for pleasure.

Even in their failure to attain pleasures, animals are still mentors. The dog I had before Issa was part Lab and part greyhound and a fiend for the rabbits that populated the desert in southern Arizona, where I used to live. She would chase them at top speed until they ducked into a clutch of prickly pear cactus, at which point she'd slam on her emergency brakes and come to a screeching stop in a cloud of dust, oftentimes with a face full of thorns to show for the effort.

But she was *not once* deterred from the chase by failure, and she had a 100 percent failure rate. If I had a fraction of that determination—of that enthusiasm just for the hunt—I'd move mountains.

And it's not only their determination but also their sheer design that keeps us endlessly fascinated, and endlessly flattering with our sincere imitations, though the critters care nothing for it. The entire field of bionics, or biomimetics (as in the mimicry of nature), is a result of our hunger to tap into nature's ingenuity and the multiform wisdoms of wild engineering to help us solve problems in medicine, materials science, even social science.

Among the wild lives that have inspired human technology are the tiny hooks on cockleburs from which we get Velcro; the wings of lowly dung beetles, which can pull water from fog and which have given rise to fog-harvesting nets used in cooling towers and dry farming regions; the mosquito's proboscis, which speaks to us of hypodermic needles; the scalloped edges of whales' flippers, which show us how to make more efficient wind turbine blades and airplane wings; and the saliva of vampire bats, which has given us an anticoagulant called, appropriately, Draculin, which is twenty times stronger than any other known anticoagulant and prescribed for heart attack and stroke patients.

And not only science, of course, but also art and architecture have drawn inspiration from nature, as far back as the bone altars and cave galleries of the Neanderthal. At every level, the natural world is shot through with magnificent design. From the atomic to the microscopic to all the kingdoms and phyla of the organic world, from the undersides of mushrooms to the pinwheels of galaxies, it's spired and spiraled, helixed and fractaled, looped, scalloped, coiled, prismed, and curvaceous in a billion billion ways.

And though extinction ensures that every year we lose a handful of opportunities to be inspired by nature, we also gain new opportunities almost every day. Scientists just discovered two new species of lemur on the African island of Madagascar in the Indian Ocean, and three new species of monkey: one in the mountains of Bolivia, one in the mountains of northern India, and one in Tanzania. We're still discovering species of primates out there. Insects and bacteria, I can understand. Fish and plants certainly. But primates?

Scientists also recently discovered a new species of leopard in Borneo, a new species of possum in New Guinea, a new species of giant cobra in Kenya, and a species of rodent in Vietnam thought to have been extinct for eleven million years. To say nothing of the two thousand species of plants discovered every year on average, and the two hundred species of yeast recently discovered hiding out in the guts of beetles.

It's hard to believe that with as much exploring as we've done on this planet, and our assumption of nothing new under the sun, we'd still be finding species we've never seen. Earth has nowhere near given up all her secrets, and the opportunities for wild encounters are nowhere close to being exhausted.

I RECENTLY WENT on a guided trek through Corcovado National Park in Costa Rica, the largest and last tract of original tropical rainforest in the

Pacific Americas and which *National Geographic* calls "the most biologically intense place on earth." The guide spent hours pointing out and plucking out animals from the jungle that I would never have seen with my untrained eye, bringing the forest to life for me, showing me what nature must have looked like before it was trammeled by humanity—filled to cacophony with wildlife. I saw monkeys, sloths, peccaries, crocodiles, scarlet macaws, boa constrictors, orb spiders the size of my hand, and all in the span of a single afternoon.

It was certainly the most biologically busy place I'd ever seen, outside of a zoo, and what struck me most was the profound *otherness* of all these creatures and all these goings-on. The old trees weren't grandfathers, the hawks weren't messengers, the clouds weren't "sky people," the frogs weren't princes waiting to be kissed, and the creatures weren't totem animals. They were only and spectacularly *themselves*, not handy vehicles for my anthropomorphisms, projections, Disneyfications, sign reading, myth making, and meaning mongering.

Not that it isn't important to feel connected, if not stewardly, toward the natural world and the creatures in it, and to practice the kind of deep democracy that gives all life-forms a place at the bargaining table. But when we're not busy disassociating from them—and therefore ourselves— we're overidentifying with them, superimposing our lives onto theirs. We dress up the animals with pants and pocket watches, assign them speaking roles, and assume that just because we humans call one another snakes, weasels, chickens, pigs, sharks, and rats, that we know something about what it actually is to *be* a snake or a shark.

People talk about the desire to touch the spirit of animals, to whisper to them and have them whisper back. But this fantasy of cuddly spirituality has its limits. The spirit of animals is as feral as the creatures themselves, and the jungle is rife with organisms that are happy to reduce visiting tourists to their organic chemicals and essential amino acids given half a chance. It is itself an organism capable of digesting meat and machines with equal gusto, with an irrepressible appetite for anything left unguarded, tearing buildings apart with its muscular roots and vines, dissolving iron with its humid breath, and occasionally driving the mortals mad.

Let's face it. Wilderness is where the wild things are. And wild things are those we don't control. Nature has a savage history that's easy to overlook in the throes of reverie about its beauty and grandeur. It's not just some humanist's dream of harmony and unity, all its roads leading to a paradise of earthly accord and good vibrations. It's also a place of bloody battle, of competition and struggle, with some dying so that others can live. And these are struggles not in the service of grand or divine harmonies but of opportunism and reproductive success. Darwin said this: "We behold the face of nature bright with gladness . . . we do not see or we forget that the birds which are idly singing round us mostly live on insects and seeds, and are thus constantly destroying life."

The evolutionary biologist Stephen Jay Gould added this: "Nature does not exist for our delectation, our moral instruction, or our pleasure. Nature simply is what she is. Therefore, nature will not always match our hopes, nor supply the answers that our souls seek." It isn't always the refuge from the stresses of civilization that we fancy, or merely a scenic backdrop for our vision quests, though if it didn't have its dangers, a lot of folks wouldn't even bother with it.

There's a prevailing coffee-table-book mentality that imagines nature as pristine and picture-perfect and ready to go all Disney in time for our vacations. The waters are always sparkling and blue, the skies always ablaze with sunset, the flowers perpetually in bloom, and the animals grazing peaceably. Which isn't to say it doesn't often look like this. It does.

But it also looks like rain and sleet blasting sideways starting on the first day of your camping trip, whole swaths of forest blighted by disease, swarms of mosquitoes clouding the air, a thirty-mile-per-hour wind with ice in its fists pushing against you during your bicycle ride through the English countryside or your canoe trip in the Boundary Waters, mud that can suck the shoes off your feet, and animals that will kill you if you surprise them on a trail or step between them and their young. And as anyone who lives along a riverbank can tell you, rivers are crocodiles that every so often lunge up onto the shore to snatch homes and drag them under.

The indigenous, too, have their own savage history, and though they can certainly inspire us in our search to reestablish contact with lost kingdoms or latent virtues and vitalities, they shouldn't be overly romanticized either. The gospel of primitive harmony that we sing to raise our spirits and our hopes for humanity doesn't always square with the facts.

The !Kung San, a.k.a. Bushmen, of the Kalahari Desert, for example, are widely believed to be pacifists, and a famous ethnography of the tribe even called them "the harmless people." But anthropologists who live among them long enough find that between raiding, feuding, and vendettas, their homicide rate is three times that of the United States, and 20 to 80 percent higher than what's found in industrialized nations—whereas the "modern" nations of Switzerland and Sweden haven't engaged in warfare for nearly two centuries.

Don't fall into the trap of assuming that what's civilized is bad and what's indigenous is good, the contemporary shallow and the primitive deep, that once upon a time we were better than we are now and more noble, and what (little) we had then is superior to what have now. The statistics on life span and disease eradication alone should make us think twice about our fantasies of golden ages and gardens of earthly delight.

And don't buy wholesale the ever-popular story of how the world lost its magic. That once upon a time there was a land of milk and honey where lions lay down with lambs and God was in all the details, where innocence was a virtue, where *virtue* was a virtue, where ideals and heroes meant something, and where children were still free-range enough to collect a jar full of fireflies before coming in for supper. When suddenly, life's doorway was darkened by science, secularism, bureaucracy, consumerism, technology, and rugged and rampant individualism.

Not that we haven't lost a lot in coming of age, in our headlong rush to civilize ourselves and raise the drawbridge before those red in tooth and claw had a chance to follow us into the compound. But our nostalgia for a golden era of peace and inner wonderfulness is in danger of turning its nose up at much that's good and right about civilization and progress. Besides, there's no generic utopia about which everyone agrees. For one thing, it depends on whom you ask. To scientists, utopias are in the future. To poets and environmentalists, they're in the past.

For another thing, civilization is a stunning achievement, encompassing the entire social heredity of humankind and the vast libraries of knowledge we've wrested from ignorance. We ought to be awed by humanity's intelligence and adaptability and offer a brow-scraping bow to the beauty of its art and music, its architecture and literature, and the gorgeously unlikely parade of evolution that took us from bacteria in brine soup to human beings whose genius is at this moment riding shotgun on a spaceship hurtling past Pluto.

With nothing more than what was lying around outside when we were first set down here—dirt, rocks, water, plants, and animals—we figured out, in a flicker of geological time, how to communicate instantly with one another from opposite sides of the planet and how to get ourselves up onto the moon. And a million generations are yet to come. Any race capable of creating interplanetary spacecraft, long-distance surgery, Chartres Cathedral, replaceable body parts, and chocolate mousse is *worthy* of a deep bow.

Sometimes, sitting in my home office upstairs, listening to the winter wind whistle in the timbers or the hawks screech in the thermals, I feel something between insulated and isolated from nature, protected from the elements and disconnected from them. I like the warmth and stillness inside, the snugness, the things to which I can put my attention other than staying warm or dry or sheltered. But I also know that this drowsy comfort seeps into me as surely as cold or wet, and fuels the somnambulist walkabout that is suburban life.

Sometimes I open the sliding glass door and step out onto the deck, letting the cold wind mess up my hair and cool the fever of forgetting, giving in to the snarky part of me that always wants to be let outside and relishes the world's enlivening discomforts. Sometimes I'm afraid that if I don't stop holding my horses, I'm going to swell and burst, or build up so much quiet desperation that I end up doing desperate things.

If one part of us wants escape from nature, another wants to escape from the culture we've built that helps us do that, "the feather bed of civilization," Robert Louis Stevenson called it. First you can't keep 'em down on the farm, then it's back to the land. One day we want a cozy fire and the company of friends, the next we want to light out for the Territories, preferring the innocent brutalities of nature to the premeditated brutalities of humanity. The walls of our houses may be barrier reefs against the roaming wet maw of the world of nature, but on the same walls where we hang our paintings and our clocks, we also hack out windows, doors, and skylights so we won't feel like prisoners in our own homes.

Most of the time we stay put, warm and dry and comfortably coifed, content to look out the windows and try to keep the trickster gods from running tire tracks across our lawns. But the way we spend our days is the way we spend our lives, and most of the time that's inside, under lighting that's artificial, air that's forced, and computers that are slowly irradiating us. As the Canadian naturalist Trevor Herriot puts it, "Table manners are little consolation when something—a vagrant restlessness, an inclination of the remnant within walls for the wholeness without—stirs [your] memory of the veldt."

As my students also occasionally remind me, there's a part of us that's always flapping against the windows, trying to get out, that simply gets hungry now and then for a break from it all. From the buildings that block the sun and wind, the city lights that block the stars, the routines that block spontaneity, the roles and rituals we continually reenact that long ago emptied of their meaning, the sound of engines and clocks and sirens and the voice in the head whispering of elopement, the straight lines and stiff suits, the chairs, the cubicles.

We want a break from looking at the world through windows and the bars on windows, through a fog of nostalgia and the psychic equivalent of a peephole. We want out from whatever keeps us in and content with being in. And all this is fueled by a kind of cabin fever, by the rage against restraint and whatever it is in us that doesn't love a wall and wants it down, panting for freedom the way dogs strain at the leash and schoolchildren count down the seconds. The principle task of civilization, Freud once said, is to defend us against nature, but as Jay Griffiths says, "the human spirit, demented by claustrophobia, hates to be cooped up."

No matter how firmly barnacled we are to the civilized life—the urban rational linear life—and to rigidities moral, mental, physical, or sexual, our language alone gives away the depth of our identification with wildness. We speak of fertile imaginations, streams of consciousness, budding geniuses, webs of life, waves of emotion, oceans of sorrow, winds of war, dark nights of the soul, seeds of change, dirty minds, soiled garments, family trees, shell games, brainstorms, a wing and a prayer, and a ground of being. All this metaphoric talk. And a metaphor has but a single purpose: to establish unity. This is that. Life is a web. Consciousness is a stream. Ground is being.

And nature is true. In the dictionary, the first definition of the word *wild* is "natural," and the word *nature* comes from a word meaning "to be born." The hunger for wildness is the hunger for our natural-born state, the "true nature" we talk about when we talk about being *authentic*. Wildness isn't about acting crazy or emotionally explosive. It isn't even about venturing into the wilderness or doing wild-man-of-Borneo dancing in your living room. Ultimately, it's about being your natural-born self.

By following your deepest enthusiasms, for example, you help to realize the gifts with which nature endowed you and become as authentic as the animals are to themselves when they climb mountain crags only they can climb, or dive to ocean depths at which only they can survive.

Trees "struggle with all the force of their lives for one thing only," said Hesse. "To fulfill themselves according to their own laws, to build up their own form, to represent themselves. A tree says: I know nothing about my fathers. I know nothing about the thousand children that every year spring out of me. I live out the secret of my seed to the very end, and I care for nothing else."

Whoever has learned how to listen to trees, he added, "no longer wants to be a tree. He wants to be nothing except what he is. That is home. That is happiness."

4

A Spark Needs a Gap

Love and Passion

SEVERAL YEARS AGO I found myself wandering around my hometown of Asheville early in the evening on Valentine's Day. I had been dancing for hours at the Mardi Gras parade, was full of energy and not ready to go home, and as I came around a corner, a brunette in a French beret and very tight blue jeans came around from the other side. As we passed each other, she turned her head slowly, appraisingly, and said, "So where are *you* going?"

I looked in the direction I was heading, then back at her. "Just wandering." I said. "Why?"

"Would you like to have a drink with me?"

Moments later, we were sitting at the curved mahogany bar of a Latin club, and at one point the conversation turned to the fact that I had separated from my wife six months earlier, after a twenty-year marriage. "Oh, that's really sad," she said. "But being a guy, you're probably not in touch with that."

At which point I slapped my palm down on the bar and said, "Now wait a minute. I don't know you, and I don't know what kind of guys you normally hang out with, but I can tell you already that I'm not one of them. This has been one of the most excruciating events of my life and the single most difficult decision I've ever made. I'm painfully in touch with what I'm feeling, and 'sad' is definitely on my radar screen."

She apologized for her presumption and then did the most extraordinary thing. In one fluid motion, she slid down off the bar stool and took a single step toward me. Pressing her pelvis against my left hip, she reached up and cradled the right side of my face in her hand, pulled it toward her, and began kissing me gently and repeatedly on the left cheek and temple.

I went into a kind of altered state. Just to be touched. Like that. After so long.

Over the next couple of hours, she did this two more times, and on the third she stood in front of me while I sat on the bar stool, and her kisses moved from my cheek to the side of my lips, to the lips themselves, and then she stopped and looked up at me. "Are you . . . not into this?" she asked, because I wasn't responding with equal enthusiasm, though I was keenly aware that, no longer being married, I was free to act on this encounter if I wanted. The taboo was lifted, the curfew repealed.

"Oh, it's not that I'm not into this," I said. "Quite the contrary. But you have to understand: you're the first woman I've kissed, other than my wife, in twenty years. So this is kind of a big moment for me."

She smiled and sat back on the bar stool and shortly afterward said she had to be getting home, had to get up early for work the next morning. We walked, a little shaky on our feet, back to her car, and sat there for a few minutes, side by side, without speaking. Then I took her hand, kissed it, got out, and walked home.

We didn't exchange phone numbers, email addresses, last names, business cards, or bodily fluids. Just an exquisite connection that would not, in my opinion, have been improved by sex. It was perfect exactly as it was, and I didn't sense that either of us was disappointed in the course it took.

In reflecting on this marvelous encounter, I realized that this bold stranger had done me a great service: helping to reactivate that part of me that, by preference—though it feels more like necessity—I turn off in deference to being monogamous. The part that oversees the sowing of wild oats and the dissemination, no pun intended, of romantic and sexual energies toward women.

She also reminded me that (heterosexually speaking) vulnerability in men is an aphrodisiac. In the proper measure, of course. Too much of it can be construed as weakness and become a turnoff. Too little of it and you become a wall that incites women to hurl themselves against.

But in the realm of relationships, I've discovered countless times, there's an intimate correspondence between vulnerability and vitality, honesty and passion. That is, there are numerous kinds of nakedness, and the one that evokes the most ardor may not necessarily be the one that involves taking your clothes off, though it may involve taking your *armor* off.

Dropping below the superficiality and self-protection that attend so many of our encounters and into the deeper reaches of disclosure can, for instance, draw not only passion from another, as my Valentine's Day encounter demonstrated, but also compassion. And trust. And often recip-rocation. My willingness to lower the drawbridge gave my companion per-mission to lower hers, too, enabling us to draw intimacy out from behind its defenses and cross the moat between us.

The link between vulnerability and passion is one of the great under-rated truths of love, in my opinion, and to the degree we're interested in the fate of passion in our intimate relationships—especially in keeping it alive—it's critical to understand what inspires it and what defeats it.

A good starting point is recognizing that passion comes from the Latin *pati*, meaning "to suffer," originating with the Passion of Christ ("Love wounds," says novelist Jeannette Winterson. "There is no love that does not pierce the hands and feet.") And nowhere is the canonical connection between passion and suffering truer than in our love lives, where our end-less hunger for passion makes us suffer through its manias and losses, as well as the kinds of surrender—the letting down of our guard—required to evoke it and sustain it.

It may be true that the danger of suffering in love is nothing compared with the danger of refusing to risk vulnerability at all, and thus to never have fully lived and loved. But in the calculus of the heart, opening to love is big, not small, and full of implications that in our soberer hours are enough to send us running for the hills—the recognition that in letting down our cloaking devices and being revealed, we're giving someone else the power to mess us up.

Vulnerability, after all, is simply the capacity to be wounded, and if you refuse to ever be vulnerable, you deny yourself the experience of passion and compassion. You also risk drawing the attention of Anteros, brother of Eros and the god of revenge against those who *scorn* love.

Ultimately it's probably true that nobody is capable of messing you up without your permission—at least in matters of love, not war—but by following the passion that leads you into love to begin with, you're putting your heart in someone else's hands and you don't know where those hands have been. As Diane Ackerman writes in *A Natural History of Love,* "We equip someone with freshly sharpened knives; strip naked; then invite him to stand close. What could be scarier?"

It's no coincidence that the word *smitten*—which so aptly describes how most people experience certainly the early stages of passionate love—comes from the word *smite,* which for its first seven hundred years or so meant "to strike a blow," and for the past four hundred has also meant "to affect with strong feeling." This tells us that we experience affection for one another as something by which we're *struck.*

The god of love, after all, doesn't use love potions or magic spells to work his will. He uses *arrows.* And to the degree they bring us both passion and, by definition, the anguish attached to it, among the heroic tasks of love is refereeing their clash in full consciousness. On one hand, raising a happy ruckus about the joy love brings, actively acknowledging and celebrating it while you can. On the other hand, offering regular and humble bows to the chaos of love, the all-your-eggs-in-one-basket, pants-down-at-your-ankles vulnerability of it, and setting a place at the table for its confusions and disappointments, its hurts and betrayals.

The truth is that beyond a certain point in life—one reached, typically, early in the game—we *all* come to the table with stories of how we've been smited by love, how we've been love-struck. We bring with us our wounded prides and clobbered egos, our shattered illusions, our fears of loss—which, if you stick with love long enough, is *guaranteed*—and our absurd Newtonian expectation that our declarations of love will be met with equal and opposite reactions, or at least an amount of tenderness equivalent to the vulnerability we feel, which is quite possibly bottomless.

I recently ran across a cartoon showing a dog lying on a psychiatrist's couch. "He pretended to throw the ball," the dog said, "but he faked me out and I made a fool of myself. It was the most humiliating experience of my life. And that's when I started chewing slippers."

We bring to love the usual misgivings and misadventures that have tutored us in how it can come to ruin: I thought you were Prince/ss Charming, but you're not. I thought you could read my mind and anticipate all my needs, but you couldn't. I thought you'd cure my life, but you didn't. I thought you'd be the missing link, but you weren't.

"Few at the altar are conscious of the enormity of their expectations," says James Hollis, author of *The Middle Passage: From Misery to Meaning in Midlife*. "No one would speak aloud their immense hopes: 'I am counting on you to make my life meaningful.' 'I am counting on you to always be there for me.' 'I am counting on you to read my mind and anticipate all my needs.' 'I am counting on you to bind my wounds and fulfill the deficits of my life.' 'I am counting on you to complete me, to make me a whole person, to heal my stricken soul.' One would be too embarrassed, if one acknowledged them, by the impossibility of these demands."

The Logic of Passion

Reason isn't typically equated with passion. Some even believe that anyone who is sensible about love is incapable of it. And it's certainly no coincidence that the Romantic era of nineteenth-century Europe followed on the heels of the Age of Reason (a.k.a. the Enlightenment) in eighteenth-century Europe. It was a kind of correction, a swinging back of the pendulum. The relationship between passion and reason is one of point and counterpoint, or perhaps punch and counterpunch.

Passion is outright opposed to reason when it involves crimes of passion or revenge, obsessive and compulsive behavior, or passions that are self-destructive. Life and literature are full of it. Macbeth has a passion for the throne of Scotland, kills the king, attains the throne, and all hell breaks loose. Madame Bovary has a passion for adulterous affairs, gets bored with them all, goes on a monster shopping spree, can't pay the bills, and kills herself. Passion may be the wind that moves the ship, and reason the rudder, but passion can rip your sails with its gusto, and reason steer you in circles, or down the drain.

The Dutch humanist Desiderius Erasmus lamented that "Jupiter . . . has bestowed far more passion on us than reason—you could calculate the ratio as twenty-four to one." Modern neuroscience, however, puts the ratio closer to two to one. Of the brain's three command centers (the reptilian, mammalian, and neocortex), two out of the three—the reptilian and mammalian, collectively referred to as the emotional brain—take none of their orders from logic and are unswayed by the cajolings of rational argument or cussed willpower.

I'm tempted, for instance, to say that getting divorced after twenty years of marriage has shattered my illusions of love—my fantasies of finding a soulmate and living happily ever after, attaining knighthood on a white stallion, committing for better, for worse, and till death do us part—and that it upended the punch line of every nursery rhyme, fairy tale, myth, movie, book, television show, and love song about the all-conquering power of love to come down the pike since the days of the troubadours, and that ever entered my impressionable brain from infancy till now. But I don't think it really has shattered my illusions.

It's put a good-size dent in them, certainly, and sent me scuttling back to the drawing board and the books to try to figure out what I missed or misinterpreted. But those fantasies are more than durable enough to withstand the onslaught of even multiple divorces and innumerable heartbreaks. I know a woman who was married eight times, four of them to *the same man*—a triumph of hope over experience and passion over reason if ever there was one.

I remember asking my mother once how she felt about having two failed marriages, and she looked at me quizzically and said, "Failed? I learned a great deal from both of them."

And I remember my father declaiming, in what surely must have struck him as the product of sane and sober deduction, that after getting divorced from my mother, he was never going to get married again, no way. Five years later he was married again, propelled, no doubt, by the two-thirds of his brain to which reason meant nothing.

And like father, like son. After ending a twenty-year marriage, straightforward logic, if not sheer exhaustion, informed me that coupling up again any time before the next ice age would be insane. But no sooner had I dusted myself off, after about a year, no sooner had the moon and stars stopped spinning cartoonlike around my head, than I was off and running again, hunting and gathering, hungry for love, if not exactly coupledom.

How much of this impulse was to connect, how much to heal, how much to neutralize the pain, how much to *forget*, it was hard to say. But it was a juggernaut. And my reasoning mind, riding high atop the emotional brain, was nothing more than a baby on the back of an elephant.

And indeed I felt as though I was being carried off by some mammalian impulse that didn't concern itself with whether I was successful at rutting last season but cared only for *this* season, and that wanted to experience *wild* love, not socialized love and domesticated passion, not the housetrained heart. That wanted to climb down from the stone tower of my mind on a rope made of someone's hair.

And meanwhile my higher brain was pacing nervously up in the study and shouting denouncements—"You've got to be *kidding* me. What are you doing? Are you crazy? Have you no common sense?"—forgetting that common sense isn't the vocabulary of longing. That's a pidgin of hunger, loneliness, impulsiveness, passion, habit, instinct, and the urge to right yourself after a stumble. And something more: the hunger even *after* a meal. The kind that makes a twenty-year marriage feel like Chinese food that leaves you hungry two hours after you're finished.

If the lyrics to all of our Top Forty tunes were merged, says Hollis in *The Middle Passage*, it would sound like this: "I was miserable until you came into my life and then everything felt brand new and we were on top of the world until you changed and we lost what we had and you moved away and now I'm miserable and will never love again until the next time."

If hope springs eternal, as they say, so, too, apparently, does knuckleheadedness. But those supposed illusions and illogics of love, those scenarios we convince ourselves are the keys to happiness, are firmly cemented in the psyche. Along with our irrepressible belief that next time—with only a little more earnestness and better communication skills, and of course the right partner for once—we'll finally make love work, finally wrestle that fire-breathing angel to a draw.

"The madman," says G. K. Chesterton, "is not the man who has lost his reason. The madman is the man who has lost everything except his reason."

Not that passion doesn't have its own internal logic. A passionate life may ultimately be the most *rational* way to live, and though love can upset our orderly lives, it also keeps our priorities in order. "The heart has its reasons which reason knows nothing of," said the French writer Blaise

Pascal, who spent the first half of his career as a mathematician and scientist, tutored by René "I think therefore I am" Descartes, and the second half as a religious philosopher—going from a life of reason to a life of faith.

Consider the concept of idealization, which tells us that our passion for someone is proportionate to how closely he or she resembles our romantic ideal. Idealization—especially its early phase of uncritical appreciation, otherwise known as infatuation—may seem unrealistic and a setup for disappointment, which it often is, as we surround our beloveds with so much celestial white light that we ourselves are blinded. But the method in its madness may be that it helps keep us in the game long enough to *begin* a love relationship, conveniently drowning out the warning signals emanating from old wounds and doubts around intimacy, and just might give us something to *revive* down the road when difficulties arise—the experience of uncritical appreciation and admiration. Or as Ethel Person in *Dreams of Love and Fateful Encounters* puts it, if there's a place for blindness in love, it's later on, when wisdom instructs us to occasionally turn a blind eye on our partner's flaws and focus instead on their merits.

Fortunately, passion and optimism are renewable resources, though patience is sometimes required. It took Scheherazade 1,001 nights—three years—to evoke it in the sultan. But if it's stubborn, even cantankerous, passion is also an assertion of that part of us that senses the limitations of rationality, doesn't always want to be reasonable, and knows that if we were, we'd never talk ourselves into romance to start with, or ever put our heart at someone else's mercy, or even bring babies into this crazy world.

A friend of mine recently told me that she's suspicious of passion in her relationships because she believes it's proportionate to how hooked she is around her "father issues" with a man, and that passion is therefore subversive, suspect just on the face of it. But she also just split up with her boyfriend of a year because she "wasn't in love with him"—i.e., didn't feel the passion, two to one.

This isn't to say that passion is only or even primarily about being "in love," about romance and sex and chemistry. This, I think, is one of the great *overrated* ideas about love. When "the thrill is gone," it isn't just the court and spark that people miss. It's the sense of being desirable and valued, and the closeness. It's emotional libido as much if not more than sexual libido.

Passion is above all the hunger to *connect*, the desire for union, the capacity for relatedness. It's your deep affinity for and abiding interest in not only a special someone, but in life itself. And with the whole world as the apple of your eye, all of life becomes an aphrodisiac, all desire becomes tantric, a vehicle for transcendence, and the archetype of the lover—the part of you that presides over passion, feeling, sensuality, and responsiveness—can spread into every usable niche. "The problem is not desire," the Indian spiritual teacher Sri Nisargadatta once said. "It's that your desires are too small."

Enlarging them, being continually eager to discover something new under the sun, is a skill you practice inside and outside of a relationship, and they're mutually reinforcing. But it's a skill you practice first and foremost for *yourself*, not for anybody else or even for the bond between you—just for your own sense of engagement with the world.

Eros, meaning "desire," was what the ancient Greeks called a primordial god—first on the scene along with Chaos, Gaia (Earth), and Tartarus (Underworld)—and represents the creative urge in nature, the lamp beneath whose light all things come into being. He is life's longing for itself, the urge toward form and fruition, and his ancient nicknames are as apt today as they ever were: "liberator," "light bringer," "thunderer," "limb-loosener," and "he who runs on a path of fire."

To the degree that Eros reflects the desire for connection, the hunger to embrace the world and the chaos of the world, and the hidden interior worlds, the god takes many forms. Love is erotic, of course, but so is language, and self-reflection, and art in every form, and prayer. In fact, the love for a deity goes through the same phases of passion and suffering as the love for a mortal: initial discovery, awe and wonder, idealization and proselytizing, devotion and the willingness to make sacrifices on behalf of it, then doubts that infect your faith, the sense of disappointment, even betrayal, the fall from grace, the attempts to be reborn, etc. In other words, love going through its usual paces.

The Spanish novelist Miguel de Unamuno summed up the connection between divinity and adversity (passion and suffering) when he said, "Those who believe that they believe in God, but without passion in their hearts, without anguish in mind, without uncertainty, without doubt, without an element of despair even in their consolation, believe only in the God idea, not God Himself."

A Marriage of Sweet and Bitter

In June 2008, police were summoned to an apartment in Mesa, Arizona, after neighbors reported a fight between a man and woman that included screaming and breaking things. When they arrived, they found only a twenty-one-year-old man simulating a fight between a man and woman by alternating a low-pitched voice with a high-pitched voice.

He was, the report noted, referred for a medical exam.

We can probably all relate to the experience of feeling divided within ourselves, occasionally against ourselves, and love will certainly induce this as handily as any of life's experiences.

A little-known fact about Cupid may help explain this. He is said to have carried in his quiver *two* kinds of arrows, gold-tipped and lead-tipped. One struck you with love, the other with hate. In retribution for Apollo mocking his powers, Cupid struck him with one of his gold arrows at the same time that he struck the river nymph Daphne with one of his lead arrows. Apollo (the god of reason) was filled with desire, and Daphne with revulsion.

It seems we each carry the broken-off shafts of *both* of Cupid's arrows in our flesh, and must learn to manage their countervailing effects. The author Nancy Friday puts it in blunter terms: "Men may love women, but they are in a rage with them, too. I believe it is a triumph of the human psyche that out of this contradiction, a new form of emotion emerges, one so human it is unknown to animals even one step lower on the evolutionary scale: *passion*."

This same tangle of love and lamentation, joy and suffering, surely goes for women as well as men, but the point is that we're pitted against ourselves, and each other. A relationship will always be both safe harbor and storm. It will always challenge us to burn without being consumed, to have and to hold without possessing. And love and passion will always be difficult to uphold in partnership because they work toward different goals. Love wants assurances, passion wants abandon. Love wants to be soothed, passion wants to be stimulated. Love wants to go steady, passion wants to be swept away.

These impulses working at such cross-purposes can spell trouble for romance because, among other things, it's hard to stay worked up over the same person you look to for safety and security, and the truth is that most people consider it a fair trade to swap heat for warmth and passion for companionship. Nor is romance even something everyone misses as time goes by. For some, respect or loyalty or friendship are the overriding virtues of love, and serenity rather than passion the state they seek to cultivate.

But the missing link in our understanding is that love isn't an either/or equation, though we've been told it is: you either have passion or serenity in a relationship, but not both. You either have sex and romance or companionable bonding, but not both. You either have freedom or commitment. You either have *Wuthering Heights* or *The Remains of the Day.*

But it's not either/or. It's both/and. There are *two* right answers to the question of sustaining desire in relationship, not one.

Try this exercise, compliments of Barry Johnson, founder of a system called Polarity Management: breathe in and hold the air in your lungs as long as possible. It feels good for a while, but then as the oxygen turns into carbon dioxide, you begin to crave air. Now exhale. It feels good for a while, but as you blow your breath out, it begins to feel suffocating.

It's the same with all the polarities in relationship. They're tensions to manage, not problems to solve. If one side wins over the other, the organism loses, and the relationship loses. In a sense, evolution itself loses. In most creation myths the world over—the stories that people of nearly all cultures have used to explain their origins and that are really about the birth of consciousness—unity inevitably evolves into opposites. If this didn't happen, life would come to a standstill. The development of consciousness, these stories tell us, requires opposition, polarity.

Nor is relationship a shuttling between only two antipodal states. It's a mosh pit of emotions. Intimate relationship flushes so many different feelings up to the surface, sometimes in rapid succession—desire, vulnerability, anxiety, aversion, anger, guilt, sorrow, ecstasy, gratitude—that to appreciate if not reap the richness of it all, we have to sit zazen with each of them and not push any of them away, immersing ourselves in the flow of it all. Now this, now this, now this.

Maintaining equilibrium, and thus passion, requires a skill I once heard described as "heroism redefined for the modern age." And that is the ability to tolerate paradox, to hold two contrary forces or impulses or ideas or beliefs inside you—and your relationships—at the same time and still retain the ability to function, if not hold on to your cookies. Security *and* passion, commitment *and* freedom, head *and* heart, love *and* hate, us *and* them.

A college professor of mine once said that the basis of every story ever written or told could be summed up in one phrase: "two worlds collide." And these two worlds don't cancel each other out. They're *both* true. And they both need to be brought to the bargaining table to hammer out a treaty that serves them both, rather than trying to stuff one or the other of them under the floorboards just for the relief of it, just to be rid of the conflict.

Besides, the ability to hold paradox builds tremendous resilience into people and their relationships and diplomacies. The ability to stretch yourself wide enough to encompass both or even many sides of an issue naturally mitigates against tyranny, both within and among people, because it refuses to elevate one side at the expense of the other. It holds them both. It tolerates the tension between them long enough to allow them to inform and educate one another, and perhaps even arrive at a treaty.

Another way of saying this is that it's critical to be able to feel *ambivalent* about love and yet proceed with it.

The poet Stephen Dunn writes that "Love at noon that was still love at dusk meant that doubt had been subjugated for exactly that long."

I saw a perfect analogy for the soar-and-dive emotional ride that is passionate relationship while I was in California last year. I was hiking in Topanga Canyon, one of the many that empty out of the coastal mountains right onto the beaches north of LA. While standing on a huge rock outcropping at the edge of a cliff, I saw a hummingbird rise up right in front of me, maybe twenty feet out past the edge of the cliff, and hover there. Then it rose higher and higher, until it was a good hundred feet above me, and suddenly dove at what scientists have clocked at sixty miles an hour straight down, past where I was standing, a hundred feet down the face of the cliff. Then it swooped upward in an aerial maneuver so sudden its g-force would easily black out a fighter pilot with its rush of blood away from the brain. Once again, it positioned itself right in front of me and hovered there in mid-courtship dance.

Then it rose and swooped again and again, a dozen times, rising straight up and diving straight down, and all the while I was whooping and hollering with the sheer thrill of it.

It seemed a perfect illustration of the pitch and roll of emotions in love relationships, the highs and lows, the rushing of blood between the heart and the brain. One moment lighthearted, the next light-headed.

But the heroic skill of holding paradox, the endless struggle between two things that are each 100 percent true and completely at odds with each other, is not some parlor game or IQ test, some pose you strike in front of a mirror to see how you look while doing it. It's ferocious and dizzying work, something you do at the edge of a cliff.

Fittingly, Anne Carson, in a book called *Eros the Bittersweet*, quotes the ancient Greek poet Sappho, who called desire not bittersweet but "sweet-bitter"—the sweet coming first, then the bitter. The kiss, then the pow.

However, Carson believes that Sappho didn't actually mean to imply that things unfold chronologically, but rather simultaneously, and that she only put *sweet* before *bitter* because it's the more obvious aspect of eros. The truth, as Carson sees it, is that if you split open any moment of desire and look inside, you'll find seeds of both sweetness and bitterness.

If you cross-section any relationship you'll find the same thing, say Charlie and Linda Bloom, who believe that the most critical aspect of a successful relationship is the ability to hold the tension between sweet and bitter. If the word *passion* means "to suffer," and *suffer* means "to bear," a truly passionate relationship is one in which the partners actively if not always gracefully bear with all that love presents. Not just the exuberant and the exultant but also the fearful and sorrowful, the unfulfilled and incompatible, the turning of interest to disinterest and knight in shining armor to couch potato who won't stop leaving his whiskers in the sink.

This is a lesson the Blooms did not learn gracefully, just determinedly, and the events that began unfolding roughly ten years into their forty-four years together are a perfect case in point.

"I thought I had picked so carefully to get a laid-back guy who wasn't going to be hard-driving like my dad," said Linda. "But when we relocated to the West Coast, Charlie became a corporate guy and had what I considered a personality transformation. This laid-back guitar-pickin' hippie who was going to help me raise the kids all of a sudden became this corporate-climbing guy walking around in a three-piece suit, and I didn't really like him very much.

"He was also on the road three weeks out of every month when the kids were small, and I was really pissed. I mean, deep fury. And it went on for years. It turned out we had some basic values differences, and our worlds were colliding. I wanted to be all about family life and sitting down to dinner together, alternating who cooked meals, and I wanted him to coach the Little League team, and I was really attached to that vision with a white-knuckle grip. Charlie was on a totally different path. It was a time of great suffering for me. I was pretty sure we weren't going to come through those years with an intact family, and it drove me up the wall that he was willing to risk that. I was upside-down about it."

Charlie was also a totally different kind of *person*, and the differences between the couple added to the stew. "In most of our personality traits," said Linda, "we were at opposite ends of the spectrum. I'm detail-oriented, Charlie is a generalist. I favor strict parenting, Charlie doesn't. I'm outgoing, Charlie is more of an introvert. I go to bed early, he stays up late. I like to get to the airport with hours to spare, whereas a fifteen-minute wait is too much for him. I believe in planning and preparation, Charlie favors spontaneity. I seek connection when I'm stressed, Charlie solitude. My strength is commitment, his is letting go. I'm a talker, he's a thinker. I manage money, he spends it."

The path that Charlie was on involved facilitating personal-growth trainings around the country, under the auspices of a company called Lifespring, dedicated, as he put it, to helping people "claim the disowned parts of themselves that were keeping them emotionally stunted." He believed it was the work he was born to do, and he was doing it on the fast track. "I told myself that I was one of the fortunate few who had the opportunity to do this cutting-edge work and that of course certain sacrifices had to be made.

"Unfortunately, Linda didn't seem to appreciate the 'realities' of our situation. She frequently reminded me how difficult it was for her and the kids with me on the road so much. My response was usually to encourage her to 'be strong' and 'use this experience as a growth opportunity' and 'be a good example to the kids.'"

Her response, which she usually kept to herself but not always: "That lousy son of a bitch. He's deserted us, abandoned us, left his children, broken his agreement with me. I should ditch the jerk. Any self-respecting feminist would have left already. Call the divorce lawyer."

This was compounded by the encouragement of a number of friends who felt she should do just that. "There are a lot of people with failed relationships," Charlie said, "who want to be right about how impossible relationships are. And some of them are marriage counselors."

Linda, however, wasn't willing to "get off of her resistance" as Charlie requested, and "get with the program." Her ongoing message was "It's not working," he said. "But despite increasing evidence to back her up, my basic response was, 'Handle it. Can't you see I'm busy?' But I wasn't just busy. I was gone."

And their marriage, nearly so.

"Almost all the trainers involved in Lifespring lost their marriages," Linda said. "We were one of only two couples in the company who didn't. The environment just didn't support marriage. The primary allegiance was to the company. And then there was all the ego inflation, the belief among the students that the trainers all walked on water. And they believed it. Being away from home and partner and family, the marriages just withered from neglect."

Then, at two separate couples retreats, Charlie and Linda each had a wake-up call, and things began to change.

The first was at a workshop facilitated by the Buddhist teacher Stephen Levine, whom Linda knew Charlie admired, and which she took him to "to get him fixed. I thought they were going to nail him to the wall: 'Look, you've got a wife and little kids. Why don't you stay home and take care of business.' But it was *me* who got nailed.

"Stephen said, 'It looks like you're pretty attached to what this family and this marriage need to look like. And I think you've got some work to do.' Maybe he thought I was just getting in my own way and reinforcing my own victimhood by seeing it the way I was seeing it. But he gave me an assignment of nonattachment and forgiveness—for myself for being irritable with the children, for being the nagging and demanding wife, and for Charlie for not being the husband of my dreams.

"My favorite fairy tale as a child was Cinderella, so when I met Charlie and fell in love with him, I thought my prince had come. But these kinds of fantasies are a setup for expectations that are impossible to fulfill, and when they don't get fulfilled, the passion can just drain out of a relationship, and the boredom and anger can set in. Some people might say there was plenty of passion in our relationship because we were fighting so much, but I wouldn't say that was the good kind to have. I was so distressed about how my life didn't look anything like I expected and wanted it to, and the fighting and resentment just eroded our goodwill.

"We argued and manipulated, blamed and shamed and threatened and carried on and screamed and didn't listen, and we weren't skilled at speaking vulnerably with each other, and we called each other names, and when you're both therapists, you can really insult people by diagnosing them. But we paid attention, and there *was* a lot of love there, and I had a dogged determination about not quitting. And what I never did was hold it inside. People get so toxic with unexpressed resentment that it finishes them off. We almost burned the relationship to a crisp, but we didn't withhold.

"Out of the fifty percent of marriages that *don't* end in divorce, you've got to wonder how many of those people are really living in fulfilling, satisfying relationships, where they're truly delighting in it. And I would guess less than ten percent. Not that they're miserable, but they're just not experiencing what they *hoped* to experience. And they often think the other person is going to bring the passion and aliveness and creative juice to their life, and they get resentful when they don't, rather than rising up to a higher level of responsibility and realizing that it's up to *them* to create it.

"The secret of a great marriage is that both people take responsibility for their own happiness and bring their happy selves to the relationship. They know what lights them up, and they're on it. Partners may not even have interests in common, but they have interests. They're engaged and impassioned with their own lives and bring that passion into their relationship and uplevel the whole enterprise.

"So ultimately I had to deconstruct that Cinderella fantasy of mine and face love as it actually was, including the concept that a relationship could die. It doesn't necessarily just get better and better and better, and the trust higher and higher and higher. It's a mixture of golden periods with dark periods, and sometimes outright tortures of the damned. But what had the most profound impact for us in keeping the passion alive might have been the switch I made in the midst of that crisis: making more room for the shadow parts, not believing that the relationship was irreversibly damaged and that I might as well just dump it and cut my losses and start over with someone new. Which is where I'd been going.

"I formed a different vision in my mind, realized I could make something good out of this, that it wasn't just a tragedy and a wreck. I learned that I could stand on my own two feet, make decisions, manage my life, and run the kids like a single mom when Charlie was gone. It was a tremendously strengthening time for me, and I created a much more realistic model for what relationship really is. It isn't all about comfort and security and happily ever after, isn't all about warm, fuzzy, feel-good pleasure. That's part of it, but if you're just going for that, you're in for a lot of trouble.

"During those years, I ran across a story that served me well and gave me a visual for what I was living. A king has a diamond that's his favorite possession, and somehow it gets scratched, and it's so deep that the lapidaries can't buff it out. So he finally sends for the most famous lapidary in the land, who lives at the far edge of the kingdom. He comes and makes the scratch down the middle of the diamond into the stem of a beautiful rosebud, and the king is pleased. And the diamond is even more beautiful than it was before it sustained the damage.

"This story helped because I had no conception of how a relationship as damaged as ours could ever be beautiful again. And my despair came from that, from not having the vision of another possibility."

The second wake-up call was Charlie's, and it took place on the Saturday before his fortieth birthday, at a couple's retreat Linda insisted they attend. "It was strange to be in the student's seat for a change," Charlie said. "Stripped of the protection of my facilitator role, I felt vulnerable and exposed, almost panicky, anticipating what I knew I couldn't control. And when it was our turn to share, Linda almost immediately dissolved into a pool of tears, and before I knew what was happening, the facilitator invited us both into the center of the circle.

"We sat facing each other, and I grudgingly reached out to take her hands at the request of the facilitator. I wanted to be anywhere else in the world than in the middle of that circle of people, who would soon be witnessing the pain, anger, and shame that we'd been dancing around for God knows how long.

"Linda went first. Looking into my eyes, as though we were the only people in the room, she talked about her loneliness, her fear that we might not make it, her concern that the kids weren't getting the time they needed with me, and the exhaustion she was beginning to feel crushed by. And for once I was listening, rather than trying to 'fix' her. I really heard her for the first time, and it didn't feel good. It felt horrible.

"Then to put the icing on the cake, the facilitator invited the men in the room who had been in my shoes to tell their stories and what they'd experienced when their day of reckoning finally came. And though I'd known these things on an intellectual level, and had been teaching about them for years, hearing these men share their stories was like hearing it for the first time, and it went straight to my heart and cracked it all the way open. I broke down like I never had in my life and wailed like a baby. And it wasn't just for all the lost and irretrievable moments, the grief and the guilt, but also in gratitude and relief. And I kept hearing the same phrase over and over in my mind: 'It's not too late. It's not too late.'

"After what seemed like hours, I looked up at Linda, who also had tears streaming down her face, and she looked more beautiful to me than I'd ever seen her.

"'It's over,' I said.'"

Two days later he gave notice at Lifespring, and he and Linda began a recovery process that would eventually lead them to begin teaching workshops called Partners in Commitment and authoring books with titles like *101 Things I Wish I Knew When I Got Married* and *Secrets of Great Marriages*. The theme of their work now is "Stronger at the broken places," a phrase borrowed, appropriately enough, from Hemingway's novel *A Farewell to Arms*: "The world breaks everyone and afterward many are strong at the broken places."

Some of those broken places showed up for Charlie in the year following his fateful decision to leave corporate life, and included a loss of income, ego gratification, and personal identity, and a deep and yearlong depression during which, he says, "I confronted some of my vulnerabilities and realized that I wasn't merely a separate unit operating independently in the world but very much interdependent if not dependent on people.

"When you're committed to growth and have a certain intolerance for anything that mutes your sensibilities and vitalities and makes you fall into complacency, this is a more dangerous path than the one that leads to security, control, safety, and predictability. Your self-image is at risk, your attachment to your belief about who you think you are, your investment in being validated. And your relationship doesn't always validate the picture you have of yourself.

"But that risk, that edge, is part of what intensifies passion. And those who keep passion alive in their relationships are not only more committed to growth than to comfort, but more in touch with the conflict between passion and security, between feeling safe and feeling challenged."

Frustration Attraction

There's a principle in Japanese garden design called *miegakure*, or hide-and-reveal, in which only a portion of any object is exposed, never the whole of it. A teahouse is partially hidden behind an arbor, a creek comes in and out of view, the main body of rocks are set deep in the ground, gardens are partly concealed by lanterns and fences.

The idea is that revealing only parts of the whole helps keep the viewer's interest peaked, teasing the imagination and giving it a little mystery to figure out, and in a sense expanding the garden beyond its merely physical dimensions.

This is the same principle that explains why partial nudity is often more alluring than full nudity—the transparent blouse that suggests the contours of her breasts, the bath towel slung low over his hipbones. It's the same principle that explains why, in the *Iliad*, the Greek poet Homer never felt the need to actually describe Helen of Troy's legendary beauty, though it was capable of launching a thousand ships. He merely tells us that as she passes, old men along the walls of Troy whisper that it is no discredit for Trojans "to suffer long anguish for a woman like that." She's otherwise left to the imagination of each reader.

In other words, what's concealed incites the imagination and stokes desire because something is withheld from us. Something we want.

If we want passion in our relationships, it behooves us to stay hungry. To build in a little anticipation from time to time, the occasional partings that make the heart grow fonder, a little healthy distance from each other, and the understanding that the essential paradox of love—and the critical ingredient in erotic relationship—is that connection requires separateness, and to not merely tolerate but celebrate that space between as well. The heart, after all, is also a private part, and is enhanced by mystery and seduction. And if cultivating separateness feels too hard-boiled, think of it as cultivating selfhood, which is the best thing you can do for the health of a relationship anyway.

My father once built a contraption in the basement of the house where I grew up, an electrical generator called a Tesla coil, crowned with two vertical copper wires between which a purple spark would jump. Whether electricity is moving between two poles or two people, the same principle applies: a spark requires a gap. If there's no gap, there's no sizzle. If there's no synapse to cross, the charge between partners can't ignite, or stay lit.

Although one of the most common insights from our spiritual traditions is the boundary-dissolving revelation that "it's all connected," a certain amount of separateness is still an operational necessity. You may feel one with Earth, but if you walk off a roof, you're still going to go splat when you hit the ground. You may feel united with humanity in a great puppy pile of love, but if you grab somebody else's girlfriend, you're likely to get a black eye. And you may romanticize togetherness—the two shall be as one; you complete me; I'm no one without you; one flesh, one heart—but fusing into an indistinguishable gob of attachment is not true intimacy; it's cannibalism. Thus the lover's refrain, "I could just eat you."

This idea of boundaryless union may appeal to the romantic in us, as well as to our spiritual visions of oneness and our prenatal memories of blissful unity, but in the rubber-meets-the-road world of grown-up relationships, it's called enmeshment. Fusion of the sort that makes it hard for people to discern where they leave off and others begin, to hang on to the singularity of their own self amid their efforts to solder two into one.

Meditators often speak of seeking "the gap between thoughts," those split seconds of silence and stillness, of inner space. And they speak of the attempt to expand these gaps, which isn't so much an expansion of absence as much as it is of *presence*. Ultimately the point is to infuse the density of daily life with more space, more elbow room amid our endless churn of thoughts, overcrowded in-baskets, and enmeshed relationships— the same way that giving yourself a little space between the main course and the dessert allows your brain to register how full it is and thus meter out how much more food it can handle without feeling bloated. Good way to lose some weight too.

But how comfortable you feel with the concept of the gap may depend on how you feel about the experience of separation generally, which at a primal level none of us are entirely comfortable with. Buried deep in the mud at the bottom of human consciousness is the memory of how to survive, and parting with the herd is not the way to do it.

It also depends on how your parents met the challenge of helping you separate from *them* (ideally, says Hollis, "offering reassurance while progressively 'abandoning'"). If your initial attempts at autonomy were met with resistance, or punished rather than rewarded, you might naturally have concluded that independence is dangerous and separation threatening to your connection with others. And this will determine how secure or insecure you'll be when it comes time to create and manage your own relationships, and how gracefully you'll balance the twin tasks of connection and separation. And for better or worse, we tend to assume that the world at large works the same way our family did.

Granted, some relationships may be characterized by too *much* gap rather than too little, as the Blooms experienced in their early years. Partners may feel like the proverbial ships passing in the night, or spend the majority of their time together but be emotionally divorced. They may feel they can't rely on each other, or feel lonely together, living parallel lives that only occasionally intersect.

In these cases, passion is continuously thwarted and turns bitter rather than sweet. In other words, that essential paradox of love (connection requires separateness) can also be the essential *power struggle* of love (that between connection and autonomy), and raise a question every couple must answer for themselves: How much space is enough? When does independence enhance passion and when does it snuff it out?

It can, of course, be difficult to even *broach* the subject of separateness with a partner—especially one with whom you're power-struggling over how much time to spend together—without it coming across as "I need some space," which most people hear as rejection, a prelude to a kiss-off. But as long as you're not enmeshed in distance-pursuer dynamics, passion is served by a little separation.

I've read that the isolation of certain of the world's islands, on which whole classes of predators don't evolve, makes them hothouses for the remaining flora and fauna, which often grow with great and exotic profusion for having fewer enemies around. The energies that would otherwise go to camouflage and self-protective behavior are turned instead toward creativity and luxuriance.

Similarly, a certain amount of decamping within a relationship, the occasional migration from togetherness, might serve love's exuberance— as long as it doesn't turn fatally inward. If our retreats are counterpoised with *advances*, and we return from them bearing the gifts of our solitude, then our leave-takings aren't likely to backfire, or turn into habits of evasion. But there's an art to intuiting when you're hiding out and when you're recharging, whether you're running from or toward someone, and when "parting makes the heart grow fonder" begins to devolve into "out of sight out of mind." And this art requires constant attentiveness, and once again the willingness to hold paradox: vigilance is stressful; long live vigilance.

THE REASON why a spark requires a gap, however, has to do with the physics of desire, which is predicated on *lack*. You want what you don't have, and once you get it, you're no longer wanting, so the desire fades. Getting what you want subverts the thrill of wanting it, and the law of diminishing returns tells us that the more you do something, the less satisfaction you gain from it. Eating your favorite meal a dozen times in a row will tend to diminish its charms, as will spending every day with the same person. It's no coincidence that the mother of Eros, god of love, was Penia, whose name means "poverty" or "deprivation" in Latin.

Part of what stokes us up about *new* love is the challenge of it, the quest for fire, but when we've reached our goal and gotten the girl/guy, the challenge evaporates, and with it some of our interest in the game. When the amphetamines of longing are no longer rushing through our bloodstreams, and are replaced by the sedatives of safety and security, or at least familiarity, we tend to let ourselves go and take our partners for granted, diminishing our returns.

One of the influential story lines of romantic love, which picks up in eleventh-century upper-crust Europe, tells that romance was sustained because the couple—usually a knight and a lady of the court—remained chaste, thus in a perpetual state of yearning. These were typically adulterous affairs, and since marriage in that time and place had little to do with love, it was a way for people to express the love not typically found in their marriages. But physical consummation was rare, and what kept the passion alive was precisely non-consummation, and of course the fact that fantasy rarely encountered the disillusionments of reality—his dishes heaped in the sink, her clothes always in piles on the floor.

I attended a psychology conference in San Francisco years ago, and during the dance party on the last night, a woman came up behind me and blindfolded me, wrapped her arms around my waist, and danced with me that way for an entire song. When it was over, she took off the blindfold but asked me to please not turn around and look for her. When I finally looked around, whoever she was was gone and no one was looking at me expectantly. It was tremendously erotic.

Desire is like the unknown. As soon as you plant your flag there, it's no longer the unknown. And though it's an endlessly self-canceling quest, you have to keep setting your sights on new horizons, new desires and challenges, because it's what you *don't* know that propels you toward discovery. This, of course, could be problematic for a relationship—and your love life in general—if you keep setting those sights *outside* it rather than inside, always toward the next and the next person, place, or thing.

But desire doesn't ultimately want to be quenched and go out, to settle for mere possession or mere contentment. It wants to be lit and relit. It's the nature of the beast. It wants yearning, not satisfaction. It wants to occupy the space between our reach and our grasp—that cleft in the rocks through which the waters pour.

I did a consultation recently with a woman who had spent the past ten years searching for her passion, her sense of calling and purpose, for what she called "the be-all and end-all." And actively searching, not passively. She'd gone to massage school, pastry school, art therapy school, written half a dozen children's books, and more. All of them had eventually ended in boredom.

At the end of our hour-long conversation, she mentioned that a friend had recently suggested she might be good at a research profession, and indeed, she said, "I seem to do my best in learning situations."

I then suggested that she'd already *been* following her calling for the past ten years, without even realizing it, by doing *research* about her passions. And that perhaps one reason she may not have found a be-all and end-all is that that wasn't what she was really after; instead, it was the process of looking for it.

Anyone who's ever played tug-of-war with a dog over a length of rope knows that the moment you let go of the rope, the dog doesn't run away with it or bury it in the backyard. He trots back to you with it. What he wants isn't the rope; it's the *tugging.*

Desire, then, must be continually frustrated and given something to tug on, must partake of an age-old dynamic in the erotic arts: elusiveness. The fan that veils the face, the sideways glance, the tease, the blindfold, the game of hard-to-get. As they say, when there's nothing left to hide, there's nothing left to seek. "The most attractive," says Alain de Botton in *On Love,* "are not those who allow us to kiss them at once . . . or those who never allow us to kiss them . . . but those who know how to carefully administer varied doses of hope and despair."

Delayed gratification intensifies desire, and this is not just an emotional fact but a biological one. It stimulates the activity of dopamine, one of the brain's natural stimulants and kin to adrenaline.

Unfortunately, the whole notion of commitment is based on the chase coming to an end, in a conquest and a surrender, and though the very sexiness of desire comes precisely in what's behind the veil and in the gratifications that are delayed, once we've settled down, we no longer really *want* anything hidden from us, or want our gratifications delayed. We don't *want* to be kept guessing anymore, wondering where we stand, wondering what comes next, tossing and turning at night. We want the veil swapped for an apron. We want to exchange roses by the dozen for slippers by the bed.

We may crave fixity from our "secure attachments," especially in a world that seems to us halfway off its hinges, but fixity comes at a price, which is often the loss of our libidos and the evisceration of our passions and life force.

Many people, including those in the psychoanalytic fields, also assume security to be a trademark of commitment, and passion and romance as passing fancies, necessary if adolescent phases on the way to "mature" love, which is characterized, somewhat antiseptically, as a steady state of companionable affection, mutual respect and trust, shared values, and common interests. Which is good work if you can get it, but it's not like you're guaranteed this state of affairs if you can just get through the romantic phase intact.

As for the widespread assumption that commitment equates with stability, does the 50 percent divorce rate tell us anything about how stable marriage is? (This is a wildly deceptive statistic, by the way. The hidden numbers reveal that eighteen-year-old newlyweds have a divorce rate close to 75 percent, blowing the curve for everyone, while those who marry in their fifties and up have a divorce rate closer to statistical insignificance.) Also, how many of us actually grew up in families that were bastions of safety and security, where our parents were paragons of maturity and dependability, and oneness reigned supreme?

A friend of mine recently told me that she longs for a long-term relationship rather than the on-and-off dating she's become accustomed to. "My heart feels ready to rest," she said. Having just come out of a twenty-year marriage, I said to her that I wasn't convinced a long-term relationship actually offered much by way of rest for the heart, even in the good years, but that I hoped she'd find what she's looking for.

Had I felt more cynical, I could have quoted to her from *Love, Etc.* by Julian Barnes: "Love leads to happiness. That's what everyone believes, isn't it? That's what I used to believe, too, all those years ago. I don't anymore. You look surprised. Think about it. Examine your own life. Love leads to happiness? Come off it."

I recently ran across an interesting commentary on the assumptions we often bring to our investments and how easy it is to overestimate our return on investment. An artist named Michael Fernandes had an exhibit in Halifax, Nova Scotia, which consisted of his placing a banana on the windowsill of a gallery. He priced it at 2,500 Canadian dollars, which is how you know it's art rather than just produce, since non-art bananas go for a modest 67 cents a pound.

Fernandes's intention was to make a statement about impermanence. In fact, he ate the banana daily, replacing it with a greener one, to simulate a reversal of the aging process. At one point, two art collectors vied for the privilege of owning this artwork, prompting the gallery owner to clarify what it is they'd be getting for their money: "It's a banana. You understand that it's a banana."

Actually it's not even that. Once the banana goes the way of all flesh, what their $2,500 will have bought is merely the *concept* of a banana, or perhaps the *memory* of a banana.

I don't mean to denounce the concept of security, or the desire to merge. Integration with others is as essential and admirable a goal as individuality, according to psychiatrist and author Peter Kramer, who speaks eloquently of what he calls "relational heroism," people who have a gift, a genius even, for reaching, understanding, and nurturing others. "To feel connected (when there is genuine give-and-take) is to feel zest, vitality, validation, clarity, worth, empowerment."

The dream of connectedness, after all, has given rise to every utopian commune and collective in human history, and as anyone who's ever been in one can attest, you need a heroic spirit to bring that dream down to earth and make it bloom in the hands of actual human beings, who are so ambivalent about connectedness and been so often wounded by it, and whose spiritual agendas routinely shipwreck themselves on their personal agendas.

Still, no matter how fixed our sense of security, no matter how wedded we are to the idea of togetherness if not oneness, the gap is a fixture of life, whether or not we acknowledge it or exercise it. To the ancient Greeks, it was the actual definition of *chaos*—a void, an emptiness, but most crucially the primordial potential from which all things arise.

In most of the world's creation stories, chaos is described as the state of the world before it was formed, meaning that *chaos precedes creation*. If you deny yourself chaos, you'll deny yourself creation. If you avoid the gap, and whatever anxieties get stirred up as you either contemplate or cultivate it, you'll deny yourself and your partner the chance to discover what's in that wide-open space—literally new worlds.

"Our ability to tolerate separateness—and the fundamental insecurity it engenders," says Esther Perel in *Mating in Captivity: Unlocking Erotic Intelligence*, "is a precondition for maintaining interest and desire in a relationship."

But humans have a kind of psychic blind spot that tends to direct our attention always toward the something rather than the nothing, the fullness rather than the emptiness, the words rather than the eloquent silences between them, the swaying boughs rather than the wind that does the moving. In his poem "The Uses of Not," Lao-tze, author of the *Tao Te*

Ching, says, "Pots are formed from clay, but the empty space is the essence of the pot."

This suggests a potentially gear-shifting insight: insecurity and empty spaces are already and always present in our relationships in the form of *impermanence,* the fact that we stand to lose our shirts in love, and that we *will* lose them—guaranteed. Therefore, a meditation on ephemerality is deeply practical and may turn into a gratitude meditation that brings passion and presence back into our lives and our love affairs.

I'm reminded of the story of a couple who, for their tenth anniversary, went to New Zealand to technical-climb a waterfall, and when they reached the summit, as they were exulting in their triumph and their love, he turned momentarily away from her, and when he turned back . . . she was gone. Just like that. She'd slipped and fallen.

Those we love will, sooner or later, slip from us forever, into the impermanence that's a natural feature of the landscape of life, the gap that's always there between them and us, no matter how much we love them, and whether we're ready or not.

Hollis begins *The Eden Project* with this line: "All relationships begin, and end, in separation"—from the moment we come squalling into this world and are severed from our mothers with a knife, through the marriage ceremony in which our starry-eyed declarations of everlasting devotion culminate in a concession to the death that do us part, right up to death itself, that uncoupling of *all* our attachments.

Even if you sought to rise above desire altogether, and cleanse yourself of the clinging that usually accompanies it—the source of much of the suffering that defines passion—you have to remember that transcendence is no cure for longing. Even the gods are full of it. The fact that desire *enthuses* us (*en-theos* means "the god within") tells us that, by definition, it partakes of the divine.

Even the singular God is often found wanting. Scripture is loaded with talk about it. "For the Lord has chosen Zion. He has desired it for his dwelling, saying, 'This is my resting place for ever and ever; here I will sit enthroned, for I have desired it'" (Psalms).

"Thus you will share the holiness of God, who saw you as slaves in Egypt and desired you to become a people of God" (Deuteronomy).

And didn't God start the whole affair to begin with by declaring, "Let there be light," and why do that unless light was lacking?

And aren't God and Adam depicted on the ceiling of the Sistine Chapel as reaching for each other, their outstretched fingers like the twin poles of a Tesla coil, between which a spark of *mutual* longing passes between them?

And if romantic love seems a lot like spiritual yearning in its goal of ecstasy and transcendence, ultimate meaning, a sense of unity and completion, it's because the Western notion of romantic love was invented as a *spiritual* path. It began as "courtly love" among the nobility in the Middle Ages, and was not between a husband and a wife but a knight and his lady. It was an idealized relationship in that it didn't typically exist in the "real life" of medieval marriages, which were based more on practical and political concerns than on love. The point was to sublimate the physical and even romantic for the sake of higher, if not religious, ideals of devotion, honor, service, and transcendence (it's often thought to have originated from the medieval veneration of the Virgin Mary), and was a way to raise knight and lady above the mundane and connect them to something greater than themselves.

To this day, what we're longing for is more than just the love of another. We're hungry for an experience of our own wholeness. We're not just looking *out there* for someone, but also looking to become the person we already know *ourselves* to be. We're not looking for the perfect partner so much as the perfection of our own selves, though the tyrannical fantasy of our own perfectibility, says British psychoanalyst Adam Phillips, becomes merely another excuse to punish ourselves: "Lives dominated by impossible ideals—complete honesty, absolute knowledge, perfect happiness, eternal love—are lives experienced as continuous failure."

What love is asking us to cultivate is *reverence*, as well as the understanding that our beloveds are, like the spiritual states we seek, mysteries that are ultimately beyond our grasp. The mortal beloved and the divine Beloved are both essentially and eternally *other*. They're apples that dangle seductively from the highest branch. And would you really want it any other way? If you sat across the breakfast table from God every morning, even God would get old.

. . .

SO HOW DO YOU cultivate fruitful frustration in relationship, a gentle procession of synapses to cross that can help keep you effortful on behalf of love?

Anyone who's been in relationship for more than ten minutes knows that you don't have to work particularly hard to find frustration there, though using it for the sake of growth and intimacy is another matter. Toward that end, the fact that desire exists only in the presence of frustration suggests one approach—a practice of deliberately "frustrating" yourself. That is, challenging your own assumptions and complacencies, confronting the things you take for granted, practicing humility, questioning your belief that there's nothing new under the sun and nothing left to learn about your partner.

For that matter, questioning the widespread belief that the prime beneficiary of love is the one who receives it rather than the one who gives it. That what it's all about is, as the title of a best-selling book puts it, *Getting the Love You Want*, rather than perhaps *Giving the Love You Want*. As the poet W. H. Auden says, "If equal affection cannot be, let the more loving one be me."

This would require that you second-guess the similarly epidemic assumption that you're the center of attention and that this fact is just cleverly concealed from everyone else, including your partner. As a minister of my acquaintance, Howard Hanger, likes to say, "Only one-seven-billionth of this is about you."

In 1990, the environmental writer Bill McKibben had a cable company tape its entire channel lineup for a twenty-four-hour period, and then spent a year watching those seventeen hundred hours of TV. "There's a very deep message coming at us through all that chatter," he concluded. "The central theme is that each of us is the center of the universe—the most important thing on Earth. We're being told we're the heaviest object around and that everything needs to orbit around our ideas of convenience and comfort—this Bud's for you."

The greatest enemy of love, insists Ethel Person, is not the routinization or institutionalization of passion but "the failure of the lovers' sense of reciprocity and mutuality . . . the wish for someone to take care of you and minister to you, but not the other way around."

To *frustrate* originally meant "to deceive," so by calling your assumptions into question, you're essentially deceiving your self-deceptions. You're undermining your illusions and expectations, and tossing the occasional monkey wrench into your machinery. And since desire is always headed in that direction anyway, you're really just getting in front of the parade.

Example: As I mentioned earlier, back in 1992, Robin and I moved from San Francisco to Taos, New Mexico, a move that started when she came to me one day out of the blue and said she wanted to move to the country. And I argued with her. "What are you talking about?" I said. "Everything's here. Our work is here, our friends are here, our income is here, our *rent-controlled house* is here, and we can get pizza and cannoli at two a.m. if we want it." And I argued with her about it for an entire year. In fact, it became one of our most frequent fights, because we polarized around it. I took the voice of no, she took the voice of yes, and we got stuck there, up to our axles in our own stubbornness.

Needless to say, this was frustrating, and not the kind that engenders desire and passion. But after a year I got fed up with the conflict and threw a monkey wrench into the works. I came to *her* one day out of the blue and said, "I'm tired of being the bad guy. Let's switch. *You* take the voice of no, and *I'll* take the voice of yes." I immediately thought it was a terrible idea, but we did it anyway, and it was very liberating, even amusing.

For one thing, she began to articulate her very legitimate concerns about moving from the city to the country, which she'd been holding back in order to balance me out. And I got to get in touch with what might be great about it, which I'd been holding back in deference to balancing *her* out. Most important, though, it brought some goodwill and affection back into our relationship, and allowed us to move on to *other* fights.

Along those lines, another version of frustrating yourself on behalf of relatedness might be to keep your mouth shut when you're ready to explode, not spraying your partner with emotional buckshot. Go to your room, tear your hair out, and don't come out till you've gotten a grip on yourself and understand where your explosive reaction came from, what wire got tripped. You work on a relationship, I was once told in couples therapy, by keeping your moods to yourself and examining them.

Or try a silent treatment. Take twenty-four hours of silence together, temporarily diverting the stream of chatter between you and providing a bit of emotional breathing room. Don't communicate with words or even written messages, except in emergencies.

Perel suggests creating new email addresses reserved exclusively for erotic exchanges and cyber seductions—with no discussion of the issues in your relationship, or any of the mundane matters of life. Only teasings and temptations, enticements and innuendos.

And here's a charming and disarming exercise brought to you by Gina Ogden, author of *The Return of Desire*: make mad passionate love to your partner for at least a half hour, but never go above the ankles.

One form of frustration that Perel considers "the seed of wanting" is uncertainty, which most people would probably prefer to cancel/clear from their relationships, but which can have a stimulating effect in the right doses. She talks, for example, of the couple whose weekly date-night consists of swapping roles as the initiator of novelty, arranging something they've never done before, somewhere they've never been, even including some unexpected guest—and without the other person knowing about it until the moment of.

She also talks about what she calls "the shadow of the third," one of the elephants in the room of relationship: our desire for the greener grass that lies on the other side of the fence, whether real or imagined. As Perel explains, just because you're committed doesn't mean you own your partner, or that he or she no longer has freedom, and the issue of fidelity is forever settled. It doesn't mean that each of you doesn't still have an active erotic life that's responsive to more than just one person, even if it's never acted out. And remembering this fact is crucial to keeping interest alive. Not focusing on it to the point of jealousy, just mindfulness and appreciation.

Rather than pretending the third doesn't exist, she says, it might be the better part of wisdom to acknowledge it, talk openly about your hidden desires and past relationships, read erotica together, give "the third" a speaking part in your sexual fantasies, point out attractive members of *both* sexes, step back and try to see your partner through the eyes of admiring strangers.

Perel has a beautiful way of framing this: "I know you look at others, but I can't fully know what you see. I know others are looking at you, but I don't really know who it is they're seeing. Suddenly you're no longer familiar. You're no longer a known entity that I need not bother being curious about. In fact, you're quite a mystery. And I'm a little unnerved. Who are you? I want you."

Granted, it can be delightful but also challenging, even threatening, to see your partner through the eyes of amorous strangers, and when it is, love is never more of a crucible, a rock tumbler in which everything gets pounded and polished, a blender in which everything gets stirred and shaken. It can flush up all your insecurities, which will parade endlessly in front of you, no matter how cool and cultivated, how *evolved*, you may appear and prefer to appear.

And yet, it can also lend an unmistakable snap to your crackle and pop, to your love if not your lovemaking, and provide a kind of antitoxin against complacency. And this is in part because the gap isn't just an abyss. It's also profoundly enlivening *because* it's an edge, even a fearful void—which makes the heart race and the breath catch, commands your attention, and fascinates the way peering over cliffs often does. You're certainly not bored.

If we were both smart *and wise*, we'd more than merely "mind the gap," as they say in the London Tube. We'd "heart the gap." We'd teach ourselves to love the gap, not just tolerate it. To love and appreciate the time apart. Love the thoughts our partners have that are not about us, and the dreams they have that are independent of ours. Love the others who love them, women and men, and in whose hearts they have a place that doesn't include us. Love the privacy they cherish, and the parts we don't understand and may never understand. Love the pillar that stands apart from ours but that helps hold up the temple of our togetherness.

And we would do all this not just to help manage our own insecurities— though the ability to self-soothe and talk yourself through fear, the way you'd calm a restive puppy by rubbing its tummy, is one of the high arts of intimacy and emotional health. We would also do it because it's what we want for *ourselves*, and what we want others to do for us. And because ultimately it's in our own best interests, if what we want isn't just a security blanket but also an exciting relationship with a strong, passionate, and *appreciative* partner who'll be inclined to demonstrate his or her appreciation in all kinds of appealing ways.

As for how you learn to heart the gap, to love what frightens you, I think the most expedient approach is what's called graduated exposure, often used to overcome phobias and anxiety disorders. You combine gradual and increasing exposure to the feared thing with relaxation exercises and self-soothing, and eventually you find yourself able to sit in the same room with snakes or spiders or scenarios of the gap and not hyperventilate and hurl your lunch.

A few years ago, I ran across a more extreme example of this approach—though every bit as applicable—while watching one of those hospital dramas on television. In one scene, a man is being told by a doctor that his beautiful young wife has breast cancer and will be undergoing a double mastectomy. The man is inconsolable, and can't conceive how he'll ever make peace with this horrible change in (his) fortune. The doctor stands up, walks over to his bookshelf, and takes down an album of before-and-after photographs of women who'd undergone mastectomies. He opens it on the coffee table in front of the man. "What you do," he tells him sternly, "is look at these photographs over and over and over until you are no longer repulsed by them."

Teaching yourself to love what you learned to fear is not for the faint of heart and will loose the hounds in your psyche. Making peace with "the third," for example, can trigger an outbreak of lifelong anxiety in us about having to share a loved one with others. A particular loved one. A mother or a father. At a literally childish level, for instance, we resent having had to share Mommy with Daddy, or with our siblings, her work, her friends, the dreams and ambitions she may have preferred to parenting, with everything and anything that didn't revolve around us, and much of it didn't. We feel threatened by this and often have great difficulty making peace with the fact that our parents had lives separate from us.

And there's that word again: separateness. That breeding ground of insecurities. That cyclotron of self-doubts. The place where the other leaves off. The space between that's simply *there* like the moon is there, and won't ever be bridged even if we write poems and love letters till we're blue in the face. Oh moon, oh thou.

Same as it ever was, though. Life and literature are rife with stories about the connection between adversity and desire—what some people call frustration attraction. There are "three structural components" in any story of eros, says Carson. "Lover, beloved, and that which comes between them." It's what keeps us turning the pages.

Some of the world's classic love stories—Tarzan and Jane, Romeo and Juliet, Porgy and Bess, Lancelot and Guinevere, Tristan and Isolde, Scarlett and Rhett—are built on the idea that what powers love is hurdles, and the strength of love is commensurate with how mightily our heroes and heroines struggle against the impediments fate throws in their path—the differences and distances between them, the disapproval of their families, the fact that her dream house is a Tudor in the country and his a tree in the jungle.

Mark Epstein, author of *Open to Desire*, believes that what mostly comes between lovers and beloveds is one very particular impediment: "clinging." Not desire, which is just life force, but the clinging to our objects of desire, which constricts our life force. In the Afghani tongue, the verb for "to cling" is synonymous with the verb for "to die."

But he also says that if we can make this obstacle into "an object of contemplation," if we can become students of this space between, then desire can become enlightening instead of just frustrating, and life full of teachable moments. Desire's secret agenda, he insists, is to alert us to the gap, but specifically the one between our expectations and the way things actually are. "As practitioners of the yoga of desire have discovered," he says, "the disappointment inherent in desire can be interesting."

The Other in Another

Were we to make our partner, too, "an object of contemplation," we would quickly discover that the closer we get to another, the more apparent it is that they are indeed an *other*, with needs and agendas that often run counter to ours as well as boundaries that no one can put asunder and no amount of merging can overcome.

Maybe love is like the moth to the flame, or the mortal to the god. You can circle around the beloved all you want, but if you dared dive straight into the light, you'd perish. You have to keep your distance.

The hunger to merge with a beloved works directly against another of the goals of love, which is to preserve and protect the beloved, whether partner, child, sibling, or friend. If we were to succeed at complete merger and become One, the very otherness of the other would disappear (as would your own). "I hold this to be the highest task of a bond between two people," Rilke once said, "that each should stand guard over the solitude of the other."

Psychologists call this highest task differentiation and consider it the basis for healthy intimacy. "It's not as cozy as togetherness, but it's not as sticky either," says David Schnarch in *Passionate Marriage.* "It can be as warm as you want, and it's psychologically clean." It's also the basis of evolution itself, which aims for diversity, not sameness. Survival depends on it.

This lesson of differentiation is one I learned a bit earlier in life than most, given that I'm a twin, and it's served me well in my other relationships. The born rivalry and entanglement that characterizes twinship is a good case study in the push-pull dynamics between any two people who are very close to each other—the wrangle between autonomy and union, competition and cooperation.

Indeed, if there's a hankering to stand apart among all people, among twins the heat is turned up, the stakes are higher, and the connection between competition and intimacy is more pronounced. After all, the closer two people are, the more likely they are to be standing in each other's shadows. And I've come to see that my brother and I compete—we all do, I think—to tell ourselves apart, and we do so precisely because we're so much alike.

For Ross and me, competition started the moment the lights winked on in the womb, though it was a competition marked by accommodation. If we weren't two gladiators tied together for a fight to the finish, we were two gymnasts attempting a trapeze act in an upended bottle. (Either way, the management never approved of our struggle for comfort.) From the very start, though, every inch he gave up was another inch for me. His losses weren't just his losses; they were my gains. And of course, my losses were his gains.

There are even medical experts who believe that as many as a quarter of all those born as single children began life as twins, and what happens, they speculate, is that in the struggle for room, position, and food, one twin "wins" and the other is literally overcome, reabsorbed into the thrum of the uterus or—in a ghoulish twist on Darwinism—into the body of the stronger twin. A friend of mine, during an operation, was found to be carrying the vestigial remains of her own twin in a mass of tissue inside her. They found vertebrae, limbs, fingers.

By degrees, though, Ross and I conspired to step away from each other's shadow, and this, I think, is the task of twinship: whereas others begin life separate and must learn intimacy, Ross and I began life intimate and had to learn separateness.

Every time someone would recklessly ask, "Which half are you?" it became clearer to us that if for no other reason than convenience, we were seen as one entity. But we were not! That's what our fighting proved. And if I could be the Older One or he the Cute One, if I could be the Smart One or he the Artistic One, if, even for a moment, I could be the winner and he the loser, then by God we were *not* one entity.

Our competition reached fever pitch during our teens, when identity crises are the order of the day anyway. Our parents had recently divorced, and perhaps facing off was a way to recapture some sense of position in our shattered pecking order. Maybe it was just girls.

Nonetheless, as we moved out into the world, our lives became a seamless web of competitive vigilance. During crucial moments of tennis, he would inevitably ask, "Gregg, do you inhale or exhale when you serve?" When we occasionally switched classes, just to see if we could get away with it (we could), I would make a point of asking the stupidest questions I could think of. When we both got new bicycle odometers for our thirteenth birthdays, we took off immediately in a frenzy to see who could rack up the most miles before dinner, thus confirming that competition had more to do with beating the other guy than enjoying the activity.

The frequent blips of animosity, however, were always tempered by fail-safe agreements. We had a rule when fighting: the only place we were allowed to hit each other was on the meaty part of the back, near the upper arm. And we stuck to it. Never once did I punch him anywhere else, no matter how angry I got.

As adults, my brother and I now have our own turfs. Mine is the Eastern Seaboard, his is the Western. I'm a writer and speaker, he's a craftsman and entrepreneur. And though I envy his community of friends, and he envies the "glamour" of writing and public speaking, it's fair to say that the competition isn't what it used to be. When we play tennis, we no longer keep score. When we ski, we no longer see who can reach the bottom first, but carve perfect figure eights in the powder, he the zig and I the zag.

And although our relationship has softened over the years, and despite feeling as strong a need now to reconnect as to separate from him, I still find vulnerability a compromising position in relation to my brother, one that goes against my instinct to compete. Once, after a weekend visit, I stood with Ross at my front door, trying to convince him to stay an extra day. In the middle of our negotiation, my then housemate, Susan, turned to him and said, "He really misses you." In the awkward silence that followed, I felt embarrassed at the tender indictment of her remark, as if she had somehow betrayed me.

Indeed, our rivalry is never far away, and given the proper stimulus, we can easily regress. I was reminded of this a few years back, when Ross again came to visit, after half a year. On our first night together, we sat in a restaurant around the corner from my house until they turned up the chairs. We talked about work, our respective love lives, and our father, who was dying. But mostly we enjoyed the attention from the people around us that each of us gets only when we're together.

Then we, very uncharacteristically, decided to split dessert.

The instant our waitress put that slice of banana cream pie on the table in front of us, Ross turned to me with a suspicious look and said, "Okay, pal. You split it, I choose it."

In that one statement, he recited the entire litany of our relationship: that our rivalry and our confederacy are inseparable and that they'll rekindle every time we reunite. Our conflicting urges to separate and to join define the competition that defines us, that orchestrates every change we've ever made, and that reanimates the first and most omnipresent relationship in both our lives. It's the relationship that, unlike all others in the world, preceded even the one we had with our parents, who always wanted us to get along without fighting and never understood that we got along despite our fighting, and maybe because of it.

It's also the coincidence of these contrary urges that seems to most accurately describe the bond between us, and explains how we're each ultimately whole: he is my most beloved friend and my bitterest rival, my confidant and my betrayer, my sustainer and my dependent, and scariest of all, my equal.

My father once told me that family is where I'll return in life when I'm most insecure, rivalries or not. And as I get older and see the effects of the years mirrored in my brother's face, I want to strengthen our remaining bond, conscious of how few lifelong ones there are. Now if I'm envious, I would never take from him the thing I envy, as I once would have. Now I'm a little clearer on where I leave off and where he begins. A little.

In a relationship baptized by competition, I'm struck by the level of intimacy we've achieved, especially in the years we've been apart. The worst I can say of it all now is that I'm spoiled rotten. It takes a monumental effort on my part to expect anything less from the other relationships in my life.

And I have a feeling that when the past is most of what there is of time, there'll be no one who can help me validate it like he can, no relationship that will encompass it like ours, and no one else who knows that when it really counts, I would gladly give him the bigger slice of pie.

WE MAY GO all gooey about the goal of oneness, but twoness is just as important, giving a tip of the hat to the boundaries that naturally encircle people, and not denying our differences or suppressing our integrity and authenticity for the sake of keeping up the appearance of oneness. An attitude of two-getherness goes against the grain, though, according to Elizabeth Gilbert in *Committed*, and certainly for couples. She argues that tradition and habit tell us our relationships should aim for four outcomes—daily, domestic, exclusive, and forever—which, as with so many aspects of culture and nature, just doesn't take the individual much into account, and we're individuals as much as we're teammates and community members. Since these romantic aspirations can compromise our ability to differentiate from our partners, they're worth a closer look.

Daily: The downside of constant togetherness is that we then have to contend with the weary familiarity dailiness often brings, which Daphne Rose Kingma calls "a drag on the radiance of love," and the fact that passion tends to tatter in the stiff winds of everyday intimacy. But rather than going to absurd lengths to replace the missing radiance (greeting your partner at the door wearing nothing but Saran Wrap, etc.), the ticket might simply be to budget in some separateness. "What we imagine will be enhanced by all this togetherness is often just diluted," she writes. Separateness, then, is like the rest in music, the vacation, the meditation. It's the pause that refreshes, the break from the routine.

Domestic: We assume that settling in under one roof will make love grow, but forget that setting up house is a flashback for most of us to our original experiences of living with others under one roof—our families—which were often fraught. But not always. For some it might even be a hard act to follow. One recent Sunday morning, I sat in the cafe of a bookstore up the street from my house and began noticing families. I was especially taken with how at ease family members are in one another's presence. The way siblings talk to each other with complete unself-consciousness, the way little girls wrap their arms around their fathers or sit unabashedly in their laps, the way mothers casually fix their kids' hair.

And *of course* we'd search for this level of intimacy ever after, in every circle of friends, in every lover's eyes—and not always successfully. It's the template most of us carry for love and belonging and the one against which we judge all other intimacies. It's the image in our souls of a matching set, whose counterpart we're always trying to find out in the grand flea market of the world.

Exclusive: We typically expect exclusivity, not just sexually but also in the sense of expecting our partner to be the sole supplier of all our needs—a surefire way to overload the circuits.

Forever: The implication here is that marriage (alone among all created things) possesses stability and permanence. But marriage is only as enduring as the people in it, and people aren't enduring, or unchanging. And before you hail the long-term committed—twenty-, forty-, sixty-year partnerships—you need to examine the state of the souls of the people in those relationships. Sometimes longevity reveals little more than the endurance people have for crippling compromise and anesthesia. Length doesn't necessarily equate with depth, nor depth with satisfaction. In *A Lover's Discourse*, Roland Barthes asks a provocative question about the hunger for longevity: "Why is it better to *last* than to *burn?*"

The sense of safety and security we feel or imagine we'll feel in relationship, and certainly the belief that the terrain of our partnership is well charted and our partner a well-thumbed book, is part reality but part apparition too. He or she has only to do or say something we don't understand for a gap to suddenly appear alongside that otherly self. It's not that our partner's behavior is illogical. Behavior always has its logic—it's psycho-logic. We just haven't figured out what it is yet. Despite our expectations, reality is often otherwise. That is, *other-wise*. There's wisdom, not folly, in another's actions, and what's required isn't judgment but inquiry. The unknown is an inescapable part of love and learning, and without it, there's little incentive to explore and little new to discover.

But forget about the other guy for a moment. How well do we even know *ourselves*? The existence of the unconscious is a testament to how much we don't know about our *own* minds. Carl Jung considered consciousness the tip of an iceberg, and unconsciousness the nine-tenths of it that's underwater. (And then there's the ocean in which the whole thing floats.)

But how well do we really know what makes us tick, our deepest motivations? What makes us react to things the way we do or set the goals we set for ourselves? How often do we understand our dreams or the genealogy of our private fantasies? What makes us choose the kind of partners we choose and wind up in the dramas we find ourselves playing out with them? What made me marry someone who has the same exact birthday as my mother—and not run in the opposite direction the moment I discovered this?

We think we know ourselves, and our loved ones, but we often don't. We think we know who they really are, what they should do, what's best for them, what they're thinking, but we don't. We take guesses. I couldn't even finish my wife's sentences accurately half the time, and we were together for twenty years.

Maybe I did it because I'm a New Yorker and she's a Californian, and New Yorkers are used to doing everything on top of other people, and if you don't interrupt them, they think you're not paying attention. Maybe it was born of the subliminal expectation that when two people fall in love, they become one, evidenced by such tender displays of fusion as feeding each other, wearing the same color clothes, and finishing each other's sentences. The problem was, my wife didn't like it when I tried to finish her sentences.

I fancied that it inferred a communion of minds and hearts, a sense of the kind of closeness people mean when they boast, "He knows what I'm going to say before I say it." It implied telepathic understanding. We used fewer words, economizing our intimacy. But it turned out that about half the time I didn't actually know what she was going to say and ended up committing the conversational equivalent of cutting in line.

My wife considered this habit, even when well intentioned, a form of trespassing, and she said it made her feel invisible. To me it was just conversation. To her it was a hostile takeover, especially in the heat of argument, when finishing her sentences took on a tactical quality—interruption carried to the level of a military maneuver, designed to throw her off balance and control the conversation. A good way to win a battle and lose a relationship.

All this, it turns out, is fairly typical, though. Women tend to use language and conversation to create rapport, men to negotiate status. One is personal, the other positional.

It was only by catching myself repeatedly—*being* caught is actually closer to the truth—that I slowly began amending this long-standing conversational colonialism. And once I started catching myself, it was like focusing on my muscles while playing tennis or the piano. I became self-conscious of something that was normally an autonomic activity like breathing, blinking, and salivating, and it threw my game off. But I suppose that was the point. To throw it off and relearn it so that I actually got what I was after in relationships: connection rather than disconnection.

Finishing my wife's sentences, though, was just one of the many unwitting encroachments we visited on each other in the name of togetherness. She turned up the radio too loud, I underlined in her books in pen instead of pencil as she requested. She snored like an eighteen-wheeler downshifting on a steep grade, I tried to strike up friendly conversations while she was painting. She was always asking me what I was thinking, I was always giving her unsolicited advice. In microcosm, these were just snippets from the wider social fabric. At one end of the continuum are the micropolitics of everyday life, with its little interpersonal imperialisms, and at the far end are invasion and war.

Changing these habits may require a rewiring of the whole apparatus of human relations, and a carving of new furrows in the brain, but it also came down to the little upgrades in attention I was able to manage in a given moment. It reminded me of the friend who once told me that he had a personal "mission statement" that went like this: "My mission is to create more peace and kindness in the world through my work, my relationships, and my actions."

Great, I said. A noble enterprise. Then I asked what happens when someone wants to cut in front of him on the freeway? (I said this knowing how he drives.) Was he going to step on the brake or the accelerator? Because one leads to more peace and kindness in the world, and one leads to less. And you can begin to see how the sheer number of opportunities to be either in or out of integrity with yourself—and the good graces of others—in the course of even a single day of driving around on the freeways of LA can pretty quickly pile up. But that's the work. It's in the small gestures, the little daily deeds. Saint Francis said, "Always preach the gospel. Where necessary use words."

Sometimes my wife and I negotiated these challenges by the skin of our teeth, but negotiation is the thing. Keeping the lines open, being willing to give an inch to make a mile, creating borders that are firm yet porous—and hardest of all, speaking up when the borders are breached: I love you, but get off my foot.

In the interests of sovereignty and peace—and with the discretion born of being endlessly confronted about it—I finally took to finishing her sentences mostly in the privacy of my own head. It cut down on conflict on the home front, braided courtesy and kindness into our relationship, and helped speed the plow.

IN A MOVIE called *The Prince of Persia*, an intense love affair blossoms between two protagonists who begin as antagonists, in accordance with that peculiar slap-kiss, frog-prince Hollywood trope that insists couples who are destined to love each other will hate each other first (*Star Wars, You've Got Mail, The King and I, Pride and Prejudice, My Fair Lady, Beauty and the Beast*, etc.), and I don't know about you, but *I* don't know any couples who loathed each other at first sight.

In any case, toward the end of the movie, our sword-crossed lovers finally allow themselves to fall in love, and amid much swirling camerawork they exchange long and piercing gazes of adoration. And as predictable as it was, I saw in that encounter what it is that people will crawl across the desert on their hands and knees for—that look in someone else's eyes. That look of love and wonder, of *recognition*. "Finally, I've found you. I've been searching for you my whole life, and now I've found you."

The moment this game-changing gaze is exchanged, we're of course back to a narrow focus on the one, the soulmate destiny has supposedly manufactured especially for you—the needle in the haystack—but the promise that look holds, even when it makes no promises, is that paradise is just around the corner.

The question, of course, is which corner? There are over seven billion people out there, in two hundred countries, spread over 150 million square miles. Your soulmate could be anywhere. And believing that only this one true love will allow you to board the glory train is, as Erich Fromm said in *The Art of Loving*, like wishing you could paint, but instead of actually learning the art, you insist that when you find just the right *object*, you'll instinctively begin painting with mastery.

In any case, much of the passion and desire we feel for a relationship is not just for the ordinary flawed human being to whom we're sending flowers and chocolates, or living with on a daily/domestic/exclusive/forever basis, but also for the dream at the heart of the whole enterprise. The dream of deliverance back to the Garden. Hollis rightly calls it the Eden Project, and what it tells us is that what we're ultimately after, what's behind all our erotic strivings and hungerings for love—including the whole crusade to create a healthy gap—is to arrive ultimately at a place of *no-gap*, no separation between us and our beloved.

We imagine that through a "magical other," we'll finally overcome the separation that defines so much of human experience, beginning with our estrangement from the natural world—call it emergence if you prefer—and moving through our individual farewells to the paradise of amniotic life, our leave-taking from mother and father, our essential aloneness in the world, and the gulf that separates us from our deities (or perhaps our deified selves). The hunger for this is captured in the very word *religion*, which, again, means to rebuild that fallen-down bridge and regain the high ground of union, whether it's flesh with spirit or flesh with flesh, whether it's the flash-fusion of orgasm, the merger of romance, or the mystical union of God-love.

Beyond our first few months of life, when we don't even perceive there to *be* any separation between ourselves and the rest of the world, we spend our lives seeking to overcome our separation from others, and experiences like falling in love offer us a grand opportunity to see the walls come tumbling down and our exile and loneliness overturned. And our natural response to this sudden breach in our isolation is to cling to the one who helps bring it on. So it's asking a *lot* of ourselves to deliberately resurrect the separation, to rebuild any part of the wall by holding that person at arm's length, however briefly or intermittently, and for whatever good and passionate cause.

We'd prefer to cleave to the idea that through love we can literally *re-pair* the damage Zeus did when he split us in two because the gods were intimidated by the power we possessed when we were one beautifully androgynous creature with two heads, four arms, and four legs, woman and man conjoined.

But the Eden Project is a bubble waiting to be popped. It's "Joy, whose hand is ever at his lips, bidding adieu," as the poet John Keats puts it. And when the less-than-magical parts of our partners begin to show through, when the conflicts commence and the disappointments pile up, when things fall apart, we're inclined to blame our partners rather than our fantasies. But our partner was never a magical other to begin with, only a fragile and imperfect mortal like ourselves, who won't stop leaving nail clippings in the sink and showing up late for appointments.

Individuality, that is, will out. He wants to have sex, she doesn't. She wants to socialize, he wants to veg out in front of the TV. He wants to spend their money on travel, she wants to put it in the bank. She doesn't like her mother-in-law, he doesn't like his. And as the boundaries resurrect themselves and partners remember that they're not in fact "one," the hard work of *real* loving begins—or doesn't. *Real* because it's an act of will, whereas falling in love is not. All you have to do there is fall, but to love, you have to *climb*.

People define this dream of paradise in different ways. For some it's the womb, whose warm waters we were flushed from by birth. The very act of coming into the world defines the first great separation in our lives, the loss of the only home we'd ever known up to that point, our mother's body, the belly of the whale who delivered us to the shore of life. Our entrance brings on our exit. The door marked "In" is also the door marked "Out." As the writer Albert Goldbarth puts it, "What is this proto-loss so grand and deeply historied inside us that it causes us to cringe at any secondary loss that even vaguely seems mnemonic of it? *Where's that damn sock?*"

Though unremembered by most of us, birth leaves its mark, says Aldo Carotenuto in *Eros and Pathos: Shades of Love and Suffering.* It becomes the antecedent of a recurring theme in our lives: the illusion that by falling in love, a structural flaw will be corrected, a fundamental loss redeemed, and we'll reenter the realm of safety and security, milk and honey.

For others, the dream of paradise points to the Garden and the supposed wholeness we had back in the primordial, before we were separated from nature. Every culture has had, as part of its creation story, the tale of a lost paradise, a time of wholeness and innocence, a time when we were as deeply natural as the plants and animals and hadn't yet plucked from the tree of knowledge and been cast—or rather, outcast—into the "civilized" life, the "conscious" life. Every birth, in fact, is a recapitulation of this narrative, a separation from the paradise of *connectedness.*

For still others, the dream takes them back to earliest parental love, to a presumed paradise based on the idea, as psychoanalyst Nancy Chodorow puts it, that "I shall be loved always, everywhere, in every way, my whole body, my whole being—without any criticism, without the slightest effort on my part."

Many people's ideal of love seems to be a throwback to infancy, when they were loved for who they were rather than what they did, and no matter what they *did*, they continued to be loved and forgiven their trespasses. No wonder we would hunger to regain this Eden. We could scream at the top of our lungs; repeatedly wake our parents in the middle of the night; urinate on them while they were changing our diapers; drain their energy, patience, and bank accounts, contribute nothing toward the household chores—and be adored.

Same with romance. For a period of time before the spell dissolves, you know you're going to be adored, worshipped as a kind of sacred object, all your shortcomings magically recast as charming eccentricities. As a character in the movie *Closer* says of an infatuation: "We're in the first flush. It's paradise. All my nasty habits amuse her."

The trouble with this imagined blueprint for all our adult love affairs, this paradise that love is said to recapitulate, is that for a whole lot of people, that wasn't their actual experience. Rather than surrounding their children with waves of oceanic bliss, their parents were self-absorbed, critical, unavailable, inconsistent, even abusive. And there were always others competing for the loaves and fishes, jealous lovers vying for their parents' attention—fathers, siblings, careers. Fidelity was seldom a given, union rarely the consoling oneness it's advertised to be.

Shame: The Hole in Wholeness

No matter how far and wide we search to complete the matching set and recapitulate paradise, no matter how many channels we flip through to find that sacred rerun, among the great clichés of both love and addiction is that we can't fill the holes in ourselves with anything or anyone from the outside, and can't love others until we love ourselves.

Actually, this last assumption isn't strictly true. I had lunch recently with a woman who told me that for thirty years she nurtured everyone in her family but herself—her kids, her husband, her friends, her parents. The truth is, you *can* love and nurture others while not loving and nurturing yourself. Lots of people offer others what they can't offer themselves—care, attention, generosity, thoughtfulness, self-sacrifice. All of them acts of love.

Nonetheless, by directing our Eden Projects not just outward but also inward, toward the ordinary flawed human being at the helm of the enterprise, toward the gap inside us that self-esteem and self-love are supposed to fill, we strengthen and expand our ability to love, which is ultimately a place we come *from*, not a place we go *to*. By exploring the holes we're led toward wholeness.

If passion is the hunger to connect and the capacity for relatedness, and we want to keep passion in our relationships, the skill of being connected to *ourselves* is crucial. If we're lacking passion for our own lives, we'll rob our relationships of that very energy. Passion is our eagerness for union, and when we're unwilling to yoga-up with our own selves, it isn't likely we'll want to do that with anyone else either.

K Smith (not her real name) recently began a life-altering and unorthodox exploration of one of the holes in her own soul, into which great reams of intimacy and happiness have fallen and disappeared.

Like many people, K has had a tempestuous lifelong relationship with her body, a relentlessly self-defeating attitude that experts call dysmorphia—an unhealthy preoccupation with her body's perceived flaws—which has tended, as it does, to generalize to her perceptions about herself. This has wreaked a certain amount of havoc on her ability to enjoy relationships and on the sense of self that she brings to them.

"When I look in the mirror, I find everything wrong," says K, a wellness entrepreneur who describes herself as "a curvy hirsute woman of size." And this, she says, has been a problem for, among other things, her love life. "My experience with intimacy has been that it was great as long as the covers were on and the lights were off. Also, I have a very high libido and adore physicality, but it was always met with disdain on the part of my husbands, as in 'too much.' Anything about my sexuality was put in its place. So this part of my life has just not been particularly well expressed or well regarded, and it just spiraled down and disappeared. I didn't even masturbate until I was forty-eight. I hope you can appreciate the significance of that statement."

What it in part signifies is something that's key to the subjugation of passion in people's lives, and the withering of intimacy between them: shame. Not healthy shame, a.k.a. conscience, which tells us when we're *doing* something wrong, but toxic shame, which tells us that our very *being* is wrong, that who we are at the core is fundamentally flawed, and that turns us away from our enthusiasms and instincts and cripples our ability to affirm ourselves. In relationships, it often shows up as a lack of intimacy, because you don't want others to get close enough to see those flaws.

Shame is the sensation of being exposed to what's called the hostile gaze, sometimes referred to as the evil eye, which in the animal kingdom usually carries the threat of attack or even death. It says, "If you step out of line, I'll kill you." The human in us may not register this, but the animal in us certainly does. Shame makes us cringe, meaning yield, and that's its agenda—my way or the highway—whether it comes at us through the thou-shalt-nots of parents and teachers, sexism, racism, or God, that ultimate alpha male. And long after our shamers have passed from the scene, the footprints they left in the wet cement of our psyches remain.

We feel it whether we're being shamed for our anger and aggressiveness, our curiosity and creativity, or for masturbating and playing doctor. And we express it in depression, addiction, perfectionism, people-pleasing, and excessive self-consciousness of the kind that makes us terrified of making a mistake, embarrassing ourselves in public, making love with the lights on and the covers off, or looking at ourselves naked in a full-length mirror.

Among the job descriptions of parenting is to model healthy behavior for children, but there are countless ways that shame creeps into the equation and begins polluting paradise: "Don't be a crybaby," "Why can't you be more like so-and-so?" "See what you made me do?" "Don't be stupid," "Don't touch yourself down there," and even just rolling your eyes at your children. And of course, all forms of criticism, contempt, abuse, neglect, ridicule, hostility, public humiliation, and emotional rigidity are based in shame.

K's father could have checked off any number of the above.

So could many of the religions and philosophies throughout human history, with their damnations and discriminations against pleasure, their insistence that the body is something to jettison on our way to the divine, their belief that sexual thoughts are a distracting impurity, a fly in the ointment of virtue, and the promulgation of ideas like original sin, which is stone-cold guaranteed to shame people to the core.

We've inherited a very combative relationship to our own natural urges and lick-the-plate sensual desires. We're endowed with over one thousand nerve endings per square inch over our entire body, ten thousand taste buds on the tongue, another ten thousand aromas we can discern with our noses, and a heavenly host of appetites toward which to apply these endowments. Our bodies were clearly *designed* for sensual experience and pleasure. But then we're often told that the supposedly intelligent designer of these gifts is disgusted by our use of them.

Pope Gregory the Great ("Opinion, not fact," as an old journalism professor of mine would say of such a title) declared, "Sensual pleasure can never be without sin." Saint Augustine argued that "nothing so casts down the manly mind from its heights as . . . those bodily contacts which belong to the married state." Gnosticism, a theology related to early Christianity and Judaism, referred to the body as "a corpse with senses, the grave you carry around with you."

Saint Jerome argued that "anyone who has too passionate a love of his wife is an adulterer." Seneca, the preeminent spokesman for Stoicism (the dominant philosophy of the Roman Empire at the beginning of Christianity) and tutor to the emperors, advised people to "do nothing for the sake of pleasure." Both Socrates and Plato viewed all forms of sexuality as inferior to abstinence because it involved the body.

The temptations encountered by Christ in Judea, Buddha under the bodhi tree, and Saint Anthony in the Egyptian desert—to name just a few of our spiritual elders who wrestled with them—are almost universally depicted in art as either naked women or demons and monsters. "The Temptation of St. Anthony," as depicted by Michelangelo, Dalí, Cezanne, Hieronymus Bosch, and many others, is described as including sensual and sexual desires, and a wide range of physical pleasures and passions, including hunger.

"Each of the creatures that people the hell of Saint Anthony," says Octavio Paz in *The Double Flame: Love and Eroticism*, "is an emblem of a repressed passion. The negation of life turns into violence, and abstinence transforms into psychic aggression against others and against ourselves."

In fact, back in the 1970s, neuropsychologist James Prescott conducted a cross-cultural analysis of four hundred preindustrial societies and found that cultures that lavish physical affection on infants and do not repress sexuality in adolescents tend to be disinclined to violence. Those with a predisposition to violence are composed of individuals who have been deprived—at least during one of two critical stages in life: infancy, and adolescence—of the pleasures of the body.

Now surely some of these "temptations" can and do interfere with our higher aspirations for ourselves and create real suffering in the world. But they're also among our greatest earthly pleasures and shouldn't be thrown out with the mortal bathwater. By doing so, we reject ourselves for being human and condemn our own desires. Besides, it was a sensual pleasure that gave each of us *life*.

More contemporaneously, and at the risk of flitting from the sublime to the absurd, in a scene from the Woody Allen movie *Everything You Always*

Wanted to Know About Sex, a man and woman are about to make love when he is suddenly struck with impotence. The camera takes us inside his head, where we see two burly security guards come bursting through the doors of Command Central in the brain, dragging a half-crazed priest who's shouting biblical injunctions against sex outside marriage. They tell their commanding officer that they found him hiding out in the subconscious.

I encountered a more subtle but no less invasive version of this at an Italian restaurant in Asheville where my girlfriend, Paula, and I were celebrating the New Year. We were seated in a quiet corner of the back room, with only one other couple. We sat, as we usually do, on the same side of the table, and were casually and affectionately draped over each other, exchanging the occasional kiss, when the manager on duty, a young woman of perhaps thirty, came over. She had a severe expression on her face, and a very serious-looking waiter standing behind her in what I can only describe as the stance of a Secret Service agent (feet planted widely apart, arms folded sternly across his chest). "I'm sorry but I'm going to have to ask you to leave the restaurant," she said.

We stared at her dumbfounded.

When I politely asked why, she only repeated herself. "I'm going to have to ask you to leave the restaurant."

I had to *guess* what the reason was, and when I finally said, "Is it because we're cuddling?" she nodded curtly and said, "This is a family restaurant."

Now, Paula and I are two professional people in our fifties, well bred, well dressed, and upstanding by at least most benchmarks of behavior. For starters, this gross overreaction struck us as ironic, given that it was an *Italian* restaurant, the Italians being world-famously passionate and demonstrative. Among the most prominent memories I have of being in Rome is the very public displays of affection among its inhabitants. Apparently, much of this is lost in translation to the American South.

Second, we were incredulous that the manager gave us no explanation, and no option to amend whatever behavior she construed as being inappropriate in a family restaurant. It was just "Out!" Had we been a family with a screaming child or ill-mannered teenagers, or talking too loudly and disturbing other customers, she would certainly have given us the chance to be more discreet—lower our voices, take the screaming baby outside, etc. But she gave us no such opportunity.

What all these people are telling us—from Pope Gregory "the Great" to our frosty restaurateur—is that our erotic passions, even when well restrained, are corrupt and corrupting. And what they're denying is the fact that our erotic passions and our spiritual passions have a great deal in common, and always have. The famous Bernini sculpture of a swooning Saint Theresa in the Santa Maria della Vittoria church in Rome—an angel about to thrust the arrow of God's love into her—is a classic example of how indistinguishable spiritual and orgasmic rapture can be. The Song of Solomon and the texts of tantra both use highly erotic language to describe union with the sacred, and they highlight the role that gazing, caressing, kissing, and embracing all play in our relations with the divine.

God and Adam gaze at each other across the Sistine Chapel, reaching to touch each other tenderly. A painting by Marc Chagall called *Rabbi* shows the eponymous holy man tenderly embracing the Torah, his lips the same bright red as the scroll. On a recent visit to the shrine of the Sufi poet Rumi in central Turkey, I noticed that someone had planted a kiss in bright red lipstick on the top of a very phallic-looking marble pedestal.

"The historical and psychological splitting of spirit and body," says Thomas Moore in *The Soul of Sex*, "of transcendence and sensuousness, virtue and desire, is a neurosis. A disturbance of the soul." And we are its descendants.

But even if we only subconsciously equate the erotic with the perverted, and the body with blasphemy, it's critical to understand that the word *perverted* means "to be turned from what's natural and normal." The erotic, sexual, and sensual are all natural and normal to humans, and technically speaking, whatever *blocks* their energies is what's perverted. And puritanical cultures, religions, philosophies, and parenting styles are expert at perverting erotic desire and expression. They specialize in separating sexuality from spirituality and pleasure from purity, and crushing the body under a load of thou-shalt-nots and nice-girls-don't. A friend of mine who was raised in a very Catholic family once told me that her mother used to refer to her vagina as her "icky," as in "Now wipe your icky."

This makes it not the least bit surprising that as an adult she thinks of her vagina as unattractive. "A weird little organ," she calls it, with all its folds and flaps and fleshy protuberances. "I can't put makeup on it," she says.

Freud once observed that "the suppression of a woman's sexuality leads to a general inhibition of desire and curiosity, a restriction on wanting and knowing that spreads throughout her life."

The most rudimentary step in undoing this spell, in unshaming yourself, according to Doug Gillette in *Primal Love*, is conducting an intervention. Catching yourself in the act of self-shaming and applying a compensating reaction, a counter-message. Let's say you introduce a new sexual position or fantasy into your love life, he says, and your partner doesn't exactly share your enthusiasm, maybe even thinks it's a little weird. Naturally you're going to feel some shame. So you might tell yourself, "There's nothing to be ashamed of. So it fell flat. I know he/she still loves me, and I know my suggestion is something I enjoy, and I'm proud of myself for taking a risk. Maybe next time he/she will be more open."

But changing your tune is a numbers game. You may have to sing yourself a different song a dozen or a hundred times before you begin to believe it, before it begins to sink in and hold sway. After all, there are easily that many messages to outshout, and you're not going to overrule them just by clicking your heels together.

The old messages also have a two-to-one advantage over the new ones because they often came from *both* your parents, who, psychologically speaking, were gods compared with your infant self. When and if you eventually come around to redressing those grievances as an adult, the voice you use to do so is not the voice of a god but a mortal, and a shamed and uncertain one at that. So you probably won't give your new commandments the same weight of authority as those of your parents. Who are you, after all, to question the received wisdom of the ages, the dictums passed down from generation to generation? Who are you not to honor thy father and thy mother?

At fifty years old, K Smith began that intervention with what a friend calls her "social experiment," a creative, confrontational, even defiant attempt to come to terms with her sense of self and her sense of shame and to look at her body-image issue in a most literal way: through the eye of a camera.

It was inspired by a very revealing conversation she'd had a few years before with a male friend who had what she calls "adoring eyes." Whenever he complimented her looks, she responded the same way: "Yeah, yeah, yeah."

"I just wasn't there," she says. "I just didn't feel attractive. Dating was horrendous. Meeting people was horrendous. My personal life was horrendous. But he would look at me and say, 'I wish you could see what I see.' So I decided to find out."

Thus began Anonymously Nude, "a journey and a journal" in which she chronicles the reexamination of her own body in photographs that she takes of herself and posts on a blog (anonymouslynude.wordpress.com), which has received over 160,000 hits in two years—often 200 to 400 a day—from people who, along with K, are bearing witness to her "self-discovering," including a handful from the Midwestern town where she lives, which she describes as "a very, very, very conservative place, where people will consider doing business with you if you join their church."

Men are the majority of her respondents, of course, but they're not the only beneficiaries of this photographic experiment. Studies have shown that when women are exposed to images of thin women, their body satisfaction decreases, but it increases when they're exposed to images of larger women. "I consider my blog a gift to others. It's also just simply very liberating and exhilarating to me, and fun. And it's strengthened my internal idea of myself; not just looking at myself but really seeing myself. And what the camera sees is very different from what my eye sees. It's very affirming and beautiful. The camera's eye is much more confident than mine."

As the poet and painter William Blake once said, "We have no body distinct from our soul, for that called Body is a portion of soul discerned by the five senses, which are the chief inlets of soul in this age." K's challenge: to see her soul in the guise of her body, and to use her senses to know it.

Sensuousness, in fact, has been one of the great surprises to come out of the project. The sensual and pleasurable experiences she's had while photographing herself in different fabrics, laces, beads, feathers, varieties of light and shadow, etc., have heightened her appreciation of her body. "That was a huge surprise to me. I was actually getting off on it, which is certainly not how I started.

"I'd never even *looked* at certain parts of my body before I began photographing it. When I first spread my legs and took photos of that part of me and uploaded them onto my computer screen, I just about died. I just screamed and hid them in my files, because it just didn't look anything like I thought it did, and certainly compared with the *Playboy* magazines I saw while I was babysitting in fifth grade. So in addition to being a full-figured woman, and also very hairy, my private parts didn't look at all like what they promote."

In blogging about one of the first photos she posted, of *that part* of her as seen through a fishnet stocking, she wrote, "I am embarrassed. This shows a part of me that I despise." Of another photo, she says: "It makes me want to crawl under a rock." Of yet another: "Did I really just post this image on the internet?

"I just didn't have a relatedness to these parts of my body—anything below the waist."

Yet soon she began finding the photos—or more to the point, her body as seen through the camera lens—"alluring." What the camera sees, she said, is "a level of beauty, and vulnerability, expression, line, shape, form that's very attractive. In a sense, the photos cherish my body, and to cherish is what I'm striving for in my life. I absolutely cannot believe that these images are me, and that I can now see how my roundness is actually inviting. Some of the images even take my breath away. How many people even know what they look like from behind? I had no idea. And now I think that's my best side. I've certainly become far more intimate with my body than most people are with theirs, even when they love their body."

Along with her nudity, she's found, her sexuality has also become bolder and more expressive. At first some of her photos were deliberately blurry because she was so shy, but soon she began describing herself and her photos as "sassy, playful, confident, and sexy." She says, "My self-esteem and personal confidence are completely altered. And the feedback I sometimes get is, 'This is stunning,' or 'I like the way this looks,' or 'I want you.'

"If nobody had said anything, I probably wouldn't have continued with the blog. But they did, and I realized I really like to be looked at. I didn't know that about myself. And I don't think I ever noticed if men were looking at me. I was just oblivious to myself. And this is why I say, 'Where have I been all my life?'

"I realized that I really need reassurance. The best way to get past despising myself was just to put myself out there and hear more of the good. Self-esteem *isn't* strictly an inside job, it turns out. It can get a serious boost from external validation too."

It's unfortunate that external validation, certainly when compared with internal validation, is often looked down on as inferior. When we were children, it was the only kind of validation there was. We couldn't give it to ourselves. It *had* to come from our parents or caretakers. But the kind of validation we got from our parents, assuming we got it, was radically different from the kind we get later in life from peers, teachers, colleagues, lovers, friends, and blog readers—even when it sounds identical. This is because of *when* we got it—when the original software was being downloaded, when the form in formative years was being set-designed.

External validation is simply more potent at that stage of the game, and the emotional process that turns it into internal validation—into self-esteem, into plain-old liking yourself and not having to spend half your life scrabbling after crumbs of confirmation from other people—is a process that loses much of its power, its translating abilities, as we age. Beyond adolescence, it's very difficult to work up the escape velocity needed to free yourself from a self-esteem damaged in childhood. Not impossible, just damned hard. It's taken K several years of concerted effort, thousands of photographs, and close to a thousand blog posts to begin turning it around.

It helps that through her experiment she's discovering whole subcultures of men who appreciate if not fetishize curvy and hirsute women of size. "These guys clan together and get all geeked out about it," she said. Someone she calls "Mr. Maryland" is the one who brought this to her attention by telling her, "Your hair is a gift. You should be very proud of it, and wear it boldly, and don't ever shave it.' And that's when I thought, maybe there's something to that. What would it be like to have someone like my hair. Not just have to get past it, but really *love* it. So there's sex, and then there's sex with hair, and that's part of it now."

Last summer, K experienced something like a graduation ceremony vis-à-vis her social experiment. She had let her hair grow out in full—"full hairy legs, hair between my breasts, hairy armpits, the whole thing, long and dark and black"—and she was attending a business-networking event. It was a particularly warm day, she was wearing a sleeveless blouse, and when she took off her jacket, a man approached her and said, "You need to put your jacket on and be a professional."

And K, looking him square in the eye, raised her arms slowly, running her fingers languidly through her hair, baring her armpits, and said,

"Really?" The man stormed off, and a moment later three strangers, two women and a man, came up to her and said, "You go!"

"I never would have had the courage to do that before. And I felt exhilarated. Brazen even. Look at me, I'm hairy and proud, proud, proud."

A comment her daughter made when K first told her about her desire to post nude photos of herself online captures the sense of liberation she felt in that moment: "Wow, Mom, how Euro."

The Fading of Passion

Warning signs that a lover is bored:

1. Passionless kisses
2. Frequent sighing
3. Moved, left no forwarding address

—MATT GROENING

The passion that characterizes romantic love is generally considered, by both practitioners and scholars, to be an unstable element, prone to degrading steadily when exposed to familiarity and commitment. It seems to serve the same purpose as a booster rocket in the space program, launching people into orbit, but then falling away once that orbit is reached.

Sometimes it happens quickly, sometimes slowly, almost imperceptibly, as when you notice that you're starting to leave the "I" off "I love you." You say to your partner, "Love you," and he replies, "Love you too." And you begin wondering if it isn't significant, if you're not taking responsibility for the feeling anymore.

Loss is romance's sad fact. It's the hard ground we do our high-wire act above, the legends of the fall we've heard so much about. And it is a fact, according to biological anthropologist Helen Fisher in *Why We Love: The Nature and Chemistry of Romantic Love.* Passion and romance didn't evolve to help people maintain stable and long-term relationships, she contends. They evolved to ensure mating, whose enormous consumption of time and energy then needed to be turned toward child rearing and community building.

In the arena of relationship, Fisher considers romantic love one of the primordial human drives. The others are lust (the craving for sex), romantic love (the elation of focused courtship), and attachment (the ideally steady state of serenity, or at least security that helps the young get reared). But the biochemistry that powers it is *designed* to fade after a few years, lasting just long enough to do your reproductive duty and get a family started. Whether your personal agenda differs from evolution's agenda or not, it then mellows into the mechanics of keeping the wheels turning and building a life together, swapping fizz for friendship, passion and desire for companionship and care.

In *Primal Love*, Gillette argues that when we climbed down from the trees and began our walkabout on the savannas roughly five million years ago, it stirred into our brewing brains the notion of coupling up, a result of the intense cooperation required to survive down on the ground where the predators were. But this was serial monogamy, pair bondings that were programmed to fail somewhere in the third or fourth year, coinciding with the time when children climbed down from their parents' hips and began foraging on their own, freeing their parents to seek new genetic mixes. Not coincidentally, Fisher has shown that it's in the fourth year of marriage that the incidence of divorce is highest, in virtually all cultures.

In the grottos of the old brain, we may still be stomping around on the savannas, but in the here-and-now, we're often devastated by the decay of passion and romance in our relationships—even when their ardors are replaced by the deeper calm that can settle over people whose lives are satisfactorily entwined—and even in our one-night stands. After Romeo and Juliet's one ecstatic night together, she tries to convince him that the birdsong they hear is not the morning lark but the nightingale, so desperate is she not to see the night, and their rapture, come to an end.

But brain wiring is only one of the reasons why romance and passion tend to fade. Another is that at some level we *want* them to—because they're destabilizing.

The fact that dancing till dawn and lovemaking till it hurts are replaced by chaste evenings with a book and reserving candles for blackouts is a salve for many people. Especially those who find love's pitch and roll unsettling, it's mad passions stressful and disturbing to their equilibrium (there must be a reason we call it "lovesick"), and especially those who grew up in chaotic homes ruled and roiled by alcoholism or divorce or constant relocation, and for whom stability is likely to be their supreme priority. Lost on them will be the charms of mystery and uncertainty, the wave-making creativity of passion, and its endless argument for the wisdom of risk over safety.

Passion and romance are rife with vulnerability, and vulnerability is scary, thus passion is scary. The danger inherent in it is nowhere more evident than in a phrase the French use to describe orgasm: *la petite morte*, "the little death." Specifically, the death of restraint, if not order. To wit: a 2006 study in the *European Journal of Neuroscience* found that orgasm decreases blood flow to that part of the brain tasked with behavioral control.

And orgasm is only one among many little deaths we submit ourselves to in the name of intimacy, certainly eroticism: taking our clothes off in front of another person, placing our bodies in their hands to gratify or frustrate, being sometimes surprised by how our own bodies respond, by what private selves come out to play, by what classified information we blurt out in the throes of ecstasy, and by simply not knowing what will happen from moment to moment.

A scintillating romance with gut-churning, mind-altering, heart-skipping, poetry-inspiring ardor may be among the highest of human highs, but for that very reason it's considered an addictive substance with its classic euphorias, cravings for a fix, pains of withdrawal, and spiralings down. Brain scans of the love-struck, science tells us, are remarkably similar to those of cocaine addicts in terms of what parts of the brain get lit up.

On the other hand, a State University of New York at Stony Brook study found that the brain scans of couples who'd been married twenty years and who claim to still be in love with their partners looked very much like those of the newly-in-love, just less lit-up in areas of the brain that register fear and anxiety. They're still in love, but without the jitters that usually accompany that experience.

Those jitters help explain why we find in ourselves a powerful countervailing urge to safely moor ourselves at harbor and steady the boat. We want to establish solidity, predictability, and ownership and to convert the unknown quickly into the known. And the more attached we become to someone, and dependent on them, the more we stand to lose and the harder we strive to make our attachment secure in any way we can, healthy or unhealthy. We try to control them, control our own insecurities, and corral the unknown, and all of these can have a distinctly anti-erotic effect.

If passion is biodegradable, it's in part because our naturally occurring insecurities prompt us to expend deliberate effort degrading it. Passionlessness in relationship is largely a consequence of the collusion of the people in it to *solidify* their relationship.

Making Love: Why Passion Takes Work

In 1910 a composer from Illinois named Leo Friedman wrote the music for a little number called "Let Me Call You Sweetheart," which ended up haunting my love life one hundred years later.

The royalties from Friedman's best-selling song eventually passed to his nephew and helped support his entire family for decades, and when that nephew died, the monies passed to his two daughters—one of whom is my ex-wife, Robin. Today the royalty checks she receives from her greatuncle's songs are a pittance, fifty bucks here, fifty bucks there, but in the 1950s and '60s the royalties were enough to support a family of four.

Robin's first husband also lived on trickle-down wealth. He was one of the descendants of the family that owned the Fisher Body Company, which sold its products to most of the major auto manufacturers starting at the turn of the last century.

Unfortunately, the pattern did not hold in her second marriage—to me—a fact that contributed a fair bit of background radiation to our conflicts around money. One of the effects of Robin's fortuitous financial history was that she inherited, along with Great-Uncle Leo's bounty, the concept of magic money. That is, money that's yours to spend but wasn't generated by your efforts. Money that comes from a benefactor. Naturally, she also inherited a somewhat relaxed work ethic, which, in addition to her profession as an abstract painter, was seldom sufficient to bring in more than a few thousand dollars a year. By and large I took up the slack.

For twenty years I also executed splendid flip-flops between love and fear, coddling and wheedling, carrot and stick, engaged in all manner of subtle and not-so-subtle maneuvering to try to change this situation and affect in her the proper stance that, in my of course humble opinion, lent itself to the making of money.

Among the unfortunate dividends of this drama over the years was a crescendoing resentment between us—toward her for insolvency, toward me for judgment, and toward each other for our respective obstinacies—which soured our goodwill toward each other and pushed a splinter into the flesh of our marriage.

As legitimate as our respective needs and shortcomings around this were, and as hard as we strained to amend them, the power struggles they engendered were corrosive, and we often came up short on a feeling of security between us that had nothing to do with money, though the confusion between emotional and financial security is understandable. The language alone that we use to describe money and commerce is strikingly similar to the language we use to describe relationships. We talk about bonds, shares, trusts, securities, support, maturity, appreciation, interest, advances, tender, partnerships, penalty for early withdrawal.

There was a conspicuous deficit of tenderness, though, in our negotiations around this issue, as we billy-clubbed each other's arguments and engaged in our debate-club tactics. "I never said that. Yes you did. No I didn't. Next time we get a tape recorder. Great way to build trust. You said you weren't going to be sarcastic. Well, you said you weren't going to slam doors. Well, I wouldn't if you weren't so mean. And I wouldn't be so mean if you weren't pushing me. I wouldn't push you if you weren't so stubborn. I'm stubborn? You're way more stubborn than I am. I am not. You are too. Quit interrupting me. I will if you quit making things up. I'm not making things up. You are too. I am not. You're being defensive. No I'm just disagreeing. Well, it sounds defensive. You're not yelling at me, you're yelling at your mother. What are you implying? I'm not implying, I'm *inferring* . . ."

Round and round and round, pushing the buttons on each other's emotional jukeboxes, letting fly all the hurled plates of our hurts and angers, trying out all the possibilities of your fault, my fault, our fault, nobody's fault, the fault of parenting, gender, religion, culture, and the big bang for having gotten the whole mess started in the first place.

Not surprisingly, the best we were usually able to muster by way of solutions were temporary treaties and grudging concessions, though on a few occasions they seemed to hold the promise of finally turning the tide and freeing us from the submerged reefs onto which we'd run aground.

I remember one such occasion in particular, fifteen years in, an event that was simultaneously mundane and catalytic.

One morning Robin walked into my office, crossed her arms, and told me that she wanted to know she was loved without having to earn it, literally. She didn't want to wonder, didn't want to jump through hoops, didn't want an answer that changed from day to day depending on which side of the bed I woke up on. "I want to stop being mad at you," she said. "I want to stop fantasizing about making a ton of money and stuffing it up your nose," though that wasn't the only orifice she alluded to.

Besides, she said, it isn't love but bargaining, and how much money will it take, anyway, and will I penalize her, like the bank does, if the balance falls below a certain amount?

Inside my head, as usual, a thousand ships were launched, bombs burst in air, men dove for cover, orders were shouted, the decks suddenly slippery with the spilled entrails of all our marital fights. I reached for the brass knuckles of argument and defensiveness, fuming and pontificating, all of which suddenly seemed like nothing more than bullying, and I saw my entire love life flash in front of my eyes, not once but repeatedly.

I felt the familiar anxiety of standing in front of a blackboard filled with the mathematical equations and hieroglyphic formulas of advanced physics, looking in vain for something I might recognize—a plus or minus sign, a fraction, a clue.

I've lost my footing on icy mountain slopes and been dragged out to sea by riptides, and I knew this sensation of going down. I have fought for leverage in a hundred arguments about love—a hundred versions of the same argument—and in that moment, pinioned in my wife's gaze, I knew the truth at the heart of every one of them. That I'm afraid of love and love's *dependence*. Afraid of being run through on its sword-point or found guilty of its meanest accusation: that I'm not *worthy* of it. And I saw not just the lie at the heart of that fear, but also the fear at the heart of the lies I've spoken every time I've negotiated love and set terms to it.

Sitting there in my office, I also saw that all my efforts to change Robin, or even just to manage my own anxieties, had failed. All my efforts to gain the security I was after with all that horse-trading had failed. And just from the standpoint of return on investment, any graduate from even a third-rate business school would have abandoned this campaign years ago. I read recently that if I yelled nonstop for eight years, seven months, and six days, I would generate enough sound energy to heat one cup of coffee, and I felt like the guy whose life was the inspiration for that statistic.

Years ago a friend told me that there was something she'd always wanted from her husband that she couldn't get, and couldn't live without; it was some way that she wanted him to be that she never did divulge to me. But at some point she realized, she *decided*, that she *could* live without it, that it wasn't a deal breaker after all, and relinquishing the struggle for it and the drama around it proved to be as profound a step toward intimacy as marrying him in the first place.

The poet Rumi writes, "There are love stories, and there is obliteration into love. / You have been walking the ocean's edge, holding up your robes to keep them dry. / You must dive deeper under, a thousand times deeper."

With those Rumi-nations in mind, I found myself easing up on my third-rate campaign. I began restraining myself from looking over Robin's shoulder so much, bean counting and scorekeeping, insinuating the threat of abandonment if she didn't pony up. And I spent a little more time in the company of my own insecurities rather than looking to *her* for a fix. It wasn't even that I could point to any specific behavior modification. It was more a *felt* shift. But we both felt it. And it lasted for the better part of a year before the tide once again turned, and eventually drained out of our marriage altogether.

INTIMACY IS HARD. Love can founder on any number of submerged rocks, and the issues that lead us onto them—and which can gouge a hole below the waterline in the passion and goodwill between partners—are *complex*. That's why psychologists call them "complexes." It's also why one of Facebook's options for Relationship Status is "It's complicated." And it's not likely to become uncomplicated in five easy steps. You're not just going to swing a sword and cut through the knots, though I wish strength to your sword arm nonetheless.

Certainly, you'll need it if what's required to breathe life back into a relationship isn't a cosmetic change but rather a profound course correction, a significant change of heart or mind—and, as the Blooms managed and I did not, one that sticks.

Resuscitating desire, for instance, isn't as simple as introducing a little novelty into your sex life, because what leads to the alienation of affections isn't just boredom and routine. Sometimes it's unaddressed conflicts or a fear of intimacy. Sometimes it's the buildup of resentments over time or the catalog of disappointments we've experienced at the hands of the other; perhaps it's the expectation that your partner will read your mind rather than you *teaching* him or her how to please you. Sometimes it's a backlog of power struggles, the compromises we keep making that haunt us, and the ways we anesthetize ourselves to them. Often it's just daily schedules that don't allow couples to get a word in edgewise with each other, no less a weekly date night—the sheer too-muchness of our lives.

These are issues that have to be addressed at the level of source, not just symptom. They're usually immune to any amount of "get the spark back" relationship exercises, and resolving them is far more involved than a trip to Frederick's of Hollywood. But a lot of couples would apparently rather forgo sex and passion than open the furnace on these kinds of issues and conversations. Understandably.

But sustaining passion doesn't just happen. There's a reason we refer to *making* love. It takes *work.* "Day labor," Rilke called it. "God knows there is no other word for it."

In a scene from the novel *Breathing Lessons* by Anne Tyler, one of the protagonists, surrounded by his problematic family members on an outing to the shore, suddenly realizes that what is a true waste of life isn't his having to support all these people and bear their idiosyncrasies, but his failure to notice how he loves them. Yet in the next instant, when one of his daughters begins complaining about something, the feeling fades and he forgets what he learned.

We're distractible around love. We tip back and forth, in and out of love with our loved ones, learning and then forgetting what we learned. And how quickly it can happen, as if love is the most precarious of forces rather than the strongest, able to conquer all. A passing whim, a thought, a memory or a mood, a single word and the subtlest tone that carries it— all are capable of conjuring love or injuring it.

How is anything that susceptible supposed to withstand the storms unleashed by intimacy—the wounds that get roused from slumber under its warming effects, the dramas you unconsciously came together to reenact, the rages it can inspire, the slow grinding-down of desire or resolve or the age-old fantasy that love is forever, a miraculously self-regenerating flower, not an interminable construction project.

But it is. That's the hard truth of it. Love doesn't build itself, and it doesn't conquer all. Maybe it should. Maybe it should prevail over the priorities we constantly put above it—our careers, our freedoms, the high-flying flags of our ideals—requiring love to compete with everything else for our attention. "Love and intimacy are not ordinary human achievements," says Thomas Moore in *The Soul of Sex*. "They're extraordinary human achievements."

Just getting ourselves to step up to the plate is an accomplishment, given the résumés of rejected love we often bring to the game. The memories we carry of how love is a bruiser of hearts and a king of clubs makes us reluctant to rush at it or let strangers into the house, reticent to allow ourselves a trust-fall into the arms of intimacy. Better to hold out until we pass beyond this life and are forever unhurtable.

There's a reason divorce comes in at number two on the famous Holmes and Rahe stress scale of life's most challenging events, second only to the death of a spouse, and, inconceivably, ahead of a prison sentence. The loss of love, in other words, is more traumatic to people than the loss of freedom.

We also bring to the bargaining table whatever lessons in love we were exposed to as children, which our developing brains distilled into a handful of guiding principles that may or may not be valid and constructive. Love is nurturing or love is suffocating; people are trustworthy or people are not; dependence is healthy or dependence is humiliating. Monkey see, monkey do. And if we get love all wrong, then, as software designers say about glitches in their programs, it's a feature and not a bug.

As for romance, we don't just hop into bed with our partners. We bring to our erotic lives the full spectrum of our feelings and experiences around being or not being nurtured, the entire history of our relationship to relationship. How trusting are you of other people? How worthy do you feel of receiving love? How well defended are your boundaries? How do you feel about letting go of control? Do you like to be touched? How naked are you willing to be with another person? How do you feel about your body? How much insecurity can you tolerate? How much pleasure? How much anger do you have around love? Around power? Around sex? What are you willing to do to be close to somebody? How much compassion can you muster for yourself? And how much for your *partner's* vulnerabilities, for his or her struggle to open to love?

When intimacy asks us to look closely at these questions, when relatedness demands that we build a better mousetrap, no matter how contrary it feels, we're being called to *work* at love. And the real work of it, the real tests, tend to come when being in love starts giving way to loving, just as the seeds of redwoods don't germinate except in the face of fire. The mythologist Joseph Campbell, popularizer of "the hero's journey," said, "Marriage is an ordeal. It means yielding time and again. It means sacrificing the ego. That's why it's a sacrament."

The heat of the marital kitchen—of intimacy in general—can be intense enough to drive a lot of people from it. Not that some don't coast along *within* their relationships, never getting to the meat of it or the heat of it—the *possibilities* of it. But the hottest part of the flame is in the middle, and it's here that we encounter the hard work of loving another person with all his or her baggage, of managing our incompatibilities, pushing our limits, wrestling with our demons and angels, and continually plying the oars. And of course the work of loving *yourself* when you fail to live up to your own standards.

What you stand to gain from all your day labor is an actual living breathing boots-on-the-ground experience of being in love, rather than outside looking in. But be aware that you can work too hard at love, and your relationships can become about being in relationship. Some couples even seem to believe that working on their relationship all the time (along with drama, intensity, and conflict) is a marker of depth. But this is like saying that you're not taking life seriously if you're not worrying about it all the time. Suffering is not necessarily deep, and joy is not necessarily shallow.

"You kids," my mother once told me, referring to my generation, "you're much more sophisticated than we ever were," referring to her generation. "Much more psychologically astute, better communicators, more emotionally thoughtful. On the other hand, you also think too much."

Adrenaline Makes the Heart Grow Fonder

The word *romance* originally referred to a story, a narrative of specifically heroic deeds. Whether that story involves two lovers, a family, or a community, a romance, to be true to itself, must involve stories of heroism and acts of courage—from the French word for "heart." In other words, courage doesn't mean backbone or balls, contrary to popular belief. It means *heart*. And the courage that matters most, that really drives the plot, is precisely the *routine* acts of heartfulness. Not the grand gestures or the flashy displays, but the daily ministrations, the everyday (not as in ordinary but as in *every day*) acts of what psychologist Robert Johnson calls "stirring the oatmeal love."

Rather than looking for the love of your life, passion might be better served by looking for the love *in* your life, and toward that end, the old idea-generating technique called brainstorming might offer a useful approach, because the question that animates that whole process is "In how many ways can I . . . ?" Or as the poet Elizabeth Barrett Browning famously put it, "How do I love thee? Let me count the ways."

The small daily acts that keep partners in each other's good graces do more for passion and intimacy than an annual Valentine's Day dinner out or an occasional fling at a motel with a heart-shaped Jacuzzi. Call to find out how his client presentation went, remember to leave the croutons out of her salad because she's gone gluten-free, slip love notes into her purse/socks/daybook/medicine cabinet/briefcase, pick up that book that's waiting for him at the library, listen to each other's dreams in the morning before hitting the treadmill, sext one another in the middle of the day.

It's hardly heroic to love others when you're infatuated with them, or when they still have their adorable baby fat and can't talk back yet, or during the big-happy-family phase of community building. Real heroism, true romance, is in the workaday narratives of keeping love alive. It's continuing to romance them even though they're as familiar to you as your furniture and you've heard it all before, and maybe especially when they try your patience. The most useful day labors may well be under those less-than-ideal conditions that human relations so often present us, since loving people when they're difficult is the best practice for loving them at all and truly.

I recently encountered—and missed—just such an opportunity when I was bicycling on a paved path through the university campus near my home, coming down a hill and fast approaching a car that had inexplicably stopped in one of the path's crosswalks. As I roared up to him, I heard myself mutter, "C'mon you idiot, move!" But he just sat there, and I had to slam on my brakes and swerve around him.

Ten seconds later I caught myself—angrily judging a complete stranger. For all I knew, he could have been buckling his five-year-old into her seat. Or talking to his wife who was in the hospital with breast cancer. Or yes, even just spacing out and not paying attention.

In that moment, I realized how often I respond that way: muttering at strangers for their various and ubiquitous idiocies, as if I myself never commit them. But we're all somebody else's jerk from time to time, and just because I have an expectation for how others are supposed to behave doesn't mean they're going to accommodate me, and when they don't, I often find myself frustrated and angry. Expectations are just resentments waiting to happen.

Romance isn't merely a phase of love; it's an *attribute*, says Stephen A. Mitchell in *Can Love Last?* And it's one of the heroic deeds that keep the story of love moving. But this requires diligence and vigilance, a continual flow of affections and intimacies, gratitudes and kindnesses, courtesies, flowers, chocolates. It takes a commitment to continue doing things together and not fall into the habit of living merely parallel lives. The law of entropy reminds us that systems tend to lose energy and that chemical bonds weaken over time. A hot cup of coffee will eventually cool down *unless reheated*. A clock will eventually run down *unless rewound*. Oatmeal will congeal without regular stirring, and soulmates will turn into stalemates. And there lies the key: we need to continually expend energy in the form of attention, affection, and appreciation.

As the novelist Jeanette Winterson says, "It's true that heroes are inspiring, but mustn't they also do some rescuing if they're to be worthy of the name? Would Wonder Woman matter if she only sent commiserating telegrams to the distressed?"

The reheating of passion happens in relationships the same way it happens in your *own* life when you're bored—by trying something new. Taking a risk. Or at least investigating what the boredom is about. The question of how to keep the fires burning is the question of how to stay interested in life itself, and among the best prescriptions for that is novelty. Doing novel things together and separately, and regularly. As I once heard someone say, "Adrenaline makes the heart grow fonder."

Manufacturing new highs and challenges together, though, doesn't mean saying, "I've got a challenge for you: help out around the house more." And it doesn't mean fighting, as much of an adrenaline rush as that can be. It means setting new and mutually satisfying goals together—working toward a vacation, taking a class together, attending a *different* church this Sunday, just for variety's sake, jumping in the car and seeing where you end up, taking occasional creative time apart, always having something to look forward to together. But perhaps most important, it means continually sharing the insights you each bring back from your own voyages of self-discovery, your own inner work.

Life's plateaus and restless patches often propel people to seek change and search for lost passion, but there are many ways to go about this. A red sports car is very different from a career change or life review, and an affair is very different from a heart-to-heart talk with your partner that reestablishes communication and commitment. Not that the plateau phases of life and love should be denigrated. Even if they're accompanied by boredom, they can also represent the well-deserved solidity that comes from a sense of mastery, the success achieved by longtime devotion to a person or pursuit.

But if we understand, as Gillette suggests, that boredom was in part invented by nature to ensure (genetic) variety, and not merely a failure to love adequately—and if we counter this dynamic with some dynamism of our own, some deliberate interventions—we can temper nature's intent and help our relationships reheat and rewind.

Novelty, though, is by definition unfamiliar, a detour from our usual haunts, and this tends to make us nervous even while it arouses us. Thus we come around full circle to the discussion of vulnerability as stimulant. I was recently reminded that novelty, vulnerability, and aphrodisia all share a border, when Paula asked me to *dance* for her.

We had come back to my place after a Thanksgiving dinner with some friends, gone upstairs to my office, lit candles, and danced to a CD of love songs I had compiled for her a few months earlier. After half an hour, she slumped in the big cushioned chair and said, "I want you to dance for me." Something I have never done in my life, for anybody. Or ever imagined I would do, for anybody.

But I just took a deep breath and went with it. I did an erotic dance for her right there in the middle of my office, to a John Mayer song called, appropriately, "Edge of Desire."

That night I dreamed of turtles being pulled from their shells.

THE CONDITIONS THAT foster passion, or the return of it, seem to begin with the willingness to go in *search* of it, even if that willingness is fueled only by desperation, and it requires that we push our edges. Security and predictability may be important parts of the succor of love, but without desire—which demands the occasional dare and seeks what's *outside* the safety net—they can become bloodless and abstract. Ultimately they can actually make love not safer but more dangerous, because we become increasingly unschooled in seeing things as they really are—in flux and mysterious—and unable to muster the resilience necessary to ride out love's inconsistencies.

Love without desire, says Mitchell, can certainly be tender, intimate, and secure, but it lacks adventure and the sense of risk that fuels romantic passion: "Homes turn into prisons; enclosures becomes confinements; the lover who was ardently courted and longed for becomes one's 'old lady' or 'old man' or 'ball and chain.'" Love without desire is also a contradiction in terms, since among the origins of the word *love* is a Sanskrit term meaning "desire."

For some couples, of course, the very magic of a relationship is in the companionable mundaneness that it proffers if you stick with it long enough, the rough stones worn smooth by time and routine. Or as Elizabeth Gilbert puts it, "Coffee, dog, breakfast, newspaper, garden, bills, chores, radio, lunch, groceries, dog, dinner, reading, dog, bed . . . and repeat."

Beyond a tolerance for trial and error, though, risk-taking is helped along, ironically, by having what psychologists call a "confiding relationship"—the kind in which you feel safe enough to approach the edge of desire (or one of sufficient brevity or anonymity that you don't care). A confiding relationship is one in which you can speak your mind and your heart, where there's a climate of trust that allows you to express your abandon and unleash your lusts, and ideally a partner who profoundly understands how much courage and vulnerability it takes to bare your soul and your naked body to another person, that we all bruise easily and therefore exquisite care is in order, and that the greatest erogenous zone isn't the one between your legs but between your ears.

The rub is that to take advantage of the healing power of a confiding relationship, you've got to actually *confide*. You've got to reveal things that many people are terrified will lose them the very love they're after. Meaning that the hunger to be safe works against the hunger to be known, which will have to fight against a stiff headwind to gain purchase in your psyche and your relationships.

One reason why people often try out their wings in a confiding relationship with a *therapist*, and why therapy is often so effective, is that love isn't just the ends there but also the *means*. Under the watchful eye of a good therapist, say the authors of *A General Theory of Love*, we learn or relearn the arts of love not by dint of homework assignments or self-help books, but by being in the presence of someone adept at modeling a healthy relationship—someone more skilled at love than you. It's not the *style* of therapy someone conducts that matters. It's the *person* of the therapist.

But make no mistake—therapy is a razor's edge too. Most people are there because the needle has gone into the red zone and gotten stuck there, and they know they need a rap on the back of the head. They're there because nothing else has worked—not all the book reading and personal-growth workshops, the affirmations and prayers and mission statements and steaming platters of self-help—and you've got that phone number a friend gave you. It means real change, scary personal change, and someone who's going to hold your feet to the fire.

But unless it's court-ordered, or the result of an ultimatum, you've got to seek it out for yourself. And this is a kind of nakedness all by itself, the admission that you *need* help, with its implication of your shortcomings, and the very common fear of being screwed for revealing your vulnerabilities. And it's especially difficult for anyone who happens to have been born a man, because the kind of vulnerability required to ask for help is generally bred out of us at a pretty early age.

A few years ago I read a story in the *Atlantic* magazine written by a waiter who works in a restaurant in Midtown Manhattan. He said that men who are choking in restaurants will sometimes, out of pride and the fear of embarrassment, hide in the bathroom, where they'll die because they can't get help.

I mentioned this story to an audience in Washington, D.C., the week after I read it, and a fellow raised his hand and said that he had done exactly that recently, and the only reason he was still around to tell the story was that someone happened to follow him into the bathroom and administer the Heimlich maneuver.

Another man a few rows back then raised his hand and said he ran a mortuary and the same is true of men who are having chest pains in public.

Then a woman behind the two of them spoke up and said that some men probably wouldn't even *make* it to the bathroom because they don't know where it is, and men of course would rather die than ask for directions.

Several years ago, my friend Pripo flew to New Hampshire to attend the wedding of a longtime buddy, and on the day before the ceremony a group of them went swimming at a nearby lake. Most were planning on swimming to the far shore and back, and though Pripo is not a strong swimmer, he decided to join them, at least for part of the crossing.

He made it about fifty yards out before realizing that he was farther from shore than he'd ever been, and though he felt a sense of pride in the accomplishment, he also felt enough anxiety that he turned back for shore. The anxiety, though, rapidly escalated into panic, and the panic into exhaustion, and the thought crossed his mind, "I could drown here."

He could also have called for help, but he didn't, though there were people swimming only twenty yards away, and more people onshore. Instead he started to go under. He remembers seeing green water above him, feeling his muscles give out, his lungs about to go out, and cursing his pride for ruining his friend's wedding.

Suddenly, the image of his wife and son flashed into his mind, and along with it came a burst of lifesaving energy, enough to get him safely to shore, where he lay on his back on the sand and hyperventilated for ten minutes.

And this is a psychotherapist, who routinely counsels people on the importance of asking for help, and makes his living from their willingness to swallow their pride and do so. Yet in the aftermath of his own near drowning, he was concerned about the self-reinforcing outcome of the incident, which proved that he didn't need help after all, that he could fend for himself.

A few weeks later, he was at home with his wife and son, standing at the kitchen counter with some take-out Chinese food, when he popped a shrimp into his mouth—and promptly began choking on it. This time, however, he *ran* for help. He ran toward his wife, turned his back to her, grabbed her by the hands, and simulated the Heimlich maneuver. She was unfamiliar with it, but following his lead, they managed to dislodge the shrimp from his throat. He was exhilarated, not only by being brought back from the brink, but also by his own willingness to, finally, ask for help.

Whether you seek help from therapists, shamans, or the wisdom of your own soul, though, the point is finding the courage to look inside and feel what you feel, and then to confront whatever blocks the natural flow of electricity between you and others, and prevents those purple sparks of passion from kicking up their heels. As Fritz Perls, the father of Gestalt therapy, used to say, awareness + risk-taking = growth.

Granted, self-awareness is often frightful as well as fruitful, and will often put the "ow" in growth and the "edge" in knowledge, and love is full of both marvelous and perilous glory. But just as Botticelli's painting *The Birth of Venus* shows the goddess of love naked on the half shell and rising fully grown from beneath the waves, the fruition of love in our lives requires that we work toward bringing our submerged passion and vitality up to the surface.

Years ago, when I lived in Tucson, Arizona, I often attended lectures offered gratis every Sunday morning by the relationship author Hugh Prather, who had just written *Love and Courage*. One Sunday, he mentioned that however character building our efforts on behalf of love may be, in the final analysis the benefits outweigh the costs. "Consider the children's song 'Row, Row, Row Your Boat,'" he said. "For every three *rows*, you get four *merrilys*."

5

The Freedoms of Expression

If you ask me what I came into this world to do,
I will tell you. I came to live out loud.

—ÉMILE ZOLA

EVERY FRIDAY NIGHT in downtown Asheville, weather permitting, a large group of drummers, forty to fifty of them, gathers in Pritchard Park and plays djembes and djun djuns, ashikos and congas, cowbells and agogos and shakers, for hours, while hundreds of people listen, dance, take pictures, and show off the more peculiar aspects of their personalities and wardrobes.

One recent Friday I saw a man wearing billowing pantaloons and an embroidered gypsy vest, and sporting a shiny purple bag over his head, of the sort you might take home from an exclusive department store, to which he had attached antennas and cut out eyeholes. I've also seen a woman who hula-hoops while reading books, a guy with a bone through his nose like a Sumatran, another with a small black Jolly Roger flying from his headband, another who plays a jumbo-size kazoo amplified with a megaphone, and a belly dancer in full regalia who dances with a sword on top of her head.

A local police officer even stops by on occasion and, while in full uniform, straps on a djembe, redefining the concept of a cop on the beat.

All of them, myself included, gather together in an unfettered display of what sociologist Émile Durkheim called "collective effervescence," the passion or ecstasy induced by communal rites, rituals and raves, harvest festivals and Burning Man festivals, trance dances, parades, religious ceremonies, and rock concerts, which help create a sense of unity and community among people, provide a counterbalance to life's dismembering and dispiriting forces, and give them a grand and inclusive opportunity to express themselves.

In a culture pressure-cooked by anxiety and fear, with so many inhibitions on authenticity and self-expression, so many of our spirits driven in and entombed, I consider it damn near a political act to give people an excuse to let their backbones slip, if "political" pertains to the affairs of state, and the state of the body-politic is as wound up as it is. In savage times, it's not just entertainment but also social action and community service to help soothe the savage beasts and give them a chance to roar.

The popularity of the drum circle attests to people's hunger for this. After ten years, the event is enshrined in hundreds of YouTube videos, tourist guidebooks, travel articles including in the *New York Times* and *Washington Post*, and coffee-table books, and it has been designated by the Asheville City Council as one of the town's six "anchor events." I've even fielded calls from other cities inquiring how to launch one.

Whether these passionate rituals are rhythmic, athletic, religious, or carnivalistic, they're fueled by what the folklorist Roger D. Abrahams (in Barbara Ehrenreich's book *Dancing in the Streets: A History of Collective Joy*) calls "the spirit of increase, of stretching life to the fullest," even to the transcendent, since they're designed to induce the feeling of being part of something bigger than yourself, surrounded by the larger hive.

Like the drum circle, they typically involve music, dancing, costuming, masking, and self-decoration, and in other cases feasting and drinking. And they're a primordial part of us. Paleolithic cave paintings from places as far-flung as Africa and Australia, Egypt and India, show portraits of conga lines, of figures who are presumed to be dancing because their postures resemble no recognizably utilitarian activity like hunting or farming—their arms high in the air, their hands held in a circle, their bodies leaping, their hair standing out from their heads as if in a stiff breeze.

And drums have been an integral part of this spirit of increase since the wild-haired sons and daughters of Bacchus played them in the Neolithic temples of the moon, helping to drive the gods into the bodies of the devotees. They're an imitation of and an homage to the rhythms of the natural world, from the sound of our mothers' blood pulsing in our prenatal ears to the proto sounds of the human world—the pounding of seeds, the knapping of flint, the clapping of hands; from the turbo-fluttering of molecules to the expansion-contractions of the universe, all the micro and macro rhythms that regulate the movement of hearts and herds, seasons and star systems, and keep bringing the swallows back to Capistrano.

But drums aren't flutes and woodwinds, proffering a white-gloved hand in request of a dance. They grab you by the tie and pull you onto the dance floor. This is music that seizes you by the brain stem, not the frontal cortex. It's not a thinking person's music, classical, erudite, something to be sipped with white wine. It's meant to be gulped down in gallon jugs and wiped from your mouth with your sleeve.

It's meant to make you sweat your prayers, and to pray with your whole body. And then to take your body—shirt untucked, hair standing out from your head, skin glistening with musk and pheromones—and join it with the bodies of others, and with the bodies of the drums, which themselves come from the bodies of trees and animals, and together to forge a jubilant trinity of plant, animal, and human.

There's a scene in *Zorba the Greek*—a work whose titular character is the ultimate Bacchanalian—in which, after a wild full-bodied dance that ends with him collapsed in a happy heap on the ground, panting like an animal, the narrator, a sober intellectual who "always held [his] kite tightly, so that it should not escape," asks Zorba what came over him to make him dance like that? "What could I do, boss? My joy was choking me. I had to find some outlet. And what sort of outlet? Words? Pff!"

WHETHER OUR SELF-EXPRESSIONS involve dancing or singing or running a restaurant, whether they're communal or personal, the hunger is the same: to get what's on the inside out. To make the unconscious conscious, the invisible visible. To let our cats out of the bag.

We have voices that want to be outspoken and bodies that want to move and shake, stories that need telling and secrets that need spilling, gratitudes and creativities to express, ideas we need to run up the flagpole in hopes that others will rally around us, and grievances we need to take out and detonate lest some innocent person stumble on them and get hurt.

In a sense *everything* you do is an expression of who you are, from the shoes you wear to the way you raise your children, the way you spend your time, the way you solve your problems, how you shop and what you read, how you react to suffering or joy, and the work you do. The question is, is it an expression of who you *really* are? Ideally, who you are should be expressed in what you do, and what you do should be an expression of who you are. You know it when there's a match and you know it when there's not.

Whatever passions and vitalities are trying to emerge in our lives are like centrifugal forces pushing out from inside us. "I hear something stamping," says a character in Virginia Woolf's novel *The Waves*. "A great beast's foot is chained. It stamps, and stamps, and stamps."

When improv teacher Nina Wise asks students what brings them to her improv classes, they talk of something missing in their lives, a longing to rekindle the spirit of self-expression, spontaneity, and play—the turbines of creativity. They want to lift the lids they've clamped over their lives, beneath which are great balls of fire—energy, emotions, expressiveness, passion, *contribution*.

What they're ultimately after, she says, is "delivering the truth." And whether we deliver it through words, images, or sounds, through art, innovation, or improvisation, we release the heat of the spirit and say yes to what wants to emerge in our lives.

To express means to push outward, to press into being. And not just to transmit but to *reveal*, the way tears reveal grief and dreams confess desires, the way you squeeze juice from an orange or press clay into shape. Expression is "e-motion." It's "pro-creation." It's giving birth to your passions, visions, and talents as well as to *yourself*, unearthing and sharing your deepest authenticity, if not the deeper voices that want to speak *through you*, which are also trying to push their way into the world—your Buddha nature, your Christ consciousness, your true self.

What, after all, are the orchestral songs of mockingbirds, the sleekness of jaguars, and the elegant whorls in seashells, the way you wear your hat, and the way you sip your tea, but expressions of a being just being what it is? It comes with the territory. And if it's not being expressed, it's being suppressed or repressed or depressed, which all imply the same thing: being forced down.

And when we draw it up, or *dredge* it up, as the case may be—what's within us, what needs expression—we also bring into being the power of self-awareness and the light of comprehension, a grasp of what we *know* in the way British educator Graham Wallas meant it when he quoted a young girl under his tutelage who said, "How do I know what I think till I see what I say?"

In fact, if you'd like a visual aid to examine how passion and dispassion express themselves in your life, have a friend interview you on camera about the dreams and visions you have in any arena—vocation, social life, health, romance. Talk about how you feel about what you're currently doing, what you'd like to be doing, what you've dared and double-dared yourself to do, the pros and cons of your various choices, what fears, fantasies, dreams, or body symptoms have attended each lately and what advice you receive from your head/heart/soul/body/spirit.

The point is to get you talking freely for at least half an hour. And you want a nice tight shot, primarily head and upper body, the interviewer offscreen and just to the side of the camera.

Then get a group of friends together on a Friday night, make popcorn, watch the video together, and let them give you feedback on what they see. Because what you'll see, in parts per million, will be an outpouring of raw data about how you truly feel about your involvements and what your body reveals about the proceedings. You'll see changes of expression, gesture, posture, and energy. You'll see the lights come on in your eyes when you're impassioned, and you'll see them go out when you're not. Just choose your friends wisely. This is intimate stuff, flying-under-the-radar stuff.

Self-expression can indeed be a most literal revelation, though it often requires that you dive deep to bring it to the surface, engaging in what some people call navel-gazing and others call mental health. The patterns of behavior, speech, and thought that hold you back from a fully lived and fully expressed life, says author and psychotherapist John Lee, become "fixed in your body like barnacles on the underbelly of a boat, and you can't see them unless you submerge into yourself and take a close look."

Lee tells the story of a man who attended one of his men's retreats in North Carolina some years ago. In his early thirties, Jeremy was slender and rugged and spoke almost in a whisper, and around a bonfire one evening he told the story of how—though doctors said there was nothing organically wrong with them that should preclude their ability to conceive—he and his wife had been unsuccessful in their attempts to have a baby.

"I think there's something inside me that isn't about the physical," Jeremy said, "but I have no idea what it could be."

When Lee asked him whether he was afraid of becoming a father, he admitted he was afraid of becoming the kind of father his father was. "The kind who left us when I was thirteen and I've never seen since. In a way I keep waiting for him to come back and tell me why he left. The only thing I have of his is this baseball cap he gave me when I was twelve." He took the hat off and held it out, gazing at it like a sacred object. "I wear it all the time."

"You're a man wearing a boy's hat," Lee gently said to him, "waiting for a father to come back and show you how to be a father. But the time for him to be a father to you has passed. It's time *you* become a father. It's time to feel the pain of abandonment. I want you to take that hat off your head again, throw it into the fire, and say, 'You left me, but I'm not you.'"

Jeremy looked at Lee, then around at the circle of men, then down at his hat. "What good will that do?" he asked. "It's the only thing I have of his." At which point he broke down in tears.

"I honestly don't know if it will do any good," Lee replied. "It's only a suggestion. Don't do it unless you feel it's right. But although a boy can't father a child, a strong, intelligent, creative, potent man will be a damn good father because you aren't anything like your dad. Your dad wouldn't be here on his best day doing the kind of work you've committed to doing for yourself and for the sake of your family."

Jeremy looked at the hat for several more minutes in silence. Then he said, uncharacteristically loudly, loud enough perhaps for his father to hear, wherever he was, "I'm not you! I won't abandon my family no matter what. You missed knowing me, and I'm a damn good man."

Then he threw the hat into the fire, and that circle of men gave him a standing ovation.

A year later, at another retreat, Jeremy went up to Lee, opened his wallet, and proudly showed off photos of his three-month-old son.

The Hunger to Make Contact

The drive for self-expression is age-old, like our communal rituals of effervescence and our spiritual aspirations, but it's probably fair to say they're all luxuries compared with those drives lower down on our hierarchy of needs: food, clothing, shelter, and security. It's not that the lack of these things, say in the guise of hunger or poverty, necessarily precludes people from having spiritual ambitions or an appetite for self-expression, but generally speaking, you've got to have a little food in your stomach before you can turn your attention to counting the number of angels that can dance on the head of a pin.

If you were tossed out on your ass in the wilderness, you'd more or less follow the survival playbook. First, you'd have to take care of finding water and food, protecting yourself from the elements, building shelter, and banding together with others. Activities like composing ballads about your adventures, searching for the meaning and purpose in it all, and whiling away the hours conferrin' with the flowers would pretty much have to wait.

But once creature comforts were checked off the list, you'd become hungry for creative expression. And you'd be driven to it in part to simply be true to yourself as the most naturally expressive of creatures, and for the sheer self-satisfaction of it. But you'd also express yourself to make contact, because we don't want to just survive; we want to be seen and heard and felt and known, and *witnessed.*

By the time Zorba came on the scene, his homeland of Crete had been fighting for freedom from Turkish rule for hundreds of years. One of his compatriots, too old to be a freedom fighter, spent his days writing letters to the kings and queens of Europe and Russia, beseeching them for help, to no avail. A friend asked why he continued to write his unreconciled letters. "Your crying is useless. No one hears you." To which the man replied, "A cry is never wasted! All the kings and the mighty of the earth, to whom I write, will one day hear. And if they do not, then their children and grandchildren. And if not these, then God. Why is God there? Why, do you think? To hear!"

Whether you get a response to your cries or not, however, the circuit isn't complete until you share them with others. Creatively speaking, what this means is that you have to first inhale life and then exhale it as expression, as writing, photography, music, speech, invention, leadership, or community building. You have to expose yourself to life, bathe yourself in it, try to capture it as you've been captivated *by* it, and then—it can't be helped, since we're products of our culture—*do* something with it. Even knowing that life ultimately belongs to itself and can't be fully seduced onto the canvas or lured into the corral of words. Even knowing that our senses, though keen, are inadequate to the task of communicating even just the *beauty* around us, no less the breadth of it all. As Virginia Wolff once said, "Nature has given you six little pocket knives with which to cut up the body of a whale."

Still, you whittle away at it, working to spread the word and make contact, working to be seen and heard and witnessed and helping others to do the same, because it's part of banding together with others, and being of service. Which is why it's so important not to keep what you know and who you are just a tidy little secret between you and yourself, hunching over it protectively as if it were the most tremulous candle flame always in danger of being blown out, but instead to let it fan out into the world and into the lives of others who, just maybe, could use the illumination themselves.

When I was in college, I majored in changing majors. I went through sociology, English, anthropology, archaeology, back to English, and psychology, before I took a course called "How to Run a College Newspaper," and boom, the light went on. I wanted to be a writer and major in journalism.

But when I informed my academic adviser that I wanted to be a writer, she said, "Excellent! A noble profession. I'm signing you up for business classes next semester."

"What do you mean 'business classes'?" I said. "I want to be a writer."

She patiently explained that in her experience, writers so often fear sullying their creative spirits with the vulgarities of business that they too often end up sullying them by *not* studying the craft of business along with the craft of writing. Without a firm grounding in how a product sells—and writing is just a product, she said, go ahead and weep—writers end up unable to make a living, or any part of a living, doing what they love. And *that*, she promised me, would have a far more vulgar and ruinous effect on my creative spirits than business ever would.

So over the next few semesters, I slogged my way through classes in economics, marketing, management, advertising, even design, in addition to my precious Survey of Western Lit, English Comp, Expository Writing, American Fiction 1912–1945, and Journalism 101. And within six months of graduating, all those business classes paid off, because I landed a job as a reporter at the *Cincinnati Enquirer*—in fact, as their youngest-ever full-time reporter and columnist. And what got me that job was my success in pitching myself to them as their first singles lifestyle columnist, backed up by insights I gleaned from those business classes, such as how to sell a product and how to position yourself in the marketplace.

Business, in other words, turned out to be the way I was able to give my gift to the world, the bellows that helped me fan the flames of my passion so that others could see it at a distance. Without those classes, I would have produced, but I might not have sold, and my Great American Writing would have sat on a shelf collecting Great American Dust.

THE IMPULSE TO share our passions finds us fanning them out into not just into the world, but into the universe. The desire to express ourselves and make contact with others isn't just personal or tribal but also planetary.

In 1977, two spacecraft, Voyagers 1 and 2, were launched from Cape Canaveral, their mission to explore the solar system before heading out into interstellar space. Still hurtling along at thirty-five thousand miles an hour, they're currently approaching the edge of what's called the heliosphere, the enormous bubble of charged particles that surrounds our solar system, inflated into existence by the sun's solar wind, which pushes out into the surrounding cosmos at a million miles an hour. Our entire solar system is like a single bubble deep in the ocean, and the Voyager crafts are approaching—and will soon pass through—the edge where that bubble meets the greater ocean.

Attached to the outside of each of the Voyagers is a gold-plated phonograph record with playing instructions written in scientific language, and on it is a message from Earth to any extraterrestrials who happen to come across it out there. Given that it will take the Voyagers forty thousand years to reach only the next star system over, the interval between sending and receiving—to say nothing of getting a response—is virtually interminable in human scale, and the chance of the recording actually being played by an extraterrestrial is infinitesimal. Its real audience is us terrestrials, and its real function, as program coordinator Carl Sagan put it, is "to appeal to and expand the human spirit."

As far back as the kings of ancient Assyria, who placed cuneiform time capsules in the foundation stones of their monuments and palaces, we've been driven by the urge to tell others, as well as future generations we'll never live long enough to meet, who we are and what we've accomplished.

Toward that end, the phonograph record contains, encoded in analog form, 117 photographs of life on Earth; greetings in fifty-four languages, including that of the humpback whale and the ancient Sumerian tongue of Akkadian, which hasn't been spoken in nearly two thousand years; and a compendium of native sounds: an elephant trumpeting, a rocket launching, a cricket chirping, a kiss, footsteps, heartbeats, laughter, and thunder.

It also includes ninety minutes of what one of the project collaborators called "Earth's Greatest Hits," starting with Bach's *Brandenburg Concerto* and ending with Beethoven's *Cavatina from the String Quartet no. 13* in B-flat, op. 130, and in between Javanese gamelan music, a Pygmy initiation song, Senegalese percussion, a Navajo night chant, Louis Armstrong's "Melancholy Blues," and Chuck Berry's "Johnny B. Goode." (In a *Saturday Night Live* sketch a year after the Voyagers were launched, Steve Martin, playing a psychic, reveals that Earth would shortly receive a broadcast from extraterrestrials saying, "Send more Chuck Berry.")

Needless to say, there were kerfuffles about what was and wasn't chosen to represent Earth, but among the more potent critiques of what was put on NASA's "Golden Record" is that we show only our good side. There are no scenes of war, famine, poverty, or devastation; no indications that life here on our little heavenly body is anything but hunky-dory, which on either a planetary or a personal level is a seriously incomplete picture.

Still, the impetus for the project, according to Sagan, was the desire to make contact. "No one sends such a message on such a journey, to other worlds and other beings, without a positive passion for the future. For all the possible vagaries of the message, they could be sure that we were a species endowed with hope and perseverance, at least a little intelligence, substantial generosity, and a palpable zest to make contact with the cosmos."

Holding Your Horses: The Force of Inhibition

The cosmos, unfortunately, is not always so accommodating to our zest—certainly not our little corner of it. Earthly life is, in fact, so full of deterrents to self-expression that what we casually refer to as "normal" behavior is really a state of arrested development. It's just so pervasive that we often don't notice it.

Through the rapped knuckles of our upbringings, for example, most of us learn early on that the full-throated expression of who we are isn't necessarily welcome, and we end up with internalized scolds telling us to sit still, pipe down, not be a showoff, not be smarter than the boys, and not let 'em see you cry. We end up suppressing whole sectors of our passion and life force to get on with the powers that be, to approximate the good boy, the good girl.

I recently consulted with a woman who told me that when she was growing up, her parents sent her to her room for any displays of "negative emotions" like tears, anger, or frustration. That is, punished her. *Banished* her. Even after she was assaulted and raped as a young woman, her father's stern advice was that she simply had to "march on" and leave it behind.

It's no surprise that at forty, after a lifetime of repressing half of her emotional repertoire, she was confronting the legacy of that stunted education by feeling blocked from being her full, powerful self, the one she needs in order to be the healer she intuits herself to be. She quite rightly refers to her mission as nothing less than "soul retrieval," reclaiming the powers and passions, the emotions, she once held in check to avoid getting an ass-whupping, but which are now the very source of her power and passion here at halftime.

The survival mechanisms of childhood work against us in adulthood, and it's one of the tragic equations of childhood that we'll readily trade authenticity for approval. And so will a great many of the adults these children become. In a short story called "My Grandmother Who Painted," Honor Moore says that at some point, her grandmother "was free and talented" and then she "married, had kids, went mad and stopped finishing her paintings at thirty-five."

Years later an old friend of her grandmother's asked what had become of her, and Moore said, "Well, she stopped painting. She was a manic-depressive. I don't know whether she stopped because she got sick or got sick because she stopped."

"She got sick because she stopped. They all did and they didn't know it."

It's not just negative emotions, either, that we're told to stuff. It's also big emotions, loud emotions, inconvenient emotions, exuberant emotions that rattle other people's calm and collectedness (and sometimes our *own*), and these begin to fill up what Robert Bly, in *A Little Book on the Human Shadow*, calls "the long bag we drag behind us."

Here's how he describes it: When we're one or two years old, we have a 360-degree personality, with energy and enthusiasm radiating out from us in all directions. That is, until our parents start sending us to our rooms for radiating certain parts of it: "Big girls don't cry." "That's not dinner-table talk." "Be nice to your sister."

Behind us, Bly says, we each have an invisible bag, and whatever parts of us our parents didn't like—restlessness, anger, high spirits, or anything that follows "Nice girls don't . . ." and "Big boys don't . . ."—get sliced off the 360-degree pie and put in the bag.

Then we get into school, and in the service of fitting in and getting along, we put more of ourselves into the bag, whole slabs of energy and individuality.

Then we enter the working world, and to continue winning friends and influencing people, we stash even more of ourselves in the bag: those parts of us that organizational life would prefer we leave out in the parking lot when we punch in, like our spiritual lives, our emotional lives, and our personal lives.

"Out of the round globe of energy we started with," says Bly, "a twenty-year-old ends up with a slice. . . . We spend our lives until we're twenty deciding what parts of ourselves to put into the bag, and we spend the rest of our lives trying to get them out again."

Which is not so easy. I was reminded just how obstinate these commandments and taboos are during a recent visit with my brother Ross in California. He and I were walking along a forest path in the Santa Cruz Mountains, and I don't recall the context of our conversation, but to make a point I dared him to hold hands with me until we reached a bend in the path maybe a hundred feet ahead. He reached out his hand, accompanied by a look that roughly translated to "I call your bluff."

There was clearly no one around, but the next ten seconds provoked an outbreak of conditioned reflexes that would have put Pavlov's dogs to shame: awkwardness, embarrassment, self-consciousness, paranoia, emotional and physical revulsion—pure conditioning. All we were doing was holding hands, barely pushing a toe across the line, and the alarm bells went off. And we didn't even dare this escapade in *public*.

And I wouldn't be a proper twin, either, if I didn't report that he broke first.

WHETHER WE'RE TALKING about the private or the public need to express ourselves, the human mind is an absolute zoo of tactics for suppressing our impulses and keeping a lid on the psyche's undesirable elements, and the possible pains thereof: denial, defense, distraction, repression, dissociation, projection, procrastination, moralizing, compulsion, obsession.

One young man told me that he'd wanted to be a teacher and a public speaker his whole life but had spent so many years biting his tongue that he literally had a pronounced scar on the tip of it. We work overtime to keep our emotions in check and our thoughts to ourselves, keeping a tight leash on them lest they misbehave and embarrass us, or worse.

I remember bringing my dog with me to a store once, and at one point she strolled around a corner, and a moment later I heard a man's voice cooing in that falsetto people usually reserve for talking to dogs and babies. I peeked my head around the corner and saw a big strapping guy with a military-style crew cut going all goo-goo over my dog. But the instant he saw me, his voice dropped two octaves and he turned bright crimson. The fear of what others will think of us is among the central reasons we keep our enthusiasms in the bag.

A marvelous example of this comes from the story of Stanley and

Livingstone. The adventurer and journalist Henry Stanley was sent by the *New York Herald* to find Dr. David Livingstone, a Scottish explorer, medical missionary, and abolitionist who had gone to Africa in 1866 seeking the source of the Nile but had not been heard from in years. In 1871, Stanley mounted an expedition and, after hacking and fighting his way across seven hundred miles of equatorial Africa, finally found the errant Livingstone in a village near Lake Tanganyika. But the climactic moment of Stanley's harrowing narrative, the now-famous greeting "Dr. Livingstone, I presume," has a bit of backstory worth mentioning.

Stanley's best-selling book about the adventure, *How I Found Livingstone*, became a foundational text for Western attitudes toward the "dark continent" and the "primitives" therein, and informed the work of such influential figures as Sigmund Freud, Edgar Rice Burroughs (author of the *Tarzan* books), and Joseph Conrad. But in the book, Stanley reveals that there was quite a bit more to that long-awaited rendezvous than was reported in the newspapers.

In the moment of finally finding Livingstone, Stanley says: "What would I not have given for a bit of friendly wilderness where, unseen, I might vent my joy in some mad freak, such as idiotically biting my hand or turning a somersault, or slashing at trees, in order to allay those exciting feelings that were well-nigh uncontrollable. My heart beats fast, but I must not let my face betray my emotions, lest it detract from the dignity of a white man appearing under such extraordinary circumstances.

"So I did that which I thought was most dignified. . . . I would have run to him, only I was a coward in the presence of such a mob—would have embraced him, only he being an Englishman, I did not know how he would receive me. So I did what cowardice and false pride suggested was the best thing. I walked deliberately to him, took off my hat, and said, 'Dr. Livingstone, I presume.'

"'Yes,' said he with a kind smile, lifting his cap slightly."

An interesting aside: up until that moment, the wilderness had been something for Stanley only to blaze his way across, something deadly and foreign, to be conquered. But in the end he wished only for "a bit of friendly wilderness" to spare him the self-censoring that seemed imperative to him in the face of feelings that were as wild as the land he had passed through, passionate emotions that he feared would undermine his dignity and enshrine in the popular imagination not the image of an intrepid gentleman explorer but a man doing somersaults and idiotically biting his hand.

Country club manners apparently pertained even in the wilderness, and reasonableness presided over passion. The result: an encounter that was forced and artificial.

In her book *Exuberance: The Passion for Life*, Kay Redfield Jamison says, "Exuberance is an abounding, ebullient, effervescent emotion. It is kinetic and unrestrained, joyful, irrepressible. . . . It is . . . at its core, a more restless, billowing state . . . a fermenting, pushing-upward-and-forward force." In its most original sense, it was an expression of *fertility*, coming from a Latin phrase meaning "to be fruitful." The earliest uses of the word in English spoke of the abundances of nature, from the profusions of harvest to the kinetics of shooting stars and waterfalls.

Exuberance is about life force, an overflowing of energy that's easier to come by in the pink of youth than the world-weariness of maturity, more readily attained at the summits of love and accomplishment, adventure and alcohol, than on the plains of everyday life. And though passionate responsiveness to the world may be an inheritance from our most ancient selves, certainly of survival value in helping us express our *attachment* to life, for all its longevity, it's also fragile stuff. A single withering look can extinguish it. To say nothing of a childhood full of withering looks.

Even under the best conditions, that is, people aren't always in the mood for our restless, billowing emotions, our kinetic and unrestrained enthusiasms, or our desire to deliver the truth. There are certainly times for pushing upward and forward and hanging like cats from the draperies, and there are times—most of the time, it seems—for settling down and hitting the mute button. Sometimes our love of life is just a bit much on people's nerves, a little too close to anarchy, which it can easily tip over into. And sometimes it only reminds others of what they themselves have lost or abandoned, and hushing us up is a way of silencing their own grief.

Another fire extinguisher on exuberant behavior is slapping labels on it that turn it into not just a problem but also a disorder. For instance, *The Diagnostic and Statistical Manual of Mental Disorders* (DSM), the bible of psychiatric symptoms published by the American Psychiatric Association, has contributed its fair share to the medicalization of problematic but otherwise normal behaviors. Since 1952 it has tripled the number of psychological disorders to nearly four hundred, encompassing almost fifty million Americans, and in some cases with little clear definition of the cutoff between normal and pathological.

The symptoms of attention-deficit/hyperactivity disorder (ADHD), for instance, which an early researcher (in the 1950s) called simply "passionateness," include "often fidgets," "often interrupts," and "often 'on the go.'"

On the go? That describes pretty much everybody I know.

The *DSM* usually associates hypomania—characterized by a high degree of energy, enthusiasm, creativity, confidence, sociability, and talkativeness—with bipolar disorder and medicates it with mood stabilizers, though it appears regularly in highly creative, and high-functioning, types.

People "affected" by histrionic personality disorder, who are also typically high-functioning, are described in the manual as "lively, dramatic, vivacious, enthusiastic, flirtatious, and egocentric."

The diagnosis of Attention Deficit Disorder (ADD) requires checking six of nine boxes from a list of symptoms that include "often doesn't seem to listen when spoken to," "often fails to pay close attention to details," "often fails to finish projects," "often loses things," and "often forgetful"—many of which accompany the natural process of *aging*.

A casual stroll through this naturalist's field guide to the troubled mind reveals countless behaviors that would surely feel familiar to most of us—behaviors including the histrionic, narcissistic, anxious, avoidant, obsessive, compulsive, depressive, passive-aggressive, delusional, self-defeating, and antisocial. We're all a little nuts, in other words, and the inmates are in fact running the asylum.

To give you a sense of the iffiness of the *DSM* (and of course the larger culture of which it's a part, if not a symptom), consider this: homosexuality was listed as a mental illness until nearly the mid-1970s. Or this: 70 percent of the current *DSM* task force members report financial relationships with pharmaceutical companies. Or this: something called relational disorder is defined as "persistent and painful patterns of feelings, behaviors, and perceptions among two or more people in an important personal relationship." But what personal relationship *doesn't* exhibit at least a couple of such persistent patterns? It's like saying that love is a mental disorder.

Or this: new additions to the 2013 *DSM* include mild neurocognitive disorder, referring to the modest decline in cognitive function that's also a natural feature of aging, and disruptive mood disregulation disorder, a diagnosis slapped on kids who sulk and throw temper tantrums, which could be a form of bipolar disorder, true, but just as likely could be the result of family trauma and developmental issues—so it's a bit of a diagnostic dumping ground for temperamental but otherwise normal kids, making it easier for health care professionals to label them with a psychiatric disorder and medicate them with psychotropic drugs.

Such squishy new labels have, in fact, provoked an intense backlash within the mental health community, and a petition signed by over thirteen thousand of them, people who may or may not be suffering from oppositional defiant disorder, characterized by the *DSM* itself as including stubborn and angry defiance of authority.

INHIBITION, HOWEVER, isn't just a reining in of the passions, or merely the triumph of will over instinct, or spirit over flesh. It's also an ordering principle in the world, one that reaches into the affairs of animal, vegetable, and mineral. It tells leaves when and when not to bud, and animals when and when not to shed. It's an essential ingredient in focused attention, the efficacy of drugs, the preservation of food and mummies, as well as in table manners, continence, and knowing when to keep your mouth shut. It's the logic behind second thoughts and software that asks if we're *sure* we want to shut down our computer.

To be house-trained, toddlers have to learn to hold their bladders and bowels. To stay on the good side of parents and peers, teenagers have to learn to hold their tongues. To stay out of jail and help maintain the general welfare, we all have to rein in some of our aggressive impulses. To put a stop to compulsive and belittling self-talk, we have to issue ourselves the occasional gag order—"Stop already!"

To survive a simple stroll through the neighborhood, consciousness itself must hide the truth from us, preventing us from seeing things as they really are. For instance, technically speaking, there's no such thing as a solid object, only masses of hyperventilating atoms. But if you were crossing the street and slowed down to marvel at a beehive of electrons moving toward you, a bolus of pure energy, you'd get run over by a car. If your senses presented the world to you as it actually is, you'd be roadkill.

And the same goes for mice as for men. At the instant of being clamped in a predator's teeth, peptide hormones are released in the hypothalamus and pituitary gland—endorphins that have the pharmacological property of opium. They attach themselves to the surface of cells responsible for pain perception, and shut them off. There is no pain. "If a mouse could shrug, he'd shrug," said physician and author Lewis Thomas.

The famous Stanford marshmallow experiment tells us that impulse control is equated with not only longer life for man and beast, but also *success* in life. At the Bing Nursery School at Stanford University in 1972, children (mostly four-year-olds) were led into a room, empty of distractions. A marshmallow was placed on a table. The children could eat the marshmallow, the researchers told them, but if they waited for fifteen minutes without giving in to temptation, they would be rewarded with a *second* marshmallow.

The coordinator of the experiment, Walter Mischel, observed that the patient children distracted themselves by covering their eyes, turning around so they couldn't see the marshmallow, pretending to play hide-and-seek, singing songs from *Sesame Street*, kicking the desk, tugging on their pigtails, even stroking the marshmallow as if it were a small furry animal.

The less patient toddlers simply ate the marshmallow as soon as the researchers left the room.

Over 650 children took part in the experiment. One third ate the marshmallow immediately, one third waited a little while before succumbing, and one third waited it out and got the second treat.

Years later, the children who scarfed up the marshmallow quickest were more likely to have behavioral problems, both in school and at home, got lower SAT scores, struggled in stressful situations, often had trouble paying attention, and found it difficult to maintain friendships.

"If you can deal with hot emotions," Mischel says, "then you can study for the SAT instead of watching television, and you can save more money for retirement. It's not just about marshmallows. You're better able, generally, to rise to the challenge."

Though inhibition can clearly be beneficial and adaptive, among the challenges we must continually rise to, individually and collectively, is the fact that anything threatening to the established order has tended to be repressed in human affairs. The spiritedness of children, the education of women, the voting rights of minorities, power in the hands of working-class people, recreational drugs, new religions, protesters. Referring to someone as uninhibited has only very recently been considered a compliment. And the word *egregious* ("out of the herd"), which originally *was* a compliment—to be outstanding, to stand out from the crowd—nowadays carries a disapproving connotation as something conspicuously bad or offensive, as in an egregious mistake.

A few years ago I visited the lovely Tuscan hilltop town of San Gimignano, which, for some inscrutable reason, is home to the Museum of Death, the Criminal Museum, and the Torture Museum, in which I saw an exhibit featuring one Giordano Bruno. He was considered the most famous philosopher of the Italian Renaissance and was burned at the stake in Rome in 1600 with what was called a mute's bridle in his mouth, constructed so that one long spike pierced his tongue and the floor of his mouth and came out beneath his chin, while another penetrated the roof of his mouth. His crime: advocating heliocentrism, Copernicus's notion that Earth revolves around the sun, rather than the other way around.

Copernicus's idea was published posthumously, because of the deadly theological repressiveness of the times. And Galileo, who touted similar beliefs, went blind after the Inquisition forced him to recant them and, for good measure, put him under house arrest for the remainder of his life.

History is rife with dangerous minds who endangered themselves in the name of self-expression and delivering the truth. There were those who trimmed our sails by exclaiming that Earth wasn't, in fact, the center of the universe. Those who shook the temples by pulling out of the ground "the thigh bone of some creature not mentioned in Holy Writ," as anthropologist Loren Eiseley put it. And those who outright kicked in the door of the establishment by proving that we descended from apes not angels, which was (and still is) perceived by many as preposterous and insulting and an assault against human dignity.

And not just cultural life but personal and social life, too, are rich with such feuds. Few of us need reminding that there can be a price to pay for speaking our minds, or simply being ourselves. Who hasn't been sent to their room, or down to the principal's office, or fired from a job, or a relationship, for doing just that? To say nothing of exile, excommunication, torture, persecution, and death. Who hasn't wished on occasion that they had just kept their thoughts to themselves?

Entire periods in history are characterized by the fear of knowledge and self-expression, and the punishing of those who trafficked in it. The aptly named Dark Ages, when monks had to hide illuminated manuscripts; the era of Nazism, with its book burning; the clandestine copying and distribution of government-suppressed literature in Soviet-bloc countries; the reign of the Khmer Rouge in Cambodia, during which anyone who evidenced stereotypical signs of learning, even just wearing glasses, would be killed.

In the second century B.C., Ch'ih Shih Huang Ti declared himself the first emperor of China, founding the Chin dynasty, from which China got its name. His first order of business was building the Great Wall to keep out the Huns (or more specifically their horses, without which these fierce nomadic tribesmen were far less effective). He then ordered the burning of all books published prior to his reign. Anyone caught hiding books was branded with a red-hot iron and made to toil on the Great Wall until the day he died, whereupon his body was used as fill.

Some twenty centuries of cultural history preceded Huang Ti's rise to power—centuries that included Confucius and Lao-tzu, the founder of Taoism—yet Huang Ti essentially declared that history would begin with him, that the past both real and mythical would be renounced. He was particularly incensed by Confucianism, which set limits to the power of rulers, and either buried alive many of its scholars, or buried them up to their necks in the ground and ordered his soldiers to swing their axes low like golfers to slice off their budding heads.

History itself, however, saw to the limits of Huang Ti's power. He had hoped to found a dynasty that would last ten thousand generations, but his ruthlessness created too many enemies. Afraid of assassination, he slept each night in a different palace, and when he died was buried with an army of seven thousand terra-cotta soldiers, horses, and chariots to protect him in the afterlife. A mere four years after his death, the dynasty collapsed, having lasted all of fifteen years.

I don't mean to suggest that as individuals we're destined to be endlessly at war with culture, that the two have irreconcilably exclusive needs, the one entity marching under the banner of control and the other flying the freak flag of freedom. The dialectic between freedom and control isn't merely foisted on us by civilization. There's endless jockeying between self-expression and self-control *within* each individual.

It's part of our deepest nature, a clash of the titans that's one of the elemental paradoxes of life, and to blame society for what holds you back is too convenient. Civilization certainly plays its part in helping to curtail our instincts and outcries, and temper our tantrums, but so does the individual ego.

Freud talked of the id and the ego, and if the id is, as he put it, "a cauldron full of seething excitations," the repository of passion and pure desire in the human psyche, the architect of immediate gratification that wants it now and wants it delivered, then the ego is the herder of cats. It's the organizing principle in the psyche that takes all those seething excitations and hitches them to the plow.

Some consider the ego nothing less than conscious awareness, the exclusive sense of self that helps distinguish you from everybody else, provides you with a personality, and drives you to *express* it in the world. In Latin it simply means "I," and in many ways it's the real engine of our hunger for self-expression, helping our passions and desires to fly in formation and thus truly accomplish things in the world.

But accomplishment and self-expression don't happen without continual negotiation between bridle and spur. I run into this on an almost daily basis just in my morning freewriting practice, which I do in part to keep the creative machinery well oiled and generate material, and in part to continually unpack that essential and elusive Voice, which is the writer's grail.

What I'm *attempting* to do is stream-of-consciousness writing, taking as my mottos "garbage is good" and "quantity leads to quality." But I'm seldom able to overcome the bad habit of editing while I write, the critic effectively steaming up the creator's glasses during the act of creation.

The critic tosses syntax, grammar, punctuation, and all the rest of Miss Thistlebottom's linguistic hobgoblins at me while I'm trying to think a decent creative thought, wags a finger at my split infinitives and sentence-ending prepositions, pesters me to consult the thesaurus and the diction-ary of etymology in midstream, and badgers me about logic, structure, even truth, when all I want is some momentum and a halfway original idea.

Sometimes I come around. I turn to the critic and say: "You. Out. When the creator is finished, *then* you can come in and do your thing, but not until then." Otherwise I'm driving with one foot on the gas and the other on the brake, and it's having a constipating effect on my work. It's the opposite of *free*writing.

Sometimes it feels like I have to silence a thousand voices and distrac-tions to bring forth a single idea worth thinking about. Sometimes I feel like I'm outfitted with a slingshot and squaring off against an army.

When I sit down to write, I hear not only a carping critic but also the whole brass section of my fears and insecurities. The doubts about my abilities; the fear of failure; the constant comparing of myself with others; the anxiety about spending so much of life sitting alone in a room, in front of a computer, looking down at the skin on the back of my hands as it slowly thins and crimples; and the bottomless gulf that separates me from the masters and geniuses in my field, the ghosts I imagine sitting around my room while I'm trying to be creative, laughing and slapping their knees. It's like I'm scattering tacks on the path in front of me.

"I set out to bring down stars from the sky," wrote Edmond Rostand, author of *Cyrano de Bergerac*, "and then, for fear of ridicule, I stop and pick little flowers of eloquence."

A rabbi of my acquaintance once told me that I should write *anyway*—despite all the arguments against—because writing, as with any calling, is ultimately a labor of love, like service; and like service, *it's not about me.* It's not about whether I'm comfortable, or whether I can measure the effect of my good deeds, or whether anybody even says thank you. "It's about some-thing you have to say that you believe the world needs to hear," the rabbi told me, "and you should say it as much because the world needs to hear it as because you need to say it."

Cleaning Your Caches

However successful we are in pulling our passions back out of the bag, should we live long enough, we may get an assist from the aging process itself, with its onset of that blessed developmental stage in which you simply don't care so much anymore what other people think of you, allowing you to regain some of your natural expressiveness and unbatten some of your hatches.

At its farther extreme, of course, is dementia, which tends to carry our inhibitions away on its ebbing tide—not always for the better, but not always for the worse, either.

A couple of years ago I spent a few days in New York visiting my mother, and as we sat over bagels, lox, and cream cheese at her kitchen table on that first morning, with little to no conversation of any real substance going on because dementia had sent her language skills the way of the dodo bird, I looked up at one point to see her gazing adoringly at me, a textbook twinkle in her eye. My initial reaction: a double take.

The next morning she reached across the table and grabbed the wrist of my right hand, placing our two palms together, and just marveled at how similar our hands were, their size and shape, the way they fit together. Then she slowly pushed her palm away from mine so that only our fingertips were touching, and then back to prayer formation.

At lunch she reached up and cupped my face in her hands like a vase and just looked at me tenderly.

The following morning, she leaned over and slowly traced the contours of my mustache with her finger, while I stared at it cross-eyed. I currently have a combination Fu Manchu and Frank Zappa mustache, and she ran her finger along each section in turn—across the top, down each side, and over the patch beneath my lower lip—saying, in a childlike singsongy voice, "You have this. And this. And this. And *this*."

What was so striking about all this was simply how unprecedented it was. My mother has simply never been the kind of person to be that emotionally or physically demonstrative, or comfortable with intimacy. I think of the photographs taken over the years of her and me together, ever since I was little, and in most of them we look like two people standing next to each other in a police lineup.

Nonetheless, I had two very contrary reactions to this sudden display of affection. On the one hand, amazement, pleasure, and appreciation that I was getting to have this experience at all with her before the curtain comes down. And on the other hand, anger. Like, where the hell has all *this* been my whole life?

I realized that after going for so long without, I'd kind of got my jaw set about it—about the kind of person my mother is, what I can expect from her, how it is. But suddenly, in a moment, it changed—and has remained changed—and this old dog is struggling to learn a few new tricks and to let go of a few old grudges.

I told myself that it was the dementia speaking, not my mother, but just as likely it *was* my mother, and had been all along. Only hidden. And now here toward the end, not too late—*never* too late—the dementia was blowing its trumpet at the walls and bringing them down. Her personality (a word that means "mask") was falling away, along with her inhibitions, and a touching-feeling person was there underneath, reaching to cup my face in her hands.

Anything can happen. Just last week I received a letter from my brother Marc, who spoke of tears and mourning about my mother's declining condition and of the "defense mechanism" of busyness that he uses to deaden those feelings and protect himself against "drowning in a sea of angst."

And once again I sat dumbfounded. Because I do not know this person, this older brother the scientist who suddenly speaks with such emotion, who uses terms like "defense mechanisms," and admits to crying. This, after all, is the same guy who once said that there are two types of people in the world, "fuzzies and techies," and clearly placed himself among the latter group, and who once, in perfect Spock-like fashion, said of fatherhood, "It's fascinating watching the consciousness come into the creature."

Novelists and children with imaginary playmates will often tell you that the characters they invent sometimes take on lives of their own, insisting on going their own way, having their own independent opinions—even about matters in the author's real life—and just generally pressing for autonomy at every turn. And these authors can end up in fits with their own creations until they let them speak their minds and go their own way.

Being the creator—whether of a novel, a universe, or an individual life—isn't a job for sissies. At some point—at many points—you've got to allow that your creations have lives of their own and free will, which they'll want to exercise. One of the special circles of writer's-block hell is the one in which you refuse to let your characters off their leashes, refuse to let them grow in their own clamorous and organic way. As E. M. Forster once said of novel-writing, "Characters arrive when evoked, but full of the spirit of mutiny. . . . If they're given complete freedom, they kick the book to pieces, and if they're kept too sternly in check, they revenge themselves by dying, and destroy it by intestinal decay."

It's tempting to think we've got everything squared away in boxes, our life stories down pat, all the actors in their places. But we often fail to take one small factor into account: evolution. People—you—evolve and change. Things don't stay the same. Inhibitions sometimes turn into exhibitions. And it's just bad science or adjudication to suppress evidence. It's dishonest. It doesn't allow you to believe your eyes that things have changed. It doesn't let people off whatever hooks you've hung them on. And it doesn't allow *you* to step outside your old narratives and grow into new stories.

This lesson was brought home to me quite clearly when I went to New York to preside over the dismantling of my mother's empire. My brothers and I had just moved her into the nursing home in California, and I was tasked with closing up shop in New York, starting with an estate sale that required that I go through all my mother's earthly possessions and clear out eighty-five years of the kind of hoarding that children of the Depression often specialize in.

At one point during this deconstruction projection, I stood before a set of olive green file cabinets that had been in my life since the day I was born, but always locked, always off-limits—my mother's version of Area 51. All she ever told me was that they contained her "personal papers." And some of them, I soon discovered, were of the sort that, had the dementia not caught up with her so quickly, I imagine she would surely have chosen to shred before anyone could read them. Or maybe not, the need to confess being what it is.

So while my mother sat in a nursing home three thousand miles away, drifting farther and farther out to sea on the outgoing tide of her dementia, I poured myself a glass of bourbon from the bar in the living room and stood before those forbidden file cabinets with their keys in my hand, with no one around to tell me I couldn't open them.

And what I found was one surprise after another, and a few good shocks. You think you know someone.

I found a four-page crush letter written to my mother by a man who was apparently in the running for her hand in marriage but lost out to my father. I found photographs of my mother naked—an acquired taste if ever there was one. I found letters my mother had written to us boys during our twenties and thirties that were in stark contrast to my story about her as being largely absent and aloof, critical and controlling, that were contrary to my narrative about how it was. Letters full of love and admiration, wisdom and support.

But the deeper I dug into those file cabinets, the darker their contents. I found a half-empty bottle of morphine in a box filled with literature about a right-to-die organization called the Hemlock Society, of which my mother was clearly a card-carrying member. She had used that bottle to help her sister, my aunt Helen, not just cope with but perhaps also die of cancer, an act of compassion that would go by the name of assisted suicide in states like Oregon and Vermont, but would go by a very different name in the state of New York.

Most disturbingly, I found a series of arrest records for domestic abuse going back to the earliest years of my mother's marriage to my stepfather, the psychologist, along with inch-thick court transcripts, photographs, and videotapes of the bruises she had sustained, and one particularly gruesome file my mother titled "Charles' Reign of Terror," in which she documented his attempts over the years, as he himself apparently said to her, "to drive you out the door . . . or out the window." He succeeded at neither, but she stayed married to him for thirty years.

Now my mother is not the type to shy away from a fight, or take life sitting down. She was one of the first women in the then-boys-only club of stockbroking, and she once bought a nutcracker in the shape of a woman's legs. So why would she put up with such abuse? Why wouldn't she just up and walk out the door?

There wasn't a clue in those file cabinets that would help me answer that question, but I do know that where there's big light, there's big shadow. And after going through my mother's personal papers, I know more clearly than ever that the stories I tell about my parents, my childhood, the things that happened to me, are sometimes made from *shreds* of evidence, cemented in place by repetition and generalization. They're a conjuring up of explanations that made sense to my childish grasp of things, which then became my philosophies of life and love, for better and for worse.

The ancient Greek and Roman marble sculptures that populate our museums weren't originally white. They were richly painted with colors, it turns out. White is simply all that was left after they'd gone through time's stomach acids. And what comes down to me from my *own* past is also whitewashed.

Going through my mother's personal papers reminded me that it's important to upgrade my files when new evidence is presented, to clean my caches, as they say in cyberspeak. It's critical to question the stories and received wisdoms we haul through time, and to consider which ones may be holding us back from seeing life as it actually is and seeing ourselves as we actually are.

Bursting the Spirit's Sleep

People don't deserve the restraint we show by not going into delirium in front of them. To hell with them!

—LOUIS-FERDINAND CÉLINE

A few years ago I was invited to dinner at the home of some friends, and for fifteen interminable minutes in the middle of the meal, they sniped at each other across the table, the way couples do when they're not having some conversation they really need to be having with one another and instead settle for passive-aggressive (or just plain aggressive) behavior—in this case a steady cannonade of criticism, sarcasm, and put-downs.

They were also doing this in front of their guests and their seven-year-old daughter, who one moment was quietly drinking her glass of milk and the next moment suddenly and explosively spitting it out in a fine atomized spray that reached clear across the table to the front of my shirt. And I remember thinking: perfect! A perfectly timed, perfectly appropriate outburst, as effective as a director yelling "Cut!" in the middle of a scene. Except that in this case, the actors turned on the director and sent her from the table. I only wished I could have gone with her.

The incident was strikingly similar to one I bore witness to only a week earlier, in a community-building workshop in San Francisco, based on M. Scott Peck's book *The Different Drum.* At one point, in keeping with Peck's general chronology of how communities form, the group—roughly a hundred people—began shifting out of the faking-it phase of community building, when everyone is mannerly and accommodating of personal differences, and toward the chaos phase, when those differences start seething under the surface but before they're openly admitted.

People began clouting one another, then trying to comb it over, then clouting some more, then smoothing it out, and this went on for a good half hour, until one man sitting on the floor suddenly yelled at the top of his lungs. No words, just a good old primal scream, which immediately split the group into two camps. Those who thought it was a weird and manipulative way of getting attention, and those, like myself, who thought it was a brilliant if unconscious way of articulating the group dynamic, all the artful dodging, and that it was no coincidence it came out as a war whoop.

The human psyche is like Earth. It's a closed system in the sense that there's no *out*, as in throwing the garbage out. There's no *away*, as in running away. There's no trash icon. You can't just delete the truth. Whatever parts of ourselves we push down—because we can't permit them expression, or can't love them, because others won't approve or they don't fit our self-image—just come up somewhere else in our lives, urgent and rebellious. As the Mexican poet José Frías once said, "I drink to drown my sorrows, but the damn things have learned to swim."

While delivering the truth has its risks, so does *not* delivering it, because the closets into which we stuff all that we refuse to express are the body and soul, and they can take only so much before bursting open and spilling their contents into the room.

At its most benign, what you suppress will simply keep coming back, curling up in some corner of your psyche and mewling. If you've ever had an encounter with someone during which you didn't express how you really felt, you're probably familiar with the way your mind keeps haranguing you afterward. What you coulda said. What you shoulda said. Why you chickened out. Maybe you should write a letter. Maybe you should just let it go. Maybe next time you'll actually speak up.

Author Patricia Hampl once wrote this: "The material I was determined to elude has claimed me. When I started at the University of Minnesota, I lost no time dumping the Catholic world my family had so carefully given me. In fact, that's why I went there. I understood that many people had succeeded in losing their religion at the University.

"For years, decades even, I considered it one solid accomplishment that I had escaped the nuns. Result: I have spent the better part of five years writing a memoir about growing up Catholic. The central character: a contemplative nun, the very figure I was determined to dodge."

It's in the nature of our secret selves to seek expression. Thought-bubbles always swim for the surface and dreams always try to press themselves into consciousness. A passion that's unlived, a gift ungiven, a secret unspoken, a wound unaddressed is something you're withholding, restraining, and it tends to build up a charge that needs discharging. Whatever has a voice can't bear being silenced, can't be anything but a caged animal that keeps rushing the bars whenever you walk by.

The psyche, though, is designed to continually give us opportunities to unleash the thing, and it does so through what Freud called repetition compulsions, the captive's way of trying to free itself. It's the lessons you've endlessly had to learn, the mistakes you continually find yourself making, the issues you've worn a footpath to and from, to and from, the dream that keeps coming back, the creativity that's constantly causing you labor pains but without a birth, the symptoms that won't go away, the kind of partner you routinely attract, the kind of fight you keep having with that partner.

And these reruns aren't opportunities to continually fail—though it often feels that way, and unfolds that way—but opportunities to finally succeed. Ultimately they work toward the good. Pathology, recall, means the logic of pain, and its logic is often that something in our lives is longing for expression and reconciliation. "We're trying to get the message, get it right," says Ann Belford Ulanov in *The Unshuttered Heart*. We're trying "to tell the story of where we're caught . . . trying to restage the original trauma to find a way through it."

For Deborah King, the message she was trying to get was simply the truth, telling the truth about what happened to her while growing up and forging from the wound at the heart of that story the gift that would define her true work in the world.

Deborah's is a harrowing tale of childhood sexual abuse at the hands of her father—whose trespasses came with the stern warning: "Don't tell!"— and at the hands of her mother, who sealed the deal with her denial, looking away and ignoring what was happening between her daughter and her husband, though Deborah vividly remembers seeing her mother more than once watching her and her father through a crack in her bedroom door.

Not surprisingly, she describes her mother as cold, cruel, and rageful. "I don't remember a single instance when she held me, kissed me, or spoke loving words to me," Deborah writes in her memoir *Truth Heals*. "I lived in constant fear of her . . . and could never take a full breath around her. . . . She was always angry, glaring at me with her infamous killer look, which she didn't, by the way, ever turn on my brother. . . . She seemed to hate both me and my father. . . . She assumed that I, a girl of six, had seduced her husband, the proverbial Eve tempting Adam and bringing about the fall of Paradise."

Nor was her mother the only one who believed that. One rainy day when Deborah was eight, she was in her favorite hiding place in the choir loft of her church when she heard Father Fitzgerald's footsteps coming up the stairs. "What are you doing up here, my child?" She darted for the stairs, but he caught her by a braid. "You little temptress," he said. "I know how you've been tempting your father, bless his soul. It's my duty to straighten you out." Whereupon he raised his cassock and pushed her down on her knees.

"I coped by shutting down, disappearing into the air," Deborah says. "My only defensive strategy as a small child was to leave, to float out of my body. . . . The fear and rage I felt . . . were kept underground. There was no speaking it, no feeling it, no acknowledging it in any way, at least not consciously. I didn't . . . know that I was suppressing the truth. I just knew that I was forbidden to say anything about what troubled me."

In the introduction of her book, Deborah says, "I was learning what I would later master—the art of bottling up and never expressing the truth. By the time I was three or four years old, the habit of lying was entrenched in the cells of my body, mind and being."

She couldn't do otherwise. Children simply can't, under those conditions. Speaking up might generally be considered a survival tactic—cry when you're hungry, bark to warn of intruders—but in some circumstances, stifling your outcries, operating by stealth, is the better part of natural selection. If you're a prey animal in a family of predators, it pays to keep a lid on it and not draw attention to yourself.

Your whole being might want to shout its anger and hurt, to call for help, but that's exactly what you cannot do. It would be hazardous to your health. The very responses with which nature endowed you for survival have to be ignored. And to some degree this is true for most children growing up. When it comes to the choice of either being true to yourself or bowing to those whose acceptance is essential for your survival and happiness, most children will opt for the sellout.

You don't have to be as egregiously abused as Deborah to feel forced to take the veil either. Alice Miller, renowned author of books on child abuse such as *The Body Never Lies*, rather disturbingly defines abuse very broadly, to include not just physical or sexual abuse but also shouting, spanking, humiliation, shaming, neglect, excessive criticism, withholding communication, and abandonment—a spectrum wide enough to include people who might not ordinarily think of themselves as having had "abusive" childhoods.

It also puts a new perspective on something that never made sense to me before reading Miller's books: the belief, so common to the generation in which I and my two brothers were raised, that spanking is not considered abuse.

If you were to slap a child across the face, that would surely be abuse by most people's standards. If you were to punch a child in the stomach or back or groin, that would be abuse. But strike them across the buttocks and suddenly it's what my mother benignly referred to as "swatting." Just because it isn't likely to damage internal organs or be visible in public, just because everyone does it and argues that it's for our own good, just because our parents claim that it hurts them more than it hurts us, doesn't mean it isn't painful and emotionally terrifying to a child.

One of the most vivid memories I carry from childhood is hiding up in the top branches of the dogwood tree in my front yard, the better to spy on the Fuller Brush salesmen who sold my mother the brushes that my father used on my backside. And just to add a bit of emotional confusion into the mix, many of my most cherished memories of physical closeness and tenderness with my father coincide with him coming into my room after spanking me, to comfort me.

But if you asked me to describe my father, I would do so in almost universally glowing terms. I would casually dismiss his occasional acts of violence as insignificant because, heck, everyone swatted their kids. I would never think to describe my father as a great guy who was sometimes violent and abusive.

Denial—along with the kind of institutionalized guilt that comes with the Fifth Commandment (Fourth among Catholics) to "Honor thy father and thy mother"—prevents people like Deborah from feeling what they actually feel and forces their bodies to bring it to their attention through the impeccable logic of illness, because the body sees through the deception far more readily than the mind does. The records of suppressed evidence aren't simply shredded; they're stored. And they're stored in the body, which doesn't have the same defenses as the mind.

From childhood on, Deborah's life was a procession of ailments. Chronic tonsillitis at five and six, teeth grinding at seven, an "accidental" fall at nine (the day after her father first raped her), and at twelve and thirteen digestive and reproductive problems, hypoglycemia, and allergies.

By the time she was fifteen, Deborah was practicing what her father had taught her on her thirty-year-old judo instructor, who, afterward, said to her, "Where did you learn to give head like that?" It was a "skill" she would use "to secure a coveted part-time college job, help score an A from a law school professor, and land that corner office at the law firm. "I climbed the ladder on my knees. From associate to junior partner to senior partner in a record two years. . . . Even opposing counsel and judges weren't immune to my charms."

She writes, "At a conference I attended, a woman's climbing team on its way to the Himalayas sold T-shirts emblazoned with the slogan: A WOMAN'S PLACE IS ON TOP. I bought several of those T-shirts and wore them until they were in tatters, never conscious of my need to make that slogan come true. . . . Like many people who are disempowered as children, I learned as a young adult that I felt safest when I was in control of others. I used seduction and manipulation to accomplish that goal. . . . As a lawyer I was a power and adrenaline junkie, and took great pleasure in slaying my opponents."

On the outside, "I was an attorney like my father: married, accomplished, successful. I was picture-perfect, or so I led everyone to believe. What I did not show others, and what I barely admitted to myself, was that I was out of control—on a roller coaster of depression and manic acting out, alcohol and drug addiction, and promiscuous affairs." And finally, at the tender age of twenty-five, a diagnosis of cancer.

"My body became a minefield full of hidden problems I chose to ignore . . . a literal expression of the pain I couldn't speak or express any other way."

The clinical explanation for this is fairly straightforward. Holding up defenses is hard physical labor, and it's *draining*. The constant self-monitoring and vigilance required to inhibit truth and self-expression weakens the immune, heart, and nervous systems and puts people at risk for disease.

So does a childhood history of abuse (which is experienced by nearly one in four girls and one in six boys, according to Safe Horizon, the largest victims' services agency in the United States). In the 1990s, a Centers for Disease Control study of over seventeen thousand Americans found a striking correlation between childhood abuse and adult unwellness. What the study showed were very strong correlates between abuse and obesity, depression, heart disease, alcoholism, cigarette smoking, intravenous drug use, and suicide—many of these clearly attempts to self-medicate.

Researchers have also identified what they call a type C coping style—contrasted with the type A style (hard-driving, rigid, impatient, aggressive) and the type B style (easygoing, reflective, right-brained). Type C people tend to be emotionally inexpressive, finding it difficult to articulate their emotions (especially anger) and even to recognize them. They're inclined toward being pathologically nice and focused on other people's needs over their own. They're also inclined toward succumbing more readily to infectious diseases, certain kinds of cancer, and HIV, as well as faster progression of these diseases.

"The strongest predictor of cancer," claims Anita Kelly in *The Psychology of Secrets*, "is an anti-emotional attitude, especially an inability to express negative emotions." And not just suppressing negative emotions, a number of studies indicate, but also positive passions as well.

Deborah's anti-emotional attitude got a significant boost during her first jury trial. She went to lunch with a colleague who, noticing her nervousness, said, "Have a drink. It'll take the edge off." Which it certainly did. But then it kept working inward from the edge all the way to the center and eventually took over her whole life. "I used drinking and Valium to handle my dread of being revealed as a fraud," she says. "I faked my whole life, pretending to be happy when I was scared, angry, hurt or devastated."

For years she lived the life of a hard-drinking, hard-driving, sexually liberated young woman who was building a legal career with no glass ceiling, and who knew her own mind and wasn't afraid to speak it. But nothing could have been further from the truth. (Old joke: How do you tell when an alcoholic is lying? When her lips are moving.)

After one of her frequent blackouts, her husband split the air with the word *alcoholic*, and that was the beginning of the end of the lies. Still, she attended her first Alcoholics Anonymous meeting dressed to kill and wearing an $1,800 pair of cowboy boots, not realizing that newcomers *usually* show up dressed to kill, in direct proportion to how much of a shambles their inner life actually is. "People were being so alarmingly honest," she says of that first meeting, "speaking the *real* truth and laying it all out there without artifice. I had never told the truth in my entire life. *Never.*"

"We all lie like hell," insists Brad Blanton in *Radical Honesty*. "It wears us out. It's the major source of human stress. Lying kills people. And the kind of lying that is most deadly is withholding. Healing is possible only with the freedom that comes from not hiding anymore."

But if we all lie like hell, we have an equally strong desire to confess, to "burst the spirit's sleep," as Saul Bellow once wrote. Most scholars of the subject consider confession a universal human impulse, the essential righting of a wrong. It's an inherent part of our religious, psychotherapeutic, and legal processes. In the Catholic Church, confession is even called the Sacrament of Reconciliation, though it's gone secular in a big way.

The rise of psychotherapy and self-help groups is a testament to people's hunger to unburden themselves and get a fresh start (Alcoholics Anonymous alone has licensed the twelve-step model to more than six hundred groups), and some believe that the true function and appeal of social media like Facebook, Twitter, and YouTube isn't to connect with community so much as to give us soapboxes from which to express ourselves, to tell others who we are and what matters to us.

There are even confession hotlines you can call to off-load your secrets and wrongdoings, and others can even call in and listen. One such hotline in Los Angeles logs two hundred confessions a day and up to ten thousand listeners. A Catholic confession hotline that was recently started in France received over three hundred calls in its first week, as well as the condemnation of French bishops, who claim that only an actual priest can preside over confessions.

To be sure, automated phone services don't offer the thing that makes confession restorative—an actual person to receive it—and you certainly wouldn't want to hear this: "Thank you for calling the Confession Hotline. We're sorry, but all of our agents are currently busy helping other sinners. However, your confession is important to us, and your call will be answered in the order it was received. Please stay on the line."

Nonetheless, it's a dubious notion that someone can simply wave the magic wand of penance over your bowed head and—*poof*—you're in the clear. Truly reconciling yourself with your shortcomings, if not with those you've harmed by them, and genuinely amending your ways, takes a lot more work than that, and it won't happen if you continually take the spiritual bypass. Ultimately we don't want to just confess, we want to *heal*. And merely downloading our misdeeds isn't a strong enough prescription. Confession is just phase one. It needs to be followed by self-scrutiny and *action*. And not onetime action, but ongoing action. There's a reason we refer to *practicing* our faith.

Another modern-day confessional is Frank Warren's PostSecret Project, in which people from all over the world mail him their secrets anonymously on postcards, some of which are then posted on the PostSecret blog. Warren has received half a million secrets since 2004, a thousand a week, and 1.5 million people visit his blog. Some of the confessions:

> "I give decaf to customers who are rude to me."
> "Everyone who knew me before 9/11 believes I'm dead."
> "I took one of our wedding invitations and wrote 'I win' in big red letters across it and sent it to your ex."
> "When I initiate sex, I do it on your side so I don't have to sleep on the wet spot."
> "Until someone abuses me, I can't love them."
> "Sometimes I hope to be hit by a drunk driver, just to teach my alcoholic father a lesson."
> "I'm terrified that I'm not in love, I'm just comfortable."
> "I flip off my wife when she isn't looking."
> "If a patient is rude to me or mean to his family I use the largest gauge needle I have to inject him. If a patient is nice I use a baby needle."
> "I sit in public and pretend to read, but I'm actually eavesdropping."
> "I hate my living room couch, so I let my dogs pee on it to force my husband into buying a new one."
> "I pretend to sneeze in public so strangers will bless me."

Whether the confessions are about sexual taboos or criminal activity, secret acts of kindness or bizarre habits, Warren believes they're inspirational to those who read them, healing to those who write them, and hope-giving to people who identify with them, helping to create a community of acceptance. And indeed, the purpose of confession is repair, a cleaning of the slate and a healing of the soul, both for the individual and the community.

But whether we step into a confession booth or turn to the Confession app on our iPhone (there actually is one), the point is that something inside us needs to be admitted, in both senses of the word. Needs to be owned up to, and needs to be welcomed in, allowed into consciousness. Whether what needs confessing is a secret, a sin, a crime, a desire, a faith, or a story to tell, it has a life force all its own, which pushes out from inside us. Ideally we begin by admitting the truth to ourselves, then to others. There's a reason therapy is referred to as "the talking cure."

In fact, nearly all schools of psychoanalytic thought are based on this: if you would be healed, in either body or mind, turn and face your wounds. To live with passion, you have to confront whatever blocks its expression, and it's a threefold strategy: confront pain, process it, and reclaim your vitality.

Squaring off with our pain, though, can readily flush old wounds back up to the surface, and this may be one reason we ignore the deeper stories our bodies are trying to tell us. One obese woman in that Centers for Disease Control study, who had been raped when she was young, said, "Overweight is overlooked and that's the way I need to be." Losing weight would naturally confront her with the prey animal's fear of being seen. But because we often encounter symptoms far downstream from the original traumas that set them in motion, we have to be willing to swim back upstream to the source to truly treat the illness.

Anyone who's stuck or inhibited at a very deep level probably intuits that what's holding them back from delivering their truth isn't so much external obstacles or practical limitations or even normal fear and doubt, but rather some core wound to their self-esteem. And just as likely, they intuit that they could talk about authenticity until the cows come home, do all the affirmations and meditations and mission statements they want, set all the intentions they want, but if they don't somehow contend with that original wound, it's going to be difficult to make the kind of progress that lasts.

Certainly not everyone has such a wound, but a lot of people do. Maybe most. Something your parents did or didn't do, something you believe *you* did or didn't do that made your parents stop approving of you or loving you unconditionally, that made you afraid to be yourself, speak your mind, follow your heart, and feel safe in the world.

And it pays, I think, to rewind the tape sometimes, to go back and touch that wound, see where it came from, and have a good cry or a good shout about it. It's striking the momentum that doing this can give to your life.

Perfect example: the movie *Good Will Hunting*, specifically the famous "It's not your fault" scene. Will Hunting, played by Matt Damon, is a genius whose genius is largely stuck inside him, along with his ability to love. There's a scene in which he's in a counseling session with a psychologist played by Robin Williams—it was either therapy or jail, for assaulting a policeman. He and the psychologist have been working together for some time, and it's become apparent that much of what holds Will back is the fact that he had an abusive childhood, the result of a foster father who regularly beat him. During one particular session the psychologist says, "It's not your fault."

Will, leaning against a wall: "I know."

Psychologist, taking a step toward him: "No you don't. It's not your fault."

Will, standing up: "Yeah, I know."

Psychologist, taking another step closer: "It's not your fault."

Will just stares at him.

Psychologist, taking another step: "It's not your fault."

Will: "Don't f— with me."

Psychologist, taking another step: "It's not your fault."

Will, pushing the psychologist forcefully backward: "Don't f— with me. Not you."

Psychologist, standing in front of Will again: "It's not your fault."

Will buries his head in his hands.

Psychologist: "It's not your fault."

At which point Will bursts into tears, along with, if I remember correctly from seeing it in the movie theater, most of the audience, myself included. Because a lot of us recognized that thing that wasn't our fault, but that we've been carrying around with us our whole life as if it were.

From that moment on—true to life, in my opinion and experience—Will's life begins to change dramatically. He begins coming into his power and his gift, and his heart.

Deborah doesn't believe it's actually necessary to remember all the disturbing details of whatever the thing is that wasn't your fault—your parents' neglect, abuse, alcoholism, intolerance, shaming, withholding, abandonment, divorce, whatever—to heal from it. But she says it is important to get in touch with "your truth." Starting with an acknowledgment that maybe your childhood wasn't the happy tale you've been telling all your life, the charming folk-art picture you've painted of it.

"We were the perfect family, starched and pressed and polished to a fine gleam," she writes. "Except the whole thing was a lie. Bad Daddy was making regular forays into my bedroom, my mother was denying what she saw, and years later when I confronted her about the abuse, she said, 'We don't talk about those kinds of things in our family.' The message 'Thou shalt not speak your truth' was etched into the welcome mat outside our front door."

The cold truth, of course, about healing from this kind of wound, no less turning it into a breakthrough, into creativity or self-expression or service, is that you've got to be willing to feel the thing. To go back and reencounter the grief of it, starting with the brute fact that you got a bum deal, that justice is beside the point and no one's going to make it up to you, and perhaps the best you can do is what the philosopher Jean Houston said of these kinds of challenges: retell the story of your life with the wound as the *middle* of the story, not the end.

Deborah's path to healing, and her path as a healer, began shortly after the cancer diagnosis, when a massage therapist helped her start to confront what had happened to her. With the guidance of one type of healer after another, over the course of twenty years of painstakingly unmasking the lies, she slowly began putting together the pieces of a devastating puzzle. And just as slowly, she began piecing *herself* back together—her authentic self, the one with a strong voice and a keen ear for the truth.

It's a work in progress. Finding the truth for herself, she says, is a daily pick-and-shovel job of "checking in and talking with myself . . . journaling . . . befriending my intuition . . . sharing with others who are trustworthy . . . and making sure I'm speaking my truth in ways that are natural and authentic.

"It took me a long time, and a serious illness, to begin expressing the truth of what I had experienced, and finally the truth of my creative self, and my intuitive self. . . . The shortfalls of my childhood put my nervous system on such high alert that I developed uncommon intuitive faculties. For survival reasons, I learned to read between the lines. . . . This capacity grew until I could read all kinds of subtle signals. I mastered the art of feeling deeply into people, sensing their hidden motives, deepest fears, and darkest demons."

All this comes into play in her work doing what's called energy healing, an ancient (though by modern standards an alternative) healing tradition that's ultimately about giving people their energy back. Its practitioners believe that imbalances in the body's energy field result in illnesses that can be treated by rebalancing energies, which are called many things in many traditions: *chi* in Chinese, *prana* in Hindi, *mana* in Hawaiian, *ruah* in Hebrew, and what Obi Wan Kenobi refers to when he says "May the force be with you." They're all akin to "soul" or "spirit" as animating forces in human affairs, all natural if not supernatural remedies for life out of balance.

Facing her own truth—not so much by *bursting* the spirit's sleep with a single blow as by waking it up slowly and in stages—has allowed Deborah's gift to be revealed. And her passion for speaking truth to secrecy has enabled her healing powers to be marshaled not only on her own behalf but on behalf of many others who also want their energy back.

For most people, such awakenings, if not revivals, come only by being stunned into consciousness, and for Deborah, cancer was the bell that finally tolled for her. It doesn't necessarily need to come to that to get our attention, though cancer certainly excels in that department. But had it not been for the cancer, the truth might have been buried indefinitely, and she along with it. "The scream that wasn't screamed," she writes, "the anger that was never expressed, the sadness that was stifled—all leave their mark."

And they all demand a voice, and though these voices can often be ignored, at least for a while, or medicated into oblivion, they're ultimately among the most authentic expressions of our true self and vitality. We can affect a great resurgence of energy and joy once that energy is no longer required for the repression and disguising of our truth, once the pain of denying the truth finally exceeds the fear of revealing it.

Setting Your Soul to Rights

There are no easy answers to the question of how to make that life-giving shift, to excavate your buried voice and the power that comes along with it, but denying your rightful suffering (passion!) and refusing to fully claim your story will short-circuit the healing that can set your soul to rights. And setting your soul to rights is not for quick-fixers and resolution junkies.

Forgiveness, of course, is good for your physical and mental health, according to countless studies, but only if you earn your stripes. It isn't a decision, but a pilgrimage. You're not going to release negative emotions, especially long-standing ones, by dropping them over the side of a bridge, and peacemaking takes hard work, as does the gaining of personal power and a merciful heart. Or as Mark Twain once said, "Habit is habit, and not meant to be flung out of the window . . . but coaxed downstairs a step at a time."

The kinds of trauma that Deborah King experienced are emotional Superfund sites, and aren't going to be cleaned up overnight, or tidied up with a hankie and a good cry. Wounds like this require the heavy machinery of our psychic technologies, all the negotiating skills we've learned from our clashes with the inner life over the centuries, and unflagging compassion and patience with ourselves.

No quick-fix approach to unraveling them is going to cut it. No amount of happy talk, herbal rescue remedies, or affirmations made in the mirror are going to suffice to trick the unconscious into believing it's been healed when it knows it hasn't. Counseling sessions, weekend workshops, and New Year's resolutions are certainly useful tools, but they're not killer apps.

Certainly we crave closure, because it brings restoration and healing, sometimes justice and a finishing of unfinished business, even a sense of the bigger picture—the *purpose* for the pain. But closure is more a verb than it is a noun, more an ongoing process than a once-and-for-all. And it can't be forced, as hungry as we often are for emotional efficiency—to turn lemons into lemonade or to forget our sufferings altogether and make the past come to heel. For one thing, there's no statute of limitations on grieving, and the past isn't always ours to project-manage.

In fact, I'm not convinced that you can completely heal a wound sustained forty years ago with *anything* you do in the present, though I've certainly put my shoulder to that wheel on many occasions. The wound also belongs to its own time, and to some degree is out of our reach. As the twelve-steppers say, we're always in recovery, always in need of being vigilant.

What we're after, understandably, is catharsis, which was originally a medical term referring to the flushing out of the body during menstruation, and means "to cleanse or purge." Aristotle was the first to use it in a theatrical sense, referring to the emotional discharge a playwright hoped to effect in an audience by the release of pent-up emotion, typically at the end of a good old Greek tragedy.

In the early days of psychoanalysis, the talking cure was sometimes referred to as "chimney sweeping." It's a cleaning out of the pipes, a restoring of the flow, but not typically clean and tidy work. Thus, catharsis must be handled with care. It's not just about blowing off steam and venting aggression, or going supernova on somebody, which has a tendency to just reinforce the venting of aggression because it temporarily feels good.

And it's not likely to happen by trying to rise above your suffering or applying artificial sweeteners to it. A few years ago, my then-wife, Robin, and I were two weeks away from moving into a new house—after our own house had already sold—when the appraisal came in well below the sale price, and the bank loan wouldn't cover us without our having to deflower our savings account. So the deal fell through, and we were faced with having nowhere to live. The people who owned the house we bid on wouldn't budge on the price and could afford to stay put until another deal came along, so to them it was nothing more than a spill in aisle four.

Not to us, despite our friends' confident assumptions of a grand scheme at work, their certainty that we lost the house in order to make room for the arrival and docking of Something Better. There are no accidents, they said. There must be a reason, they said. It's all for the best. God has a plan. You'll be fine. None of which helped.

Only one person said, "Man, that sucks." Which *did* help.

The health benefits of catharsis require that you actually *feel* your emotions, not just vent them or circumvent them. You might argue that you're definitely feeling anger while you're venting it, but what about the sorrow that's below it? And the vulnerability that's below that? And the love that's below *that*? Ironically, getting closure requires opening up, though there's an even chance that doing so will make you feel worse before it makes you feel better. Before it kicks in, catharsis will immerse you in whatever disturbing emotions have accompanied your troubles and traumas.

Also, passion encompasses fury and grief, jealousy and greed, as surely as it does joy and exuberance. Ask Ahab, Macbeth, Medea. It's not necessarily something to just let fly, and self-expression is not always a happy circumstance. The ruins of every civilization are the marks of men trying to express themselves and make an impression on the world.

But the darker emotions are also not something to chloroform. Talk-show host Larry King was once asked who makes a great guest for his show? His answer: "You have to be articulate, funny, self-deprecating, and you have to have a chip on your shoulder." Something you care passionately enough about that, with only the slightest provocation, you're ready to go to the mat. Or as I heard a novelist say recently, "Nice people with common sense do not make interesting characters, though they do make good former spouses."

Improv teacher Nina Wise believes that the darker impulses should be not only acknowledged but also played up and played *with*. She reminisces about a "depression party" she once hosted. Guests had to wear black, they lit black candles, served black food—black caviar, black sesame crackers, black bean dip, black coffee, dark chocolate. They ate on black plates, wiped their downturned mouths with black napkins, and when anyone asked, "How are you," the partygoers had to say they were terrible, horrible, awful, and complain volubly about all the depressing and demoralizing things that had befallen them lately: heartache, heartburn, weight gain, financial loss, romantic breakup, mental breakdown, car trouble, appliance malfunction, career off the rails, and the world generally going to hell in a handbasket.

Finally, having exhausted themselves with the rigors of kvetching, and feeling better for it, they put on loud music and danced.

Many years ago I, too, made peace and moved on from a sore spot in my life, and in the process freed up energies that had long ago gotten snagged on a rock.

I have a long-standing chip on my shoulder about sports—specifically team sports. I've avoided participating in them ever since I left high school forty years ago, almost never attend organized sporting events, and whenever there's a football or baseball strike, I find myself muttering "Good!" with the kind of umbrage I normally reserve for when they throw drunk drivers in jail.

So it was with no mean irony that one summer I joined a men's softball team, though I probably did it for the same reason that forty years after a war a soldier returns to the battlefield where he lost a leg.

I didn't start out soured on team sports. In fact, my first taste of it came about because my family had the biggest yard in the neighborhood when I was growing up. With two sets of trees, apples and elms, at either end to act as goalposts, we had the best soccer field around. I don't remember the winnings or losings of any of those games, only that it was *my* yard, and for a few indomitable years before my parents split up and I had to move, I felt like I lived in the best of all possible places. After my parents' divorce, something happened to my budding sense of team spirit. It faltered.

Once I hit elementary school, it downright fell on its face. This was largely a function, I believe, of all-boys gym class, where sports—which were defined from elementary school on as football, basketball, and baseball—were administered with a certain cutthroat economy, epitomized by what I call the Lineup. Two captains, invariably the most athletic, were picked by the coach, a former Marine who was now a math teacher pressed into service as a phys-ed instructor for ten-year-olds. These captains would then alternately pick team members from a lineup consisting of the rest of the boys, until everyone was teamed up.

It wasn't just the indignity of being last on line, or even second or third to last, that I would remember with a wince all those years later. It was that the captains would sometimes *argue* about who had these designated losers the last game—mostly the skinny kids, the fat kids, and the short kids—and who had to take them this game. As one of the first yardsticks against which I measured myself out in the world, sports were thus sorely lacking, although at the time I thought it was just me.

Out on the playing fields, things weren't much improved. The baseball diamond behind my old elementary school was popular with dirt-bikers and gophers, and in baseball you couldn't count on a ground ball doing anything more predictable than jumping erratically and possibly knocking out a few of your front teeth. Even out in right field, where I usually bided my time trying to talk myself out of sitting down, going after one felt like throwing my body onto a grenade.

By the time a grounder did get to me, it had often passed through at least one infielder's legs, or even two, with howls attending each. The air seemed to gel with the collective anxiety of my teammates. If the ball went through *my* legs, which it did with some regularity, the field exploded with disgusted and disbelieving groans, accompanied by the sound of mitts thudding against the dirt.

The few moments of victory I did experience in those games were so gratifying and infrequent that in my mind they still seem larger than life. I recall the time I hit a ball over second base, driving home three of my teammates. The astonished expressions on everyone's faces said it all: I was Ulysses returning from sea, who, disguised as a beggar, recaptured his sovereignty in a house full of insolent braggarts.

I don't doubt that these comeback memories may have had something to do with my return to the sport—and to team sports—after all those years. As I get older, I sense the urge to reexperience old glories, forgetting, or perhaps forgiving, that they were attended by a disproportionate amount of pain. And back in the game after my extended leave of absence, I did indeed rediscover some of these old glories. At bat, for example—it was all coming back to me—I remembered that in no other arena did being a lefty command such respect. Stepping up to the plate, I quietly reveled in watching the entire opposing team shift ten paces to the right, and this time without taking any paces *in*.

On the other hand, some things hadn't changed at all, and it seemed that we were just bigger versions of the way we were. There was still a kid swinging at balls after they had already hit the catcher's mitt. There was still a captain whose repertoire of exasperated gestures took half the fun out of the game. And there was still a deep anxiety, which I kept to myself.

But there was no Lineup.

The closest thing to it was the batting order, and once it became evident that I had honed my grudge into a fairly consistent line drive, I was not last, or even second or third to last, at bat. During one particular game, I had the great satisfaction of hitting a line drive that knocked the short-stop's glove right out of his hand. The captain, in a decision he couldn't possibly have known the significance of, changed the batting order after that and put me in the coveted position of fourth at bat.

In that moment, I knew I had gotten what I came back for, and began to understand *why* I had come back. What I proved by making that pilgrimage back to team sports was simply that the war was over. In literally playing out my unreconciled emotions, I was able to finish some unfinished business and finally make peace with some hard feelings I had about myself.

MOST PEOPLE HAVE heard of the "fight or flight" response, but there's a third reaction to threat that's seldom mentioned, and which people like Deborah understand only too well. It's called the freeze response, as in playing possum, and understanding a bit about it might help in our efforts to purge the past and regain momentum, to thaw our numbed-out emotional and creative energies.

Here's how it generally works in the animal kingdom: In the face of threat, an animal's body will rev up to fight or to flee—muscles tensed, senses on red alert. But if it can't do either, it will often freeze, hoping this strategy of playing dead will allow it to survive. If it does, the animal will then typically shake and tremble, shiver and quiver, to bring itself back to normal mobility and functioning and let the trauma go.

Humans, on the other hand, blessed but also cursed with that "higher" brain of ours, complicate this process by going into mental overdrive, triggering ourselves over and over in the face of subsequent events that feel like the original threat but aren't—getting your buttons pushed again and again by a string of men who only *remind* you of your father, or flying off the handle at any situation that makes you feel out of control the way you did during your childhood.

If you're unable to blow off the accumulated steam, shake out the muscles and the tension, it often gets stuck in the body, and over time you become a neuromuscular mess. The result is that an acute state of arousal congeals into a chronic state of arousal and vigilance, whether you're traumatized by childhood abuse, alcoholic parents, bullying, poverty, combat, natural disaster, domestic violence, employment discrimination, serious illness, or sudden loss.

Peter Levine, author of *Waking the Tiger*, believes that animals have something to teach us about getting unstuck and that healing from post-traumatic symptoms—anxiety, depression, hypervigilance, emotional numbing—requires completing the incomplete survival response and discharging the energy. Finding ways, as it were, to fight or to flee. But we activate this by turning to the body, not just the mind.

You have to work at the level of feelings, muscles, sensations, and sounds, exploring in very subtle ways how emotions get expressed or repressed in your body, how they get frozen or thawed, how they *move* inside you. Depending on the level of difficulty you're dealing with, this might be one from the "Do not try this at home" department. It might be best to do this kind of healing work with someone well trained in emotional bodywork.

Catharsis is often best handled in not only caretaking situations but also in small doses rather than large ones. And people are better off having a few confidants and a few practices at hand to help them *regularly* release the daily pressures that build behind the dam, rather than waiting for an outburst and a flood. If inhibition builds up enough internal pressure, the situation will tend to resolve in favor of a breach, because, like all things that flow, life seeks its own level, wants to go from a region of higher pressure to one of lower pressure. We need to routinely decompress, so the proverbial small stuff stays small and we court expression rather than explosion.

I recently saw an example of this process.

A retreat center at which I've presented workshops was celebrating the retirement of its director after forty years at the helm. There was a computer glitch in its invitations to the bon voyage event, resulting in everyone on that event list being spammed with emails from those who apparently hit "Reply All" instead of just "Reply," or had questions, or wanted to unsubscribe from the list.

Fifty or sixty emails piled up in our in-boxes over the course of a single day, and irritation swiftly gave way to aggravation, then anger, then, for some, a kind of panic. "Yikes. Please stop all these emails from coming," one woman wrote.

"OMG, people, stop!" exclaimed another.

"I'm being inundated. Take me off this list ASAP."

"Are you f—ing kidding me. Get me off your goddam list."

"Help! Please stop this deluge."

"You have created a nightmare."

"I agree. This is a nightmare."

"For the love of God remove my email from this awful nonsense."

"I think I might go to this event, if only to punch the director in the face. Ask around about me. I'll do it."

Then at some point, one of the spamees, bless her levelheaded soul, pointed out that while it was certainly annoying and inconvenient, this episode hardly constituted a "nightmare." The Holocaust was a nightmare. Being sold into sexual slavery is a nightmare. Getting spammed a few dozen times by mistake is not.

And from that email on, people seemed to come to their senses a bit. "I second that emotion," someone piped in.

"God how spoiled we've become. This is obviously an aberration," said another.

"Cool down everyone. It's just a mistake."

"Let's laugh at ourselves and find the learning here, shall we?"

"OK, I hereby promise *not* to slug the director when I attend his retirement party."

The fact that so many people—especially those on the email list for a spiritual center—could so easily be knocked off balance, and go so quickly to anger and attack, is ironic at the least, and indicates that spiritual centers have their work cut out for them.

It also suggests that a lot of folks are getting by at a level of coping with life that's only a single provocation away from a meltdown, are set to overheat at a moment's notice, and have a very tenuous hold on their tempers. They appear to be in dire need of a dose of equanimity and perspective, the kind that's helped immeasurably by, say, a meditation practice or a retreat at a spiritual center. Or a heart attack.

The Link Between Revealing and Healing

It's not by accident that Native American medicine men put
these questions to the sick who are brought to them:
When was the last time you sang? When was the last time you
danced? When was the last time you told your story?
When was the last time you listened to the stories of others?

—MARK NEPO

Writers often claim that to truly lay someone or something to rest, to shoo the ghost, it's necessary to write about them. "In polite society," writes Sylvia Plath in her *Journals*, "a lady doesn't punch or spit. So I turn to my work." Later in the *Journals*, she says, "Fury jams the gullet and spreads poison, but, as soon as I start to write, dissipates."

The psychic core of trauma, or any experience that overwhelms your system, according to Carol Gilligan in *The Birth of Pleasure*, is a loss of voice, the inability to tell your story. And recovery means recovering your ability to tell that story.

In a series of workshops called In Our Own Voices, conducted during the 1990s, Gilligan and Kristin Linklater, who teaches in the theater department at Columbia University, worked to free what Linklater calls the natural voice—the voice that carries rather than covers a person's inner world—the voice that's "in direct contact with emotional impulse, shaped by the intellect but not inhibited by it, in which the person is heard, not the person's voice."

Unfortunately for most of us, this natural voice, this access to our ancient sources of passion, sorrow, anger, and laughter, to the roar of pain or pleasure, has either been civilized or brutalized out of us, and reclaiming it takes a bit of doing, if not *un*doing. The intention of the workshop, according to Gilligan, was to encourage people to find in themselves "a resilience, a sense of adventure, a directness of expression, an energy, and a voice that they had forgotten or not heard with clarity for years. I was drawn by the sound of an unmediated voice, a voice that broke free, a wild voice."

She wanted to help participants pick up the subtlest manifestations of the impulse to speak, and through voice, theater, and writing exercises to connect those impulses with breath and sound. The process helped reconnect people with both their bodies and parts of their own history that they had split off from consciousness. And because it was a journey back to a time of dissociation, an associative process was necessary. "What is dissociated or repressed—known and then not known—tends to return," Gilligan writes. "The brilliance of dissociation as an adaptation to trauma is that it keeps alive what had seemingly been lost."

Studies of the biological and psychological nature of trauma, she says, reveal that coming out of dissociation and into consciousness are linked through the recovery of a person's *voice*. When you're able to tell your story, you're able to come into awareness of what's been forgotten and wants to be known. The workshop took participants through a six-step associative process:

Step 1: Free-association writing, beginning with the statement "I am going back to find her/him."

Step 2: Visualizing: closing your eyes and imagining yourself as you were when you were nine or ten, drawing a picture of your child-self, then imagining this child saying to you, "I want to take you on an adventure."

Step 3: Recording the journey s/he takes you on, in some form.

Step 4: Listening: doing a free-write starting with the phrase "And s/he came to tell me . . ."

Step 5: Resonating: freewriting from the phrase "And I heard you say . . ."

Step 6: Composing: writing "A Poem to My Voice."

Interestingly, during the 1990s, Gilligan and Linklater also co-facilitated theater workshops that brought together actresses with girls nine to thirteen years old. They found that bringing women into the company of girls led to "a release of voice and energy that inspired fresh, original, and at times brilliant work. In the presence of girls who will speak freely and say what they're seeing and hearing, thinking and feeling, women begin to know what they know." Or as one of the participants said, "Do you want to know what I think? Or do you want to know what I *really* think?"

What Gilligan and Linklater's workshop and a host of studies have demonstrated is that there's a well-documented connection between recovering your voice and healing, in both body and soul. It's no coincidence that the ancient word *pneuma* means both "breath" and "spirit," or life force. The breath that plays over our vocal chords, the wind that carries the word and allows our spirit to speak and our life force to be expressed, is also the air we breathe in order to live. Finding your voice tends to fill your sails.

James Pennebaker, a pioneer in what's called writing therapy, conducted a study at Southern Methodist University in the 1980s in which he had students write about either traumatic or superficial experiences.

Those who wrote about their deepest thoughts and feelings related to a trauma showed a 50 percent drop in visits to the university health center compared with the other group, benefits that accrued in direct proportion to how reluctant a student had previously been to disclose these emotions. The more resistance, the more relief.

Writing in depth is essentially a form of confession and brings with it a drop in blood pressure and heart rate and a boost in immune function, mood, and general outlook. Even employment. Another of Pennebaker's studies showed that those who kept a journal about losing a job were more likely to find reemployment in the months following the study. And this outcome didn't seem to be caused by increased motivation or job-seeking efforts. These people didn't make more cold calls, send out more résumés, or pound more pavement. Their willingness to reveal their emotions set up something like a magnetic field that simply drew things to them, like attracting like.

It apparently works for insomnia, too, as Pennebaker himself discovered. Rather than continuing to toss and turn one sleepless night, he got up, found a tape recorder, lay down on the couch in his living room, closed his eyes, and talked stream-of-consciousness. Within ten minutes, he was sound asleep. He conducted a follow-up study with university students broken into three groups. One group just went to bed and tried to fall asleep, a second group talked their thoughts out loud, and a third counted sheep. Only the second group got to sleep and stayed asleep.

To test whether writing was unique among the expressive arts in its healing properties, Pennebaker tested three others: singing, drawing, and dancing. He found that in all three forms of art therapy, clients are ultimately encouraged to *talk* about their emotional experiences, and putting them into words, into language, is primarily where the healing happens. The refusal to talk to anybody about problems is linked with a higher incidence of illness, he believes, and those who seldom become sick are those who live in ways that allow them not only to be themselves but also to *disclose* themselves.

SOME YEARS AGO I ran across the story of "Alex," a thirty-two-year-old man who had witnessed his father plan the murder of a beloved relative, a crime his father subsequently committed. Alex was overwhelmed by fear that he would be called to testify against his father, and eventually repressed the entire event.

Perhaps not coincidentally, he developed throat cancer, but during an intense psychotherapy session the night before an operation to remove it, he broke down and recounted the whole episode, with all the emotion he felt at the time, complete with weeping and wailing, shaking and trembling.

Within four hours, he finished the first meal he had been able to eat without pain in a week, and within four days he presented to his doctor one of the great surprises of his medical career: an X-ray showing that the tumor had completely disappeared.

I came upon this story in the archives at the Institute of Noetic Sciences in Sausalito, California, founded in 1973 by Apollo 14 astronaut Edgar Mitchell for the purpose of studying "human potential." It is one of thirty-five hundred case studies included in the world's largest database of spontaneous remissions, what are called remarkable recoveries from disease, those that can't be explained by medical treatment.

Far from being the flukes portrayed by a medical community reluctant to even document them (typically dismissing them as misdiagnoses), spontaneous remissions point to the extraordinary self-repair capacities with which we're endowed. In fact, even the term *spontaneous remission* betrays an underlying bias. These recoveries are not spontaneous. They all have a cause, just not necessarily a medical one.

Among the most consistent causes of these remarkable recoveries is a profound and affirmative personal change just prior to the remission. It could be a reconciliation with a long-despised parent, a revelatory experience, or the radical assumption of responsibility for your own life. It could be a significant confession or admission, allowing a long-buried and essential part of you to finally emerge and be expressed. Or it could be the pursuit of a long-denied passion, the reclaiming of what poet W. H. Auden called your "foiled creative fire."

This isn't to suggest that all disease is psychosomatic, or that we can simply *talk* our way out of illness. Nor is it a foregone conclusion that making a radical change guarantees a radical recovery, and healing your life necessarily heals your body, though the body-mind literature certainly points to a strong correlation between the two.

People who experience these kinds of turning points, say Marc Ian Barasch and Caryle Hirshberg in *Remarkable Recovery* (quoting a physician who had worked with "spontaneous remitters") aren't usually shooting for a cure anyway, only "to live congruently at long last with their inner values." This may begin, for any of us, they say, "with a single instance of self-listening, a few small acts of affirmation, and the tiniest mustard seed of faith in the deeper self."

"For some of those who walk the path of healing," the authors say, "disease seemed to have forced a moment that arrives for most of us all too infrequently, when life itself depends on us becoming authoritatively, powerfully, even crazily, the person we were meant to be."

If you're not used to expressing yourself, creatively or emotionally—and in the absence of an illness pressing you toward authenticity at gunpoint—you're probably going to have to start by *forcing* yourself. To get up from the couch, put on some music, and dance. To doodle in the margins and drum on your desk. To write poetry on restaurant napkins and sing in the shower. To say what's really on your mind. To do your true work in the world.

Start with those subtle manifestations of the impulse to express yourself and build from there, slowly unharnessing yourself from the yoke of inhibition and conventional conduct, which is a fairly narrow band of behavior, a thin slice of human potential that offers little room to really stretch out. It doesn't truly allow us to experience our full range of motion or our full vocal spectrum from soprano to basso profundo. But don't leave this body and soul behind without knowing what they can do, and know that at the heart of whatever unnerves you is probably the restorative you need.

If you have to, fake it till you make it. Once you become accustomed to cutting loose, maybe even enjoying it, you won't have to force yourself anymore. Then it's a matter of enchantment.

The Dangers of Overexpression

On a flight from Tucson to Los Angeles last year, a fellow sat next to me who had the body of an ex–football player and a latticework of broken blood vessels on both cheeks, and despite my concerted effort to exude solitary vibes, he wouldn't stop talking to me. First, he looked over my shoulder and asked me what I was reading and then launched into an homage to spy thrillers and detective novels. I tried a trip to the bathroom, but he was waiting for me when I got back. I tried bringing the woman sitting in the aisle seat into the conversation, but she wasn't interested.

In a momentary lull, I buried myself in a newspaper, holding it up around my head like a Japanese folding screen, but he asked me a question and my cursed civilized upbringing forced me to speak when spoken to. I even resorted to subterfuge, pulling out of my briefcase the notes for a lecture I was giving in Los Angeles and telling him that I had work to get done, but he said, "You're not getting rid of me, so you might as well talk to me."

I'm not ordinarily a curmudgeon, and it isn't misanthropy that propels me to turn from my fellow man and radiate the warmth of a boarded-up building. It's a defense mechanism against frequently finding myself in the company of serial talkers.

Linguists call them conversational narcissists, talkaholics, and high verbalizers, and what they're verbalizing so highly is largely chitchat, short for "chittering and chattering," both synonyms for incessant talk. It's small talk in large liquid doses and is rightly referred to as verbal diarrhea—running off at the mouth.

Psychologist Sidney Jourard in *The Transparent Self* refers to it as "irresponsible self-expressiveness," in which the passion to communicate goes into overdrive if not warp-drive, and if my own experience is any indication, there's quite a lot of it going around. It's probably no coincidence that all cultures have a word for *vampire*, for a creature so needy it sucks the life force out of others. If passion means "to suffer," this is a case of one person's passion becoming *another* person's suffering, and a profile in how passion can get out of hand.

I'm routinely stupefied by the number of people I run across whose idea of conversation—perhaps our primary arena of self-expression—is a rampaging monologue, and for whom I'm just a bucket in which to drain all the clutter and piffle from their minds, audience for whatever long-winded soliloquy or emotional drama they feel like getting off their chests, and they're there to strut and fret an hour or two upon the stage while waiting for the plane to land. To them, it was "great talking to you," and undoubtedly they leave with the impression that I'm a fine fellow. I, on the other hand, am left feeling like someone just picked my pockets.

This goes doubly for people who *pretend* to conversation, interrupting their data dump long enough to ask a question about me, only to use it as a form of in-air refueling before turning the conversation back to themselves. Their questions are like boomerangs; they mean for them to come back around quickly.

The writer Jane Campbell once observed that overcommunicators regard life as a talk show on which they're the star guest. "If you ask, 'What's the capital of Venezuela?' they hear, 'So tell us a bit about your early years, Bob.'"

They're oblivious to, or ignore, a basic principle of human relations, something that's really kindergarten stuff: taking turns. I'll do you, then you do me. They make great use of an attention-getting tactic called shift response (constantly shifting the focus back to themselves) and minimum use of an attention-*giving* tactic called support response (encouraging the other guy to talk).

If you tell someone you're having a hard day and she says, "Me too," that's shift. If she says, "How come?," that's support. It's the subtle difference between giving and taking, curiosity and indifference. It's the difference between a conversation that's actually interactive—two people's self-expressiveness swapping juices—and one that's merely additive, one story piled on top of another; mine, then yours, then mine, then yours, the conversation really two elbowing monologues.

It probably doesn't help that we (Americans at least) live in what sociologists call a "therapeutic culture," one devoted to personal development and self-help, and one in which people often confuse conversation and psychoanalysis. Ordinary dialogue becomes a talking cure, the autobiographical impulse gets stuck in the On position, and others are cast into the role of spectators.

It's an inheritance from Freud's most important insight: that patients already know everything they need to know but can't access it without help. The therapist is essential for them to display what they know to themselves. In other words, they need a catalyst, a witness—a role you probably wouldn't mind filling if they were paying you a hundred dollars an hour for it.

Some conversational researchers believe there's no such thing as people who talk too much. There's only subject matter you're either interested in or not, and if you're not, then any amount of it is too much. If someone were to talk endlessly about your shining qualities, you probably wouldn't feel put upon.

Flashback: In 1984 I moved from Cincinnati to Berkeley, and one night, a few months after moving, I was reading in bed when a woman called, said her name was Linda, and that she was responding to my ad in the *Bay Guardian* looking for people interested in swapping magazines. I had subscriptions to half a dozen of them at the time, and rather than tossing them when I was finished, I concocted the idea of exchanging them with people who had subscriptions to half a dozen *different* magazines.

When she asked me what I looked like, though, I sensed she wasn't interested in magazines. This was confirmed when she asked if I liked blondes, described herself as a model with blue-green eyes, 114 pounds, and said, "Men come on to me quickly in bars." She asked if I ever fantasized about swinging or ever had a threesome, segued into a vivid description of her participation in one, and wrapped it up by inquiring if I was getting turned on.

Let's just say I realized in that moment that Berkeley was going to be the antidote to Cincinnati.

"So tell me," she said, "what would *you* want to do to me?"

At which point I stretched my leg out and closed the bedroom door with my foot, so my housemate Joan wouldn't hear.

I'm sure I talked nonstop for ten or fifteen minutes—a genuine blue streak—but it was the *content* of what I talked about that kept Linda on the line. I was doing all the talking, but *she* was the center of attention. I figure if someone can bring you to an orgasm just by talking to you, you're probably not going to be bored.

In our virtual postcoital reverie, Linda told me I was terrific, said she wanted to call me again sometime, and then, of all things, recommended a book: *The Road Less Traveled*.

At the beginning of my speaking career someone told me that if I was going to presume to be a public speaker and take up people's precious time, I'd better damn well be entertaining, and I feel the same way about other people's public displays of expression—and the sharing of passion in general. This goes especially for the evangels, the people with such an intense wallop about some subject or project or vision that they live only to spread the gospel about it, serenely insensible to the fact that people may be slipping into comas around them.

From a purely entertainment standpoint, they usually lack a few of the elemental sensory and sensitivity skills that make for engaging interaction and willing participants. One is an understanding of the basic requirement of a story: something should happen. Another is an eye for the cues that signal whether people are engaged in your passionate exhortations or not, and a feel for when to knock off. Astute conversationalists notice when their listeners have left the building—their eyes have a remote look, their nods and uh-huhs are sluggish.

A promising bit of research being conducted at MIT might be just the ticket for the less astute conversationalists. Folks in the Media Lab there have developed a device—originally designed for people with autism, who have difficulty picking up on social cues—that alerts users if the person they're talking to starts showing signs of boredom or annoyance. It's a kind of prosthetic device for people with low emotional intelligence that consists of a camera small enough to be mounted on a pair of eyeglasses, connected to a handheld computer that runs image-recognition software. If you fail to engage your listener, the computer vibrates.

An acquaintance of mine, Tebbe Davis, who counts himself among the talkaholics, has devised a different feedback mechanism, which he calls Code 17. When someone says "Code 17" to him, that's the signal that he's overdoing it. For example, at a weekly business networking meeting, two friends come armed with an index card with "Code 17" emblazoned on it, which they flash at him when he's talking too much.

Among the verbose, lack of editing is another problem. Every story is told with mind-numbingly inessential details, useless digressions, and self-interruptions to fuss about accuracy. Those who have little of interest to say often seem to spend the most amount of time saying it. Especially when they're drunk. Nothing inflames talk like alcohol (or being paid by the word for it, as any author will tell you). The writer Diane McWhorter, an avowed "motormouth," once wrote that she went out for martinis with a friend who asked, "What are you like when you drink them?"

She answered, "I'm the same, except I talk more."

She waited for him to calculate this, then said, "Does that help you understand the definition of 'infinity'?"

It's also simply more entertaining to tell our own stories than to listen to other people's, which is why it's boring to listen to people talk shop, gossip about people we don't know, or recite their dreams. The cast of characters is unfamiliar, the settings and lingo alien, the can of worms not our own. W. H. Auden's poem "Musée des Beaux Arts" beautifully illustrates this estrangement in commenting on a painting by Peter Brueghel's called *Fall of Icarus*. In the painting, Icarus plunges toward the Aegean, while causality rushes up to meet him, and Auden writes that "Everything turns away / Quite leisurely from the disaster; the ploughman may have heard the splash, the forsaken cry, / But for him it was not an important failure."

Talkaholics may think of themselves as linguistically well hung, but the rest of us think of them as merely narcissistic, which, granted, is immensely hard to undo and not necessarily their fault. It's a holdover from that original egocentric stage around one or two years old, when children naturally feel grandiose and at the center of the universe. But it's supposed to be a *transitional* phase, after which we face the inconvenient realization that the universe includes other people and that if we want our report cards to say "Gets along well with others," we have to learn to make the small sacrifices of self that lend themselves to mutuality.

Like so much of communal life, the *sharing* of passions—in this case in the form of conversation—requires a decentralizing of self, an extending of awareness beyond our own borders, into the spaces we share with others, into others themselves, and ideally we push it outward as far as possible. The more of the world we can identify with and the wider our field of affections, the bigger we are and the less we have to try to prove it.

The theologian Martin Buber talked about the difference between an I-It and an I-Thou relationship to others. One treats people like things, the other treats them like extensions of the self, expressions of the Unity that carries us all on its hip. To Buber, *I-Thou* is a word pair that he considered a single word, and one that can no more be workably split apart than a pair of pants. But he also said that as soon as you add to any dialogue what he called an object of thought—an assumption, a judgment, an agenda, even an opinion—you immediately turn the relationship into an I-It.

Significantly, he placed a hyphen between *I* and *Thou*, which not only connects them but also divides them, separating them by the slightest pause, room enough for an edgewise thought or a wedge of opinion, an atom of hesitation that, split, would reveal the history of our sundered Oneness, the unabridged biography of the Fall. In it we would read of all that has ever kept people apart and to themselves: competition, autonomy, ignorance, self-preservation.

Buber understood that I-Thou is an ideal, the attainment of real communion, not imagined or pretended, not Christ in a cracker, and something you're lucky to achieve a handful of times in life, no less sustain. But in a single moment of paying genuine attention to someone, a split second of being self-forgetful like the swamis, the space between people can be straddled.

Ever since I was first read fairy tales, I've been captivated by the concept of "magic words," the abracadabras and alakazams and open sesames that grant wishes, break spells, reveal the truth, and leave the bad guys eating dirt—the words that can transform us and make our dreams come true.

Maybe people who overexpress are after the same thing, running through all the volumes they know, hoping that some combination of words, some incantation, will crack the code and grant them whatever treasure they're after. It reminds me, though, of the old debate about whether an infinite number of monkeys given an infinite number of typewriters (and time) would eventually produce the complete works of Shakespeare. Statisticians assure us they would, but a recent test of the theory suggested otherwise. Researchers at England's Plymouth University left a computer in the primate enclosure at a zoo. The monkeys attacked the machine and failed to produce a single word.

We ourselves are descended from monkeys who descended from trees, and some linguists think language evolved as a substitute for the grooming behavior of our primate ancestors, which afforded us an intimacy that became more and more difficult to maintain as the animal groupings grew in size and we lost easy physical contact with the members of our tribe. So we began vocalizing these bonds in the linguistic equivalent of delousing each other.

Maybe all our towering babble is proportionate to how badly we need that lost intimacy, how desperate we are to run our fingers through one another's hair.

Maybe this is what we need to bring back to the tribe: the sort of fine-tuning, the *feel* for each other, that we had back when we were nitpicking each other for real. The feel for how to really touch each other so that communication turns into communion and our conversations are more than just storms with the dry heaves—lightning and thunder but no rain; information and knowledge but no wisdom.

Unfortunately, the Age of Information is synonymous with the Age of Words—most information comes to us as language—and it's a world already in the times of flood. Words fill up the newspapers that fill up the garbage trucks that fill up the landfills. We have twenty-four-hour-a-day talk comin' atcha through radio, television, telephone, print, internet, mail, and movies, to say nothing of cocktail parties full of small talk and tall talk, sweet talk and trash talk, straight talk and double talk. Humanity currently churns out roughly five exabytes of new information a year on print, film, magnetic, and optical media—the equivalent of thirty-seven thousand libraries the size of the Library of Congress, which has seventeen million books.

Science even tells us that we have roughly one hundred trillion cells in our bodies, with six feet of DNA in each cell, and if we could unpack each packet of DNA and lay its alphabet in single file, it would reach from here to the sun twelve hundred times. We're a wordy bunch, in the very fiber of our being.

If talk is for the purpose of establishing connection, though, then given the amount of talking many of us do, we ought to be pretty well interbred by now. But the degree of alienation among people suggests otherwise. We shout back and forth over the castle walls instead of lowering the drawbridge, and our talk, our self-expression, becomes barrier rather than connector, a shell around soft underbellies.

Like arms proliferation, the metastasizing spread of yammer is detrimental to the bonds between people—if not to life. Breath is life; and when talk is futile, we say, "Don't waste your breath." We cover our mouths when we yawn because of the age-old belief that a gaping orifice is an invitation for the soul to escape and evil spirits to enter. Among the animals, too much talk can be lethal. The chattier the animal, the easier it is for predators to find it.

Unfortunately, the means we use to satisfy our need for communication sometimes create the opposite effect. "The single biggest problem in communication," George Bernard Shaw once said, "is the illusion that it has taken place." The cruel irony is that overexpressers seldom attain the thing they're after—receivers—because most people take to their heels, or tune them out like the boy who cried wolf, or develop covert signaling systems to indicate to others across a room: save me.

Conversation comes from a word meaning something like intimacy, but abused it's antisocial, and talkers wind up constantly sowing seeds that don't bear fruit. They want to ingratiate themselves but end up annoying people instead. To paraphrase Plutarch in his essay *On Talkativeness*, they don't have companions so much as conscripts.

The Physics of Communion

Don't surround yourself with yourself.

—YES, "I'VE SEEN ALL GOOD PEOPLE"

Ever since my high school guidance counselor, Ms. Transue, offered me the chance to participate in a weekly rap group, which I jumped at, I've been involved in groups designed to immerse me—educate me—in the how-to of communication, designed to break the crust of superficiality that attends most social encounters and drop people into the deeper waters of relationship, into what is abstractly referred to as being *real*.

Men's groups, community-building workshops, theater improv classes, personal development trainings, drumming classes, therapy groups—all of them have taught me the power of listening, the first rule of which is to stop talking. We were given two ears and one tongue and should utilize them proportionately.

They've also helped me examine the thoughts behind my thoughts, the assumptions behind my opinions, the active ingredients in intimacy and alienation, and the peculiar alchemy that turns stranger into friend.

They've taught me that personal problems are also cultural problems, and that both require the incremental (re)building of trust, which often runs aground on the derelictions of love and power that most of us have encountered if not committed.

Most important, all the groups have *ground rules* that allow for both speaking and being heard—rules that, unlike in everyday conversation, are both explicit and enforced. One person talks at a time, everyone gets to talk, no interruptions or advice, and, to cut down on generalizations and projections, "I" statements only, no "You" statements, though I once heard an extremely inventive end-run around this rule when two men in one of the groups were arguing and one said "F— you!"

"Hey!" the other guy said, "'I' statements only."

"Fine," the first guy shot back. "Eat me!"

These groups have been tutorials in communication as well as silence, which can be either a hole that people fall into and so constantly try to fill, or a Roman candle that illuminates a far broader landscape than merely the words that people speak. And it's often in silence that we figure out what it is we actually have to say to the world, and get a bead on what our passions are, and the source of those passions.

Silence is formidable and paradoxical stuff. It's hard to find, and once found, it's hard to tolerate. It's a blessing in solitude and a curse in conversation. It can be an intimate part of fellowship, or it can be used to dismantle it. People often associate silence with loneliness and isolation, with the Nothingness that brackets life on both sides, beginning and end—we refer to "dead silence"—and talking tells them they're not alone, that someone is listening. "I'm heard, therefore I exist."

But this is a belief that's also been taken advantage of since Paleolithic times in a practice called "shunning," a means of punishment for breaching the social order, a way of forcing people back into line, like the woman whose parents sent her to her room for displays of "negative emotions."

It's kept alive today primarily through religious communities such as Mennonites and Jehovah's Witnesses, who call it disfellowshipping. Those shunned, for violations of faith or doctrine, are ignored completely. No one talks to them or listens to them. They're treated, even by family members, as if they don't exist and are looked right through. It's a form of excommunication, which means "out of communion." It's the silent treatment amplified to the point of an existential crisis, and sometimes a psychotic break.

But silence can also be used to create and communicate the deepest passions and affinities, something I saw writ large in an experience I had in the aftermath of the World Trade Center bombings in 2001. I was in Scotland at the time, had finished up some work in Aberdeen and driven to the west coast for a stay in the tiny town of Ballachulish. I was walking upstairs with my second glass of sherry from the bar when I thought I heard, through the door of someone else's room, something about a jet crashing into the World Trade Center, and I thought it was some tasteless BBC routine. I had settled into a nook in the bay window when my wife turned on the television and all that awfulness came pouring out.

The next day, the entirety of Europe, eight hundred million people, stopped whatever they were doing in the middle of their day, for three minutes of silence and commiseration. The TV showed scenes from every country in Europe—the chambers of British Parliament, city streets in Madrid, department stores in Paris, financial offices in Germany—with everyone stopped in their tracks.

But when we're not using "a moment of silence" for prayer, contemplation, or the emotional equivalent of flying our flags at half-mast, we're wary of silence. If even a little of it is dropped into a conversation, for example, suddenly it's all hands on deck. Eyes dart nervously, sweat beads in unseen places, file cabinets in the brain are ransacked looking for something to say. Even nature lovers and meditators fall to jabbering when the silence of their beloved meadows and meditations slips into a conversation. Suddenly we feel naked, and in the rush to clothe ourselves, we occasionally speak without thinking, blurting out whatever desperate thought crosses our minds first. Sometimes we just replace feeling awkward with feeling stupid.

As a writer and reporter, I've conducted several thousand interviews and have seen in myself a desire to rescue people, including myself, from this awkwardness, by rushing to fill silences with questions. Eventually I learned to rein myself in (while on assignment anyway), because somebody always breaks the silence, and if that somebody isn't me, it's going to be them, and they'll sometimes break it with something juicy and revealing, which may not necessarily be matched to their better judgment.

With what Henry James called the "terrible fluidity of self-revelation," people sometimes reveal things they wish they hadn't. I've had my share of irate phone calls on the morning an article of mine appeared in the newspaper, from people claiming that they never said such-and-such, and when I send them a tape of the interview, they say well, they didn't *mean* to say that. Their mouth was in Drive, but their brain was in Park.

Silences may be revelatory, useful for reporters, therapists, and contemplatives—one person's abyss is another person's vista—but in purely social situations, we seem to routinely come up short on the grit necessary to ride these silences out.

This has something to do with Western civilization being full of what linguists call "word cultures" in which silence in conversation is usually treated as a failure of rapport, a breakdown in communication, a lack of expressiveness, and where the more someone talks, and the faster, the more he or she is perceived as intelligent, credible, and possessed of leadership qualities. Intuition tells me that the more people *listen*, the more effective their leadership, and the more intelligent, at least if intelligence is judged by its original definition: the capacity to understand.

In "silence cultures" like the Japanese, Apache, Navajo, and Paliyan (India), which are far less loquacious and consider verbosity abnormal, even offensive, silence is perceived as evidence of trust, agreement, and harmony, and it says you're at ease with people. Among the Scandinavian Lapps, entire minutes of silence can pass between a simple request and a simple reply. Time enough for a couple of quick cell phone calls where I come from.

At the least, forcing words into conversational silences strikes me as a failure of faith, if not emotional intelligence—we don't trust that we'll speak when we're moved to speak. We think that silence means nothing is happening, when what scares the daylights out of us is that actually something very profound is happening: presence. Just our presence with one another, which we react to like radio DJs react to dead air.

I remember a vivid demonstration of this in a seminar I attended back in 1983 with 165 other people in a Cincinnati hotel ballroom. In something called the danger exercise, the facilitator instructed each row of people, perhaps thirty to forty to a row, to stand up and file onto the stage. Once there, we were to do nothing but stand quietly and face the audience. No hands in your pockets or on your hips, no crossing your arms or shuffling back and forth from one leg to the other, no playing with your hair, no drink or cigarette in your hand. And no talk. Just stand there in your body in front of other people.

It took *moments* for the nervous throat-clearing to start, then the ragged breathing, the shuddering and shaking, the crying. I glanced down the line and saw men and women—grown-ups, professional people—their faces tight with strain, their bodies trembling at a dozen different places. True, we'd been primed by a day of emotional "processing" and were more vulnerable than if we'd just been pulled in from the street. But still. "Is this the way human bodies are supposed to look," the facilitator asked, "all bent out of shape?"

I thought the exercise would be a cinch for me, since I'm a public speaker and used to being stared at, but without my speeches, without the power of polished oratory and the theatrics of gesture and expression, without the anchor of a lectern or a sense of purpose, my legs began to quake. Also, I couldn't maintain eye contact with people, which is normally easy for me. I stared instead into the middle distance.

I've often noticed that the moment words stop in a conversation, even momentarily, eye contact breaks off. It's simply too intimate to just stand there looking at each other. It's like trying to keep your eyes open during a sneeze. Even when silence is the *rule* and people expect it, it still makes us squirm. I've spent time at Trappist monasteries and in silent retreats, and I've noticed that when people are sitting directly across from each other at narrow tables during meals, no one makes eye contact. Everyone looks down at their plates or up at the ceiling. If it doesn't accompany talk, eye contact becomes excruciating, even invasive.

I sometimes find myself staring at small children, even infants, who stare back unabashedly, unblinking, their smooth faces betraying not a hint of opinion or valuation, only the rudimentary sensing that dogs and cats have to friend or foe. But it took me some time and conscious effort to allow myself to do this, because I'm habituated not to stare at other people, and I had to regularly remind myself that infants do not, yet, possess the capacity to judge, or be embarrassed.

So now I look right back at them and hold their gazes, bathing myself in the experience of exchanging intense eye contact with another person, without a shred of awkwardness, taking in and being taken in by another in an atmosphere of zero scrutiny and judgment, simple and absolute presence.

Interestingly, a week after the danger exercise, I was sitting in a Laundromat around the corner from my apartment when a little girl, no more than seven, started dancing in front of me, though I quickly realized she wasn't just dancing in *front* of me. She was dancing *for* me. I have no idea why, but she did a ballet dance, utterly unself-consciously, simply immersed in the delight of movement and make-believe and somebody to watch her.

At first I was embarrassed. People were looking and I felt put on the spot. But suddenly I stopped thinking about the others, and about myself. My strained smile fell away and beneath it was a real one. I just sat at that funky old table, piled with magazines and empty detergent boxes, watching my tiny dancer. We didn't take our eyes off each other. When she finished, with a flourish and a bow and an ear-to-ear grin, I clapped and clapped, with all those people looking.

THERE ARE INUIT tribes in which two people will sit facing each other and one will open his mouth in the shape of an O and the other will blow his breath across the bottle top of the other's mouth, and together they'll imitate the wind singing in the rocks or whistling across the chimneys.

Dialogue, the physicist David Bohm says, is a stream of meaning flowing through and between people, and that stream doesn't necessarily have to be made of words. A Quaker doctrine, in fact, says that what's required to apprehend the spirit of God is a suppression of self that's best got to through silence—or more to the point, through presence and attention, a deep listening that is the hatch that leads to communion. How much of ourselves—of our essence and emotions, our passions and compassions—can we express just through our presence? And how much can we learn of others' through *theirs*?

Ironically, in theological terms, communion is something one *receives*, so in conversational terms, communion would go to the receiver—the listener, not the talker. It would go to the one who takes in the other, and who is increased in grace by doing so.

Talkaholics attempt to do what lovers do—make a connection—but they go about it through promiscuity, which fails from its sheer quantity, overzealousness, and the sense of shame that often propels it. The goal is union, to be touched in a place that fingers can't reach, but sex isn't necessarily intimacy, and lots of sex isn't necessarily lots of intimacy.

The power of wordless communion—and the exchange of passion—is seldom made more obvious to me than through my participation in Asheville's drum circle, a group that gets together every Friday night but whose members speak hardly a word to one another.

I saw this crystallized in an encounter there last summer when a big guy emerged from the crowd and lurched toward the drummers, possibly drunk, possibly not, but definitely disheveled and disturbed about something, the look on his face somewhere between angry and crazy. He stopped abruptly in front of one of the drummers, who, out of conditioned response, looked off to the side and kept drumming. The wildman stood rigidly over him, his head cocked, the muscle between his eyes knotted in a burl. Then he suddenly stepped in front of the next drummer and then the next and the next, all the way down the line, like some half-mad composer searching for a sour note in the score.

When he neared the end of the line, though, something came over him. His features changed in slow motion from hard to soft. The corners of his mouth rose up in a smile, his eyes closed, his face turned up and caught the moonlight in his perspiration. He stood there for a long time, restored, mollified, rocked by the drums and lit by the moon, while all around him dancers stirred the thick air with their bodies.

It was the same rapture I've seen come over the *whole* crowd every time—and it happens several times a night, when all the drummers, even if only by coincidence, get onto the same wavelength, and the sound and the spirit soar, accompanied by a chorus of tribal yahoos.

The technical term for the process by which a group of individuals achieves this quality of elation through synchronized movement or activity is phase entrainment. This rhythmic conformity brings with it a deeply satisfying experience of boundary loss, which, at its farther reaches, becomes ecstatic trance, with the drum as the shaman's horse ridden into and out of this altered and exalted state. Musicians call it the groove, scientists describe it by saying things like "a slow recovery variable interacting with synaptic time scales to produce phase-locked solutions in networks of pulse coupled neural relaxation oscillators," and soldiers call it lock-step, which, despite its seeming mindlessness, fits the description for many. In *Keeping Together in Time: Dance and Drill in Human History*, William H. McNeill describes the hours of military drills and close-order marching he had to do in boot camp during World War II. "What I remember now, years afterward, is that I rather liked strutting around, and so, I feel sure, did most of my fellows. . . . Words are inadequate to describe the emotion aroused by the prolonged movement in unison that drilling involved. A sense of pervasive well-being is what I recall; more specifically, a strange sense of personal enlargement; a sort of swelling out, becoming bigger than life . . . a state of . . . emotional exaltation."

I've read that two heart cells in a petri dish will synchronize with each other over time, like menstrual cycles in a sorority house or pendulum clocks in a room, and this certainly resonates with the local newspaper's headline for a story about the drum circle: "The Heartbeat of Downtown."

Entrainment speaks to a kind of force field, a "co-respondence" that can be generated between and among people without a word being spoken. It highlights that there are forces at work down in Pritchard Park far subtler than anything the tourists are picking up in their photographs, far below the threshold of conscious awareness, at the level of the unseen influences that operate in the universe—electromagnetism, gravity, attraction, the binding forces and deep structuralities that hold nature and the cosmos together, forces you can't see though you can see what they do.

The definition of *communicate* is "to make something common," and all communication, human and animal, verbal and nonverbal, is predicated on shared understanding, on the answer to the question "Do you read me?" It can be anything from a chemical powwow among bacteria to a general assembly meeting of the United Nations. But communication is neither the signal nor the response. It's the relationship between the two. True dialogue keeps the focus not on one person or the other, but on both, on mutuality. Chinese proverb: "Tell me and I'll forget; show me and I may remember; involve me and I'll understand."

IWannaBeFamous.com:
The Commodification of Passion

For three months after the publication of my second book, *Callings*, in September 1997, I kept a copy of that month's *Life* magazine propped up on a bookshelf in my office, facing conspicuously outward. On the cover was a picture of Oprah Winfrey, and a title that declared her "America's most powerful woman."

I could work day and night for thirty years and not achieve the kind of success she could administer with a single abracadabra. And talk about having a platform for your "palpable zest to make contact," a stage from which to share your passions with the world.

Early that December, one of the producers at the *Oprah Winfrey Show* called my publicist at Random House and said she wanted to conduct what she called a "pre-pre interview, a chance to see how he handles himself on the phone." Robin and I were sitting in my office when the publicist called. My mouth must have dropped open wide enough to drive a semi through, judging by the look on her face, and when I pointed sharply at the copy of *Life* on the bookshelf, *her* mouth dropped open.

The publicist said that the *Oprah* producer would call me in the next day or two.

She didn't. Nor did she call in the next week or two. Or three. Or four.

What began as a shock of excitement quickly devolved into pacing and muttering and prayer that sounded suspiciously like begging. Every time the phone rang, for weeks, I cleared my throat and tried to say hello with charming confidence, even though it was likely some guy wanting to sell me storm windows. And I was largely unsuccessful at hiding my disappointment from whoever *was* calling, though it did make a convenient excuse to get off the phone when I wasn't in the mood to talk, which is most of the time: I'm waiting for Oprah. Can't tie up the lines.

It doesn't take much to bring out my superstitious side—wagers, bumpy plane rides, annual physicals—and my brush with Oprah more than sufficed to have me knocking on wood and blowing on dice, when I wasn't filling my time with distracting busywork and trying to figure out *why* the producer wasn't calling.

This was hard to get sympathy for, though. Through the media coverage alone that I enjoyed during a two-month book tour subsidized by the publisher—complete with appearances on network television and major metropolitan bookstores, lodging at high-class hotels and chauffeuring—I reached a larger audience than Julius Caesar did in his entire lifetime. In Greek mythology, those who insult the goddess of earthly plenty are usually punished with hungers that cannot be satisfied.

A month later, the producer from the *Oprah Winfrey Show* finally called. I remember thinking, the instant I picked up the phone and said hello, that it was a good hello. I was on the phone for forty-five minutes with the producer, who conducted an interview more rigorous than anything I'd experienced on CNN or NPR. The next day a *different* producer called, said they like to get second opinions, and we were on the phone for *another* forty-five minutes. She ended by saying, "Great answers," and noted that my appearance on the show still had to be approved by a senior producer.

Once again I found myself lying awake at two in the morning wondering what I could tell myself in that moment while the coin was being tossed, what words of wisdom I had for myself? I ran through my options. The philosophical: you call this a problem? The spiritual: relax, it's out of your hands. The creative: win or lose, it's all writing material. The physical: just keep breathing. And the existential: in the big picture, the whole human drama from beginning to end is a skirmish of microbes on the surface of a dish in the sink, so who cares?

I once heard someone say that even if you set your toothache in a perspective of light-years and parallel universes, the toothache continues to hurt as though it had not heard. So, as the days of waiting once again turned into weeks, I found myself prowling back and forth like something caged, trying to channel my frustration into constructive behavior that wouldn't fill the house with profanity and junk food. But it was a pose, a pretending not to think about Oprah, Oprah's the furthest thing from my mind. Oprah who?

I even contemplated calling the producers instead of waiting for them to call me, but I'd tried that once with a magazine editor who had taken months to get back to me about a story I'd pitched. When I finally caught up with him, he was irritated. "Look," he said, "if you need an answer now, it's no. If you're willing to wait, it's maybe."

One night, in the midst of all this, my older brother called from California and during the conversation mentioned that one of my nieces had just auditioned for the role of Beauty in an elementary-school production of *Beauty and the Beast* and wouldn't know whether she got the part for at least a week, which to a seven-year-old is something like eternity.

We've all got our hands on the wishbone.

WHEN I WAS TWELVE, my father and brothers and I went on a ski trip to Gore Mountain in upstate New York. For a reason that still eludes me, I decided, as we passed under a bridge on the New York State Thruway, to lock the image of that bridge in my mind forever. Just to see if I could do it. If I could remember that bridge for the rest of my life. If one random, ordinary moment in time could be singled out.

To my amazement, I still remember that bridge. Over forty-five years later, I can still picture the girders and grime on its underbelly, still see it receding from view out the back window of the station wagon. In fact, I've thought of it often over the years, and each time it's a complete non sequitur, a random neuronal firing, the image just appearing in my mind's eye like a moth at the window and gone.

Maybe I was trying to test my mental powers. Or maybe I was starting to notice the passing of time, and freeze-framing that moment was a way to try to stop the slide. But I suspect that at the heart of the fantasy of fame—if not the nod of posterity—is a similar desire: to take a random, ordinary person and carry him through time on memory's shoulders, keep at least the *image* of him alive in somebody's mind.

The passion to express ourselves, to make contact and get what's on the inside out, will (if we act on it) lead us out into the world to share it with others, just as our personal callings typically lead us toward service somewhere along the line. And in doing so, we'll encounter our desire for, at the very least, feedback and recognition, if not remuneration and renown. In a starstruck and highly commercialized and internetted world, virtue isn't so likely to be its own reward. It now prefers an audience. It's not enough anymore to be good or great at something. Now we want to be *seen* as being good or great.

Though some aspects of fame-seeking are uniquely modern, the enterprise as a whole surely derives from an ancient impulse, the primordial fear of disappearing from sight, being forgotten and left behind out there. So we wail that others will turn around and see us, which of course makes good biological sense for the wee and helpless, as does the understanding that whatever we want can only be gotten through other people, so we'd better stay in their good graces.

Evolution also bundles into every creature a desire—a *drive*—that predisposes us to behaviors like trying to get on the *Oprah Winfrey Show*: the urge to spread our seed, to bequeath something of ourselves before taking our eternity leave, whether that legacy is flesh and blood or a $24.95 hardcover. Natural selection tells us that impressing others is good for our genes.

This absolute need to be seen and heard, though, moves along a continuum from simple attention to recognition to approval to respect to admiration to renown and ultimately, I believe, to love. And would you complain if they also named a constellation or at least a cologne after you?

We all look for the limelight and jockey for attention. And we all have our own stages, private and public, on which we play the part, from the fishbowls of family, friends, and job, to the arenas of politics, sports, and entertainment. Frankly I don't believe anybody, short of a saint, who claims indifference to praise and recognition and whose commitment to self-expression is *purely* for authenticity's sake and not also for attention. Even my electronic piano has a built-in setting for "applause."

And because the desire to be seen and heard is part of our motivation to express ourselves—not just art for art's sake, as it were, but for the sake of exhibition—it's very effective at prodding our passions. The prospect of fame is a stimulant to growth, spurring our ambition to create, invent, publish, and perform. When it's backed up by a market economy, fame is adept at exchanging praise and profit for passion and performance, and is an excellent case study in the ways in which our hunger for self-expression—all our passions—can be commodified.

And though fame can tempt us to become hooked on the dangling carrot of other people's attention and approval, and become just another kind of materialism, it can also benefit individuals as well as the culture, motivating participation in public life, stirring all kinds of achievements in science, business, and the arts, and goading people to reach higher and take the kinds of risks that ultimately enrich *everybody's* lives.

Consider Carl Linnaeus, a Swedish botanist and the father of taxonomy. He helped turn the hunger for renown to good scientific use by spreading the word that if you discovered a new plant or animal, you could name it after yourself, thus encouraging thousands of amateur sleuths to help add to the store of human knowledge.

Whole professions of people thrive on attention—entertainers, politicians, athletes—but it's also writ small in a thousand daily ways. Boasting has a chip of it on its shoulder. So does blogging, posting videos of yourself on YouTube, dressing up, misbehaving, showing off, playing victim, any kind of performance, and vying to be the center of attention at dinner parties.

There's even a website called IWannaBeFamous.com, where anyone can send in a photo and tell the world why you want to be famous. People's reasons for wanting fame run the gamut:

Rikki: "I wanna be famous because I want to be wanted."

Amy: "I wanna be famous to make my ex-boyfriends jealous."

David: "I wanna be famous because I think that pharmacists should have groupies, too."

Tania: "I wanna be famous because if Jeff from second-floor daycare can be famous then I definitely can, and because I have nice cleavage."

Angela: "I wanna be famous because I'm a single mother going to school and working at the same time, and if that's not reason enough, I don't know what is."

Monica: "I wanna be famous because I'm bored with an ordinary life."

Meredith: "I wanna be famous so I can prove to my family and friends that I can be something other than a high school dropout."

Kahlin Kelly: "I wanna be famous because people are starting to figure out that Gene Kelly and Grace Kelly aren't really distant second cousins and I need a new gimmick."

Shenan: "I wanna be famous because I don't want to have to wait till I'm dead for my art to be valuable."

The hunger for attention illuminates the chasm that exists between how we view ourselves as individuals and how society and nature view us, which is as indistinguishable from the wriggling masses. Fame, whether small or large—and self-affirmation, whether subtle or aggressive—is our conception of how to separate ourselves from the hordes and confirm that we're the unrecognized sons and daughters of the elect. "Let us build a city and a tower, whose top may reach unto heaven," Genesis instructs us, "and let us make a name, lest we be scattered abroad upon the face of the earth."

It seems we already *are* scattered abroad upon the face of the earth. But in the face of our relative insignificance in the universe, which only grows with each new discovery from the astronomers, it makes sense that we'd look to glory to deliver us from obscurity and give us a taste of the immortality that (we forget) drives the gods to boredom and mischief and making up rules like "You shall have no other gods before me," which sounds like Somebody has issues.

Anyway, the gods have always intruded on our turf, so why not we on theirs? Fame is one way we aspire to live a god's life: everlasting and out-size, able to live anywhere we want, and possessed of a personal grandeur that separates us from mere mortals and permits us to be worshipped by them. In fact, one of the questions routinely provoked in people who are outside the fairy ring of fame is "Can I touch you?" The implication is that some of it might rub off or give them a contact high, that the famous are glory-bearers who transmit that glory, Midas-like, to anyone whose shoulder they sling their arm around. To put it crudely, fame (we believe) puts the lie to the supposedly self-evident truth of equality. It's proof that we *aren't* all created equal.

At the very least, fame is a law of nature, a thermodynamic principle: the order of things is not fixed! Change is possible, hope justifiable, and the universe always expanding. It's one of our dearest dreams of transcendence, its presence in the world proof that the mighty can topple and the meek can inherit the earth.

Actually, you can bank on it. The story of Earth, scientific models tell us, will end the way it began: hot, sterile, and inhospitable to life, with bugs at the top of the food chain. The sun, in its final phase as a star, will turn from its familiar yellow to red, will swell and swallow the orbits of all the inner planets, including ours, becoming hot enough to melt the surface of Earth and return us to the molten world of prehistory. At the end, photosynthesis will have stopped, animals died off, the oceans long since evaporated into space, the temperature near seven hundred degrees Fahrenheit, and the only life left to inherit the earth: single-cell bacteria, which will once again have the place to themselves, as they did for the first three billion years.

The moon will spiral slowly in on its orbit and end in a colossal impact with Earth, an event no poets or lovers will be around to witness and lament, which is a shame, because it will be a reunion like no other. The moon, once part of Earth, its prima materia gouged from Earth's flank during a collision with another planet five billion years ago and sent into cold exile from the motherland, will now return.

I WAS in the green room at the Toronto studios of the *Dini Petty Show*, Canada's equivalent of the *Oprah Winfrey Show*, sitting around with the other guests: the actor Daniel Baldwin and a boy band called VIP. We were all staring at the television mounted high up, hospital-style, in the corner, watching Petty do her opening monologue, tell stories, and introduce the lineup of guests. When she got to me, she held up a copy of the *Callings* book in front of five million viewers and said that this was the book she was going to buy all her friends and family for Christmas.

One of the guys in the band looked over at me and said, "Cool." Daniel Baldwin gave me a thumbs-up.

It was actually a considerably toned-down version of the commentary she'd made about the book when we'd first met, a half hour before the show. I was sitting in a barbershop chair in the makeup room, getting my nose and forehead powdered, when she walked in, sat down in the chair next to mine, and said, "Are you Gregg?"

I nodded.

"F—ing great book," she said.

"You'll say that on the show, won't you?" I asked.

Daniel Baldwin was supposed to be on the show for three segments and I for two, but somewhere in the game plan, Petty decided to switch the batting order, and I ended up on the show for three segments instead of him, and the thought crossed my mind that I didn't want to run into that bad boy in the parking lot.

Just before I went on, I stood in the wings with the stage manager, who held a clipboard and wore the kind of earpiece that Secret Service agents wear. I noticed that he was grabbing on to the back of my sports coat, lest I, drunk on my statutory fifteen minutes of fame, lurch onto the set prematurely.

In the moments before I went on, standing there behind the curtain of what Joni Mitchell called the star-maker machinery, I saw that it's a set. Manufactured, furnished, arranged, floodlit, and stage-struck, and behind it all the ropes and pulleys and urgent dreams of everyone involved, from the eponymous star of the show and the guests in the green room waiting like gladiators for their triumphal entrance, to the audience members who get to toke on fame's secondhand smoke. I remembered reading somewhere that television studio audiences are often coached in what's called the superclap, a technique by which fifteen people can sound like fifty—everyone holding their hands in front of their faces, prayer-style, and clapping in triple time.

On cue, the stage manager said, "You're on," and gave me a push. I walked around a curtain and onto the set of a major national television talk show, with robotic moving-cameras everywhere, banks of what looked like stadium lights, a live audience clapping in triplicate, and Dini Petty standing in her faux living room waiting to shake my hand.

The hunger for renown may go way back, but fame has changed more in the past hundred years than in the previous two or three thousand. It used to be that renown depended on what caste you were born into, whether you had a face that could launch a thousand ships, who you knew, how well you could work a room, how much financial and institutional support you had, whether you had fortunes to throw at publicity, and how many degrees of separation there were between you and Lady Luck. Not so much anymore.

For one thing, fame has become democratized and industrialized, fed by an ever-ballooning number of ways to get your name, your face, your teachings and preachings, your fashions and passions in front of people: newspapers, magazines, books, radio, television, teleclasses, webinars, websites, movies, museums, galleries, theaters, CDs, DVDs, audiotapes, blogs, billboards, spray paint.

In contrast to aristocratic cultures, democratic ones also have much greater freedom of movement, encouraging and rewarding—inciting—personal initiative and big dreams. It's one of the promises imbedded in democracy's promotional literature: it's the land of opportunity, and anything is possible. So whether you were born in a castle and your arrival heralded by trumpets, or you were born in a hut while the drums beat all night and the dingoes ate your afterbirth, the field is wide open.

And nowhere wider than in the United States, home to over three thousand Halls of Fame, including ones for pickle packers, dog mushers, snowmobilers, and "queer martial artists of color." And it's understandable that fame is a national obsession, given that America itself was suckled on fame and self-consciousness, its entrance onto the stage watched by all of Europe, certainly all of England.

We live in what some people call a celebrity culture, "half vacuum cleaner and half sausage maker," a *TV Guide* reporter once called it, sucking people in, giving them a spin, and spitting them out encased in a thin wrapping of celebrity. It's a machine model of heroism, an assembly-line approach to "celeb-rating" people and creating, often out of the flimsiest materials, the stars by which the rest of us fix our positions and gauge our progress and our passions. But famous people are just like the rest of us, only advertised a lot better and made into leading brands, similar to deodorant and dog food.

Reality shows like *American Idol, America's Got Talent, The X Factor, Star Search, America's Next Top Model,* and *Sports Illustrated Swimsuit Model Search*—all of which represent a mere smattering of the genre—are also proof that the making of celebrities is becoming as much an object of fascination as the celebrities themselves, and, in fact, the shows are far more successful than any of the contestants. Just as it's architecturally hip and postmodern to reveal the pipes and duct work in new restaurants and clothing stores, it's all the rage now to make transparent the creation of Franken-fame, to turn it inside out so the stitching shows.

And it's not peculiar to the United States, or even the western hemisphere. It's gone global. There's *Malaysian Idol, Albania's Got Talent,* and Slovakia's very own *Slovensko hladá SuperStar.*

But if fame once took winning a war or ascending a throne, or at least hailing from aristocratic stock, your place already set before you got to the table, what increasingly distinguishes the modern-day fame-game is that even do-it-yourselfers can gain an audience if their YouTube or music videos, for instance, go sufficiently viral. (Still, these people are often quickly co-opted by commercial enterprises, which may undermine the DIY nature of it, but can also send their exposure into the stratosphere. I'm thinking of a young fellow who's in the news as I write this, a musician named Jessie Rya, who was videotaped playing his guitar outside a Dallas grocery store, and within weeks was appearing on Jimmie Kimmel Live!)

But even in the age of DIY, *sustaining* an audience's attention for more than the time it takes to flip channels will probably require not just a certain amount of commercial prowess, but ultimately hard work. Fame, after all, comes from a Latin word meaning "manifest deeds," though in order to perpetuate themselves these deeds need the added propellant of determination, passion that may even border on obsession, on what D. K. Simonton in his book *Greatness* calls a "monomaniacal preoccupation," which tends to distinguish the greatest figures in every field of human endeavor. These are people who've made their passions not merely the focus of their lives but also the *point* of it, and who wouldn't know work-life balance if it dropped on them from a third-floor window.

An equation called the Price law highlights the role that voluminous productivity plays in noteworthy success. It states that if you take the number of people most active in any given field, the square root of that number will give you the percentage who are responsible for 50 percent of the contributions in that field. Example: 250 composers are responsible for most of the classical music repertoire. The square root of this number is 15.8, and it turns out that 16 composers have their names attached to half of all the pieces performed and recorded. The Price law holds for every major domain in the arts and sciences.

John Ball and Jill Jonnes compiled a detailed analysis of success in America for their book *Fame at Last*, basing it on a database of almost ten thousand obituaries from the *New York Times* over the course of six years (roughly 2.5 million Americans die every year, and about 1,800 of them, or 1 in 1,400, get an obit in the *New York Times*). What they found was that 99 percent of the famous fell into the arenas of arts and media, higher education, sports, and executive business, while fewer than 30 percent of the American workforce fall into those categories. The famous weren't chronic track jumpers but had lifetime careers, they were five times more likely to have had a college education than the general population, fewer than 2 percent were millionaires, 80 percent were men, and 95 percent were white.

Significantly, though, fewer than 20 percent of the obits made any mention of these people's qualities as human beings, or the kind of emotional and spiritual achievements that, for many people, *are* the greatest accomplishments of their lives, not the professional and public ones. So the loving family you helped create, the faith you forged in a dark night of the soul, the forgivenesses you finally came around to, even the thousands of small kindnesses you bestowed on others, these don't generally count in this particular brand of scorekeeping.

But just because a couple of academicians have come up with a seating chart for fame doesn't mean it isn't also incredibly arbitrary. In Geoffrey Chaucer's *House of Fame*, Fame sits on her throne before a line of people that stretches out the door and around the corner, all of them waiting to plead their cases, and the fates that Fame doles out are completely irrational. One person steps up, a genius who serves his country honorably with his gifts, and he gets obscurity. Another wants only fame and glory and is doing nothing to achieve it, and she gets wildly famous. One after another, the hopeful are subjected to the whims of this moody, capricious yo-yo of a goddess.

Fame's distribution isn't anything like fair, and nothing is easier than working yourself into a foaming lather about who gets famous and why, while whole armies of genuinely talented people, like yourself, live out your life on the margin, working away under the laughably old-fashioned illusion that the way to gain recognition is to become extremely good at something. What talented and struggling singer hasn't occasionally driven herself crazy thinking about Britney Spears? What writer, working diligently for years on some complex and courageous novel, hasn't checked into the local bar for a bender on discovering that *101 Uses for a Dead Cat* has hit the best-seller list?

My own first-ever celebrity sighting confirms the often absurd and self-canceling nature of fame. A group of students from Charlie Gaines's writing class at New England College drove a van down from New Hampshire to New York City to attend a symposium during which a young Arnold Schwarzenegger—highlighted in Gaines's book *Pumping*

Iron—was spinning slowly around on a giant turntable, oiled up and striking he-man poses, while a panel of experts debated in front of an audience whether bodybuilding was art.

I don't remember a thing they said, but the image of Mr. Olympia rotating like a kebob in the atrium of the Whitney Museum of American Art stuck with me. It was fascinating and cheesy all at once.

The way the cards are stacked could certainly make a very handy excuse to throw up your hands and not to pursue your passions in life, or to complain bitterly about the world's seeming lack of interest in them, or the lack of reward for your hard work. But better to quit wasting good umbrage and spittle on the unfairness and folly of it all and to try getting your hands on what Alexander Pope called "one self-approving hour," which is worth all the cheers of an anonymous public.

The question is, which is harder to attain: fame or one self-approving hour?

The Social Version of Love

During the writing of this chapter, whenever I told friends that part of it was about the hunger for attention, among the expressions that flickered across some of their faces I thought I saw a look of pity. Translation: what private little hell don't we know about you?

The subtext is that what underlies the desire for attention, and the occasional granting of large doses of it that we call fame, is a kind of psychological frailty, one of those core wounds to self-esteem that we think is going to be healed by *other* people's esteem. It's a making up for what you didn't get, the hunger for it in direct proportion to the lack of attention you got as a kid. The less attention, the keener the deficit. And the appetite. As Madonna said when informed that she was tied with Elvis Presley for having the most Top 10 singles, "Me and Elvis? Are you kidding? I'm gonna tell my dad. Maybe that will impress him."

It's fame as the social version of love, and an example of the connection between shame and grandiosity, between a belief that you're defective material and the strategy you reflexively devise to camouflage it as superiority: a defensive crouch honed into a swagger.

Like elevator shoes, attention seeking becomes something we use to make up for what's lacking, perhaps compensation for a tenuous sense of legitimacy in the world, a wounded sense of belonging here at all. We want whatever we were denied, so fame becomes the righting of a wrong. Saint Augustine said that the loss of God is the loss of the loved one *looking at you*—God as audience—and if so, the desire for God and the desire for attention share a common ambition: the desire to be *seen*.

Compensation theory doesn't explain people who were starved for attention in their formative years and grew up to be accountants and librarians rather than actors and rock singers. Or people who are exhibitionists because they were *rewarded* for doing their shtick in front of the dinner guests. But the competition for attention is still one of the key contests of social life, and it follows the same set of rules that money does in the economy: people are hungry for attention and suffer its absence. Unfortunately, it's distributed like wealth: unevenly. There are those who are rich in it and those who are poor in it, and the poor suffer the hunger pangs of a kind of attention-deficit disorder.

Attention is also not distributed to nearly the degree people imagine. Most people are actually too busy worrying about what *we* think of *them* to really care all that much about us. Studies show that people pay about half as much attention to us as we think they do. In one study of what's called the spotlight effect (where you overestimate the amount of attention you're getting), college students were instructed to attend a large introductory psychology class while wearing an embarrassing bright yellow T-shirt emblazoned with a picture of Barry Manilow. When they were subsequently asked to guess how many of their fellow students had noticed the T-shirt, they figured that twice as many students saw it as actually did.

But to focus on getting attention is to focus on what only *other* people can give you. Thus the flip side of craving people's attention is living in fear of the power they have over you, and of their judgment, though it makes a kind of brutal sense to crave it anyway if you look inside for validation and don't find any—if the sound track of your life is an endless recitation of crappy self-talk.

Still, if there's a moral issue around fame, says Leo Braudy in *The Frenzy of Renown*, it's not the uncoupling of fame from merit but the definition of achievement as something *external* to us. The belief that it's not how we feel about ourselves that matters, but how *other* people feel about us, and that self-esteem is just unicorns and yetis until it's authenticated by the greater authority of other people's recognition, which makes it real.

At the end of the *Wizard of Oz*, the wizard says to the Tin Man, "Remember, my friend, that a heart is not judged by how much you love, but by how much you are loved by others," and my whole life I've been baffled by that statement, because intuition tells me it's the other way around.

If recognition can have a liberating effect on people, it can also have a paralyzing effect, epitomized by Pulitzer Prize–winning authors who can no longer scribble so much as a sentence fragment on a matchbook cover without wondering if it's Pulitzer material. Louis de Bernières, author of *Captain Corelli's Mandolin*, which was made into a Hollywood blockbuster starring Nicolas Cage and Penélope Cruz, said that writing for him is now like being stood stark naked in Trafalgar Square and being told to get an erection.

One of the drawbacks of renown is that you're always in danger of becoming a victim of your own success. Often it happens, for instance, that after people become celebrities, they struggle like hell to become artists again, because catering to an audience can be a creativity killer, constantly inducing you to try to figure out what the audience wants and track its endless flights of fancy, doing whatever it takes to keep the goodies rolling in.

Often this is exacerbated by the public demanding to hear the same old songs at every whistle-stop on the concert tour, or art reps who tell you to keep painting with the same colors as the paintings you've been selling lately. Once people discover a formula that works, there's an irresistible urge to encase it, assembly-line it, and repeat it endlessly.

A Harvard study conducted by creativity researcher Teresa Amabile compared artworks created by two groups of artists: one commissioned to produce with the expectation of public scrutiny and the other with no expectation that their works would ever see the light of day. The collected works were then reviewed by a panel of experts (gallery owners, art historians, museum curators, etc.) who were told nothing about the artists. Though no different in terms of technical skill, the commissioned works were consistently rated as less creative than the non-commissioned works.

This is a subset of a larger handicap: fame tends to encourage the false self and discourage the true. It can be literally *self*-destructive. Under its influence, you're tempted to do what the producers of NASA's Golden Record did—show only your good side—because in the light of fame, your human imperfections seem more shameful compared with the idealized version of yourself that's being projected onto the public screen, and you live in dread of exposure. When we had fights, my ex-wife sometimes asked how I would feel if my audiences could see *this* side of me?

To say nothing of trying to be yourself in the onslaught of fame's scrutinizing attentions: everybody wanting a piece of you, the inflationary effect of sudden power, the calcifying effect of years of smiling and saying "cheese," the temptation to trip out on the light fantastic and start believing your own hype, and the nagging paranoia of the imposter syndrome warning you that your fame was fraudulently got and you will soon enough be found out.

We want fame on *our* terms—focused on our public self but not our private self, on our talents but not our flaws—and it doesn't work that way. Fama was the monster goddess of gossip, with a thousand prying eyes, a thousand wagging tongues, and a trumpet, who flew around spreading and entangling fact and fiction with indiscriminate glee, and coming home at the end of a busy day to a house made of reverberating bronze. She was the bringer of both rumor and reputation. She was the patroness of word of mouth and the architect of the tipping point. But she took no instruction from mortals.

ONE FRIDAY NIGHT at the drum circle, I stood in the middle of the plaza playing a djun djun, a large African drum that, by its nature as the biggest drum there, commands attention and sets the pace, and could only be more attention-grabbing if the person playing it happens to be wearing a lurid Hawaiian shirt capable of being seen from outer space with the naked eye.

But I was new to the djun, and every time I looked up at the crowd, or caught someone's eye—every time I diverted my attention from the drumming to the audience—I lost my concentration and along with it the beat.

"For the most part," said Tolstoy, "all the external side of life must be neglected. One should not bother about it. Do your work!"

Psychologists talk about primary and secondary motivations, doing something for its own sake or doing it for the sake of a payoff (attention, power, money, sex, fame). There's a simple test to determine which one is in the driver's seat: when the secondary payoffs dry up, do you still do the work? Are your passions still intact?

Something called the intrinsic motivation principle of creativity says that people are most likely to keep doing the work, and are at their most creative and expressive, when they're motivated primarily by the challenge and charge of doing a thing, not by external evaluations, which tend to be nerve-racking and have a strangulating effect on creativity. Interior motives are a lot more likely to keep you going during dry spells, dark nights of the soul, and the inevitable turning of the spotlight onto the next contestant.

Fame is like heroism and happiness. Ideally, you don't go looking to do something heroic or looking to be happy. These come riding on the back of something *else*, like passion or service. *Happy* comes from a word meaning "chance," as in "happenstance," and it happens when you shift your focus, even minutely, from secondary to primary motivation, from external reward to internal satisfaction. You have to stay close to your passions and keep your head down so you don't get clipped by the constantly incoming flak of other people's opinions.

I don't know if this would quench anybody's thirst for earthly approval, but it would be a turning toward the only thing we really have any control over: our own actions rather than the actions of others. It would be a filling-up from inside rather than a waiting around on alms for the poor, and a shift of attention from the future to the present.

People talk about looking for love in all the wrong places. Fame seeking is the materialistic urge applied to popularity, and like any materialistic urge, it's a focus on and a compulsion toward getting an external fix. Tim Kasser, in *The High Price of Materialism*, concludes that materialism causes unhappiness and that unhappiness causes materialism, which ripens best among those least secure in matters of love, self-esteem, competence, and a sense of control over their lives, and most afraid of death.

To get painfully specific, people with strong materialistic urges report less vitality, more physical symptoms, less satisfying relationships, and less investment in love and community, and they tend to have been raised by parents who were less than nurturing and poorly satisfied their needs for security and safety. Simon Cowell, the former *American Idol* judge, said that a lot of those who appeared on the show had a Napoleon complex, the result of "a pretty bad adolescence where no-one's taken much notice of them."

On the other hand, Kasser equates well-being with nonmaterialistic goals like personal growth, self-acceptance, service, and intimacy. "If what you're after is feeling good about yourself," he says, "figure out more direct paths!"

Start by cultivating a healthy cynicism about the celebrity culture that pits you against yourself in a never-ending game of comparison, constantly elbowing you in the ribs to look outward rather than inward for validation. If you understand only that much, then even without ever having read the confessions of Saint Augustine or the Olde English mouthfuls of Chaucer, you'll understand the crux of those teachings, and what fame is actually worth in terms of what it is we *truly* seek.

The Nobel Prize–winning biologist George Wald once said, "How do you *think* one gets to be a Nobel laureate? Wanting love, that's how. Wanting it so bad one works all the time and ends up a Nobel laureate. It's a consolation prize."

The first time I visited Los Angeles, in my twenties, I saw one of the ubiquitous billboards for Hollywood icon Angelyne—featuring just her picture and her name—above one of Hollywood's avenues of broken dreams. She was wearing fluffy pink lingerie that barely contained preposterously enormous boobs, onto which spilled cascades of bottle-blonde hair, and she was lying coquettishly atop a pink Corvette.

Angelyne—whose billboard is one of the first landmarks to be obliterated by molten lava in the movie *Volcano*, and in the cartoon *Futurama* is one of the first things the hero sees upon waking from a cryogenic sleep in the year 3000—is, in reality, a nice Jewish girl from Idaho named Renee

Goldberg and a classic example of someone who's famous for being famous, kicked off with a personally financed billboard blitz in Los Angeles, New York, and Washington, D.C.

In an interview she conducts with herself on her fan-club site, she poses the question, "What do you do?" and answers, "I don't do—I AM!"

It's cheesy, but doesn't it cut to the broken heart of what we're all after? To be known and loved for who we are, not what we do.

When I think about it, the people who send their photos to IWannaBe-Famous.com have it right. They want to be famous because they deserve it. It's not pathetic; it's profound. And it's true. People shouldn't have to bloody their noses on the grindstone for a little attention. People shouldn't have to crawl on their hands and knees to get a little love in their lives. It should come with the territory, an inheritance you get when you're born, the mint under your pillow when you check in. You shouldn't have to beg for it.

If what's at the bottom of fame seeking is the desire for love and attention—if what drives us toward it is the belief that if only we were better (no, perfect!), we'd get the love we didn't get—the truth is that we *do* deserve it. That's a given even when it's not given.

Anyone who's gotten close enough to fame to feel its hot breath and its addictive appeal has probably gotten close enough to read the fine print too. Not just the clauses reminding you that tenure is tenuous and that it's far easier to obtain brand recognition than to *retain* it, but the one reminding you that the adoration of the public isn't capable of affirming you in the way you really want to be affirmed: for being *yourself*. It doesn't tell you whether you're loved for who you are. You'd need to be anonymous—what fame calls "a nobody"—to find that out.

During a swing through New York City on my book tour in 1997, I was standing outside an Italian restaurant in Greenwich Village called Grandpa's, when the proprietor, Al Lewis, stepped out to smoke a cigar. I instantly recognized him as Grandpa Munster—the vampire patriarch of the 1960s television show *The Munsters*. But when I told him I grew up on his show, he waved his cigar dismissively and said, "So did one hundred million other people. What difference did it make? It means nothing." Then he stubbed out his stogie and walked back into the restaurant.

I was stunned by his casual dismissal of not only my loyalty but also his own fame, though I now understand that he was just giving voice to phase three of the age-old sequence of Ambition, Attainment, and Disgust that's so familiar to the literature of fame—maybe to *all* our worldly conquests and seductions—and articulating one of life's thorny truths: the error of clinging and the inevitable slide of attachment into suffering.

It reminds me of the closing scene in *Raiders of the Lost Ark*, in which the Ark of the Covenant is wheeled down a long corridor in some anonymous government warehouse, to be stored indefinitely. The camera slowly pans back until the colossal size of the building becomes apparent, along with the vast and sepulchral anonymity to which the Ark is being consigned.

It's one of the recurring nightmares of the famous. That and the thought that the world will, inconceivably, just keep going after they're gone. People will go about their business, shops will open and close at their usual hours, children will bicycle past their house (or their statue) on their way to school, and for some time even their mail will continue to be delivered. As an idle rumination, I sometimes picture, in place of the Ark, the audio cassette of a lecture I once gave at the Smithsonian Institution, which is buried somewhere in the bowels of the museum, among the dinosaur bones and the jars of pickled Amazonian toads and the handwritten ethnographic notes about extinct Siberian tribes.

A simple principle of perspective works against the best-laid plans to be remembered, certainly in perpetuity: the farther away you are from something, the smaller it appears.

From the crown of the pyramidal Luxor Hotel in Las Vegas, a shaft of light is nightly beamed into space. At forty billion candlepower, it's the brightest light on Earth, and from low Earth orbit—the zone in which space shuttles and the International Space Station operate—you can read a newspaper by its light. Naturally, the man who turns the light on and off is proud of his job and the dash of fame that comes with it. "I work on the brightest light in the world," he says in John D'Agata's *Halls of Fame*. "The Brightest Light! I mean, man, this thing *rules*. I go into a bar and people know. And the chicks love it. I tell them I'm the guy who turns the light on and . . . BANG."

Across the Nile River from the *real* Luxor—a city in Egypt that is home to the Valley of the Kings, resting place of pharaohs—is a massive fallen statue, one of many. Once sixty feet tall, it depicts Ramses II, considered the most powerful of all the pharaohs of Egypt and believed to have been Moses's nemesis in the book of Exodus.

An inscription at the base of the statue was immortalized by the poet Percy Bysshe Shelley in his poem *Ozymandias*, in which a traveler comes upon "two vast and trunkless legs of stone" standing in the desert, and nearby a shattered stone face lying half sunk in the sand. At the base of the statue are these words: "My name is Ozymandias, King of Kings. Look on my works, ye Mighty, and despair."

No doubt Ramses's fame got him laid too—he had two hundred wives and concubines—but whether you're the man-god who built the pyramids or the custodian who turns the lights on and off in the amusement-park replica, no one is a match for time, which readily devours individuals and their accomplishments, as well as even memories of them.

I remember wandering the catacombs beneath a church in Lima, Peru, a few years ago and looking into an old well dating back to the sixteenth century. It was three stories deep, twenty feet across, and filled to the brim with the bones of twenty-five thousand wealthy Spaniards, arranged like a huge platter of hors d'oeuvres. A cluster of skulls in the center, femurs radiating out from them like spokes on a wheel, a ring of pelvises, another fan of ribs, and sprinkled among the brown bones a variety of candy wrappers and other flotsam.

If the wealthy and powerful can wind up with their bones arranged like carrot sticks and cauliflowers for the amusement of tourists, what about the rest of us? If Pharaoh can end up facedown in the dirt, what about *our* ambitions and passions? If Rome can fall, what of New York, London, and Tokyo?

When middleweight boxing champion Marvin Hagler lost his title to Sugar Ray Leonard in Las Vegas in 1986, through a still-debated referee's decision, he moved to Rome to begin a career in Italian action movies after a stint as an alcoholic. "I was angry as hell when they took away my title," he said. "But when you stand in the Pincio Gardens at sunset looking down on the whole of Rome, across centuries, it sort of puts things in perspective." As Christopher Woodward remarks in his book, *In Ruins*, Hagler was merely "the last of many proud kings who have come to Rome and been consoled by the sight of a far greater fall."

. . .

I'VE OFTEN THOUGHT that fame is best delivered late in life, after a nice long stretch of obscurity. By then you're more likely to have a grip on your ego and a working familiarity with perspective. Fame isn't automatically destructive, but it's a strong brew, and as long as it's metered by conscience and self-awareness, you'd probably do all right with it.

I'm not lobbying for patience, though. Patience is still based on the assumption that something is going to happen, and you're probably better off not fostering that expectation. Relinquishment is the better bet, a gentle turning of your attention (again and again and again) away from the limelight and toward the lamplight and the work to be done, the passions to nurture, the soul to keep.

And even if you do manage to become famous, the trajectory of most human lives, as novelist Julian Barnes puts it, will still look like this: "We live, we die, we are remembered, we are forgotten." And if your response to this is despair, don't stop there. Do what the doctor prescribed: look at it over and over and over until you are no longer repulsed by it, but rather are inspired to get on with living, and loving, and getting what's on the inside out, even knowing that nothing you do will ultimately be earthshaking— that even if all seven billion of us jumped up and down at the same moment it wouldn't shake Earth.

I've now been waiting seventeen years for Oprah to call, seventeen years of standing outside the gate harrumphing and calling disappointment "spiritual growth." It's like waiting for a missing person to come home. It's been seventeen years, and I figure the case is closed, but there's no body, so the doubt lingers, lodging itself in a corner of my mind, in an old hatbox labeled "You never know."

Since then, Earth has spun on its axis over six thousand times, and I've had all the atoms in my body replaced twice, or so science tells me, been remade in the image of God twice, or so religion tells me. Since then, my hair has grown whiter and I'm longer in the tooth, I've written a new book, gotten divorced, bought and sold three homes, lost my dog, and taken the copy of *Life* magazine down from my shelf.

Since then, I've moved from a desert to a forest, and when I walk barefoot along the creek that purls through my backyard, I'm eye-level to broadleaves on whose green streets insects play out their insect lives. I've seen dragonflies hooked together like planes fueling in midair, and gnats walking across the wings of butterflies.

Sometimes I look up through the trees in my backyard, at the crosshatching contrails of jets, and imagine looking back down on myself from a window seat, down through miles of hazy Appalachian air, down through the forest canopy, down along the toothpick trunks of trees, and I appear less substantial than a bug on the forest floor, to say nothing of the avid scribblings in my notebook.

I sometimes have to guard against being stunned into inertia by these observations, but precisely by showing me my relative position in the vastness, they remind me what's worth doing and what's not, and to live in such a way that the ephemeral nature of things (or more precisely of *me*) inspires rather than defeats me, and doesn't diminish my passion for life— or for telling it on the mountain—but amplifies it.

6

The Passion Is in the Risk

Life should not be a journey to the grave with the intention of arriving safely in a pretty and well preserved body, but rather to skid in broadside in a cloud of smoke, thoroughly used up, totally worn out, and loudly proclaiming "Wow! What a Ride!"

—HUNTER S. THOMPSON

BACK IN MY LATE TWENTIES, I had a dramatic if not melodramatic confrontation with one of my longest-standing fears: the fear of the dark, which I consider a subset of the fear of the unknown and which I'd had since childhood. Too many monster movies before bedtime, too vivid an imagination and not enough ability to distinguish it from reality, and perhaps too many secrets in my family. There was also that tree that scraped against my bedroom window on windy nights, and car lights that launched fearful shadows across the walls.

Fear of the dark may be native to childhood, if not humanity, but in a grown-up who'd lived most of his life in the suburbs, in clean, well-lighted places, it wasn't exactly a biologically useful fear. It was a deformity, a misshapen version of something that *was* once useful, and still is if we're talking about wandering around in dicey neighborhoods after dark or camping out in places where you're not the apex predator.

But if we're talking about sleeping in our suburban homes and gated communities, or going down into the basement to fix a broken bulb, then darkness is just the absence of light. It doesn't suddenly spring tentacles and teeth the moment we turn off the light switch. There are no bogeymen. It's just *us* in there, making up monsters—though apparently 40 percent of grown-ups still do it, according to a British study on the fear of the dark.

Fears have always been profoundly useful to us, and they tend to swarm at the smell of both danger and daring. But fears were generally designed for *short* tours of duty, temporary triggers for the old fight-or-flight response that's helped keep us on guard and out of harm's way. They were never meant to get stuck on continuous play.

Studies of stress tell us that the four horsemen of fear, anxiety, anger, and depression are toxic emotional states if kept up over time. Short-term they're not so bad and can be useful and adaptive, keeping us on our toes, getting us moving, and, in the case of depression, maybe even giving us a much needed retreat from the world. But long-term they're toxic and plunge us into a *parody* of our survival instinct, shutting down intelligence and creativity as well as health.

Still, most of us, myself included, are painfully familiar with the kind of chronic and often learned fears that limit our ability to take on life stoutheartedly and exuberantly, to make good on the transformative risks our lives are crying out for, leaving us paralyzed at the top of the diving board or the starting line. Fears of the unknown, of failure and success, intimacy and commitment, ridicule and rejection, our own power and passion.

The confrontation occurred in the third-floor attic loft of an old Victorian on a quiet street in Cincinnati, where I lived while working for the newspaper. In the bedroom was a large walk-in closet with no door, directly opposite the bed, and one night I bolted out of sleep at the sound of a thump that seemed to come from inside the closet. I sat up wild-eyed, staring into its open maw, holding my breath. As the cool night air poured in over the windowsill, and a faint moon cast shadows around the room, I tried rationalizing the origin of the sound. Probably an old pipe in the wall. Maybe a beam cracking down, or a coat falling off its hanger.

I wanted to leap from the bed and hit the lights without even touching the floor, lest it grab me and pull me under. But I didn't move. And nothing happened next, except that I slowly became aware of a pounding in my throat, followed a few long minutes later by a growing sense of exasperation, a rising temper that I slowly realized was directed toward *myself*. The next thing I heard was a voice in my head: "I'm sick of being scared." And not just of the dark.

Not coincidentally, I was at that point in my life in conniptions about whether to quit my job as a newspaper reporter to become a freelance writer, swerving back and forth on an almost daily basis between determination and fear. It was a passion, a calling, that had announced itself a half decade before, but I was simply too afraid to act on it. It had stolen enough sleep from me as it was, and that night it came to a head.

Staring unblinking into the closet, I slowly drew back the covers, trying not to let a slasher movie take hold in the back of my mind, and stood momentarily beside the bed, one hand on the wall. Then, matching each footstep with a deep breath, I walked over to the closet, knelt on the floor in front of it, and crawled in.

In the pitch-blackness, I thrust my bare wrists into every corner of the closet and held them there. Then I rolled my head back and exposed my throat.

When I crawled back out twenty minutes later, I was ecstatic, triumphant. A yell welled up from my solar plexus, from the pit of my stomach, which a friend once referred to as my power chakra, a shout that I stifled only in deference to my sleeping housemates and neighborhood. I faced out into the room, which now looked comparatively bathed in light, and on the wall along my bed were flickering shadows of the tree outside the window.

The next morning, reading the newspaper over breakfast, my eye fell on a comic strip called *Bloom County*. That day's episode featured a knight on a stallion who comes charging out of the "anxiety closet" of one of its characters, a ten-year-old named Binkley, and invites him on a great quest. But Binkley demurs. His bedsheet pulled up to his chin, he excuses himself from adventure because he has a school report on *snails* due in the morning. When the knight departs with a shrug and a puzzled look, Binkley says to himself: "Someday, when I've got kids, a dog, a mortgage, liver paté rotting in the fridge and a Chrysler mini-van in the garage, I'll say to myself, 'Binkley, you poor, miserable, bored Yuppie . . . you never went for the gusto.'"

. . .

IN *THE REBEL*, Albert Camus speaks of a kind of rebellion that's a deep metaphysical protest against whatever negates us, up to and including the central fact of life—that it ends, and we along with it.

A rebel, Camus argues, is anyone who says no. No to any condition of life that's finally unacceptable. No to any intrusion that's intolerable and oppressive. No to living under the heel of someone or something that grinds the life and dignity out of us. A no that is also a yes. A yes to something within us that we perceive to be inalienable, God-given, an absolute right. A yes that is loyalty to ourselves, an argument in favor of our own integrity and potential. And by that simple and declarative yes, we pick a fight. The kind that isn't really about whether we win or lose, but about the principle of the thing: better to die on one's feet than to live on one's knees.

Shortly after crawling out of that closet, I made the fateful decision to say no to my job and yes to my passion. Not without some lingering fear of the dark—though it wasn't ever as acute after that night—and not without some fear of the unknown. Courage isn't fearlessness. It's doing it anyway. You're afraid of the dark and you're going in anyway. You're afraid of love and you're going in anyway. You're afraid of death and you're going in anyway.

The dangerous edge is also the cutting edge, and it shares a border with thrill. Cliffs speak to us of the leap into space. Raging waters electrify us with their roar. The unknown tempts us with discovery. Vulnerability offers the chance for love. Rebellion offers the possibility of freedom.

Embedded within the dangerous is the liberating, and within the fearful is the heroic, and risk-taking is just the name we give to the work of moving from where we are to where we *want* to be, the mechanics of making dreams come true even while they make us tremble. Within us is what Edgar Allen Poe called the imp of the perverse. "We stand upon the brink of a precipice. We peer into the abyss—we grow sick and dizzy. Our first impulse is to shrink from the danger. Unaccountably we remain." Sometimes we even leap. Other times we crawl in on our hands and knees.

We do so because we recognize that the passion is in the risk, and it's only by taking risks that whatever passion is in us truly comes alive. The horse-and-cart equation isn't necessarily that we find our passions and *then* begin taking risks on their behalf, but that through the act of taking risks—making decisions, putting ourselves on the line—we begin to discover our passions and bring them to fruition. If we have a passion for something but we're not acting on it, it's in a state of suspended animation. It's only potential energy, not kinetic energy. It's lifeless. It's only when we actually move toward it that it awakens.

I recently consulted with someone who had convinced himself that he needed clarity about what form a particular passion would take before he could commit himself to pursuing it, but I suggested that the clarity he seemed intent on finding he might only find *by* taking action.

We also recognize that if courage inspires passion, passion in turn fuels courage. Our passions—for life, for an ideal or a cause, a person or place, a field of study, a vocation—inspire us to take risks, push against barriers and press our case, because we want them to come alive, bear fruit, and change the world. We want to tell it on the mountain and listen for its echo in other people's lives. We want to create a life that doesn't leave the best of us out in the cold.

A risk has the power to reignite us and jump-start our engines. Whatever we've been holding ourselves back from, daring and double-daring ourselves to do, in that danger is the medicine we need, the spirit of wakefulness that's capable of rousing us from our slumbering life and our sleeping gianthood. The risk itself is the bugle at sunrise, the piper at the gates of dawn.

In fact, risks are a bit like a nighttime phenomenon called myoclonic jerks, those jolting muscle spasms that people often experience as they're falling asleep. Researchers speculate that they happen because our heart and breathing rates slow down, and our muscles relax, and the old mammalian brain perhaps interprets this as a prelude to disaster—to losing our grip and falling out of a tree—and tries to snap us to attention. Similarly, risks are wake-up calls that help bring us around when we've begun falling asleep at the wheel.

"The secret for harvesting from existence the greatest fruitfulness and greatest enjoyment," said Nietzsche, "is to live dangerously. Build your cities on the slopes of Vesuvius! Send your ships into uncharted seas!" It's his reminder that the most exuberant experiences don't grow out of a well-protected life in which risks are anxiously kept at bay, but out of "a courageous exposure to the forces and conditions of life that activates the best of a person's powers.

"A good horseback rider will not beat a spirited horse into submission to have an easy ride, but rather learn how to handle a difficult mount. Similarly, a strong and healthy person will not shun the dark and often dangerous sides of the world by retreating to some metaphysical realm of comfortable peace, but rather embrace life in its totality, its hardships and terrors as well as its splendors and joys."

Among the principles of Outward Bound—a nautical term referring to a ship's departure from harbor—and by extension the whole field of outdoor education, is this one: people discover their passions, abilities, values, and responsibilities best in situations that offer them adventure and the unexpected.

It's important to remember, though, that adventure isn't just about sending your ships into uncharted seas, and even to the degree that it is, its real psychological purpose is to amplify your heroism more than your conquests, is more about inspiration than about planting flags on mountaintops. The original definition of *adventure* was that of "something about to happen"—as in Advent celebrating the coming of Christ. So a sense of adventure is related to a sense of *anticipation* about life, the prospect of new growth, which is helped along immeasurably if you always give yourself something to look forward to, whether it's a gathering with new friends over the weekend, a workshop to attend, a new trail to explore up in the mountains, a road trip with your camera at the end of the month, or at least some light at the end of whatever tunnel you've been boring through lately.

The appeal—the beauty—of adventure is that it brings on arousal, and all that implies by way of stimulation and awakening. There's of course good arousal (excitement) and bad arousal (anxiety), and adventure can bring on a flow state or a fear state. But because it naturally has a bit of both in it, it can help increase your threshold for both, and thus your overall resilience.

The science of immunization is based on the wisdom that one way to strengthen the human body is to shake it up, to introduce a little chaos into the system for the sake of helping it evolve and adapt, grow stronger and more resilient. Adventure and risk-taking have a similar effect on the human psyche, so it might be instructive to ask yourself what act of boat-rocking you could introduce into your life right now that would have the effect of shaking you up and helping you evolve.

If you have plenty of chaos in your life as it is, thank you very much—your daily life is already on avalanche alert, your schedule always at fever pitch—perhaps "chaos" would be taking something *out* of your in-basket, declining a project or social engagement, slowing down, simplifying. When you're standing at the edge of a cliff, progress can be defined as taking a step backward. "I have a 'Carpe Diem' mug," the children's book author Joanne Sherman says, "and, truthfully, at six in the morning the words do not make me want to seize the day. They make me want to slap a dead poet."

In her book *A Big New Free Happy Unusual Life*, Nina Wise relates a story that captures how inactivity, not just hyperactivity, can be a chaos and adventure all its own—and a practice as rigorous as any spiritual discipline. She was participating in a ten-day retreat with the Buddhist teacher Thich Nhat Hanh, to explore the relationship between art and social action. On the first morning, everyone gathered under a big oak tree. Thay (as his followers call him; pronounced "Ty") sat before them in his brown robes, was silent for several minutes, then said, "Do nothing today. Be quiet. Tomorrow we will meet again."

Sighs of disappointments, grumbles of frustration, but he was the master, so they did as requested.

The following morning, they once again gathered beneath the oak tree, Thay composed himself before them, sat silently for several minutes, then said, "Do nothing today. Be quiet. Tomorrow we will gather in the morning."

Louder sighs of disappointment, deeper grumbles of exasperation. They were *activists*, after all, and wanted to act. But again, they followed the advice of their revered teacher.

On the third morning, they assembled in their customary spot, Thay once again silently arrayed before them, listening deeply to the mood of the group. He said, "Do nothing today. Be silent. Don't write in your journal and speak only when it is absolutely necessary."

An audible wave of anger and protest spread through the group. They had given up ten days of their lives to sit at the master's feet and stoke their spiritual fires. Couldn't they just do some formal meditation practice? But he forbade even that.

At midmorning, Wise reports, "I found myself perched on a hillside overlooking the golden rolling hills. The days of quiet had calmed me. I had no impulse to do anything aside from observing the patterns of grasses moving at the mercy of the wind. Delight struck me. The inner stillness I had cultivated had carved out the possibility for wonder."

On the fourth morning, the group yet again gathered beneath the oak, Thay yet again before them in his flowing robes, his inscrutable silence, his antenna tuned to their mood and rhythm.

"Today we will begin a formal schedule," he said. "We will do meditation practice three times a day, walking meditation at eleven, and I will give a dharma talk at three. Now you are ready."

CHAOS AND RISK are similar in that they both have questionable outcomes, and for that reason, life itself would have to be categorized as a risk, though ultimately we know how it ends. During the writing of this chapter, two friends of mine had the struts kicked out from under their lives—one was diagnosed with stage-two breast cancer that necessitated a double mastectomy, and the other had a love affair blow up in his face right before he was going to propose marriage—reminding me that life is a car capable of turning on a dime, and sometimes that dime is in your front pocket when it happens.

Risk, however, is utterly relative. It's whatever scares *you*. Whatever is capable of rousing *you* from torpor and amnesia. Whatever brings a little excitement into *your* life. I was sitting around with a few friends one recent evening when one of them said, "You know what the problem is? We're not outrageous enough." When I asked him what he would do if he were to be outrageous, he thought for a moment, then reached up and swept his hair from middle-parted and slicked-back to side-parted with a cowlick dangling rakishly over his forehead—instantly transforming him from Richard to Ricardo, from Ph.D. to matinee idol. "I'd come into work like this," he said.

One person may feel adventurous simply asking someone out on a date, or riding in a New York City taxicab, or wearing a hat with a feather in it, and another may need the kind of adrenaline rush that comes only from an activity in which the result of a mistake could be injury or death—big-wave surfing, skiing down Mount Everest, even criminal behavior. I once heard an inner-city teenager say that he felt the most alive when he was running from the cops.

Some people can barely get out of bed in the morning without feeling overwhelmed by the dangers of life; some love to dangle from ropes on mountainsides, and their day wouldn't be complete without leaping off a tall building in a single bound and waiting till the last possible second to pull their ripcord (otherwise known as base-jumping).

For some people, having an extra crumpet with their tea feels terribly rash and makes them giggle with reckless delight. For others, it's sitting down to a meal of fugu, the Japanese puffer fish whose natural toxins have no known antidote and a lethal dose of which can fit on the head of a pin, but if cooked just right will leave a near-death tingle on the lips—a meal that's considered the Medal of Honor among thrill-seeking gastronomes, and the weapon of choice among Japanese fishermen playing Russian roulette.

Obviously, courage, like risk, is also relative and a matter of perception. What looks like bravery could be rashness or even stupidity, and what looks like cowardice could be courage. An old college roommate of mine told me that when his father began experiencing the unmistakable signs of dementia, he committed suicide rather than submit himself to the long, slow decline. Cowardice or courage?

Sometimes courage is unrecognizable because you don't know the backstory. I presented a workshop at a women's prison once, and at the end of it one of the women came up and gave me a hug. There's nothing unusual about workshop participants giving me hugs at the end of presentations, except that in this context, as I found out later, it could have gotten the woman more prison time, because hugging visitors is forbidden. It's one of the ways contraband is exchanged. The woman took a hell of a risk just to express her gratitude to me.

We tend to think of adventure as involving physical risk, but it could also be financial, creative, or emotional—a business venture, a book project, a marriage proposal, a plunge into psychotherapy. For some people, their most outrageous adventure is simply learning to love another human being, an undertaking full of precipitous drop-offs, fierce natives, and sudden storms, though also grand vistas and great heroisms.

We also tend to overlook adventures that are close to home and every bit as capable of lighting our fires—if not raising a little hair on the backs of our necks—as jumping out of an airplane or traveling the world. Taking your poems or jokes to open-mic night. Joining a theater company. Being the first to make up after a quarrel. Making love with your eyes open or the lights on. Spending a little more and getting what you *really* want. When someone asks how you are, telling them how you *really* are. Saying yes to something you've been saying no to, or saying no to something you've been putting up with for too long—a toxic job, a self-limiting belief, a grudge, or a power struggle with someone over something that long ago lost its meaning, isn't worth the fight anymore, and is just riding on the *fumes* of principle.

Sometimes the riskiest thing you can do is to simply sit for an hour a day and do your writing/painting/piano playing/business planning/_____, thereby putting your talents to the test and discovering the true dimensions of your gift. To say nothing of risking feedback.

Or take on a serious creative project into which you throw yourself body and soul and bank account, not just pick at the way children pick at their vegetables. The kind Barbara Ehrenreich took on in writing *Nickled and Dimed*, working nothing but minimum-wage jobs for a year to report on America's unskilled laborers. The kind Morgan Spurlock took on with his film *Supersize Me*, in which he subjected himself to McDonald's cuisine for a month.

Unless you have absolutely everything you desire in life and have no need to reach for anything, risk is not only inevitable but also essential, because in no arena of human ambition can you win, or grow, without taking a risk. And yet sometimes the most heroic risk is just your willingness to *participate* in life, to keep daring to show up, to continually return to the coin toss of life even in the face of all its odds and obstacles, all the forces that would have you pulling the covers up over your head.

An acquaintance told me years ago that he was once arrested at an antiwar sit-in and given a suspended sentence with fifteen hours of community service. The judge told him that he could perform any kind of community service he wanted, so when they let him go, he went right back to the sit-in. He said to me, "I was *doing* community service when they arrested me."

Those who are larger than life, argues Jean Houston in *A Passion for the*

Possible, aren't necessarily heroic or influential, physically imposing or charismatic, living their lives on grand stages or at the vanguard of revolutions and mass movements. Her definition is far more quotidian: they're people who are "profoundly present to the stuff of their lives. . . . They use and enjoy their senses more than most, they inhabit with keen awareness their bodies as well as their minds . . . and they explore the world of imagery and imagination. Quite simply, they are cooking on more burners."

The Mach 1 Experience

I recently saw a gravestone in a local cemetery for one W. C. Stradley, 1855–1904, who, according to the epitaph, had "a spotless life, a triumphant death." And it struck me that, personally, I'd prefer it the other way around: a triumphant life, a spotless death.

A spotless life doesn't really strike me as something to aspire to. If you don't depart this life with a few grass stains on your pants, a little blood on your knuckles and knees, some passionate indiscretions under your belt, a few hearty tales to tell about your adventures with the seven deadlies, it seems to me you've missed the boat, and maybe the point, which is not to rise above it all, to keep your shoes clean and your thoughts pure and wear your Sunday best all week long, or to live only for the next life but not this one.

It's to sink your teeth into it and let its juices dribble down your chin, spill some wine and stain yourself with tears now and then, jump into it up to your eyebrows. A friend has a postcard on her refrigerator with a picture of a woman on her hands and knees scrubbing a bathtub and the caption, "A clean house is the sign of a wasted life."

Step One of what mythologist Joseph Campbell called the hero's journey is "The Call to Adventure," but Step Two is "The Refusal of the Call." And though we all have different thresholds for how much of this journey we're inclined to take and how far we want to go with it, most people's initial response to the call to live heroically is to refuse to live heroically. If it's any consolation, this is fairly universal.

Another universal is that intermediate step between refusing the call and finally answering it, when we convince ourselves that we're going to take the required risks . . . when our ducks are lined up. This is an exalted state of alignment, which in some mollified corner of our mind we know will happen roughly around the same time . . . the cows come home.

Especially as we begin to fathom the *dimensions* of the call to adventure, and the price that will be exacted from us in following it, we're likely to suffer a kind of sticker shock, letting this cup pass from us and singing the praises of the status quo—it's familiar, warm, and cozy. No really, it's fine. And even when it's *not* fine anymore, even when its coziness has turned to anesthesia and its safety has become suffocating, it's still the hell we know rather than the hell we don't, and we find ourselves "backing away like lobsters from free-swimming life into safe crannies," as Peter Matthiessen puts it.

We tell ourselves that adventure is for adventurers, gambling is for gamblers, thrill is for thrill seekers, daring is for daredevils—all of them descriptors of people who are not us. But if you attempt to drain life of its thrill, minimizing all daring and danger and playing it safe, you're gambling with your life anyway, taking the chance that you won't live to regret it. Just because you're safe doesn't mean you won't be sorry. As Clint Eastwood once said, if you want a guarantee, buy a toaster.

Ironically, the best thing I ever did for my sense of security in the world was take a flying leap of faith and quit my job as a reporter to become a freelance writer, because by doing so, I learned a lesson I couldn't have learned any other way: that I can live close to the edge and not just survive but also thrive. And it's given me a quality of security that those who are employed will never possess: the knowledge that I can never be fired.

In the movie *The Right Stuff*, about the Mercury astronaut program, there's a scene in which test pilot Chuck Yeager is attempting to break the sound barrier for the first time, and just before he reaches that illustrious Mach 1—roughly 750 miles an hour—the plane starts shaking and shuddering violently and threatening to bust apart in midair. But then *at* Mach 1 he breaks through the sound barrier, people on the ground hear the world's first sonic boom, and Yeager's jet suddenly goes into a perfectly smooth ride. He described it later by saying, "Grandma could be sitting up there sipping lemonade."

In any attempt at a breakthrough—whether physical, psychological, creative, social, or spiritual—there's going to be a Mach 1 experience. There's going to be shaking and shuddering before things smooth out, and it's not opposed to the breakthrough; it's part of it. But we've got to push past it if we want to reach the boom times. Abraham Maslow even believed that self-actualizing types are "those who make the growth choice instead of the fear choice a dozen times a day."

Part of what we're pushing past, or at least against, is our own internal wiring. The old brain that's helped get us through the evolutionary maze comes equipped with a worry meter set somewhere near the middle of the spectrum. Too much of it would have been constraining, too little would have incited foolhardiness, but either way we're wired to be cautious.

Our brains have also clocked quite a bit more time focusing on danger than delight, on negative than positive stimuli. Brain imaging studies conducted at the University of Iowa have demonstrated that when people are shown pictures that are either pleasant (an ice-cream sundae, puppies, mountain scenery, a couple on the beach at sunset), unpleasant (a garbage pile, a rotting dog carcass, a dead soldier with part of his face missing, an unflushed toilet, a sink full of dirty dishes), or neutral (a fire hydrant, an umbrella, a dustpan, a blow dryer), the unpleasant pictures activated ancient subcortical parts of the brain that scientists call the danger-recognition system, while the pleasant pictures lit up a much younger part of the brain, the prefrontal cortex.

Maybe this helps explains why it's so much easier to focus on the negative than the positive in challenging situations, on what could go wrong rather than what could go right. Maybe it even explains why psychology textbooks have devoted twice as much space to negative emotions like depression and phobia than positive ones like joy and happiness, and why cross-cultural language studies have found that nearly every society has a great deal more words and concepts for negative than positive emotional states.

Furthermore, at any stage of the game, from infancy on, if someone has a choice between satisfying the need for security or the need for growth, security will generally win out. When toddlers venture beyond the protected harbor of their mothers to explore their surroundings, even just an unfamiliar room, that odyssey is dependent on their mothers being there when they look back over their shoulders. If she suddenly disappears, the urge to explore is short-circuited and the toddler returns to port, and might even regress to crawling back rather than walking.

There are repercussions either way, whether we choose security or passion, but at the end of the day most people prefer to be moored safely at harbor rather than pitching around on the open sea. My brother Marc once compared himself to me by saying that he's an oil derrick high above the waves and I'm a boat down on the surface. His life is stabler, more secure, and without all the tossing around, while mine is wilder, more exciting, but with more ups and downs, more volatile and intense. He wasn't suggesting one was necessarily better than the other; just observing, he said.

Although anxiety makes evolutionary sense—prompting us to consider the consequences of our actions, concern ourselves with the fate of our offspring, and anticipate what dangers might lie around the next bend—the trick is finding a workable middle ground between inhibition and recklessness, and keeping an eye on the more modern brain's tendency to grind us to a halt sweating the small stuff and spinning out fearful scenarios. That is, we worry not just because we come from a long line of worriers, and been tutored in the arts of worry since childhood, and certainly not because we always have good *reason* to worry, but because that's what happens when you mix fear with abstract thinking, fear with the question "What if?"

You end up with a whole grab bag of strategies to avoid risk-taking and fears disguised as logic. At the end of Julian Barnes's novel *The Sense of an Ending*, the protagonist, looking back on his life, says, "We thought we were being mature when we were only being safe. We imagined we were being responsible but were only being cowardly. What we called realism turned out to be a way of avoiding things rather than facing them."

Sometimes what we find ourselves pushing against in trying to break through to a passionate life isn't just our own wiring but *other* people's wiring. Sometimes sending your ships into uncharted seas ends up troubling other people's waters, though it's critical to understand that in their attempts to turn you back to port they're often just using you to argue with themselves.

Despite his identification with being an oil derrick high above the chop, Marc recently wrote me to announce that he had decided to retire from Stanford to work for Google, where he'd spent the past two years on a partial leave of absence from the university, working primarily on the Google Glass project. He described it as the single-hardest decision of his life, and one that's irrevocable—he can't ever return to being a tenured professor there. But in the final analysis he faced two inarguable truths: he was having more fun at Google, and he was enjoying fresh challenges.

I'm particularly impressed with the fact that his decision is based in large part on the desire to have *fun*, which, certainly as the basis for a momentous and irreversible career decision, would almost seem frivolous and emotionally light on its feet, yet is anything but. His decision to give up a job that doesn't get much more prestigious than a tenured professorship at Stanford, and for someone as *logical* as he is—in order to have *fun*—strikes me as profound validation of the importance of that precious commodity.

In his letter he said that one of the "pivotal" factors in his decision to move on was, of all things, a newspaper clipping I had sent him when he first started at the university, and which he had kept pinned to the center of his bulletin board ever since. It said, "How fossils are formed: 1) get tenure, 2) teach for 20 years."

"I swore that would never happen to me," he wrote, "and by the time I wrap things up at Stanford in a few years, it will have been exactly tenure + 20 years. Thanks for sending me that clipping."

He also wrote that his fellow faculty members have promised that between now and the time he departs, they will "gang up on me and try to convince me to reverse my decision." To which I said, "Bring it on! It'll only help clarify your decision and your conviction, and their doubts will undoubtedly be ones you've already entertained till you're blue in the face and will probably just be projections of their *own* fears and fantasies about life outside Stanford, extensions of the arguments they've probably had with themselves about the prospect of leaving for greener pastures—i.e., big grain of salt and all that."

I know this one firsthand. Shortly before leaving my job at the Cincinnati paper to go freelance, I played a memorable game of racquetball with my regular partner, a guy I worked with at the paper who, ever since I told him I was contemplating the freelance life, seldom missed an opportunity to draw my attention to all the risks and ramifications of leaving behind a steady job, a regular paycheck, and medical benefits (never mind that the only reason I was *using* those medical benefits was that my job was making me sick), and remind me that freelance writers have really boring annual company picnics.

At the beginning of the game, he strode onto the court and declared that if *I* won, I could leave, but that if *he* won, I had to stay.

I don't think either one of us ever played so hard, and the game went into the kind of overtime that had us neck-and-necking for half an hour, neither of us more than a point ahead of the other guy. I finally won with a dink-shot that hit the front wall two inches above the floor, too low for him to reach. I punched the air hard in triumph, and we both slumped against the back wall.

When he finally caught his breath, he said, "I can't believe you're going to leave me here alone at this crummy job." Which immediately put his years of naysaying into perspective. He had apparently debated endlessly with *himself* about moving on, but couldn't get himself to do it.

As for that deciding match, it wasn't that I was passionate about winning so much as I was about *leaving*. I was overdue for new challenges, overripening and rotting on the vine, and time was flying by. I wasn't playing to win the game, but to win my freedom.

Coda: a year later, my old racquetball buddy—I like to think inspired at least a little by *my* willingness to pursue my passion—left the paper for a job at the *Miami Herald*, and two years later a job at the *Washington Post*, where, as the editor of the *Washington Post Magazine*, he conceived and edited two Pulitzer Prize–winning stories.

Just saying.

AS MY RACQUETBALL partner discovered, we probably have more limited influence over others than we like to think, and even if we manage to sway them for a time, ultimately they are who they are and have to do what they have to do. Sometimes we're trying to talk them *out* of their passions, but sometimes we're trying to talk them *into* their passions.

A few years ago I had a conversation with my mother that illuminated this dynamic and provided me with a wake-up call in the process. My mother had been at loose ends for a good twenty years about how to spend her time since retiring from being a stockbroker, and the conversation began when she asked—very uncharacteristically—what I thought she should do with her time. So I made a few suggestions.

How about taking some art lessons again?

"I did that already," she said, as if art is something you do once and check off a list.

How about enrolling in one of those music-appreciation courses at the university that take you on field trips to the opera and the symphony (she could no longer drive)?

She made a sour face and shook her head. "Those are for old people," she said, prompting me to bite my tongue.

What about a trip? I know you can't do the adventure travel anymore, but what about a barge tour of Provence or a cruise up the Inside Passage? At least you'll get out of Dodge.

She just shrugged.

What about volunteering with the Service Corps of Retired Executives (a national mentoring program)? You have so much experience you could share with younger folks.

"Oh please," she said. "*Volunteering?* That counts for absolutely nothing on a résumé." To which I said, "Mom, you're eighty-two. Are you really still building your résumé? Are you still climbing the ladder? Not that you should give up the good fight, but Jesus."

In that moment, I realized that I had to give up my *own* good fight, the one in which I continued to encourage, cajole, inspire, chide, and nag my mother to take on new challenges, make new friends, get out of the house, do the jig of generativity, shake the rat race out of her system, and submit herself to some of the deeper calls that come in this later phase of life. To reengage with the world and come back to life after what I perceived to be the dual de-motivators of retirement and a second divorce, or as she once put it, "no one to do it for anymore."

She had simply lost the will to participate, to explore and create and contribute, and all she had left were her excuses. She had stopped investing herself in life, stopped investing in *herself*, and you can't *make* someone do that. And you can't unbind the spells they put on themselves.

I would even venture to guess that some if not much of the rapid decline in my mother's functioning in the past few years—both cognitive and physical—is a result of her self-suffocating inertia, her decision to opt out of active *engagement* in life, her characteristic passion for it becoming the victim of neglect rather than natural entropy. She just withdrew from most of her involvements, outings, and friends, into a shell. Or more specifically into her apartment in New York, which was once like an outtake from *Architectural Digest*, or at least *Good Housekeeping*, but slowly became dingy and ill-kept, the upholstered chairs threadbare, the carpeting criss-crossed with footpaths of filth running between rooms, the bedspread frayed and held together with duct-tape, linen closets mildewed, shower stalls half off their runners.

This wasn't a function of frugality, and certainly not penury. It was a profound sort of detachment and passivity, the kind that renders people effectively sightless and senseless. My mother just slowly caved in on herself, collapsing in around her exhausted core. And as for the dementia that quickly overtook her, in a matter of just a few years, I think she was literally bored out of her mind.

"She should have quit New York fifteen years ago," her best friend, Joan, told me, "and moved out to California where you boys were. She should have stopped insisting on staying in her own home as long as humanly possible. She stopped making good decisions on her own behalf a long time ago."

It's well known that social isolation is detrimental to elders—to anybody—contributing to increased depression and disability, which then increase the social isolation, which studies show is as bad for your health as cigarette smoking. (On the other hand, passion tends to compel people to seek out others who share their passions, stretching them beyond their comfort zones, even their isolation. "Passion trumps inhibition in the service of new connections," say the authors of *The Power of Pull*. "Connecting with our passions can help us recover our natural sociability.")

In the year before my mother's dementia hit the fan, Ross visited her and reported that "her world has gotten so small," reduced to a monotonous back-and-forth shuffle between the bedroom and the kitchen. When I asked her in-home aide what my mother *did* all day—this dynamo of a woman who was a role model for living boldly and to the hilt, who seldom sat still and would have been bored on a roller coaster, who was a ground-breaker, world traveler, expert skier, sculptor, pianist, published poet, fashion model, opera lover, reader of the *New York Times* from cover to cover, mother of three boys (four if you include my father), outspoken, strong willed, competent, intimidating—the aide said "mostly nothing. Sometimes she picks lint out of the carpeting, or collects dead leaves from the houseplants." And I was left incredulous, though I suddenly had a better grasp of incomprehensible concepts like Earth standing still or a perfect vacuum in space.

Ross recently sent me an article about the mother of a mutual friend of ours, whose résumé reads a lot like our mother's—both of them, in fact, among the first women stockbrokers. In telling the interviewer about her strategy for remaining engaged, she said, "You get up in the morning, get out, and stay active." And that, to me, speaks volumes about why she's still in the game in her mid-nineties, still going to work part-time and sharp as a tack.

Studies show that active engagement in life, whether physically, socially, creatively, or productively—a prime indicator of passionate living—is associated with health and longevity, as well as overall life satisfaction. According to a recent Scottish study, the engaged are 60 percent more likely to report good health than the disengaged (assuming the social activity isn't something like gambling, which is associated with alcohol abuse, depression, and other adverse health effects).

Passion isn't just something that *generates* engagement—a force that pushes us to create and contribute, as in "following your passion"—but something that's also generated *by* engagement; the sense of aliveness we gain from our immersion in life, from staying in the game. And while you can't redeem the failures of your parents, you can use them as cautionary tales. In fact, I think one of the greatest forces operating in our lives, whether we're aware of it or not, is the *unlived* life of our parents. The dreams they had that never came true, the callings they had that went unanswered, the sword they refused to pull from the stone, and which only they could.

Sometimes these dramas get passed on to one's children to remedy and compensate for—"You do what I could not do!"—and sometimes, if those children have a similar dream, their parents will try to talk them out of it lest they suffer the same disappointment. Either way, what we resist persists, if not in our own lives, then in the lives of our offspring, our families, our circles of friends, and the company we keep. All of them are affected by our passion and courage, as well as by our passivity and detachment.

Sometimes what our elders model isn't so much detachment as overattachment, which can also have a debilitating effect on our initiative and our spirit of adventure. If you were raised by hyper-parents, for instance, who continually snowplowed the road in front of you lest you slip and fall, or have to dig a path for yourself, this will tend to have the effect of preventing you from gaining the self-reliance that's so essential to living up to your own potential and following your passions; learning how to deal with failure, rejection, disappointment, and boredom; learning to not only cope with life but also to find out what you *can* cope with.

The trend toward handing out trophies to any kid who shows up for a ballgame is a good case in point. There's nothing wrong with helping kids build self-esteem, but it ought to be realistic. Giving every kid a trophy may make some of them feel like winners, but what happens when life doesn't hand them a trophy just for showing up? It's likely to puncture a hole in their determination and undermine the kind of risk-taking and stick-to-it-iveness required for trophy-winning behavior in the real world, where those who sit on the sidelines *don't* get the same glory as those out on the field, and where there *is* a distinction between "winners" and "losers."

Certainly, there's something to be said for encouraging participation and teamwork, rewarding kids for improvement and not just winning, and letting them know they're loved whether they win or lose, but not at the price of a false sense of merit. And if they don't learn to handle failure, and expect that life will bestow trophies on them for their merest efforts and swoop them up in its arms whenever they stumble, they may opt to shy away from challenges, sticking close to the sidelines and all but guaranteeing themselves a zestless life.

Fear typically makes people stick to their comfort zone and try to build up their resistance to what's outside it, and a passionate life requires just the opposite. It requires challenge and the knowledge that we can cope with it.

I recently went bowling with some friends and surprised them, I think, with my umbrage around the presence of gutter-guards, which prevent children from suffering what's presumed to be the emotionally scarring effect of getting gutterballs, or tallying up low scores. Call me a curmudgeon, but if you prevent kids from ever getting a gutterball, they won't learn how to bowl. And they won't learn how to manage the vagaries of real life, which has gutters and requires aim.

If we constantly engineer success for kids, they won't learn the resilience or humility to handle failure. And if you micromanage their every effort and emotion, they won't learn self-reliance, what it takes to achieve excellence, or how to become successful at managing failure while still maintaining their enthusiasm for the Game. In fact, we should be encouraging them, and ourselves, to make *more* mistakes, so we temper our fear of them.

David Bayles and Ted Orland, in their book *Art and Fear,* relate the story of a ceramics teacher who divided a class into two groups. One would be graded solely on the quantity of work produced, the other on the quality. At grading time, the works of highest quality were all produced by the group being graded for *quantity*.

"It seems that while the 'quantity' group was busily churning out piles of work—and learning from their mistakes," say the authors, "the 'quality' group had sat theorizing about perfection, and in the end had little more to show for their efforts than grandiose theories and a pile of dead clay. If you think good work is synonymous with perfect work, you're headed for big trouble. Art is human; error is human; *ergo* art is error. . . . To require perfection is to invite paralysis."

Just prior to quitting my job as a reporter, I had lunch with a mentor of mine, and when I mentioned my fear of failing at self-employment, he said, "Gregg, if you're not failing *regularly*, you're living so far below your potential that you're failing anyway." Which reminded me why I had lunch with this guy maybe once a year.

That's a bar set pretty high, but it's in line with the old baseball analogy people like to invoke in praise of the virtues of failure: a .300 batting average puts you at the top of the game, but what it actually means is that you only hit three balls out of every ten that cross the plate. You fail seven times out of ten and you're at the top of the heap. The more failure, the more success.

Granted, failing to get a hit in baseball isn't life threatening, and the baseball analogy doesn't hold up in other arenas where the risk factors are considerably higher. Failing to properly secure a piton seven times out of ten would give you a very short mountain-climbing career. Same with failing to adequately scout big rapids before rafting them, or to research the marketplace before rolling out your products and services.

Not that you want to stop taking swings at life, but in certain arenas you certainly don't want to *aspire* to fail regularly. ("It seems only yesterday I used to believe / there was nothing under my skin but light," writes former poet laureate Billy Collins. But now when I fall upon the sidewalks of life, I skin my knees. I bleed.") You just want to understand that setbacks and obstacles, going back to the drawing board, are all part of the path, part of the gaining of wisdom and mastery—part of the Mach 1 experience.

I *easily* struck out seven times in ten as a magazine freelance writer, sending query letters to editors in hopes of landing assignments. In fact, I was *delighted* to eventually attain that batting average, given that I started out failing *nine* times out of ten. Rejection is so fundamentally a part of freelancing that if you don't have a very high threshold for it—and be willing to learn from your mistakes—you're going to be working for somebody else again within a year. The only way to avoid rejection is to stop putting it out there, though by doing so you avoid rejection but not failure.

Although in most cases rejection slips are just people saying, "No thank you," and writers are counseled not to take them personally, this is easier said than done. It *is* personal. It's your writing, your ideas and visions, your heart and soul poured onto the page, your delicate shoots of optimism sent out into a world that wears big dirty boots. And when editors hide behind standard rejection forms ("This does not meet our editorial needs"), which they do, understandably, for the sake of expediency, it robs us of the right to face our rejectors, if not the chance to find out *why* our writing does not meet editorial needs.

Rejection and failure hurt. There's no way around it. And if it doesn't hurt, there's something fishy. But I say, let it hurt—curse and pout and mutter about the indignity of it all—and then let it go. Get yourself right back out there, preferably the same day. Rejection by its very nature makes you feel out of control, and the best way to regain that sense of control is to send your work out to the next client on your list. Fall down seven times, stand up eight.

For that matter, someone telling you no isn't rejection. Rejection is the conversation you have with yourself *afterward*. The way you beat yourself up, the flaws you believe that no confirms.

And take solace from history. It's full of the miscalculations of editors/teachers/parents/judges/talent agents/admissions officers/etc. Here's a smattering of examples from a compendium called *Rotten Rejections*, which I used to keep on my reference shelf during the freelance years, right next to the dictionary and the thesaurus. These famous kiss-offs from literary history, many of them from editors who undoubtedly lived to regret it, routinely helped me manage the failures endemic to that line of work:

> *The Diary of Anne Frank*: "The girl doesn't, it seems to me, have any special perception or feeling which would lift the book above the curiosity level."
>
> *Catch-22*, Joseph Heller: "A continual and unmitigated bore."
>
> *Lady Chatterly's Lover*, D. H. Lawrence: "For your own good, do not publish this book."
>
> *Lord of the Flies*, William Golding: "It does not seem to us that you have been wholly successful in working out an admittedly promising idea."
>
> *A Portrait of the Artist as a Young Man*, James Joyce: "It is not possible to get hold of an intelligent audience in wartime."
>
> *The Fountainhead*, Ayn Rand: "It is too intellectual for a novel. It won't sell."
>
> *Mankind in the Making*, H. G. Wells: "Only a minor writer of no large promise."
>
> *Animal Farm*, George Orwell: "It is impossible to sell animal stories in the U.S.A."

A Ropes Course for the Soul

In Arthur Conan Doyle's *The Lost World*, Professor Challenger declares, "It is only when a man goes out into the world with the thought that there are heroisms all round him, and with the desire all alive in his heart to follow any which may come within sight of him, that he breaks away as I did from the life he knows, and ventures forth into the wonderful mystic twilight land where lie great adventures and great rewards."

To this gusty proclamation, another character, a reporter, replies, "I'm afraid the day for this sort of thing is rather past. The big blank spaces on the map are all being filled in, and there's no room for romance anywhere."

Even if this were the case—and those big blank spaces are certainly more filled in now than when *The Lost World* was written more than one hundred years ago—it still raises the question, "Filled in with what?" With someone *else's* experience? With a few more pages of ethnographic notes, a few more little blue lines on the map? Someone may have planted a flag or hacked a runway out of the jungle or written a rousing adventure story about their journey to some empty quarter, but if you yourself have never been there, it's as good as undiscovered. It's not like the adventure has been had, so move along, folks, there's nothing to see.

Besides, there are other kinds of worlds every bit as lost and undiscovered as Conan Doyle's, with big blank spaces just as full of the potential for heroism and passionate exploration. But these aren't worlds you go *out* to, as Professor Challenger did. They're worlds you go *into*—the inner wildernesses of the human psyche, imagination, and unconscious, of the soul and spirit. The places where, as Gary Snyder said, there's a bobcat *right now*.

Yet, as with any adventure, journeying to these interior realms requires preparation and courage and has its dangers and vulnerabilities. The sought-for goal may not be reached, may even prove to be inaccessible, and a return to "normal" life not always guaranteed. But the true heroism of these kinds of journeys may lie not so much in what happens while in these "mystic twilight lands" but instead in your willingness to simply go there.

Such sojourns may demand more ardor and bravery of you than any expedition to the Mountains of the Moon or twenty thousand leagues under the sea. Jumping out of airplanes, climbing deadly peaks, being a war correspondent or a corporate buccaneer—these are often playing patty-cake compared with the guts it takes to head downriver into that heart of darkness inside your own head. Interior adventures are real adventures, with real risks and real consequences.

"Why should we honor those who die upon the field of battle," the poet Yeats asked, "when we may show as reckless a courage in entering into the abyss of ourselves." I've known people who wrestle alligators, chase after tornados, and motorcycle-jump over rows of school buses but who wouldn't be caught dead in a therapist's office or on a ten-day meditation retreat.

Or at a workshop like the Max.

The Max is, by most accounts, the single scariest of the more than five hundred personal-growth workshops offered each year at a retreat center called the Esalen Institute in Big Sur, California—ground zero for the human potential movement, which *specializes* in pushing people to their limits.

Facilitated by Paula Shaw, a Vancouver actress most famous for her role as the mother of Jason in the slasher movie *Freddy vs. Jason* (a crossover between the *Nightmare on Elm Street* and *Friday the 13th* franchises), the Max, like the movies, is not for the fainthearted. Its write-up in the Esalen catalog even mentions its own scariness, saying that if it tightens your bowels just thinking about it, it's probably the right workshop for you.

"The game is risk," it says, describing its "extremely challenging" combination of hot-seat work, stage performance, role-playing, improvisation, and dress-up assignments. "You're going to turn yourself inside out," engage in "a rigorous exploration of your emotional limitations," and have a former est trainer hammer at your defense mechanisms. Oh, and you're going to do public speaking about your most intimate issues.

Naturally, this is a fairly off-putting advertisement for most people. But not all.

Paula describes much of what she does in the weeklong workshop as "breaking and entering": breaking through people's resistance to living to the max and experiencing an expanded sense of themselves and their possibilities. Helping them get out of their own way and confront the deals they've made to keep themselves tucked away from trouble. People come with "the need to move," she says, to move something in their lives that's blocking their energy and potential. "They're so uncomfortable, can't stand being where they are, and feel like they're going to explode. The Max is just an opening, bringing them up to being present and noticing it.

"I don't know how you get to the place of being willing to move—why some people get there and others don't. Being desperate helps, from being so miserable, from the cost exceeding the payoff, when the cost of being where you are, who you are, how you are, is greater than what you're getting out of being that way." That and being driven by what Abraham Maslow called metamotivation, the innate urge that compels us to go after growth the way plants go after light.

The turning yourself inside out typically begins the moment you sign up for the Max (or any workshop devoted to personal growth). It doesn't wait until you get there. I myself endured an onslaught of physical symptoms in the weeks leading up to it, including diarrhea, insomnia, and acne, and in the transition from the workshop back to the ordinary world, I got a rip-roaring cold, in the throes of which I had to teach two full-day seminars back to back, which sucked, though they were among the best presentations of my career—more spontaneous, more passionate.

Paula calls these anticipatory symptoms "little explosions in the foundation of your house," a kind of immune response to the prospect of having someone messing with your *stuff*.

When I got to Esalen, my room was, appropriately, situated at the very edge of a cliff overlooking the ocean, and when I walked out onto the back deck I saw, on the porch of an adjacent building, a skeleton hanging from a hook. Undoubtedly a prop for one of Esalen's bodywork classes, but a skeleton, looking casually out to sea right alongside me. Try not reading too much into *that* one.

Paula's acting teacher, Uta Hagen, a three-time Tony Award winner, taught that actors must learn to face themselves, to hide nothing from themselves, and that to do so takes an insatiable curiosity about the human condition, and of course courage. "You look," Paula said. "When something comes up, you look at it and don't push it away."

Toward that end, and because being fully present is essential to the experience of aliveness, Paula spent a considerable amount of time during the week minesweeping for defense mechanisms while people were onstage doing their emotional work (in front of the rest of the class). She constantly told us to stop fidgeting, stop playing with our hair, crossing our arms, tapping our feet, closing our eyes, putting our hands on our hips—all the nervous energies we devote to avoiding the situation and whatever we're feeling. Her most common refrain was "Come baaaaaack."

She wanted us to notice how we ran away from being present, from what was really going on—from our aliveness—which comes down to one thing: consenting to be exactly where you are in the moment and seeing what happens. The operative question then changes, as Ann Belford Ulanov says in *The Unshuttered Heart*, from "How can we be safe and secure" to "How much lightning can we stand?"

Paula even made a point to encourage us to stay with our discomfort throughout the week. "Don't meditate, don't transcend, don't hug and comfort each other." She even said, only half-jokingly, "You can do the baths, but don't relax too much." Her concern was our tendency to use these kinds of activities to keep ourselves away from the growing edge that's critical for this kind of work, keeping us a little too calm and collected.

It reminded me of a workshop I'd participated in years before in which the facilitator strategically placed boxes of tissues around the room, in anticipation of emotional outpourings. During one of the exercises, the woman next to me started crying copiously, and though she herself didn't reach for a tissue, everybody else stared at me fixedly, as if willing me to hand her a box of tissues. But I ignored them because I didn't want to short-circuit her emotions. I wanted to witness their raw and marvelous display, and didn't want either her or myself succumbing to the cultural conspiracy to wipe it away.

Despite the edginess of the Max, Paula insists that people there are "safe." Yes, you're scared out of your wits, but you're also safe, as in "it's a safe space." And as forgiving an audience as you could ask for.

It's like a ropes course. You're experiencing clinical fear if not terror, and from a purely neurological and hormonal point of view, it's as big an adrenaline rush as parachuting and running Class V rapids, but you're also tethered and harnessed and ultimately you're safe. You're not going to die (your chances are roughly one in twenty million, according to a Project Adventure study). You might even get liberated, might even walk out of there larger than when you came in, with more options for moving forward, more choices in terms of your responses to life, and more passion for it.

One of the highlights of the Max for me was an encounter between Paula and a tough-talking twentysomething named Vanessa, who bartended for a living, so you knew she'd been around the block perhaps a few too many times for being so young, and one of those orbits was taken with a guy who'd recently broken her heart and left her volubly bitter about it.

One of our assignments during the week was to do a performance piece in front of the class, one to three minutes of a song, poem, skit, or monologue. Hers was a Disney-ish ditty about an affair between two toothbrushes.

"Delightful stuff," Paula said when she was finished. "Really. Very cute. But I want more. You're a singer, aren't you? You must know a love song. How about singing a love song?"

The young woman exhaled sharply and shook her head, her jawed cocked sideways. "You don't know who you're dealing with."

"Yes I do," Paula said.

A light sweat broke out on a roomful of foreheads. Each of us knew we would eventually be in Vanessa's shoes, if not that day then the next. There was no "There but for the grace of God go I." We shared a boat, a bond of anxiety, and commiseration, and Vanessa's anguish was our own.

A wave, a pulse of feeling, radiated through the room, and I sensed that it was our collective desire for Vanessa to break down and break through, because that's why we had all come to the single scariest workshop at Esalen. To push through whatever was holding us back from living out loud. To let loose a flood of tears and snot and profanities, the kind of medicine that tastes like hell going down but is profoundly healing.

We could see her right on the edge of letting it loose, but still holding it in. Her eyes darted around the room, like she was an animal that can't get away from its shape and can't get air. She looked past the stage lights into the far corner of the room, then into the opposite corner, like she was searching for a way out, while the muscles below her cheekbones twitched uncontrollably, visible from the third row back. Then she looked down at her feet, then straight at Paula, who was looking straight back.

Then Vanessa began to sing. A love song. One she had clearly written herself, achingly and obviously autobiographical. And suddenly there it was, only a motion away: her heart. The sound of her heart knocked loose from its secure riggings and rattling audibly, but alive and beating hard with grief and passion.

She could barely get through the song for all the crying, the stuttering inhales and wracking shoulders, the rictus of grief that pulled her face tight—the kind of crying most of us haven't done since we were children. But when she dropped her pretense of not feeling anything, her tough-guy stance, and just wept, just sang her love song and wept, it broke everybody's heart wide open. There wasn't a dry eye in the house. And whatever judgments we might have had about her dissolved in compassion.

And from that moment on—as it had been for all those who preceded

Vanessa onstage and gotten themselves to drop into whatever emotions they were resisting—she suddenly *landed*, suddenly showed up with her full personality rather than the narrow slice she'd been struggling to present. For the rest of the week, she was more present and available, more transparent, less guarded, more joyful, and the work she did onstage ended up explaining a lot about our first impressions of her.

FACING INTO THE CYCLONE winds of your own self, and not hiding from it—in fact, tackling most kinds of risk and adventure—requires a skill, a kind of seamanship, that's famously misunderstood, and which we all struggled with that week: vulnerability.

If passion is engagement, and a passionate life one of radical *participation*, we can't hope to be truly open to the experience of living if we insist on sticking to the shelter of the sidelines and not stepping onto the field, if we refuse to show up and risk the vulnerabilities inherent in a full-blown life. But vulnerability is not a weakness. It's a strength.

Granted, if your castle were being besieged by an enemy army and you had a breach in the walls, that kind of vulnerability would, in fact, be weakness. But we're not talking about warfare, even if you believe life to be a battleground. We're talking about the kind of vulnerability that's life affirming rather than life threatening. We're talking about living with a minimum of defenses so that we're capable of taking on life "wholeheartedly," as Brené Brown puts it in *Daring Greatly*, which she defines as "living from a place of worthiness," and making the journey from "What will people think?" to "I am enough."

"There is no equation," she insists, "where taking risks, braving uncertainty, and opening ourselves up to emotional risk equals weakness. Vulnerability is life's great dare. It asks, 'Are you all in?'"

But don't start with the big risks. "Please" and "Thank you" are perfect examples of vulnerabilities that are strengths. One confesses the desire for help and is a reaching-out; the other is an acknowledgment that someone has met that need and that we're momentarily beholden to them. And both help build bridges, strengthening the bonds between people.

So, too, "I'm sorry." I vividly remember the look of satisfaction, if not astonishment, that bloomed on my mother's face when my grandmother,

her ex-mother-in-law, apologized for "all the things I did to you" during the years my mother was married to my father. They were standing at the front door of my uncle's house, where we had all gathered after my father's funeral, and my mother's mouth dropped open, her eyes welled up, and she said: "I never thought I'd live long enough to hear you say that." Vulnerability as strength—peacemaking, ice melting, soul restoring.

Same with "I don't know." As a public speaker, I'm keenly aware that the willingness to say "I don't know" boosts my credibility in people's minds, rather than diminishes it, and allows me to turn my energies toward learning rather than pretending to know. And every speaker can appreciate the power that sharing vulnerabilities has to help build trust and rapport.

By acknowledging our "failures," too, we open ourselves to learning from them. I read a story about someone who had made a multimillion-dollar mistake at his job, and in a fit of contrition went into his boss's office to resign. The boss, however, had other ideas. "Why would I let you go now, after having spent millions of dollars training you?"

Similarly, in the weeks following the 9/11 bombings, when the fiction of American invulnerability was so shockingly revealed, many of us found ourselves acting a little differently. We held doors open for strangers, spent more time with our kids, paid the tollbooth fare for the driver behind us, honked less, listened more. Passions and loves were released. Parts of us that were frozen thawed a bit. Emotions rose to the surface for a gulp of air. Our involvement in life intensified. In other words, life's fragility, our fragility, woke us up.

And I don't have a shred of doubt anymore that taking the risk to lower my defenses and reveal vulnerability builds strength into my relationships, is a liberation of love, not a defeat. Despite my long-standing assumption that I would get skewered for revealing any chinks in my armor (and indeed people sometimes do take advantage of it and I get hurt), my usual experience, far and away, has been that's it's worth it, that safety *and* passion noticeably deepen when I let down my guard and my pretense of invincibility.

There's a reason that when we feel love or adoration for someone, we talk about having a *soft spot* for them. We reflexively equate love with vulnerability. In order to love, we're telling ourselves, we need to have a soft spot. And in this sense, strength is not necessarily power, if it's the kind of strength we muster to push our emotions down and cover our soft spots. Usually the far more empowering thing—and for our health the safer thing—is to let them rise. "What happens when people open their hearts?" asks writer Haruki Murakami. "They get better."

Not that they won't sometimes get worse *before* they get better. A friend of mine who's normally a very private and guarded person recently disclosed to me something particularly vulnerable, and the next day came down with a cold. I guessed that her confession must have registered with a seismic jolt of vulnerability inside her, and it was no coincidence that she got sick. Stress, after all, tends to undermine people's immune systems—my friend's *immunity* to the world was temporarily compromised—and what a cold triggers is precisely a rallying of *defenses.*

It was a perfect emotional metaphor for her vulnerability. But it was also, I sensed, part of a larger healing, a symptom of her readiness to take more risks and reveal herself to others.

The willingness to be on speaking terms with your emotions—to admit you have them, be able to name them when they arise, understand that they have power, sometimes *over* you, and share them with others—is often the better part of valor. And defending yourself against any emotions and experiences that could lead to pain is tantamount to locking yourself in a tower and calling yourself safe.

But being detached is not the same as being unafraid. You'll still have to contend with the fear that propelled you to lock yourself away to begin with. You'll still have to toss and turn your way through dreams at night, where whatever you repress is bound to make an appearance. And you'll set yourself up for the pain and regret of missed opportunities, of the life you could have lived and the person you could have been—the daring young man on the flying trapeze, the girl with the dragon tattoo. "My nights are spent in a vicious fury at the life which I've let slip away from me," says the title character in Anton Chekhov's play *Uncle Vanya.* "I could have enjoyed everything in life. *Everything.* I enjoyed nothing. And now I'm too old."

Life is lived out in dualities. Conscious and unconscious, passive and active, passion and reason, give-and-take, creation and destruction. In fact, polarization defines our very "indivi-duality." And each side needs its opposite to give it balance, to give it something to push against and test its theories, and so come to know its own strength and its own boundaries.

Thus, vulnerability requires courage, and courage—to step into the arena and wholeheartedly take what comes—requires vulnerability. As a Persian proverb says, "A jewel that never leaves the mind never acquires polish."

The Tiger and the Cage: Intelligent Risk-Taking

What constitutes intelligent risk is hard to discern when you consider that as far as risk-taking goes, most of us are still swinging by our tails from the trees. Our brains are prehistorically programmed to shoot first and ask questions later, to fear first and think second, and brains that were designed to respond knee-jerkily to predators in the grass are not always adept at gauging present-day risks—driving versus flying, a heavy intake of social media, quitting your job to pursue your passions.

Also, when you're in the throes of risk-taking—especially those that involve the body—you're taking orders more from your "animal" intelligences than from your "human" intelligences. When you're rock climbing or even lovemaking, it isn't the "higher" brain alone or even primarily that's running the show—not language or creative skills, not planning or reasoning, but reflexes, electrical impulses, and chemical reactions. And given the language we use to describe courage, in a sense *all* risks involve the body; putting ourselves on the line in the most personal way. The word *courage* itself means "heart," but we also refer to being courageous as having guts, nerves, balls, backbone, a stiff upper lip, intestinal fortitude, and a strong stomach. When we take a risk, we stick our necks out and put skin in the game.

It's certainly of survival value to anticipate danger and consider what *could* go wrong, but not at the continual expense of quality of life, and the ever-pressing metamotivation to grow and thrive. Just because you have afterimages of saber-toothed tigers—or childhood traumas for that matter—flickering in the back of your mind, for instance, doesn't mean they still exist. An imagined or remembered fear is not necessarily a real and present danger that requires you to take to the battlements.

Sometimes it's important to second-guess your own risk perceptions. Not to override your instincts and intuitions, not to make light of the traumas you have experienced, but to temper your involuntary assumptions and wild imagination. I have a Doris Lessing book called *Prisons We Choose to Live Inside*, and on the title page, a previous reader had written, as if in summation: "Don't believe everything you think."

For example, we're safer and healthier now than at any time in the history of life—take a spin through any Victorian-era cemetery to be reminded of this—yet we're more worried about injury, disease, and death than ever. And it's not that the world is necessarily more dangerous, but that, among other things, there's money to be made by promoting fear. For all their sincerity, groups as varied as corporations, politicians, activists, the media, nongovernmental organizations, and even charities routinely traffic in mis- and disinformation in the name of profit and power, ratings and votes.

For example, the media's portrayal of death—bundled with the age-old human penchant for lurid storytelling—focuses disproportionately on the dramatic, violent, and catastrophic rather than the mundane, which is by far the more common. Cancer and diabetes take out considerably more of us than murder, car crashes, shootouts, and drone strikes. The deadliest plane crash in history—two jumbo jets that collided on a foggy runway in the Canary Islands in 1977—took 583 lives, but the death toll from heart disease worldwide reaches that number roughly *every eighteen minutes*.

But chronic rather than catastrophic events aren't going to grab the attention of people flipping through newspapers and magazines in the dentist's office. Thus the old journalistic tropes "If it bleeds it leads" and "If it scares, it airs," both of which lend themselves to what's called "mean world syndrome," whereby the violent content of mass media makes viewers believe the world is more dangerous than it actually is.

It isn't just the sensationalizing of death, either, that skews our perceptions of risk, but the failure to put it in *perspective*, to pose a question that's critical to our understanding of any risk: how likely is it? The *Times of London* once ran a story claiming that the number of Brits murdered by strangers had increased by a third in eight years, from 99 to 130. That's certainly dismaying, but what the article failed to mention is that there are roughly 60 million Brits. Thus their chances of being killed by a stranger increased from .00016 percent to .00022 percent. Hardly reason to lock yourself in an underground bunker and stock up on canned soup and shotgun shells.

Disease-awareness campaigns—which are sometimes underwritten by drug companies that profit from diagnosis and treatment, and sometimes by public-health advocates—do the same thing. Breast cancer activists routinely point out that one in eight American women will get breast cancer in the course of their lifetime, but what they routinely leave out is the fact that you'd need to live to be ninety-five to face that full risk. The statistic looks very different when viewed from different ages. Your chance of getting breast cancer by age seventy is one in 14, by age fifty is one in 50, by age forty is one in 217, and by age thirty is one in 2,525.

Similar to our assessment of the likelihood of mishap in risk-taking is our cost-benefit analysis—what we stand to lose compared with what we stand to gain—and we routinely play it safe in this department. Safer than we often need to. And we routinely focus only on the prospect of short-term pain and not on the prospect of long-term gain.

Ever since becoming self-employed, I've spent roughly 50 percent of my time working to get work, to drum up writing assignments and speaking engagements, and I'm routinely surprised how often I have to push myself to do follow-up with people, because I'm afraid of coming across as pushy or desperate, afraid of annoying them.

But I do it anyway, because follow-up falls squarely in the category of risks in which I have *nothing to lose, only to gain*. This would appear to be a no-brainer, but it's appalling how often my brain intervenes and prevents me from hitting the Send button. It's not like I already have the assignment or speaking gig and am at risk of losing it, and people generally understand that following up is part of doing business. They typically respond by saying, "Thanks for reminding me," or "I'm not in a position to move on this now," or "We can't swing it." But whether they respond with a yea or a nay, I regain my momentum.

It's the same with asking someone on a date. Worst-case scenario: a onetime embarrassment. Best-case scenario: a soulmate. Same with asking for a raise. Worst-case: you're turned down. Best-case: a bigger paycheck every week. Same with arranging an informational interview with someone who does something you're thinking of doing with your life. Worst-case: losing an hour of your time. Best-case: a new career, and possibly a new mentor.

I went kayaking on the Snake River in Idaho a few years ago, accompanying a group on a raft, and the put-in was immediately upstream of a large and long Class IV rapids, which was a bit off-putting right up front. I was given the option of riding that first set of rapids in the raft, my kayak strapped to the back. But when I asked one of the guides for her recommendation, she said this: "Most people talk themselves out of kayaking this first rapid, but once we're through it, most of them also say, 'I could have done that.'" (Translation: I *should* have done that.) I decided not to be one of those people, and it was among the great thrill rides of my life.

How much of a sense of *control* you have over a given risk, too, will help determine how likely you are to take it on, despite the odds. We may fear the experience of falling, for instance—an inheritance from our arboreal ancestors—but we get a kick out of a *controlled* fall, à la skydiving, bungee jumping, roller coasters, and even, sometimes, falling in love. My chances of making a decent living as a freelance writer have probably been equivalent to my chances of a skydiving accident, both of them remote, but I'd much rather strap myself into my desk chair than into a parachute. I feel far more in control, the consequences of failure are far less dire, and should I begin to fail, I'd at least have numerous opportunities to self-correct on the way down, compared with skydiving's singular Plan B: one reserve parachute.

Besides, my passion for it tends to diminish my perception of its risks, and amplify my perception of its rewards, even my sense of control over it. Perhaps my eagerness and determination translate into optimism, helping see me through the fear and doubt—*insisting* on finding a way through. In a curious way, risk may be a kind of reward for the passionate, as it's the surest way to make new discoveries and explore new territories.

We usually equate intelligence with reason rather than passion, but sometimes the most *reasonable* thing you can do is precisely to follow your passions, if you define *reason* as "sound judgment and good sense."

I recently received a letter from a woman who described being an attorney as something that she hates "deep down," is "soul-killing," makes her feel like she's "living in a cage," "living someone else's life," and only "half a life" at that. She said she's "always held back" from what and who she truly wants to be, and meanwhile her "well has totally dried up."

Now given this state of affairs, would it make sense for her to continue practicing law, since it's certainly a sensible career—the paycheck, the prestige? Would it be *sound judgment* for her to ignore other passions that make her feel fully alive rather than half alive? And is it a *coincidence* that there's an organization in San Francisco called Lawyers in Transition, specifically devoted to helping people get the hell out of that profession, and a popular blog called Lawyers With Depression, for those still in it?

This isn't to suggest that passion is all-powerful and gut feelings infallible, or that feeling in control is a guarantee of success. It was gut feelings, after all, that prompted so many people to quit flying and start driving in the year after the 9/11 bombings—imagining that just because they felt more in control, it was safer, when statistically it is not—and this ended up adding almost twenty-two hundred traffic fatalities to the average that year, according to a Cornell University study.

Sometimes we're less concerned about risk than we ought to be—people who choose driving over flying, smokers who shrug off their chances of getting lung cancer, people who've had a few drinks insisting that they're fine behind the wheel of a car—but just as often we *overestimate* risk and consequences and so shrink from opportunities.

Sometimes the antidote is simply thinking things through rather than going on pure gut or trusting whatever seemingly plausible conclusion comes quickly to mind. You won't make truly informed decisions, or take truly *intelligent* risks, if you don't apply thinking to feeling.

For instance, you may refuse to send your creative works out into the world because you're terrified of rejection, believing you'll be devastated by it and it will only prove your worthlessness. But you have to think through how your life might unfold, or fail to unfold, if you never take the chance, if you keep your gifts and passions locked in a drawer. You have to think through not only how you'd feel about yourself if you got rejected (and *why* you'd feel that way), but how you'd feel about yourself if you never tried—or if you got *accepted*.

For that matter, you're probably better off not even thinking in terms like failure and success. Rather, think like a scientist. Life is an *experiment* and there are only results.

ONE THING WE CAN do to improve the results of our risk-taking, and our tolerance for it, is to increase what Michael Apter in *The Dangerous Edge* calls our protective frames, mechanisms we put in place to convince ourselves that we can do it, and help us not only manage our anxiety but also turn it into exuberance.

"Think of looking at a tiger in a cage," he says. "Both the tiger and the cage are needed in order to experience excitement. The tiger without the cage would be frightening. The cage without the tiger would be boring. Both are necessary. In order to experience excitement, then, we need both the possibility of danger and something we believe will protect us from it."

This could be the psychological bubble provided by well-honed skills, advance preparation and rehearsal, proper equipment, a support network, a sense of confidence, and an emergency parachute. It could be rituals and routines that help ground you and keep you balanced while you do your high-wire work—a regular writing schedule, a daily meditation practice, a cuppa coffee before and a jog in the park after your peak creative hours. I knew a freelance writer who, to take himself seriously and convince himself that he was "going to work," got showered and dressed every morning, left the house through the side door, came back in through the front door, walked upstairs, and began writing.

It could even be an act of *reframing*. "Don't call it uncertainty—call it wonder," suggests Osho in his book *Courage: The Joy of Living Dangerously*. "Don't call it insecurity—call it freedom."

Sometimes it helps to build a case for yourself, to convince yourself that you're courageous by remembering those times when you were courageous. Make a list if need be. The time you finally got yourself to jump off the high diving board, to act in a play, to end a relationship that wasn't working, to get back into a *new* relationship, quit a job for something better, unfriend someone on Facebook, correct someone who mispronounced your name, share a vulnerability with a friend, ask for help, let your kid ride his bike alone for the first time *downhill*, ask someone out on a date.

For roughly half my decade-long tenure at the *Cincinnati Enquirer*, I kept hearing a call to quit and become a freelance writer, a decision that's not exactly designed to reassure your parents, or your partner, or your creditors—and one I largely ignored anyway, because it was Scary Stuff. Freelancing is considered by many to be akin to an extreme sport in its level of risk and lack of security. To balance out the fear factor—and not risk living with something I knew I'd always regret *not* having done—I followed Apter's prescription, and Louis Pasteur's advice that "chance favors the prepared mind." I created a plan to help skew my perceptions back in my favor and to build some courage into the enterprise.

I began with a pep talk to remind myself that I'd been told that my chances of landing a job as a reporter at a big-city newspaper right out of college were close to nil, and I did it anyway; and before that, I'd been told that my chances of convincing the college I'd been attending to allow me to take the internship that had brought me to Cincinnati to begin with, when they didn't even have an internship program, were also close to nil, but I did that too.

Then I committed to spending each Thursday night for one year studying the life I wanted to live, becoming a disciple of its details. (There's nothing sacrosanct about Thursdays; it just happened to fit into my schedule.) So instead of taking the bus back uptown on Thursdays after work, I stayed downtown, and my first order of business was to take myself out to dinner—at a restaurant with tablecloths.

Then I went to the public library from six to nine, when it closed, and studied as well as practiced the freelance life. I read books about it, brainstormed story ideas, queried editors, researched and wrote articles, conducted interviews, fielded rejection letters, rewrote articles, and sometimes just slept (and inevitably got woken up by the security guard who would bang on the bottom of my shoe with his nightstick, because you're not allowed to sleep in the public library—something about the vagrancy laws).

I also met with freelance writers to pick their brains. I asked them what they liked about the life, what they hated, how they got into it, what kind of job they left, how much preparing they did, how long it took for them to start making decent money, what advice they had for a neophyte, what they wished someone had told *them*. And one of the things they frequently told me was that I'd better have two years' worth of savings in the bank, which was a bummer, because I didn't have that kind of money in the bank at the time, and what it made me do was extend my deadline another year, as well as my employment at the newspaper.

Two years is a long time to be doing something when you'd rather be doing something else, but it's not twenty. And at least I was actively moving toward my goal rather than actively talking myself out of it. And the cumulative effect of two years' worth of Thursday nights spent preparing was what gave me the running start I needed to carry me through my leap of faith. And by the time I leapt, I leapt into work, not into an abyss. I had relationships up and running with editors, assignments in the queue, published freelance clips, and confidence I didn't have two years earlier.

Another example of framing: for as long as I can remember, I've told myself and others that I won't partake of any sport that involves the sensation or the possibility of falling—hang gliding, parasailing, mountain climbing, bungee jumping, skydiving, even riding a roller coaster. My very first nightmare, and for many years during my childhood the most recurring one, was of falling. Not falling *from* anything or *toward* anything—just falling.

So when my girlfriend, Paula, asked if I wanted to go paragliding with her while on a trip to Turkey a few years ago, I declined, and we more or less shelved the idea. But one afternoon we visited a village on the Turquoise Coast called Ölüdeniz, considered among the world's top spots for paragliding, and I spent a solid hour behind my binoculars, watching paragliders come off the mountains along the coast—one after another, sometimes twenty in the sky simultaneously. My conclusion was that it looked like smooth sailing, and the landings soft. So backed up with this new protective frame, this reinforced cage around the tiger, I changed my mind on the spot, as well as my story.

It helped that I also had, as I always do on such adventures, the additional frame of travel insurance, up to and including helicopter rescue to airlift me out of some inaccessible canyon where I could have broken my leg or worse.

The next day, in an act of not just courage but also paradigm busting—and in what would become the most literal high of the entire trip—I went paragliding.

Our base of operations was a small harbor town on the Mediterranean called Kas, founded by the Greeks twenty-five hundred years ago and backed by enormous mountains that plunge down to the sea. The venture began with a twenty-minute drive up a hairpin mountain road that one of our pilots said was statistically riskier than the flight itself.

After being harnessed in tandem with a pilot, we each took off by essentially jumping off a two-thousand-foot cliff and catching a thermal, which took us up to thiry-five hundred feet. I looked between my legs and there was nothing between me and the ground but empty air. To borrow an expression from whitewater kayaking, it may have been Class II rapids, but it had Class V consequences.

Naturally, my instinct for survival was going off like a siren in my skull, reminding me that jumping off cliffs is not generally in keeping with the agenda of staying alive. But we not only jumped off the cliff; we actually *ran* toward it, the better to catch the wind in our parachutes. The only other inner narration I heard was that incredulous and electrified voice that so often accompanies taking a flyer: "I can't believe I'm actually doing this."

But for the most part, in keeping with the data I had collected down in Ölüdeniz the day before, it was a very smooth ride, unless you opt for the option of "acrobatics," which the pilots will gladly accommodate, swooping and corkscrewing and generally doing their unlevel best to bring your lunch back up for reconsideration. For this reason, I do not recommend eating lunch before such an adventure, or for that matter breakfast, or possibly even dinner the night before. In fact, a three-day fast leading up to it doesn't seem like an unreasonable protective frame to me.

We spent a good forty minutes aloft, gliding out over the Turquoise Coast and the tiny Greek island of Meis, a twenty-minute ferry ride from Kas harbor, and our landing, right onto a concrete jetty down at the harbor, was as gentle as stepping off a curb, though the rush of adrenaline I experienced at having done it, having survived it, raised my blood pressure more than anything I experienced on the ride itself.

The whole thing from beginning to end was also captured by the pilots in photographs and videotapes, which they were of course happy to sell to us for an exorbitant fee back at the office, and which, in our triumphant state, we bought.

Playing the Edge

In the natural world, the edge is where the action is. The zone between two ecosystems—water and land, or field and forest—is where the greatest diversity and productivity are found, as well as the most predation. This is fitting, as the Greek word for this region, an ecotone, means "tension." But it's characterized by a fertility that biologists call the edge effect.

In human affairs, the ecotone between the life we have and the life we want, between our present condition and our potential, is equally fruitful if not fitful, full of passion and suffering, productivity and predation. The exercise of pushing beyond our assumed limits into this zone of intensity and virility, in search of fulfillment and new possibilities, is rightfully referred to by sociologists as edgework.

It's a kind of personal anarchy, an affirmative revolt against our own stuckness, as well as the entrapments and overdetermined nature of everyday life (they don't call it the "beaten" path for nothing). It's not loss of control, though, but an acute sort of self-control, says Jeff Ferrell, a professor of sociology at Texas Christian University quoted in Stephen Lyng's book *Edgework: The Sociology of Risk-Taking*. "It's self-control in place of control by church, state or job, based on the understanding that if you don't control yourself, somebody else will. . . . It's self-control for the sake of self-determination. Self-control in the interest of holding on to your life while letting go of it. . . . Self-control that gets you hooked on the autonomy of self-invention. . . . It's a defiant disavowal of secondhand living."

When days, weeks, and months, even years, can pass without consequence, without registering so much as a blip on the ontological Richter scale, it's in our best interest to push a few boundaries and risk making some trouble, if not engage in some of those activities that guarantee it will matter *greatly* how the next few seconds or minutes unfold. There's no shortage: skydiving, whitewater rafting, bull-riding, competitive sports, asking someone on a date, coming out of the closet, or any fierce conversation in which whatever you say next could have a make-or-break effect.

I used to have a silver ring that a high school girlfriend gave me, which I wore well into my thirties, and was in the habit of using in a peculiar game of chance. From time to time I would slip it off and twirl it in my fingers while dangling it over some precipice—the edge of a cliff, the balcony of a high-rise apartment, the side of a boat—just to play the edge and give myself a little thrill.

Once, while in college, I was standing with Ross on a covered bridge in New Hampshire, twisting the ring over the railing when it—finally, inevitably—slipped from my fingers and dropped into the Contoocook River. We both looked down at the spot where it hit the water, and Ross matter-of-factly said, "Well, that's the end of *that* game."

A week later, he and I were swimming in the river, a quarter mile downstream from the bridge. I was sitting on a large granite rock at the water's edge when Ross swam up, climbed out, sat next to me, and held out his fist, palm up. "Does this by any chance look familiar?" he said, while simultaneously opening his fist and revealing the ring.

Sometimes you're just plain lucky. Luckier than life would normally allow, luckier than you have a right to be. The odds against such good fortune may be astronomical, but there you are anyway, with a fistful of four-leaf clovers and an ear-to-ear grin, a batter with three balls and no strikes against him. Sometimes it's just the way the dice roll.

Not often enough, of course, that most people would bet on those kind of odds if what was at stake was truly valuable or irreplaceable (certainly your life), and granted, the consequence of this particular gamble were negligible—an acute but temporary sense of loss. Still, I think my penchant for playing I-dare-you with the ring all those years was a small attempt to keep life interesting, keep my hand in the game, stay practiced at taking risks and involving myself in those activities where the next few moments really do matter (or at least living in such a way that I remember that every moment *matters* and every second *counts*).

The desire to explore the edge, to gain the rim and push ourselves out of our dried-up wells, certainly helps explain the popularity of thrill-seeking, which may just be courage adapted for monotonous times, for an era when the demands on our physical courage are few.

Civilization is designed to minimize natural risks and stabilize the instabilities of not just nature but human nature as well. And as the screws have been tightened over time through legal and moral strictures, social and religious sanctions, urbanization and suburbanization, and litigiousness, risk takers have been compelled to devise ever more outlets for their enthusiasms, what Paul Zweig in *The Adventurer* calls "small vertical escapes from the chain gang of our days."

Thus we see, among other things, the rise of thrill sports, though the tension between civilization and risk-taking goes quite a bit farther back. How much of the British Empire, Zweig muses, was built by people trying to escape the strangulating conformity of Victorian England? And how much of the fact that developing countries have a conspicuous *lack* of thrill sporting is a function of their intimacy with those natural risks that developed countries have minimized? Where death and disease are everyday occurrences, such contrived risks are redundant. Who needs bungee jumping when you have malaria?

Thrill sports are the kinds of adventure whose primary goal is a push toward the Limit. This is not literary adventure, not armchair adventure, not family adventure, not a vacation into which you throw a little surfing or a zip line. This is the hunger to feel yourself vividly alive by stepping right up to the cage with the tiger in it. Or as I heard an ice climber once say: "I open the door, see the Grim Reaper right there, but instead of just slamming the door, I push him back a few steps."

Among my most memorable encounters with the Limit was a helicopter skiing trip I once took with Ross in the Wasatch Mountains of Utah. It was a full-day venture involving seven long runs down seven different mountaintops, the day after a storm that left three feet of the kind of light, dry snow that skiers reverently refer to as champagne powder, which rolls away like bow waves in front of you as you ski.

Our sense of being close to the Limit was heightened by being far off the beaten track and thoroughly immersed in the elements, as well as being shuttled from peak to peak by a former Vietnam War pilot with a possible death wish, who roared just above treetop level and banked sharply off canyon walls. It was also clarified by being fitted with an avalanche beeper, a constant reminder of the element of danger, of the fine line that exists between life and death. That grim beeper was the only thing between us and the absolute quiet of those remote mountains—with the exception of our ecstatic hollering.

The proximity of danger and excitement, and the urge to put your life on that line, may explain the adrenaline rush of war too, and why men in combat (and increasingly women) speak of it as a peak experience, and lament its passing because along with it goes the most passionate time of their lives. They felt the most alive, right there at the edge of death, all their senses and capacities on full alert, all their scattered attentions and ambitions tapered to an absolute clarity. Their sense of purpose is never again so single-pointed, their sense of camaraderie never again so emotional, and they often spend the rest of their lives looking for an experience, any experience, that might help them recapture that lost grandeur, which is like a forest fire, or cancer under a microscope—deadly, but beautiful.

It may explain the appeal of cigarette smoking for some people too. I saw a billboard a few years ago for Newport cigarettes, featuring a couple of youthful smiling faces and the slogan "Alive with pleasure!" You might wonder why anyone would partake of something that's advertised as "Alive with pleasure" but whose small print says it can kill you. Yet the same could be said about thrill sports.

Precisely *because* death tends to make us shrink, timid and fearful, it can provoke in some people the desire to push back, to stalk the stalker. They refuse to be in*timid*ated. They refuse to allow their courage and vitality to be worn threadbare by the clinging to comfort and security. The desire for adventure becomes the desire for revolt, not just against the fear of death or the understimulated life, but also against a scaredy-cat culture that hides behind gates and guardrails, bailouts and subsidies, schools that eradicate playgrounds and dodgeball, and manufacturers that put warning labels on their products saying "Do not iron clothes on body" and "Wearing this Superman costume does not enable you to fly."

And it seems that for every uptick in secondhand living, there's a countervailing attempt to make the edge even edgier. Consider this ever-expanding list of thrill-sports: hurricane sea-kayaking, unicycle hockey, underwater rugby, chess boxing (alternating a round of boxing with a round of chess), fireball soccer (dousing a soccer ball with lighter fluid, setting it aflame, then playing ball with bare feet), and extreme ironing, in which you take an ironing board into a dangerous situation—rock climbing, scuba diving, even combat—and iron clothes, which, as its aficionados like to say, combines the thrill of an extreme sport with the satisfaction of a well-pressed shirt.

I remember watching a television program a few years ago on extreme parachuting. A group of four jumpers sat in a convertible that had just rolled out the back of an airplane. They sat calmly in the car as it plummeted to the ground, and on cue pulled their ripcords and rocketed upward out of their seats, while the car hurtled downward and smashed into the ground at terminal velocity.

There's even a company in New York City that offers "designer kidnappings" for a few thousand dollars each, an idea cooked up by one Brock Enright, who earned an MFA from Columbia University in "new genres," and whose website (www.semagoediv.com; *videogames* backward) is discreet to the point of obscurity.

One minute you're standing at the bus stop or showering in your apartment, and the next you're stuffed into a duffel bag, tossed into the trunk of a car, duct-taped, and hauled to the roof of a warehouse in the Bronx or a creepy hotel in the Meatpacking District and subjected to the terrors or thrills of your choice, as designated on your intake questionnaire.

Custom kidnappings, though, may be more than just the latest distraction for the rich and bored. They echo an idea put forth in a G. K. Chesterton short story from the turn of the last century titled "The Tremendous Adventures of Major Brown," from a collection called, appropriately, *The Club of Queer Trades*.

At one point in the story, Major Brown is being addressed by the proprietor of an outfit called the Adventure and Romance Agency, to which people pay a quarterly or yearly fee in return for being subjected to "startling and weird events."

"Major," asks the proprietor, "did you ever, as you walked along the empty street upon some idle afternoon, feel the utter hunger for something to happen—something, in the splendid words of Walt Whitman: 'Something pernicious and dread; something far removed from a puny and pious life; something unproved; something in a trance; something loosed from its anchorage and driving free.' Did you ever feel that?"

"Certainly not," said the major.

Not so Brock Enright's clientele, which has grown sufficiently to enable him to consider opening franchises in other cities and begin pitching the idea as a reality show to the cable networks.

SOME PEOPLE ARE THRILL seekers not because they have a hunger for something to happen, but because they have that migratory gene variant that some call "gene wild."

There are roughly fifteen hundred genes on chromosome 11, and one of them is the human dopamine D4 receptor gene (DRD4)—dopamine being a brain chemical implicated in pleasure and stimulation seeking—and it's referred to as the thrill-seeking gene, in addition to acting as something of a teaching aid to the brain in the acquisition of new behavior. (If you don't possess the gene, or the inclination toward risk-taking, and want to increase your threshold for it, you can change the way your brain perceives risk by introducing it to a lot of small risks on a regular basis and building a tolerance for it.)

There are a number of variations of the gene, though, and which version you possess will determine whether you're more at home with a thirty-year mortgage or a parachute-jump, more likely to build your house on a golf course or on the flanks of a volcano. As I noted earlier, one of these variations is the exon III 7-repeat allele, which predisposes people to such behaviors as risk-taking, novelty seeking, and ADHD.

If you inherited this variant, everyday life is likely to be more problematic since your threshold for the everyday will be lower than others'. Having a Wilder Gene also predisposes you to boredom, job dissatisfaction, alcohol and drug abuse, gambling, promiscuity, crime, a passion for horror movies, and political liberalism.

People diagnosed with ADHD are twice as likely to have the gene variant, but some of what we consider ADHD symptoms, like rapidly shifting focus and quick movements, may actually be survival traits that were selected for during our migration out of Africa. Evolution, it appears, may have latched onto a gene linked to risk-taking and adventurousness.

In fact, the primary evolutionary advantage of these behaviors, says Apter, comes down to exploration. Some members of any tribe, especially in new environments, have to investigate what's dangerous and what's not, and test the limits so that others will know what they are and either avoid them or exercise caution in approaching them. The explorer and aviator Charles Lindbergh rightly asked, "What civilization was not founded on adventure? . . . Our earliest records tell of biting the apple and baiting the dragon, regardless of hardship or danger, and from this inner drive, perhaps, progress and civilization developed."

Thus the importance of supporting the dragon baiters, both in society and in ourselves. Of keeping alive the role of edgewalker, outlier, provocateur, and imagineer—the one who stands outside the shop window looking in and questioning; who lives in the liminal zone between civilized and wild, conformity and rebellion; who dives beneath the surface of life to its depths.

The philosopher Alfred North Whitehead said that "civilized" society is defined by having five qualities: beauty, truth, art, peace, and *adventure*, and that it preserves its vitality only as long as "it is nerved by the vigour to adventure beyond the safeties of the past. Without adventure, civilization is in full decay." And the same goes for its civilians.

The same goes for business too. Interestingly, what's missing from that Gallup poll of "engaged," "not engaged," or "actively disengaged" workers worldwide, which I mentioned in the Introduction, is a category for those who are "actively engaged," i.e., passionate. Not just emotionally committed to corporate goals and showing up on time but also impassioned about their own and the company's potential, about pushing the edge and continual growth. A 2012 study conducted by the appropriately named Deloitte Center for the Edge (part of the Big Four consulting firm Deloitte) found that 30 percent of American workers were "engaged," but only 11 percent possessed what they called "the passion of the explorer."

A friend recently told me that her therapist gave her an assignment to break one rule a day for two weeks, as long as it benefited her work. By "rule," he meant the assumptions and formulas that orchestrate her relationship to doing business. He wanted her to step outside the comfort zone and take some chances, do a little edgewalking, and realize that habits are habits because they tend to work, but that they're not the *only* way things can work, and they sometimes work against us. The rules, even the laws, we live by, need occasional upgrading when they fail to deliver on their promises.

For instance, there are rules of engagement that are widely believed to make relationships work and that we only break at our supposed peril: never go to bed angry, always be 100 percent honest, the children come first, fighting is bad for love, marriage will end your loneliness, and having a baby will bring a couple closer. But anyone who has spent time in actual relationships knows it ain't necessarily so, and there are plenty of exceptions to these beliefs and bylaws, some of which are in fact better off broken.

There are rules of engagement that are also believed to make businesses succeed but that are sometimes bent to great effect. An example of this— and of the link between risk-taking and passion—is the corporate practice, utilized by firms as large as 3M and Hewlett-Packard, of what's called "20 percent time": one day out of the workweek, employees are allowed to pursue any project their heart desires, as long as it benefits the company.

Google's 20 percent policy is known to have contributed to roughly half of its innovations and billions of dollars in revenue, and has inspired the use of 20 percent time as an educational model, which isn't surprising given that Google's cofounders credit their implementation of the policy to their experiences attending Montessori schools, where students are assumed to be capable of self-directed learning and learn best through discovery.

Twenty percent time helps ensure that employees are passionate about their work, and passion equals productivity. It also highlights the power of intrinsic versus extrinsic motivation (and tends to work best for companies that are in the business of innovation and creativity, as opposed to, say, mass production; are not understaffed or rigidly hierarchical; and don't have a "failure is not in our vocabulary" approach to doing business).

Asking people, whether employees or students, what turns them on and what they truly *want* to learn—and (here's where the risk comes in) releasing them from their scripted and commissioned routines to pursue those things, to explore and innovate—helps them clarify their passions, which can then be put in service of the general welfare.

In *The Charge*, business trainer Brendon Burchard contends that real change, progress, and accomplishment come only when we choose causes we deeply believe in and refuse to let ourselves be "neutered of any real desire or ambition by heeding the advice of the 'realists,' who tell us to set SMART goals (specific, measurable, attainable, relevant, and time-bound). But these types of attainable goals never spark the imagination or fire the will. You want to change? Then do not, under any circumstances, allow yourself to settle on a vision or calling that is uninspiring."

The parameters placed on our behavior by everything from the Code of Hammurabi and the Ten Commandments to the admonitions of our parents, teachers, employers, and lawmakers, are rules of conduct designed to ensure the smooth functioning of society, if not the say-so of those in power. But some of these strictures are far less defensible than others, and do more damage to the individual. It's not that rules are necessarily made to be broken, but that the constraints some of them put in place end up doing as much harm as good. Like all decrees and doctrines, they need to be filtered by conscience and efficacy.

Take the 613 commandments listed in the Torah, the first five books of the Old Testament and collectively referred to as "the Law." Among these laws are do not marry outside your religion, create no artistic representations of God, "follow not the whims of your own heart," no tattoos, no blowing on dice, no talking to the dead, no working on Saturdays, no sex with menstruating women, and no rebelling against your parents or "trying" God's patience.

How about a show of hands: all those who've ever tried God's patience?

It's one thing to legislate theft and murder, but another to legislate "idolatry" or "blasphemy." For starters, these are, and always were, extremely relative terms. One person's blasphemy is another's religion. One person's abomination is another's love life. And of course the breaking of rules is at the very heart of the creative act itself, and of living creatively. It was only by breaking with tradition and coloring outside the lines that certain artistic, political, and social movements became *liberation* movements for people, and whole classes of people—the civil rights movement, gay rights movement, women's rights movement, anticolonialism, the scientific revolution, the Renaissance, impressionism, Beat poetry, gonzo journalism.

"I submit that an individual who breaks a law that conscience tells him is unjust," said Martin Luther King, "and who willingly accepts the penalty . . . in order to arouse the conscience of the community over its injustice, is in reality expressing the highest respect for law."

What he's saying is that there are *two* orders of law, a higher and a lower. Higher laws are those that uplift the human spirit. Lower laws are those that degrade it. And just because it's a law doesn't make it right, or uplifting. "A meteorite on a collision course with New York City might be obeying all the laws of the universe," said Mihaly Csikszentmihalyi in his book *Flow*, "but it would still be a damn nuisance."

And there are plenty of laws still on the books that are damn nuisances and are only there because no one has bothered to challenge or repeal them. For instance, in Alabama it's illegal to wear a fake mustache that causes laughter in church or to carry an ice cream cone in your back pocket. In Connecticut you're not permitted to walk across the street on your hands. In Arizona it's illegal to own more than two dildos. In Oklahoma it's a punishable offense to have a sleeping donkey in your bathtub after seven p.m. In Missouri you can't drive down the highway with an

uncaged bear in your car. In Iowa a kiss may last no more than five minutes. And in the appropriately named Normal, Oklahoma, there will be no
teasing dogs by making ugly faces.

A Matter of Life and Depth

One day in 1979, just shy of his thirtieth birthday, Jerry Wennstrom stood
looking out the window of his seventy-five-dollar-a-month loft in Nyack,
New York, across the Hudson River from Sing-Sing, the maximum-
security prison that gave us the expression "sent up the river," referring to
criminals sent up there from New York City.

It was early morning and he was watching a garbage truck pull away
from the curb in front of his building, in the belly of which, mashed
together with the crumpled soda cans and pizza boxes, was his entire life's
work as an artist—over one hundred large canvasses.

He was thinking to himself, "My God, what have I done?"

This sentiment was echoed a few days later when television filmmaker
Mark Sadan, whose crew had by then spent a year making a documentary
about Jerry's life and work, came by to visit. "What the hell have you
done?" he said. "Are you crazy? You blew it. What were you *thinking?*"

When Jerry told him, his reaction changed from incensed to inspired
and he decided to make it the postlude of his film.

At that point, Jerry was what some were calling a rising star in the
New York art scene, his subject matter the kind of images that populate
the nightmares of surrealists—the tempestuous faces of lunatics, demons,
and insane asylum patients; a macabre amalgam of the paintings of Hieronymus Bosch, the photographs of Diane Arbus, and the drawings of gonzo
artist Ralph Steadman. It was accomplished work, critics agreed, if not
exactly something you'd want to hang above your couch.

"I felt I could see the beauty, the divinity in those subjects," Jerry says,
"and even felt I could change the world somehow by painting them, that I
could get people to feel about these things what I felt about them, see
what I saw. Our tendency is to look away from the things that disturb us,
but I wanted to look at them. It was my attempt to penetrate beneath the
repulsive surface of things."

This, it turns out, would be preparation for his eventual decision to drop out of "the scene," with its sometimes misshapen values, in search of a more abiding vista—an apprenticeship for his role as one of those edge-walkers who dives beneath the surface of life to its depths and brings fist-fuls of silver back to the rest of us.

In a bit of foreshadowing, the famed Austrian actress and singer Lotte Lenya, who had helped him financially as a young artist, gave him a copy of a reading she did of Franz Kafka's *The Hunger Artist*, about a man whose art form is fasting (or as some see it, suffering)—starving himself for the entertainment of the masses. Kafka felt that hunger was analogous to spiritual yearning, and it was a central theme of his writing: "The anguish and perplexity of modern man in search of God." The question the story posed for Jerry was "How far would you go for the sake of your art?" But behind that was the question "How far would you go for the sake of the larger life in which your art is merely a puzzle piece?"

"I've always believed that the one thing you hold back from God is the one thing God is going to demand of you," says Jerry. "I could eat or not eat, have relationships or not have them, but the one thing I couldn't do, wouldn't do, was not paint. That was my identity. Everything in my life was about painting. If you got in the way of that, you were out. I would do *anything* to keep painting.

"But I also sensed that I was worshipping the *vehicle* to God rather than God. In this case, my art. And everything was telling me that I was larger than my art, that the journey was more than this. The art was becoming too small, and since art was everything to me, everything in my life started to feel dead.

"I sensed that there was a larger life and that I would have to live like a coward if I wasn't willing to put everything on the line for it, and I knew that to live creatively meant I had to do that. Wherever I gave in to fear, life got small, and wherever I went with the spiritual, life got larger."

It may be that many of us have, at certain junctures in our lives, entertained such thoughts. What would it mean to put everything on the line for our beliefs? What would happen if we got off the merry-go-round altogether, left it all behind, risked everything? What does "giving it all up to God" really mean? What would it be like to set our lives on a completely new course, guided by entirely different values and reference points, to make one of those radical changes that completely redefine who we are and how we go about life? Or as Jerry puts it, "decide how much faith and courage we're willing to give ourselves to, and then give ourselves to it."

For most of us these are idle musings, the kind of what-ifs we entertain when we're at wit's end or life hasn't lived up to its hype and we suspect we've been sold a monster bill of goods about what really matters. We're both fascinated and repulsed by the idea of giving it all up, quitting the game, refusing to buy into the System. Jerry, however, did it. He took that famous leap. He destroyed all his art, gave away everything he owned, dispersed all his money, and lived that way for the next fifteen years.

The tipping point was a public lecture he attended at a friend's urging, given by a spiritual teacher in New York City named Hilda Charlton, a former dancer who now held forth weekly at the Cathedral of Saint John the Divine. He sat in the far back, in his paint-spattered clothes, and at one point Charlton closed her eyes and began speaking of someone in the audience who was hiding behind a veil, with "a bright light ready to shine."

This, of course, could refer to almost any of us, but then she opened her eyes and looked directly at Jerry, bit a piece of candy in half, and tossed him the other half, commanding him to "Eat it!" Then she continued with her lecture. "It was clearly a challenge," he says. "She was a fiery, wild woman, like a witch, and it was almost like she was inviting me to meet her halfway to that wild place."

When the lecture was over, he walked out the back door of the church, around the corner, and suddenly stood face-to-face with a startling synchronicity: a wooden frame leaning against the side of the church, its painting cut out. In that moment he had an intuition that he would soon be letting go of his own art in some radical way, a process that started that night when he began fasting and stopped painting for a month, contemplating a choice, as he put it, between fear and God.

As a spiritual path, as worship, he felt that art had taken him as far as it could on the shoulders of sheer discipline and ambition. An old Hindu parable counsels that when you take a boat across the river and reach the other side, don't keep dragging the boat with you beyond that point.

That month ended with a classic dark-night-of-the-soul during which Jerry struggled with despair, indecision, and "an inspired new vision," and come morning he stood by his window watching garbagemen loading his life's work into the business end of a dump truck.

"There are pivotal moments in our lives," he says, "when we have the choice between life and death, between a living death or some radical change whose outcome . . . we have no idea. For me, this was a choiceless choice. I could not have done otherwise and survived in terms of my life force. I had been so driven, had done so much, and couldn't push it one bit more. I could have chosen cowardice, to stay in the safe place of the art scene, but it was no choice. It was death.

"I was very excited about this abstract and intuitive sense of something greater. It was irresistible, and acting on it, I knew, meant everything. Or nothing. Just that I was bringing the idea of the Holy Fool down from the chalkboard into real life, acting on the understanding that being open to life is more rewarding than trying to control it.

"I was completely ready for that moment, and completely terrified. Everything that looked and felt like life to me, however outrageous, was in making that leap. The only inspiration anymore was my life asking me to walk away from it all. And this was not about *dabbling* in inspiration. This was about all or nothing. You want a creative life? OK, then, do it with *all* of your life. Fear-based comfort can become deadly safe—the agent of a slow, sorrowful death—and to position your life so that nothing happens requires an enormous amount of attention.

"But I wouldn't have destroyed all my art, wouldn't have given away all my money and my possessions, if I didn't have a sense that I was going to be saved, that something intelligent was unfolding. Yogananda (Paramahansa Yogananda, Indian yogi and guru) once said that he didn't think Christ would have climbed up on that cross if he didn't know he was going to be saved. At some level, I sensed I was going to be saved, whatever that means. And I knew from the history of art and art movements that radical departures are part of entering new territory.

"And I'd read a lot about the lives of saints and great individuals, and radical departures were part of their stories too, though I kept thinking, 'Who the hell am I? I'm no saint.' But I knew the template, which was radical departure, with no more reference points, unless you consider Jesus and Buddha to be reference points. Ultimately I don't think there are any bushwhackers out there, because these people have already cut the way."

In addition to relinquishing his art, his loft, his money, his furniture, and his car—he kept an old hot plate and a few changes of clothes—he also made a retreat from language (for a year), sexual activity, and socializing. It was the kind of withdrawal that's a well-known motif in art and spiritual life, and which guarantees, as Jerry put it, that "everything comes up" and that "people just won't get it."

For years he ate only what supermarkets threw away, brought boxes of produce to poor families in the neighborhood, relied on the kindness of both strangers and friends, and moved around a lot.

Fasting, silence, and reading defined his life for many years thereafter, along with a lot of intuitive wandering and a lot of time at the dump. And the fact that he spent not a single night on the street in fifteen years was a testament to his ability to create genuine friendships, or simply the kind of goodwill—a spirit of generosity and a generosity of spirit—that translated to a roof over his head and at least a fairly regular meal.

"I ate when I had food and fasted when I didn't. I gave to people unconditionally and expected nothing in return. I'd made a conscious choice to leap into the void, so I didn't have the luxury of asking for sympathy when the journey became frightening.

"My work was to maintain a clear sense of direction in a state of complete dissolution. I maintained navigational clarity only by staying attentive to the creative, defining moments of grace as they presented themselves and pointed out the next step I was to take. It was terrifyingly simple. And whether you're releasing the world or receiving it, the task is exactly the same. How clear and well you communicate with your whispering God is all that really matters."

The experience reminded him of a passage in Annie Dillard's book *Holy the Firm*, in which she describes seeing a golden female moth fly into a candle, her wings igniting like tissue paper, her legs curling and blackening, her head crackling like gunfire. All that was left was the shell of her abdomen stuck upright in the wax, which became a wick. The wax rose through her thorax and widened into a saffron flame, by whose light Dillard read a book for two hours—about the poet Rimbaud frying his circuits in Paris—until she finally blew the moth out.

"I was just a shell with spirit flowing through it," says Jerry.

"I also knew at a cellular level that I had done the most important thing

I could ever have done, destroying my work and letting go of the life I knew. It was the single most important event of my life. And though the filmmakers were initially very upset, they were also very moved by the experience, and it was when they decided to have me tell the story that the film became about something archetypal and larger than just about 'art.'

"Death and rebirth is nice in theory, but it's a whole different story when it's *your* butt's on the line, and though 'death' still scares the hell out of me, what has stayed with me is the memory of how to do it. The gift has been the ability to do it over and over again, to live a truly creative life. Whatever the death is, you can turn it into life. That's the essence of my story." (And it's a story, ironically, about someone becoming more famous for *destroying* his art than he ever became for creating it.)

It's also the essence of what he calls his "usefulness" to others. By stepping over the edge into that terra incognito that would surely leave most of us behind, he's able to offer people trust in what could easily be perceived as only devastation and loss, if not foolishness. "Trust that when you're asked to let go of everything you think you are and all you think you possess, and if you can truly give yourself to this process—and you have to really mean it; you can't fake it—what will emerge will be a truer self in a truer world."

This is the kind of trust that the Spanish call *duende*—the authenticity and aliveness that come from the knowledge of death; the pain at the heart of all love songs, the understanding of evil at the core of goodness, Christ's crucifixion between two criminals. The dictionary defines *duende* as both a kind of goblin and a kind of charm or magnetism, and it reminds us not to refuse the struggle required to keep the soul on the path of truth.

"People often come to me to talk, sometimes people in million-dollar jobs whose friends are all telling them they're crazy to consider leaving it behind, but they say, 'I'm dyin' here,' and I'm someone who gets it and one of the few voices that will tell him or her it's okay to leave that situation."

His willingness to jump into insecurity in its most raw form has made him a role model for the taking of quantum leaps, the deaths that are rebirths, and those times in our lives when we're called to let go of whatever no longer works—success that feels empty, roles that no longer suit you or serve you, if they ever did, and a life path that's going in circles.

"However beautifully you can stand alone in what feels like death is how beautifully you can stand in the new life," he says.

For Jerry, that new life began when he moved from the East Coast to the West Coast in the late 1980s, from New York to Whidbey Island, near Seattle, where, for a change, people "got it." They understood what he had done, and why, and the cycle he'd set in motion in that walk-up flat in New York began to come around. "Like a tide, it goes out and everything goes out with it," he says, "then there's the slack tide, and then it begins to come back. Very naturally."

He began making art again after finding a stamped envelope on the sidewalk. The stamp was the head of some important personage, to which he attached a body, then an environment, then an entire scene—and so began the Return. He started doing public speaking, the filmmaker did another movie about him, and he was asked to write a book about his experience (*The Inspired Heart*). He now has a home, possessions, an art studio, land, and a car. And he got married.

His art has also gone from two-dimensional to three-, from painting to sculpture. In other words, he's added a whole new dimension—that of depth. He describes it as becoming "larger bodied." The sculptures are elaborate and interactive coffin-shaped mechanical marvels, part arcade machine, part crypt, part Russian nesting dolls. Coffin, as in the epitome of death and detachment, but hidden within are other realities, and the insides of each sculpture are whimsical, surprising, and full of life.

Ready, Fire, Aim

All you need is twenty seconds of insane courage,
and I promise you something great will come of it.

—BEN MEE (PLAYED BY MATT DAMON),
FROM THE MOVIE *WE BOUGHT A ZOO*

After being unceremoniously dumped by a girlfriend, Danny Wallace went into a slow spiral that became a lifestyle of staying in and avoiding the world. "Pottering about and tinkering with things, slouching, napping, channel hopping. And soon that was all I wanted to do. And so I became the man who could wriggle out of any prior engagement. Who could spot an invitation coming a mile away and head it off at the pass. The man who'd gladly swap a night down at the pub for just one whiff of an episode of *EastEnders*. The man who'd send an email instead of attend a birthday, text instead of call, and call instead of visit. I became the man who mastered the white lie. The man who always had an excuse. The man who always said no."

One day, while riding a double-decker bus in London, he sat next to a man who, in reply to hearing Danny's story about living in no-man's-land, simply said, "Say yes more."

"The people without passion," he'd said, "are the ones who always say no, but the happiest people are the ones who understand that good things occur when one *allows* them to."

And that was it. That one remark from a stranger on a bus was the philosophical bombshell that changed Danny's life and set him on the road to becoming a yes-man, and author of a book called *Yes Man*, the inspiration for a movie of the same name starring Jim Carrey. He made a commitment that night to say yes to everything and anything that came his way until the end of that year, three months away.

"I wanted to do *all* the things I'd missed out on. I wanted to turn the clock back and shout yes to all the things I'd mumbled no to. Not just the big nights or the main events or the frantic celebrations, but the little things. The normal things. The things that sometimes matter the most."

He writes, "I was angry at myself. I had wasted half a year. Half a year *gone*. Thrown away. Swapped for toast and evenings in front of the telly. It was all here—or, rather, it *wasn't*—in black and white. Every dull nonentry was a sharp slap in the face. . . .

"I would say yes more. Saying yes would get me out of this rut. It would rekindle my love for life. It would bring back the old me. The me that had died a little the day I'd been dumped. I just needed a little kick-start. A little fun. A chance to live in a completely different way. I could treat it like an experiment. A study in my own behavior. A study in positivity and opportunity and chance."

A study that immediately revealed its ramifications when he got a telemarketing call later that same evening from someone wanting to sell him double-paned windows, and the next morning a spam email asking if he'd like a bigger penis, and if so, "the new Penis Patch Technology now means that thousands of men just like you can . . ." Both of which he said yes to.

But he also said yes to spontaneous and unexpected travels, meetings with remarkable people, experiences that were marvelously out of his box, a new job opportunity, folks who shared his newfound enthusiasm for life, even new love and a winning lottery ticket. He learned the power of not just saying yes but also of the well-considered no, and that there are *yeses* that are really saying no to yourself—as when you say yes to something you really don't want—and *nos* that are really saying yes to yourself.

The willingness to say yes to risk and take *action* is vital to the passionate life because it keeps you on your growing edge, trying new things, taking initiative, and leaning into life rather than away from it. Where there's action, there's movement and energy, kinetic and catalytic force. And though movement isn't necessarily progress, it's still movement, and for anyone stuck in the doldrums, it offers at least a breeze.

At best it offers what's referred to as the flow state, in which you're so involved in an activity that nothing else seems to matter and all the troubling distractions of daily life and the usual discombobulations of mind— even, blessedly, your preoccupations with yourself—are swept aside by the sheer structuring of attention that the activity demands.

The best moments of our lives are not typically the passive but the active. Not the times when we're lounging on the beach with a good mystery novel, but the times when body and mind are stretched to the limit in an effort to accomplish something difficult and worthwhile. Not when the mountain comes to Muhammad, but when you strap on your climbing gear and head for the heights.

It's the moments you *make* happen—the ones that give you the feeling of participation in determining the course and content of your life—which bring you as close to what is meant by happiness as anything you can imagine in a universe not designed with human happiness in mind.

A huge part of courage is just accepting—no, *taking*—responsibility for your life, understanding that *you're* the mover and the shaker, the one who calls the shots. *You're* the place where the buck stops. No one is holding you back.

Certainly there are consequences in un-choosing the choices you've made in your career or partnerships or social life, or making the choices you've steadfastly refused to make. But those choices are yours to make or unmake, and you could do it *today*. You could give notice at your job today, could put a deposit on an apartment in the city and move out of your toxic marriage today, could start taking art lessons, begin a walkabout, buy a plane ticket to one of the far corners, today.

The essence of living an improvisational life, says Nina Wise—of not only going with the flow but also *creating* flow—is action. "We act in order to discover what comes next. For the improviser, it is ready, *fire*, aim. We begin before there's a plan. What we do moves us forward and gives us more information about how to proceed."

I remember my brother Marc once deciding on the destination for a vacation by spinning a globe beneath his finger and wherever it stopped was where he would take his vacation. Lucky for him he landed on British Columbia, and he went.

So try an experiment, says Wise. For a period of time, say yes to everything. Accept all offers. Affirm other people. Go along with the plan. Practice acting on your passions and desires in a moment here and a moment there. If you feel a yearning, let yourself act on it, just a little, and look at the feedback your life gives you. Follow what you want to do, where you want to go, who you want to be with, what your intuition tells you, what you need to say, what you *long* to say, what you're curious about, what *moves* you. Not as a five-year plan, but as a daily practice.

"And here's the password," says Wise. "It is *yes*! Yes starts the juices rolling. Yes expands your world. Those who say yes are rewarded by the adventures they have. Those who say no are rewarded by the safety they attain."

Saying no, she says, is a habit for many people, a lifelong unconscious tactic of blocking experience, maintaining position and status quo, minimizing intrusion and upset, and it's often disguised as an analytical, intellectual or academic perspective whose hallmark is skepticism, and whose ironic effect is to put a lid on inquiry and innovation.

Not long ago I became aware of a little naysaying habit of my own, and have been working to undo it. In the liminal zone between sleeping and awakening each morning, the slow stirring-up phase of my day during which I drift tidally between dreaming and consciousness—which I get to enjoy because I don't get woken up by an alarm clock (it helps to be self-employed)—some singular thought will usually come forth, solidify, and propel me out of bed. Often it's a thought about something I have to get done that day, an approaching deadline, sometimes an anxiety, an unpleasant sound outside, a disturbing dream image, or a rebuke for allowing myself to sleep late. In other words, a negative motivation.

Lately I've been experimenting with a new approach. Rather than allowing a negative or worrisome thought to be the first thing that goes through my mind when my feet hit the floor—thereby literally grounding myself, and my day, in that disposition—I've decided to wait until a more affirmative thought enters my mind before letting my feet hit the floor, and starting my day on that note. An upswing rather than a downer. It helps me rise as well as shine.

"Real change happens on the level of the gesture," says Cheryl Strayed in *Tiny Beautiful Things*. "It's one person doing one thing differently than he or she did before."

A FEW YEARS AGO, I shaved my mustache off, not realizing at the time that it was a kind of rehearsal for a more penetrating disclosure, if not exposure, that I was readying myself to make—writing again after a five-year moratorium. In retrospect, it reminded me of the time I signed onto a Class V whitewater rafting expedition in (unconscious) preparation for quitting a job I was terrified to quit—an adventure that had the effect of giving me a critical boost in courage.

On the morning of, I stood before the bathroom mirror, my hand trembling noticeably. After all, I'd had the mustache since high school, ever since I was *able* to grow facial hair, and didn't know what I'd find under there after all that time, whether I'd like it, and whether I'd feel like I was coming out of hiding with my hands up.

It came off in seconds, floating like ash into the sink, and I was struck by how little hair actually went into making what I always thought of as a rather substantial mustache. Not a Mark Twain mustache, not a handlebar mustache, not the kind I had to keep reined in the way I kept the lawn throttled back so it wouldn't turn jungly and overtake the flower beds. But a mustache that could still hit the floor and do push-ups.

I just didn't like the way it looked. Or rather, the way I looked without it. Though Robin claimed it improved matters in the kissing department, and seemed stirred up by the fact that it made me look like another man, she also described that suddenly exposed stretch of skin between mouth and nose as looking "surprised," and that it lent me a slightly "orangutan-like" look. A friend said it made me look Pennsylvania Dutch. A third raved. I went back and forth. Mostly back. Within a couple of weeks I'd regrown it.

During that time, though, I'd also come out from behind my writing hiatus—which actually felt more like a boycott, prompted as it was by burnout—and began writing again.

Large ships have large rudders, but attached to the large rudder is a smaller one called a trimtab, which is used to turn the big one, which then turns the ship. The application of a small amount of energy can have an effect disproportionate to its size. In fact, it seems to me the only goals with any power are the little ones that you can put on tomorrow's to-do list, because they're the only goals you can really get your hands on. The big ones are, in a sense, out of your control. There's nothing wrong with visioning, but you've probably heard the expression "The best way to make God laugh? Declare your five-year plan."

Or declare your mission statement. I attended a business conference in Mexico a few years ago, and sat in on a session presided over by a management consultant named Richard Whiteley, who told a story about asking a client of his, a CEO, whether he had a mission statement. The guy, being the CEO of a company, said, "Sure we do." When Richard asked him to recite it, however, the guy didn't have a clue. He shuffled around with the papers on his desk and finally said, "Oh, hell, I don't know. It's around here somewhere." He got on the intercom and said to his secretary, "Dorothy, would you bring in that vision thing for me."

Unclear on the concept. A mission statement is visceral, one sentence, easy to remember. Especially if you *care* to remember it. But most important, it isn't just "a vision thing" you slap up on a plaque in the lobby. It comes to life, becomes real, and means something more than just a high opinion you have of yourself, only in the choices you make day to day to day and sometimes hour by hour.

The small-steps approach to risk-taking will also give you a sense of accomplishment early in the game, a sense of *momentum* that will make you much more likely to keep going—rather than making all the goals and goodies long-term and all the problems and obstacles short-term. Anyone who's ever dieted probably knows this by heart. The ideal figure is always out there somewhere, but the chocolate chip cookies always seem to be right under your nose.

"It's like driving a car at night," the novelist E. L. Doctorow once said. "You can only see as far as your headlights. But you can make the whole journey that way."

I recently read the remarkable story of a young Canadian man, Kyle MacDonald, who traded a red paperclip for a house. He had bills to pay, a live-in girlfriend who was slowly losing patience with his status as perpetually between jobs, and the dream of making it up to her by buying her a house. So he put an ad on Craigslist to trade a red paper clip for something "bigger and better." And in fourteen trades over the course of a year, "each a key to adventure," as he put it, he actually managed to trade up from a paperclip to a house. It was an object lesson in the power of starting small—"where you are and one step," as a friend of mine used to say—and the understanding that ships don't come in; you build them and take them out.

His first trade was the paper clip for a pen shaped like a fish. His second trade was the fish pen for a doorknob. His third: the doorknob for a camping stove. Fourth: the camping stove for a portable generator. Subsequent trades included a snowmobile, a small moving van, a recording contract, a year's rent on an apartment in Phoenix, an afternoon with goth rocker Alice Cooper, a role in a movie produced by Corbin Bernsen of *L.A. Law* fame, and finally—the climax of a story in improbability and a willing disposition—a house. On Main Street in Kipling, Saskatchewan, with 1,100 square feet, two stories, one and a half bathrooms, and a new roof.

And along the way, millions of hits on his redpaperclip.com website and appearances on just about every major television and radio show in North America.

As for how you know when it's high time you started trading up and giving your passions their entrance cues, consider the following from Christine Kane, a folk singer and founder of a motivational company called Uplevel You: "You've said, 'At least I have benefits' more than once in the last month. You think to yourself, 'I need to just learn to surrender to this place and be present and grateful,' and a few seconds later, you think, 'Don't I?' You've used any of the following words or phrases when referring to yourself: 'Stuck.' 'Can't.' 'Shouldn't.' 'Should.' Or 'This is just how I am.' There are more than three empty Ben & Jerry's Cookie Dough Ice Cream containers in your trash this week. You're waiting to be discovered, rather than committing to discovering yourself, and you check your email regularly to see if you've been discovered yet. You think that 'getting out of your comfort zone' means getting out of bed in the morning."

Of course, by its very nature as a counterforce to inertia, passion will move you out of the comfort zone and into the rumble, which can scatter your well-mannered ducks and fill the air with loose feathers. The desire to live out loud will upset your inner couch potato. The hunger to travel will rock your worldview. The desire to connect more deeply with people will reveal the false intimacy of most of your social-media relationships. The urge to become an entrepreneur could cost you your regular paycheck.

A friend of mine recently had an opportunity to take her business to a whole new level by collaborating with a new partner, and on the morning of her initial meeting with him, she woke up puking. "A big fat upper limit," she said of it.

In other words, a self-sabotage, one of those mechanisms we've all devised—probably for security reasons and probably unconsciously—to flip the circuit breaker when we have too much juice running through the system, or we're too close to the proverbial flame, the one the moth goes around.

One of mine used to be blurting out some newfound enthusiasm to my most cynical family member. I might as well have just disemboweled myself on the spot, because what typically happened was that the cynic then did what cynics do: found all the problems, focused on all the obstacles, and asked all those devil's-advocate questions that tend to be a little heavy on the devil and a little light on the advocate. And I was always left feeling abandoned and betrayed when I probably should have known better, given that I was *raised* by that person.

At the very least you should know that when taking risks to share your passions with others, you need to start with the *easy* customers and work your way up to the tough ones, not the other way around. Unless your unconscious objective is to sabotage yourself, in which case it'll work just dandy.

Not that you even have to say a peep in order to sabotage yourself; the whole thing can be done in pantomime. Simply refusing to open a door for fear of closing another is a time-tested tactic. I met a woman at a conference in Denver last year who told me that she was one of those people who have a lot of passions, a lot of talents, could go in *so* many creative directions, but didn't know how to choose among them.

I had an intuition that her "embarrassment of riches" might have been a strategy of avoidance—playing jack-of-all-trades as a way to avoid becoming a master at any of them, playing dilettante and not putting her talents to the test by focusing her attentions. Mastery comes only with focus. Not that she has to gain mastery, and not that she has to be excellent or her pursuits are a waste of time. But I sensed her dissatisfaction with skating around on the surface, flitting among all these talents and not settling down to drink deeply the nectar of any one of them.

Sometimes, though, it isn't even action that brings on the shift we need, and the vitality attached to it, but simply the *decision* to take action: when it drops from your head to your gut, when there's one of those *felt* shifts, a sense of inevitability, a sense that it's no longer a matter of if, but when.

The political commentator and comedian Jon Stewart was interviewed on *60 Minutes* some years back, and at one point the interviewer, Dan Rather, asked what his big break was. Stewart's answer: when he made the *decision* that this was the life he was going to live.

The Enzyme of Our Passions

Warning: dates in calendar are closer than they appear.

—BUMPER STICKER

During a Callings retreat at Esalen a few years ago, the conversation came around to the subject of sacrifice. What we have to let go of in order to move forward with our lives and follow our passions. People talked about their fears around letting go of jobs, paychecks, their sense of identity, familiarities and securities of one sort or another, etc. And as a visual aid to this decisive discussion, I pulled a skeleton out of a closet—literally.

We were in the building named for Ida Rolf (as in the deep-tissue bodywork called Rolfing), and while setting up the room earlier in the day, I'd found, in the supply closet, one of the model skeletons used in body-work seminars. With the skeleton now standing next to me at the front of the room, I pointed out that eventually we're going to be called to sacrifice *everything*. Not just our paychecks and reputations and the lifestyles to which we'd become accustomed, but our very lives. Everything we hold dear, everything we've worked for, all our possessions, all our loved ones, our bodies, the world. We all owe God a death, Shakespeare said, so we owe it to ourselves to practice for the occasion whenever possible.

When I went to put the skeleton back in the closet, several people said, "Leave it here in the room for the rest of the retreat." Which we did.

All risk could be said to be an encounter with death—with the passage into the unknown and the prospect of loss, if not liberation. Risk is about our skirmishes with our own fragility and insecurity, and what more perfectly captures these states than death? But what more powerfully reminds us that we have a use-by date and the time to live is now? In an old *Peanuts* cartoon, Snoopy is conversing with a fruit fly, whose life span is only twenty-four hours, and who confides his one regret: "I wish I knew at nine o'clock what I know now."

Among *The 7 Habits of Highly Effective People*, by Stephen Covey, Habit 1 is "be proactive." Take responsibility for your own life; make it happen. Habit 2 is "Begin with the end in mind," by which he means having a clear sense of where you're going. And I don't think it's morbid, but life-giving, to keep the end in mind. The reality of death defeats us, but the idea of death liberates us. Also, by acknowledging the fears we have of aging, sickness, and death, we can regain the vitality we lose by repressing them, which takes a great deal of energy.

Our acceptance, even our welcoming, of vulnerability, of chaos as potential and boat-rocking as evolution, extends all the way up to the ultimate vulnerability and chaos, which is also the ultimate clarifier—and that is mortality. And I'm a big believer in the power of a regular mortality meditation to help clarify what's important and how to best use our precious time.

The transience of almost *anything* tends to increase our enjoyment of it. When you knew you had only fifteen minutes before you had to stop playing and come in for supper, it intensified your play. When you're on your last day of vacation, in those minutes before you turn around and head back to the hotel and it all becomes about return, you set your soul on wide-angle and really take it in. When you remember that your loved ones are all going to pass away, love strengthens.

The philosopher Martin Heidegger considered the contemplation of one's own death not morbid curiosity but an act of genuine courage, one that leads to a state of being that he almost ecstatically describes as "passionate anxious freedom." A state in which you strip yourself of any illusions of immortality, refuse to be tranquilized into witlessness about the fact of death, and are thus free to live your life to the fullest.

Or not. The knowledge of your own mortality is no guarantee that you'll suddenly begin seizing the day. Even those, myself included, who are keenly aware that someday there'll come a last call, still manage to squander plenty of precious moments and waste perfectly good days fretting about this or that, or just plain lose sight of what's important. We're thickheaded and habit is habit-forming. Even the most potent awakenings can easily doze back to sleep in the onslaught of day-to-day routine.

To say nothing of the complications that would ensue from living each day as if it were your last, a thought experiment that's useful for putting life into clearer focus but that would probably bog you down quickly were you to actually put it into practice. Think about it. What would you do if you knew you were going to die tomorrow, or even next week or a month from now? You'd almost certainly quit your job, or if you're self-employed, you'd certainly quit busting your entrepreneurial hump. You'd probably stop paying bills, reading books, going to movies, working out, cleaning the house, and fixing the leaks, and you'd probably never let your loved ones out of your sight, which would become tremendously annoying to them if *they* weren't going to die tomorrow and had errands to run.

Not that the understanding of your mortality shouldn't translate into action, otherwise nothing would change and you'd continue letting the days slip by absentmindedly and life would come and go before you knew what hit you. But perhaps you do the next best thing to actually living each day as if it were your last, by routinely asking yourself, regarding as many decisions and goals as possible, "What really matters to me? And does this activity take me toward it or away from it?"

Really, any encounter that offers you a look at the bigger picture and your place in it—mortality being but one of them—will help you, ironically, to focus. To remember that this is your time in the game and to make the most of it. The health of the eye demands a horizon, Emerson once said, and I think the same goes for the spirit. Something to counter nearsightedness. Something that makes us feel expansive and humble all at once.

That something could be, as Emerson meant it, the enormities of the natural world. Or it could be the immensifying study of history, geology, archaeology, anthropology, paleontology, mythology, cosmology, spirituality. And ideally *field* study, because the more tangible an experience of the big picture, the better. Turn fossils over in the palm of your hand. Stand on the platform of an observatory and look through a telescope at Saturn and its rings and understand that what you're looking at is *real*. Press your nose to the glass of a diorama at a natural history museum that shows heavy-browed hominids standing at the edge of a forest and staring out across grasslands that will one day be the skyline of a city shimmering in mathematical grandeur, though the stone ax is still a million years in the future. Stand before cliffs and see huge slabs of time at a glance—epochs, not calendar pages. Walk through the ruins of a city come and gone, or stroll down the aisles of vast libraries.

To be sure, these inquiries can be a bit like waving ammonia under your nose, because among the challenges of submitting yourself to the big picture is that the individual is more or less lost to sight. But once you get over the dismay of that revelation, it can be quite redemptive. In a commencement speech to the 1989 graduating class at Dartmouth College, the Russian poet Joseph Brodsky said, "The most valuable lesson of your life . . . is the lesson of your utter insignificance. . . . It puts your existence into its proper perspective. . . . The more you learn about your own size, the more humble and the more compassionate you become. . . . The more finite a thing is, the more it is charged with life, emotions, joys, fears, compassion. . . . Because it is the anticipation of that inanimate infinity that accounts for the intensity of human sentiments. . . . Passion is among the privileges of the insignificant. Passion, above all, is a remedy against boredom."

In John Gardner's book *Grendel*, the beast of Beowulf fame, lonesome and considering getting out of the monstering business, seeks counsel from a dragon, who says to him, "You improve them, my boy! Can't you see that yourself? You stimulate them! You make them think and scheme. You drive them to poetry, science, religion, all that makes them what they are for as long as they last. You are, so to speak, the brute existent by which they learn to define themselves. The exile, captivity, death they shrink from—the blunt facts of their mortality, their abandonment—that's what you make them recognize and embrace! You *are* mankind, or man's condition: inseparable as the mountain-climber and the mountain. If you withdraw, you'll instantly be replaced. . . . Stick with him! Scare him to glory!"

The kinds of glory that the blunt facts of mortality can provoke in us tend to fall into familiar categories, the core of which was captured by the painter Pierre Bonnard in his habit of waiting to paint picked flowers until they wilted a bit, because that way, he said, they had more *presence*. What mortality can teach us is a deeper gratitude for life, a keener appreciation for the beauties and pleasures of the world, a greater commitment to keeping our priorities in order, less time spent doing things we don't want to do, sweating the small stuff, and worrying about what other people think, and maybe most of all a deeper communion with the people we love.

At the end of *The Lord of the Rings* trilogy, Sam Gamgee, Frodo's faithful friend, gets married soon after returning to the Shire. Now that he'd been to Mordor and faced the terror of death, he was ready to take on the big guns: marriage. It's as if facing death were merely a novitiate to the great work of love. And in fact, in addition to purely anecdotal evidence of this, studies have demonstrated that there's a direct link between the two. One such study, out of Florida State University, showed that just being physically near a cemetery affects how willing people are to help a stranger. Those who walked through a cemetery were 40 percent more likely to help someone than those who walked only a block away. Their conclusion: the awareness of death can motivate increased expressions of compassion, tolerance, egalitarianism, empathy, and pacifism.

Enduring the *wilting* process, however, so that it helps us bring more presence, passion, and compassion to our experience of life, is demanding work, and I myself have been employed at it since my late twenties, when a switch flipped in my genetic command center and alerted my hair follicles to pump out an enzyme by the painfully appropriate name of reductase, which began pouring into the roots of my hairs, stunting their growth and shortening their life span. What were once thunderclouds are slowly and unavoidably becoming wisps of cirrus flitting irresolutely overhead.

My hair, which once guarded my scalp with a sunup-to-sundown guarantee, has become like a sunscreen that with each passing season loses another sun-protection factor. What started out as a total sunblock is now down to an SPF of roughly two, affording me barely an hour in the noonday sun before I'm persuaded to run for cover by the inarguable logic of sunburnt skin.

The hat I initially bought as a concession to this unfortunate turn of events looked like a fedora but felt more like a yarmulke, a sign of deference to a higher power. It was to hatwear what bifocals are to eyewear, and its purchase marked a rite of passage into that depilatory scourge known as middle age.

As my hairs fall in battle, there are simply fewer and fewer recruits to replace them, and I increasingly find myself picking up the bodies of the fallen from the sink and the shower drain—each a little reproach, each a small piece of threading. And in the pattern left by those hairs in the bathroom sink, like tea leaves before a fortune-teller, I begin to read the presentiments of my own demise and feel the special anguish that resides at the heart of youth and beauty: the certainty of their decline, the knowledge that they'll be carried off by time's hired muscle and go nowhere that I can follow.

My mother once told me that you can tell what you looked like ten years ago by lying on your back on a bed and looking up into a mirror, and what you'll look like ten years from now by lying over the edge of a bed and looking down into a mirror. (I mentioned this at a party once, and one of the middle-age women listening in said, "That's it. I'm never going to be on top again.") My version of this dispiriting little exercise takes place in the bathroom mirror. Tilting my head down, I look into the past; tilting it up, with the light streaming in from a window behind me, I see into the future, and it looks like a tire low on tread.

On bad days, I try to remind myself that what's really important is inner beauty not outer, or that having love in my life will console the failings of the flesh, or at least that I'm balding like Jack Nicholson, William Hurt, and Bruce Willis. I try to count the benefits of balding: I save on shampoo, my hair takes no time at all to dry, and eventually I'll have one less thing to obsess about.

The worst of it, though, is that if I hate losing my hair, then I'm going to hate looking at my own self in the mirror, hate myself for being human, and that is certainly not going to make it easier to grow old gracefully, which, like wearing a hat, one hopes to carry off with panache.

I begin to understand why those in the clergy so often shave their heads entirely—the better to get a grip on their priorities.

I suppose that as I age, I'll become more concerned with health than beauty, less concerned with what others think, and perhaps someday I'll even allow myself a good sniveling cry over the loss of my hair and what it portends. As with life, I've loved having it, have caressed it a hundred thousand times, and am now grieving over the loss of a relationship every bit as real as any I've had with a person, place, or thing. Then, after a proper lamentation, and with a tip of the hat to the Fates, I'll redouble my efforts to squeeze everything I possibly can out of life, and leave it the same way I entered it—naked, bald, and complete.

EARLY LAST SPRING a friend of mine, Philip, died of lung cancer after a six-month—well, I wouldn't exactly call it a battle, since he and his wife, Judith, are longtime dharma teachers in the tradition of Thich Nhat Hanh and were committed to not raging against the dying of the light but to going at it with the old nonattachment thing firmly in place. And in fact it was as beautiful and "conscious" a death as you could ask for. Full of love and grace and family and friends, and of course sorrow and grief and painkillers.

After he died, he lay "in state" for three days so that friends and family could come and view the body, and one late afternoon I went to say goodbye. Unexpectedly, I got to spend half an hour alone with him. And there it was: the one and only Death. Up close.

My first reaction on entering the room was a jolt, partly a visceral response to seeing a dead body in the course of an otherwise average day, and partly the shock of seeing Philip so gaunt-looking compared with his normally robust self. He'd lost a lot of weight in the six months since his diagnosis, and especially in the final eight days, during which he neither ate nor drank a drop. Otherwise, he just looked like he was sleeping, except that there was no rising and falling of the breath. And the room was cold, because Judith had opened the windows and placed his body on a bed of ice to keep the decomposition process at bay for those three days.

I spent much of that half hour touching him tenderly, mostly his face, which felt cold and a little rubbery, clearly missing the essential ingredient of life force—and Philip himself, who was so obviously Somewhere Else. And it was strange to touch someone so intimately and not have him respond, or feel it, or even open his eyes.

I was also vaguely aware that my very hands-on approach to my friend's death was partly to rectify a mistake I had made long ago when my grandfather died. He lay in an open casket at a mortuary and though I wanted very much to touch him, I refrained, thinking it inappropriate. Years later, I mentioned this to my mother and asked her if it would have been all right for me to have touched Papa. "Of course," she said. "He's *your* family. You grieve any way you want." Whereupon I burst into tears.

And though Philip was not family, he was friend and at this age friends are family, and the passing of a friend hits close enough to home that it becomes a mortality meditation, if you're so inclined. What struck me with this one is that what frightens us about death isn't so much the dying as the prospect of not *living* rightly. Not doing whatever you were meant to do or being who you were meant to be, in which case death becomes a constant threat, though not one you need look nervously over your shoulder to find, as if it's gaining on you. It's in *front* of you.

"Of all the footprints, that of the elephant is supreme," said Buddha. "Similarly, of all mindfulness meditations, that on death is supreme."

But a meditation on death may not be for everyone, and you might ask why anyone would want to go *looking* for such trouble when life is plenty rife with it as it is, full of good scares that bring mortality right up close to rub its bristly face against our own—the death of loved ones, the routine physical that goes bad, the test results that come back positive, a near miss, a close call.

But it's one thing to merely get two-by-foured, to pick yourself up and try to get back to "normal" as quickly as possible, and it's another to use these experiences as genuine wake-up calls, allowing them to truly reorient us. After all, a dead end is also a turnaround. Or as the musician Warren Zevon said on *The David Letterman Show* just before he died of cancer, "Enjoy every sandwich."

For mortality's payload of insight and perspective to be delivered, it's got to be a close encounter, either imaginal or physical, not just a casual look-see—a little rubbernecking at the scene of an accident, squirming your way through horror movies, skimming other people's obituaries. Death is something we know all about but don't really know at all. On one hand, we've heard it all before: life is short, here today gone tomorrow, ashes to ashes and dust to dust, out out brief candle, death and taxes, to be or not to be. On the other hand, many of us know it intellectually but not emotionally. It hasn't really penetrated to the level where it impacts behavior and decision making, and frankly, I think, the more in-your-face, the more impactful it will be, the more likely to sink in.

Still, whatever routes you take toward acclimatizing yourself to mortality, to *your* mortality—reflections on impermanence, time spent with the dying, contemplative strolls through the church graveyard, a building up of the skills of risk and loss, even what Buddhists call a decomposition meditation (which is exactly what it sounds like)—they require courage, time, and patience, a lot of deep breathing, and perhaps a strong stomach and the willingness to weep.

Same with this very simple death-awareness meditation, referred to as the Five Daily Recollections, brought to you by Buddha: "I am of the nature to grow old; I am of the nature to sicken; I am of the nature to die."

Same with visualizations like the following, from Larry Rosenberg's book *Living in the Light of Death: On the Art of Being Truly Alive*: Picture yourself on your deathbed. Imagine the person you love most in the world coming to your bedside, and imagine saying good-bye to that person *forever*.

Same with a simple breast self-exam.

Same with a contemplation of your own children, because, as Jerry Seinfeld once observed, "Make no mistake about why they're here. They're here to replace us."

Same with this graphic little exercise I ran across in a workshop: look in the mirror, hook two fingers into both sides of your mouth, and pull your lips out and to the sides as far as you can, exposing your teeth and gums—and then move your jaw side to side and up and down and look at your *skull*.

Same with an experience I had years ago while working for the Cincinnati paper: watching an autopsy—a word that means to look within. It was an experience that, contrary to what you might expect, helped me fall back in love with the miracle of my own body, and the miraculousness of life.

I was there compliments of a friend who worked at a county coroner's office and who counseled me to skip lunch that day and come on an empty stomach. But it turned out that nausea was the furthest thing from my mind, though I was mightily impressed that one of the young attendants was able to punctuate his postmortem work with frequent bites of a tuna fish sandwich.

Besides the sheer amazement of getting to peer inside the human body—a backstage pass of the highest order—what made the experience so compelling was the fact that the body in front of me was of my *own* species, not roadkill or bug spatter but one of my own. He was a long-distance trucker who had died sitting in the cab of his truck, and when I first saw him, he was rigor-mortised in a sitting position on the examining table, necessitating that the doctor cut the tendons on the insides of his elbows and knees to enable him to lie more or less flat.

The most vivid image I carry of this experience was after the man's ribs were spread open, when the doctor snipped the esophagus and lifted his internal organs out of his chest in one fell swoop, all the way down to his intestines—all the organs connected to one another—leaving his chest cavity empty like the hull of a boat.

For days afterward I became acutely aware of the most casual movements of my own body—the swallowing of food, the stretching of muscles, the vibration in my throat when I talked, the delicate rhythmic pulsing of a vein in my wrist or ankle, and I stared for long minutes at a time at the tendons in the back of my hands as I drummed them on tabletops and armrests. I have never looked at my body the same since then, nor taken it for granted the way I used to. The experience triggered a quantum leap in my sense of awe and gratitude for life.

This is exactly the revelation that Bonnie O'Brien Jonsson hopes to elicit in the participants of the Year to Live groups she facilitates in the San Francisco Bay Area. Bonnie is a health educator who teaches the

Mindfulness-Based Stress Reduction program at the Osher Center for Integrative Medicine at the University of California, San Francisco, and since 1998 has led over seventy of the yearlong classes, designed to gently and communally confront people with the reality, and the benedictions, of mortality, "to bring death up close so that we wake up and live!"

Waking up from trance was the reason she started the groups to begin with, she says. "I had been scared to death of death my whole life. I remember once going with my aunt to a cemetery and being terrified. I couldn't imagine people being underground and not being able to breathe. During a meditation retreat in which we focused on the breath, I realized that ever since I was a little kid, I often felt like I couldn't catch my breath. I had a kind of air hunger in which you can't get a full breath into your lungs. All my life I had a fear of drowning, of suffocating, and I was diagnosed with asthma later in life. But I know all this wasn't just physiological. It was all that grief getting stuck in my breath."

The grief she's referring to, which was instrumental to the genesis of the Y2L groups, stemmed from the defining ordeal of her childhood: the disappearance of her father during the Korean War. It was what bereavement counselors call "unresolved grief," and it haunts families like hers, who experience something like a feeling of suspended animation. "You always feel up in the air. You wonder, but you never know. You make up stories that maybe he's living in China and has another family and doesn't want to come home. But of course we never talked about death, or even about him, though an oil painting of him hung in the living room all those years, his eyes following me wherever I went."

He was officially listed as missing in action, and Bonnie describes "waiting for him all the years of my childhood." And adolescence. And adulthood. And it wasn't until she and her sister attended a POW/MIA meeting in 1998 that they finally learned what had happened to him—a very belated result of the Russian government, which had orchestrated the North Korean side of the war, coming forth with old records on the fates of missing soldiers. It turns out her father's plane had been shot down over North Korea in 1952, when Bonnie was two years old. They found scattered wreckage, a machine gun whose serial number matched the one on her father's plane, and they found a foot.

The meeting was attended by about one hundred, mostly daughters of

Korean War soldiers and widows of Vietnam War soldiers, and the grief that poured out was as if the soldiers had just died. Decades worth of unresolved grief suddenly came flooding to the surface, and through that experience, Bonnie says, "I really began to understand how people are affected by war. I saw how much my own life has been affected, and how that affects all the people I meet. I saw how that wound, that trauma, radiates out—multiplied by millions of people, by billions, really, as those wounds spread through the world and through time.

"When I was six and my sister was eight, we wrote letters to Daddy, asking him to come home, which we put on the top stair leading to the attic, because we figured that was the closest we could get it to heaven. When the letters disappeared, we figured he must have received them, but we soon found out that my mother had hidden them in her jewelry box without saying anything to us about them, and we understood that this had probably hurt our mother. When she died many years later, she had with her a folder called Important Papers, and those letters were in the folder."

At the end of her first Y2L group, which was attended by a dozen women, Bonnie wrote an article about the experience for the *Marin Independent Journal* and then headed off on a trip to India, a place she wanted to visit before she died. Bodgaya, specifically, where Buddha was enlightened, which is considered the great pilgrimage for students of Buddhism, as Rome was for Christian pilgrims and Mecca is for Muslims.

"India has a much more in-your-face relationship with death than we do. It's much more integrated into daily life and more out in the open, as is their spirituality. It's all woven together. Death, life, peeing, pooping, animals, garbage, colors, smells, sounds, sights. I've never felt so alive as I did in India."

The newspaper article appeared the day she returned, and she received *hundreds* of phone calls. She started six Y2L groups, $650 per person, groups of eight, the age range from twenty-four to ninety. There are twelve meetings, three hours each, and one full day at the end of the year. There's only a 10 percent attrition rate.

"I make it clear upfront, though, that this isn't a death-and-dying group. It's a *living* group. It's about waking up and living. Most of those who attend want to be more engaged in life, more fully alive, to look at what's most important to them in life. I also remind people that we're letting death be a guide, but without calling death to us. It's a practice and a process, but not a self-fulfilling prophecy."

Still, they keep their primary focus on the one-year (you'll pardon the expression) deadline, using it to continually clarify their intentions. If group members talk about making plans for a year down the road, Bonnie reminds them that there won't be a next year, that the purpose is to live as if this were their last year.

The most moving phases of the yearlong process, she says, are the first meeting—when people first open up to the conversation, share stories about why they're there, and share their wishes for their own lives, which they may not have even acknowledged to themselves up to that point—and the last meeting. At that final day, the group meets for eight hours, beginning with a guided meditation on dying, a full life review, the making of a death mask, and the sharing of a last supper together, featuring their favorite foods.

They end up at the beach, where they spend several hours just observing the world and recognizing that it will go on without them, that Earth will continue to spin, that the universe in which Earth is a grain of sand and each of them a grain of sand within that, will continue to expand for billions of years, without them in it.

Each person is then given a hunk of clay to make into something symbolic of his or her life, and afterward they form a circle on the sand and they each talk about their life, about the clay figure and what it means, and then they either bury it, put it in the ocean, or leave it to the elements. It's a symbolic letting go of the body, Bonnie says, of the primal clay out of which the gods of many religions are said to have made us.

Each person then says good-bye to the others, one at a time, telling each what they've meant to them, and in silence they all return to the meeting place for two final exercises: a rebirth meditation and the sharing of the deepest intentions each of them has for however many years they have left.

In between the first and last meetings, Bonnie says, they also have numerous field trips—they read their eulogies in a cemetery, visit a cremation chamber, go to a funeral parlor—and of course have numerous life changes. People have gotten married, quit their jobs, started new businesses, moved from one coast to the other, and gotten divorced. Bonnie herself was diagnosed with breast cancer a couple of years ago, and went through her surgery, chemo, radiation, the whole bit, with the people in her groups. She's also no longer daunted by the prospect of teaching. "Before doing the groups, I was afraid to teach. I'm not anymore."

The most consistent benefit of the year seems to be acceptance, she says. "Accepting yourself, the life you've lived, the things you can't accept, and accepting that you can't accept them and bearing with it anyway. It's not about self-improvement but self-acceptance. Another common experience of the groups is a sense of deep gratitude for life. That we're alive at all.

"Afterward, people typically find that they experience less bickering and contentiousness with people, that many of their reasons to be annoyed are reduced, and their relationships either improve or end. When you're feeling deeply alive, there just doesn't seem to be the same block between you and others; there's a brightness to life, to looking at the world. And in that light, people see the deepest, purest intentions for their lives emerge."

ONE OF MY OWN most important mortality meditations is ruin wandering, and as I've learned repeatedly in the course of that most literal "pasttime," all empires—personal, civic, and mythic—eventually come tumbling down. Rose Macauley ends her marvelous book *The Pleasure of Ruins* by stating their primary counsel: "There is no security, which is what we always knew."

We've known it from the moment we came squalling into the world with a mammal's brain evolved just enough to awaken in us the knowledge of our own death, which is denied nearly every other creature, though death may not be what frightens us most but insignificance, the fear that we'll die without leaving a mark on the world, or even so much as a pile of picturesque rubble—and though we're no less wise for fearing death. Even spiritual masters choke back tears in the face of it. "Confucius wept," writes Annie Dillard. "Confucius, when he understood that he would soon die, wept."

This is actually part of the appeal of ruins, part of their emotional impact, and what makes them such profound mortality meditations. Here are the remains of a life once lived, a city once lived in, which sends through us a shudder at how ambition is wrecked by time, and the certainty that we, too, will be overtaken before our projects are finished. And here is the standard-issue revelation on ruins, and the main tent pole of wisdom: all things come to an end. It's a fact we roll around in our mouths like hot food, waiting till it cools enough for us to swallow.

And it fills us, as it did the Arabs, with an awe that's equal parts terror and amazement, suffering and passion, saddening us and spurring us to live all at once, to take our chances while we have the chance. It's a somewhat self-abnegating fascination with the passage of time; a bit like wanting to know the future. We want to see it but we don't. It's a pain/pleasure thing. A love/hate thing.

And fittingly. The Greek god of wonder, Thaumas, was the father of utterly paradoxical daughters: the rainbow and the Harpies, those demons of the whirlwind, snatchers and grabbers of people, who were themselves bifurcated, half human and half bird, and tormented by insatiable hunger. Maybe we're hungry for the tangled wisdom inherent in mortality, the reminder that we're "fearfully and wonderfully made," as the Psalmist tells us.

And maybe, like the future, it's death's unattainability that provokes our passion. It's something that's not attainable in life, and its very out-of-reachness incites the mind and the soul.

At the National Electric Exhibition in New York City in 1896, men and women stood in line for hours to see a new wonder, the "fluoroscope," or X-ray machine, just to get a glimpse at the bones inside their hands, which are not just a marvel but also a revelation. There it is, right below the surface—the skeleton. Horrible and divine. Fearfully and wonderfully made. Ruins of a very personal nature.

There is death, the source of meaning, the enzyme of our drives and passions, the brute existential fact that gives urgency to love and work and what the poet Philip Larkin calls the "million-petaled flower of being here."

There is the rationale behind the ancient Egyptian custom of bringing the skeleton of a dead man to feasts and festivities—to serve the guests as a reminder of their condition, how short-lived—and the ancient Roman tradition of parading victorious military heroes through the streets on chariots pulled by white horses, but accompanied by a slave holding a laurel wreath above their heads and continuously whispering in their ears, "Memento mori." Remember, thou art mortal.

There are the terms of our agreement with nature, whose agent will one day come around to collect. There the river that both buoys us and carries us off. And though death is a deep mystification to most people, the ultimate conjunction of awe and terror, it's really not the slightest bit unusual, perfectly mundane and perfectly safe. Humans have done it a hundred billion times already, that being roughly the number of people who've ever lived, the dead outnumbering the living 15 to 1. On the day we each die, 150,000 others will go with us.

Perhaps this is no consolation, though perhaps you could take some of the sting out of it—and tingle your spine in the process—by considering death in the context of deep time. The British scientist Richard Dawkins suggests an imaginative exercise:

Spread your arms wide. The tip of your left hand marks the beginning of evolution and the tip of your right hand marks today. The span from the tip of your left hand all the way to your right shoulder brings forth nothing more than bacteria. The first invertebrates make their entrance near your right elbow. The dinosaurs appear in the middle of your right palm, and die out near your outermost finger joint. *Homo erectus* and *Homo sapiens* appear at the white part of your fingernails. And all of recorded human history—the Cro-Magnon caves of Europe, the neolithic Fertile Crescent, the god kings of Assyria and Mesoamerica, all the spreading trade routes and codified laws and languages of the world, the rise of nation-states and the fall of the Roman Empire, right up to the Rolling Stones and reality TV—all of it would be erased by the single stroke of a nail file.

This is certainly sobering and highlights our relative position in the scheme of things, but it also reminds us that we're part of something vastly greater than ourselves, an endlessly unrolling tapestry of history that preceded us by billions of years and will proceed without us for billions more, but that includes us.

It reminds us that we're of the same stock that went from caves to cosmic travel in the geological bat of an eye, the same lineage that built the aqueducts of Rome and the pyramids of Giza, painted the caves at Lascaux and wrote the *Odyssey* and the *Mahabharata*, and spun the World Wide Web. We are, each of us, the descendants of all the world's Adams and Eves, the founding fathers and mothers, related to them all. We're always at the throne.

The contemplation of the awe-full fact of death is a reminder of the awesome fact of life, and that it's astonishing *any* of us are here, given the utter billion-to-one implausibility of our turning up at all out of the wild farrago of fire and brimstone and inorganic elements that preceded our entrance onto the scene, and to which we bring an understandable jumble of bewilderment and bedazzlement.

The astronomer Fred Hoyle once said that the probability that life would appear on Earth is roughly equivalent to the chance that a hurricane sweeping through a scrapyard would manage to assemble a Boeing 747 in its wake. But whether life came about through accident or intention, through natural selection or God, whether we believe every atom in the universe is saturated with infinity or divinity or lime-green Jell-O, it doesn't diminish the fact that it's amazing any of it is here. And equally amazing that each of us is connected to the passionate force that put it all here. That the same power which fills the east with light every morning also puts the gleam in our own eyes. We're the wake of the hurricane, the living buckshot from the big bang.

Gratitudes

This book has been blessed with the passionate and compassionate touch of a lot of people, and for each of them I'm exceedingly grateful:

Joel Fotinos, Gabrielle Moss, and Maureen Klier at Tarcher/Penguin, for so expertly shepherding this book into the world.

My agent Ned Leavitt, for both supporting me and challenging me, and sometimes helping me get a grip.

Those friends, family, and colleagues who so generously read and offered feedback on early chapters of the book, helping shape my thinking around it: Robin Samuel Sierra, Elizabeth and Richard Garzarelli, Kathleen Osta, Sylvia Haskvitz, Tim Lewis, Robert Gerzon, Leslie Cancilla, Ernest Izard, Deben Tobias, Bill Kauth, Bill Jamieson Jr., and the inimitable Ross Levoy.

The people who very openly shared with me their stories of passion lost and found, and helped the rubber meet the road.

The editors of magazines and newspapers that originally published portions of the book: *New York Times Magazine, Psychology Today, Longevity Magazine, Christian Science Monitor,* and the *San Francisco Chronicle.*

Paula Hanke, for your exuberant love and being my fellow adventurer.

Pripo Teplitsky, for your beloved friendship and great good laughter.

My father, Barton Levoy, for giving me the gift of wonder.

And, finally, my mother, Phyllis Chesler, for being a consummate role model in living a passionate life.

Bibliography

Abram, David. *The Spell of the Sensuous: Perception and Language in a More-Than-Human World*. Vintage, 1997.

Abrahamson, Eric, and David Freedman. *A Perfect Mess: The Hidden Benefits of Disorder*. Little, Brown & Co., 2006.

Absher, Tom. *Men and the Goddess: Feminine Archetypes in Western Literature*. Park Street Press, 1991.

Ackerman, Diane. *Cultivating Delight: A Natural History of My Garden*. HarperCollins, 2001.

———. *A Natural History of Love*. Vintage Books, 1994.

Adams, Cass, ed. *The Soul Unearthed: Celebrating Wildness and Spiritual Renewal Through Nature*. Sentient Publications, 2002.

Amato, Joseph. *Dust: A History of the Small and the Invisible*. University of California Press, 2000.

Anderson, Rob, Kenneth Cissna, and Ronald Arnett, eds. *The Reach of Dialogue: Confirmation, Voice and Community*. Hampton Press, 1994.

Apter, Michael. *The Dangerous Edge: The Psychology of Excitement*. Free Press, 1992.

Aurandt, Paul. *Destiny: From Paul Harvey's The Rest of the Story*. Bantam Books, 1984.

Ball, John, and Jill Jonnes. *Fame at Last: Who Was Who According to the "New York Times" Obituaries*. Andrews McMell Publishing, 2000.

Barnes, Julian. *Flaubert's Parrot*. Alfred A. Knopf, 1985.

———. *The Lemon Table*. Alfred A. Knopf. 2004.

———. *Love, Etc*. Alfred A. Knopf, 2001.

———. *Nothing to Be Frightened Of*. Alfred A. Knopf, 2008.

———. *The Sense of an Ending*. Alfred A. Knopf, 2011.

Barron, Frank, ed. *Creators on Creating: Awakening and Cultivating the Imaginative Mind*. Tarcher/Putnam, 1997.

Barthes, Roland. *A Lover's Discourse: Fragments*. Hill and Wang, 1977.

Bauman, Richard, and Joel Sherzer, eds. *Explorations in the Ethnography of Speaking*. Cambridge University Press, 1989.

Bauman, Zygmunt. *Liquid Love: On the Frailty of Human Bonds*. Polity Press, 2003.

Becker, Ernest. *The Denial of Death*. Free Press, 1997.

Bellah, Robert. *Habits of the Heart: Individualism and Commitment in American Life*. Harper Perennial, 1985.

Bellow, Saul. *Henderson the Rain King*. Penguin, 1958.

Benford, Gregory. *Deep Time: How Humanity Communicates Across Millennia*. Bard, 2001.

Bennett, Jane. *The Enchantment of Modern Life: Attachments, Crossings, and Ethics*. Princeton University Press, 2001.

———. *Thoreau's Nature: Ethics, Politics, and the Wild*. Sage Publications, 1994.

Benson, Arthur Christopher. *Escape and Other Essays*. University of California Libraries, 1915.

Berman, Laura. *The Passion Prescription: Ten Weeks to Your Best Sex—Ever!* Hyperion, 2005.

Berman, Morris. *Wandering God: A Study in Nomadic Spirituality*. State University of New York Press, 2000.

Bernard, Andre. *Rotten Rejections: A Literary Companion*. Pushcart Press, 1990.

Berns, Gregory. *Satisfaction: The Science of Finding True Fulfillment*. Henry Holt & Co., 2010.

Bernstein, Peter. *Against the Gods: The Remarkable Story of Risk*. John Wiley & Sons, 1996.

Biswas-Diener, Robert. *The Courage Quotient: How Science Can Make You Braver*. Jossey-Bass, 2012.

Blanton, Brad. *Radical Honesty: How to Transform Your Life by Telling the Truth*. Sparrowhawk Publications, 2005.

Bloland, Sue Erickson. *In the Shadow of Fame: A Memoir by the Daughter of Erik Erickson*. Viking, 2005.

Bloom, Charlie, and Linda Bloom. *Secrets of Great Marriages: Real Truth from Real Couples About Lasting Love*. New World Library, 2010.

Bodanis, David. *The Secret House: The Extraordinary Science of an Ordinary Day*. Berkley Trade, 2003.

Bohm, David. *On Dialogue*. Routledge, 2004.

Borges, Jorge Luis. *Labyrinths*. New Directions, 2007.

Bradshaw, John. *Healing the Shame That Binds You*. Health Communications, 1988.

Bratton, Susan Power. *Christianity, Wilderness, and Wildlife: The Original Desert Solitaire*. University of Scranton Press, 1993.

Braudy, Leo. *The Frenzy of Renown: Fame and Its History*. Vintage, 1997.

Breton, Denise, and Christopher Largent. *The Paradigm Conspiracy: Why Our Social Systems Violate Human Potential—And How We Can Change Them*. Hazelden, 1998.

Briggs, John. *Fire in the Crucible: The Self-Creation of Creativity and Genius*. Jeremy Tarcher, 1990.

Brown, Brené. *Daring Greatly: How the Courage to Be Vulnerable Transforms the Way We Live, Love, Parent, and Lead*. Gotham Books, 2012.

Brown, Kurt, ed. *The Measured Word: On Poetry and Science*. University of Georgia Press, 2001.

Brown, Tom. *The Tracker*. Berkley Books, 1986.

Bryson, Bill. *A Short History of Nearly Everything*. Broadway Books, 2004.

Buber, Martin. *I and Thou*. Touchstone, 1971.

Burchard, Brendon. *The Charge: Activating the 10 Human Drives That Make You Feel Alive*. Free Press, 2012.

Burke, Peter. *The Art of Conversation*. Cornell University Press, 1993.

Capacchione, Lucia. *The Art of Emotional Healing*. Shambhala, 2006.

Carol, Shawna. *The Way of Song: A Guide to Freeing the Voice and Sounding the Spirit*. St. Martin's Press, 2003.

Carotenuto, Aldo. *Eros and Pathos: Shades of Love and Suffering*. Inner City Books, 1989.

Carse, James P. *Breakfast at the Victory: The Mysticism of Ordinary Experience*. HarperOne, 1995.

Carson, Anne. *Eros the Bittersweet*. Princeton University Press, 1986.

Carson, Rachel. *The Sense of Wonder*. Harper, 1998.

Chabon, Michael. *Gentlemen of the Road*. Del Ray, 2008.

Chatwin, Bruce. *Anatomy of Restlessness: Selected Writings 1969–1989*. Penguin, 1997.

———. *The Songlines*. Penguin, 1988.

Chaucer, Geoffrey. *The House of Fame*. PIMS, 2013.

Child, Craig. *The Animal Dialogues: Uncommon Encounters in the Wild*. Little, Brown & Co., 2007.

Chopin, Kate. *The Awakening*. Prometheus Books, 1996.

Cohen, Stanley, and Laurie Taylor. *Escape Attempts: The Theory and Practice of Resistance in Everyday Life*. Penguin, 1976.

Coles, Robert. *The Call of Service: A Witness to Idealism*. Mariner Books, 1994.

Collins, Billy. *Ballistics*. Random House, 2008.

———. *Horoscopes for the Dead*. Random House, 2011.

———. *Sailing Alone Around the Room*. Random House, 2001.

———. *The Trouble with Poetry*. Random House, 2005.

Connolly, Cyril. *The Unquiet Grave: A Word Cycle by Palinurus*. Viking Press, 1945.

Connor, Janet. *Writing Down Your Soul: How to Activate and Listen to the Extraordinary Voice Within*. Conari Press, 2008.

Cook, Charles. *Awakening to Nature: Renewing Your Life by Connecting with the Natural World*. Contemporary Books, 2001.

Cotlow, Lewis. *In Search of the Primitive*. Little, Brown & Co., 1942.

Coville, Bruce, ed. *Half-Human*. Scholastic Press, 2001.

Cowen, Tyler. *What Price Fame?* Harvard University Press, 2002.

Csikszentmihalyi, Mihaly. *Flow: The Psychology of Optimal Experience*. Harper & Row, 1990.

Cumes, David. *Inner Passages, Outer Journeys: Wilderness, Healing, and the Discovery of the Self*. Alfred A. Knopf, 1999.

D'Agata, John. *Halls of Fame: Essays*. Graywolf Press, 2003.

Dalai Lama. *Art of Happiness: A Handbook for Living*. Riverhead Books, 2009.

Davidson, Sara. *Leap: What Will We Do with the Rest of Our Lives*. Random House, 2007.

Dawkins, Richard. *Unweaving the Rainbow: Science, Delusion and the Appetite for Wonder*. Mariner Books, 2000.

de Botton, Alain. *The Art of Travel*. Vintage International, 2002.

———. *On Love: A Novel*. Grove Press, 2006.

Degler, Teri. *The Divine Feminine Fire: Creativity and Your Yearning to Express Your Self*. Dreamriver Press, 2009.

DeGraaf, John, David Wann, and Thomas Naylor. *Affluenza: How Overconsumption Is Killing Us—and How to Fight Back*. Berrett-Koehler, 2005.

Dennis, Carl. *Callings*. Penguin, 2010.

———. *New and Selected Poems*. Penguin, 2004.

Derber, Charles. *The Pursuit of Attention: Power and Ego in Everyday Life*. Oxford University Press, 2000.

De Waal, Frans. *Our Inner Ape: A Leading Primatologist Explains Why We Are Who We Are*. Riverhead Books, 2005.

Dillard, Annie. *For the Time Being*. Alfred A. Knopf, 1999.

———. *Pilgrim at Tinker Creek*. Harper, 2007.

Dispenza, Joseph. *The Way of the Traveler: Making Every Trip a Journey of Self-Discovery*. John Muir Publications, 1999.

Dodes, Lance. *The Heart of Addiction: A New Approach to Understanding and Managing Alcoholism and Other Addictive Behaviors*. William Morrow, 2002.

Dubos, Rene. *A God Within*. Macmillan, 1973.

Ducornet, Rikki. *The Monstrous and the Marvelous*. City Lights Publishers, 2001.

———. *The Word "Desire."* Dalkey Archive Press, 2013.

Dunn, Stephen. *Different Hours*. W. W. Norton, 2002.

———. *Landscape at the End of the Century*. W. W. Norton, 1991.

Dyja, Thomas, ed. *Awake: Stories of Life-Changing Epiphanies*. Marlowe & Co., 2001.

Eberhart, Mark. *Why Things Break: Understanding the World by the Way It Comes Apart*. Broadway Books, 2004.

Eckermann, Johann Peter. *Conversations of Goethe*. De Capo Press, 1998.

Edgerton, Robert. *Sick Societies: Challenging the Myth of Primitive Harmony*. Free Press, 1992.

Eggers, Dave. *How We Are Hungry*. McSweeney's Books, 2003.

Ehrenreich, Barbara. *Blood Rites: Origins and History of the Passions of War*. Holt Paperbacks, 1998.

———. *Dancing in the Streets: A History of Collective Joy*. Henry Holt & Co., 2006.

Eigen, Michael. *Psychic Deadness*. Jason Aronson, 1996.

Eiseley, Loren. *All the Strange Hours: The Excavation of a Life*. Bison Books, 2000.

———. *The Firmament of Time*. Bison Books, 1999.

———. *The Immense Journey: An Imaginative Naturalist Explores the Mysteries of Man and Nature*. Vintage, 1959.

———. *The Invisible Pyramid*. Bison Books, 1998.

———. *The Lost Notebooks*. University of Nebraska Press, 2002.

———. *The Night Country*. Bison Books, 1997.

———. *The Unexpected Universe*. Mariner Books, 1972.

Englander, Nathan. *For the Relief of Unbearable Urges*. Alfred A. Knopf, 1999.

Enright, D. J. *The Oxford Book of Death*. Oxford University Press, 1983.

Epstein, Mark. *Open to Desire: The Truth About What the Buddha Taught*. Gotham Books, 2005.

Erlich, Gretel. *Islands, the Universe, Home*. Penguin, 1992.

———. *John Muir: Nature's Visionary*. National Geographic Society, 2000.

Ewans, Andrew, and Glenn D. Wilson. *Fame: The Psychology of Stardom*. Vision, 2001.

Farley, Wendy. *The Wounding and Healing of Desire: Weaving Heaven and Earth*. Westminster John Knox Press, 2005.

Ferber, Michael. *Romanticism: A Very Short Introduction*. Oxford University Press, 2010.

Ferris, Timothy. *The Mind's Sky: Human Intelligence in a Cosmic Context*. Bantam Books, 2009.

Feynman, Richard. *Surely You're Joking, Mr. Feynman!: Adventures of a Curious Character*. W. W. Norton, 1997.

Fields, Jonathan. *Uncertainty: Turning Fear and Doubt into Fuel for Brilliance*. Portfolio/Penguin, 2011.

Fisher, Helen. *Why We Love: The Nature and Chemistry of Romantic Love*. Henry Holt & Co., 2004.

Fisher, Philip. *Wonder, the Rainbow, and the Aesthetics of Rare Experiences*. Harvard University Press, 1998.

Ford, Richard. *The Lay of the Land*. Alfred A. Knopf, 2006.

Franzen, Jonathan. *The Corrections*. Picador, 2002.

———. *How to Be Alone: Essays*. Picador, 2003.

Frazier, James. *The Golden Bough: A Study of Magic and Religion*. Oxford University Press, 2009.

Freedman, Marc. *Encore: Finding Work That Matters in the Second Half of Life*. PublicAffairs, 2007.

Freeman, Lynn. *Express Yourself: Discover Your Inner Truth, Creative Self, and the Courage to Let It Out*. SoundStar Productions, 1999.

Freud, Sigmund. *Civilization and Its Discontents*. W. W. Norton, 2010.

———. *The Future of an Illusion*. W. W. Norton, 1989.

Frey, William. *Crying: The Mystery of Tears*. Winston Press, 1985.

Fried, Robert L. *The Passionate Learner: How Teachers and Parents Can Help Children Reclaim the Joy of Discovery*. Beacon Press, 2001.

———. *The Passionate Teacher: A Practical Guide*. Beacon Press, 1995.

Friend, Tim. *Animal Talk: Breaking the Codes of Animal Language*. Atria Books, 2005.

Fromm, Erich. *The Art of Loving*. Harper & Row, 1956.

Gaiman, Neil. *American Gods*. HarperCollins, 2002.

———. *Anansi Boys*. William Morrow, 2005.

Gallagher, Winifred. *New: Understanding Our Need for Novelty and Change*. Penguin, 2012.

Gamson, Joshua. *Claims to Fame: Celebrity in Contemporary America*. University of California Press, 1994.

Gardner, Dan. *Risk: The Science and Politics of Fear*. Virgin Books, 2009.

Gardner, John. *Grendel*. Vintage, 1989.

Garreau, Joel. *Radical Evolution: The Promise and Peril of Enhancing Our Minds, Our Bodies—and What It Means to Be Human*. Broadway Books, 2006.

Gaylin, Willard, and Ethel Person, eds. *Passionate Attachments: Thinking About Love*. Free Press, 1988.

Genova, Lisa. *Still Alice*. Pocket Books, 2007.

Germain, Gilbert. *A Discourse on Disenchantment: Reflections on Politics and Technology*. State University of New York Press, 1993.

Gilbert, Daniel. *Stumbling on Happiness*. Vintage, 2005.

Gilbert, Elizabeth. *Committed: A Love Story*. Viking Press, 2010.

Gill, Libby. *You Unstuck: Mastering the New Rules of Risk-Taking in Work and Life*. Solas House, 2009.

Gillette, Douglas. *Primal Love: Reclaiming Our Instincts for Lasting Passion*. St. Martin's Press, 1995.

Gilligan, Carol. *The Birth of Pleasure*. Alfred A. Knopf, 2002.

Glendinning, Chellis. *My Name Is Chellis and I'm in Recovery from Western Civilization*. Shambhala, 1994.

Goldbart, Stephen, and David Wallin. *Mapping the Terrain of the Heart: Passion, Tenderness, and the Capacity to Love*. Addison-Wesley, 1994.

Goldbarth, Albert. *Budget Travel Through Space and Time: Poems*. Graywolf Press, 2005.

———. *Dark Waves and Light Matter: Essays*. University of Georgia Press, 1999.

———. *Great Topics of the World*. David Godine Publisher, 1995.

———. *Griffin*. Essay Press, 2007.

———. *Pieces of Payne: A Novel*. Graywolf Press, 2003.

———. *Saving Lives: Poems*. Ohio University Press, 2001.

———. *Sympathy of Souls*. Coffee House Press, 1990.

Goleman, Daniel. *Emotional Intelligence: Why It Can Matter More than IQ*. Bantam Books, 1995.

Goode, William. *The Celebration of Heroes: Prestige as a Control System*. University of California Press, 1979.

Gottman, John. *The Seven Principles for Making Marriage Work: A Practical Guide from the Country's Foremost Relationship Expert*. Crown, 1999.

Gould, Stephen Jay. *I Have Landed: The End of a Beginning in Natural History*. Harvard University Press, 2011.

Green, Michelle. *The Dream at the End of the World: Paul Bowles and the Literary Renegades in Tangier*. HarperCollins, 1991.

Greene, Richard, and K. Silem Mohammad, eds. *The Undead and Philosophy: Chicken Soup for the Soulless*. Open Court, 2006.

Griffiths, Jay. *Wild: An Elemental Journey*. Jeremy Tarcher, 2006.

Grout, Pam. *Living Big: Embrace into Passion and Leap into an Extraordinary Life*. Conari Press, 2001.

Guinn, Jeff, and Douglas Perry. *The Sixteenth Minute: Life in the Aftermath of Fame*. Tarcher, 2005.

Hall, Kathryn. *Reclaiming Your Sexual Self: How You Can Bring Desire Back into Your Life*. John Wiley & Sons, 2004.

Hampl, Patricia. *Blue Arabesque: A Search for the Sublime*. Harcourt, 2006.

Hart, Mickey. *Drumming at the Edge of Magic: A Journey into the Spirit of Percussion*. Harper, 1990.

Hayes, Charles, ed. *Tripping: An Anthology of True-Life Psychedelic Adventures*. Penguin, 2000.

Healy, Sean Desmond. *Boredom, Self, and Culture*. Associated University Presses, 1984.

Hedges, Chris. *War Is a Force That Gives Us Meaning*. Anchor Books, 2002.

Helferich, Gerard. *Humboldt's Cosmos: Alexander von Humboldt and the Latin American Journey That Changed the Way We See the World*. Gotham, 2004.

Henry, Pat. *By the Grace of the Sea: A Woman's Solo Odyssey Around the World*. International Marine/Ragged Mountain Press, 2004.

Herriot, Trevor. *Jacob's Wound: A Search for the Spirit of Wildness*. McClelland & Stewart, 2004.

Hesse, Herman. *Narcissus and Goldmund*. Bantam Books, 1971.

———. *Siddhartha*. Bantam Classics, 1981.

———. *Steppenwolf: A Novel*. Bantam Books, 1969.

———. *Wandering: Notes and Sketches*. Paladin Books, 1988.

Hirshberg, Caryle, and Marc Barasch. *Remarkable Recovery: What Extraordinary Healings Tell Us About Getting Well and Staying Well*. Riverhead Books, 1995.

Hodgkinson, Tom, and Matthew De Abaitua. *The Idler's Companion: An Anthology of Lazy Literature*. Ecco Press, 1977.

Hogan, Linda. *Dwellings: A Spiritual History of the Living World*. W. W. Norton, 2007.

Hollis, James. *The Eden Project: In Search of the Magical Other*. Inner City Books, 1998.

———. *The Middle Passage: From Misery to Meaning in Midlife*. Inner City Books, 1993.

Hooks, Bell. *All About Love: New Visions*. William Morrow, 2001.

Hotchkiss, Sandy. *Why Is It Always About You: The Seven Deadly Sins of Narcissism*. Free Press, 2003.

Housden, Roger. *Seven Sins for a Life Worth Living*. Harmony Books, 2005.

Houston, Jean. *A Passion for the Possible: Guide to Realizing Our True Potential*. Harper, 1997.

Hubbell, Sue. *Waiting for Aphrodite: Journeys into the Time Before Bones*. Mariner Books, 2000.

Huxley, Aldous. *The Doors of Perception: Heaven and Hell*. Harper Colophon, 1963.

Jacoby, Mario. *Longing for Paradise: Psychological Perspectives on an Archetype.* Inner City Books, 2006.

Jaggard, Jason. *Spark: Transform Your World, One Small Risk at a Time.* Waterbrook Press, 2012.

James, Muriel, and John James. *Passion for Life: Psychology and the Human Spirit.* Dutton, 1991.

Jamison, Kay Redfield. *Exuberance: The Passion for Life.* Alfred A. Knopf, 2004.

Jasper, James. *Restless Nation: Starting Over in America.* University of Chicago Press, 2002.

Johnson, Robert. *Ecstasy: Understanding the Psychology of Joy.* Harper & Row, 1987.

———. *We: Understanding the Psychology of Romantic Love.* Harper & Row, 1983.

Jourard, Sidney. *The Transparent Self.* Van Nostrand Reinhold Co., 1971.

Kant, Immanuel. *Observations on the Feeling of the Beautiful and Sublime and Other Writings.* Translated by John T. Goldthwait. University of California Press, 1965.

Karen, Robert. *Becoming Attached: Unfolding the Mystery of the Infant-Mother Bond and Its Impact on Later Life.* Warner Books, 1994.

Kasser, Tim. *The High Price of Materialism.* Bradford Books, 2003.

Kazantzakis, Nikos. *Freedom or Death.* Simon & Schuster, 1956.

———. *Zorba the Greek.* Simon & Schuster, 1952.

Keen, Sam. *Apology for Wonder.* Harper & Row, 1969.

Kelley, Charles. *Life Force: The Creative Process in Man and in Nature.* Trafford, 2004.

Kelly, Ania. *The Psychology of Secrets.* Plenum Publishers, 2002.

Kelly, Franklin. *Frederic Edwin Church.* National Gallery of Art and Smithsonian Institution Press, 1989.

Keoghan, Phil. *No Opportunity Wasted: Creating a Life List.* Rodale Press, 2004.

Kerouac, Jack. *On the Road.* Penguin, 1998.

Kimmelman, Michael. *The Accidental Masterpiece: On the Art of Life and Vice Versa.* Penguin Press, 2005.

King, Deborah. *Truth Heals: What You Hide Can Hurt You.* Hay House, 2009.

Kingma, Daphne Rose. *Coming Apart: Why Relationships End and How to Live Through the Ending of Yours.* Conari Press, 2000.

———. *The Future of Love.* Doubleday, 1998.

Kingsolver, Barbara. *Animal Dreams: A Novel.* HarperCollins, 1990.

Kolakowski, Leszek. *Freedom, Fame, Lying and Betrayal: Essays on Everyday Life.* Westview Press, 1999.

Kowalski, Gary. *The Souls of Animals.* Stillpoint Publishing, 1999.

Kramer, Peter. *Should You Leave?: A Psychiatrist Explores Intimacy and Autonomy—and the Nature of Advice.* Penguin, 1997.

Krauss, Nicole. *The History of Love.* W. W. Norton, 2006.

Kroeger, Brooke. *Passing: When People Can't Be Who They Are.* PublicAffairs, 2003.

Kuhn, Reinhard. *The Demon of Noontide: Ennui in Western Literature.* Princeton University Press, 1976.

Kushner, Harold. *Living a Life That Matters.* Anchor Books, 2002.

Lamothe, Ryan. *Becoming Alive: Psychoanalysis and Vitality.* Routledge, 2005.

Lamott, Anne. *Help Thanks Wow: The Three Essential Prayers*. Riverhead Books, 2012.
———. *Traveling Mercies: Some Thoughts on Faith*. Anchor Books, 2000.
Lawrence-Lightfoot, Sara. *The Third Chapter: Passion, Risk, and Adventure in the 25 Years After 50*. Sarah Chrichton Books, 2009.
Lee, John. *The Half-Lived Life: Overcoming Passivity and Rediscovering Your Authentic Self*. Lyons Press, 2012.
Lessing, Doris. *Prisons We Choose to Live Inside*. Harper & Row, 1987.
Levine, Peter A. *Waking the Tiger: Healing Trauma*. North Atlantic Books, 1997.
Levine, Stephen. *A Year to Live: How to Live This Year as If It Were Your Last*. Bell Tower, 1997.
Lewis, Thomas, Fari Amini, and Richard Lannon. *A General Theory of Love*. Random House, 2000.
Lightman, Alan. *A Sense of the Mysterious: Science and the Human Spirit*. Vintage, 2006.
Linklater, Kristin. *Freeing the Natural Voice: Imagery and Art in the Practice of Voice and Language*. Drama Publishers, 1976.
Lipnis, Laura. *Against Love: A Polemic*. Pantheon Books, 2003.
Loeb, Paul Rogat. *Soul of a Citizen: Living with Conviction in Challenging Times*. St. Martin's Griffin, 2010.
London, Jack. *The Call of the Wild*. Macmillan, 1963.
———. *Martin Eden*. Penguin Classics, 1994.
Loporto, Garret. *The Davinci Method: Break Out & Express Your Fire*. Media for Your Mind, 2005.
Louv, Richard. *Last Child in the Woods: Saving Our Children from Nature-Deficit Disorder*. Algonquin Books, 2005.
LoVerde, Mary. *I Used to Have a Handle on Life, But It Broke: Six Power Solutions for Women with Too Much to Do*. Touchstone Books, 2002.
Lyng, Stephen, ed. *Edgework: The Sociology of Risk-Taking*. Routledge, 2005.
Macdonald, Kyle. *One Red Paperclip: Or How an Ordinary Man Achieved His Dream with the Help of a Simple Office Supply*. Three Rivers Press, 2007.
Madson, Patricia Ryan. *Improv Wisdom: Don't Prepare, Just Show Up*. Bell Tower, 2005.
Malchiodi, Cathy. *The Soul's Palette: Drawing on Art's Transformative Powers for Health and Well-Being*. Shambhala, 2002.
Mallinger, Allan, and Jeannette DeWyze. *Too Perfect: When Being in Control Gets Out of Control*. Ballantine Books, 1993.
Mandell, Fred, and Kathleen Jordan. *Becoming a Life Change Artist: 7 Creative Skills to Reinvent Yourself at Any Stage of Life*. Penguin, 2010.
Mander, Jerry. *Four Arguments for the Elimination of Television*. William Morrow & Co., 1978.
Marchesani, Robert, and E. Mark Stern, eds. *Frightful Stages: From the Primitive to the Therapeutic*. Haworth Press, 2001.
Maslow, Abraham. *The Farther Reaches of Human Nature*. Penguin, 1976.

———. *Toward a Psychology of Being*. D. Van Nostrand Co., 1968.

Matthiessen, Peter. *The Snow Leopard*. Penguin Classics, 2008.

Maugham, Somerset. *The Razor's Edge*. Blakiston Co., 1945.

May, Gerald G. *Addiction and Grace: Love and Spirituality in the Healing of Addictions*. HarperOne, 2007.

———. *The Wisdom of Wilderness: Experiencing the Healing Power of Nature*. Harper, 2006.

McCarthy, Barry, and Emily McCarthy. *Rekindling Desire*. Brunner-Routledge, 2003.

McCorduck, Pamela. *The Edge of Chaos*. Sunstone Press, 2007.

McNeill, William. *Keeping Together in Time: Dance and Drill in Human History*. Harvard University Press, 1997.

McPhee, John. *The Control of Nature*. Farrar, Straus & Giroux, 1990.

Mendenhall, Doug. *Spark*. Spirit Press, 2005.

Mercogliano, Chris. *In Defense of Childhood: Protecting Kids' Inner Wildness*. Beacon Press, 2007.

Midgley, Mary. *Man and Beast: The Roots of Human Nature*. Cornell University Press, 1978.

Miller, Alice. *The Body Never Lies: The Lingering Effects of Hurtful Parenting*. W. W. Norton, 2005.

Miller, Donald. *A Million Miles in a Thousand Years: How I Learned to Live a Better Story*. Thomas Nelson, 2009.

Miller, Henry. *The Colossus of Maroussi*. New Directions, 1941.

Miller, Ian. *The Mystery of Courage*. Harvard University Press, 2000.

Miller, William, and Janet C'de Baca. *Quantum Change: When Epiphanies and Sudden Insights Transform Ordinary Lives*. Guilford Press, 2001.

Mitchell, Stephen, trans. *Gilgamesh*. Free Press, 2004.

Mitchell, Stephen A. *Can Love Last: The Fate of Romance over Time*. W. W. Norton, 2002.

Moore, Lorrie. *Birds of America: Stories*. Alfred A. Knopf, 1998.

———. *Like Life*. Alfred A. Knopf, 1990.

———. *Self-Help*. Vintage Books, 2007.

Moore, Thomas. *The Re-enchantment of Everyday Life*. Harper Perennial, 1997.

———. *The Soul of Sex: Cultivating Life as an Act of Love*. HarperCollins, 1998.

Moravia, Alberto. *Boredom*. New York Review of Books, 1999.

Nachmanovitch, Stephen. *Free Play: The Power of Improvisation in Life and the Arts*. Tarcher/Putnam, 1990.

Nadis, Fred. *Wonder Shows: Performing Science, Magic, and Religion in America*. Rutgers University Press, 2005.

Nepo, Mark. *The Exquisite Risk: Daring to Live an Authentic Life*. Harmony Books, 2005.

Newberg, Andrew, and Eugene D'Aquili. *Why God Won't Go Away: Brain Science and the Biology of Belief*. Ballantine Books, 2001.

Oates, Joyce Carol. *The Faith of a Writer: Life, Craft, Art*. HarperCollins, 2003.

————. *I Lock My Door Upon Myself*. Ontario Review Press, 2002.

————. *New Heaven, New Earth: The Visionary Experience in Literature*. Vanguard Press, 1974.

Oelschlaeger, Max. *The Idea of Wilderness: From Prehistory to the Age of Ecology*. Yale University Press, 1991.

Ogden, Gina. *The Return of Desire: A Guide to Rediscovering Your Sexual Passion*. Trumpeter Books, 2008.

Oliver, Mary. *Thirst: Poems*. Beacon Press, 2006.

O'Neill, Nena, and George O'Neill. *Open Marriage: A New Lifestyle for Couples*. M. Evans & Co., 1972.

Osho. *Courage: The Joy of Living Dangerously*. St. Martin's Press, 1999.

Ozick, Cynthia. *Fame and Folly: Essays*. Vintage, 1997.

Parrott, Les. *The Control Freak*. Tyndale House. 2001.

Pasternak, Charles. *Quest: The Essence of Humanity*. Wiley, 2004.

Paz, Octavio. *The Double Flame: Love and Eroticism*. Harcourt Brace & Co., 1993.

Pearce, Joseph Chilton. *The Biology of Transcendence: A Blueprint of the Human Spirit*. Park Street Press, 2004.

Peck, M. Scott. *The Road Less Traveled: A New Psychology of Love, Traditional Values and Spiritual Growth*. Simon & Schuster, 1978.

Pendergrast, Mark. *Mirror, Mirror: A History of the Human Love Affair with Reflection*. Basic Books, 2004.

Pennebaker, James. *Opening Up: The Healing Power of Confiding in Others*. William Morrow & Co., 1990.

Percy, Walker. *Lost in the Cosmos: The Last Self-Help Book*. Farrar, Straus & Giroux, 1983.

————. *The Moviegoer*. Alfred A. Knopf, 1999.

Perel, Esther. *Mating in Captivity: Unlocking Erotic Intelligence*. HarperCollins, 2006.

Person, Ethel. *Dreams of Love and Fateful Encounters: The Power of Romantic Passion*. W. W. Norton, 1988.

Petersen, David. *Heartsblood: Hunting, Spirituality and Wildness in America*. Island Press, 2000.

Phillips, Adam. *Darwin's Worms: On Life Stories and Death Stories*. Basic Books, 2001.

————. *Houdini's Box: The Art of Escape*. Vintage Books, 2001.

Pink, Daniel. *Drive: The Surprising Truth About What Motivates Us*. Riverhead Books, 2009.

Pinker, Stephen. *The Blank Slate: The Modern Denial of Human Nature*. Viking, 2002.

Platt, Peter G., ed. *Wonders, Marvels, and Monsters in Early Modern Culture*. Associated University Presses, 1999.

Plotkin, Bill. *Nature and the Human Soul: Cultivating Wholeness and Community in a Fragmented World*. New World Library, 2008.

————. *Soulcraft: Crossing into the Mysteries of Nature and Psyche*. New World Library, 2003.

Porter, Eliot. *In Wildness Is the Preservation of the World*. Sierra Club/Ballantine Books, 1962.

Powter, Geoff. *We Cannot Fail: The Fine Line Between Adventure and Madness*. Constable & Robinson, 2006.

Preston, Douglas. *Dinosaurs in the Attic: An Excursion into the American Museum of Natural History*. St. Martin's Griffin, 1993.

Quammen, David. *Wild Thoughts from Wild Places*. Scribner, 1999.

Quinn, Daniel. *Ishmael: An Adventure of the Mind and Spirit*. Bantam, 1995.

Quinn, Robert E. *Change the World: How Ordinary People Can Accomplish Extraordinary Results*. Jossey-Bass, 2000.

Rako, Susan. *That's How the Light Gets In: Memoir of a Psychiatrist*. Harmony Books, 2005.

Raymo, Chet. *The Soul of the Night: An Astronomical Pilgrimage*. Cowley Publications. 2005.

Reade, D. *Superheroes, Saviors and Sinners without Secrets: Untold Twists and Tales of Life on Earth with Christ*. iUniverse, 2007.

Redmond, Layne. *When the Drummers Were Women: A Spiritual History of Rhythm*. Three Rivers Press, 1997.

Rezendes, Paul. *The Wild Within*. Jeremy Tarcher, 1998.

Rilke, Rainer. *Letters to a Young Poet*. Translated by Stephen Mitchell. Vintage Books, 1984.

———. *Rilke on Love and Other Difficulties*. W. W. Norton, 1975.

Robbins, Tom. *Jitterbug Perfume*. Bantam Books, 1984.

Robinson, Marilynne. *Gilead*. Picador, 2006.

Ropeik, David. *How Risky Is It, Really? Why Our Fears Don't Always Match the Facts*. McGraw-Hill, 2010.

Rosenberg, Larry. *Living in the Light of Death: On the Art of Being Truly Alive*. Shambhala, 2000.

Ross, Andrew. *The Celebration Chronicles: Life, Liberty, and the Pursuit of Property Value in Disney's New Town*. Ballantine Books, 2011.

Roszak, Theodore, Mary Gomes, and Allen Kanner, eds. *Ecopsychology: Restoring the Earth, Healing the Mind*. Sierra Club Books, 1995.

Roth, Phillip. *American Pastoral*. Vintage, 1998.

———. *The Counterlife*. Farrar, Straus & Giroux, 1986.

———. *Everyman*. Vintage Books, 2006.

———. *The Ghost Writer*. Vintage Books, 1995.

———. *Zuckerman Unbound*. Vintage, 1995.

Rothenberg, David, ed. *Wild Ideas*. University of Minnesota Press, 1995.

Rushdie, Salman. *Midnight's Children*. Random House, 2006.

Sagan, Carl. *Billions and Billions: Thoughts on Life and Death at the Brink of the Millennium*. Ballantine Books, 1998.

———. *Cosmos*. Ballantine Books, 1985.

———. *The Demon-Haunted World: Science as a Candle in the Dark*. Random House, 1995.

———. *Murmurs of Earth: The Voyager Interstellar Record*. Random House, 1978.

Sagan, Carl, and Ann Druyan. *Shadows of Forgotten Ancestors*. Ballantine Books, 1993.

Salamensky, S. I., ed. *Talk, Talk, Talk: The Cultural Life of Everyday Conversation*. Routledge, 2001.

Saltz, Gail. *Anatomy of a Secret Life: The Psychology of Living a Lie*. Morgan Road Books, 2006.

Sanders, Scott Russell. *The Force of Spirit*. Beacon Press, 2000.

———. *A Private History of Awe*. North Point Press, 2010.

———. *Staying Put: Making a Home in a Restless World*. Beacon Press, 1994.

Sandra, Jaida N'Ha, and Jon Spayde. *Salons: The Joy of Conversation*. New Society Publishers, 2001.

Sark. *Succulent Wild Woman*. Simon & Schuster, 1997.

Scarre, Chris, ed. *The Seventy Wonders of the Ancient World: The Great Monuments and How They Were Built*. Thames & Hudson, 1999.

Schaef, Anne Wilson. *When Society Becomes an Addict*. HarperOne, 1988.

Schnarch, David. *Passionate Marriage: Keeping Love and Intimacy Alive in Committed Relationships*. Henry Holt, 1997.

Schneider, Kirk. *Awakening to Awe: Personal Stories of Profound Transformation*. Jason Aronson, 2009.

———. *Rediscovery of Awe: Splendor, Mystery, and the Fluid Center of Life*. Paragon House, 2004.

Seaman, Donna, ed. *In Our Nature: Stories of Wildness*. Dorling Kindersley Publishing, 2000.

Sedaris, David. *Dress Your Family in Corduroy and Denim*. Back Bay Books, 2005.

Sedlar, Jeri, and Rick Miners. *Don't Retire, Rewire*. Alpha Books, 2007.

Sendak, Maurice. *Where the Wild Things Are*. HarperCollins, 1963.

Sharp, Daryl. *Getting to Know You: The Inside Out of Relationship*. Inner City Books, 1992.

Shepard, Paul. *Coming Home to the Pleistocene*. Island Press, 1998.

Shields, David. *The Thing About Life Is That One Day You'll Be Dead*. Alfred A. Knopf, 2008.

Simonton, D. K. *Greatness: Who Makes History and Why*. Guilford Press, 1994.

Smith, Huston. *Forgotten Truth: The Common Vision of the World's Religions*. HarperOne, 1992.

Smith, Roger. *Inhibition: History and Meaning in the Sciences of Mind and Brain*. University of California Press, 1992.

Snyder, Gary. *The Practice of the Wild*. North Point Press, 1990.

Solnit, Rebecca. *Wanderlust: A History of Walking*. Penguin Books, 2000.

Solomon, Robert C. *Spirituality for the Skeptic: The Thoughtful Love of Life*. Oxford University Press, 2002.

Spacks, Patricia Meyer. *Boredom: The Literary History of a State of Mind*. University of Chicago Press, 1995.

Spiegel, Maura, and Richard Tristman, eds. *The Grim Reader: Writings on Death, Dying, and Living On*. Anchor Books, 1997.

Stegner, Wallace. *Crossing to Safety*. Modern Library, 2002.

Steinberg, David, ed. *The Erotic Impulse*. Jeremy Tarcher, 1992.

Stevenson, Robert Louis. *The Lantern Bearers and Other Essays*. Cooper Square Press, 1998.

Strayed, Cheryl. *Tiny Beautiful Things: Advice on Love and Life from Dear Sugar*. Vintage Books, 2012.

Swimme, Brian, and Thomas Berry. *The Universe Story: From the Primordial Flaring Forth to the Ecozoic Era*. HarperOne, 1994.

Talbot, Michael. *The Holographic Universe: The Revolutionary Theory of Reality*. Harper Perennial, 2011.

Terkel, Studs. *Will the Circle Be Unbroken: Reflections on Death, Rebirth, and Hunger for a Faith*. Ballantine Books, 2002.

Thomas, Lewis. *Lives of a Cell: Notes of a Biology Watcher*. Penguin, 1978.

———. *The Medusa and the Snail: More Notes of a Biology Watcher*. Penguin, 1995.

Thomson, Hugh. *The White Rock*. Overlook Press, 2003.

Tolstoy, Leo. *The Death of Ivan Ilyich*. Vintage, 2012.

Toohey, Peter. *Boredom: A Lively History*. Yale University Press, 2011.

Torgovnick, Marianna. *Gone Primitive: Savage Intellects, Modern Lives*. University of Chicago Press, 1990.

———. *Primitive Passions: Men, Women, and the Quest for Ecstasy*. University of Chicago Press, 1998.

Trafford, Abigail. *My Time: Making the Most of the Rest of Your Life*. Basic Books, 2004.

Treasurer, Bill. *Right Risk: 10 Powerful Principles for Taking Giant Leaps with Your Life*. Berrett-Koehler, 2003.

Tuan, Yi-fu. *Escapism*. Johns Hopkins University Press, 2000.

Turner, Jack. *The Abstract Wild*. University of Arizona Press, 1996.

Tweedie, Jill. *In the Name of Love*. Pantheon Books, 1979.

Tyler, Anne. *The Amateur Marriage: A Novel*. Alfred A. Knopf, 2004.

———. *Breathing Lesson: A Novel*. Alfred A. Knopf, 1988.

Ulanov, Ann Belford. *The Unshuttered Heart: Opening Aliveness/Deadness in the Self*. Abingdon Press, 2007.

Updike, John. *Toward the End of Time: A Novel*. Random House, 2009.

Urry, John. *The Tourist Gaze: Leisure and Travel in Contemporary Societies*. Sage Publications, 1990.

Vaillant, George. *The Wisdom of the Ego*. Harvard University Press, 1993.

Valusek, Jay. *The Secret Sorrow: A Memoir of Mourning the Death of God*. iUniverse, 2010.

van den Haag, Ernest. *Passion and Social Constraint*. Stein and Day, 1963.

Vidyadevi, Ed. *Reflections on Wildness*. Windhorse Publications, 2000.

Viorst, Judith. *Imperfect Control: Our Lifelong Struggles with Power and Surrender*. Free Press, 1999.

Volney, C. F. *The Ruins, or Meditation on the Revolutions of Empire and the Law of Nature*. Bibliobazaar, 2006.

Voltaire. *Candide*. W. W. Norton, 1966.

Walker, Matthew. *Adventure in Everything: How the Five Elements of Adventure Create a Life of Authenticity, Purpose, and Inspiration*. Hay House, 2011.

Wallace, Danny. *Yes Man*. Simon & Schuster, 2005.

Wallace, David Foster. *A Supposedly Fun Thing I'll Never Do Again*. Little, Brown & Co., 1997.

———. *Brief Interviews with Hideous Men*. Little, Brown & Co., 2007.

Walsh, Roger, and Frances Vaughan, eds. *Paths Beyond Ego: The Transpersonal Vision*. Tarcher, 1993.

Ward, Peter, and Donald Brownlee. *The Life and Death of Planet Earth: How the New Science of Astrobiology Charts the Ultimate Fate of Our World*. Holt Paperbacks, 2004.

Warren, Frank. *PostSecret: Confessions on Life, Death, and God*. HarperCollins, 2009.

Watts, Alan. *This Is It: And Other Essays on Zen and Spiritual Experience*. Vintage, 1973.

———. *The Wisdom of Insecurity: A Message for an Age of Anxiety*. Vintage, 2011.

Wennstrom, Jerry. *The Inspired Heart: An Artist's Journey of Transformation*. Sentient Publications, 2002.

Weschler, Lawrence. *Mr. Wilson's Cabinet of Wonder: Pronged Ants, Horned Humans, Mice on Toast, and Other Marvels of Jurassic Technology*. Vintage, 1996.

Wheatley, Margaret. *Turning to One Another: Simple Conversations to Restore Hope to the Future*. Berrett-Koehler, 2009.

Wilkes, Paul. *The Art of Confession: Renewing Yourself Through the Practice of Honesty*. Workman Publishing, 2011.

Williams, Brooke. *Halflives: Reconciling Work and Wildness*. Island Press, 1999.

Wilson, Cintra. *A Massive Swelling: Celebrity Re-examined as a Grotesque, Crippling Disease and Other Cultural Revelations*. Penguin Books, 2001.

Wilson, E. O. *Biophilia*. Harvard University Press, 1984.

———. *On Human Nature*. Harvard University Press, 2004.

Wilson, Peter. *The Domestication of the Human Species*. Yale University Press, 1991.

Wilson, Sule Greg. *The Drummer's Path: Moving the Spirit with Ritual and Traditional Drumming*. Destiny Books, 1992.

Winter, Richard. *Still Bored in a Culture of Entertainment: Rediscovering Passion and Wonder*. InterVarsity Press, 2002.

Winterson, Jeannette. *Art and Lies*. Vintage Books 1994.

———. *Gut Symmetries*. Vintage Books, 1997.

———. *The Passion*. Vintage Books, 1987.

———. *Written on the Body*. Vintage Books, 1992.

Wise, Nina. *A Big New Free Happy Unusual Life: Self-Expression and Spiritual Practice for Those Who Have Time for Neither*. Broadway Books, 2002.

Woodward, Christopher. *In Ruins: A Journey Through History, Art, and Literature*. Vintage, 2003.

Yalom, Irvin. *Staring at the Sun: Overcoming the Terror of Death*. Jossey-Bass, 2008.

Yeshe, Lama. *Introduction to Tantra: The Transformation of Desire*. Wisdom
    Publications, 2001.

Zamyatin, Yevgeny. *We*. Avon, 1972.

Zerubavel, Eviatar. *The Elephant in the Room: Silence and Denial in Everyday Life*.
    Oxford University Press, 2006.

Zweig, Connie. *The Holy Longing: The Hidden Power of Spiritual Yearning*. Tarcher/
    Putnam, 2003.

Zweig, Paul. *The Adventurer: The Fate of Adventure in the Western World*. Basic Books,
    1974.

Index

Page numbers in *italics* indicate drawings.

About the Author

GREGG LEVOY is the author of *Callings: Finding and Following an Authentic Life* (Random House)—rated among the "Top 20 Career Publications" by the Workforce Information Group—and *This Business of Writing* (Writer's Digest Books). A former columnist and reporter for *USA Today* and the *Cincinnati Enquirer* and a former adjunct professor of journalism at the University of New Mexico, he has written for the *New York Times Magazine*, the *Washington Post*, *Omni*, *Psychology Today*, *Reader's Digest*, and many other publications, as well as for corporate, promotional, and television projects.

As a lecturer and seminar leader, he has presented at the Smithsonian Institution; the Environmental Protection Agency; Microsoft; British Petroleum; National League of Cities; National Conference on Positive Aging; American Counseling Association; Esalen Institute; Omega Institute; and universities across North America; and has been a frequent guest of the media, including ABC, CNN, NPR, and PBS.

He lives in Asheville, North Carolina, and his website is www.gregglevoy.com.